Working with
ROOSEVELT

A Da Capo Press Reprint Series

FRANKLIN D. ROOSEVELT
AND THE ERA OF THE NEW DEAL

GENERAL EDITOR: FRANK FREIDEL
Harvard University

Working with
ROOSEVELT

by

SAMUEL I. ROSENMAN

DA CAPO PRESS · NEW YORK · 1972

Library of Congress Cataloging in Publication Data

Rosenman, Samuel Irving, 1896-
  Working with Roosevelt.
  (Franklin D. Roosevelt and the era of the New Deal)
  1. Roosevelt, Franklin Delano, Pres. U.S.,
1882-1945. 2. Authorship — Collaboration. I. Title.
II. Series.
E807.R73   1972   973.917   75-168391
ISBN 0-306-70328-9

This Da Capo Press Edition of
Working with Roosevelt is an unabridged
republication of the first edition published
in New York in 1952. It is reprinted by
permission of Harper & Row, Publishers, Inc.

Published by Da Capo Press, Inc.
A Subsidiary of Plenum Publishing Corporation
227 West 17th Street, New York, New York 10011

Printed in the United States of America

Working with
ROOSEVELT

Working with
ROOSEVELT

by

SAMUEL I. ROSENMAN

HARPER & BROTHERS, PUBLISHERS
New York

To My Wife

Contents

The illustrations, grouped as separate sections, will be found following pages 144 and 336.

Acknowledgments

When I began to write these pages I had no belief or intention that they would be a book. They were intended to be only a general introduction to the thirteen volumes of *Public Papers and Addresses of Franklin D. Roosevelt*. In an introduction to those volumes I wanted to provide some historical background about the way the President—in the exercise of his democratic leadership in domestic and world affairs—worked and thought and lived.

I started to dictate this introduction during a leisurely vacation in the California desert—without benefit of documents of any kind. The recollections of seventeen years of association and labors with Governor and President Roosevelt, the calm peacefulness of the desert, and the quiet efficiency of my recording machine—all seemed to produce an abundance of words which went far beyond the space limitations of an introduction. Friends and associates who had helped me in the preparation of the *Public Papers* persuaded me to expand into this present book the material that had outgrown its original purpose as an introduction.

To write a book in the midst of a rather busy professional life is not easy. I would never have finished this one had it not been for the constant urging and encouragement of two or three people. They were convinced that it might provide some interesting historical sources to help in understanding and evaluating Roosevelt—the leader, the statesman, the man—and the epoch which he had a substantial part in producing.

First among them was my wife, who had lived through all these stimulating and absorbing years and experiences with me. She not only encouraged; she helped immeasurably—in refreshing recollection, in reviewing the manuscript in its many drafts from the very beginning, in thousands of helpful suggestions and criticisms, in continuous editorial assistance and copy reading. Without her, the book would not have been started; and certainly would not have been completed.

Professor Kenneth W. Hechler, formerly a member of the faculty at Columbia and Princeton Universities, now a member of the White House staff, who had helped me so much on the *Public Papers and Addresses*, was another who constantly prodded me to finish this book. I am grateful to him too for his helpful research on this project, for his invaluable and innumerable suggestions of ideas, and for his scholarly checking of facts in the manuscript.

Others who, from time to time, had served the great President with me have taken the time and trouble to read the manuscript in order to insure as full and accurate an account as possible, where so much depends on human recollection. Robert E. Sherwood, Bernard M. Baruch and Benjamin V. Cohen have done so; and I am grateful for their many suggestions and ideas for improvement. I acknowledge thanks also to Albert Lasker and Arthur Schlesinger, Jr., who have read this manuscript and made valuable criticisms and recommendations.

I have received many helpful ideas, in personal interviews or through correspondence, from Adolf Berle, Jr., Stanley High, Thomas G. Corcoran, Donald Richberg, Archibald MacLeish and Felix Frankfurter—each of whom had an active part in some of the speeches of the President.

There were others who were good enough to read and check the manuscript or specific parts of it, and refresh my recollection on certain events, or furnish information that was new. I should prefer to give personal acknowledgment for each, but space does not permit. I apologize for this inadequate record of my gratitude to them: Paul Appleby, Milton H. Biow, Charles E. Bohlen, William C. Bullitt, Margaret Donnelly, Stephen Early, Max Freund, Edward S. Greenbaum, Joseph Grew, Luther Gulick, Robert Hannegan and Mrs. Hannegan, William Hassett, William J. Hopkins, Harold Ickes, Herman Kahn, Esther Lape, Ernest K. Lindley, Anne O'Hare McCormick, Leland Olds, Mrs. Gifford Pinchot, Michael F. Reilly, William M. Rigdon, Anna Roosevelt, Franklin D. Roosevelt, Jr., James Rowley, Richard S. Salant, George Schreiber, Margaret Suckley, Myron C. Taylor, Rexford G. Tugwell, Grace G. Tully, Frank C. Walker and Sumner Welles.

And for invaluable help, encouragement and editorial assistance I am deeply grateful to Miss Marguerite S. Hoyle of the staff of Harper & Brothers, whose ability to rearrange, edit and cut a manuscript would be useful to any team of speech writers; to Evan Thomas of the same firm who helped in so many ways; and of course to Cass Canfield and Frank S. MacGregor of Harper's who from the beginning insisted that there was a book in the material which I handed in as an introduction.

If, in spite of the assistance of all these people, any errors have crept into this book, I take sole responsibility for them.

Foreword

This is a partisan book. It is written by one who believes that Franklin D. Roosevelt, with all his faults, ranked with Washington, Jefferson and Lincoln as one of our greatest Presidents, and that he was a very great human being besides.

One measure of him as a President and as a man is what he said and wrote in his public life. More than any other president—perhaps more than any other political figure in history—Franklin D. Roosevelt used the spoken and written word to exercise leadership and to carry out policies.

This book is essentially a story of his words, of the ideas behind them, and of their translation into policy and action. But since the words necessarily involve the man himself, this story must tell something of the sort of man Roosevelt was, the kind of leadership he furnished, the imprint he left on the national fabric and world pattern. The story of his words involves also the men who helped him shape those words and ideas and policies. Finally, it is the story of the circumstances under which the words were written, what the President hoped to accomplish by them, and how far he was successful.

This book is written in the belief that such a story is important, not only as a footnote to history, but as an aid to a better understanding of the leadership exercised by Franklin D. Roosevelt. It is not intended in any sense to be a history of the times through which he lived. Nor is it intended to be a full biography of him, or the complete memoirs of one who knew him. It covers only a portion of the President's life and activity, and only a part of my own association and work with him.

During the lifetime of the President, there were widespread interest and much public speculation about how his speeches were written, what their backgrounds were, what assistants and collaborators and advisers helped in their preparation. Numerous articles and books, published both during his lifetime and since his death, have presented some curious —almost ludicrous—versions of their genesis. These pages may help to dispel some of the misconceptions and give a more accurate account of how the President's messages and speeches came into being.

In the course of the story, I shall make frequent reference to speeches and messages themselves, and to an occasional press conference. These speeches, messages and conferences, covering the period from October, 1928, to the date of his death, have been gathered together and published in thirteen volumes entitled *The Public Papers and Addresses of Franklin D. Roosevelt*.[1] Readers who wish to study in detail the messages and speeches to which I shall refer and from which I shall quote will find them set forth in full in those thirteen volumes. I regret that space limitations prevent fuller or more frequent quotation here.

[1] The first five volumes were published by Random House, Inc.; the second four by The Macmillan Company; and the last four by Harper & Brothers.

Working with

ROOSEVELT

Chapter I

Speech Writing and Speech Writers

The room used for the meetings of the President of the United States and his Cabinet is probably the simplest and least ornate room in the world used for any similar purpose. It is separated from the President's private office by a tiny secretary's office. The President enters the Cabinet Room from his own office through the secretary's office. There are two additional entrances from a main hall running through the White House office wing. The Cabinet members enter through one of these, and whenever the President is in the room, a Secret Service agent is stationed at each door.

The walls of the room are white, and during Roosevelt's tenure were unadorned except for portraits of Jefferson and Jackson on the west wall and a portrait of Woodrow Wilson over the simple fireplace at the north end of the room. It is a small room, as such rooms go—say, about the length of an ordinary Pullman car and four times as wide. The east wall consists almost entirely of French windows opening onto a paved covered walk leading a hundred feet or so to the residential part of the White House. Through these windows, draped in red damask, there is one of the prettiest scenes in all Washington. Out over the rose garden enclosed by a tall green hedge you look toward the south entrance of the White House with its beautiful curved balcony and the famous winding stairs leading up to it. The white walls of the house are relieved by the large magnolia tree planted there more than a century ago by Andrew Jackson, which now towers up above the balcony itself. A little to the right, the south lawn of the White House stretches majestically down toward the Washington Monument, lined with the magnificent old elms and oaks which are the wonder of all visitors to the Capital.

From the windows of the Cabinet Room you could watch President Roosevelt coming along the covered walk at a speed which made you fear he could not possibly continue to hold on to his armless little wheel chair. In his hand, there was nearly always some document he had been reading. In his mouth was his cigarette holder tilted at the usual jaunty angle. Fala, his Scottie dog, ran along at his side. A Secret Service agent raced alongside also; and a messenger followed, holding a large wire basket containing the mail and memoranda on which the President had worked in his bedroom the night before or that morning. A bell had been rung three times to alert the White House police that the President was on his way; and officers were stationed at several different points along the path.

I used to stand at the windows frequently after the bell rang, waiting to say hello to him, and he would smile and wave when he passed. Sometimes he was so engrossed in his reading or so occupied in thought that he never looked up until he had been wheeled past the Cabinet Room and into his own office.

Ordinarily, all was very orderly and decorous in the Cabinet Room. An unbelievably large mahogany table in the center of the room took up more than half the floor space. It had eight unequal sides, but, being four or five times as long as it was wide, it seemed almost rectangular. The purpose of this strange octagonal shape was to enable the President to sit in the center of one side and have a clear view of the Cabinet members on each side of him as well as those opposite him. On this highly polished and impressive table, there were ordinarily only a telephone with a long wire and a few reference books, such as the Congressional Directory and Government Manual, in front of the President's place. The rest of the table was bare, except just before Cabinet meetings when a large yellow pad and several pencils were laid before each Cabinet officer's place. During the war, the table got a little crowded because extra chairs were placed around it for the heads of some of the new wartime agencies. There was a plain carpet on the floor, some chairs and small tables along the wall, a clock which chimed each quarter hour, a large globe of the world at one end near the fireplace—and that was all.

Most of the time the room was the quietest place in wartime Washington. Even in peacetime, visitors to the White House are not shown that room except under extraordinary circumstances. Sometimes an "off-the-record" visitor, who had been admitted through one of the side doors to avoid the press, was shown into the Cabinet Room to await his time to see the President. Otherwise the room was empty and silent, and somber.

But on occasions, say for about four or five days each month, the room was a mess! For it was in the Cabinet Room that nearly all of Roosevelt's famous speeches and messages were put together. Quiet and secluded, efficiently air conditioned, it was the best room for that kind of work; and the large table was the most convenient place for all the papers and documents which had to be used. Moreover, the President could conveniently be wheeled in and out with the least disturbance to anyone.

If a visitor, familiar with the appearance of the Cabinet Room on an ordinary day, were to have looked into it, say about midnight of February 21, 1942, he would have been quite startled.

All the lights were burning. But there were black curtains pulled across the windows now; we were at war, and it was blackout time. The shining surface of the large table was hardly visible, for it was covered from one end to the other with papers, books, telegrams, letters. At one end of the table was a large tray; on it were a big thermos pitcher of coffee, two piles of sandwiches covered by a damp napkin, a large number of bottles of beer, Coca-Cola, ginger ale, and plain charged water, some cups and saucers and large glasses, a bowl of cracked ice, and a bottle of whisky.

Seated around the table were three men. They were all in their shirt sleeves and were obviously tired, for they had been working all day on a speech. They had just said good night to the President in his study in the White House, and had then walked over to the Cabinet Room to do some more work on the speech. The tray of food and drinks had come over from the pantry of the White House at the direction of the President.

Robert E. Sherwood poured himself a whisky and soda; Harry Hopkins helped himself to a cup of black coffee and a sandwich; I took a bottle of Coke and two sandwiches. I phoned upstairs to the four stenographers who had been asked to report for duty at 11:00 P.M. to work with us.

"There are some sandwiches and coffee and soda down here in the Cabinet Room. Come on down and help yourselves."

They did, and after some pleasantries they returned upstairs carrying their food and drink with them.

Harry had stopped at the map room on the way over.

"What's the war news like?" I asked.

"It's all terrible—we're getting one hell of a licking all over the Pacific, and it certainly looks as though it's going to get worse instead of better," Harry said as he stirred his coffee, carrying it around with him as he nervously paced the floor.

"If the American people ever needed a shot in the arm, this is the time," said Bob. "I hope this speech can do it. If they could only look into that room across the way and see the magnificent spirit and confidence of the President, as we did just now, it would do them a world of good."

"They can't see it," I said, "but if I know the Boss, they'll feel it in his voice next Monday. But they won't unless we get to work—he expects the next draft with his breakfast."

Grace Tully, in her own office, had been typing some inserts and corrections which the President had dictated during our recent session with him. By this time she had brought some of them in, each on a separate piece of paper labeled "Insert A, p. 2," or "Insert B, page 15." She silently gave a copy to each of us, helped herself to some coffee and a sandwich, and went back to her room to type the other inserts and to wait.

As we drank, we huddled over the new inserts she had brought in.

We were working on a fireside chat the President was to deliver on Washington's Birthday, 1942 (celebrated on February 23rd because the 22nd fell on a Sunday that year).

"Let's see now," I said, "this is draft six"—so I took a carbon copy of draft five, which the President had just gone over with us, and changed the "five" to "six." I also kept before me the original of draft five, on which he had made deletions and corrections in his own hand.

"He certainly has the geography and strategy of this war at his finger tips," I said as I reread some of the pages. "He makes it sound as simple and understandable as he did the banking crisis back in 1933. It was damned smart of him to ask the people to spread out their maps of the world and follow him when he speaks—that's the way they'll get it and understand what the strategy is all about. A lot of the newspapers are going to print maps of the world on Monday so their readers can have them when the President speaks."

This was the first fireside chat by the President since December 9,

1941, right after Pearl Harbor. Our armed forces were being beaten and forced back at every point. The consistently disastrous news had produced an atmosphere of defeat and despair. The President had decided to make a fireside chat explaining the global strategy of the war, pointing out the exact position of the Allies and the reasons for the bad news, and encouraging Americans—and people all over the world—to the belief that victory and liberation could be won. He had dictated parts of a first draft several days ago, and had just carefully read over and revised the fifth draft. We had each written some inserts for this fifth draft which had been submitted to him. Some had found their way into the draft—and some into the wastebasket.

"Too bad, Bob, he cut out that stuff of yours on page three; it sounded pretty good to me as he read it out loud. I wonder why," I murmured as I reached for another sandwich.

"I think he thought it was too optimistic and promised too much good news too soon," said Harry, pouring himself a highball. "One thing the President does not want to do is to kid the American people into believing that this is anything but a tough son-of-a-bitch of a war against the toughest and cruelest bastards on earth. He wants them to realize right at the start what they are up against."

I do not remember whether Grace was in the room during this outburst, but if she was, she would not have been surprised—everyone was used to Harry's frequently picturesque and blunt language.

I always consumed coffee and Coca-Cola in great quantities at these late sessions, mainly to keep awake. Bob and Harry insisted that bourbon had the same effect on them; although, strangely enough, it might make other people drowsy.

"Well, no one is as good as the President in fixing the line between keeping up morale and confidence on the one hand, and being too optimistic on the other. I'd take his judgment any time. But," Bob said longingly as he reread the words that had been cut, "it was a purple passage all right. I'll save it—maybe some day I'll use it myself in a speech."

He grinned. Although he had been doing this kind of work only a little over a year, he had already become quite accustomed to seeing passages that had taken hours to write ruthlessly discarded in a minute.

"I'm glad we were able to convince the Boss to cut out those pages eight and nine that he dictated yesterday," I said as I read through the draft. "That kind of vindictiveness about the old isolationists is out of place now, even though they did often say that there was no chance of Germany or Japan ever attacking us."

"Yeah," said Harry, "it took a lot of arguing. But I think this insert D of his tonight is almost as bad. Let's leave it out of this draft and try to talk him out of it in the morning."

I looked at Bob; he approved; and so I carefully set it aside in a folder to take up with the President when we discussed the next draft with him.

Now we started at the beginning, going over the draft again sentence by sentence, word by word. A suggestion for a change would come from one or another. An idea would pop up which we all would think fine.

"Bob, suppose you write a couple of paragraphs on that," I asked, "while I dictate something to take the place of those two pages the Boss said we ought to 'boil'" (his favorite expression for shortening).

Bob went up to the end of the table with a pad and fountain pen, while I went into Miss Tully's room for a few minutes to dictate a new and shortened version of the two pages. Harry, in the meantime, wrote out a few paragraphs for some other part of the speech, based on something the President had said that evening.

Whatever the speech, the general pattern of our collaboration was always the same. When Bob had finished, he would silently pass to me what he had written; and Harry and I would read it together. We might say "O.K." or "fine" and clip it in the right place; or we might say "try again—that's too complicated or too oratorical for the Boss"; or we might suggest a few changes here and there. The same thing would happen with what I had dictated to Grace, and with what Harry had written.

The inserts the President himself had dictated got the same close scrutiny. We changed his language and often cut out whole sentences. When there was some dissent among us, we made a note to talk to the President about it the next day.

There was no pride of authorship; there was no carping criticism of each other. We were all trying to do the same thing—give as simple and forceful expression as possible to the thoughts and purposes and objectives that the President had in mind. Whatever language and whoever's language did it best was the language we wanted.

"Here is a suggestion from Berle which is O.K. and one from Marshall which is a peach," I said that evening, passing them around. By common consent, they went into the next draft, each marked as an insert and clipped to the right sheet.

After a few pages of the carbon copy of draft five were corrected and added to in this way, I pushed a button in the table near the President's chair. It was a bell connected with the messenger room. A messenger came in and took the pages to the girls upstairs to make six copies. This draft would be number six. From then on we sent the new draft up page by page, so that almost as soon as we were finished they could send it down retyped, and we could immediately begin working all over again on the seventh draft—polishing, correcting, adding, deleting.

One lengthy insert the President had dictated two days before had caused a long argument. I have a carbon copy of it before me now, called insert D. (No page was indicated—the President had merely said, "Stick it in somewhere, boys.") It was an attempt to explain how three German cruisers had escaped from the British fleet in the English Channel a few days before. This incident had occurred shortly before Singapore fell and was part of a long series of British disasters. Churchill and the British were feeling the humiliation. Roosevelt wanted to stiffen the morale of the British people. However, as we read what he had written, it seemed to us too apologetic; none of us liked it. We spent some time that night rounding up our arguments— and our nerve—to go after him again on it, although he had already told us several times that he wanted it in. It took us several days, chiefly because he had promised Churchill that he would make the explanation; but he finally was convinced, and the insert was dropped.

By two o'clock we had finished sending up the sixth draft; it was down again in a few minutes, and we were ready to begin the seventh.

Harry excused himself, for he had not been well recently. Bob and I plugged along. By three o'clock, we had finished the seventh draft— also the coffee, sandwiches, soda and a good part of the bourbon.

The seventh-draft original we left in a sealed envelope at the usher's office to be delivered to the President with his breakfast. One copy we left for Harry. The rest we put in our brief cases; and, after getting a White House car to take the girls home, we started to walk over to the Willard Hotel where we shared a small apartment. That was the only bit of fresh air we had had since breakfast.

"We'll take another look at it in the morning at breakfast," I said as we prepared for bed, "and I'm going to send a copy over to General Marshall as soon as I get to the office."

"Good," said Bob, "I've got a new idea for a peroration."

We did not know, as we went to sleep that night, that a Japanese submarine was then on its way to the California coast. It had orders to get close to shore at night and to open fire on some obscure and unimportant target near Santa Barbara at the very time the President was delivering his speech. This attempt to "steal the headlines" and to counteract the effect of Roosevelt's speeches, which the Axis tried frequently to do whenever Roosevelt spoke, was eloquent proof of how highly the enemy rated the power and propaganda of Roosevelt's words.

This was the grind—and the glamour—of what was known as "ghost-writing" for a President of the United States.

In 1942 it was chiefly Harry and Bob and I who did it. But there had been others before Harry and Bob: Moley, Tugwell, Johnson, Corcoran, Cohen, Berle, Bullitt, Richberg, High, MacLeish. In these pages their names will appear time and again.

I seem to have been used the longest and the most. In 1928, I worked with Roosevelt on one of his first campaign speeches for Governor of New York; in 1945 I worked with him on his last major speech, when he reported to the Congress on the conference at Yalta seven weeks before he died. In between those two dates, spanning seventeen years, I had something to do with a very substantial number of his major speeches and messages.

Is it important to know who the people were who helped in the preparation of speeches? So far as routine speeches are concerned—for example, a Red Cross drive speech, or a short message to the Congress transmitting some report—no, it is not important.

But nearly every major speech of a President is, in one way or another, a policy-making speech, and those who are around when it is being prepared and while it is going through its many drafts, with numerous changes and insertions and deletions, are in a peculiarly strategic position to help shape that policy.

Very often they may have prepared the first draft themselves. That first draft may contain an important statement of policy. Of course, the President can immediately reject it; indeed, I have seen Roosevelt do just that, many times. Nevertheless, when the draft is physically before the President, those who have helped prepare it have the great advantage of being right at his elbow ready to argue their point of view.

And so much depends on the choice of words and phrases, on shadings of meaning and emphasis. Language enunciating a policy may be made bold and forthright; or words may be used that obscure, understate or circumscribe the policy. For example, if some of the officials in the State Department during 1939 and 1940 and the early part of 1941 had been given a free hand in drafting the President's speeches, the tone would have been much more cautious, the approach more timid. The President was extremely impatient with some of the drafts that came over from the State Department during those years, and with some of the suggested corrections in the drafts he had sent over to them for consideration. He felt that they were too apt to use "weasel words" (a favored phrase he had borrowed from Theodore Roosevelt); that they made too many reservations and were too diplomatically reserved. If the men helping the President on speeches at that time had been more in sympathy with the point of view of the State Department, the spirit and shading of the speeches would have been quite different—assuming that the President would have kept using such men, which is quite doubtful. And the effect of the speeches on world events might have been quite different also.

I do not mean to imply, of course, that any of the people who helped in the preparation of speeches would try to impose their own views on the President or to slip them in. Even if they had tried, they would have failed. We always informed him of any contrary view expressed to us by one of his associates, and it would be fully and frankly discussed.

"Hull does not agree with this statement on page blank," was a frequent admonition we gave him, or "Henderson does not think that this paragraph goes far enough in controlling the economy."

"Why not?" he would ask.

"Well, he says," etc., etc.

The President would listen and he would argue. When the reasons had all been given, and he had heard all our own arguments, it was he who would make the decision. Sometimes it would be final; sometimes he might say, "Well, let's leave it the way it is in this draft, and I'll think about it overnight." Or he might say, "Ask Leon whether he thinks this would do," and proceed to dictate a new suggestion. But the final decision was always his—and his alone.

The President had strong views of his own regarding any suggestion that was made, or he would develop them quickly. Anyone who knew him well knew how stubborn he could be. One reason that he changed the make-up of his speech-writing team from time to time was that he found that the views of this or that person were becoming too sharply different from his own basic convictions. Those who stayed with him knew that he had certain fundamental principles which would never alter. A hundred isolationist speech writers could never have changed his views on foreign affairs after 1937. No speech writer could ever have made him compromise on the fundamental principles of social security or water power development.

On the other hand, those who helped with his speeches would have been useless to him if they had been mere yes men. One of the most difficult tasks a President of the United States has is to find assistants who are not yes men. A smart President knows that such a man can do more harm than good. The President looks to his assistants for candor and frankness, for helpful criticism and suggestions. A yes man merely confirms and encourages whatever errors the President might make. The same is true of a man who assists the President in writing speeches. As soon as he is ready to accept as sacrosanct or immune from criticism anything that the President has written, he might as well go home—he is going to be of no use to the President. If he is to be helpful to him at all, he has to feel free to criticize, and even to urge a complete discard of the material that the President has dictated. President Roosevelt understood this very well; he expected us to criticize and argue with him, and to suggest changes in language and ideas.

Of course, as I have said, the time would come in any speech when the President, after debate pro and con, made up his mind that he would say a certain thing in a certain way. Then, it generally became useless to keep arguing for a change.

We learned when was the best time to battle with him. Often we would give way and strategically retreat in draft three, only to return again in draft six with greater success. Or we might be successful in draft five, and the President, after a night's reflection, might change it again in draft seven. Of course there are no traces in the finished speech of this kind of development or argument. Some day, scholars and research students will examine in detail the originals of the successive drafts of the speeches, nearly all of which are now in the Franklin D. Roosevelt Library at Hyde Park, New York; there they will find the detailed changes that were made from draft to draft. In some of them they will find paragraphs which were dropped in one draft reappearing in a later one. This means that the speech-writing team reinserted something that the President had taken out, and tried again to persuade him to keep it in. Sometimes we succeeded; sometimes we failed. There will be no effort made in this book to trace these specific changes from draft to draft. It would require a detailed study more interesting to the specialist than to the general reader, and would take much more space than this account contemplates.

If the preparation of speeches is so important in the development of policy, why did not the President write his own speeches; why did he have people help him?

Basically, the answer is this: the speeches as finally delivered were his —and his alone—no matter who the collaborators were. He had gone over every point, every word, time and again. He had studied, reviewed, and read aloud each draft, and had changed it again and again, either in his own handwriting, by dictating inserts, or making deletions. Because of the many hours he spent in its preparation, by the time he delivered a speech he knew it almost by heart.

But if the question is: Why did not the President sit down and from the beginning write the whole speech himself so that all the words were his alone? the answer is this: there just is not enough time in a President's day.

The preparation of some of the speeches or messages took as many as ten days, and very few took less than three. That does not mean actual writing time. But there were long memoranda and proposed drafts to be read, and information and statistics to be gathered. Irrelevant data had to be separated from relevant data. Many people had to be interviewed, sometimes a dozen or more for a single message. Some were consulted during the preparatory period before the speech began to take shape, others during the actual writing of the speech—either to check data or to canvass views on questions of policy. The President often asked that a full draft of a speech or certain paragraphs in it be checked by several departments and agencies. Sometimes a speech went through as many as twelve or thirteen drafts before the President was finally satisfied. Obviously, for him to undertake so exhausting and time-consuming a task from beginning to end was impossible if he wanted to continue to carry on his other duties. As it was, a major speech invariably set his schedule back a full day or two.

So, when in these chapters I say that this person or that one worked on a particular speech or message, I mean that—and only that. I do not mean that any particular speech was Bob Sherwood's or Ray Moley's or mine. Because it was not. No matter how frequently the speech assistants were changed through the years, the speeches were always Roosevelt's. They all expressed the personality, the convictions, the spirit, the mood of Roosevelt. No matter who worked with him in the preparation, the finished product was always the same—it was Roosevelt himself. And nothing I write here should obscure that fundamental fact.

Chapter II

The First Campaign for Governor, 1928

It was in the fall of 1928 that I happened into the business of helping on speeches. Alfred E. Smith was then the Governor of New York and the Democratic candidate for President. He wanted Franklin D. Roosevelt to become the Democratic candidate for Governor.

Although Roosevelt had not been personally active in the details of New York State politics for fifteen years, he was very popular within the party. He had built up a fine reputation in his own right, and had great appeal to the people of the state. He had the best trade name in American political life. As an upstate Protestant, he would serve to attract to the support of the ticket those who might otherwise shy away from Smith, the New York City Catholic. He had defied and successfully fought Tammany Hall during his early days in the New York Senate. In short, he provided exactly the proper balance to the ticket, and his presence on it might help Smith even outside New York.

The story is well known how Smith begged Roosevelt to run for Governor, and how Roosevelt finally yielded to his old friend whom he had twice nominated for the Presidency. It will not be repeated here.

Roosevelt, recognizing that he was not adequately familiar with the details of the recent legislative history of both parties in New York State, asked Maurice Bloch, his campaign manager and the Democratic leader in the Assembly, to find someone to go with him on his campaign trip who could give him such information, and also help him in the preparation of his campaign speeches. Bloch suggested me; and, I learned later, so did Mrs. Belle Moskowitz, who was one of Governor Smith's close advisers for many years. As a member of the New York Legislature for five years and of the Bill Drafting Commission for three, I had acquired considerable experience with recent legislative and political history in Albany. However, aside from my own campaign speeches as a candidate for the Legislature and my speeches as a member in the years between 1921 and 1925, all of which were extemporaneous "off-the-cuff" talks, and apart from college debating and public speaking, I had no experience at all in the preparation of speeches.

The conservative Republican-controlled Legislature during the decade before 1928 had been in almost constant conflict with the liberal policies of Governor Smith—a fact that made our campaign strategy in 1928 quite obvious, for Roosevelt was definitely classified as a progressive and liberal. I have never been able to learn to my own satisfaction the original sources of Roosevelt's unwavering liberalism. What was there in his home environment, education or experience to account for it? He was born into a rich and aristocratic family; he was educated by private tutors in the patrician environment of a Hudson River Valley estate. He attended the most exclusive of Eastern preparatory schools, and was a member of the best clubs at Harvard. His friends and family nearly all belonged to the privileged and conservative class. By the time Roosevelt, at the age of twenty-eight, ran for the Senate in 1910, one would have expected him to be a reactionary in politics, or at least a confirmed conservative.

I have tried from time to time to find the reason for his early liberalism by looking into his college experiences, into his early legal practice which took him a great deal into the East Side of New York, into the rural life of Dutchess County. I tried in conversation with Roosevelt himself. I have asked his old friends and members of his family. I have never found a satisfactory and complete answer. I conclude that there were none of the usual outside influences. The reason was born when he was born: it was in the heart and soul of the man, in his love of people, his own sense of social justice, his hatred of greed and of exploitation of the weak, his contempt for the bully—whether it was a Hitler or Mussolini or an owner of a sweatshop or an exploiter of child labor.

Of course, his veneration for the earlier Roosevelt—Uncle Ted as he called him, his experience under Wilson, and his association with the liberals in that administration did much to encourage and cement his progressive thinking. I have no doubt that the suffering and pain and physical handicap of many years of paralysis intensified his understanding of the problems of those suffering from the pain of hunger and destitution, and deepened his sympathy for those handicapped by poverty and ignorance and suffering from social injustices. But the seed was there long before, and it had flowered long before the disease struck.

Despite his reputation, I did not know the full extent of Roosevelt's liberalism when I first met him. Indeed I was a bit afraid that after the work I had done on some of Smith's program, Roosevelt was going to be a letdown for me and for all Smith liberals. I knew Roosevelt's family and cultural background; and I was skeptical.

As soon as I was told that I was to go on the campaign trip, I proceeded to gather together the material we might need. The issues of the gubernatorial campaign of 1928 were essentially not very different from the issues of each of Roosevelt's later Presidential campaigns. They included in general such matters as labor legislation, questions relating to old age pensions, unemployment insurance and other forms of social security, better housing, education and health, the development of water power and other natural resources, improvement in the administration of justice, farm relief, minimum wages, regulation of public utility corporations, cheap electricity.

As I collected the material, I separated it into large red manila envelopes, each properly labeled by subject matter. Eventually I had several suitcases full of these envelopes. I mention this otherwise minute detail because the arrangement seemed to make a great impression upon the candidate when he saw it. He remembered it so well that eight years later when he began to make ready for his first campaign for re-election to the Presidency, he asked that the campaign material be arranged in exactly the same way, including even the size and color of the envelopes. His was not by nature the orderly kind of mind that separates material into individual compartments; so it was understandable that he should have been impressed by that sort of arrangement and should have recognized how useful it could be to him.

We started the campaign that year on October 17, crossing the ferry from New York City to Hoboken, and taking the Erie Railroad up through the southern tier of New York counties. I had seen Mr. Roosevelt once before. It was during his gallant performance at Madison Square Garden in New York City four years earlier when, thoroughly crippled by infantile paralysis, he led the forces fighting for the nomination of Governor Smith for the Presidency. That time I had watched him from the upper recesses of the third balcony. Not until this 1928 trip had I personally met the man with whom I was to spend so much time for so many years. He was sitting in his automobile on the ferry-boat, smoking, chatting informally, and watching the activity on the river. Maurice Bloch took me over to shake hands with him. I was young then—thirty-two—but I had already had eight years of experience in district politics and in public office. The only Governor I had known was Smith. This man was different—different in bearing, in speech, in personality. He was cordial, but not gruffly so. He spoke impeccable English with a cultured accent and inflection. He was obviously not the self-made man risen from city streets; he was the country squire, dressed carelessly—soft collar, loose-fitting tweed suit, well-used felt hat. He was friendly, but there was about his bearing an unspoken dignity which held off any undue familiarity.

I had heard stories of his being something of a playboy and idler, of his weakness and ineffectiveness. That was the kind of man I had expected to meet. But the broad jaw and upthrust chin, the piercing, flashing eyes, the firm hands—they did not fit the description. Though those stories were never finally and universally dispelled in the public mind until the startling "hundred day" period following his first Inaugural in 1933, for me they became a joke within a week after I met him.

I had quite a detached, indifferent feeling toward this man at first. After all, I was going along just to do a chore—to give him all the helpful information I could. I did not expect actually to write any speeches for him. That was not what I was supposed to do. I had helped Governor Smith on speeches in Albany once or twice; but Smith almost always spoke extemporaneously from prepared notes which he held in his hand. Helping Smith on speeches usually meant merely gathering the material for those notes. As the weeks went on, however, Roosevelt's warm, genial personality, his friendliness and cordial informality, drew me close to him. Nearly everyone who worked intimately with him had the same experience. Roosevelt loved people, and they learned quickly to return that affection.

After our meeting on the ferry, he ignored me completely for the next three days except pleasantly to pass the time of day. The territory through which we were then campaigning—the counties along the border between New York State and Pennsylvania—was all strongly Republican. One of these counties had been a particular stronghold of the Ku Klux Klan. Mr. Roosevelt's first major speech of the 1928 campaign was in that county, in the city of Binghamton. It was an extemporaneous, impassioned speech against the forces of religious prejudice which were then bitterly fighting Governor Smith's candidacy for the Presidency.

As he went through that part of the state for the next three days, he continued to devote his speeches almost exclusively to the candidacy of Smith. Once in a while, he lapsed into a state subject with which he was familiar, such as agriculture or local rural government. They were all extemporaneous speeches; so by the time we reached Buffalo I had just about decided that I and my suitcases of red envelopes were excess baggage.

At Buffalo I received a telegram from Bloch: "Tell the candidate that he is not running for President but for Governor; and tell him to stick to state issues."

Luckily, I did not have to show this to the candidate—and probably at that time I would not have dared to—because when we arrived at the hotel in Buffalo, he told me he was going to deliver a speech on labor the next night.

I now began to feel of some use.

"I've got several files of material on labor," I said. "That's one subject on which you can lambaste the Republican leaders all night."

I hastily pulled several envelopes out of one of the large suitcases of material I had, and passed them to him.

He looked through the material for some time, calmly smoking his cigarette, his chin resting on his right fist in a position I was later to see thousands of times. He rarely said anything when reading a document, and he disliked being interrupted during the process. He could read fast; sometimes you wondered whether he was reading at all, he flipped the pages so quickly. But when he started to talk about what he had read, you knew that he had absorbed most of it. He generally preferred to get his information orally; he could interrupt and ask questions; it was easy for him to get the gist right away. However, when he was too busy or was unwilling to see people, he would ask for memoranda, which he could read at odd moments—in bed or between appointments or during lunch.

When he had finished reading, he handed me back the files. I expected him to take paper and pencil and jot down an outline of the points he wished to make. He had only that evening and the next day to prepare the speech, and I could see that he was on ground that was then less familiar to him than rural affairs and national subjects.

"Sam," he said—he called his working associates by their first names very soon after meeting them—"I've got to run now and meet some of the local political brethren. I'm afraid I'll be busy most of the evening. Suppose you knock out a draft of what you think I ought to say tomorrow night, and let me have it in the morning. We'll go over it together tomorrow."

He must have seen the look of consternation on my face, for he smiled encouragingly as he called for his valet to get his wheel chair and take him into his bedroom.

He added as he was being wheeled out: "Don't stay up all night—do the best you can."

"Any particular line you want me to follow?" I asked, as I nervously followed the wheel chair out.

"No, just put something together so we can look at it in the morning," and, for the time being, the speech was dismissed from his mind.

I gathered up the papers and, with considerable misgiving, went to my own room. I was not much impressed by his judgment in placing that much confidence in a comparative stranger.

Now, for the first time, I was in business for myself as a ghost writer, and I was pretty nervous and worried about it. I sat down at the small desk in my bedroom with the material I had selected. It was hard to get started—it always is. I had no instructions, no leads from the candidate. This seemed strange to me at the time; I was to get used to it in later years. I did not know much about Roosevelt's style. What I had heard in the past few days was extemporaneous, almost informal, speechmaking. I had brought along a copy of his famous "Happy Warrior" speech nominating Smith for the Presidency in 1924, and also his speech nominating Smith in 1928. I got them out and read them again for style. Then, nervously, I plunged in.

I recounted all the promises to labor that had been made during the past decade by Republican platforms and Republican candidates, and how the promises had been broken. I listed all the things that the Democratic party had pledged itself to do and what it had done. It was all well documented, for I had the facts. But as I read it over, it was inexpressibly dull. I tried to pep it up a little in the next draft; but as I crawled into bed early that morning after slipping the last draft under Roosevelt's door, I felt despondent about my first effort of this kind.

I had been asked to join him at breakfast, and as I came in he was sitting up in bed, reading the draft. He greeted me, motioned me with his cigarette holder to a chair, and kept on reading. It seemed to go on forever.

Finally he laid it down on the bed and quickly began his breakfast. It was on a tray; and he motioned me to go ahead with a tray that was on the table.

"You've got all the stuff in there we need, and it's pretty good but a little on the dull side. It makes a telling story, and I can use most of it. All it needs is something to hold it together. Some of the statistics will have to come out—we'll get in a stenographer right after breakfast."

This was a fair appraisal. There was no attempt to salve my feelings, but there was a ready acceptance of the parts that he considered good. I was to get used to this too; it was the way he always worked.

"You know," he said reminiscently, "things today are not very different from the days when I was in the Senate back in 1911 and 1912. Al Smith and Bob Wagner and Jim Foley were there then, plugging for social and labor legislation as I was. I remember they used to call us socialistic and radical in those days. I remember how furious my poor mama used to get to think that her son had become a socialist."

This got to be one of his favorite themes whenever his later programs were called socialistic or communistic. What had been socialism in 1911 had become solid Americanism by 1928. In the same way, much of the essence of the "communist and radical" New Deal of 1933 was to become a part of the Republican platform in 1944.

"I think I'll use that happy thought in the speech," he added. "Happy thought" was an expression he used frequently to refer to an original good idea which had popped into his head—or any other head.

When the breakfast trays were cleared away, he started to dictate some inserts and corrections. I got my first lesson in how to pull a speech together and pep it up. For example, preceding my long and boring dissertation on unfulfilled Republican promises to labor, he dictated the following graphic paragraph:

And so tonight I am going to tell you all about it, tell you the facts, go back in my own mind and in your mind into the history of this State. Somewhere in a pigeonhole in a desk of the Republican leaders of New York State is a large envelope, soiled, worn, bearing a date that goes back twenty-five or thirty years. Printed in large letters on this old envelope are the words, "Promises to labor." Inside the envelope are a series of sheets dated two years apart and representing the best thought of the best minds of the Republican leaders over a succession of years. Each sheet of promises is practically the duplicate of every other sheet in the envelope.

But nowhere in that envelope is a single page bearing the title "Promises kept."

After several other amendments he turned, and said almost apologetically: "I'm going to take one more crack at religious bigotry. If Al is licked, that's what will do it. I know some of the boys at my campaign headquarters won't like it, but I'm more interested in electing Al than in anything else."

So he dictated a very moving passage about his experience in World War I, watching stretchers of wounded American boys being carried to the rear.

. . . somehow in those days people were not asking to what church those . . . American boys belonged. . . .
And I want to say to you very simply, very solemnly, that if there is any man or woman whose mind can go back ten years; if there is any man or woman who has seen the sights that I have seen, who knows what this country went through; any man or woman who knows what Germany, Poland, France, Austria, England went through—even more than we did— in those years; if any man or woman, after thinking of that, can bear in his heart any motive in this year which will lead him to cast his ballot in the interest of intolerance and of a violation of the spirit of the Constitution of the United States, then I say solemnly to that man or woman, "May God have mercy on your miserable soul."

As I reread that paragraph today, I am struck by its similarity to the things he had to say fifteen years later about religious and racial intolerance during the course of a more devastating war.

The speech went through several drafts that day. He worked on each one carefully, word by word. When the final reading copy was completed, many of my original sentences and even paragraphs, I noted with pride and satisfaction, were still intact—but many had fallen into the basket. And so much had been added!

I listened to the speech that night from the back of the big auditorium. When applause came, I was more uplifted than the speaker. When a point was made, I thought of all the changes and discussion that lay behind it. Although I knew the speech almost by heart, I hung on every word as though I were hearing it for the first time. And no one applauded more vigorously than I. Even though I was to go through this experience scores and scores of times, I never lost completely the original feeling of excitement of this first occasion. In later years my wife often teased me about my rapt attention to words which I knew so well. I used to watch others who had worked on speeches with

Roosevelt; their reaction was the same. I frequently saw Bob Sherwood actually forming the words with his own lips as they were being spoken by Roosevelt.

That night after the speech, I joined Roosevelt and some of the local political leaders in his suite at the hotel for some light refreshments. There were loud congratulations from his guests on the speech; they talked about it in detail; I went up to congratulate him on his eloquent, effective delivery.

When we were finally alone, and he was making ready for bed, he said, "It went over fine, Sam—good work."

I felt repaid for the sleepless night I had spent on it. But the luxury of reflection and conversation about a speech that had already been delivered was soon over.

"Now let's see," said Roosevelt, "what shall we speak about in Rochester?"

Jolted out of my complacency, I realized there was a lot of work for me to do before I could go to sleep.

After some discussion, we decided on the subjects. He gaily went off to bed, and I—a little more confidently this time—went to my room to knock out a first draft of the speech for the next night.

That campaign was a difficult one. After the first two days by train, Roosevelt decided that he would continue the rest of the trip by automobile. This would enable him to make speeches at the scores of crossroads and villages all through the state that he could not reach if he traveled by train. Two large buses accompanied the automobiles. One was used by the newspapermen who were covering Roosevelt's campaign. In the other bus were the stenographers, mimeograph machine operators and their equipment. The speeches had to be typed and mimeographed for the press while the bus was actually speeding along the road.

After a speech had been delivered in one city, I sat up and prepared a draft of the speech for the next night. It had to be ready for the candidate to look at the next morning during his breakfast when we would go over it together.

After breakfast, the cavalcade of cars and buses would start the journey to the next city. I would get into the bus where the typewriters were, and, with Roosevelt's corrections and suggestions, would work on the draft. As each page was finished I would give it to the typists, and they would knock out a clean copy while the bus was in motion.

That is not an easy thing to do, especially on a country road. Every once in a while the procession stopped at the center of some village, where Roosevelt would make a short informal talk to the crowd. Afterward, he would sit in his car, chat with some of the people in the crowd, and engage in general handshaking. I would get into his car at one of these stops, and, after we started off again, we would discuss some of the changes in the draft or some suggested inserts which I had prepared or which he had dictated during breakfast that morning. Sometimes he stopped his car at the roadside and did some writing on the draft, or sent for one of the stenographers and dictated some new material. As soon as he was finished with me, I would return to the bus and get to work on the next draft.

Generally at noon we stopped an hour or so in a village or small city where local party leaders had arranged a luncheon. After his impromptu speech following the lunch, we usually had an opportunity to go into a private room and turn out the final draft.

When we started off again, I would ride in the working bus, where a reading copy was prepared for him to use that night and also about a hundred mimeographed copies for the press.

It was not easy for a crippled man to carry on this kind of campaign. It was a strenuous physical ordeal for him to get in and out of automobiles and hotels. He made his daytime speeches standing in the back of his car. The simple job of getting up and sitting down several times was almost as much exercise as the ordinary man takes during an entire day. He could not climb stairs, and often we had to carry him up some back stairs of a hall and down again. He always went through this harrowing experience smiling. He never got ruffled. Having been set down, he would adjust his coat, smile, and proceed calmly to the platform for his speech. I marveled at the courage of this man as well as at his physical stamina. In later years I was to see the same kind of courage and stamina time and again; but my wonder never wore off— nor my admiration.

As the trip progressed, my respect grew. I had never met anybody who could grasp the facts of a complicated problem as quickly and as thoroughly as he. He could listen attentively to a brief statement of the facts, and then dictate them into a speech; or, then and there, walk onto a platform or rise at a banquet table and talk about them before an audience as though he had had a lifelong familiarity with them.

At Syracuse I got another lesson in how to hang the details of a speech on to a central dramatic theme. He had decided that his subject would be water power. I had prepared for him the details of how the Republican leaders had several times tried to turn the water power of the state over to private interests for private development and profit. The Democrats had blocked those attempts, and had insisted on public development. He listened as I read him the facts. Then, interrupting me, he turned to the stenographer and said, "Take this as the opening paragraph on the section about water power:

"Tonight I am going to talk about a very wet subject—water power. While it may not be quite as soul-stirring a subject as the other wet one I discussed last night [prohibition], in some ways it goes just as deep to the roots of our democracy.

"This is a history and a sermon on the subject of water power, and I preach from the Old Testament. The text is *'Thou shalt not steal.'*"

That was more telling than all the pages of detailed facts which followed that introduction. I still remember the way he read those words that night, and the thunderous applause he got.

He was such a fine, natural orator that he could make the commonplace sound important. No matter how badly you had written, when you heard him speak, the words seemed suddenly to be endowed with force, emphasis and charm. His voice and his delivery more than made up for any deficiencies in the substance and style of the pages he was reading.

It was easy to work with him. I discovered that almost immediately. He went out of his way to see that his visitors were at ease. I remember when a new, young, substitute stenographer was sent to his study in the White House to take dictation in the absence of both his regular secretaries, Marguerite A. LeHand and Grace Tully. I could see how painfully nervous the poor girl was. She confessed to me later that as she came into the room she was "scared to death," and that her knees nearly caved in under her. She managed to get to the chair he asked her to take. He saw her nervousness immediately, and instead of starting off to dictate he casually asked her her name and what part of the country she came from. Then he started to talk about that part of the country (he seemed to know something about every part) and got her to talk about it too. After a bit he talked to me, and let her alone for a while. In ten minutes she was composed and smiling, thoroughly at home with him. He recognized this, too, and started to dictate. She never felt ill at ease with him again.

He made people feel he was deeply interested in their own lives and in their families; for he encouraged them to talk about themselves, and he always listened with deep attention. He was interested! By the warmth of his greeting, he could make a casual visitor believe that nothing was so important to him that day as this particular visit, and that he had been waiting all day for this hour to arrive. Only a person who really loved human beings could give that impression.

I had heard that this Roosevelt was aloof, reserved, lacking in humor, hard to get to know. He was just the opposite. He was friendly and affable; he was anxious to have people like him. He had an infectious sense of humor. He knew how to laugh, and he loved to laugh. He knew how to stop work, even when hardest pressed, for a joke or an anecdote or a minute of light conversation or gossip. Those working with him were never afraid to interrupt and tell him a joke or a funny story, even during a serious discussion. He knew the benefits of that kind of brief relaxation—how it relieved the strain and tension of hard, concentrated work. On this 1928 campaign I got to know that characteristic very well, and it made the tough job of campaigning a real joy.

Above all, I learned quickly to respect and admire the sincerity of his liberalism and tolerance and human brotherhood. He was not concerned with distinctions of wealth or social position or religious beliefs. This was a new kind of man in politics for me: one who did not seem to care—or even know—whether you were a Catholic, Protestant or Jew. He believed in the liberal cause because he believed in the dignity of man and in his right to a self-respecting life and to protection against exploitation. This became apparent very early in our acquaintance, not only from his speeches, but from conversations with him in his car, at breakfast, and at night over a glass of ginger ale before he went to bed.

When we arrived in New York City for the last week of the campaign, my task became easier because instead of working in a moving automobile or bus we worked at Roosevelt's residence on East Sixty-fifth Street. During the trip upstate I had been alone in this work; after we came back to New York City, Louis Howe joined us.

Louis Howe was the strangest person I met around Roosevelt. He had only one loyalty in life—and it was a kind of religion—Franklin D. Roosevelt. To promote the interests of Roosevelt was his main, if not sole, mission in life. He had known Roosevelt since the early Albany days in 1911, and practically ever since he had been associated with him and his family. His own family and his own private life had been completely submerged in the service of his hero.

The greatest service he rendered, though the least conspicuous, was during the years of Roosevelt's tragic illness. It was largely he and Eleanor Roosevelt who during that period kept Roosevelt's political urge alive; for they brought all kinds of people to see him, and insisted on his keeping in touch with Democratic party leaders all over the United States. Ever since then Howe had occupied a position of great intimacy in the Roosevelt family, living with them for long periods. He spent all his time and energy working to enhance Roosevelt's political fortunes. He was one of the handful of people who called the President "Franklin"; and he lived at the White House from March 4, 1933, until he died in 1936.

Howe had no great concern with large issues of policy or political philosophy, except only as they might serve to make Roosevelt President. His chief ambition was to be the manager of this President-making campaign, and to be the man closest to his idol. Like a faithful watchdog he showed his teeth at anyone who came near Roosevelt, and if a person was welcomed too heartily or got too close, Howe became his jealous enemy. He did not really like me from the very start—and he liked me less the more work Roosevelt gave me to do. However, during these campaign days of 1928 he was friendly enough to me at least outwardly, for I am sure he considered me only a temporary worker who would disappear after the campaign.

He loved Roosevelt, but he never hesitated to argue with him when he thought "Franklin" was harming his own political advancement. He probably said No to Roosevelt more frequently and loudly than anyone else, and stuck to his position longer. His mission in life was fulfilled on March 4, 1933, when Roosevelt was inaugurated and he became Secretary to the President. Except for Roosevelt himself, Howe did more than anyone else to help him into the White House. From then on, Howe was no longer of comparable service. Roosevelt was extremely fond of him, but Howe did not play an important part in framing major policies.

Up to election day in 1928, I spent a good part of each day and night with Roosevelt. I sat up with him at his headquarters at the Biltmore Hotel on election night, getting the returns. It was a custom I was to follow each election night, right through the last one in 1944. Partly because no other election was quite so close as this one, and partly because this was my first, the excitement and tension of the later election nights were never quite so great, even though they involved the Presidency.

As the returns came in from the Republican strongholds in upstate New York it seemed certain that Roosevelt was beaten. By midnight it was definite that Smith had lost New York and the national election.

At one point, as he handled some bad returns from upstate, he said, "We'll stay around until it is over. I have an idea that some of the boys upstate are up to their old tricks of delaying the vote and stealing as many as they can from us."

His jaw was set—quite the way I saw it, years later, the day after Pearl Harbor. He picked up the phone and put in a call for the sheriffs of several upstate counties. He spoke himself to all he could reach.

"This is Franklin Roosevelt," he said. "I am watching the returns here at the Biltmore Hotel in New York City. The returns from your county are coming in mighty slowly, and I don't like it. I shall look to you, if they are unduly delayed, and I want you personally to see that the ballots are not tampered with. If you need assistance to keep order or to see that the vote is counted right, call me here at this hotel and I shall ask Governor Smith to authorize the State Troopers to assist you."

This was a bluff because there was really little that Roosevelt could do if those instructions were not followed, especially if he were not elected. But it worked—the returns began to come in more quickly. And they were better.

The early editions of the papers the next morning carried the news of Roosevelt's defeat; but the final returns showed that he had won, but only by 25,000 votes out of a total of 4,000,000. Roosevelt for two years referred to himself jocularly as the "one half of one per cent Governor." Hoover defeated Smith by over 100,000 votes in New York, and by a landslide in the rest of the nation. I have often wondered what the course of American history would have been during the depression and during the war if in 1928 only 13,000 voters had switched from Roosevelt to his opponent, Ottinger!

As the Governor-elect left the headquarters very late that morning, his joy of victory was diluted by distress over Smith's overwhelming defeat; he knew how large a part in that defeat had been played by religious bigotry. Before he went home, he invited several of us to visit him at Warm Springs later in the month, to help him map out a legislative program and to discuss prospective political appointments.

"And, besides, I'd like you to see Warm Springs. It will be a nice vacation, and we'll all have a fine time over some Brunswick stew. Good night—get some sleep."

I took him at his word, and went home to sleep for two days and two nights.

Chapter III

The Genesis of the New Deal: The First Term as Governor, 1929-1930

A few weeks after election a gay group went to Warm Springs. There were Maurice Bloch and Bernard Downing, who were to be respectively the Democratic leaders of the New York Assembly and the New York Senate. The newly elected Lieutenant Governor, Herbert H. Lehman, went too, and the Democratic State Chairman, William Bray. I was delighted to be along, and assumed that the reason I had been asked was that it would be my job—as the Democratic Legislative Bill Drafting Commissioner of the state—to draft the legislation to carry out the Governor's program.

On the way down we naturally speculated on the kind of governor Roosevelt would make. How well was he? Would he have to take much time off? How much would Al Smith continue to "run the show"? How about his Cabinet? How far would he go in taking political recommendations in making appointments? Would he "high-hat" the political leaders and the rank and file of the party, or would he be a "regular guy" politically? Strangely enough, none of us ever asked each other or gave any thought to the question, Would this man ever be in the running for the Presidency? Two years later, this question was on the lips of everybody interested in politics.

At Warm Springs, we were comfortably lodged in a small cottage. We spent several days there, and had our first glimpse of Roosevelt on vacation. There, for the first time, I met Miss Marguerite A. LeHand. She had been Roosevelt's private secretary for several years, but had been ill during the gubernatorial campaign and therefore had not taken any part in it. She had long been a friend of the Roosevelt family and they all called her "Missy." That is the name by which she soon came to be known by all Roosevelt's friends and associates. She was to play an important role in the history of the nation in the next thirteen years —but an anonymous one.

I saw how easily and completely Roosevelt could throw off all cares and problems, and then suddenly get down to earnest work and discussion. I also learned to respect the firm set of his jaw when, for example, he discussed political appointments—making it clear that although he would be willing to take political recommendations for minor places, the policy-making and top-ranking positions were going to be filled on the basis of ability and of his own personal confidence in the appointees.

His routine in Warm Springs showed that, apart from his legs, Roosevelt was healthy—far above the average. The fatigue of the campaign was all gone; he was buoyant in spirit and mind, enthusiastic over the prospect of the Governorship. One thing became certain very early: Roosevelt was going to be his own Governor and take full charge. Any thought anyone of us might have had that Smith was going to run things was almost immediately dispelled.

During our stay in Warm Springs there was an old-fashioned barbecue in Roosevelt's honor at Chipley near by. One of the speakers referred to Warm Springs as the "Summer White House after 1932." There was loud applause, and *The New York Times* reported the incident as a lead in its Warm Springs story of December 4, 1928. No one, however, took it seriously; it was merely some oratory in behalf of a favorite son—an adopted one.

The conferences we held with the Governor-elect in Warm Springs dealt with two matters. The first was the adoption of a sound, progressive program of legislation; the second was the building up of the Democratic party organization, especially in upstate New York where it had been traditionally and notoriously decadent.

In later years Roosevelt taught me how closely these two subjects were intertwined, how important both were to success at the polls— a good affirmative liberal program and a good party organization. He knew how to use this combination perfectly. In Roosevelt the practical politician and the humanitarian statesman worked together.

He once said to me many years later in connection with some idealistic course which was being urged on him but which was hopeless of early accomplishment and also dangerous politically:

"You know the first thing a President has to do in order to put through good legislation? He has to get elected! If I were now back on the porch at Hyde Park as a private citizen, there is very little I could do about any of the things that I have worked on. So don't throw votes away by rushing the gun—unless there is some good sound reason. You have to get the votes first—then you can do the good work."

And I have heard the converse from him too. When a course of conduct was urged upon him as good politically, he looked first to see whether it would hurt or help the objectives he was seeking to attain. A very striking example was the invasion of North Africa by American troops on November 8, 1942. The Congressional elections were to be held on November 2. We had been fighting on the defensive all through 1942, and many people were criticizing the conduct of the war. The result of the elections was doubtful. Obviously if our first great military offensive could be announced in advance of the elections, it would have a striking political effect. This fact was pointed out to the President— needlessly, I am sure, for it must have been apparent to him. He would have none of it. He dismissed the idea summarily. The invasion job was to be done when the military commanders thought it best to be done. It was done several days after election, too late to have any political effect at all.

One day, during this 1928 visit to Warm Springs, the Governor called me aside and said, "Sam, I shall want you to act as the Counsel to the Governor—we will have a fine, stimulating time together."

Taken by surprise, I hesitated. Under Governor Smith, the position of Counsel to the Governor had not been much more than a political sinecure. Smith had assembled a small group of intelligent, able and energetic advisers in a sort of "kitchen cabinet." This group performed for him many of the tasks that were properly the Counsel's. When I mentioned this, Roosevelt said, "I do not expect to continue to call on these people whom Al has been using. I shall expect the Counsel to do much of the work they have been doing."

I discussed the duties of the office with him very carefully, and told him that I would make up my mind in a week or so.

While I was deliberating the matter and discussing it with my friends, the afternoon papers one day suddenly carried the story on the front page that I had been appointed by Governor-elect Roosevelt as his Counsel. This was a complete surprise to me, and I might add quite a shock, because at no time had I said I would accept the appointment. I immediately put in a phone call to the Governor, and asked him whether it was true that he had announced my appointment. He laughed and said "Yes," and added, "I made up your mind for you."

There was nothing I could do about it. As time went on I was very thankful that he had not waited for me to make up my own mind. I remained as Counsel—and loved it—until nearly the end of his Governorship.

After I had been sworn in, I told Roosevelt of my wonder that he should have filled a place of such close and confidential relationship with a young man whom he had known for such a short time.

He said, "I get to know people quickly and I have a pretty good instinct about them. Sometimes that instinct is better than a long and careful investigation."

During the first two years of Roosevelt's Governorship, my family and I lived in Albany during the Legislative Session. After the Legislature adjourned each year, and my family returned to New York, I continued to spend at least three days a week in Albany. In 1931, the Governor and Mrs. Roosevelt invited me to move into the Executive Mansion and to live with them there, which I did for the rest of the time I was Counsel.

Constant association with him during these years—at the office by day and at his home during the dinner and the evening, and our many hours of discussion about state issues and later about national issues—taught me a great deal about the way Roosevelt spoke and wrote and thought.

After Roosevelt became President, writers and commentators expressed surprise at the rapid succession of legislative proposals urged by him during the "first hundred days" of his Presidency in 1933. Many have spoken and written of those proposals as though they suddenly sprang from Roosevelt in 1933 as a new kind of political philosophy. Many have wondered where they all came from in such a short time. The fact is that the basic philosophy and social objectives of the New Deal proposals can all be found in Governor Roosevelt's speeches and messages during the four years *before* he became President. The details are different, because the proposals in 1933 were framed for national rather than state action. But, as an examination of the earlier documents will show, the concepts are basically the same.

In those messages and speeches from 1929 through 1932 you will find proposals for appropriate state action in the same fields in which he later urged action by the Congress: minimum wages and maximum hours, old age insurance, unemployment relief through public works and other means, unemployment insurance, regulation of public utilities, stricter regulations of banks and of the use of other people's money, improved housing through the use of public subsidies, farm relief, public development of water power, cheaper electricity especially in rural areas, greater use of state funds for education, crippled persons and the mentally and physically handicapped, repeal of prohibition laws, reforms in the administration of justice, reforestation and proper land use.

You will also find extended discussion of many of the themes that he was later to use so frequently that they came to be well known as a part of the Roosevelt philosophy: the interdependence of all groups of the population—city and farm; subsistence homesteads and the resettlement of population; regional planning; bringing industry into rural areas; conservation of natural resources; separation of legislative from executive functions.

In style and form, as distinguished from substance, the speeches were not given so much attention and effort when he was Governor as when he became President. However, even in style and general composition you will find a substantial similarity between these earlier documents and the later ones.

By the time he became Governor, his basic philosophies and principles had been pretty well formed. In a general way he had thought a great deal about nearly all the subjects on which he later proposed legislative reforms. His ideas became more specific and concrete through assiduous reading and long hours of conversation with experts whom he invited to come to see him—usually for dinner and to spend the night.

He used to love, as he put it, to "bat ideas around" with people who were sympathetic to his general philosophy and objectives. And he learned fast—so fast that he amazed the people from whom he learned. He could quickly squeeze every bit of information he wanted from a visitor. And he was able to retain it, although he seldom made notes other than a few words on a pad, which he soon threw away.

During the Albany days there was usually a steady stream of visitors from all parts of the state and indeed from other parts of the country. The Roosevelts liked to have the guest rooms in the Executive Mansion occupied as much as they did later in the White House. The occupants of those guest rooms contributed many ideas.

To take one example in detail—Roosevelt, time and again, had come out strongly for the public development of water power. Closely allied was the whole problem of the adequate regulation of public utility companies, especially electric and gas companies. The New York Public Service Commission was not doing the job of consumer protection which had been envisaged when it was first created in 1907. From the way Roosevelt talked about the subject in public and in private, it was easy to see that he had thought about it a great deal, and that he had discussed it with many persons. His general objective was clear, and he had stated it several times very plainly: to get cheap electricity for the consumers of the state and particularly to get it into the homes and farms. He knew that electric rates were too high; that until they were drastically reduced, the benefits of electricity would never reach as many people as they should. He felt he could accomplish a reduction in two ways: first, by development of cheap electricity through the state's water power, especially on the St. Lawrence River; and second, by a militant, affirmative regulation of the existing electricity companies. But he wanted advice on how best to do it.

So during 1929 and 1930, he invited to the Mansion people who had spent many years in the field: Milo R. Maltbie, an expert adviser to municipalities in rate cases, who was later to become his appointee as Chairman of the Public Service Commission; Leland Olds, a public-minded student of the subject, who was later to become his appointee on the Federal Power Commission; Julius Henry Cohen, an experienced lawyer in this field, who had worked with Governor Smith on water power and who was to become the counsel to the St. Lawrence Water Power Commission; Professor J. C. Bonbright, of Columbia University, who was an acknowledged expert and instructor in the subject.

Leland Olds, invited to meet Roosevelt for the first time, was quite nervous and excited as he was shown to his room in the stately old Executive Mansion one late afternoon. I went up to his room to greet him, since I had already spoken to him on the phone several times. After a while, we wandered downstairs to meet the Governor as we heard his car, which had called for him at the office, come to a stop at the back door.

The Roosevelt greeting made Olds think that the Governor had been waiting for this opportunity all his life, and that his whole legislative program depended on what Olds was going to tell him. This never failed. As experienced as I was with it, I used to get the same impression as he greeted me when I would come down in later years from New York to Washington to do some work for him.

Then, as he got out of the car, "How about joining me for a swim in the pool?" he asked. It was midwinter, but a heated pool had been constructed in the old hothouse, and in it the Governor took his water exercises quite faithfully. A bathing suit was the last thing Olds had thought to bring along to Albany in February; but he came over and watched us in the pool.

At dinner there were just four of us, Missy acting as the hostess. There was not a word of the business for which Olds had come. Everything was discussed except water power and utility regulation. That was typical of Roosevelt on such an occasion. He liked to give his full attention to the main subject, undiverted by dinner-table conversation. And Roosevelt enjoyed the small table talk of dinner so much that unless time was terribly pressing he hated to discuss any business at that time. Also, he wanted to make his visitor feel perfectly at ease before they began serious discussion.

When dinner was over, I got his chair and wheeled him from the dining room to his comfortable couch in the small study where we all had coffee. Roosevelt had been doing most of the talking at dinner, and continued to do so until the coffee cups were removed. Finally:

"Mr. Olds, it was nice of you to come up here. I've been thinking about this problem for many years. Back on one of the dirt roads of Dutchess County, about ten miles from Hyde Park, I know an old farm family who settled there in 1828"—then came some history of the farm family, with rather minute details down to 1928.

"Now they have been watching electricity come along in Poughkeepsie and Rhinebeck and even in Hyde Park more and more each year. And they have tried for years to get electricity out where they are, and they just can't. They and the other farmers are willing to pay, but the damned old electric corporation won't listen; says they can't afford the expense of the line. Of course, that's nonsense. I know something about their stock"—then came a long description of the finances of the local electric corporation, whose bonds Roosevelt's grandfather had bought many years ago.

"Now that farmer's wife still has to pump her water by hand, and sew by oil lamp, and cook by wood. The farm chores and household chores take so much time that they have no chance for rest and leisure.

"I want to get cheap electricity out to that farm."

Roosevelt thought of social and economic problems and reforms not in the abstract but in terms of people and how people would benefit.

Most often it was people whom he had met in his life around Hyde Park or in Poughkeepsie or down in Warm Springs. Sometimes the people were real; sometimes he made them up to illustrate a point. But even though he made them up, they became real to him after a while because he was so deeply interested in the effect of his actions on people. When he talked about the benefits of cheap electricity he did not think in terms of kilowatts; he thought in terms of the hired hand milking by electricity, the farm wife's pump, stove, lights and sewing machine going by electricity; he thought of the difficulty that confronted the small shopkeeper competing with the large chain store without being able to afford electricity.

"I know generally what lies at the basis of the breakdown of regulation we have now," he continued. "It's the complicated and outworn valuation procedure which we still follow; and it's the failure of the Commission to be forceful in protecting the consumer. And I know all the problems of transmission lines and distribution lines for public power development. But we've just got to find a way."

Olds had tried to interrupt, but unsuccessfully.

"Now," Roosevelt went on, "I've been thinking that the whole reproduction cost theory of valuation is the bunk and that overvaluation is as bad now as overcapitalization was in the old days. Tell me what you think about the prudent investment principle as a basis of rate making."

I pulled out my pad and pencil to take notes as Olds began to answer. I knew I would have to prepare the first draft of a speech or message on the subject, and I was not able to absorb and retain it all the way the Governor could.

Roosevelt interrupted Olds frequently and courteously. If he did not quite understand, he frankly said so, and asked him to repeat.

"Yes, but what do you think the courts would do about it—what has been the latest trend of the decisions?" he asked.

And a long series of other questions:

"Isn't the accounting of these companies questionable; shouldn't there be a uniform system of accounts?

"Shouldn't the function of the Public Service Commission be less judicial in nature and more administrative and forceful?

"What do you think of a People's Counsel to protect the consumer in rate cases?

"Don't we need a real club in the closet that we can use to make the companies behave decently—like municipal power plants?"

Some of these questions I had heard him put to other people. Some were new and had been suggested by his talks with the others, and by some things which Olds had said.

By eleven o'clock, the Governor rang for refreshments. He usually took what is called a "horse's neck"—a long glass of ginger ale with lemon peel in it. Later, after the repeal of prohibition when good beer returned to the market, he would, at this late hour, take beer.

So it went, question and answer, until after midnight. And then, the frequent final question:

"Tell me, what would you recommend if you were Governor?"

When the time came for bed, the Governor expressed his thanks, and, as usual with his overnight guests, he asked Olds to come into his bedroom in the morning after breakfast to say good-by. By this time Olds—as nearly every other visitor who came up on a similar errand— was a little the worse for wear but completely "sold" on Roosevelt, on his sincerity of purpose and on his determination to fight for his objectives.

Many of the ideas expressed that night found their way into a series of messages which the Governor sent to the Legislature in 1929 and 1930—a complete, well-formulated program of utility regulation.

After he had finished with several visitors like Olds, Roosevelt had a good working grasp of a subject, and his conversation showed it.

The same kind of process was followed in many fields of his legislative program. He did the same thing later in Washington.

Even in the early Albany days, I was amazed that he never seemed to worry. He would think a problem through very carefully. Having come to a decision, he would dismiss it from his mind as finished business. He never went back to it to worry about whether his decision was right. As I heard him put it on one occasion:

"Once you've made a decision, there's no use worrying about whether you were right or wrong. Events will soon prove whether you were right or wrong, and if there is still time you can change the decision. You and I know people who wear out the carpets walking up and down worrying whether they have decided something correctly. Do the very best you can in making up your mind, but once your mind is made up go ahead."

To the men who worked around him and who were prone to worry a great deal about all the momentous decisions that Roosevelt had to make, this was one of his most amazing traits. It persisted down to his death. Even when a decision concerned hundreds of thousands of lives, as on D-Day in 1944, for example, the President, although deeply concerned and anxious and tragically worn down by the prospective casualty lists, did not continue to debate in his own mind whether the decision had been right to attack across the Channel instead of another way.

Even less did he seem to worry about his physical infirmity. The first physical thing that struck you on meeting Roosevelt was that huge, powerful body without the use of legs. As you got to know Roosevelt, it was also the first thing you forgot. The wheel chair, always present in the background, soon became a normal part of the furniture of the room. Wheeling him in to dinner or to bed became as routine as offering your arm to your dinner partner. It was something that he himself seemed never to think much about. In fact, when he wanted to end a conversation or a visit, he frequently would say: "Well, I'm sorry, I have to run now!"—and I am sure it never struck him as a strange thing to say, even though he had not been able to walk since 1921.

I do not recall ever hearing him complain about his inability to walk, or ever refer to it in sadness or self-pity, except on one occasion. A number of us at Hyde Park were going out to look at some trees he had had planted deep in the woods many years before. He could not drive his car close enough to see them, and as we got out to walk into the woods, he said: "I'm sorry, I can't go with you, I'd like to see those trees again after all these years, but"—and he sadly pointed to his wasted legs.

Certainly his disability had no effect upon his energy and the amount of hard work of which he was capable. Although from the day of his first nomination in 1928 down to the day of his death in 1945 there were questions raised about his physical vigor, I never saw a man who worked harder. The loss of the full use of his legs deprived him of many of the diversions and amusements of other persons; the time he might so have spent he put largely into work. The campaign of 1928, for example, tired out every one of us except him; on one day he made as many as fourteen speeches. No public office except the Presidency imposes so heavy a burden on a man as the Governorship of New York. Roosevelt added to the burden by traveling more, by making more speeches and public appearances, than any Governor before him.

He generally followed the same daily work routine in Albany that he did later in Washington. He had breakfast in bed at about eight, during which he read papers, talked with his immediate staff, and laid out the work for the day. Then about ten in the morning to the Capitol, where he worked without stop, with lunch at his desk, until five in the afternoon. Then home for a swim and some tea, frequently with visitors on official or political business. Dinner was often with one or more friends, public officials or official guests, seldom alone. After dinner—except for a rare social evening—he was wheeled into his study, where he continued to work on papers, speeches, bills; he even carried memoranda and reports to bed; frequently he continued to discuss business with me or others after getting into bed. And he always had to read several late newspapers before finally turning out the light.

There were exceptions, of course, to this routine, but they were rare. He believed in frequent vacations, but even on vacation work was sent to him by mail or wire or radio. I doubt whether—from the time he was first nominated for Governor until his death—a single day ever passed without some part of it being devoted to public affairs. I got used to this routine and, when I lived at the Mansion, I became a part of it, leaving for the office with him and returning home with him. It was a difficult pace to keep.

By 1930 Roosevelt was recognized as a confirmed and relentless liberal, and he had shown that behind his aristocratic bearing there were plenty of "guts." It was a series of fights with the conservative Republican Legislature that did more than anything else to bring him national prominence. In tangible results, many of the fights were unsuccessful; but even the unsuccessful ones dramatically advertised Roosevelt and his policies to the whole nation. Some of the fights he won; they resulted in progressive legislation which spread his reputation as a progressive Governor and as an effective leader. At the end of the very first Legislative Session in 1929, labor organizations, farm organizations and consumers organizations—liberals of all classes and groups—joined in his praise.

During his first term as Governor, the Republican leaders fought him bitterly on nearly every progressive measure he recommended—

and wound up by grudgingly passing a good part of his program. There were several reasons for his striking victories. New York State—like the nation as a whole—was liberal in its political thinking. The Republican leaders stupidly opposed much that Roosevelt suggested simply because it was he who had suggested it and they were fearful of the political advantage to him if they passed his measures.

But the most potent reason was Roosevelt's adept use of what came later to be known as the fireside chat. From time to time during each session of the Legislature he delivered a very simple, direct, chatty radio talk in which he told the people of the state what was currently going on in Albany, and appealed to them for help in his fight with the Legislature. He also did this after each session, reporting on the failures and accomplishments of the year. A flood of letters would deluge the members of the Legislature after each talk, and they were the best weapon Roosevelt had in his struggles for legislation. For these radio speeches I used to gather the material, but most of the talks were prepared by the Governor himself. As he showed later in his Washington fireside chats, he was a master at presenting the most complicated matter in the most understandable terms.

In the first of his annual reports (1929), for example, see how disarming and effective he was right in his opening statement:

As a statewide elected official, I feel I have a distinct duty to keep the people of the State informed as far as possible as to what goes on in the State Government. And I am very mindful of the fact that I am the Governor not just of Democrats, but of Republicans and all other citizens of the State. That is why this talk . . . will be just as much as I can make [it], nonpartisan in character. I want merely to state facts and leave the people of the State to draw their own conclusions.

He proceeded to show how the Republican leaders had violated every one of their major platform pledges, and how he had tried to carry out the Democratic pledges, only to be blocked by a hostile Legislature. And he did not hesitate to appeal to the people to repudiate legislators who refused to carry out their will.

That speech was typical of the others. He delivered them from his study at the Mansion, in the same informal conversational tone that the rest of America was to hear so many times from his "fireside" in Washington.

He was not satisfied with radio contacts with the people, however. Each summer, he made informal inspection trips around the state, meeting and speaking to thousands of people, telling them what he was trying to do and what the Republican leaders were doing to block him. Never did he use words more successfully to build up popular support than during 1929 and 1930. The election results of 1930 showed what he had accomplished during the two years since the dangerously close election of 1928.

After the 1930 legislative bills were disposed of, the Governor as usual went to Warm Springs for a rest. From there he sent me a letter after a week or so which I quote in part because it discloses one of the secrets of Roosevelt's fine public relations. There he was in Warm Springs on a vacation. All editorials and important news items were clipped and sent to him (especially those from papers upstate, where he was trying to build up a strong Democratic party). He busily singled out those that were unfavorable, such as the one mentioned in the letter, and was ready to go to no end of trouble to correct any misunderstanding or error of fact. He did this constantly—sometimes about subjects that seemed to me quite trivial, and often with very unimportant newspapers. But, in terms of public understanding and approval, it always seemed to pay.

I am enclosing an editorial from the Binghamton Press in regard to the Lord-Bentley grouse bill. Will you have a talk with Alec Macdonald in regard to it and suggest to Alec that he write me a letter for me to send to the Binghamton Press to show to them that there is no intention of creating an open season for grouse this year, and that their editorial is based wholly on misinformation. Further, that he, the Conservation Commissioner, will keep the season closed, as he has a right to do, by a department order. He ought to be a little indignant at the thought that the Conservation Department will encourage the extinction of ruffed grouse. . . .

Roosevelt's opponent in the fall of 1930 was Charles H. Tuttle, who had been the United States Attorney for the Southern District of New York, which included New York City. By this time, the great depression which had struck the United States in October, 1929, was beginning to have a devastating effect all through the country, including the State of New York. Unemployment was rising rapidly and the distress of the unemployed was becoming acute.

There were two factors that cast doubt on Roosevelt's re-election in November. First, during the spring and summer of 1930 there had been many disclosures of graft and corruption in the government of the City of New York. Second, prohibition had become a major issue in the campaign, for the Democratic party had adopted a platform calling for its outright appeal. The Republican platform was something of a straddle. Upstate New York was regarded as normally dry territory, and it was feared that the Democratic plank would hurt us very seriously in those counties, especially since Roosevelt had taken a strong personal position for repeal.

The campaign of 1930 was as strenuous as the campaign of 1928. It was conducted in much the same manner. Constant advice and assistance, and sometimes drafts of campaign speeches were furnished by Louis Howe and Basil O'Connor, who was a law partner, close friend and able and astute associate of the Governor. O'Connor worked on speeches very frequently with me, especially when Roosevelt was in New York City; he had a very effective and forceful manner of writing.

By this time I was pretty thoroughly familiar with the Governor's style of writing. I had worked on so many speeches and messages during the last two years, I had seen so many of his corrections and had heard so much of his own dictation, that it was easier for me to imitate him. Consequently he had to make fewer corrections, and my drafts were not so badly mutilated as they used to be.

The issue between liberalism and conservatism was even more sharply defined this year than it had been two years before. The bitter legislative struggles of the two sessions of 1929 and 1930 had highlighted and emphasized the differences between the two political parties. In his speeches the Governor concentrated on this issue. But he knew that if he was to win by a substantial majority, he would have to get the votes of many hundreds of thousands of normally Republican voters. He did not want to alienate them by attacks on "Republicans" or even on the "Republican party," so he followed a practice that he continued through all his Washington days—centering his attack on the Republican *leadership* and *leaders*, rather than on the Republican voters.

"There are thousands of people who call themselves Republicans," he said to me once, "who think as you and I do about government. They are enrolled as Republicans because their families have been Republicans for generations—that's the only reason; some of them think it is *infra dig* (another common phrase of his) to be called a Democrat; the Democrats in their village are not the socially 'nice' people the enrolled Republicans are. So never attack the Republicans or the Republican party—only the Republican *leaders*. Then any Republican voter who hears it will say to himself: 'Well, he doesn't mean me, I don't believe in the things that Machold and McGinnies and Knight and the other reactionaries up in Albany believe in either.' "

This seemed incredible to me at first. But after years of experience in talking with Republican friends, I have been amazed at how many of them reacted to this simple bit of psychology exactly as Roosevelt said they would.

This paragraph from his acceptance speech in 1930 is typical of the way he would phrase it:

Let me make it perfectly clear that in my judgment this Republican leadership does not represent the great rank and file of the men and women of this State who call themselves Republicans. Let me make it perfectly clear that I am confident that they, in large numbers, will recognize this autumn, as they have recognized before, that Government at Albany must be and shall be progressive, and that they are still as out of step with the leadership of their own Party as they have been in the past.

In his acceptance speech, on which Howe and O'Connor and I all worked with him, he struck a new note—a note that was soon to grow in volume and develop into a forceful attack upon the Hoover Administration:

"Lack of leadership at Washington has brought our country face to face with serious questions of unemployment and financial depression. Each State must meet this situation as best it can. . . ." In only a few months Roosevelt was going to lead his own state into definite action against the distress of unemployment.

During the campaign, he blamed the Republican Administration (1) for not putting brakes on the speculation orgy of 1928 and 1929, (2) for concealing from the people the seriousness of the situation after the crash and for issuing false, optimistic statements about it, and (3) for failure to take quick and decisive action—"nothing happened but words." He said he was making these points only to prove an old thesis of his that "no political party has any monopoly on prosperity," although the Republican party had for many years preached that it had.

As another main thesis of the campaign, he hammered home what he had done in two short years on labor legislation, old age pensions, hospitals, public works, cheap electricity, regulation of public utilities, prisons and the other items of his program.

His knack of homely exposition enabled him to get across to the people in forceful and understandable language his ideas about cheap electricity. Instead of talking about kilowatt hours and technical machinery for developing and transmitting water power, he dwelt on how much it cost a woman in Toronto, Canada (where water power was developed publicly), to use electric appliances like a stove, refrigerator, iron, toaster, vacuum cleaner, waffle iron, etc., as contrasted to a woman in Syracuse or Brooklyn or Utica, who had to pay six or eight times as much per hour. Some graphic campaign material was devised that used the same theme and showed the same contrasts. The speeches and campaign pamphlets got so much attention and circulation that many people referred to the 1930 campaign as a "waffle iron" campaign. It was very successful, and got the Governor widespread support from the women of the state.

This year a political situation prevailed upstate that was quite unprecedented in the history of New York. As a result of the Governor's comprehensive program of farm relief—which the Republican leaders had not quite dared to reject—the farmers, who were traditionally Republican voters, had become his staunch supporters. Hundreds of thousands of people who lived by agriculture were going to vote for a Democrat for Governor for the first time in their lives.

His position on all these state issues was piling up more upstate support for him every day as the campaign progressed; and his stand on prohibition was giving him unusual strength in the large cities. The Republican Administration in Washington was getting scared. An overwhelming victory for Roosevelt in 1930 would be a Republican disaster not only in New York but in the whole country. And if Roosevelt was to be stopped for 1932, the time to do it was in 1930. So, in their desperation, the Washington Republican leaders made the mistake that Roosevelt always avoided (except for the ill-fated "purge" of 1938): they decided to come into New York and campaign against him.

Three high Cabinet officers appeared on the stump in New York: the Secretary of State, Henry L. Stimson; the Under Secretary of Treasury (later Secretary), Ogden L. Mills; and the Secretary of War, Patrick Hurley. Most of their attacks, especially Stimson's, were directed at the charges of Democratic corruption in New York City. The weight of these gentlemen was beginning to be felt in the campaign.

How to handle this? Roosevelt decided on ridicule, and gave O'Connor and me instructions to center the attack on federal interference in state elections. We saved our ammunition for the last speech, the big speech in New York City, to give it the widest publicity. O'Connor drafted this part of the speech and, after the Governor had revised it, it was a most effective kind of *ad hominem* argument. It is hardly remembered now; but in its way it was comparable in its use of ridicule to the "Fala" speech of 1944:

Before we look into the soundness of the instructions given to the people of this State by these representatives at Washington we have a right to demand that they show their credentials. Of these three estimable gentlemen, one comes from that great State of Oklahoma, which we all respect. He has never lived in New York State; he knows nothing of the problems of New York State; he knows nothing of the situation in New York City; he knows nothing of the requirements and necessities of the twelve million people of this State. Whatever information he has, has been given to him obviously by the members of his own party. It can hardly be said that he has been impartially informed on our affairs. And yet he comes to us presumably only by virtue of his great office. Well may the people of New York State resent this, as would the people of Oklahoma if the tables were turned.

The other two gentlemen of this triumvirate, the Secretary of State and the Under-Secretary of the Treasury, are both citizens of this State. The credentials that they present to the people of the State as authorizing them to give instructions are the same in both cases. Both of them have run for Governor in campaigns based largely upon the same kind of tactics as are being employed in this campaign. Both of them were *defeated* at the polls by the people of this State. The people did not believe in them or in their issues then, and they will not believe in them or in their issues now. . . .

And now . . . let us examine into the soundness of the instructions which they have given us. The substance of their instructions to us is this: That the only issue in this campaign is judges in New York City, and nothing else counts.

Then he heaped ridicule on them for not discussing the real issues: prohibition, water power, old age insurance, farm relief, etc.

And he concluded:

They and their party, this present national Administration, came before this State two years ago soliciting the votes of its people on representations, promises and prophecies. They represented themselves as the creators of the prosperity of the country. . . . Under them prosperity had always prevailed, and only under them could prosperity continue. Poverty was on its way to be abolished. There is no need for me to demonstrate to you how false were those representations, those promises and those prophecies. There is no need for me to point out to you what has been unfortunately experienced by almost every man, woman and child in the Nation.

I say to these gentlemen: We shall be grateful if you will return to your posts in Washington, and bend your efforts and spend your time solving the problems which the whole Nation is bearing under your Administration. Rest assured that we of the Empire State can and will take care of ourselves and our problems.

Right on the eve of election, the speech had a telling effect.

In the same speech he dealt with the damaging charges that had been hurled at him all through the campaign of corruption and bribery in the appointing of judges in New York City. Although he was doing all that he could in this purely local situation—which had nothing to do with state issues—the charges were blown up and exaggerated by nearly all the state newspapers, and seemed to be threatening seriously his chances for re-election.

Roosevelt was a firm believer that a candidate should pick his own battleground in a political campaign, as a general does in a military campaign. By the same token, he said: "Never let your opponent pick the battleground on which to fight. If he picks one, stay out of it and let him fight all by himself."

Since in this campaign the Republican strategy was to use New York City corruption as the chief battleground, Roosevelt spoke about everything except New York City. The more Tuttle talked about New York City judges, the more Roosevelt talked about water power and old age pensions. He completely and consistently ignored the Republican charges—until he got down to New York City at the end of the campaign. Here he had decided to meet them once—and meet them head on. This was not an easy matter to handle. Roosevelt told O'Connor and me how he thought it should be done:

"The important thing is not to be apologetic or defensive. We in Albany have nothing to be ashamed of; we have done all the law allows us to do to uncover graft in the City of New York. Unless they can show some neglect on my part, this has nothing to do with state issues. We must drive that home to the people, but at the same time make it plain that we are just as anxious as anyone to get rid of and punish corruption."

When the Governor had finished correcting the draft O'Connor and I had prepared, reciting everything he had done and could do to find the facts and punish the crimes, this is the way it read:

The Republican candidates and a small section of the local press have sought . . . to make the people of this city believe: (1) That the greater part of the 220 judges in this city are corrupt; (2) that as a result the judiciary as a whole is no longer worthy of the confidence of the people; (3) that neither I nor the Democratic Party in city or State would lift a finger to restore confidence in the courts and punish the guilty.

I, as a citizen of the State and as Governor, resent this campaign, as every person in this State who knows me, and who believes in honest and decent government, resents it. . . .

If there are corrupt judges still sitting in our courts they shall be removed. They shall be removed by constitutional means, not by inquisition; not by trial in the press, but by trial as provided by law.

If there is corruption in our courts I will use every rightful power of the office of Governor to drive it out, and I will do this regardless of whether it affects or may affect any Democratic or any Republican organization in any one of the five counties of New York City, or in any one of the fifty-seven other counties of the State. That is clear. That is unequivocal. That is simple honesty. That is justice. That is American. That is right.

Now we have come to the close of the campaign. I ask the electorate of the State of New York for their support. I ask this as a rebuke to those Republican national and State leaders who, substituting false charges and deliberate misrepresentation, have had the cowardice to ignore the great problems and issues before the whole State. . . .

The New York City speech was successful in both objectives he had in mind: to remove by ridicule the effect of the speeches of the Washington Cabinet officers, and to meet the attacks arising out of New York City corruption.

The results of the 1930 campaign made new political history in New York. Election night was quite different from that close call in 1928. From the very first return there was never any doubt. Roosevelt was elected by the unprecedented plurality of 725,001 votes. The highest Democratic plurality before that had been 386,000 for Smith in 1922. Upstate New York, which for generations had been conceded to be safely Republican, gave Roosevelt a plurality of 167,784 votes, and a plurality in 41 of the 57 upstate counties.

What were the reasons for this extraordinary outcome? It was not principally the depression, for there was no similar Democratic trend that year in the New York Congressional elections. It was the work of the last two years of Roosevelt the statesman and liberal leader: his program of help to the farmer, the laborer, the aged, the consumer, the housewife.

It was also the work of the last two years of Roosevelt the politician and political strategist: his build-up of the Democratic party upstate, his constant trips around the state, his radio speeches, his ability to put complicated problems of state government into the A B C category.

It was the warmth of Roosevelt the man and the orator, who knew how to convey his personality and charm to the people he met and to the people he talked with over the air.

Chapter IV

The Second Term as Governor: Washington Horizons, 1930-1932

Overnight, the election results—especially those upstate—made Roosevelt a leading contender for the Democratic nomination for the Presidency in 1932.

The next day, I was among those who rode up to Albany with him on the noonday train from New York City. There was a lot of joking about the Presidency. Roosevelt only laughed. He was with intimate friends on this trip—O'Connor, Howe, Missy, Grace Tully, me—and yet I do not recall his saying seriously even once that he was interested in 1932—or that he was not. We all took for granted that he was, and I am certain that by that morning, if not before, he had concluded that he would become a candidate for the nomination of the Democratic party in 1932.

And so, very shortly after the election of 1930, we were embarked on another campaign. It was a campaign for the nomination for the Presidency.

As is customary, it was not an open campaign. It was conducted by the friends of the candidate rather than by the candidate himself. But he was always consulted on strategy; and he knew that everything he said or did from that time on would be interpreted in the light of his candidacy and would affect it.

This was the period when James A. Farley first began to be closely associated with Franklin D. Roosevelt. At the suggestion of the Governor, Farley had become the chairman of the Democratic State Committee for the election of 1930. He did a splendid job during that year and in the two years that followed. No one could have equaled him.

As a practical politician and organizer, he showed then what a master he was. During this period, Louis Howe also rendered Roosevelt great political service. Both of them used to make weekly trips to Albany to go over political strategy with Roosevelt; and while they did not take any major part in advising on state policy as distinguished from politics, they were right in the center of all the political maneuvering. They were partners in this enterprise; neither could have done as great a job as they did without the other. Frank Walker was also very active on behalf of Roosevelt at this time, and later served in his Cabinet and in other positions of great responsibility.

Roosevelt's national prominence was accentuated by a dramatic and decisive step which he took in the summer of 1931. The depression had now become a national catastrophe. The people of New York—like those of all states—looked to their federal government for some action to relieve their distress. No action came. President Hoover and the Republican leaders had taken the position—and had maintained it stubbornly throughout the depression—that direct relief for unemployment distress was no function of the federal government, but had to come exclusively from local charities and local government. The only action that came out of Washington was the establishment of the Reconstruction Finance Corporation. But it was not set up for the purpose of granting any relief to starving or homeless people; its purpose was to make loans to railroads, financial institutions and other large corporations.

The paralysis that had overtaken the federal government in the matter of relief spread to the various states. The first one to take action was the State of New York. In the winter of 1930 Roosevelt had started a small public works program, and had taken steps to co-ordinate the relief work of various municipalities and private agencies. In March, 1931, he had recommended that the Legislature establish a commission to study the question of unemployment insurance. But the immediate needs quickly grew beyond the scope of this program, and the Governor became more and more worried. He talked about it a great deal, and kept saying privately that the time was soon coming when the states would have to do something if Washington kept to its policy of doing nothing. Finally, after waiting through the dreary winter and spring and most of the summer of 1931 for some action or leadership from Washington, he decided to assume leadership himself and to take action for the State of New York.

It happened that about this time the legislative committee which had been investigating the affairs of New York City asked the Governor to convene the Legislature in extraordinary session in order to pass a technical statute authorizing the committee to grant immunity to witnesses. The Governor said that he would comply with the request; but he had in mind other matters for the Legislature to consider far more important than this minor legal amendment. Under the New York Constitution the Legislature in an extraordinary session can consider only matters that are specifically submitted to it in writing by the Governor.

Consequently, he instructed me to draft the necessary proclamation, and said: "This is the time to get some direct action on unemployment relief. Suppose you take a try at a first draft of a message."

I had a fairly clear idea of what he had in mind. I knew that he had come definitely to the conclusion that the state should go the whole way and appropriate a large sum of money to help the unemployed directly. This kind of direct government action seems quite natural now in 1952—almost routine—but in 1931 it was an extraordinary and startling proposal.

He had told me several times that he was opposed to payment of money by dole, that he thought the state should provide public work for its unemployed citizens, and that if no work could be found for them, they should be given food, clothing, and shelter from public funds.

"The important thing to recognize is that there is a duty on the part of government to do something about this—it just can't sit back and expect private charity or even local government to take care of it entirely."

The message was written largely at Hyde Park, and was sent to the Legislature on August 28, 1931, a date which is important in the history of governmental social thinking in the United States. It contained one of the underlying concepts of the New Deal—that it is the duty of government to use the combined resources of the nation to prevent distress and to promote the general welfare of all the people:

What is the State? It is the duly constituted representative of an organized society of human beings, created by them for their mutual protection and well-being. . . . Our Government is not the master but the creature of the people. The duty of the State toward the citizens is the duty of the servant to its master. The people have created it; the people, by common consent, permit its continual existence.

One of these duties of the State is that of caring for those of its citizens who find themselves the victims of such adverse circumstance as makes them unable to obtain even the necessities for mere existence without the aid of others. . . .

While it is true that we have hitherto principally considered those who through accident or old age were permanently incapacitated, the same responsibility of the State undoubtedly applies when widespread economic conditions render large numbers of men and women incapable of supporting either themselves or their families because of circumstances beyond their control which make it impossible for them to find remunerative labor. To these unfortunate citizens aid must be extended by Government, not as a matter of charity, but as a matter of *social duty*.

Pointing out that local charities and local government could not meet the new burdens, he recommended that the state immediately appropriate $20,000,000, to be raised by new taxes, to provide useful work for the needy where possible, and where such work could not be found, "to provide them with food against starvation and with clothing and shelter against suffering."

To emphasize the importance of this message, he went up in person to deliver it to the Legislature.

In the State of New York and all through the nation, the message was a breath of fresh air in the stagnant, depressing fog of inaction and indecision which had come from Washington.

In 1952 it seems unbelievable, but the Republican leaders at Albany in 1931 decided to oppose Roosevelt on this recommendation. He had offered to let Republican legislators introduce the necessary legislation and thus share the political credit with him. Roosevelt the politician did not make such a noble gesture to his political opponents except in times of extraordinary crisis, such as 1941. His offer in 1931 showed how anxious he was that some direct relief be provided quickly. Intelligent leadership in the Republican party would have eagerly seized his offer. But Governor Roosevelt was blessed politically with bitter and unintelligent opposition. His political luck did not fail him this time.

The Republican leaders rejected his offer. Instead, in a stupid attempt to stop Roosevelt's bold, far-sighted program, they introduced some ineffective, "wishy-washy" legislation (another common expression of Roosevelt). In spite of almost universal condemnation, they stuck to their guns, prepared with their majority of votes to put through their own program and to adjourn. Roosevelt publicly explained the vital defects of their program, threatened to veto their bill, and stated that he would call the Legislature back again into a second extraordinary session to pass an effective bill. Finally, at the very last hour, the Republican leaders capitulated. They incorporated practically all his ideas in their bill, passed it and adjourned. Their actions in first opposing Roosevelt and then yielding to him increased his national stature and prestige almost as much as the merits of the legislation itself.

The message and the victory which followed increased Roosevelt's lead in the race for the nomination to oppose President Hoover in 1932. Between these two men a fundamental issue of political and economic philosophy had been drawn in precise and dramatic fashion. On the one hand was the laissez-faire doctrine of Hoover that the problem of the depression would finally work itself out, and that it should be allowed to do so no matter what the cost might be in human misery. On the other hand was the doctrine of Roosevelt that the government had an affirmative duty to step in with bold action, and to use the resources of the nation to stop the distress and prevent ultimate disaster.

The activities of Governor Roosevelt's friends in his behalf now became more strenuous. As the depression became worse, and as the leaders of the Republican party in Washington continued to refuse to take any substantial action to meet the emergency, President Hoover's chances of re-election rapidly faded. Spurred on by the scent of victory, a great many candidates for the Democratic nomination appeared.

In Roosevelt's favor were a number of tangibles and intangibles. His continued fight for the liberal social and economic objectives, his energy and physical stamina, which had reduced public concern about his crippled condition, his successful struggles with the New York legislative leaders—and even his unsuccessful ones—had increased his reputation throughout the country for boldness, initiative, aggressiveness, and spirited leadership. He enjoyed a good fight, and the people liked a fighter. His smile was becoming a national picture—and the people liked a leader who could smile. He seemed to be on terms of close relationship with all the 12,600,000 people of his state—and the contrast to Hoover in this respect was dramatic. The sound of his resonant, persuasive voice was becoming known by radio outside New York; and his audiences all over the nation felt, as they listened, that they were in the same room with him, beside the same fireplace.

He knew how to talk to politicians and political leaders. When local or national leaders visited him at the Executive Mansion—and he saw to it that such visits were frequent—they came away impressed. They had met a reformer, true; but they had also met a practical fellow who knew their problems and was willing—almost anxious—to discuss them frankly. As Governor, he had corresponded personally with political leaders all over the country; and his two chief political workers, Farley and Howe, had carried on an enormous correspondence with them.

Roosevelt, as Governor and later as President, recognized the value of political organizations and the contribution they could make toward electing good men to office. He knew how necessary it was to work with political organizations on matters of patronage in order to keep them strong and effective. He was often accused of too active co-operation with politicians, especially those in the larger cities. But he recognized that successful practical politics required the leadership of political specialists who could and would spend part of each day of the year in political activity, and that no political party or candidate could rely for success exclusively on those who spent only election day and primary day on politics. That is why he encouraged and helped the growth of political organizations. That is why, on many occasions, he sought their help, took their advice, and followed their recommendations for appointments.

He was sure that politics could be an honorable, as well as a necessary, profession. He abhorred the tendency of many Americans to look upon practical politics as something dirty and dishonest, feeling that this attitude kept out of political and public life many qualified and conscientious men and women who could have rendered great service to their country.

He had raised the level of public understanding of government issues by his frank and simple talks about them to the people of the state. He had also raised the level of debate in the Legislature itself.

Early in the first session of 1929 he said to me:

"I'm going to arrange to have the Democratic leaders in each house meet with us at luncheon every Monday to go over the legislative program for the week. There has been too little contact between the third floor [where the New York Assembly and Senate meet] and the second floor [where the Executive Chamber is located]. They don't understand fully what I am trying to do, and their debates show it. So next Monday I'm going to have the leader in each House, Herbert [Lehman, the Lieutenant Governor], and you to lunch for a long talk, and we'll do it every Monday during the session."

"Governor, I think you ought to expand the list a little," I said. "I've been in the Assembly myself for five years and the leader can't carry the ball himself all the time. You ought to let each leader bring two of his colleagues with him and perhaps change them every couple of weeks or so. Then they can all help in the debates; and, besides, the more of them who can meet you and talk to you personally, the more enthusiasm there will be in the debates."

And so it was. Each Monday during the legislative sessions, we met at the Executive Mansion at lunch. These luncheon meetings lasted as long as three hours.

The news of the luncheons soon leaked out, and the improved standard of debate on the floor of each House showed how effective they had been. Because at the first few lunches the main dish was roast turkey, the group got to be popularly known as the "Turkey Cabinet."

Many years later, when relations between Roosevelt as President and the Democratic members of the Congress became strained, as they did periodically, I urged him to revive this practice. I know that others used to urge him also, including Mrs. Roosevelt. But we were all unsuccessful.

"I just haven't got the time," he protested, "and besides, there are so many of them that we could never get around to all."

I was never convinced that these were the true reasons. In the Congress the Democratic leaders are much less disposed to follow the Chief Executive than are those in the Legislature in Albany. The Governor commands more support from members of his party in Albany than the President does in Washington. Roosevelt was convinced that a Turkey Cabinet in the White House would not produce the same results that it had in the Executive Mansion. I think also that he was so angry and shocked at the voting record of some of the men he would have had to include that the meetings would have been personally distasteful to him. Roosevelt hated to talk about government affairs with people who had offended him deeply or whom he disliked. He would at times carry this feeling to extremes—for example, refusing to see a committee of the Congress that had requested an appointment, because of his deep dislike of one member of the committee.

Roosevelt had shown by 1932 his mastery of the intricate game of politics, especially where rough-and-tumble tactics with political opponents were required. He had enough experience and understanding of politics and government to know that a good compromise bill today —so long as it did not sacrifice principle—was better than the hazy prospect of a perfect bill in the indefinite future. This willingness to compromise on small matters was a part of his general distaste for details —and his inefficiency in dealing with them. He was fond of looking at what he liked to call the "whole picture," and if its composition was good and its general effect was what he wanted, he did not worry about two or three badly executed lines in the painting.

The national political atmosphere in 1932 seemed to shout for a progressive Democrat who liked bold action—the very antithesis of Hoover. Roosevelt fitted the bill perfectly. If being a progressive means the willingness to advocate change in order to meet changing conditions, that was the very foundation of Roosevelt's political thinking. The dictum of Macaulay, "Reform if you would preserve," was one of Roosevelt's maxims, which he quoted frequently and observed always. That is why he was always so receptive to new ideas; that is why in administering affairs of state he believed so strongly in "bold persistent experimentation."

In physical appearance, he had the dignity and the bearing that Americans like to see in their Presidents. He disdained any attempts at pretentiousness. He did not seek to impose respect toward himself on visitors or friends or servants; like all natural-born leaders, he seemed to command respect and affection unconsciously.

His campaigning of 1928 and 1930 showed what a great campaigner he could become in 1932.

So it was no wonder that, aided by Farley's services in corralling delegates, Roosevelt by the spring of 1932 had forged way out in front in the political race.

Chapter V

The Brain Trust, 1932

On January 22, 1932, Roosevelt publicly declared his candidacy. Thereafter, he had to become more and more concerned with matters beyond the boundaries of the state—with the whole field of national and international affairs. While his basic philosophy and objectives in meeting national problems would be the same as they had been in state affairs, his specific handling of the new problems was going to be far different.

I personally was beginning to get worried about this new field of activity. The issues involved reached beyond my own experience. We had used experts freely in particular fields in state affairs, but the job that had to be done on the national scene required more than just expert, specialized technicians. The whole American economy seemed to be going rapidly to pieces before our eyes. Technicians and financial experts were being called down to Washington almost daily to consult with President Hoover; but things kept going from bad to worse.

One evening in March, after we had finished the business in hand and as we were about to retire for the night, I told the Governor what was on my mind, and added:

"The time has come, I think, to get together some up-to-date information about the troubles with our economy and the worst danger spots—and some ideas on what to do about them. If you were to be nominated tomorrow and had to start a campaign trip within ten days, we'd be in an awful fix. You would be without a well-defined and thought-out affirmative program. It would be pretty hard to get up intelligent speeches overnight on the many subjects you would have to discuss."

He was interested at once. It was easy to tell when he was listening out of politeness and when he really wanted to listen. There was always something about the eyes, about the tilt of the head, the outthrust jaw, that seemed to say: "Go ahead, I'm listening."

"I think we ought to get some people together to discuss the national problems of today, and see whether we can come up with some answers or at least with some good new intelligent thinking, pro and con, and some new ideas."

"Do you have anyone in mind?" he asked.

"Well, no one in particular, but I do have a strong feeling about the kind of people they ought to be and the kind they ought not to be."

He looked up expectantly.

"Usually in a situation like this," I went on, "a candidate gathers around him a group composed of some successful industrialists, some big financiers, and some national political leaders. I think we ought to steer clear of all those. They all seem to have failed to produce anything constructive to solve the mess we're in today. Now my idea is this: Why not go to the universities of the country? You have been having some good experiences with college professors. I think they wouldn't be afraid to strike out on new paths just because the paths are new. They would get away from all the old fuzzy thinking on many subjects, and that seems to me to be the most important thing."

"What would you have them do—exactly?" he asked cautiously.

This was something new, and he was deeply interested. But he wanted to get nominated and elected—that was the important thing—and he was not sure whether this kind of group would help or hinder.

"I don't know exactly. We'll have to kind of feel our way as we go along. My thought is that if we can get a small group together willing to give us some time, they can prepare memoranda for you about such things as the relief of agriculture, tariffs, railroads, government debts, private credit, money, gold standard—all the things that enter into the present crisis; the things you will have to take a definite stand on. You'll want to talk with them yourself, and maybe out of all the talk some concrete ideas will come."

After a pause and several puffs on his cigarette, his eyes on the ceiling, he said, "O.K., go ahead."

"The first one I thought I would talk with," I said, "is Ray Moley. He believes in your social philosophy and objectives, and he has a clear and forceful style of writing. Being a university professor himself, he can suggest different university people in different fields. Is that all right with you?"

The Governor nodded. I was not quite sure, as I wheeled him to his bedroom and talked of other things, that he was too enthusiastic about the whole idea. But I knew that he needed help then, just as he did, in a much less important way, during the gubernatorial campaign of 1928.

"We'll have to keep this whole thing pretty quiet," he said as he shifted to his bed from the wheel chair. "Do you think these professors can be trusted not to talk about it on the outside? If it gets into the papers too soon it might be bad."

Then he thought awhile—and, as his mind probably dwelt on the speeches he was already committed to make fairly soon on national subjects, he said:

"Well, we'll just have to take our chances on that."

And thus was born a peculiar institution in American political life, and a new phrase in American political jargon: the "Brain Trust."

I had come to know Professor Raymond Moley of Columbia University through his association as a member and executive director of the New York State Commission on the Administration of Justice. The commission had been set up on Roosevelt's recommendation and the Governor was very interested in its work. At that time, Moley seemed to agree with the social and economic philosophy of Roosevelt, and had told me repeatedly that he would like to be helpful in the pre-convention national campaign. Here was a place where he could be most useful. I called him on the phone and asked him to come up to Albany, which he did.

I explained to him what the Governor had in mind, and he was enthusiastic. I told him that I had suggested him as one who might get together a group of college instructors, and that Roosevelt had approved.

"The first thing is for you to talk to several of them and see whether they would be willing to do this for Roosevelt. Maybe some of them have other candidates whom they would prefer. The people we use must be strongly for Roosevelt. They must be discreet, and not talk to people about what they are doing. We have no money to pay them with, so it will have to be done on the basis of willingness to promote the progressive policies of the candidate. Do you think you can find such men who are equipped to do what we have in mind?"

He felt sure he could.

"Well, suppose you think about some of the people, and the next time I get down to New York I'll ask Doc O'Connor [as Basil O'Connor was familiarly known] to meet you and me at my apartment, and we'll discuss them."

Our first meeting took place shortly thereafter. Moley had prepared a list of subjects and a tentative list of men.

Agriculture was on the list—and the name of Professor Rexford G. Tugwell of Columbia was suggested. Tariffs was on the list—and Professor Lindsay Rogers of Columbia was the name recommended. The name of Adolf A. Berle, Jr., of Columbia was opposite the subject of Credit.

Doc and I looked over the list. I had heard of these men, but did not know any of them. We all liked the idea of getting men from universities in New York City, because they would be more readily available for conferences.

"Let's meet these men, one by one," Doc said. I suggested Tugwell first. Roosevelt wanted to lay great emphasis on the sad plight of those who lived by agriculture, and it was a subject I knew practically nothing about nationally.

Moley brought Tugwell to meet us the next day at my apartment; he talked to us at length about the farmers' problems and the kind of action that ought to be taken to help them.

In rapid succession Moley introduced us to the others: to Rogers and Berle, to Professor Joseph D. McGoldrick of Columbia, an expert on government finance who later became Comptroller of New York City under Mayor La Guardia; and to Professor Howard L. McBain of Columbia, an expert on constitutional and administrative law. There were others whom Moley asked merely for memoranda on their particular specialties, without bringing them personally into the group.

While this was going on, a turning point in my own life separated me from official association with Roosevelt for over ten years, until World War II brought us officially together again. My unofficial and informal association, however, continued unbroken.

A vacancy occurred on the Supreme Court Bench of the State of New York at the end of December, 1931.

Ever since I had been admitted to the bar, my ambition, like that of many young lawyers, had been to become a justice of the Supreme Court of New York State. I never dreamed that the opportunity would come in 1932, when I was only thirty-six. However, Roosevelt knew about my ambition, and some of my friends in Albany urged my appointment. I also told him I should like to have the position. He said that he would prefer me to go with him to Washington, if he went;

but I was not anxious to take a post in Washington, for I dreaded the intrigues and personal jealousies of the Capital. He decided to appoint me, but said that he wanted me to stay in Albany with him through the current Legislative Session and the thirty-day bill period.

In order to make that possible he would send my name to the Senate on the last day of the session, which was two months off. In the meantime we were to keep it a secret, for John F. Curry, the leader of Tammany Hall, would soon be making recommendations for the place, and there would be general speculation about the long delay in filling the vacancy. It was an embarrassing secret. The Governor had been accustomed to sending messages down to Curry through me—especially the unpleasant kind of message, such as that he was not going to follow Curry's recommendation for some political appointment. Conversely, Curry frequently used to send confidential messages to the Governor through me. He did submit recommendations for the vacancy and kept pressing for action. As time went on, the situation became more embarrassing, as Curry became more and more anxious. On the last day of the session, March 11, 1932, the Governor sent my name to the Senate, which immediately confirmed the appointment. I stayed on with the Governor through the thirty-day bill period, and did not take my judicial office until April 15.

At my induction ceremonies, the Governor asked Mrs. Roosevelt to represent him and make a little speech. During the course of her speech, she handed me a longhand letter signed by the Governor, which she asked me to read later in private. It was in reply to a letter of farewell which I had written him expressing my appreciation and pleasure at the opportunity to work with him during the crowded and exciting years of his Governorship. I am printing his letter in reply as showing the warmth and generosity of the man; he was not, contrary to the picture painted of him by some writers, an ungrateful or unappreciative person.

State of New York
Executive Chamber
Albany

Franklin D. Roosevelt
   Governor   April 14th, 1932

Dear Old Sam—

That letter of yours is not only the finest token of real personal and deep friendship I have ever had—but it also makes me feel that public service can & does have a personal relationship which compensates one for the merely official elements which carry little of humanity.

I don't need to tell you that you have lightened the burden for me in so many ways that already, though you've only been gone a day, I have that "harried" feeling of many things left undone! The result will be that you will be assigned to Special Term to hold my hand, & do all my chores, soon & often—in fact, it would be a very pious & Kosher idea if you'd come up here on Friday P.M. the 22nd & go with me to N.Y. (via H.P.) the next day.

Do you know that I hate to see you sitting on that Supreme Court Bench? . . . But I suppose we can best consider it a "grand experience" which in the long run will fit you for higher things & an opportunity for greater service—

In any event I miss you now a lot—& some day, some way I want this old partnership of ours renewed—the quicker the better—

Affectionately your old friend

FRANKLIN D. ROOSEVELT

Meanwhile, on April 7, 1932, the Governor made a short radio speech which threw down a challenge to all his conservative rivals for the nomination. It created a great deal of discussion at the time; in many quarters, it evoked the epithet "demagogue"—but it kept him in the forefront as the outstanding liberal fighter.

I was busy working on the 825 bills the Legislature had left on the Governor's desk, so I did not do much work on this speech. Moley had submitted an excellent draft, including the phrase "forgotten man."

It was only a ten-minute speech but it was beautifully written, for Moley could write brilliantly. And it contained the germ of several projects that Roosevelt started right after he became President—some of the projects then being discussed among the members of the Brain Trust.

The general theme of the speech was that sound prosperity depends upon plans "that rest upon the forgotten, the unorganized but the indispensable units of economic power . . . that build from the bottom up and not from the top down, that put their faith once more in the *forgotten man* at the bottom of the economic pyramid."

"Forgotten man" was a phrase that had been used by William Graham Sumner in an essay in 1883. But as used by the Governor, at Moley's suggestion, it referred to a wider group in American society than Sumner had had in mind. The "forgotten man" was a living person to Roosevelt, not merely an oratorical abstraction. He was the man without money, power, or social position. He was the worker in the sweatshop; he was the small farmer who had to face the problem of high debt and low income; he was the little businessman struggling against ever-growing monopoly; the housewife beset with high prices and a light pay envelope; the rural youngster who had no good local school; the child laborer, the unemployed, the destitute aged, and the handicapped. These were the people who were to receive Roosevelt's major attention and concern during his terms as President.

The philosophy of the "forgotten man" speech was entirely contrary to the philosophy that had prevailed in Washington since 1921: that the object of government was to provide prosperity for those who lived and worked at the top of the economic pyramid, in the belief that prosperity would trickle down to the bottom of the heap and benefit all. Roosevelt believed that prosperity did not "trickle" that way; that it too often ran dry before it reached the lower strata where it was needed most.

Into this ten-minute speech Roosevelt crowded all the following suggestions, based on that general philosophy:

1. Increase the purchasing power of the half of our population who live by "farming or in small towns whose existence immediately depends on farms." The interdependence of the "city worker's employment" and the "farmer's dollar" makes this essential. (Here was the germ of the AAA.)
2. Prevent foreclosures of homes and farm mortgages. (Here were the germs of the HOLC and the FCA.)
3. Assist local little banks who lend on homes and farms as well as the great city banks miles away. (Here was the new policy which was to govern RFC after 1933.)
4. Reduce tariff walls in order to enable us to sell our surplus manufactures abroad and to provide "a reciprocal exchange of goods." (Here was the germ of the Reciprocal Trade Agreements Act.)

And, foreshadowing his First Inaugural Address, in which he said he would not hesitate to ask the Congress for war powers if necessary to meet the emergency of the depression, he said: "It is high time to admit with courage that we are in the midst of an emergency at least equal to that of war. Let us mobilize to meet it."

The Brain Trust was now beginning to function actively. The small group was jocularly first referred to by the Governor as his "Privy Council"—but only when he was with us. He was careful not to discuss us or our work with other people.

From time to time, we—Moley, O'Connor and I—would take one or more of the new men up to Albany to talk with the Governor. Usually we would catch a late afternoon train after court hours, and get there in time for dinner. Roosevelt would talk generalities during dinner, sizing up the new recruit by casual questioning and conversation. Then, after we had retired with coffee to his little study, the barrage would begin.

Moley or I would start the session going by telling the Governor something about the visitor we had brought up and about his qualifications to discuss the subject we had in mind. Roosevelt had nearly always read something on the subject, and usually had some undigested opinions about it. He would not hesitate to express them and to invite criticism. If the visitor were embarrassed about criticizing, we would all encourage him to be as outspoken as he wanted. Sometimes the visitor had prepared a memorandum which he would read aloud. Always there were scores of questions by Roosevelt. The process of milking the visitor dry of ideas would go on for hours. Roosevelt did not make notes, for he knew that we would later get the man to prepare a full memorandum for him.

It was not the purpose of this group to try to work out any blueprints for the future and to lay them down for the Governor to accept or reject. That is not the way Roosevelt functioned. Sometimes we differed among ourselves. Then our ideas and arguments, pro and con, would be "batted out" before him, discussed and debated. New lines of thought would be stimulated. It was the kind of "homework" in governmental thinking which Roosevelt enjoyed, which he used a great deal in the White House, and from which he always profited. Out of it his own thinking was brought into sharper focus. Sometimes it knocked down newly formed ideas of his own; sometimes it opened up entirely new avenues which would later broaden into action.

When it got to be near midnight, we would have to dash to catch the sleeper back to New York. Sometimes the questioning and discussion and argument would get so intense that the session would last past our train time and we would have to spend the night at the Mansion.

I always had to take the sleeper or a very early morning train in order to be back in court by ten o'clock the next morning. Most of my evenings and week ends were given to the work of the group; but the day-by-day supervision was furnished by Moley, whose time was not so restricted as mine.

Toward the end of April, the Governor left for his annual Warm Springs holiday. Before he left he talked with me about the work of his "Privy Council."

"I'm getting an awful lot of good ideas out of this group. I hope my being away in Warm Springs will not stop any of you from going right ahead. When I get back, we'll need a lot of material. Do you think you could come down, say in about three weeks, for a week end, and bring with you all the material you have prepared? We can go over it together down there."

"I'll phone and let you know when I'm coming," I said.

We all redoubled our efforts. Moley, Tugwell, Berle and I frequently spent the late afternoons and evenings together working, sometimes with other people. We did not attempt to put the material into the form of speeches; there was not enough time. Saturdays and Sundays, Moley and I would read over the long memoranda submitted by others —cutting, amplifying on the basis of conversations we had had, re-arranging, simplifying.

Finally, I was set to go; and on May 19th, with several large envelopes of material in a suitcase, I took the train for Warm Springs. Moley came down to the station to see me off. We were both pleased with the result of our work, and hoped that the Governor would be too. We had gotten together enough to constitute a rather specific program for Roosevelt to consider and upon which he could build. It was not that he lacked a program of objectives or that he did not have a clear idea of the kind of action necessary to attain those objectives. But he did need specific thinking about specific methods and projects and legislation—that was what we were trying to help him formulate.

For example, he knew that he wanted to get unemployed young men off the city street corners; that many of them had lacked decent food for years, and that they were going morally to pieces under long periods of enforced idleness; that what they needed more than anything else was work; that it was the duty of the federal government to find work for them which would provide food and shelter and clothing. At the same time, he recognized that proper conservation of our natural resources included long overdue work in our forests—fire prevention, cutting and logging, reforestation, care of trees. Part of the answer to all these needs was found in the Civilian Conservation Corps (CCC), which Roosevelt set up almost immediately after his inauguration. That is an example of the type of specific remedy that

Roosevelt was looking for to apply to his general objectives. To help him arrive at such proposals and to help in the formulation of them were the purposes of the Brain Trust.

I reached Warm Springs on the 20th, evading the reporters' questions about why I was down there. To show how closely our work had been kept secret, I quote excerpts from a *New York Times* dispatch from Warm Springs dated the day I arrived.

Supreme Court Justice Samuel I. Rosenman arrived this evening from New York. Governor Roosevelt and Miss Marguerite LeHand motored forty miles to Newnan, Georgia, to greet him and drove back to the Pine Mountain cottage, where the justice will be a guest until Sunday.

When Justice Rosenman served as Counsel to the Governor at Albany, he was generally looked upon as the liaison officer between Mr. Roosevelt and Tammany. Whether the current visit has any connection with the stand of Tammany on the New York votes in the Democratic National Convention was not learned. Members of the Roosevelt party insisted that the visit was purely social.

I was there only two days. Roosevelt was scheduled to make a speech at Oglethorpe University at Atlanta on the 22nd, but he found time to read carefully all the material I had brought down. He asked many questions about the memoranda and about the people who had prepared them. He was satisfied, and said that he was most anxious that our work go on.

The Oglethorpe speech turned out to be a very important one. The draft of that speech was prepared under unique circumstances. One day the small group of New York newspapermen in Warm Springs with the Governor—Walter Brown of the Associated Press, the late James Kieran of *The New York Times*, Louis Ruppel of the New York *Daily News* and Ernest K. Lindley, now of *Newsweek*—were off on a picnic with the Governor and Missy. They were all having a good time. After a while the newspapermen began ribbing Roosevelt about some of his recent speeches. He said, good-naturedly:

"Well, if you boys don't like my speeches, why don't you take a hand at drafting one yourselves."

Lindley said, "I will"—and he did.

The other newspapermen did some prompting and editing, but it was chiefly Lindley's draft. The Governor made very few changes in the language; a reading will show a style quite different from his usual style. The theme of the speech was that "the country needs . . . the country demands bold, persistent experimentation." It became a kind of watchword for the New Deal program.

"It is common sense to take a method and try it: If it fails, admit it frankly and try another. But above all, try something."

The speech forecast another basic part of the Roosevelt program for recovery and economic stability: emphasis on purchasing power for consumers rather than accumulation of capital for the producer:

"Do what we may have to do to inject life into our ailing economic order, we cannot make it endure for long unless we can bring about a wiser, more equitable distribution of the national income."

It was an address to the graduation class at the University, and his final word to the young graduates indicated, perhaps in somewhat exaggerated form, the great social objective that he was to seek:

We need enthusiasm, imagination and the ability to face facts, even unpleasant ones, bravely. We need to correct, by drastic means if necessary, the faults in our economic system from which we now suffer. We need the courage of the young. Yours is not the task of making your way in the world, but the task of remaking the world which you will find before you. May every one of us be granted the courage, the faith, and the vision to give the best that is in us to that remaking!

No one can say that Roosevelt did not try to lead in that task.

Chapter VI

The Chicago Convention: The "New Deal," 1932

After Roosevelt returned from Warm Springs, the Brain Trust continued its work with renewed energy. Howe had never taken part in any of the meetings of this group either with or without the Governor. I do not know how much he knew about our work; but he was not consulted on it until Roosevelt was nominated and the group became somewhat more formally organized.

On the basis of the memoranda which had been shown to Roosevelt in Warm Springs and the conversations we had had with him over the past few months, a draft of an acceptance speech was being gradually prepared. It was being written chiefly by Moley, with some occasional suggestions from others of the group. Moley consulted frequently with Roosevelt in writing this draft. When it was finished, Moley left the original with Roosevelt and took a copy with him to the Democratic Convention at Chicago. O'Connor and Berle and Tugwell left for Chicago too.

The Governor invited Mrs. Rosenman and me to come to Albany and spend the period of the convention with him at the Executive Mansion.

"Better bring a lot of pencils along," he added over the phone. "We have to whip the acceptance speech into final form."

"Well," I said, "after all the work that has gone into that speech, I hope we get a chance to use it."

"We will," he said confidently.

Many times during the convention, it seemed that the speech would land in the wastepaper basket.

Things got to be exciting at the Mansion even before the convention opened. A direct telephone wire had been set up between the Governor's little study in the Mansion and his headquarters at the Congress Hotel in Chicago. There it was connected to a loud-speaker so that the Governor could talk to the members of each of the state delegations as Howe and Farley brought them into the headquarters. Because of his long experience in national politics and the wide personal acquaintance that he had built up, he was able to call many of the delegates by their first names, and even to ask about their wives and children and other relatives by their first names. This was a feat of memory that he displayed on many occasions, to the bewilderment of those around him and to the amazement and delight of the person to whom he was talking.

Throughout the convention he kept in constant touch with the proceedings, and participated in practically all the important decisions of his leaders in Chicago.

The major mistake the Roosevelt forces made was the attempt at the start of the convention to abrogate the two-thirds rule and substitute the majority rule. Roosevelt had a majority of the delegates, but not two thirds of them. It was unfair to try to change the rules, for our own benefit, in the middle of the game. The attempt created great resentment in Chicago; it was responsible for much hard feeling which, had it persisted, might have cost Roosevelt the nomination. Fortunately, Roosevelt decided in time to drop the effort, and the two-thirds rule continued in force.

There came the day for the nominating and seconding speeches, June 30. The list of candidates seemed interminable, and the nominating speeches were not finished until about 3 A.M. the next morning. At that very late hour, it was decided to proceed immediately with the balloting. Three ballots were taken, but no candidate received the required two-thirds vote. Each ballot took so long that they were not concluded until after nine o'clock in the morning.

This all-night session, following several close votes on other issues earlier in the convention, made some of us at the Mansion a little doubtful of the outcome. As the session went on and on, dimmer and dimmer to me became the prospect that the acceptance speech—into which had gone so many weeks of work and thought and writing—would ever be used. As originally prepared, it would have taken almost an hour for delivery. The Governor and I had been working over the draft from time to time, but had not drastically shortened it. In the years that followed, President Roosevelt held firmly to a resolve never to talk for more than thirty minutes. However, this was an extraordinary occasion. The speech was to express the new kind of political philosophy and social thinking that Roosevelt would bring to the national scene—and there was just too much ground to cover.

Although the address had been put in rather final form, no one had yet taken the trouble to prepare a draft of a peroration. Perorations usually add nothing to the context of the speech; they are more inspirational than informative. Every oration needs one, however, and a well-written peroration can clinch an argument or inspire confidence or lift morale. The writing of the peroration had been put off until the main body of the speech was completed. And in the midst of all the excitement and turmoil of the convention, it had not yet been written.

As the night of nominating and seconding speeches wore on into the morning, the monotony of the oratory became oppressive. The Governor announced that he was going to take a hand at writing a peroration. He started several. However, there were so many interruptions by telephone from Chicago and from other parts of the country that he could not concentrate on the job. He did finish one, and read it aloud to us. We unanimously said it was terrible, so he sadly tore it up.

I remember one of those interruptions very well. The telephone operator announced that Senator Huey Long of Louisiana was on the telephone in Chicago, and wished to speak with the Governor. The Governor and the Senator had never met each other; but as soon as the Governor got on the phone, Long said, "Hello, Franklin—this is the Kingfish."

Roosevelt laughed and said, "Hello, Kingfish, how are you?"

Long said, "I'm fine and hope you are. I have a suggestion for you which will clinch the nomination."

The Governor was all attention.

Long continued: "I think that you should issue a statement immediately, saying that you are in favor of a soldiers' bonus to be paid as soon as you become President."

"Well," said Roosevelt guardedly, "I'm afraid I cannot do that because I am not in favor of a soldiers' bonus." [As a matter of fact, in 1935 Roosevelt vetoed the soldiers' bonus bill; and again in 1936, when it was passed over his veto.]

"Well," said the Kingfish, "whether you believe in it or not, you'd better come out for it with a strong statement, otherwise you haven't got a chance for the nomination."

The Governor thanked him for his interest, but repeated that he did not feel that it was possible for him to make any such statement.

"Well," said the Kingfish as he hung up, "you are a gone goose."

As the evening progressed, and as the balloting on the first, second and third ballots rolled on, we all began to think, although none of us dared say so, that perhaps the Senator was right.

We presented a strange picture along about three o'clock in the morning there in the small sitting room of the Executive Mansion. The Governor, his wife, his mother and I sat listening to the radio. He was in his shirt sleeves, silent, puffing on one cigarette after another. The phone was at his side, and he used it frequently. He seemed deeply interested in the convention oratory, nodding approval of some parts, shaking his head in disapproval of others, laughing aloud when the eloquence became a little too "spread-eagle" in tone.

I have a keen recollection of Elliott, his son, leaning back in a chair with his ear next to the radio—sound asleep. My wife was sitting on the floor, dozing against my chair. Missy and Grace were both asleep on couches.

Out in the garage in the back yard the press associations had set up their wires and typewriters. They had a radio blaring out the news of what was going on in Chicago. Every once in a while the kitchen of the Executive Mansion would send them pots of steaming coffee to keep them awake, and Mrs. Eleanor Roosevelt made some scrambled eggs to go with their coffee.

As one ballot followed another, the President's mother, who naturally thought that her son should have been nominated on the first ballot by acclamation, was dismayed not only at the lack of acclamation but at the lack of the required vote. The bitterest cup for her to swallow was to hear over the radio that some of her "nice" friends in the delegation from New York were actually voting against her Franklin and for Alfred E. Smith. When they did this, not only on the first ballot but on the second ballot, she announced with grim determination that this was more than she could stand and that she was going to return immediately to Hyde Park. She was thoroughly disgusted with the proceeding, and wanted no more of it.

The rest of us stayed on, of course, and early in the morning I asked one of the attendants at the Mansion to drive to a delicatessen store downtown and buy some frankfurters. We went into the kitchen and boiled them, passing them around in the garage for the newspapermen and in the Mansion for the tired group around the radio.

Taking several frankfurters and a small pot of coffee into the little informal dining room, I decided to try my hand at that missing peroration. I was by now half convinced that it would be labor lost; that the acceptance speech for this nomination would be delivered by some one other than Roosevelt. However, I thought the speech might as well be complete, whether delivered or not. I suspect also that I was restless and nervous, and looking for something to do while we were waiting for something definite to happen in Chicago.

I mention these details because the peroration I drafted had in it two words to which I gave little thought at the time, but which within a week became accepted as symbolic of the whole new philosophy and program of the Democratic candidate. Intended to epitomize the program of "bold, persistent experimentation" on behalf of the "forgotten man," the phrase was in the sentence "I pledge you, I pledge myself, to a *new deal* for the American people."

I had not the slightest idea that it would take hold the way it did, nor did the Governor when he read and revised what I had written. In fact, he attached no importance to the two monosyllables. Many articles were written about the phrase after it became popular. Commentators have attributed to it shades of meaning that never existed either in my mind or in the mind of the Governor when he delivered it in Chicago. Some have said that it was intended to be a combination of the Square Deal of President Theodore Roosevelt and the New Freedom of President Woodrow Wilson. There was no such intention when it was written or when it was delivered. It was intended to indicate that the old kind of political and economic thinking which had persisted in Washington during the last twelve years would come to an end if Roosevelt were elected; that no longer would the chief concern of government be the financial and corporate power at the top of the economic pyramid; that the primary concern of government was henceforth to be the great mass of humanity at the bottom of the heap; that for the "forgotten men," women and children of the nation the cards were to be redealt to give them a better chance in economic competition and in the pursuit of happiness.

I am sure that the Governor thought no more about it than this, because when I handed him the scrap of paper on which the few paragraphs had been written he said that he thought they were all right as a peroration. There was no discussion about New Freedom or Square Deal, or even about the phrase "new deal" itself; I do not recall that it was even mentioned between us.

I have often tried to find the reasons why those two simple words became so quickly and so universally symbolic of the great program of social revolution which was ushered in by President Roosevelt. I have never been able to do so to my own satisfaction. It was simply one of those phrases that catch public fancy and survive—short, concise, and yet comprehensive enough to cover a great many different concepts.

At eight o'clock that morning, after the second ballot was taken, there was a motion to adjourn. The anti-Roosevelt forces, thinking that they now had Roosevelt definitely stopped, blocked adjournment, but after the third ballot the motion was carried.

At the Mansion, we all tried to get a little sleep. However, quite early that day I had to awaken the Governor to take several phone calls which had been coming in from the convention in rapid succession. Trading and negotiation went on all during that day, and the results are now a matter of history.

Just before dinner a call came in on the direct Chicago wire. We could only hear the Governor, who simply muttered: "Good—fine—excellent." He hung up, grinning. His air of importance during the call and his air of mystery afterward told us that the development, whatever it was, was significant. But he would not say a word about it.

He asked that the dining-room table be moved a little down the room toward the serving pantry, so that he could sit at his usual place at the head of the table and still use the Chicago wire, which otherwise would not stretch to his place. He said he was superstitious, and "did not want to change his luck" by changing his place at the table. He did not have to tell us—we knew his superstitions. He was superstitious about the weather and about some other small things. He disliked, for example, lighting three cigarettes on a single match, or having thirteen at table, or starting a voyage on the thirteenth.

He was obviously waiting for a very special call. Missy commented: "F. D., you look just like the cat that swallowed the canary."

He nodded, and smiled broadly and tantalizingly, but he wouldn't talk. He enjoyed this kind of childlike teasing. It was very provoking to the rest of us, and he thoroughly enjoyed being provoking. He ate his dinner in silence.

Then *the* call came through. And we learned that the earlier call before dinner had been only the curtain raiser for this one. For this second call brought the definite news that on the next ballot the California and Texas delegations were going to switch from Garner to Roosevelt. That shift would mean the nomination.

When dinner was over, we went into the study again. This time we waited and listened with expectant certainty. And very soon came the climax we were expecting. As soon as California was reached and Senator McAdoo began to speak, we knew, and the whole nation knew, that the deadlock was over—that Roosevelt was the choice.

Certainly the City of Albany knew because, almost simultaneously with the second paragraph of Senator McAdoo's speech, automobiles began to arrive in front of the Mansion. People congregated on the front lawn, to cheer and to show their approval of the nomination. Pretty soon the large rambling house, which, except for our small group had been practically deserted for five days, became a confused, busy center of activity. Friends and associates crowded in to shake the hand of the candidate. There were no guards, so anybody who wanted to just walked in. Floodlights were set up in the large ballroom for pictures. The newspaper reporters crowded in from their uncomfortable quarters in the garage, seeking to describe the local color of the scene and to get a few words from the candidate himself. Roosevelt was pretty tired from his preceding night's vigil and from the long day of activity that had followed. But he was laughing and exchanging gay remarks with the reporters, photographers and visitors. He was happy, and he made no effort to hide it. He asked me for some paper and, during all the excitement, wrote out in longhand two personal telegrams, one to Garner and the other to McAdoo.

The acceptance speech was going to be used after all! Howe phoned me, and said that he wanted to read it in its present form before the Governor arrived at Chicago. So, before I went to bed, I asked Grace Tully to read the text of the entire revised speech over the private wire to a stenographer in the Roosevelt headquarters in Chicago. In Chicago it was transcribed and given to Howe. It must have been late when Louis finally was able to read it. I learned the next day that he did not like it, or any part of it.

While it had become generally known that the Governor intended to break tradition and go to the convention to accept the nomination immediately, there was much good-humored mystery about his means of transportation. It was originally believed that he was going by train before the actual balloting began, and would remain in Chicago waiting for the nomination. Some of the rival candidates were already there.

But Roosevelt would have none of such prosaic arrangements. He knew the value of drama in public office and in public relations, and he understood the psychology of the American people of 1932. He felt that the dismayed, disheartened and bewildered nation would welcome something new, something startling, something to give it hope that there would be an end to stolid inaction. He wanted to let people know that his approach was going to be bold and daring; that if elected he would be ready to act—and act fast. It was in that spirit that the whole trip to Chicago was conceived. It was a break with tradition, with in-action and procrastination, and a symbol of new, bold and direct action.

News shortly began to leak of the presence of a new trimotored plane at the Albany airport; and the newsmen, with their uncanny ability to put two and two together, predicted that the Governor was going to fly to Chicago.

The following excerpt from the Associated Press story which went out of Albany, June 29, is typical of some of the banter between the Governor and the press during these days. When the press asked him whether the waiting airplane was to take him to Chicago, he neither affirmed nor denied:

He only laughed. "Now, I'll tell you what I'm going to do," he said with pretended seriousness. "I'm going to bicycle out to Chicago.

"I'm going to get one of those quintets—you know, five bicycles in a row.

"Father will ride in the first seat and manage the handlebars. Jim will ride second, then Elliott, then Franklin Jr., and then John.

"Sam (referring to Supreme Court Justice Samuel I. Rosenman, his close friend) will follow—on a tricycle."

The traditional procedure had been for the candidate to wait until about two months after the convention, when a committee of the convention would descend upon him and solemnly notify him that he had been nominated some sixty days before. Then, and not until then, the acceptance speech was delivered.

The trip to the convention to accept the nomination in person was not the only precedent that Roosevelt established. The means of trans-portation was also new. Airplane travel was not as common in 1932 as it is now, and this was the first time that a Presidential candidate had ever made a campaign trip in an airplane.

The morning after the nomination we drove out to the airport to board the plane for Chicago. The airplane party consisted of the Governor and Mrs. Roosevelt; their sons Elliott and John; Missy; Grace; Guernsey Cross, the Governor's secretary; two bodyguards, Earl Miller and Gus Gennerich; and myself. Mrs. Rosenman remained behind. She had been given the job of asking some of Smith's friends to discourage him from giving vent to pique and disappointment by making an unfriendly statement which might later embarrass him or the new candidate. One of the people to whom she spoke was Justice Bernard L. Shientag, an old friend and associate of Governor Smith. The Justice, at her suggestion, went to Harmon, New York, to board Smith's train as it came in from Chicago. He rode with Smith down to New York City, and was largely instrumental in persuading him to remain silent in the face of his defeat for the nomination.

In those days long-distance flights without stops were rare and dangerous stunts. Our flight plan called for stops for refueling at Buffalo and Cleveland. We planned to arrive at the Chicago auditorium at about 2 P.M. By that time the Vice-Presidential nomination would be out of the way, and the delegates would be ready for the acceptance speech. But we did not keep up with our schedule. Strong headwinds delayed us, and made it a very rough flight.

Shortly after we started on our journey, we went to work to polish the acceptance speech for delivery. We were in radio communication with the convention hall, and learned that the delegates were becoming impatient at our delay; some of them had started for home. We had to cut the speech drastically. Out at the convention hall, all kinds of devices were improvised to keep the delegates amused until the Governor's arrival. Song writers played the piano and sang songs, the band played overtime; and although many delegates' seats became vacant, the parts of the hall into which the public was allowed became more and more crowded as the day wore on.

With each radio report, we were falling further and further behind schedule; and more and more paragraphs came out of the acceptance speech. This lopping off of material on which we had worked so long and so hopefully was a painful process. I know that there were some jewels dropped on the airplane floor that day. It is likely, though, that the cutting process hurt us more than it did the speech.

The President did not seem to mind the bumpy ride; as he explained to the convention in his opening extemporaneous paragraph, "I regret that I am late, but I have no control over the winds of Heaven and could only be thankful for my Navy training."

Once, between Buffalo and Cleveland, I looked up from my work toward the Governor; and what I saw convinced me that here indeed was a man of steel nerves, who could shake off worry and excitement and deliberately take rest when necessary. The Governor—on his way to accept a nomination that was almost tantamount to an election to the Presidency of the United States—was sound asleep.

When we finally reached Chicago at about 4:30 P.M., there was a tremendous crowd at the airport. I saw Farley, Howe and some of my colleagues of the Brain Trust. As I stepped out of the plane, relieved to be back on solid ground again, Moley pulled me aside. He was quite agitated.

"You've got to do something about this," he said. "Louis [Howe] has read the acceptance speech, and he says it's terrible. He stayed up all last night and dictated a brand new one; and he is going to try to get the Governor to deliver it instead of the speech which you telephoned in last night. I have tried to tell him how foolish that would be, but it's no use; he is over there talking to the Governor about it now."

I went over to the car in which the Governor had now settled himself. Howe was saying, "I tell you it's all right, Franklin. It's much better than the speech you've got now—and you can read it while you're driving down to the convention hall, and get familiar with it."

"But, Louis," said the Governor, "you know I can't deliver a speech that I've never done any work on myself, and that I've never even read. It will sound stupid, and it's silly to think that I can."

Louis persisted.

"All right, Louis," said the Governor, "I'll try to read it over while we are riding down to the convention hall." He smiled in a way that made me sure that he would handle the situation without offending his old friend Louis, but that at the same time he would not do what Louis wanted.

I have a vivid recollection of Roosevelt, as his car sped through the streets of Chicago lined with hundreds of thousands of people, waving his hand and tipping his hat in friendly greeting, shouting "hello," first to one side and then to the other. From time to time he would glance down at Louis's manuscript on his lap. In later years, I heard him many times describe this episode with great glee, and with many gestures showing how he waved his hat and read the speech at the same time. With each telling, the wave of the arm would be wider and the "hellos" more numerous.

Later that night in his hotel suite after the speech had been delivered, he told me what he had decided to do as he rode through the crowded streets. He saw from a few quick glances at the first page of Louis's manuscript that that page could easily be substituted for the first page of the speech he had brought with him. He decided to do this; the rest of the speech he left intact. I, of course, did not know any of this until later. When we arrived at the convention hall and he started to read his speech, after ad-libbing an apology for his late arrival, I was dismayed to hear, for at least a minute, some brand-new sentences. After the few opening paragraphs, however, I began to hear the words with which I had become thoroughly familiar.

Howe was the only person who used to work on Roosevelt's speeches who ever openly expressed pain and resentment when his material was discarded. But in this instance, he seemed to be satisfied by the use of his first page, for he said no more about it.

Apparently, the President thought this feat of oratorical legerdemain worthy of recording, for he dictated a short memorandum which is now attached to the original reading copy of the speech in the Roosevelt Library at Hyde Park:

March 25, 1933

This is the original manuscript of the Acceptance Speech in Chicago which was used in the Auditorium.

The speech was put into final shape in the Executive Mansion in Albany at 1 A.M. the night before and I took it with me on the plane early Saturday morning, correcting it on the way to Chicago.

On arrival at the Chicago Airport, Mr. Howe had ten or twelve pages of a suggested speech, based on a review and amplification of the Democratic platform. I discarded all of this except the first page which seemed better than what I had prepared. It worked into the rest of the speech and expressed the same ideas. Hence it was used in place of my first page.

FRANKLIN D. ROOSEVELT

The acceptance speech was received at the convention with thunderous applause, and throughout the nation there was clear understanding that if Roosevelt were elected there would be a new kind of thinking and action in Washington.

It epitomized many of the things our group had discussed with the

Governor over the last three months. It was a discussion of progressive government and liberal thought, the interdependence of all groups in the economy, prohibition, public works to provide employment, reforestation for better use of land and to provide employment, reduction of farm surpluses, planned agricultural production to reduce oversupply, reduction of interest on farm mortgages and home mortgages, reduction of tariffs and negotiation of reciprocal trade agreements, federal responsibility for the relief of unemployment distress, and the right of all people to a more equitable opportunity to share in national wealth.

Perhaps the best exposition of the general philosophy of the speech is contained in the last four paragraphs:

Never before in modern history have the essential differences between the two major American parties stood out in such striking contrast as they do today. Republican leaders not only have failed in material things, they have failed in national vision, because in disaster they have held out no hope, they have pointed out no path for the people below to climb back to places of security and of safety in our American life.

Throughout the Nation, men and women, forgotten in the political philosophy of the Government of the last years look to us here for guidance and for more equitable opportunity to share in the distribution of national wealth.

On the farms, in the large metropolitan areas, in the smaller cities and in the villages, millions of our citizens cherish the hope that their old standards of living and of thought have not gone forever. Those millions cannot and shall not hope in vain.

I pledge you, I pledge myself, to a new deal for the American people. Let us all here assembled constitute ourselves prophets of a new order of competence and of courage. This is more than a political campaign; it is a call to arms. Give me your help, not to win votes alone, but to win in this crusade to restore America to its own people.

The day after the acceptance speech was delivered there appeared in one of the newspapers a Rollin Kirby cartoon. It showed a farmer leaning on his hoe. He seemed symbolic of the nationwide misery caused by the depression. With a look of bewilderment mixed with hope, he was watching an airplane flying overhead—Roosevelt's airplane. On the wings of the airplane were the words "New Deal." This was the first indication that a popular phrase had been coined; but none of us even then had any idea of the extent to which it was to be used. So far as I know, or have been able to discover, there was never any attempt by the Roosevelt forces or the Democratic National Committee to publicize or exploit the phrase. However, it was soon adopted as a two-word summary of the Democratic platform and of the principles of the Democratic candidate. Within a short time it became a commonplace—the watchword of a fighting political faith.

It still is.

Chapter VII

Campaign Promises and Fulfillment: The First Term as President, 1933-1937

Shortly after the acceptance speech the Brain Trust set up its own head-quarters in the Roosevelt Hotel in New York City. The headquarters consisted of a living room, working office, and one bedroom where we used to put up visitors who came to see us from out of town. In this suite we used to gather for dinner three or four nights a week to discuss various issues. From time to time we invited people in Washington of practical experience in government to come to talk with us about national subjects. Senator Key Pittman of Nevada and the Senator from South Carolina, James F. Byrnes, were among our visitors. Hugh Johnson became one of the regular group after the convention. We did not always see eye to eye on all issues; often the discussions became very heated, lasted far into the night, and had to be adjourned to the next night. Robert K. Straus acted as secretary of the group and spent most of his time there during the day, co-ordinating activities, supervising mail, taking care of all the mechanics.

My own part in the work of the group was limited by my court en-gagements, and Moley continued to act as chairman and supervisor. That summer he was a frequent visitor at my home in Dutchess County, where we used to go over things together before driving over to Hyde Park, a short distance away.

Our headquarters were kept quite separate from those of the Demo-cratic National Committee, which were across the street in the Bilt-more Hotel. We did not attempt to participate in their political activi-ties, and they scrupulously refrained from interfering with us in any way.

It was after the nomination that the group acquired its strange name, which like "new deal" was to catch popular fancy and become a common phrase. News of our activities had spread among Roosevelt's friends and associates, although the general public had heard little or nothing of it. Howe knew all about it by this time, and he did not like the idea. One day, in conversation with the Governor, he referred to the group as "your brains trust." Shortly thereafter on a day when we were expected at Hyde Park for a conference, the Governor told the newspaper men that a group was coming up to see him. Although Howe's reference to us had been derisive, the Governor in talking with the newspaper men referred to the group by the same term, "brains trust." One of the reporters used the phrase in his news article the next day—and it stuck. The "s" of "brains" was soon dropped, and the phrase Brain Trust continued to be applied to advisers of the President even after the original group had been completely disbanded.

It was in that little suite in the Roosevelt Hotel that a good part of the spadework, gathering of material and initial drafting of campaign speeches was done. From here the material was forwarded to Roosevelt's campaign train or taken up to Albany for discussion with him.

The following letter, which the President took the time and trouble to write long after the campaign, on March 9, 1933, when the banks were all closed, when he was as thoroughly busy and occupied as at any time during his Presidency, shows what he thought of the work of the Brain Trust and the assistance it had been to him.

THE WHITE HOUSE

WASHINGTON, March 9, 1933

DEAR SAMMY:—

I am waiting to hear what the Congress will do with my first bill. We worked until two o'clock this morning preparing it and it seemed queer to do this kind of work without you. After four years of such close association it is not easy to work with others.

I want you to know how grateful I am for the fine loyalty you have shown and for the unselfish service you gave me during the campaign. Even though you were not with me all the time I knew how hard you were working behind closed doors in smoke-filled rooms, and your contribution of Ray and Rex was probably the best that anyone made during the whole campaign.

I hardly need tell you that I want you to feel perfectly free to telephone or come to see me at any time. If I can be of help to you please let me know. I do hope that we will see you and Dorothy here in Washington often. Our contact has been too close to need constant correspondence or conversations. I just want you to know of my feeling toward you and my gratitude for all that you did.

As ever yours,

/s/   FRANKLIN D. ROOSEVELT

During the 1932 campaign, the Governor was once more beset by troubles with Tammany Hall and by charges of corruption in New York City. These troubles were also to affect me in a personal way.

The climax of the work of the Joint Legislative Committee Investigating the Affairs of New York City had been reached before the convention in Chicago. The Committee had filed charges with the Governor against the Mayor of the City, James J. Walker, seeking to have him removed from office. Tammany Hall hoped that the Governor would dismiss the charges right away or at least take no action on them. The Governor promptly sent the charges to the Mayor to answer, thus making it apparent that he was going to give them his serious attention. The Tammany Hall leader, John F. Curry, and his henchmen served notice that it would be a fight to the finish, and it was.

But the finish was not what Curry had hoped for. He was not the most astute of the leaders of Tammany Hall. In 1932, he had an opportunity to become one of the most powerful political leaders in the United States by supporting Roosevelt. But Curry had a blind loyalty to Walker, knew and cared little about political or social philosophies, and was willing to go to any length to save Walker from being removed. He stupidly thought that the way to save Walker was to frighten Roosevelt by threatening not to support him in Chicago. He was ready to sacrifice the Democratic organization of New York City—and his own political future—in the attempt. He succeeded in sacrificing both, and he did not save Walker.

Most of the city delegates, except those from the Bronx under the leadership of Edward J. Flynn, did vote against Roosevelt and for Smith at Chicago. Walker, who was himself a delegate, made it a point to be recorded personally against Roosevelt's nomination. But the Curry followers did not have enough votes in the convention to do anything but show their defiance. If they thought that this gesture would intimidate Roosevelt—and I am sure that Curry did think so—they soon learned otherwise.

Walker's answer to the charges filed against him came in on July 28, 1932. Replies to that answer were filed by Judge Seabury, the Committee's counsel, on August 2. Two days later, Roosevelt set the matter down for public hearing before him personally, to be held on August 11 at the Executive Chamber in Albany. The hearings were continued on fourteen subsequent days down to September 2, 1932. Walker tried to stop them by a court order, but failed.

Roosevelt could well have used all the time that the hearing took to work on his speeches for the coming campaign. But he was determined to finish the hearing before the campaign actually began, so that he could not be charged with playing politics with the situation.

Nationwide attention was focused on the Executive Chamber in Albany. What would Roosevelt do? Would he brave the chance of losing New York in the election by removing Mayor Walker, or would he find some reason to keep him in office—perhaps with a censure and warning?

The Roosevelt supporters were fairly excited, of course. The Walker hearings had nothing at all to do with any of the vital national issues before the electorate; yet it was possible that the national election might turn on New York State, and that the identity of the next President of the United States might depend on the outcome of this purely local matter.

Roosevelt was not excited. He listened with great attention to all the testimony. He appointed an eminent New York lawyer, Martin Conboy, as his special counsel. I am sure that he was becoming persuaded by the testimony that Walker should be removed, and that he was getting ready to do so.

We were discussing the proceedings one night in his little study in the Mansion—O'Connor, Moley, several others, and I—when a telegram came in from Walker. It was his resignation. The hearings were over. We were all relieved. The resignation was hailed as the result of Roosevelt's strong stand against Tammany Hall. Just as his fight in 1911 with the Hall helped launch him on his political career, his fight in 1932 with the Hall helped his election to the Presidency.

Under the Constitution of New York my appointment to the bench by the Governor was effective only until the following November, when I would have to stand for election. As a part of the fight on Roosevelt, Curry decided that the Democratic organization would not nominate me, despite the unbroken rule that it would automatically nominate anyone appointed by a Democratic Governor to fill a vacancy. Resentment against Roosevelt made Curry decide to break this rule for the first time in the political history of the City. He must have known that this gratuitous insult to the Governor—who was pretty clearly on the way to becoming President—would not be too cordially received. But he even carried his venom far enough to start a movement against the gubernatorial nomination of Herbert H. Lehman, who had been an outstanding Lieutenant Governor for four years. Smith and Roosevelt together prevented that by appearing at the state convention and insisting on Lehman's nomination.

Roosevelt was on a campaign trip when he heard of Curry's action against me. He sent me the following telegram from Milwaukee, Wisconsin, September 30, 1932:

> The fellow who is behind in the first quarter mile is very likely to finish first. I am nevertheless terribly disappointed, but you will remember that I have a long memory and a long arm for my friends.
>
> F. D. R.

Within less than a year, I was reappointed to the first available vacancy on the Supreme Court of New York by Governor Lehman. And Roosevelt's "long memory and a long arm" worked effectively to remove Curry from the leadership of Tammany Hall, which his ineptness had by this time badly weakened.

The wire from Roosevelt was typical of the man. He was most generous and forgiving about human weaknesses; but he was implacable and vindictive toward those who deliberately were unfair to him, especially in political matters.

Sometimes that aspect of Roosevelt's make-up led him into political difficulty. For example, in 1944 the President was convinced that Jesse Jones was one of the behind-the-scenes leaders in a movement to have the Texas delegation in the Democratic convention vote against Roosevelt's nomination for the fourth term—although Jones denied it. Roosevelt said very little about it at the time, but I could see his face harden as he talked about the reports which came to him about Jones' political activities in Texas. He did nothing about it until after his inauguration. Then, without talking to anyone, he suddenly sent Jones a letter asking for his resignation as Secretary of Commerce and Federal Loan Administrator so that he could appoint Henry Wallace to both those posts. It was politically wrong to ask Jones to quit in that fashion. He had never done a thing like that to such a high official before. It was even more inadvisable politically to name Wallace to those positions. The bitter fight in the Senate over Wallace's confirmation showed what a mistake it had been. Roosevelt would never have made it under ordinary circumstances, but the vindictiveness aroused by the reports of Jones' activities impaired his usually clear political insight.

He occasionally had to be ruthless with friends who had done something that embarrassed him and made it impossible for him as President to continue close association with them. Obviously he took no pleasure in this; it was a matter of cold duty. I remember his remarking to me on one such occasion that while the President of the United States has many luxuries—a fine house, special railroad train, private yacht, a fleet of automobiles—there is one luxury he does not have, the luxury of loyalty to his friends; that sometimes the public interest does not permit it, and the public interest must prevail.

The 1932 campaign has long since become a chapter in history. It was more like a triumphant tour than a campaign for Roosevelt. To an anxious nation he brought a fresh personality, fresh ideas, and fresh hope.

There is not room here to discuss in detail each of the campaign speeches. It can be said, however, that—except for the NRA (National Recovery Act) as an expedient for swift recovery and except for deficit spending to fight unemployment—every major project of the first term, every important part of the New Deal program, was foreshadowed in one or more of the speeches:

At Columbus, Ohio, August 20, 1932: reciprocal trade agreements and reduced tariffs, supervision of sales of securities, securities exchanges and bank deposits, separation of investment banking from commercial banking.

At Sea Girt, New Jersey, August 27: repeal of the prohibition amendment.

At Topeka, Kansas, September 14: a program of agricultural relief, planned land use, refinancing of farm mortgages.

At Salt Lake City, September 17: a program for relief of the railroads.

At Portland, Oregon, September 21: public development of water power and supervision of public utilities; control of public utility holding companies.

At Detroit, Michigan, October 2: social justice through social action.

At Albany, October 13: government responsibility for relief of unemployment distress, public works to lessen unemployment, unemployment insurance, better housing, health as a concern of the federal government.

At Pittsburgh, October 19: balancing the budget.

At Springfield, Illinois, October 21: relief for agriculture by raising farm prices, reducing its taxes, and lightening its burden of farm mortgages.

At St. Louis, Missouri, October 21: plans for helping the eight great credit groups of the nation.

*At Boston, Massachusetts, October 31: comprehensive program for unem-
ployment, emergency relief, temporary public works, permanent public
works, employment exchanges, reduction of work day and of work week,
unemployment insurance.*

Certainly, when the campaign was over, no citizen who heard or read
the speeches had any reason to be surprised at any part of the Roosevelt
New Deal program.

The one exception was the Pittsburgh speech on October 19. The
President frequently complained in later years that this speech was one
of the few he ever made—even in the heat of a campaign—without
adequate time for discussion and consideration. He had in mind particularly the part of the speech that indicated that he expected to reduce
government expenditures. A cut in expenditures was a definite pledge
of the Democratic platform of that year; but Roosevelt, even early in
the campaign, began to lay out many projects to relieve distress that
were bound to cost large sums of money. I am sure that if there had
been time to give the issue more thought the speech would not have
been delivered in the form that it took at Pittsburgh. He would not
have so definitely committed himself. As it was, he went out on a
long limb.

During 1935 and 1936, while the federal budget was constantly
increasing and becoming more and more unbalanced, his political opponents quoted from this speech frequently and accused the President of
breaking his word.

The charge was quite true. But it would have done irreparable harm
to the nation had he stubbornly stuck to his Pittsburgh promise,
ignoring the dangerous conditions which arose. For obviously it would
have been impossible to do any of the things that he did to put the
stricken country back on its feet unless he continued deficit spending.

Nevertheless, the criticisms of that Pittsburgh speech rankled in the
President's mind for years. Four years later, just before the start of the
campaign of 1936, he said to me:

"I'm going to make the first major campaign speech in Pittsburgh
at the ball park in exactly the same spot I made that 1932 Pittsburgh
speech; and in the speech I want to explain my 1932 statement. See
whether you can prepare a draft giving a good and convincing explanation of it."

By that time the details of the 1932 speech had become a little vague
in my mind; so I got a copy of it and read it again very carefully. That

evening I went in to see the President in his study and said that as long
as he insisted on referring to the speech, I had found the only kind of
explanation that could be made. He turned to me rather hopefully and,
I think, with a little surprise, and said, "Fine, what sort of an explanation
would you make?"

I replied, "Mr. President, the only thing you can say about that 1932
speech is to deny categorically that you ever made it."

We both laughed. It was hopeless to try to explain it away, but he
did the next best thing. Without mentioning the speech at all, he did
explain why the budget had not been balanced during the last four
years. He explained that the expenditure of money had been necessary
to save the economy of the nation and maintain its democracy, and was
fully justified in view of human needs and human suffering.

Getting the election returns in 1932 was not very exciting because
there was no doubt of the result. Mrs. Rosenman and I were invited
to a buffet supper at the Roosevelt house on Sixty-fifth Street with
some of his friends. During the early evening, I noticed two strange
men come into the room unobtrusively and take positions near the
Governor. I asked who they were, and learned that they were members
of the United States Secret Service. That man having his supper so
gaily with his friends might turn out tonight to be the President-elect,
and the United States of America was taking him under its watchful
protection. He was not to be free of that guarding watchfulness a
single moment for the rest of his life.

Roosevelt carried 42 states; he was elected by a popular vote of
22,821,000 to 15,761,000, with a plurality of 7,000,000, and an electoral
vote of 472 to 59.

After the election, the President asked me, among others, what I
thought should be done about the Brain Trust. I suggested that it be
kept intact for the purpose for which it had been organized and for
that purpose only—as a staff to gather materials for study and for
speeches, as a group with whom the President could, as formerly, "bat
around" ideas from time to time, and who could "bat around" ideas
among themselves.

I said that it would be particularly unfortunate if the members of
the Brain Trust were to be given administrative jobs in Washington
to which each would have to devote his major time and attention. No
matter how large the particular job might be, it would be only a small
part of the over-all picture with which the President would have to

deal, and these men could be more helpful in advice and discussion within that larger framework. If they were to be genuinely useful, it was important, I felt, that they have no personal or departmental axes to grind. In administrative posts, inevitably they would each become the spokesman for one small segment of federal interest. They would start worrying about the trees when their job should be to help the President in his concern about the forest.

The President did not agree. Moley was appointed Assistant Secretary of State; Tugwell became an Assistant Secretary of Agriculture; Berle did some work for a while with the Reconstruction Finance Corporation, then became a city officeholder in the La Guardia administration, and finally an Assistant Secretary of State. Johnson became the NRA administrator. I decided to remain in New York, since Governor Lehman had indicated that he would reappoint me to the Supreme Court, which he did in September, 1933. I remained on the Bench until October, 1943, when the President asked me to resign and devote my full time to helping in the war.

I still think that it was a mistake for the President to break up the original Brain Trust and change the functions of its members. Acting together in a consultative and advisory capacity, they could have been of great help. Acting individually, without the natural restraint and check which came from group discussion, some of the members of the Brain Trust who did take administrative positions in Washington in 1933 eventually caused the President embarrassment in one way or another. Ultimately their paths and the President's separated. The later careers of Moley, Tugwell and Hugh Johnson, for example, indicate that there is something about administrative power along the Potomac that excludes the concept of anonymous helpfulness which was the basis of the success of the original Brain Trust.

The only function performed by the original Brain Trust which was continued after 1933 was that of helping on speeches. But the old group never again did that job as a team.

As the months went by after the election the term "Brain Trust" was applied not only to the original members of our group but also to many new people who came to Washington—Harry Hopkins, Dean Acheson, Tom Corcoran, Ben Cohen, William Woodin, Joseph P. Kennedy, Felix Frankfurter (before he became a Justice of the United States Supreme Court) and many others. Soon anyone not in government service upon whom the President relied for advice or assistance, or even persons in government who had frequent access to the President on general problems, came to be labeled a member of the Brain Trust.

The first year of his Administration the President himself has called a "Year of Crisis." But he understood "crisis" to mean more than just the stalled economic machine and the unemployment, poverty and hopelessness. It was in his mind a crisis in American democracy itself, a time for the American people to decide whether they "would have been willing to accept any form of specious glittering guarantee of a chance to earn a livelihood."[1]

His conception of the task of leadership in 1933 was clear. It was to "correct the immediate material illness." But it was much more: it was "to remove the sore spots which had crept into our economic system, if we were to keep the system of private property for the future." These objectives he considered as interdependent—to be accomplished simultaneously.

His twofold aim was set out in his First Inaugural Address, March 4, 1933.

The purpose of that speech the President himself later described: "I sought principally . . . to banish, so far as possible, the fear of the present and of the future which held the American people and the American spirit in its grasp. . . . I promised a program of action: first, to put people to work; and second, to correct the abuses . . . which had in great measure contributed to the crisis."

This was one of the President's truly great speeches, not only in form and substance but in accomplishment. It contained one of those immortal statements which have since become so closely associated with him: "The only thing we have to fear is fear itself . . ."

The speech was a fine example of his ability to instill courage and lift morale by showing courage and fixed purpose on his own part. Its effect throughout the country was electrifying.

It was a short speech, but it contained all the elements of his program —a program he promised to urge upon the Congress at once in a special session. And he stated he would ask for "broad executive power to wage a war against the emergency, as great as the power that would be given to me if we were in fact invaded by a foreign foe."

The speech was one of those very few of which the President wrote the first draft in his own hand. He wrote it on yellow legal cap paper,

[1] Introduction to 1933 Vol., *Public Papers and Addresses of Franklin D. Roosevelt*, p. 3.

sitting by the fire at Hyde Park on the night of February 27. The original manuscript is now in the Roosevelt Library at Hyde Park, and has attached to it this typewritten note by the President:

March 25, 1933

This is the original manuscript of the Inaugural Address as written at Hyde Park on Monday, February 27th, 1933. I started it about 9:00 P.M. and ended at 1:30 A.M. A number of minor changes were made in subsequent drafts but the final draft is substantially the same as this original.

The President's original longhand draft does not have in it the famous "fear" sentence. The first paragraph of that draft reads as follows:

"I am certain that my fellow Americans expect that on my induction to the Presidency I will address them with a candor and a decision which the present situation of our nation impels. This is no occasion of soft speaking or for the raising of false hopes."

From this longhand draft a typewritten copy was made. After the President-elect arrived in Washington he revised this typewritten copy in his suite at the Hotel Mayflower. The final draft was typed on March 3, the day before it was delivered. In that last draft the paragraph quoted above had been strengthened by the President, had been made positive and affirmative instead of negative, and the "fear" sentence had been inserted. The way it was changed was typical of what the President could do with a speech—even in the great rush and excitement of those days just before his first inauguration:

I am certain that my fellow Americans expect that on my induction into the Presidency I will address them with a candor and a decision which the present situation of our Nation impels. This is preeminently the time to speak the truth, the whole truth, frankly and boldly. Nor need we shrink from honestly facing conditions in our country today. This great Nation will endure as it has endured, will revive and will prosper. So, first of all, let me assert my firm belief that the only thing we have to fear is fear itself—nameless, unreasoning, unjustified terror which paralyzes needed efforts to convert retreat into advance. In every dark hour of our national life a leadership of frankness and vigor has met with that understanding and support of the people themselves which is essential to victory. I am convinced that you will again give that support to leadership in these critical days.

While the President was waiting inside the Capitol to go out onto the steps to deliver his address, he wrote in longhand on his reading copy a new sentence—an impulsive demonstration of what his thoughts must have been as he sat there waiting to take the helm of the wallowing ship of state:

"This is a day of consecration."

And as he read it he ad-libbed the word "national" before "consecration."[2]

Exactly where the idea of the "fear" sentence came from I have been unable to learn—and strangely enough I never asked the President about it. I just assumed that it had been in the first draft he had written at Hyde Park and that it had been one of his "happy thoughts." Not until recently when I examined the longhand draft carefully did I see that it had been inserted later, after he had arrived in Washington.

I have inquired of many people who were in a position to know. It was the President's own sentence, and it might well have been completely original with him. However, it bears a striking resemblance to a statement about fear written by Henry David Thoreau: "Nothing is so much to be feared as fear." Eleanor Roosevelt has told me that one of her friends had given the President a copy of some of Thoreau's writings shortly before the day of inauguration, and that it was in his suite at the hotel while this speech was being polished. Roosevelt frequently picked up a book at his bedside for brief reading before turning out the lights. It may be that in this way he came across the phrase, it stuck in his mind, and found its way into this speech.

The phrase served as a guidepost for the President in many later emergencies, as it had served him personally all his life. Although he was criticized on a great many scores, I have never heard it said that he was ever timid about taking action in an emergency. Bold and courageous leadership is what he gave to the people of the nation immediately upon his inauguration, and it was that kind of leadership they came to expect whenever domestic or international crises arose. The reins of resolute leadership which the President took up on that March day in 1933 he never dropped or even slackened until the day

[2] The copy printed in the *Public Papers*, Vol. II, p. 11, does not have this opening sentence. It was not in the official copy given to the Congress for printing, and through oversight it was not subsequently included. When I edited the first set of *Public Papers* in 1937 I used the official copy, without checking with the reading copy. This oversight was not repeated in later speeches, because all the President's later speeches were taken down stenographically; and the texts of the speeches in the volumes of *Public Papers* were all taken (as edited) from the stenographic record as well as from the official copy given to the press.

of his death. Sometimes he got out too far in advance, as in the "quarantine" speech of 1937. But never was he content merely to follow.

A different kind of speech—a type that the President used to make in Albany and was to make quite frequently in Washington—was his first fireside chat of March 12, 1933. The President hit upon this type of speech as a means of talking directly to the people of the nation—or rather to each person in the nation. The function of the fireside chat was to explain by the use of simple, everyday language and homely analogy the complex problems of government.

He believed that if the people understood the facts, if they understood the reasons behind a government action or policy, if they were taken into the confidence of their government and received a full and truthful statement of what was happening, they would generally choose the right course. And he felt it was part of his job of leadership to give them those facts. There lay the greatest source of the President's strength. He was able to explain to the people the most intricate problems of government. He could do it by the use of simple language and by the clear, confident, and persuasive tone of his voice.

The first chat, eight days after the President took the oath of office, dealt with the banking crisis which had immobilized the entire nation. A bewildered and frightened people had watched the great financial institutions of America, which to them had come to be clothed with Gibraltar-like stability, one after another close their doors. For millions of Americans those closed doors had behind them a lifetime of hard-earned savings.

On March 6, two days after his inaugural, the President had taken the drastic step of closing all the banks, so that they might reopen gradually on a sound basis. This was bewildering even to those who had some experience in traditional finance. To the great mass of American citizens it was as understandable as the theory of relativity or nuclear fission. The President decided to go on the air to explain to the people what was going on and what he intended to do.

The Treasury Department prepared a scholarly, comprehensive draft of the speech. The President saw that it would be meaningless to most people, tossed it aside without any attempt at rewriting, and proceeded to write his own instead. He dictated it in simple, ordinary language—he looked for words that he would use in an informal conversation with one or two of his friends. He found the kind of language that everyone could understand. And everyone did understand. Confidence was restored. And in those dark days, confidence was essential, for a panic of bewilderment could have meant chaos and collapse.

The atmosphere in which the fireside chats were delivered bore little relationship to the quiet and secluded atmosphere generally associated with a real fireside. There happened to be a real fireplace in the room, but it was empty. At it the President sat before a desk on which were bunched three or four microphones, a reading light, a pitcher of water, and glasses. Equipment and machinery had to be brought in which would enable sixty or seventy million people to join in the scene and hear what was being said. There were some thirty uncomfortable folding chairs for those who had been invited to listen—usually friends, house guests, and selected public officials. The audience was seated about ten minutes past ten for a ten-thirty broadcast (the usual hour), and the President was wheeled in at about ten-twenty, carrying his reading-copy book and the inevitable cigarette.

Radio announcers for the major broadcasting chains would huddle about, testing their microphones. The radio engineers would test their equipment, which was spread all over the room from wall to wall, making it difficult to move about. The renovated White House will have an adequately equipped broadcasting room, but the basement room which had to serve the purpose for Roosevelt had never been intended or constructed for such use.

The President, once seated at his desk, exchanged greetings and pleasantries for a few moments with the guests and the announcers. As the minute of ten-thirty approached, the atmosphere got more tense. The President would put out his cigarette, arrange his reading copy, and take a drink of water, as nervously as when he was about to address a visible audience. Then, on signal, complete silence, a nod from the chief radio engineer, the usual announcement from each announcer stating tersely that the broadcast was coming from the White House and introducing "The President of the United States"—and finally the clear, resonant voice: "My friends."

The President's nervousness quickly disappeared; everyone sat back and listened; some of us followed the speech from mimeographed copies.

When he had finished, we all rose as the radio stations played "The Star-Spangled Banner." Then, at the signal showing the President was off the air, we went up to talk with him. There was a general hum of conversation, congratulations and good-bys, and the audience gradually drifted away.

The President remained behind to let the newspaper and movie photographers take pictures of him reading certain passages. He would select these himself. When this was over he would go upstairs to the Oval Room for a drink and a sandwich, a post-mortem discussion of the speech, the reading of the usual telegrams, which would begin to come in almost immediately, and then to bed.

During his first term as President my visits to Washington were almost exclusively social. Mrs. Rosenman and I were invited down to occasional formal dinners; we were invited for week-end and holiday visits; we accompanied the President on some of his boat trips down the Potomac River; but seldom was I called upon to do any work. He did ask me to help prepare the veto message of the soldiers' bonus bill, May 22, 1935, while we were cruising on the *Sequoia* on the Potomac earlier that month, and to help polish the language of his Annual Message of January 3, 1936.

Outside of those two isolated instances, I had nothing to do with any of the speeches or messages of the first term until the acceptance speech of 1936.

As long as Moley was officially in Washington, i.e., during 1933, he was generally in charge of speech preparation. After he left Washington at the end of the year he still used to go down frequently to help. Even when others worked on speeches, they generally cleared them through him. Donald Richberg, Louis Howe, William Bullitt, Felix Frankfurter (then at Harvard Law School), Hugh Johnson, and Rex Tugwell all worked with him at various times during 1933 and 1934; and most of them continued to work on speeches from time to time after he no longer did so. Tom Corcoran and Ben Cohen were brought in in 1934, first with Moley as a screen, supervising and directing them; and, beginning in early 1935, they continued on their own without Moley.

Since I have no personal knowledge of the preparation of the speeches and messages before 1936, I shall not attempt to discuss them in any detail.

The first year, 1933, was characterized by a quick succession of messages to the Congress—bold, direct, simple, asking for legislation needed to carry out his pledges of a New Deal:

March 9: Legislation to reopen the banks on a sound basis.

March 10: Legislation to effect economies in government.

March 13: Modification of the Volstead Law to permit light wines and beer.

March 16: Legislation for relief of agriculture (AAA).

March 29: Legislation for supervision of sale of securities (SEC).

April 3: Legislation to save farm mortgages from foreclosure (FCA).

April 5: Civilian Conservation Corps created (CCC).

April 10: Legislation for Tennessee Valley Authority (TVA).

April 13: Legislation to save small-home mortgages from foreclosure (HOLC).

May 4: Legislation for relief of railroads.

May 17: Legislation to establish the National Recovery Administration (NRA).

May 20: Legislation for relief of the oil industry.

For the most part, the Congress passed the bills which he requested one after another, in quick succession.

After the fireside chat on the banking crisis, the President made three other fireside chats during 1933. These chats not only informed; they cemented the relationship between the people and their President. They created confidence in Roosevelt's leadership; they explained his objectives so clearly that the people as a whole were ready to forgive the mistakes he made in his "bold experimentation" to reach those objectives.

In his second chat on May 7, he explained what had happened in banking since his first chat, and he described the other steps being taken: the new Civilian Conservation Corps, the proposed TVA, the legislation to save homes and farms from foreclosure, the direct unemployment relief appropriations, the proposed public works program, farm relief, the railroad bill, the action on gold, the international money and disarmament conferences then going on with ministers from abroad. All of these were crowded into a half-hour speech, and were summed up by Roosevelt as "a wise and sensible beginning."

Again, on July 24, the President took to the air to explain "the simple purposes and the solid foundations upon which our program of recovery is built." He wanted to explain that the "crowding events of the hundred days which had been devoted to the starting of the wheels of the New Deal" had "not been just a collection of haphazard schemes, but rather the orderly component parts of a connected and logical whole." He discussed the various acts and executive orders and showed how each fitted into a scheme to obtain his twin objectives of recovery and reform.

In his last chat of the year, October 21, he could begin to point out some of the beneficial results of his program. It was a cautious estimate; but he did speak of reduced unemployment, reduced foreclosures, increased farm income, abolition of child labor and sweatshops, increased soundness of banks, the increase in commodity price levels.

By 1934 there were no traces left of the panic and fear of March 4, 1933. There was complete realization, as the President himself put it, "that the Legislative and Executive branches of their government were willing and ready to use all of the power and resources of the nation to alleviate suffering, prevent further disaster, and rebuild the structure of economic life upon firmer foundations of social justice."[3] And with it had come general acceptance and approval of his program of reform.

Nineteen hundred and thirty-four was a year of continued recovery and continued reform. But in 1934 voices began to be heard against the reforms. There was "definitely a lining up of those on the one hand who wished to stop the New Deal in its tracks, and those on the other hand who wished to see it go further along the lines it had laid down."[4] Therefore, in the 1934 speeches and messages Roosevelt began to express himself forcibly against the opponents of his program. He was making a record, for in November, 1934, the Congressional campaigns would place before the people the issue of the New Deal.

During the year he made many requests for additional legislation and issued many executive orders, but made only two fireside chats. The first one followed the end of the session of the Congress, June 28, 1934.

It was more argumentative than explanatory. But it was simple, direct —almost unanswerable—argument. It was built around three simple questions: "Are you better off than you were last year?" "Have you as an individual paid too high a price for these gains?" And referring to the charges of "plausible self-seekers and theoretical die-hards" that individual liberty was being lost in the process of recovery: "Have you lost any of your rights or liberty or constitutional freedom of action and choice?"

He accused the "Doubting Thomases," the opponents of his program,

[3] Introduction, 1934 Vol., *Public Papers*, p. 3.
[4] *Ibid.*, p. 6.

of being moved by a desire for special privilege, and boldly laid out the program for the "larger future": better homes, better land use, development of water resources, social insurance. He anticipated the attacks to come:

> A few timid people, who fear progress, will try to give you new and strange names for what we are doing. Sometimes they will call it "Fascism," sometimes "Communism," sometimes "Regimentation," sometimes "Socialism." But, in so doing, they are trying to make very complex and theoretical something that is really very simple and very practical.
> I believe in practical explanations and in practical policies. I believe that what we are doing today is a necessary fulfillment of what Americans have always been doing—a fulfillment of old and tested American ideals.

His next fireside chat was three months later, September 30. The thesis of the speech was simple: "We are moving forward to greater freedom, to greater security for the average man." But the attacks on the program had been growing, and the President paid his respects to the "reactionary lawyers," "political editors" and to their "awesome pronouncements concerning the unconstitutionality of some of our measures of recovery and relief and reform."

The New Deal went to the polls in November, 1934, in the Congressional elections, and the resounding victory surprised even Roosevelt. His party gained seats in both Houses of the Congress. Obviously the people did understand and did approve his leadership and his program. He continued in 1935 to send recommendations to Congress for additional legislation—social security, conservation of national resources, regulation of public utility holding companies, work relief appropriations, tax revision. Executive orders set up the Resettlement Administration, the Rural Electrification Administration, the National Resources Committee, National Labor Relations Board, and the National Youth Administration.

But although Roosevelt had beaten the opposition to his program at the polls in 1934, the Supreme Court began in 1935 to take the program apart by judicial decisions. The decisions not only nullified much that had been done but also cast doubt on the possibility of doing anything effective in the future to bring about the New Deal.

Chapter VIII

The Second Presidential Campaign, 1936

||||||||||||||||||||||||||||||||||||||||||||||||||||||||||||||||||||||||||||||||||||||||||||||||||||||||||||||||||||||||||||||||||||||||||||||

For the Decoration Day week end, 1936, the President invited Mrs. Rosenman and me to accompany him on a trip down the Potomac. I assumed that this was to be another social cruise with no work to do. Once we were under way, however, the President began to talk about the coming campaign for re-election.

Although the President was to carry every state but Maine and Vermont in 1936, in the spring the prospects for re-election did not seem quite that bright. Political opposition had begun to crystallize. The close Democratic unity had begun to dissolve; many of the old-line Democrats, especially from the South, had come to feel that the New Deal was a little too strong for their tastes. The American Liberty League had been organized, and it included among its prominent members a number of national leaders of the Democratic party. Its purpose was to prevent the President's re-election; it proclaimed that much of his program threatened fundamental American liberties and freedoms. In later years, the majority of the people came to look upon such charges as ridiculous. But when this line of attack was first vigorously pushed in 1936—and with such men as John W. Davis and Alfred E. Smith, both former Democratic candidates for the Presidency, acting as its leading proponents—Roosevelt's friends took the charges seriously. So did he.

There were other factors that made the outlook for the coming election less rosy than it turned out to be. With the country getting on its feet again, the old fear which had paralyzed the nation four years before had disappeared. Many of the sick patients of 1932—big industrialists and businessmen, financiers, and others—were ready in 1936, as Roosevelt put it during the campaign, to "throw their crutches at the doctor"; and they were raising the cry of "communism," as they were going to each four years thereafter.

I talked to the President rather lugubriously on this trip about what seemed to many Democratic political leaders to be a definite popular trend away from him. He refused to be excited or worried.

"This is only May," he said, smiling. "Lots of things can happen before November. Tides turn in politics; the sentiment of the voters changes very quickly. Wait till October comes around when we really get a chance to tell the people the facts—which they're not getting now from their newspapers."

At least 85 per cent of the press was against him, and most of the papers were disturbingly articulate and vehement in saying so.

The other guests on the *Potomac* on this trip were Stanley High and his wife. The President introduced High to me as one who had helped him on several speeches in 1935 and 1936, and as one of the people whom he had asked to help in the coming campaign.

High had been active in Republican circles four years earlier in 1932. In 1940, 1944 and 1948 he was again to take an active part in behalf of the Republican candidates against President Roosevelt and President Truman. It would appear, therefore, that 1936 was rather a political aberration for High, but I was to find him an excellent writer and a very congenial collaborator. He had a happy facility of expression and phrasemaking, perhaps a better one than anyone else with whom I worked on Roosevelt speeches. He was very easy to get along with, and relatively immune from the ordinary occupational diseases of speech writing—argumentativeness and stubbornness. There is something about helping in the preparation of a speech for the President of the United States—perhaps the realization that it is going to be a part of history and may indeed help shape history—that tends to make people argue over every little phrase and every shade of meaning. With some collaborators, valuable time was lost in argument over whether a particular paragraph should go in a speech as it was written or whether a few words should be changed or whether it should go in at all. With Stanley High there was no such difficulty.

On my first meeting with High, however, the President did not suggest that I was to do any work with him in the campaign. I later realized that he had arranged for Stanley and me to meet so that I might tell him about some of our experiences and problems in the gubernatorial campaigns in New York. The President talked about my first meeting with him on that Hoboken ferry in 1928 and about the various red manila envelopes of campaign material which I had with me. The Hoboken ferry on the Hudson River was a far cry from the *Potomac* on the Potomac, but those red manila envelopes seemed to bridge the gap. The President said that for the coming campaign trips he wanted to take along the same kind of material, prepared in exactly the same way.

I thought that was the end of it, but in June, a few days before the Democratic Convention, Missy telephoned and said that the President wanted me to come down and stay at the White House with him during the convention period. I told her that I was doubtful about how useful I could be. Having had so little to do with the Administration during the intervening four years, I did not have the kind of day-to-day firsthand knowledge that I felt was necessary to be helpful to the President. Missy answered that the President needed some help during that trying period, and that I always seemed to be able to work quietly with him without getting him nervous. He had given her the same reason back in 1932 for asking me to stay at the Executive Mansion in Albany during the national convention.

On the Sunday before the 1936 Democratic Convention was to begin I arrived at the White House and was assigned to one of the guest rooms opposite the President's study. Until Pearl Harbor, when the White House became too busy and too full to take care of many overnight guests, I usually occupied one of these bedrooms on overnight visits, although at one time or another I have slept in each of the White House guest rooms. It is doubtless ungracious, but nevertheless factual, for me to report that all the guest-room beds were equally uncomfortable. From time to time, I secretly checked my appraisals with other guests and they agreed. Of course, no one thought of mentioning this to anyone connected with the household. As a result nothing was done about it until word came in 1939 of the projected visit of the King and Queen of England. Someone must have spoken about the beds to Mrs. Roosevelt, for immediately she took steps to remedy the difficulty all through the house. After that, thanks to King George and Queen Elizabeth and some unknown but courageous complainant, sleeping in the White House became a more comfortable experience.

By arrangement Stanley came over and met me in one of the White House offices and we started to work on a draft of an acceptance speech. After lunch, the President asked us to come into his study, where we found Senator Alben Barkley, who was to make the keynote speech as temporary chairman of the convention, and Senator Joseph T. Robinson, who was to be the permanent chairman. He wanted us to hear the speeches they proposed to make at the convention. This was the way to make sure that there were no major variances in policy declarations at the convention, and is not an unusual procedure. There was some discussion about the contents of the speeches, and also about what was to go into the platform.

After Barkley and Robinson left, the President told us that a group working on the platform was coming over after dinner to bring a first draft, and he invited us to join them.

It is no secret that the first draft of a platform on which a President is to run for re-election is generally prepared at the White House and not at the convention. As finally adopted, there are, of course, differences from the draft written at the White House—sometimes major differences. But obviously the platform for re-election must, in the main, conform with the President's views and with his course of action during the preceding four years.

The group that evening consisted of the President, Senator Wagner, who was to be the chairman of the Resolutions Committee, Assistant Attorney General John Dickinson, William Bullitt, High, Missy, and me. Dickinson had prepared a long draft which he read to the group. There was considerable criticism of both its substance and form. The President wanted a shorter and simpler platform.

I knew that no document could possibly be drafted with so many people in the room. In my experience in drafting documents, I have never seen one prepared satisfactorily with more than three or four persons present. The larger the number of participants, the more argument and discussion go on, and the less thinking and writing.

The evening progressed, but the drafting of a platform did not. There were stenographers waiting to take dictation, but when midnight came they did not have very much on paper.

Finally, a little past midnight, Bullitt said, "We'll never get anywhere this way. My suggestion is that we have someone sit down and spend the rest of the night getting up a draft of the platform which we can look at tomorrow. My nomination for this job is Sam Rosenman."

The President and the others acquiesced, and the meeting rapidly broke up. Everybody was hot and tired and wanted to get home as quickly as possible. High and I were left alone with the President and

Missy. I suggested that High and I go over to the Executive Offices of the White House and see what we could do in the way of a draft. I must say that I considered myself wholly inadequate to the task, having been thrust into it without any notice and without any preparation. I had hardly made a practice of reading party platforms, let alone writing them. But there we were, and the job seemed to be up to us to do, if it was ever to get done. The President told us to go ahead; and just before being wheeled off to bed, said:

"I have one thought which I would like to leave with you. I would like to have as short a platform as possible this year, and as I said during the discussion this evening I would like to have it based on the sentence of the Declaration of Independence, 'We hold these truths to be self-evident.' Here are all the drafts which have been submitted by Wagner and some others. Try to put all the ideas together into one short one."

With those few instructions, Missy, High and I went over to the executive offices. Missy soon retired, leaving High and me alone. We went to work—High at the typewriter, I sitting alongside him—and together we knocked out a draft that night. It was as short as the President had desired, and it was based on the language of the Declaration of Independence. It was a brief but full statement of the tenets of the New Deal, and a pledge of action in accordance with them.

However, there were parts still missing on which we would require further policy discussion. Most pressing was what to suggest about the recent Supreme Court decisions which were nullifying the most important recovery and reform measures of the New Deal. Nor did we have time to draft a foreign affairs plank or a peroration.

High and I worked nearly all that night. This was to become a frequent practice of the speech-writing teams in order to have a draft ready for the President to read at breakfast time. The stenographers and night watchmen at the White House were quite accustomed to activity in the Cabinet Room late into the night whenever a major speech was in preparation. So, fortunately, were the people in charge of the kitchen at the White House.

On this occasion, however, there were no sandwiches or coffee; the custom had not yet been started. So, at about three-thirty in the morning, High and I decided to go over to Childs, not far from the White House, for breakfast. I remember that in order to get out of the White House we had to wake up one of the guards. We returned to put the finishing touches on the platform, and the draft was typed and on the President's breakfast tray the next morning.

High went to his hotel, and I went to my room. We had an hour or so of rest and a shower.

Stanley came over for breakfast early Monday morning and we went into the President's bedroom. There we met Donald Richberg, who had been asked by the President to prepare a plank on the recent Supreme Court decisions and on proposals for dealing with them. The President read our latest draft aloud and approved it. We discussed the plank that Richberg had submitted and after a few minor changes it was incorporated in the proposed platform.

We went into my bedroom and were in the process of arranging a new draft when Bullitt came in and gave us a draft of a plank on foreign affairs, and Harry Hopkins came in with a suggested peroration.

A little later in the Oval Room the same group gathered that had met the night before, with the addition of Richberg and Hopkins. After more discussion and changes, the group finally approved the draft and broke up. A new clean draft was made ready, and was about to be sent over to Senator Wagner to take to the convention in Philadelphia, when Robert La Follette called me on the phone.

"I think you ought to know that that peroration which Harry gave you and which I understand the President is using was given to Harry by me, and it is practically the same peroration which my father used back in 1924 when he ran for President on the Progressive ticket. I don't know whether anyone will discover it or not but you ought to know."

I thanked him and we went in to tell the President. He said to strike it out and get up a new one. So while Wagner waited, we quickly prepared a new one, which the President approved, and the platform went off to Philadelphia.

But this platform draft met the same literary fate that befell later platforms which were drafted in the White House. A great many new provisions were inserted at the request of different groups or delegates. Except perhaps for literary reasons, such additions are highly desirable. For above all, a platform is, and should be, the work of the convention rather than of the White House or the candidate—provided, of course, that it does not conflict with the candidate's own views.

After we had finished our chores on the platform, the President asked High and me to prepare a rough first draft of an acceptance speech. This time—unlike 1932—Roosevelt's nomination was certain, and he had decided again to go to the convention and accept the nomination on the spot.

At the same time, and unknown to us, Roosevelt had asked Moley and Thomas G. Corcoran to prepare a first draft for him. This was unusual in speech writing. On other matters Roosevelt had developed a habit of asking two different people to do the same thing for him at the same time. Sometimes he had forgotten that he had asked one person to do the job by the time he asked the second. Sometimes he did it, I am sure, in order to have one check on the other—without either knowing it. Invariably the two persons working on the same project would run into each other in their research or would soon hear about each other. Those who were unfamiliar with the President's method of working would get irritated; those who worked with him for any length of time grew accustomed to this strange and inefficient practice and did the best they could. Although the President was apologetic whenever it was called to his attention, he never fully dropped this habit.

But the only times I have known him to do this with speech writers were where Moley was concerned. And, knowing Roosevelt as I did, I can understand it. Since the inauguration Moley had been the person most constantly at his side in connection with speeches. Roosevelt's great failing was his inability to fire people who had been close to him. He was loath to tell Moley that he was about to use other people for help on speeches. But he did want to make a change because by this time he felt that Moley's political and economic views were no longer close enough to his own. He thought that Moley had swung too far and too definitely to the right. It would have been a painful and embarrassing process for them to try to work together on ideas and words when they were no longer together on purposes and objectives. But Roosevelt hated to make the break cleanly and definitely as he should have.

As was inevitable, we all learned what was going on. After a while the President told us that a draft had been prepared by Moley and Corcoran and gave us a copy of it, asking us to try to work it into the draft that we had prepared, which he liked. This was not an easy thing to do. The Moley-Corcoran draft was a very moderate, conciliatory speech based on the theme of faith, hope and charity as the foundation of a "nation fighting the fight for freedom in a modern civilization."

Our draft, on the other hand, was a militant, bare-fisted statement of the necessity for economic freedom to supplement the political freedom the people had won in the past. It was intended to give battle to the reactionaries in both parties who were now out in full force to stop the New Deal. And there was very little in it that was conciliatory.

How to work these two themes into one speech presented a problem that was never really solved—as a reading makes evident. However, we did the best we could with occasional help from Don Richberg.

Three days before the speech was to be delivered, Roosevelt had the four of us—Moley, Corcoran, High and me—in to dinner. That night in the small family dining room, for the first and only time in my life, I saw the President forget himself as a gentleman. He began twitting Moley about his new conservatism and about the influence of his "new, rich friends" on his recent writings, which had been very critical of the Administration. Moley responded with what I thought was justifiable heat. The President grew angry, and the exchanges between them became very bitter. We all felt embarrassed; Missy did her best to change the subject but failed. Their words became more acrimonious. Roosevelt said that Moley's criticisms would not have received any attention but for the fact that, like Hugh Johnson's, they came from a former intimate of the Administration. Moley resented this, and said something to the effect that Roosevelt's inability to take criticism was leading him down the wrong paths. While I knew how deeply Roosevelt had been stung by the unfriendly attacks on his policies by Johnson and Moley, I thought that his temper and language were particularly unjustified, not only because there were other people present, but because they were all his invited guests. It was an ordeal for all of us, and we were relieved when dinner finally broke up. I am sure that Roosevelt soon felt sorry for what he had said; but I could not see how the two of them could ever resume their earlier relationship. They never did.

After his final break with the President, Moley became quite vehement in his opposition to Roosevelt and to his policies. In magazine articles, and later in a book, he bitterly attacked his former friend. The same course was later followed by others who had been powerful in the Roosevelt Administrations: Hugh Johnson, James Farley, William C. Bullitt, Jesse Jones.

Nearly all these men owed their high public position entirely to Roosevelt. In all probability none of them would ever have been known to national history were it not for Roosevelt. Somehow they all seem to forget that the only reason their attacks received as wide circulation as they did was that at one time they had been selected by the man they were vilifying to be his associates in great causes. It is hard to understand, as one reads the writings of Jesse Jones, for example, how Jones could have been so anxious to continue to serve for almost thirteen years with the kind of man he describes Roosevelt as having been.

Jones was opposed to Roosevelt's nomination in 1940. Yet in 1940 he was willing—if not anxious—to be nominated as Vice-President with this man whom he now criticizes so harshly. And he stayed willingly and actively in Roosevelt's Administration for four years thereafter in spite of his feelings. In 1944 he was again opposed to Roosevelt's nomination; yet he was willing to remain in his Administration until he was finally dismissed. I have said—and repeat—that the method of his dismissal was unfair and unlike the Roosevelt I knew; but I think that Jesse, in view of his presently expressed opinion of Roosevelt, should not have waited for the dismissal. For some reason or other, these bitter critics never seemed to discover Roosevelt's heinous faults until he had to dismiss them or refused to acquiesce in their ambitions.

In his 1936 acceptance speech, the President attacked the reactionaries of the nation, to whom he gave, for the first time, the name of "economic royalists." He pointed out that in the eighteenth century full political freedom had been attained in the United States in spite of the efforts of royalists or tories to prevent it. But, he said, the new age of "machinery, of railroads; of steam and electricity; the telegraph and the radio; mass production, mass distribution—all of these combined to bring forward a new civilization and with it a new problem for those who sought to remain free."

The "economic royalists" were the same kind of tories now using economic power to block equality of economic opportunity for the ordinary citizen. The New Deal was "committed to the proposition that freedom is no half-and-half affair. If the average citizen is guaranteed equal opportunity in the polling place, he must have equal opportunity in the market place."

The phrase "economic royalist" was suggested by High, and it is another one of those which have been frequently quoted. It expressed vividly the President's feeling about the concentration of economic power in the hands of those who sought to control the lives of less fortunate persons, and to direct the action of government itself. The

President liked that phrase, and rolled it off at the Philadelphia Convention in great style.

In his annual message of January, 1936, Roosevelt had devoted much time to a discussion of foreign affairs, pointing out the dangers from aggression and totalitarianism abroad. Now, in his acceptance speech, he again took cognizance of the rising dictatorships abroad, referring to the people "in other lands" who have "grown too weary to carry on the fight. They have sold their heritage of freedom for the illusion of a living. They have yielded their democracy." The President then expressed a conviction that he felt deeply: that only by making democracy work here at home could we revive it in those parts of the world where it had died.

"We are fighting," he said, "to save a great and precious form of government for ourselves and for the world. . . . This generation of Americans has a rendezvous with destiny."

"Rendezvous with destiny" is another famous phrase which has come down through the years. It was suggested by Corcoran.

The President did not have a restful summer vacation that year. Instead, he made a number of those "nonpolitical" trips around the country which are, of course, the most effective political trips a President can make. His speeches, however, were generally nonpolitical. Corcoran, Cohen, Bullitt and High worked on these, either alone or in collaboration.

One of them—his speech at Chautauqua on August 14—deserves special comment, for it was a forerunner of many that he was to make a few years later. It was devoted almost entirely to foreign affairs. The President was beginning to see clearly the crisis which was shaping up abroad, and long before his public expression of concern he had expressed privately his very deep worry.[1]

As things got worse in Europe, Roosevelt's anxiety grew and he decided at Chautauqua to make further and bolder reference to the storm he saw coming.

He pointed out how in the field of world policy he had tried to dedicate this nation to the policy of the good neighbor. He remarked again on the long period of friendship between the United States and Canada without guns or soldiers or barbed wire at the frontier—a

[1] See for example his letters to Colonel Edward M. House, Ambassador William E. Dodd, and Ambassador Jesse I. Straus in Elliott Roosevelt (ed.), *F.D.R.: His Personal Letters* (New York: Duell, Sloan & Pearce, 1947), pp. 472, 543, 555.

frontier which he described as "3,000 miles of friendship." Propheti
cally he said: "We are not isolationists except in so far as we seek to
isolate ourselves completely from war. Yet we must remember that so
long as war exists on earth there will be some danger that even the
nation which most ardently desires peace may be drawn into war."

The keynote of the speech—perhaps the keynote of the President's
whole foreign policy in the long years before Pearl Harbor—was
summed up in the famous and heartfelt words:

"I have seen war. I have seen war on land and sea. I have seen blood
running from the wounded. I have seen men coughing out their gassed
lungs. I have seen the dead in the mud. . . . I have seen children
starving. I have seen the agony of mothers and wives. *I hate war.*'

The speech was a direct bid—but a wholly unsuccessful one—to the
nations of the world to join with the United States in its efforts to
maintain the peace.

The draft of the speech was prepared by Bullitt. Bullitt has told me
that the phrase "I hate war" was one he had carried in his memory
since 1917. During a private talk with President Wilson soon after the
declaration of war by the United States, Wilson, with tears in his eyes,
had dramatically seized Bullitt's hands and, in great emotion, had used
that phrase.

President Roosevelt thought this one of his important speeches.
Indeed, the gift he sent to many of his friends on the following Christmas was a specially printed and inscribed copy of it.

The speech was the beginning of many addresses and statements in
the years to come that were designed to warn the people of the United
States and the world of the dangers which lurked in all dictatorships.

It is idle to speculate now how history might have been altered if the
President's words at Chautauqua had fallen on more fertile ground, or
if he had pressed the theme more insistently. He was later to come back
to the theme—at Chicago in 1937, in the famous "quarantine" speech.
But even that speech was too much and too early for the people. They
were still a long way from being ready to follow on a path of stern
resistance to the rising dictatorships.

I did no work on the Chautauqua speech or on any of the others that
the President made that summer. I assumed that my chores for 1936
were completed, and that I would have only a strong rooting interest
in the 1936 campaign. I was mistaken.

As his opening gun in the campaign, the President was to speak at the

Democratic State Convention at Syracuse, New York, on September 29, where Governor Herbert H. Lehman was to be renominated. By this time, the relations between Moley and the President had become even more strained. It seems, however, that at the suggestion of Frank Walker, Moley had been invited to Hyde Park to discuss the campaign generally and this speech in particular. At the same time, Corcoran, High and I had been asked to prepare a draft and to be ready for further work. The President had gone to Hyde Park, and we were asked to come up there.

I remember that High and I went up together by train after working for a couple of days on the speech. We had not had enough time to type a few inserts which we had discussed. We asked the train conductor whether we could use the baggage car; and between New York and Poughkeepsie, using a trunk as a table for High's portable typewriter, we wrote some paragraphs that survived through to the reading copy.

When we got to Hyde Park, we saw that the President was about to repeat his performance of last June. He did not want Moley to know that he had called us in. It was another example of his well-known weakness—his desire to please the people around him and to avoid personal conflict among them. Instead of telling Moley frankly that he wanted other people to work on the speech, he gave him the impression that he was working on it alone. Maybe he hoped to put off the final break and make everybody happy and nobody angry. Anyway, he asked the rest of us to remain out of sight while Moley was in Hyde Park. We did; but Hyde Park is not big and it was not too easy to find a hiding place for our group, which included High, Corcoran, Corcoran's secretary (now his wife), Mrs. Rosenman and me.

Mrs. Roosevelt moved us out of the house for a day or two to an apartment over a tearoom about two miles away from the President's residence. The following letter from her is interesting, for it has to do with our involuntary stay at the tearoom:

DEAR SAM

I was humiliated beyond words when I learned from Nellie Johansen that she accepted money from you and Mr. High and Mr. Corcoran for your meals. That place belongs to me and I use it for my guests when the house is full. Nellie simply didn't understand and if I don't tell her each time, she gets confused.

I hope you were comfortable and found everything pleasant. I am enclosing my check for $8.00. Will you please reimburse the other two for their share?

Tell Dorothy I am looking forward to seeing her on Monday at the United Neighborhood dinner if I don't see you both before that time.

Very cordially yours

/s/   ELEANOR ROOSEVELT

Fortunately, there were few experiences like that game of hide-and-seek with Moley, so it could be borne in good humor—even jocularly. It was not until Moley had left after a day's stay that we were again permitted to come out into daylight. By this time we had finished our first draft and the President went to work on it.

The purpose of this speech was that of any first speech of a well-conducted campaign—to lay out the general issues which were going to form the basis of the debate between the candidates. The Republican leaders and the right wing of the Democratic party had decided to base their campaign upon the charge that the New Deal was an "alien" form of philosophy, that it was undermining the American constitutional system, that it was endangering the liberties and freedoms of the people —and that it was the forerunner of communism, if not communism itself. The Hearst newspapers enthusiastically took up that hue and cry. Much of the anti-Roosevelt press followed suit.

The President, instead of "ducking" or ignoring the issue, decided to meet it head on, and at once, in the very first speech of the campaign:

I have not sought, I do not seek, I repudiate the support of any advocate of communism or of any other alien "ism" which would by fair means or foul change our American democracy. That is my position. It always has been my position. It always will be my position.

In that speech there was an excellent example of the vivid imagery that President Roosevelt knew so well how to use to make a point. Recalling the situation in 1933 when the American economy was crumbling, he referred to the "powerful leaders of industry and banking who came to me in Washington . . . pleading to be saved."

I remember very well the President's whimsical smile as he dictated the following insert, which, when delivered, made his audience howl:

"In the summer of 1933, a nice old gentleman wearing a silk hat fell off the end of a pier. He was unable to swim. A friend ran down the pier, dived overboard and pulled him out; but the silk hat floated off with the tide. After the old gentleman had been revived, he was effusive in his thanks. He praised his friend for saving his life. Today, three years later, the old gentleman is berating his friend because the silk hat was lost."

For the rest of his Presidency, Roosevelt was to be constantly attacked by those who believed it was still possible to find and retrieve that old silk hat.

Another example of the President's keen feeling for words and his use of a homely and effective phrase to describe a complicated situation occurred in 1935 when the Supreme Court declared unconstitutional the National Recovery Act. One morning as he was dressing to go over to the office for his first press conference since the decision, Stephen Early, his press secretary for many years, came in as usual. In the course of conversation Steve remarked that he had driven down that morning with his brother-in-law, George Holmes, and that they had talked about the Court decision. He added casually,

"George says that those boys up there think that this is still the horse-and-buggy age."

The President never said a word as he slipped on his coat and motioned that he was ready to be wheeled over to the office. But he immediately recognized the phrase as one that everyone could understand, and that would be clearer in its implications than the most learned constitutional treatise on the effect of the decision.

So, in the midst of a twenty-page press conference in which he discussed the opinion point by point, he said:

"The whole tendency over these years has been to view the interstate commerce clause in the light of present-day civilization. The country was in the horse-and-buggy age when that clause was written and if you go back to the debates on the Federal Constitution you will find in 1787 that one of the impelling motives for putting in that clause was this: There wasn't much interstate commerce at all—probably 80 or 90 percent of the human beings in the thirteen original States were completely self-supporting within their own communities."

It was the "horse-and-buggy age" that made all the headlines in the newspapers. It was the phrase people used most in discussions at the time—in parlors, cracker-barrel grocery stores and street corners—in arguing with each other about the controversy. It is the phrase that people still remember when they talk about Roosevelt's fight with the Court.

In this speech at Syracuse in 1936, the President made the point—which he made time and again—that it was the liberal, progressive program of the New Deal that saved the country from communism by eradicating the domestic conditions "congenial to communism." Quoting a sentence from Macaulay, he said, "The voice of great events is proclaiming to us: 'Reform if you would preserve.' Wise and prudent men—intelligent conservatives—have long known that in a changing world worthy institutions can be conserved only by adjusting them to the changing time. . . . I am that kind of conservative because I am that kind of liberal."

After this speech the President returned to Washington only to leave soon on a short campaign trip through West Virginia and Pennsylvania. Missy called me in New York and told me that the President wanted me to meet him in Washington to work on the major speech of that trip, scheduled for Forbes Field, the baseball park in Pittsburgh, the night of October 1. That was where, in 1932, he had made the speech promising to curtail federal expenditures and balance the budget. And it was in discussing the preparations for the 1936 speech at Forbes Field that he asked me to draft an explanation of his earlier speech (an incident that I have described in Chapter VII).

When I got down to Washington, I found that no one had prepared even a rough draft of a speech for Pittsburgh, and that there was apparently no material in hand. The President wanted to talk about the finances of the nation, and especially to meet the charge that the extravagance of the New Deal was forcing the country into bankruptcy. Several representatives of the Treasury, including Secretary Henry Morgenthau, attended the first conference in the Oval Room at which the speech was discussed.

Since the campaign train was to leave two days later, there was a sense of rush and urgency in the meeting. The President had not found time to think much about the speech. He had been kept busy passing on the innumerable arrangements that always had to be made before a campaign trip. They included nice questions of protocol which might seem trivial but, as Charles Evans Hughes had learned in 1916, might make quite a difference. For in 1916 Hughes had neglected to see Hiram Johnson, and partly as a result thereof lost California by a narrow margin—and with it the Presidency. Which local politicians would ride on the campaign train from one station to another; whom the President would talk with between and at various stops; who would be on the rear platform with him when he made extemporaneous speeches at stations—these and a host of similar delicate problems had to be considered and decided. These little details never occur to the newspaper reader who sees a picture of the President on the rear platform of the train surrounded by six or seven people, or who reads that State Committeeman John Jones got on at one station and got off at another in order to make way for Congressman James Smith. All this, however, is carefully prearranged, and President Roosevelt used to take a keen personal interest in the arrangements; whenever he had the time, he would participate in them himself.

After the plans were made and the details settled, the President entrusted the execution of them to his secretary, Marvin H. McIntyre. "Mac," as he was known around the White House was a marvel of tact and firmness in these matters. It is a most difficult thing to have to say politely and without giving too much offense that Messrs. A, B, D and F, who were on the station platform alongside the campaign train, might go in to see the President or ride for several hours on the train or stand with him on the rear platform—but not C and E.

At that evening meeting in the White House there was much talk about the subject matter of the Pittsburgh speech; and as time went on without much practical result, the Secretary of the Treasury finally said: "Mr. President, a speech has been prepared for me to be delivered at a dinner next week at a bankers' convention. It deals with the finances of the nation. Why don't you use that speech and deliver it at Forbes Field?"

While the President was quite sure that the kind of speech a Secretary of the Treasury might make at a bankers' dinner was not quite the kind of speech a Presidential candidate could successfully make in a baseball park at night, he wanted to be polite and settled back to hear the draft read to him.

We all listened attentively for a few minutes. The President realized right away that it would never do; however, he apparently was steeled to hear it to the end. Missy was not quite so polite. At the end of the second page she stood up and with great firmness announced: "By this time all of the bleachers are empty, and the folks are beginning to walk out of the grandstand."

As she sauntered out of the room, we all burst into laughter, including the Secretary of the Treasury himself. Further reading of the draft was discontinued.

Of course, as I have pointed out earlier, the President gave up trying to "explain" his 1932 Pittsburgh speech in 1936.

After the Pittsburgh speech there was a lull for a few days. Then on October 8 the President began his main campaign trip through several of the Midwestern states. He asked Mrs. Rosenman and me to go with him. Senators Burton K. Wheeler, Joseph O'Mahoney, and Key Pittman; Breckinridge Long of the State Department; and Secretary of Agriculture Henry A. Wallace, had also been invited.

Wallace accompanied us for a good part of this trip because we were passing through some of the most important agricultural territory of the United States. His intimate knowledge of the farm community was very helpful, though he later lost his close touch with the agricultural voters. In 1936 he was a popular figure with the farmer. At least the President thought so—and that was the reason for his presence on the train.

I assumed that all these men had been asked to come along to advise on speeches and political activities, for each of them was from one of the states the trip was to cover. But the fact is that they did little or no work on the speeches, except to read them over and make a few suggestions here and there. However, they were invaluable to the President in meeting and talking with the many political leaders who boarded the train at different stops to ride for a few hours.

The 1936 campaign trip was the most strenuous I ever took with the President. I was the only member of the speech-writing team on the train; the others—High, Tommy Corcoran and Ben Cohen—had stayed in Washington to prepare material which they were to send along for us to use in the speeches. It came either by wire, or in the mail pouch which met the train at various stops.

As I explained earlier, Corcoran and Cohen had been brought in as speech writers by Moley in 1934. They had met him originally in connection with legislation to regulate securities exchanges and public utilities. Starting in 1935 they had begun to work directly with the President on speeches and legislation, and gradually they became two of the most important handymen and trouble shooters the President had.

When I first met them, it was on a purely social basis; it was not until the campaign of 1936 that we began to work together intensively.

Each of these two men was remarkable in his own way; together they constituted a unique team. For four years—from 1936 to 1940—I would say that they were as intimate and important a part of the Administration as any Cabinet officer or Presidential adviser—and much more so than most of them. I got to know them both very well during those four years. They are in different pursuits now, but in those days they worked together as one of the most effective mainsprings of the New Deal.

Tommy, as almost everyone in Washington used to call him, was a young, stalwart and enthusiastic worshiper at the shrine of Roosevelt. Over the years, he introduced into many of the departments and agencies in Washington a number of young lawyers who were his loyal friends, so his contacts with the administration of government reached all over Washington.

He was in those days a New Dealer without one per cent deviation. Disloyalty or opposition to the principles of the New Deal was to him a serious offense; no one who was guilty could be a friend of his.

He was the aggressive partner of the team, fighting, cajoling, threatening, ready to do almost anything to advance the program. He had warmth and wit, and a keen and exuberant mind. Ben was more resourceful, a more careful and astute lawyer and a more philosophical thinker—but shy and reserved and constantly in the background. Tom stormed in and out of the White House with all sorts of news and ideas; but when he wanted a bill drawn or an order dressed up it was to Ben he turned, and Ben did it. Tom blew in and out of a Senator's office demanding a vote for a New Deal measure, having a good reason at the tip of his tongue to overcome any and all objection. But if the Senator wanted a documented brief for the bill or a scholarly statement of its merits, it was Ben who furnished it. Each had his own peculiar usefulness: Tom's was action; Ben's was thought. Each admired, adored, and respected the other; and each would claim that the other was the more important member of the team. In fact, each was the supplement of the other.

Everyone admired Tom's great ability; nearly everyone liked him personally. He could entertain in any kind of group—he played the accordion and the piano equally well; he could sing and had an inexhaustible supply of diverting songs. He loved life and people and action and laughter; and he was welcome in nearly all homes not only as a political power in Washington but as a great social asset at a party. He did not like to go to social affairs unless he might meet someone from whom he could get some information or some action. At parties and from his far-flung group of friends he got all the latest gossip and serious information about anyone of importance.

One of Roosevelt's very human qualities was his fondness for homey, friendly gossip. He loved to tell old family anecdotes and reminisce about personalities and old friends—what they were now doing, whom their children married, where they were living. He was always eager to hear about the latest goings-on in Washington social life. And he would lay aside work eagerly for a few minutes if anyone came in with a new story about someone prominent in the Washington political scene. Tommy always had plenty of these stories.

In his zeal for the New Deal Tommy was ready to "slug it out" directly if necessary; but he preferred to get things done indirectly. He knew how to put great political pressure on Congressmen and on others.

He could always be counted on to insist on fighting words in a speech wherever opponents of the New Deal were concerned. He did not give up easily on his views about what should go into a speech. He was always ready with quotations. There was one particular thought which he tried time and again in the 1936 campaign to get into one speech after another. The President had spoken of the way interlocking directors and interlocking bankers were used to concentrate industrial control in a small group of corporations, and Tommy wanted to add the phrase "interlocking lawyers." For some reason the President did not like that phrase. He would cross it out in one draft after another, and then in one speech after another. It soon got to be a standing joke among us, for it began to appear in a slightly different form each time. It was not a very important matter, but the incident shows Tom's "stick-to-itiveness" on all things. It finally did get in—at Chicago—and Tommy sent me a wire at once reading in part as follows:

Speech came over fine. Thanks for interlocking lawyers. Mail at Grand Rapids. Wired you statement as requested.

TOM CORCORAN

Ben was not always at our White House sessions. He preferred to stay in his own office long past midnight, reading, studying and writing. For years we urged him fruitlessly to join us, and it was not until the President himself insisted that he began to come regularly. But even by this kind of remote control, his contribution to the thought in many speeches was as great as Tom's. He, too, was a 100 per cent New Dealer; but he could more easily see the other side of a question, and he was much less vitriolic in discussing it.

These two men, working together during the second term, took many burdens from Roosevelt's shoulders. They left their liberal, progressive imprint on nearly all the major public utterances of the President during that term.

Stanley High would have continued to be of even greater assistance than he was in 1936 had he stayed on for the rest of the term. More and more he contributed fine phrasing and ideas for the speeches. I have spoken of his "economic royalists." I have also always admired another bit of imagery which he contributed to the Chicago campaign speech October 14, 1936:

> Some of these people [industrialists opposing the New Deal] really forget how sick they were. But I know how sick they were. I have their fever charts. I know how the knees of all of our rugged individualists were trembling four years ago and how their hearts fluttered. They came to Washington in great numbers. Washington did not look like a dangerous bureaucracy to them then. Oh, no! It looked like an emergency hospital. All of the distinguished patients wanted two things—a quick hypodermic to end the pain and a course of treatment to cure the disease. They wanted them in a hurry; we gave them both. And now most of the patients seem to be doing very nicely. *Some of them are even well enough to throw their crutches at the doctor.*

Unfortunately, Stanley was a professional writer, and could not resist the temptation to write for publication on current public affairs. That is always a dangerous practice for anyone known to be close to a President. Whatever opinion or course of conduct he proposes, it will almost always be attributed to something he must have heard the President say. Although the attribution may be wholly unjustified, the President is bound to be embarrassed by it. In Stanley's case, his writings also caused hurt feelings among people in very high places, including Vice-President Garner. One of his magazine articles predicted that Roosevelt would eventually get rid of the conservatives in his own party. Undoubtedly, like others of us, High had heard Roosevelt frequently complain of the conservative millstone about his neck in the form of some of the Southern Democrats. But it was impossible for him to write about such things publicly, and at the same time remain a part of the intimate White House group. Anonymity is always helpful for a speech writer; public utterances about current political affairs are a mistake. So, after what I thought was too short a stay, Stanley was withdrawn from the group.

He seemed during the short time he worked with us a thorough progressive; many of the very liberal passages of the campaign speeches of

1936 came from his pen. After our close collaboration it seemed strange in the later campaigns that we should be on rival campaign trains. I do not fully understand how he was able to join Roosevelt's opponents in 1940 and 1944. As a professional writer he seemed to be able, like an experienced lawyer, to argue for either side. But it was quite noticeable that in the campaigns in which High worked against Roosevelt, there appeared no phrases or paragraphs equal in quality to those for which he was responsible during the time he worked with Roosevelt. The inspiration of a Roosevelt, the direction which Roosevelt gave our thinking and our writing, were absent—and when High no longer had these, he did not do as well.

Other men helped on the 1936 campaign speeches with suggestions, drafts and memoranda. Among them was Donald Richberg, who was then completely in sympathy with the President and who was very helpful. But the main burden fell on us four: High, Corcoran, Cohen and me.

The campaign train of eleven cars carrying about one hundred people started from Washington on October 8, 1936. My wife and I had a compartment—theoretically. Practically the entire compartment was occupied by stacks and stacks of those red manila envelopes containing all kinds of campaign material. I did not use the compartment much for sleeping, for I did not get much sleep. I was able to announce proudly when the trip was over that I had lost twelve pounds. But the hard work that can produce that happy result on a campaign train is seldom a source of complaint or annoyance. The excitement and exhilaration are too absorbing for you to notice that you are not getting enough sleep, or that you never get your food at the right time, or that you do not get a chance to take a bath, or do not even have time to read the newspapers thoroughly. It is impossible to describe to one who has not been on a trip of this kind the thrill of crowds of cheering people station after station, city after city, the applause of ten thousand enthusiastic rooters inside an auditorium or the shouts of a hundred thousand people in a ball park, the mounted police holding back the crowds as the cars parade through the streets, the excitement and rush of getting out one speech and starting almost immediately on the next, the few precious minutes of kidding and laughing as you gulp your food—and, in 1936, the look of hope and confidence on the faces of people who four years before were despondent and desperate.

As I reread the speeches[2] of that campaign—one hundred printed pages of them—especially the prepared speeches, I am struck by the thoroughness with which the issues were all covered. The central theme of the campaign was simple and clear: this Administration has rescued industry, farming, labor and banking from complete collapse; it has corrected abuses in our social and economic system; this program of recovery and reform will continue if the Democrats are elected, and it will be scuttled if they are not.

Once the trip actually got under way, it was almost impossible for the candidate himself to spend any prolonged periods of time on speeches. He had to talk with officeholders, political leaders and other prominent citizens at every stop, and even during the run from one station to another. He had to read and act on many official dispatches which came from Washington and, in later years, from all over the world. For the business of government had to go on.

To add to the burden, he had to make an appearance and a short talk at all station stops. These "whistle-stop speeches" were usually very effective. The crowd would gather from all over the countryside hours before traintime. By car and wagon, on bicycle and on foot, they would come, children and all, to see the President. The children would be lifted onto the shoulders of the men—wide-eyed in attention. The speeches were either a short rehash of the major speech he had delivered the night before or a few remarks of purely local interest.

[2] St. Paul, October 9: Agriculture, farm co-operatives, reciprocal trade agreements.
 Omaha, October 10: The agricultural program, past, present and future; crop insurance.
 Denver, October 12: What has been done for industry, agriculture and mining.
 Wichita, October 13: The general accomplishments of the New Deal, especially in agriculture.
 Kansas City, Missouri, October 13: The Administration's accomplishments in behalf of the youth of the country.
 Chicago, October 14: The Administration's accomplishments in behalf of business.
 Flint, Michigan, October 15: Work relief vs. a dole.
 Hamtramck, Michigan, October 15: "Boondoggling."
 Detroit, October 15: Effect on industry of federal spending—prevention of future depressions.
 Cleveland, October 16: The unity of interest between business and labor.
 Buffalo, October 17: Public works—responsibility of federal government for unemployment relief.
 Rochester, October 17: Social and progressive economic legislation.

From the talks Roosevelt made at these short stops, he seemed to have been everywhere in the United States; for he nearly always prefaced his remarks by saying that he had been at that particular little place before. There was usually some local celebrity whose name could be dragged in; that always caused a swelling of local pride, and some cheers. A few examples:

At Fort Warren, Cheyenne, Wyoming, October 11:

"I am glad to come back here. As you know, I am not a stranger. I think it was in 1920 that I first came to Fort D. A. Russell. I was here four years ago after the name had been changed in honor of a very old friend of mine, Senator Warren. I am glad to come back here today, not only because it is Sunday, and a day off, but also because it is an anniversary. This happens to be Mrs. Roosevelt's birthday. So I am having a very nice home party."

At Greeley, Colorado, October 12:

"Good morning. I have just got through breakfast; and I am glad to come back here to be introduced by Fred Cummings, who is an old friend of mine.

"The last time I stood here, I think, was with Mrs. Roosevelt in 1920 when I was running for Vice-President. A lot of things have happened since that time."

At Pueblo, Colorado, October 12:

"I go back a good many years, to the campaign of 1920, when I spent most of a day and evening in Pueblo; and I remember that I spent a good part of the evening trying to beat Alva Adams in bowling at the 'Y.' But I think he was a better bowler than I was."

And so it went—all around the country.

When he had not been at a place before, he said so, but he tried to work in some local color or personality:

At Dubuque, Iowa, October 9:

"My friends, I am glad to come to Dubuque. I had planned this visit way back last spring. I planned it with a very great citizen of this state and of this city, and I am only sorry he cannot be with us today.

"Louis Murphy was a great and kind man, a close friend of mine. Instead of talking politics, I want to read to you a few sentences from a very wonderful tribute which was paid to Louis Murphy at the time of his funeral here. I want to read them to you because these words are not political, and yet they are concerned with better government all over the United States."

At Creston, Iowa, October 10:

"I am glad to get into this section of the state. I understand that you good people were pretty hard hit by the drought this year. As you know, I have been going around the United States trying to get first-hand information in regard to drought conditions and a lot of other conditions.

"I am glad to come here for another reason. I understand that Henry Wallace was born about fourteen miles from here."

At Pacific Junction, Iowa, October 10:

"We have had an awfully interesting couple of days. I can see by looking at your corn that you people out here in this corner of the state have been through a drought. As you know, we are doing all we can by the principle of co-operation between local government and state government and Washington to improve drought conditions all through this area from here west. I think we are getting somewhere."

Sometimes, but quite rarely, the President might unexpectedly say something that had nationwide rather than purely local interest. This would cause a great flurry of excitement among the newspapermen. They tried, if possible, to send off some dispatch while the train was waiting at the station. Sometimes it was a close call, and we would see a reporter dash out of the telegraph office and run down the platform to catch the train as it was just beginning to move.

Since all these campaign chores left the President very little time for concentrated work on the major speeches, we had prepared three or four in advance before leaving Washington. On these he had been able to spend some time. But most of the speeches delivered during an extended campaign trip had to be written one after another while the train was making its way around the country. Often we had only twenty-four or, at the most, forty-eight hours to prepare a speech—and with pressure like that every hour seemed to be much shorter than sixty minutes.

Time was further cut by the fact that we generally could not resist the temptation to go with the President from his train to the hall or park to hear him speak. His speech was preceded by a tremendous parade arranged by the local party chiefs, in which he rode in the second open car, right behind the Secret Service. The excitement of riding through the streets and seeing the cheering crowds sometimes trying to break through the police lines to get closer to the President was too much for us to resist.

The President loved crowds, whether they were in a convention hall or along the streets. From them he drew strength and determination in the continuous fight he waged for liberal causes. Crowds gave him too a deep thrill and a comforting feeling that the people were with him in his objectives and in his methods for attaining a better life and a world of peace.

After the speech, the Presidential party would return to the railroad station. The local leaders and dignitaries usually rode back in the long procession of automobiles to say their "good-bys" and "good lucks" at the train side. The President pulled himself up the long ramp which was always carried on the train for him to use when he got on or off. As he slowly got up the ramp to the platform of his railroad car, there was generally a hush among the crowd around the train—including even hard-boiled newspapermen who had been traveling with him for many years. Friend or foe, those who saw him at this moment could not help being moved at the sight of this severely crippled man making his way up with such great difficulty—really propelling himself along by his arm and shoulder muscles as his strong hands grasped the rails at the side of the ramp.

And as he finally reached the door of the car, one last wave, one last flash of the calm smile the American people had come to know so well, one last cheer from the crowd, and he was back in the little sitting room of his private car. The shades were drawn, the noise of the crowd in the station was shut out by the thick windows, and the President was alone with his friends and staff.

He could now relax. Thoroughly experienced public speaker though he was, he was generally very nervous as the time to get up to deliver his speech drew near. He seldom found any pleasure at a meeting or at a banquet until his speech had actually begun. He would nervously smoke cigarette after cigarette. His hand would shake as he drank water. While waiting to be introduced, he would fidget in his chair. Once he had gotten to his feet and said, "My friends," he was a changed man—relaxed, in perfect touch with his audience, every fiber concentrated on what he was saying and in the effect it was producing—all traces of nervousness gone.

Now back in the quiet of his train, there was usually a half hour or so of chatter and banter. The President would have either a glass of beer or a "horse's neck." Because someone had once written a magazine article exaggerating my fondness for chocolate sodas, the President one night had the car steward prepare one for me. It was a good joke—and, I must admit, a welcome one to me—which I am glad to say was often repeated. And it never failed to draw a laugh from the others in the car.

We would talk about the crowds and the speech just delivered—a particular passage that had gone over well, or one which, contrary to our expectations, had proved to be a dud—and any other incidents of unusual interest. There was nearly always something new happening in the crowded streets we could talk about, like the time an elderly lady came close to the President's car and dropped in her wrist watch as a gift (which we afterward had a lot of trouble returning); the struggle of some man or woman to get close enough to the President to shake his hand; the little group of people perilously clinging together on a rooftop ledge to get a better look.

The President would repeat to us what the local leaders had just told him about election prospects. At each stop he always tried to get the truth—whether good or bad—about the prospects for the national and local tickets. He did not always get the truth because there were many who liked to tell him only good news. There were some, however, on whom he could always rely for frank and accurate appraisals, no matter how brutal they might be. Edward J. Flynn, then one of the most competent and intelligent of the political leaders in the United States, was one; Ed Kelly of Chicago, Frank Walker, and James A. Farley were others. The President tried to check one source of information with another. We too would talk to the local politicians and to as many local citizens as we could, and naturally we would get a franker —and usually less optimistic—report than he did. All of us tried to get any information that would help determine what mistakes had been made and how to correct or avoid them in the future, and we would compare notes on what we had learned.

There was the usual amount of small talk; and, as the train sped along through the night, there were also a few minutes of serious talk about the contents of the speech for the next night. The President might look at some of the documents in the large "speech material file," or, if he were not too tired, dictate a few pages to Grace as he sipped his drink. Then with a cheery "good night, sleep tight, I'll see you children in the morning," he would hoist himself onto his little wheel chair, which could barely get through the corridor of his private car, and be wheeled to his room. There, before turning out the light, he would go through the stack of newspapers that had accumulated since breakfast.

As he said "sleep tight," he would smile, because he knew that that benevolent wish was the height of optimism. A speech had to be delivered the next night, and some kind of draft had to be put in shape for him to get his "teeth into" the next morning at breakfast.

Instead of sleeping tight, we would proceed to one of the compartments in the next car and go to work. There were usually three or four stenographers on the train, snatching whatever sleep they could, operating in relays to type the drafts one after another. Grace Tully, Dorothy Brady, and Roberta Barrows were always on campaign trips; they worked around the clock with a minimum of sleep. During the night we usually made at least one trip into the always open dining car to get some coffee to help us stay awake. There we would run into the reporters writing their stories about the speech that had just been delivered. I never missed a chance to exchange views with them, to get their reaction to what the President had said and their opinion on what the editorial comment and the popular reaction would be. These talks with the newspapermen were always very helpful. A few of the men were so strongly anti-Roosevelt that anything they said could be discounted. A few others were so idolatrous that anything they said was colored by their admiration for Roosevelt. But, as a rule, most of them would tell us frankly how they thought the campaign was going, and would offer advice on the line of attack in future speeches. Most newspapermen assigned to campaign trains of Presidential candidates are experienced, intelligent, and discerning observers of public opinion. Politics is their business. I always found that I could learn as much about public reaction from talking with five or six seasoned political newspapermen as I could from any group I knew.

We soon learned to distinguish politically between the newspapermen and the papers they represented. A great majority of the papers were hostile to the President; but many of the men employed by rabidly anti-Roosevelt papers were on our side and, in confidence, would tell us so.

On long campaign trips, except on Sundays, the speech workers rarely got to bed before three or four in the morning. The stenographers had to stay up even longer because they had to transcribe inserts or, perhaps, entire new drafts before the breakfast deadline. Often some of the stenographers did not get to bed much before seven or eight o'clock. They worked in shifts, and could sleep through most of the morning; but at least one of them had to be on hand when the President went over the draft in the morning.

We gathered in the President's bedroom after his breakfast; by that time he had read the draft and was ready to tear it apart. We worked in his room, or waited until he was dressed and worked in the sitting room. Some of the draft he would strike out, dictating substitute inserts sometimes several pages long. Often he suggested additional points which he thought should be covered and asked us to prepare a page or two on them. After perhaps an hour so spent, the speech would begin to assume a Rooseveltian character.

The President then would get ready to meet some of the political leaders and other people who had already crowded onto the train and who were waiting in the next car to come in to see him. We would go to work to prepare a new draft in the light of his comments and suggestions. Sometimes we would have to get in touch with the White House in order to obtain certain statistics or to check some date or quotation or general bit of information. At each important stop, a telephone wire was strung into the President's car from the station, over which he could talk directly with the White House switchboard. We would take advantage of this arrangement to ask for the information we needed, and often would find it waiting for us at the next stop. This procedure was greatly simplified and speeded up in the campaign of 1944, when a car was attached to the President's train that could send and receive messages while in motion.

Usually the next time we could see the President was during or immediately after lunch. As a rule he would be able then to spend a couple of hours on the speech, and by midafternoon it would begin to take final shape. The deadline was about five-thirty. Then Grace would type the final reading copy, and as each page was typed and proofread the carbon was sent to the mimeographing crew, which could turn out several hundred copies in incredibly short time. We tried, if possible, to get the entire mimeographed speech into the hands of the press before 7 P.M. so that they could immediately put it on the wires to their respective papers and press services. It was our aim to get it into the offices of papers like *The New York Times* in time to make their first edition, which provided their out-of-the-city circulation. The later the speech was given to the newspapermen the less time they had to study it, and the less news coverage it received.

We would then try to snatch an hour's sleep before dinner, and be prepared to leave with the candidate to hear the speech. After it was over, the same procedure would start for the next day.

It is illustrative of the kind of material that passed between the 1936 campaign train and Washington to quote a few of the scores of messages and telegrams which I received on the train:

1. A letter from Corcoran which came by pouch:

DEAR SAM:
Herewith:
(1)   Trade statistics for Michigan and Ohio.
    (a)   Clippings from the Department of Commerce for Grand Rapids, Jackson, Bay City, Pontiac and Flint, Michigan, and Dayton, Springfield, Columbus and Cincinnati, Ohio. . . .
    (b)   Paraphrases of other newspaper reports from Ohio and Michigan—absolutely accurate—earlier prepared for the Democratic Committee by people in my office. I know they are all right.
    (c)   Lubin is going to wire you more Michigan statistics. I'll get some of them in this envelope if I have time.
(2)   Relief.
    (a)   A ribbon copy of the relief speech I prepared for Aubrey Williams and which he did not use—of which I have told you before. I think there are some very good, fresh ideas on the relief program in this speech; particularly "There but for the grace of God go I"; the Shipping Board, the dole as "suspended animation"; the fact that only 5% of the workers are picked by an agency with which the Federal Government has anything to do; the Gilbert and Sullivan at the end (too fawncy, I suppose).
    (b)   Some data from the WPA on how the federal assumption of the relief burden took off the backs of three rural counties in ten representative western states what otherwise would have been a burden on the only tax sources available to those counties, i.e., the land. The President has thought it would be a good idea to point out that Landon's proposal to turn relief back to the states means turning the burden of relief back on the state sources of taxation, i.e., land and sales, and taking it off the Liberty Leaguers who have to pay big federal income taxes.
    (c)   Reference to Fortune's recent article on WPA.
    (d)   An excellent article in the "Nation" of November 27th by Stuart Chase on the spending program and national income— really very swell stuff, albeit a bit high hat.
(3)   Securities Commission.
    (a)   A speech prepared by Landis which begins to bite on page 4.

(b)   An earlier draft of a speech prepared by Jim Fayne—more colorful than Landis' but not so accurate—good for phrases.

(4)   The editorial in which the Scripps-Howard came out for Roosevelt (today). Remember this will have run in the papers in Columbus, Cincinnati, Akron and Toledo. It's awfully good.

Yours,

TOM

2. A letter from High which came by pouch:

October 16, 1936

Honorable Sam Rosenman
Aboard the President's
Special Train—
DEAR SAM:

I am sending herewith more material.

After a careful day-to-day reading of the speeches, etc., on both sides, I am convinced that there are one or two emphases which the President still needs to make. Those emphases concern 1. Relief and relief politics and waste; 2. Taxes; 3. The interests in and the plans for the average business man. I do not think that any of those three subjects has, as yet, been adequately covered.

I have no suggestions, here, for Massachusetts except this—I don't think the President ought to talk about relief in Massachusetts, because there, under Curley, the scandal is probably at its worst.

Chicago was glorious.

Please tell the boss that we've got bang-up business men's dinners on the way in 15 cities. It will be the greatest demonstration of its kind ever staged.

Outside of that, I've nothing to do.

As ever,

STANLEY HIGH

3. A wire to the campaign train from Isador Lubin, then head of the Bureau of Labor Statistics, checking on some figures I had sent him:

Samuel I. Rosenman.

Seriously recommend that you omit sentences relative to city residents in section dealing with food prices and incomes. The figures on city inhabitants will not hold water. Suggest you substitute for them the following, "The income of all wage and salaried earners of the country fell by 41 percent from 1929 to 1932. Between 1932 and 1936 the income of all wage and salaried workers increased by 31 percent."

These income figures are the total amount paid out in salaries and wages to all workers in all branches of economic activity in the United States. They are the official figures as published by the Department of Commerce. Figures for 1936 are Commerce estimates.

ISADOR LUBIN

At Omaha, Nebraska, on this trip, Roosevelt showed in dramatic fashion how much more interested he was in liberalism than in empty party labels. Against the urgings of his own political leaders he had decided to endorse Senator George Norris, the old-time liberal fighter, a lifelong Republican. He had tried to get a Democratic endorsement for Senator Norris in Nebraska but had failed.

The Omaha speech was on agriculture, and had been prepared in Washington before we left. But the opening paragraphs, endorsing Norris, were prepared separately by Roosevelt himself. With his keen sense of the dramatic, the endorsement was kept secret until actually released to the press. I think that Norris himself was the only one outside the White House group who knew that it was coming. As the President delivered these words in the presence of the Democratic leaders of Nebraska, I could see how much he enjoyed the surprise and drama of the occasion:

> On this platform sits a man whose reputation for many years has been known in every community—a man old in years but young in heart—a man who through all these years has had no boss but his own conscience—the Senior Senator from the State of Nebraska, given to the Nation by the people of Nebraska—George W. Norris.
>
> Outside of my own State of New York, I have consistently refrained from taking part in elections in any other State.
>
> But Senator Norris' name has been entered as a candidate for Senator from Nebraska. And to my rule of non-participation in State elections I have made—and so long as he lives I always will make—one magnificently justified exception. . . .
>
> Nebraska will be doing a great service not only to itself, but to every other State in the Union and to the Nation as a whole, if it places this great American above partisanship, and keeps George Norris in the Senate of the United States.

In this campaign, as in all subsequent ones, the President adhered to his policy of never mentioning his opponent by name, and seldom even by any allusion. There were several reasons for this deliberate practice. Since he was the President running for re-election, an attack by him could only result in giving his opponent more publicity than he otherwise would get. It would give his opponent a chance to answer him, and the very fact that he was answering a President would build up publicity for the answer. One of the best ways of making the front page is to say something unfavorable about the President of the United States. Roosevelt did attack Hoover frequently in the 1932 campaign when the roles were reversed; when he was the contender running against the President then in office.

Another practice that the President followed scrupulously in his campaigns, which I have already discussed in connection with his campaigns for Governor, was never to make an attack upon Republicans as such. His criticism was always directed at the principles or actions of the Republican leaders rather than at the rank and file Republicans generally. Many enrolled and independent Republicans who violently opposed his national domestic policies enthusiastically endorsed his foreign policies—especially in 1940 and 1944—and on balance, cast their votes for him. He was aware of this, and made every effort to avoid alienating these supporters. His opponents in campaigns were not always so tolerant or astute.

To show how closely Roosevelt liked to adhere to these political campaign rules I quote a private memorandum he sent to James A. Farley on May 22, 1936.[3] In a speech Farley had predicted that "the governor of a typical prairie state" would get the Republican nomination for President—meaning of course Alfred Landon of Kansas. It created quite a furor, and the Republican orators thought they could make political capital out of what they called a snide reference to Landon and to Kansas. The President wrote:

THE WHITE HOUSE,
May 22, 1936

Memorandum for J.A.F.:

I thought we had decided any reference to Landon or any other Republican candidate was inadvisable.

Now that the water is over the dam, I told Michelson that possibly a somewhat facetious reference to Frank Knox, between now and June ninth, by you might soften the effect of the Landon reference. Another good rule which should be passed down the line to all who are concerned with speech material is that no section of the country should be spoken of as "typical" but only with some laudatory adjective. If the sentence had read "One of those splendid prairie States," no one could have picked us up on it, but the word "typical" coming from any New Yorker is meat for the opposition.

F. D. R.

I think that the best speech of this 1936 Western campaign trip was delivered in Chicago. It was one of those drafted in Washington before the trip, although shortly before we got to Chicago a new

[3] *F.D.R.: His Personal Letters*, pp. 591-592.

draft reached us on the train. It was largely the work of Corcoran, Cohen and High; it was a fighting New Deal speech—an affirmative statement of the underlying philosophy of the New Deal, what it had accomplished in the way of recovery and reform, and a pledge of future action along the same lines.

In the speech, Roosevelt compared the Chicago of 1936 with the Chicago of 1932 in which he had accepted the first nomination. It was a graphic way of showing what the New Deal had done:

Four years ago I dropped into this city from the airways—an old friend come in a new way—to accept in this hall the nomination for the Presidency of the United States. I came to a Chicago fighting with its back to the wall—factories closed, markets silent, banks shaky, ships and trains empty. Today those factories sing the song of industry; markets hum with bustling movement; banks are secure; ships and trains are running full. Once again it is Chicago as Carl Sandburg saw it—"The City of the big shoulders"—the city that smiles. And with Chicago a whole Nation that had not been cheerful for years is full of cheer once more.

Conscious of the growing attacks upon him and the New Deal by business, he showed what the New Deal had done for business—but note that he did it not by dry statistics but in terms of human beings:

Do you have a deposit in the bank? It is safer today than it has ever been in our history. It is guaranteed. . . .

Are you an investor? Your stocks and bonds are up to five- and six-year high levels.

Are you a merchant? Your markets have the precious life-blood of purchasing power. Your customers on the farms have better incomes and smaller debts. Your customers in the cities have more jobs, surer jobs, better jobs. . . .

Are you in industry? Industrial earnings, industrial profits are the highest in four, six, or even seven years! . . .

Are you in railroads? Freight loadings are steadily going up. Passenger receipts are steadily going up—have in some cases doubled. . . .

Are you a middleman in the great stream of farm products? The meat and grain that move through your yards and elevators have a steadier supply, a steadier demand and steadier prices than you have known for years. . . .

Some people say that all this recovery has just happened. But in a complicated modern world recoveries from depressions do not just happen. The years from 1929 to 1933, when we waited for recovery just to happen, prove the point.

But in 1933 we did not wait. We acted. Behind the growing recovery of today is a story of deliberate Government acceptance of responsibility to save business, to save the American system of private enterprise and economic democracy—a record unequaled by any modern Government in history.

He reiterated his insistence on continuation of the system of private property and free enterprise, and pointed out that it was the New Deal which saved that system from destruction back in 1933.

I believe, I have always believed, and I will always believe in private enterprise as the backbone of economic well-being in the United States. . . .

You good people have heard about . . . fairy tales and bogey-men too. You have heard about how antagonistic to business this Administration is supposed to be. . . .

The answer to that is the record of what we have done. It was this Administration which saved the system of private profit and free enterprise after it had been dragged to the brink of ruin by these same leaders who now try to scare you.

The campaign trip through the Middle West had just ended when almost immediately a swing into New England was begun. All the speeches for that trip were prepared in Washington with the help of the current speech-writing team—Corcoran, Cohen, High and me.

The prospects for victory seemed very bright by this time, and during the preparation of these speeches the President was confident, genial and lighthearted. At dinner one night and in the course of some general bantering and teasing, Stanley (who never could get used to Roosevelt's easygoing humor and gaiety in the midst of serious business) said to him:

"Mr. President, I don't suppose there ever has been a Presidential contest in which preparations and campaigning went forward with so much kidding and hilarity."

The President laughed and then with mock seriousness said what I had often thought to myself, "Can you imagine what it must have been like to campaign with Hoover or Coolidge?"

On another occasion over cocktails before dinner, he said to us:

"You know, boys, I had a lovely thought last night. I thought what fun it would be if I could now be running against Franklin D. Roosevelt. I don't know whether I could have beaten him or not," he hastened to add cautiously, "but I certainly would have given him a close race—a darned sight closer than Landon is doing.

"First, I would repudiate Hearst. Then I would repudiate the Du Ponts and everything they stand for.

"Then I would say: 'I am for social security, work relief, etc., etc. But the Democrats cannot be entrusted with the administration of these fine ideals.' I would cite chapter and verse on WPA inefficiency—and there's plenty of it—as there is bound to be in such a vast, emergency program.

"You know," he added reflectively, almost longingly, "the more I think about it, the more I think I could lick myself."

Since the New England speeches were completed in Washington, none of us went on the trip; instead, we began work on the remaining speeches of the campaign.

Businessmen's dinners had been arranged in different parts of the country for October 23, and the President by radio from the White House made a short, spirited speech to these dinners in defense of his policy toward business.

When these dinners of business men throughout the country were first organized, I was asked to talk specifically for the business men of the nation. But I said that it was impossible to make a speech for business men as members of a separate and distinct occupation from the rest of the people in America. . . .

We have no separate interests in America. There is nothing to say to one group that ought not to be said to all groups. What is good for one ought to be good for all. We can make our machinery of private enterprise work only so long as it does not benefit one group at the expense of another.

The speech also again boasted that the system of free enterprise was saved—not hurt—by the New Deal:

It was this Administration which dragged it back out of the pit into which it had fallen in 1933.

If the Administration had had the slightest inclination to change that system, all that it would have had to do was to fold its hands and wait—let the system continue to default to itself and to the public.

But a warning! The New Deal would not tolerate a return of abuses:

But as your profits return and the values of your securities and investments come back, do not forget the lessons of the past. We must hold constantly to the resolve never again to become committed to the philosophy of the boom era, to individualism run wild, to the false promise that American business was great because it had built up financial control of industrial production and distribution in the hands of a few individuals and corporations by the use of other people's money; that Government should be ever ready to purr against the legs of high finance; that the benefits of the free competitive system should trickle down by gravity from the top to the bottom; and above all, that Government had no right, in any way, to interfere with those who were using the system of private profit to the damage of the rest of the American citizens.

The last major speech of the campaign was in Madison Square Garden in New York City. It was, I think, the best of the speeches of that campaign. We four—Corcoran, High, Cohen and I—spent more time on it than on any other, and so did the President.

He had become very indignant at some of the tactics of the Republican leaders in the campaign. Many of the big employers, in an effort to block the President's social security plan, had embarked upon a campaign of fear propaganda, inserting printed broadsides in the pay envelopes of their workers. The propaganda was intended to create the impression that employees alone were going to pay for their unemployment and old age insurance and would not reap corresponding benefits. Indeed, it intimated that the reserves might in future be diverted to some other purpose.

I was at Hyde Park when John G. Winant, a Republican, who was then chairman of the Social Security Board, came up to see the President, and with great indignation resigned so that he could go out as an individual Republican, publicly fight this flood of propaganda of intimidation, and expose the falsehood of these "pay envelope" charges.

The whole campaign of propaganda proved to be a boomerang, and was much more harmful than helpful to the Republican candidate. The workers of the nation refused to be fooled or intimidated, and turned out a tremendous vote for Roosevelt. There may have been a time in the late nineteenth or early twentieth century, as, for example, in the Bryan campaigns, when the workers of the nation, either willingly or unwillingly, took political advice from their employers; by 1936 they were voting on their own.

The President had already denounced this "pay envelope propaganda campaign" in a speech at Wilkes-Barre, Pennsylvania, October 29, when he said:

"No employer has a right to put his political preferences in the pay envelope. That is coercion even if he tells the whole truth. . . ."

But he became more indignant as the campaign continued, and he told us to take off all gloves in the final speech at Madison Square Garden. We did—and if there was a trace of a glove left when we got through, the President himself removed it.

The speech summed up the campaign, and also summed up the last four years:

Tonight I call the roll—the roll of honor of those who stood with us in 1932 and still stand with us today.

Written on it are the names of millions who never had a chance—men at starvation wages, women in sweatshops, children at looms.

Written on it are the names of those who despaired, young men and young women for whom opportunity had become a will-o'-the-wisp.

Written on it are the names of farmers whose acres yielded only bitterness, business men whose books were portents of disaster, home owners who were faced with eviction, frugal citizens whose savings were insecure.

Written there in large letters are the names of countless other Americans of all parties and all faiths, Americans . . . whose consciences were burdened because too many of their fellows were burdened, who looked on these things four years ago and said, "This can be changed. We will change it."

He lashed out at those whose hatred he said he welcomed:

For twelve years this Nation was afflicted with hear-nothing, see-nothing, do-nothing Government. The Nation looked to Government but the Government looked away. Nine mocking years with the golden calf and three long years of the scourge! Nine crazy years at the ticker and three long years in the breadlines! Nine mad years of mirage and three long years of despair! Powerful influences strive today to restore that kind of government with its doctrine that that Government is best which is most indifferent.

For nearly four years you have had an Administration which instead of twirling its thumbs has rolled up its sleeves. We will keep our sleeves rolled up.

Then he repeated his attack on the pay-envelope campaign, and ended with a final challenge based on the famous words of one of his heroes, John Paul Jones—"I have not yet begun to fight."

This is our answer to those who, silent about their own plans, ask us to state our objectives.

Of course we will continue to seek to improve working conditions for the workers of America—to reduce hours over-long, to increase wages that spell starvation, to end the labor of children, to wipe out sweatshops. Of course we will continue every effort to end monopoly in business, to support collective bargaining, to stop unfair competition, to abolish dishonorable trade practices. For all these we have only just begun to fight.

He repeated the same pledge about all the things he had promised to do for the farmers, consumers, unemployed, home owners, slum dwellers and many others—adding each time, "for all these things we have only just begun to fight." The repetition of this phrase was Roosevelt's own idea, and it proved to be very effective.

There was one statement in the speech—at a point where the gloves were clearly off—which caused a last minute flurry of substantial proportions. The opposition immediately seized upon it in a final desperate effort to stop the tide running against Landon. I remember some nervous politicians on our own side who thought that it was going to be as damaging as the historic "rum, Romanism and rebellion" of the Cleveland campaign of 1884. In speaking of the forces of reaction which during the last four years had sought to block his program, the President said:

> Never before in all our history have these forces been so united against one candidate as they stand today. They are unanimous in their hate for me—and I welcome their hatred.
>
> I should like to have it said of my first administration that in it the forces of selfishness and of lust for power met their match. I should like to have it said of my second administration that in it these forces met their master.

Immediately the wires began to hum, the columnists began to shout, the editorial writers began to scream, and the Republican campaign orators began to orate. They cried that the President was seeking to make himself the "master" of the American people. Many of the President's friends called him and asked him to issue an explanatory statement. Some of the Democratic political leaders, becoming panicky, sent in wires asking that the President do something about it. The President said that to answer such an absurd charge would give it a dignity to which it was not entitled, and a degree of publicity which it could not itself attain. He did not answer the accusation; he did not retract the statement. Indeed, there was nothing whatever for him to retract. All that he meant was exactly what he said. There was nothing sinister in his words or his meaning. He intended to carry on his program of reform until reactionary political thinking in the United States was conclusively discredited at the polls. Recent political history proves that the President was to a large extent successful in that aim. The Republican platforms and speeches of 1940 and 1944 and 1948 fairly completely abandoned—at least for election purposes—the reactionary policies of the Old Guard. In fact, with some exceptions, they embraced the major philosophy and principles of the New Deal—always with the reservation, of course, that the Republicans could carry them out more efficiently and more economically and with no "loss of American liberties."

The final speech of the campaign was delivered on the night before election from the President's home at Hyde Park. This became a quadrennial custom. It was not a political speech; it was rather a nonpartisan appeal urging the voters of the nation to come out and vote.

On the Monday before each election day he used to go out in an open automobile to renew his acquaintance with the voters on both sides of the Hudson River near where he lived. He would make an all-day tour through the villages, towns and small cities in the counties in which he had begun his political career as a candidate for the New York State Senate. In the cold November air, he would speak from the back of his open car to groups of people standing in the village squares. Many of these neighbors he knew by their first names.

Coming home in the late afternoon he would go over the final draft of the speech that he was to deliver that night. The speech was finished in the dusk of the evening at the fireside in the large library of the President's home at Hyde Park. Tea was served while the President worked at the blazing fire which tempered the chill of the November evening. Between the turning of pages he munched pieces of cinnamon toast, his favorite at teatime. The crumbs usually spotted up the drafts and created quite a mess, which did not bother the President as much as it bothered the rest of us. He interrupted his work now and then to tell of some funny incident that had happened that day during the tour among his neighbors. His mother sat quietly sipping tea, admiring her Franklin with loving eyes. Missy and Grace hovered around, and took each page of the manuscript, as he finished it, out to the little office to be retyped and taken down to the temporary White House office in Poughkeepsie for mimeographing. It got darker; the shades were drawn; soon the job was finished.

Tom and Stanley and I, who worked with him on this speech in 1936, then wished him good luck; he thanked us for our labors in the campaign; and we went home to vote the next day.

In 1936, 1940 and 1944 the President received the election returns in Hyde Park, instead of at campaign headquarters as in 1932. Election night we would go up to Hyde Park to hear the returns with the President. Some forty or fifty Dutchess County neighbors and relatives were usually invited. A buffet supper was laid out in the large library, where the guests sat quietly in small groups talking or listening to the radio. As soon as the returns began to come in, the President retired to the dining room two doors up the hall from the library. He insisted on keeping a tally of the returns himself. Several of his secretaries and one or more of his children kept him company. An Associated Press ticker and a United Press ticker in the dining room noisily knocked out the election returns on a long roll of paper, which was cut in sections and brought to him to read, and he tallied the votes on a large chart whose preparation he always supervised personally. An extra telephone, especially installed, enabled him to communicate directly with the Democratic headquarters in New York City.

I never could understand the necessity for this elaborate news-gathering setup. The President seldom got his returns much earlier than any citizen who paid close attention to the radio. Only the telephones accelerated some of the information coming in, for through them the President could get quick flashes from any particular state through the national headquarters. Of course, keeping track of the returns and making entries on the chart provided a mounting excitement and gave him something to do to relieve the tension of waiting. I used to wander in and out of the dining room, but I found that I could get quicker and more satisfactory information by going upstairs to join a small group which gathered in a bedroom around a radio.

From time to time one of the group in the dining room with the President would come out into the library and announce some late bit of information which had been received. Some of the elderly friends of the President's mother had spent their lives in an atmosphere quite foreign to this; they were entirely unaccustomed to listening to election returns and wholly unfamiliar with national politics. I remember some of them receiving with great glee the news from the dining room that Alabama and Mississippi were going "for Franklin" with a fine majority.

As the returns began to come in in 1936, it seemed that all the forty-eight states were "going" that way. From the very beginning, there was no doubt of the President's re-election. Early in the evening the report came in that he had carried New Haven by 15,000. He refused to believe it and asked someone to check it on another phone. When the check proved the report accurate, he leaned back in his chair, blew a ring of smoke at the ceiling and exclaimed: "Wow!" He knew it was over, and at ten-thirty came down the hall to the library for some sandwiches. The only states in the Republican column that year were Maine and Vermont.

Along about midnight there was a torchlight parade composed of several hundred of Roosevelt's neighbors and friends from Hyde Park and Poughkeepsie. They called themselves the Roosevelt Home Club. Headed by a brass band and carrying red torchlights, they came marching down the long driveway to the house, singing and cheering—like the old-time torchlight parades on election nights in the days before radio—and gathered on the gravel area in front of the open uncovered porch. This celebration—repeated in 1940 and 1944—gave the Secret Service men guarding the President great concern; it was very difficult in the darkness to tell exactly who had joined the parade. As soon as Roosevelt heard the music of the band at the entrance, he called for his braces, put them on, walked out on the porch and greeted the paraders as they spread out in front of the porch. All of us in the house went out to hear the few brief remarks with which he greeted and thanked them. It was generally a very homey sort of talk, the kind the President used to describe as a "Howdy do."

On election night in 1936, Roosevelt's son and daughter-in-law, James and Betsy, and their two children were house guests. The grandchildren had apparently been awakened by the band. I remember looking up at their bedroom window from the porch and seeing the two little faces pressed to the window. They were breathlessly watching the proceedings below; their eyes were fairly popping in the red light; they were straining to make out what their granddaddy was saying to all those strange people.

The President felt very warm toward the people of the Hudson River Valley counties, and liked to think that they felt the same way toward him. On election eve, he used to talk with visitors and friends about the local election prospects. In every one of his elections he was most anxious and tried very hard to carry his home county of Dutchess and, particularly, his home town of Hyde Park, though they made little or no difference in the Presidential or gubernatorial races. They were, of course, strongly Republican, and though he carried both in 1930, he never succeeded in carrying either of them in any election after that.

After his remarks to the paraders, the President would shake hands

with a few of the leaders. I could not help remarking the great contrast between this neighborly scene and what we knew was going on
in Europe at this very time, when Fascism and dictatorship were beginning their march over the entire continent. Here was the duly elected
leader of 130 million people, the strongest and most powerful nation
in the world, celebrating his victory—not by the marching goose step
of armies or the flight of thousands of planes or by the prearranged
applause of 100,000 people in a vast, flag-bedecked stadium. There
were no salutes; there were no *heils* or blaring of trumpets. Here was
the President dressed in an old—a very old—tweed suit, chatting with
some friends who had come in to wish him well as an old neighbor.

Chapter IX

The Second Term as President: The Court Fight, 1937

A few weeks after his election, the President made a trip to South America in connection with the Inter-American Conference for the Maintenance of Peace. The speeches he made there were intended for consumption in Europe and Asia as well as in South America. The purpose of the conference was to create solidarity among the nations of the Western Hemisphere, "to show its unity to the world," and also to "offer hope for peace and a more abundant life to the peoples of the whole world." The material and drafts for these speeches were prepared in the State Department, and the President was able to give a great deal of attention to them on his trip to the conference.

Upon his return, he went to work on his annual message to the Congress (January 6, 1937). He had devoted deep thought to the problems which he was to face after election, and how he could meet them. Much of the New Deal legislation that had been passed since 1933 had been declared unconstitutional by the Supreme Court. Some of the decisions indicated that many of the acts of the federal government were in fields in which only the several states themselves could act. The President knew how impossible it was to expect the forty-eight states to take the concerted action that national conditions made necessary. Indeed, the decisions in some cases went so far as to indicate that even the states could not validly act within those fields either. The President studied the subject thoroughly, reread some of the books about the origins of the Constitution and the debates in the original Constitutional Convention, and discussed the problem from every angle with a number of qualified people.

The entire tenor of his Annual Message of 1937 reflects his anxiety over the impasse between the executive and judicial branches of the government; it indicates how hard he was thinking about what he could do to break the deadlock. He pointed out that the objectives that had just been approved by the American people at the polls could not be attained by "simultaneous action by forty-eight states." He was convinced, he said, from rereading the old debates in the original Constitutional Convention that those who framed the Constitution "were fully aware that civilization would raise problems . . . which they themselves could not even surmise . . . [but] that a liberal interpretation in the years to come would give to the Congress the same relative powers over new national problems as they themselves gave to the Congress over the national problems of their day." But the Court had repudiated this promise of a liberal interpretation.

And he said pointedly that while the legislative and executive branches would continue to meet the demands of democracy, "the Judicial branch also is asked by the people to do its part in making democracy successful."

Tom, Stanley, Don and I worked with the President on that message —the last one on which we had the benefit of Stanley's help. We had all noted the President's preoccupation with the subject of the Court's recent decisions, and before he left on his South American trip we had talked with him about the various methods that had been proposed to cope with it. Something had to be done—and quickly. When we submitted our draft to him upon his return we told him that we had tried to outline the problem, but had not attempted to suggest the method of attacking it.

I now know that his mind was fairly well—though not completely—made up by then, that he and Attorney General Homer Cummings had had several meetings to canvass the various proposals, and that the President was leaning very heavily toward the one he finally used. Even as we were working on this annual message, the Department of Justice was preparing the legislation and message and compiling the statistics that were to form the basis of the Supreme Court plan of the next month. But we knew nothing of this at the time.

"Leave the whole thing very general for now," he said. "Let's just point up the need and when we get ready we'll submit the solution. I'm not quite ready yet."

Maybe he had not finally determined what he would do; maybe he wanted to make sure that there was no premature discussion even among us. Whatever his reason, he did not consult us about it; he did not even tell us about it. As will be seen, he was more anxious than usual to make his plan a dramatic surprise. Up to this point, he had not consulted with any of his Cabinet or with any of the Congressional leaders or with any of the other men to whom he might normally have turned, except the Attorney General and the Solicitor General. His silence about it with us while we were working on the annual message was strictly compatible with his conduct throughout.

After sounding the first warning bell in his annual message, the President said nothing more about the Court problem publicly for a few weeks. But he kept working on it with the Attorney General.

His next major address was the Inaugural Address of January 20, 1937.

Donald Richberg had submitted a draft of a complete speech, which was used as a basis for a first draft for the President. Richberg, Tom and I worked with the President on it. I recently re-examined the original drafts of this speech, which are now in the Roosevelt Library; they show probably more work, corrections, inserts, substitutions and deletions by the President than any of the other speeches.

His theme was that since 1933 we had come a long way in the program of recovery and reform; that the country in the last election approved what had been done; that the job was unfinished; that we could not stop now and say that we were satisfied; we had to move forward—through a sound, democratic process.

To make his point, he wrote a passage which was another characteristic example of his use of imagery. After pointing out our great progress in material recovery and in the reforms of abuses—reforms which he called a "change in the moral climate of America"—he painted the people of the United States as travelers who were looking for a pleasant valley in which to settle, and who might be tempted to rest in the place where they had already arrived.

"Shall we pause now and turn our back upon the road that lies ahead? Shall we call this the promised land? . . .

"Many voices are heard as we face a great decision. Comfort says, 'Tarry awhile'; opportunism says, 'This is a good spot.' Timidity asks, 'How difficult is the road ahead?' "

Then, as if to answer the question, he said: "Here is the challenge to our democracy"; and listed some of the social injustices that still existed and still needed correction. He listed them again not in terms of cold statistics but in terms of human beings.

"I see tens of millions of its citizens" denied the "necessities of life"; "I see millions denied education, recreation, and the opportunity to better their lot and the lot of their children"; and there followed several other examples of what "I see."

I had written on the original of the second draft a summation of all the "I sees" with a final "I see." I do not remember nor is there a record of what that summation of mine was, for the President rubbed out all I had written in pencil after that final "I see" and after a moment's reflection substituted in his own hand his own summation: "I see one-third of a nation ill-housed, ill-clad, ill-nourished."

And he read aloud what he had written, with great satisfaction. He was very pleased with the sentence; so were we; so was his audience.

I saw this kind of thing happen frequently over the years. Going over a draft, the President would suddenly lay down his pen, lean back in his large swivel armchair, throw his head back, and look up at the ceiling intently. This might continue for two or three minutes, although it would seem longer as we sat around quietly waiting. Then he would sit up and start writing or, more often, start dictating. Sometimes he would preface his dictation by turning to Grace and saying, "Grace, take a law." This phrase came from a bit in a Broadway musical success entitled *I'd Rather Be Right*. In this play George M. Cohan, impersonating the President during the hectic period of the first hundred days when laws were being passed very quickly at his recommendation, would dictate statutes to a stenographer rather than ask the Congress to pass them. The actor would turn to his secretary, who on the stage was supposed to be Marvin McIntyre, and say, "Mac, take a law." The President had never seen the play himself, but always enjoyed hearing about it. "The law" he would dictate to Grace was often a gem which found its way into a speech or message.

Frequently and continuously in the process of speech writing he would make copious corrections of language in his own hand—shortening a sentence here or making a phrase there more pungent and striking than it was. He had marked ability to contract a long sentence into a shorter and more effective one. He preferred a short sentence to a long one, and a one- or two-syllable word to a four- or five-syllable word. He preferred simple, direct, forthright statements to fuzzy, ambiguous or devious language. He preferred a simple everyday expression to a flowery oratorical one.

Having summed up with his pithy "one-third of nation" sentence the reasons for not tarrying, for not concluding that the traveler had "reached his happy valley," the President said he was sure that the men and women of this Republic would insist on going forward. "They will insist that *every* agency of popular government use effective instruments to carry out their will. . . ."

The Chief Justice of the United States, who had just delivered the oath of office to the newly elected President, sat closely behind him on the porch of the Capitol as Roosevelt read this sentence with great emphasis. I watched his face as the President stood there in the driving rain. There was no doubt that the Chief Justice understood what the President meant when he emphasized the word "*every*."

The President said later when we were talking about the ceremonies: "When the Chief Justice read me the oath and came to the words 'support the Constitution of the United States' I felt like saying: 'Yes, but it's the Constitution as *I* understand it, flexible enough to meet any new problem of democracy—not the kind of Constitution your Court has raised up as barrier to progress and democracy.' "

The reading copy of this speech in the Roosevelt Library at Hyde Park—all wrinkled from being exposed to the driving rain that day—illustrates rather amusingly how much attention the President paid to his delivery and how carefully he went over his speeches beforehand to make sure that his reading would be correct and effective. There was a sentence reading: "Hard-headedness will not so easily excuse hard-heartedness." In reading one draft aloud he had inadvertently transposed the "head" and the "heart." He wanted to make sure that he would not confuse the two when he delivered the speech. So, above the word "head" he drew on his reading copy a head, and above the word "heart," he drew a heart with a neat little arrow through it. He frequently marked his reading copy to indicate emphasis, timing, pauses, etc.

By the end of January, 1937, the President's thoughts had completely crystallized on the steps to take concerning the Supreme Court. Many plans had been submitted to him for his consideration, before and after the election. Some of them required a constitutional amendment; others merely required legislation. The overriding necessity was

Governor Roosevelt signs the "Water Pollution Bill." Albany, 1931. Samuel I. Rosenman on his left. Other interested witnesses include Fiorello H. La Guardia.

MR. ROSENMAN

Fiftieth Birthday Luncheon

January 30, 1932

HYDE PARK
NEW YORK

WHO TURNS THE PARDON CASES DOWN?
AND VIEWS PAROLE WITH ANGRY FROWN?
WHO KNOWS HIMSELF TO BE AN ORACLE
ON ELOQUENCE AND THINGS RHETORICAL?
WHO CAN WRITE MESSAGES THAT FLOW
LIKE HOMER OR LIKE CICERO?
WHO CAN DO THIS AND KNOWS HE CAN?
WHY — MODEST SAMMIE ROSENMAN.

The author's place card at FDR's fiftieth birthday luncheon.

The "Missus" at work aboard the *Sequoia*, 1935.

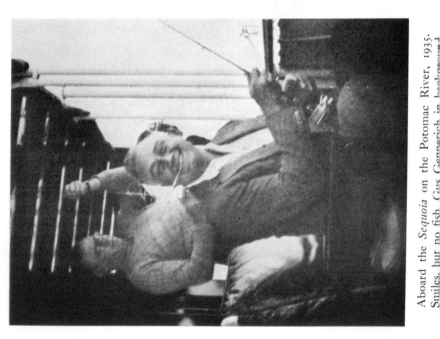

Aboard the *Sequoia* on the Potomac River, 1935.
Smiles, but no fish. Gus Gennerich in background.

Work comes aboard the *Sequoia*, 1935.

Relaxation aboard the *Potomac*, 1936. Missy Le Hand, Dorothy Rosenman, the President—all reading.

On the top deck of the *Potomac*, May, 1936. Dorothy Rosenman, Stanley High, Missy Le Hand and the skipper.

The President gets the news aboard the *Potomac*. May, 1936.

Voters crowd around the candidate's car. 1936 campaign.

1936 campaign train. Senator Joseph C. O'Mahoney, Samuel I. Rosenman, Secretary of Agriculture Henry A. Wallace.

The President loved a picnic in the country, August, 1942. (Photo by Margaret Suckley)

In the living-dining room of the President's cabin at Shangri-la, 1942. The author with Archie MacLeish. (*Photo by Margaret Suckley*)

Dinner at Shangri-la, 1942. The President tunes his portable radio. Archie MacLeish, Dorothy Rosenman, FDR, Grace Tully. Hidden from view next to Miss Tully are Mrs. MacLeish and the author. (*Photo by Margaret Suckley*)

The Commander-in-Chief gets the war news at Shangri-la. Summer, 1942.
The author listens with him.

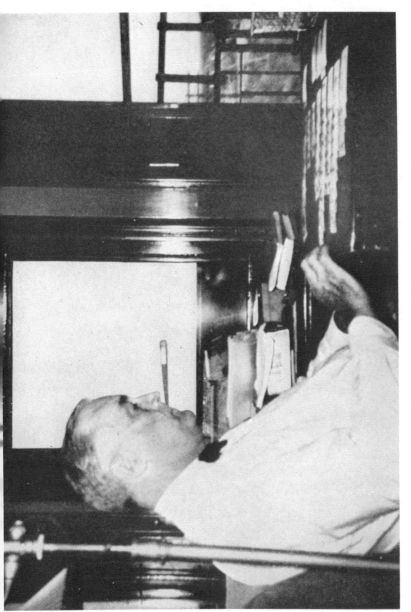

On the train—the President in one of his favorite means of relaxation.

A cartoon from the Washington *Star*, 1942.

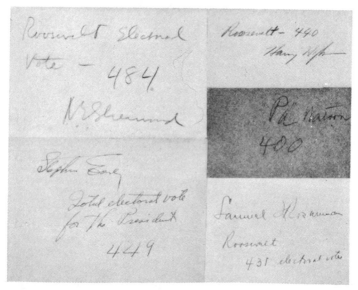

Sherwood, Hopkins, Early, Watson and Rosenman bet on
FDR's total electoral votes—in 1944. (Actual vote: FDR 432,
Dewey 99.)

The President and friend go for a drive. Hyde Park, 1944. (*Photo by Margaret Suckley*)

A cartoon from the Portland *Oregonian*. March, 1944.

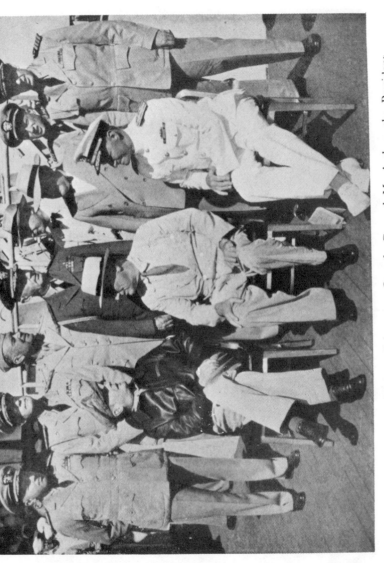

Aboard the USS *Baltimore*, July, 1944. Seated: General MacArthur, the President, Admiral Nimitz. Standing: Admiral McIntire, Admiral Brown, General Watson, Admiral Leahy, Elmer Davis, Judge Rosenman, Lieutenant-Commander Bruenn, Captain Chester Wood.

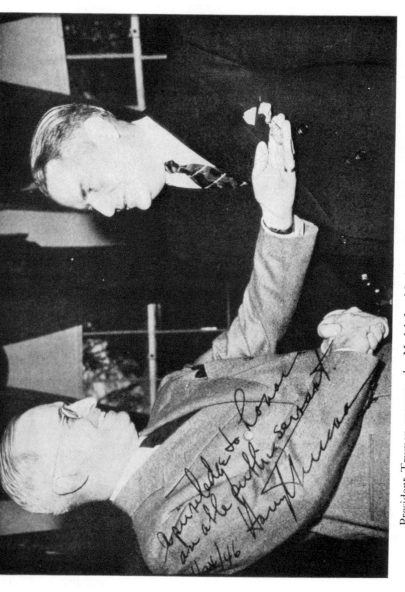

President Truman presents the Medal for Merit to "Samuel I. Rosenman, for exceptionally meritorious conduct in the performance of outstanding services to the President to get something done in a hurry to overcome the paralysis imposed by the Court upon the legislative branch of the Government. The plan that was finally adopted was the one recommended by the Attorney General.

I did not keep a diary during the years of my association with Roosevelt. On one or two occasions, however—largely for the purpose of being able to look back on them in later life—I made fragmentary notes of some of the things that I had seen and heard and done. I wish I had made them more frequently. In looking through my records, I find that within a short time after the delivery of the Message on the Judiciary, I wrote out in longhand some memoranda about the circumstances of its preparation. A detailed account of the Congressional fight itself can be found in *The 168 Days*, by two experienced and well-equipped Washington reporters, Joseph Alsop and Turner Catledge.

I had been invited to come to the White House on January 30 for the President's "cuff-links" birthday party. This was my first year of attendance at this famous annual celebration; I looked forward to it, as I did each year thereafter. I had been given my cuff links after the 1936 campaign—two oval-shaped gold discs connected by a link. On one of the discs were the initials FDR and on the other, the initials of the recipient.

I had intended to go to Washington late in the afternoon only in time for the cuff-links dinner. However, the night before, Missy phoned and asked whether I could get to Washington before lunch for a very important conference. I arrived at the White House just as the movie stars who had come to Washington for the annual Birthday Ball were gathering downstairs for their luncheon with the President.

I was told that the President was not going to have lunch with them this time, but that lunch had been set for him and some others, including myself, upstairs in the Oval Room. I knew that only a very important conference would make the President miss that lunch, for he always enjoyed it, so I rode upstairs in the elevator with considerable wonder and expectancy. The table in the Oval Room was set for five. The conferees were the President, Donald Richberg, Solicitor General Stanley Reed, Attorney General Homer Cummings, and I.

Richberg was then a practicing lawyer in Washington. He had been general counsel for the National Recovery Administration since its beginning, and after General Johnson's resignation had become its administrator. As a railroad labor lawyer and as a public official, he had become a well-known liberal. He was a frequent visitor at the White House. In later years, however, his views became much more conservative, and he drifted away from close contact with the President and from the speech-writing team.

I had not the faintest idea of the purpose of the conference; nor was I enlightened during the course of the luncheon, for conversation was general. As we ate, the President remarked that this quiet, peaceful lunch reminded him very much of the story of a certain combat ship during the first World War—the "Q-ship" or *Santee*. This ship had been camouflaged to look like an ordinary merchantman. Whenever stopped by a German submarine it would docilely obey the orders of the submarine commander. Then as the submarine closed in, a false side wall of the ship would come down, uncovering its guns, which would open fire on the surprised submarine. While this story made the others laugh it only made me wonder more, for I could see no connection whatever between the combat ship and this pleasant, rather aimless luncheon for five.

After the dishes had been cleared away and the doors of the room closed, the President moved over to his chair behind the desk. He announced, with a side glance at Cummings, that he had received a letter from the Attorney General to be attached to a proposed draft of a message to be sent by him to the Congress. He said that he wanted to read them both aloud. It was obvious that he and the Attorney General and the Solicitor General had been discussing the subject of the letter and message for some time.

In late December, 1936, Richberg had suggested legislation that would have retired a Supreme Court Justice automatically at the age of seventy from *active* service. He would then be subject to duty as a Special Master or to take the place of a disqualified Justice. Richberg had actually prepared a bill that the President had turned over to the Attorney General. The Attorney General had advised the President that the bill would not be constitutional and the President had so informed Richberg. So Richberg also knew what was coming. I was the only one of the five still in the dark.

The President read the two documents aloud, slowly and very seriously. Although he had dropped hints that some action would soon be coming, the course which he was now proposing to take was a complete surprise to me—contrary to many "dope" stories which appeared in the newspapers a few weeks later.

The message contained a series of recommendations for a general reorganization of the judiciary of the United States from the Supreme Court down to the district courts. Nearly all the recommendations were noncontroversial and ultimately became law. But one—the real purpose and the heart of the entire message—became the most controversial proposal Roosevelt ever made during his twelve years as President, and cost him much in prestige, particularly in party prestige. It dealt with judges in any federal court—including the Supreme Court—who had reached the age of seventy. It provided, in essence, that whenever a judge of that age in any federal court refused to avail himself of his existing statutory opportunity to retire on a pension, an additional judge should be appointed to that court by the President with the approval of the Senate.

There was a general discussion among the five of us concerning the message and the plan as a whole. Some of the proposed alternative plans were discussed and discarded—as they had been by the President for the last three months. The President had finally made up his mind once and for all.

The message placed great emphasis—almost the major emphasis—on the fact that all the federal justices were overworked, and that as a result calendars were clogged and decisions delayed. We had a lengthy discussion of the advisability of using that approach rather than the direct one that because of the age of the present justices, the Court needed and could be given a fresh and more resilient outlook by the addition of younger men. Richberg, Reed and I thought that that should be the major approach. But Cummings was confident of his facts and of the reasons—overworked judges. The whole plan appealed to Roosevelt as a subtle device for getting what he wanted without being charged with "packing" the Court because of disagreement with the trend of its decisions. It was hard to understand how he expected to make people believe that he was suddenly interested primarily in delayed justice rather than in ending a tortured interpretation of the Constitution; but the cleverness, the too much cleverness, appealed to him. In subsequent drafts, there was added further reference to old age and its natural conservatism. But the emphasis even in the final message remained on the delay in justice by overworked judges and crowded calendars in all United States courts.

We all agreed that the message, which was still in draft form, would have to be given considerably more popular appeal than it had. As the President put it, it would have to be "pepped up."

The next question was the date when the message should be sent to the Congress. One factor to consider was that the White House Judiciary Dinner had been set for February 2—just three days off. To that dinner, in accordance with custom, all the members of the Court had been invited, and with one or two exceptions probably all would be present. Obviously, it would be embarrassing if the message were sent up before the dinner. On the other hand the Solicitor General was scheduled to argue several cases before the Court on Monday, February 8. These cases involved the National Labor Relations Act and several other important New Deal statutes. The President wanted the message to go up to the Congress before the argument. The date of February 5 was finally decided upon.

The conference broke up at about 4 P.M., and after the others had left the President said to me, "The message in its present form leaves me cold. We will have to rewrite it. I wish you would try to get up another draft."

I worked on the language in the Cabinet Room until it came time to dress for the birthday party that night. After dinner was over the ladies separated into different groups, either to play bridge or to sit and talk, and the "cuff-links gang" went upstairs to play poker.

The President thought he was a good poker player. That opinion, however, was not shared by all those who played with him—and some of them should know. He lost more often than he won. All of us took particular pride and joy in winning from him, and nothing pleased him more than to win from us. As the President grew older, Doc McIntire insisted that the number of hours of card playing on his birthday be cut. From the all-night sessions which used to take place in Albany, they gradually shrank to 4 A.M., then to 2 A.M., and finally, much to the President's disgust, to midnight. He would complain about quitting early, but on a glance from Doc we would all insist, and if necessary just get up and quit.

About 11 P.M. on this date each year, the game was interrupted. Everybody—the poker game and the ladies too—assembled in the broadcast room in the basement, where the President made a short fireside chat thanking the people for their contributions on his birthday to the fight against infantile paralysis. After the speech, the card players would return upstairs to continue, and the ladies would generally go home.

My notes indicate that on this particular occasion I lost $12, that the President lost $16, and that the game broke up at 4 A.M.

The next day was Sunday, and I spent part of the morning working on the proposed message. After lunch, the President himself put in some more work on it. I left Washington that night for Philadelphia, where I was scheduled to make a speech, and returned on February 2. That afternoon another conference was held with the same people present. The President read aloud the new draft. Suggestions were made; the President from time to time dictated insertions, made deletions, and proposed new ideas. Again it was suggested that the major basis for the drastic proposal might well be changed—that it should be based frankly upon the course of judicial decisions in the last two years.

This was one of the rare occasions when the President deliberately avoided making a frontal attack on a problem. He insisted on his chosen course in spite of the fact that in press conferences and in speeches he had openly criticized the Court for what it was doing to the New Deal program. He came soon to realize that a more direct attack would have been better, and said so four years later in his introduction to the 1937 volume of his *Public Papers and Addresses:*

> I made one major mistake when I first presented the plan. I did not place enough emphasis upon the real mischief—the kind of decisions which, as a studied and continued policy, had been coming down from the Supreme Court. I soon corrected that mistake—in the speeches which I later made about the plan.

He certainly did. But this did not come until later. At the conference, he was unwilling to make the change. When the change did come it was too late. The original basis had been too firmly planted in the American people's minds. And they were not allowed to forget it, for the opponents of the plan kept referring to it all during the fight.

After the conference, with the President's consent, I talked with Corcoran about the proposed message. This was the first Tom had heard of it. Working with Tom on this project had its own complications. For once again, the President was willing to go to great wasteful lengths to keep conflicting personalities apart while the work was going on. The Attorney General and Tom at this time were very angry at each other. I do not know what Cummings had said to the President, if anything, about Tom in connection with this message; but the President told me that Tom should stay out of these conferences. He also told me to make sure that Cummings did not know that Tom was taking any part in the discussion or preparation of the message. I told Tom this; like me, he had grown used to this weakness of the President.

That night Mrs. Rosenman came down to join me for the Judiciary Dinner. Before the guests began to arrive, a very small group gathered as usual for cocktails in the President's study—the President, Mrs. Rosenman, Missy, and I. Later we were joined by Mrs. Roosevelt. The President made quite a ceremony out of this daily cocktail hour, mixing the drinks himself from various ingredients brought to his desk on a large tray.

People who were more accustomed to drinking than I, and who knew more about the mixing of drinks, were a little nonplused at the nonchalance with which the President, without bothering to measure, would add one ingredient after another to his cocktails. To my unpracticed eye he seemed to experiment on each occasion with a different percentage of vermouth, gin and fruit juice. At times he varied it with rum—especially rum from the Virgin Islands.

The President liked to press a second, and at times a third, cocktail upon any guest who was at all willing. His usual expression, on noticing an empty glass held by one of his guests, was: "How about another little sippy?" Fortunately, because of an episode which had occurred during the Albany days, he had learned not to press me for more than one drink. I happen to dislike liquor; so it was quite a chore for me to be polite and swallow even the first cocktail. One night, in Albany, after the Governor had insisted on refilling my glass for a second drink, I wanted to dispose of it without drinking it but without seeming to be ungracious. I hit upon an old but effective device. There were some plants and shrubs in the study of the Executive Mansion, so I walked nonchalantly around the room and quietly poured my cocktail into one of the flowerpots. The President, thinking I had swallowed the drink, tried to hide his surprise and admiration at my newly developed capacity. For several evenings I was successful in this method of disposal without being caught; but I suspect that Missy finally noticed me misplacing my drink. She must have mentioned it to the Governor. The next evening during the cocktail-mixing ceremony the Governor turned to me with great mock seriousness and said:

"You know, Sam, a peculiar thing has been happening to the plants in the Executive Mansion. Some time ago, the leaves of some of them began to change their color. Whitehead [the steward at the Executive Mansion in Albany] got worried about them and asked one of the experts from the Department of Agriculture to come over and take a look at them. The expert said he had never seen such a strange condition before, and would like to take the plants over to his laboratory for analysis of the soil. The report has just come back, and what do you think they found? They found that the soil was filled with a large percentage of alcohol. Whitehead is thoroughly mystified as to where we ever got that kind of soil."

We all laughed, and I said, "Well, Governor, if you don't want to lose all your plants, you'd better pass me up on seconds." In the later days at the White House, the President used to repeat that story to his guests to explain why he never offered me a second drink.

The President got great pleasure always out of this informal pre-dinner cocktail period. It was usually scheduled to last a half hour before dinner, but it often passed very quickly to a full hour—until a White House usher would come in to suggest for the third time that dinner was ready to serve. The President seldom discussed serious matters during this period; he seemed to find complete relaxation in light conversation with his guests and friends.

I never saw him take more than two cocktails on any of these occasions. He lingered long over each one, sipping it very slowly, spending a lot of time mixing drinks and offering them to the guests, and doing most of the talking as usual.

He would tell anecdotes which some of us had heard time and again, but which always seemed to gather additional embellishments as well as additional charm in the telling. In telling stories of the past the President never bothered to remember whether or not he had told them previously to the same audience. Some of his anecdotes I have heard at least five times, and I am sure that Missy and Grace must have heard them twenty times. But I cannot ever remember being bored even the fifth time. He usually invented or, as he would say, "remembered," some new detail, and with each telling the anecdote seemed to become livelier and more personal. He had a fine sense of humor, and a sure instinct for the dramatic; he could tell an anecdote well, timing the punch perfectly, and keeping the suspense alive even for those who had heard the story before and knew what the end was going to be.

Sometimes in telling stories the President's imagination and sense of the dramatic got the better of his recollection. For example, during my days as Counsel to the Governor one of my duties was to sit with him during extradition hearings. On one occasion, Roosevelt was in Hyde

Park; the matter was urgent and he asked me to hold the hearing in Albany without him. Two Chinese had held up and shot a man in Boston. Two Chinese were arrested in New York and held as suspects. Their extradition had been demanded by the Governor of Massachusetts. At the hearing the only evidence of identity came from one witness who said that he had obtained a fleeting glimpse of the two men running away from the scene of the crime in Boston, and he identified these suspects as the fugitives.

The defense counsel asked the witness to leave the room, and lined up in front of me some twenty Chinese whom he had brought to Albany. He placed the two defendants among the twenty, and then asked that the witness be called back. Although during the hearing I had taken a good long look at the two suspects, I must admit that I could not have picked them out of the other twenty Chinese in line. The witness came back, and of course he could not identify them either.

After the hearing I drove down to Hyde Park to report to the Governor and to recommend that extradition be denied on the ground that the identity of the fugitives had not been sufficiently established.

Roosevelt in later years used to tell that story quite frequently to visitors. I heard him tell it accurately—once. The next time I heard him tell it, I learned to my surprise that it was he who had conducted these proceedings in Albany, not I; and that it was he who had been unable to identify the suspects in the long line of Chinese in front of him in the Executive Chamber. I was a little startled at first; but I heard the story told many times that way. I am sure that the President did not consciously misstate this incident; he had so vivid an imagination, he had become so engrossed and interested in the anecdote itself and in the telling of it, that he had come to believe he was actually present during the hearing. Every time Missy and Grace and I heard him tell the story we would smile and wink at each other, but we never killed his fun by correcting him.

Usually the group at cocktails were close friends and associates. When there were other house guests with whom he was not on terms of intimacy, they would not be asked to join the cocktail group, but would gather with Mrs. Roosevelt in the West Hall of the White House. There they would talk and wait until the President was ready to come down for dinner.

He would then be wheeled out of his study and into the West Hall.

where he would greet the other guests. Together they would all go down in the elevator to the family dining room on the first floor.

The evening before the Judiciary Dinner the discussion at cocktails was a little more serious than usual. We were all impressed with the seriousness of what was coming. We felt it more deeply because we knew that even then the Justices were gathering downstairs in the East Room, and because the whole thing had been kept such a secret among a small handful of people.

We drank a toast to the Supreme Court as it was, and as we hoped it would be after the President's recommendation had been adopted. The President said with mock glumness that he was not looking forward with great pleasure to this dinner, but the rest of us knew that he really was enjoying the occasion very much. Several times he repeated the same thought: "The time for action with respect to the Supreme Court really cannot be postponed, and unpleasant as it is, I think we have to face it."

Mrs. Roosevelt came in during cocktails and joined in the conversation. She smilingly but firmly reminded the President that he needed a new dinner suit since his trousers were beginning to show signs of wear. She added that she was going to call in the tailor and have one made. The President plaintively bemoaned the fact that he could not afford a new dinner suit. The incident caused considerable merriment, especially since a newspaper story a few days earlier had listed the President among the ten best-dressed men in the United States. Whenever he appeared in a very old suit or sweater or hat—which was not infrequently—and Mrs. Roosevelt would say something about it, he would proudly recall the fact that he had made this exclusive sartorial list.

The dinner that night stands out in my memory above all the other formal dinners I attended at the White House. When we got down to the East Room and were announced, the guests were nearly all assembled; there were about ninety, the usual number. All the Justices of the Supreme Court were there, except Justice Louis Brandeis, who never attended evening social functions, and Justice Harlan Stone, who was recovering from an illness. Chief Justice Charles E. Hughes was in a jovial mood. Justice McReynolds, as usual, was morose and taciturn. There were many other "big names" present, for this was always one of the important annual social affairs: Mrs. Woodrow Wilson; Senators

William E. Borah, Pat Harrison, Henry F. Ashurst; Judge Irving Lehman of the New York Court of Appeals, and others, including Homer Cummings, Stanley Reed and Donald Richberg. Cummings came over and whispered to me: "I wish this message were over and delivered. It makes me uncomfortable; I feel too much like a conspirator." Looking at his tall, lanky, thin figure and comparing it with my own rotund body, I said, "General, you certainly look more like the traditional conspirator than I do. But I wish it were over too."

After dinner, in accordance with the usual custom, the ladies retired to the Blue Room and the Green Room. The gentlemen moved up closer around the President at the head of the dining table, or sat in small groups smoking cigars and drinking coffee. I chatted with Justice Cardozo and with Joseph A. Broderick, who had been the New York Superintendent of Banks when Roosevelt was Governor. From time to time I glanced over to watch the President and the group around him. He seemed to be having a grand time, completely at ease, puffing on a cigarette. The Chief Justice and Justice Van Devanter had moved over next to him; there was a lot of laughter and conviviality.

I am sure that except on rare occasions the President found these formal White House dinners rather boring, as his predecessors probably had, too. He complained that because of the strict observance of protocol, he found himself seated next to the same people time and again. However, I never saw him at any of these dinners with even a fleeting look of boredom on his face. He so much enjoyed talking to people— almost all people—that on nearly any occasion he could find something interesting to talk about, and if the people with him had nothing interesting to say he would do all the talking himself. This Judiciary Dinner he seemed really to enjoy. The difficult question of what to do about the Supreme Court had bothered him for more than a year. Now that the decision had been made, he felt relieved.

All through the next day the President worked on the Court message. The same group was present. Although some of the judicial statistics still had to be checked, by nightfall the message was practically completed. As I was preparing to leave for New York, Missy called me aside and said, "The President is terribly nervous about this message. I think it would be helpful and comforting to him if you stayed over until the thing is finally completed and put to bed" (a phrase we used to indicate that the speech had gone to the mimeographing room).

I mention this because it shows the President's state of mind just before the final step was taken. It was not the offhand, cavalier action that some writers have called it, but a carefully thought-out and thoroughly considered plan, the momentous nature of which he thoroughly appreciated. While he was convinced he was right about the step he was taking, he was nervous. It is the only time I can recall that he seemed worried after once deciding upon a course of action.

Perhaps the depth of conviction that was customarily his was the reason that Roosevelt inspired such deep security in the American people. They seemed to lean upon him with a feeling that in some way he would be able to weather any storm with safety. That was particularly noticeable during the dark days of the war in 1942. In spite of all the news of defeats and losses, there was a feeling of confidence in the nation that somehow everything was going to come out all right. He felt keenly that there were few if any problems impossible for human beings to solve. He realized that it might take a long time and call for many trials and errors; but he was sure that there was an answer to all human problems, and that sooner or later the answer could be found if only the will to find it was strong enough.

On the following day, we finally had the message completely checked and in finished form. At about five in the afternoon, the President asked his secretary, Marvin McIntyre, to call a Cabinet meeting for the next morning at ten to precede the regularly scheduled press conference. He asked Mac to invite to the meeting Senator Ashurst and Congressman Sumners, who were the chairmen of the Senate and House Judiciary Committees; Bankhead, the Speaker of the House; Senator Robinson, the Democratic Senate leader; and Sam Rayburn, the Democratic House leader. The President was so anxious to keep this whole matter a secret, that although it was unusual to invite Congressmen to a Cabinet meeting, he did not even then tell Mac what it was all about.

He did ask Steve Early, however, to come over to the study; and that afternoon he handed Steve a copy of the message to read in our presence. Steve was completely surprised, for the President had given him no inkling that action was this near. The President wanted him to know about it before the press conference the next day so that if the newspapermen asked him any questions afterward he would be in a better position to answer them. Steve was told to arrange for part of the White House staff to come to work at the unheard of hour of six-thirty the next morning in order to mimeograph the message, so that there would be less danger of a leak. These were unprecedented precautions although it does not seem now that secrecy was so important.

By this time the President was feeling quite confident. I said good-by to him, and then with several others—Missy, Grace, Tommy and his present wife, Peggy—went out to Betsy Roosevelt's for dinner. All of us there knew of the message, and that was the sole topic of conversation at dinner. Tom kept talking about the terrible effect it was going to have on "old Isaiah"—meaning Justice Brandeis.

"I've got the Boss' O.K. to go down and tell him in confidence what's coming," he said. "He sure won't like it." Tom was right; he did not like it.

The next day the Cabinet met, together with the Congressional leaders who had been invited. The President read the message to them. He asked for no advice or suggestions. It was a hurried meeting; the newspapermen had been waiting for some time for the press conference scheduled after the Cabinet meeting. At the press conference, which lasted until the message was literally on its way to the Congress, the newspapermen asked him about the Cabinet meeting:

QUESTION: Was that [referring to the message which the President had read to the Press] the reason for the special Cabinet meeting?
THE PRESIDENT: Yes.
QUESTION: Can you tell us what the reaction was this morning?
THE PRESIDENT: I did exactly what I did here. As soon as I finished I came in here. There was no discussion.

I am sure that even if there had been discussion, the President's mind could not then have been changed.

Commentators and historians have already written much, and will doubtless write much more, about the Court fight. Its details have no place in this book, nor has any extended discussion of the events that followed the President's message. But to the extent that the controversy was reflected in the President's speeches and actions, it does have a place here.

The moment the President's message became public, there was a strong reaction. Opposition came at once. It came from the Congress, from the Court itself, from almost the entire press of the nation. Congressional opposition was carried on more violently and bitterly by members of the President's own party than by the Republicans. The strategy of the Republican leaders was to encourage the Democratic opposition, while they remained scrupulously silent but terribly interested. For this fight might well have meant the political end of Roosevelt, the New Deal, and, for many years, Democratic Presidents.

As the fight developed, the President abandoned the artificial position he had taken in the message—that Court reform was needed because of calendar congestion. Instead he concentrated as he should have in the first place on the kind of decision that had been coming from the Court. He delivered two major addresses in an effort to rally public support.

In the first—at a dinner of Democrats on March 4 noisily celebrating the victory of last November—the President pointed out that by the time of his second election it had become apparent that the New Deal was being frustrated in its effort to make the democratic process work for the benefit of the people as a whole. He pictured the government as a three-horse team. This simple, graphic figure of speech was part of a paragraph dictated by the President while he was going over one of the drafts:

"If three well-matched horses are put to the task of ploughing up a field where the going is heavy, and the team of three pull as one, the field will be ploughed. If one horse lies down in the traces or plunges off in another direction, the field will not be ploughed."

He asserted that many of the major efforts of the New Deal had been aborted by recent decisions of the Supreme Court—and that by these decisions the power of the federal government to achieve nearly all its objectives had been cast in great doubt. And he added:

"We gave warning last November that we had only just begun to fight. Did some people really believe we did not mean it? Well—I meant it, and you meant it."

There were already whispered charges that the President was toying with the idea of a third term. Ridiculous as they were in 1937—I am certain that nothing was further from his mind—he took advantage of them in telling how he wanted to clear the road for action:

A few days ago, a distinguished member of the Congress came to see me to talk about national problems in general and about the problem of the Judiciary in particular.

I said to him:

"John, I want to tell you something that is very personal to me—something that you have a right to hear from my own lips. I have a great ambition in life."

My friend pricked up his ears.

I went on: "I am by no means satisfied with having twice been elected

President of the United States by very large majorities. I have an even greater ambition."

By this time, my friend was sitting on the edge of his chair.

[And, I might add, so was the audience at the Hotel Mayflower in Washington.]

I continued [the President went on]: "John, my ambition relates to January 20, 1941." I could feel just what horrid thoughts my friend was thinking. So in order to relieve his anxiety, I went on to say: "My great ambition on January 20, 1941, is to turn over this desk and chair in the White House to my successor, whoever he may be, with the assurance that I am at the same time turning over to him as President, a nation intact, a nation at peace, a nation prosperous, a nation clear in its knowledge of what powers it has to serve its own citizens, a nation that is in a position to use those powers to the full in order to move forward steadily to meet the modern needs of humanity—a nation which has thus proved that the democratic form and methods of national government can and will succeed. . . ."

The President had a lot of fun dictating that passage. We who heard him dictate it to Grace were a little nonplused ourselves as he began talking about not being satisfied with having been elected twice. He had even more fun delivering it to a hushed audience. The Congressman "John" was about the same kind of character as the garage mechanic and the other assorted characters who, according to his speeches and press conferences, "visited" the President from time to time to discuss problems—and give him a chance to explain in a homely, conversational way some point he wanted to bring home.

The President was of course furious that the opposition to the Court proposal was coming from the members of his own party with whom he had just won an overwhelming victory at the polls on an all-out liberal platform. His bitterness was apparent all through the fight. He gave an indication of it in this speech when he said:

"If we do not have the courage to lead the American people where they want to go, someone else will."

The speech did not win the popular support for his plan that the President expected, and for which he was now working.

He tried again—this time in a fireside chat on March 9. The same team helped: Corcoran, Cohen, Richberg and I. I think it was the last speech on which Richberg did any substantial work. Although he became quite conservative in his point of view after that, I missed his calm judgment and deliberate thinking in our later work. The strongest argument of the opposition was that the proper way to meet the problem was by a constitutional amendment. It was an appealing argument and the President had been urged to answer it. He did. In this fireside chat he explained in simple terms his reasons for the Court proposal:

There are many types of amendment proposed. Each one is radically different from the other. There is no substantial group within the Congress or outside it who are agreed on any single amendment.

It would take months or years to get substantial agreement upon the type and language of an amendment. It would take months and years thereafter to get a two-thirds majority in favor of that amendment in *both* Houses of the Congress.

Then would come the long course of ratification by three-fourths of all the States. . . . Thirteen States which contain only five per cent of the voting population can block ratification even though the thirty-five States with ninety-five per cent of the population are in favor of it.

A very large percentage of newspaper publishers, Chambers of Commerce, Bar Associations, Manufacturers' Associations, who are trying to give the impression that they really do want a constitutional amendment, would be the first to exclaim as soon as an amendment was proposed, "Oh! I was for an amendment all right, but this amendment that you have proposed is not the kind of an amendment that I was thinking about. I am, therefore, going to spend my time, my efforts and my money to block that amendment, although I would be awfully glad to help get some other kind of amendment ratified." . . .

And remember one thing more. Even if an amendment were passed, and even if in the years to come it were to be ratified, its meaning would depend upon the kind of Justices who would be sitting on the Supreme Court bench. An amendment, like the rest of the Constitution, is what the Justices say it is rather than what its framers or you might hope it is.

He then turned to the charge of "packing" the Court—a charge which was very appealing to popular opinion:

What do they mean by the words "packing the Court? . . ."

If by that phrase "packing the Court" it is charged that I wish to place on the bench spineless puppets who would disregard the law and would decide specific cases as I wished them to be decided, I make this answer: that no President fit for his office would appoint, and no Senate of honorable men fit for their office would confirm, that kind of appointees to the Supreme Court.

But if by that phrase the charge is made that I would appoint and the Senate would confirm Justices worthy to sit beside present members of the Court who understand those modern conditions, that I will appoint Justices who will not undertake to override the judgment of the Congress on legislative policy, that I will appoint Justices who will act as Justices and not as legislators—if the appointment of such Justices can be called "packing the Courts," then I say that I and with me the vast majority of the American people favor doing just that thing—now.

The President was extremely sensitive about the charge of "packing"; the foregoing paragraphs he dictated himself.

It was no use. He was unable to get the people to back him up and get the action he wanted from the Congress.

Some writers have suggested that if the President had been less stubborn, less blind to realities, he could have obtained a compromise which would have served his purpose. Since I did not take part in the fight other than to give what help I could on the two speeches, I do not know whether that is true. I do know that the President felt very confident—almost "cocky"—that he could win, and was in no mood for compromise. On the other hand, as he wrote in his Introduction to the 1937 volume of his *Public Papers:*

I received . . . no reasonable guarantee or assurance that some other definite method would obtain Congressional approval. Rumors of compromise were plenty; but never a definite agreement or offer. . . . And the best legislative advice which I could get from the Congressional leaders was that my own suggestion would ultimately be approved. . . . Had any satisfactory compromise been definitely offered which would have been effective in attaining the objective, and which would have been capable of quick passage, it would have been accepted by me.

On July 22, the Supreme Court plan was finally and definitely rejected by the Congress, although practically all the other recommendations in the Judiciary Message were adopted.

Why did it fail? Some have said that it was because many of the leaders in Roosevelt's own party were opposed to it. Others have said that it was because of the overwhelmingly hostile press comments; the deep veneration in which the people of the United States held their Supreme Court; inept fumbling in the Congress by those in charge of the bill; the untimely death of the majority leader of the Senate, Senator Robinson; the refusal of the President to accept some compromise.

While each of these things contributed to the defeat, they were not the decisive factors. The plan, in my opinion, was defeated by the

Court itself. The plan was defeated because the decisions of the Court changed—without the addition or substitution of a single Justice.

The first shift which turned the minority into a majority in the Court came on March 29, within eight weeks after the President's message, when, by a five to four decision, the Court—completely reversing its prior decision just nine months previously—held that a state could constitutionally pass a minimum wage law for women. We now know that Justice Roberts, whose change of position turned the majority of the Court into a minority, had really changed his vote in conference in December, 1936. But no one outside the Court knew of any change until it was announced on March 29. The following month the Court upheld the constitutionality of the National Labor Relations Act—a sharp departure in approach and reasoning from several prior decisions. As a climax, the Court upheld the constitutionality of the Social Security Act. By the time the Court recessed for the summer, it was obvious that the liberal dissenting views of the minority in 1935 and 1936 had in large measure become the majority views of the Court. As a contemporary wag put it: "A switch in time saved nine."

In retrospect, perhaps it would have been better tactics if the President had withdrawn the legislation as soon as the switch became apparent, for in the face of the Court's changed attitude it was impossible to arouse the American people to the immediate necessity of Congressional action.

It was not until June 2, 1937, that the President, by the retirement of Justice Van Devanter, got his first opportunity to select a Justice of the Court. Van Devanter was seventy-eight years old and one of the most conservative members of the Court. His retirement made completely certain the death of Roosevelt's Court plan.

The battle had been lost; but the war had been definitely won. That is why I believe that the President's message of February 5, 1937, was among the most important of his domestic utterances. So did he.

What about the President during this fight and defeat? It was a bitter pill for him, so soon after the glorious victory of the re-election. That it came largely from his own party made it more difficult to swallow. I do not think he ever did completely swallow it. Many mistakes were made during this fight: the mistake of overconfidence, the mistake of refusing to discuss the measure in advance with Congressmen, the mistake of stubbornness, the mistake of not personally leading the fight, as he did other fights. I think he later realized all the mistakes he had made. His defeat contributed directly to another grave mistake: the purge of 1938. It seemed to crystallize the President's feelings about the need for a realignment of the liberal forces in the two major parties. That the fight went deeply into his sensibilities was clear to anyone who heard him talk about it.

Chapter X

Foreign Quarantines and Domestic Purges, 1937-1938

During the late spring and summer of 1937 I was not called upon to do any work with the President. He was occupied primarily with the Court fight, and with pushing additional New Deal legislation: a program to reduce farm tenancy, February 16, 1937; a program of crop insurance, February 18; a permanent Civilian Conservation Corps, April 5; a comprehensive flood-control plan for the Ohio and Mississippi rivers, April 28; legislation for minimum wages and maximum hours, May 24; development of water power on the St. Lawrence River, May 25; closing up loopholes in income tax laws, June 1; regional planning and development of natural resources through seven regional authorities, June 3; new farm program, July 12, to take the place of AAA, declared unconstitutional in 1936.

He did not make any important speeches after the Court fight speeches until the celebration of the 150th Anniversary of the Constitution on September 17, 1937. Tom and Ben and I worked on that speech. During the Court fight, the President had been often and loudly accused of ignoring the Constitution. He wanted to use this opportunity to explain what he thought the Constitution was. The general theme of the speech was Tom's idea: that the Constitution was not a lawyer's contract, strict and inflexible, but a layman's document, appropriate to a layman's broad and flexible construction.

The President accepted that theme. But with Hitler and Mussolini on the march in Europe, he was beginning to emphasize a note that he had sounded before and that was material in the Court fight.

In our generation, a new idea has come to dominate thought about government, the idea that the resources of the nation can be made to produce a far higher standard of living for the masses of the people if only government is intelligent and energetic in giving the right direction to economic life. . . .

That ideal makes understandable the demands of labor for shorter hours and higher wages, the demands of farmers for a more stable income, the demands of the great majority of business men for relief from disruptive trade practices, the demands of all for the end of that kind of license, often mistermed "Liberty," which permits a handful of the population to take far more than its tolerable share from the rest of the people.

The President made a full-dress comparison between our democracy and the concept of government held by the rulers of Germany, Italy, Russia, and Japan. Although he did not mention those countries by name—because this was still the period of diplomatic silk gloves—it was quite clear about whom he was talking. He warned that they were gradually building up the danger of a new world war, and said that although "the people of America are rightly determined to keep that growing menace from our shores . . . it takes even more foresight, intelligence and patience to meet the subtle attack which spreading dictatorship makes upon the morale of a democracy."

That statement was the natural forerunner of the "quarantine" speech at Chicago on October 5, 1937, delivered on the return leg of a trip to the West Coast.

Sumner Welles, who was Under Secretary of State at the time, has written me as follows in response to my inquiry about the "quarantine" speech:

At that time he was, I think, more immediately concerned with the situation in the Pacific than with conditions in Europe. As you undoubtedly remember, he was talking with the Navy about drawing an actual line in the Pacific to be maintained by the United States, if the British would agree to cooperate, beyond which Japan would be told she would not be permitted to trade or to expand in the event that she persisted in the policy of military conquest of China upon which she at that time seemed bent. I remember very well indeed upon at least two, and I think three, occasions when I was with the President in his office in the White House that he had me walk over to the large map of the Pacific that he had on a stand in the rear of his office in order that I might follow point by point the various lines that he had under consideration. . . . The President used the word "quarantine" in connection with that line and the talks to which I refer took place in the earlier part and in the middle of the summer of 1937. . . . He did not discuss with me the so-called "quarantine" clause before the

Chicago address was delivered. Harold Ickes has upon several occasions told me that he was responsible for the inclusion of that clause. All that I can be certain of, however, is that it was a word that the President had used several times in talking with me long before the speech was drafted.

During September the President had also been talking about the state of the world to Norman Davis, then in the State Department. Davis had prepared a draft which was the basis of the Chicago speech. The Davis draft had the phrase "War is a contagion," but did not use the "quarantine" idea.

Ickes used to talk to Roosevelt frequently about matters outside his own department, especially foreign affairs. Ickes has written me that at lunch just before the President started West on his trip he told the President that the only voice left in the world that could effectively be raised for democracy was Roosevelt's. Ickes criticized the weak attitude of the State Department; Roosevelt agreed, and said that he was going to run the Department himself when he got back from his trip. Then Ickes talked about the international situation as a disease, saying that a neighborhood has a right to "quarantine" itself against a threatened infection. The President interrupted him, says Ickes, and wrote the word down, saying he would use it some time.

The speech at Chicago was devoted entirely to foreign affairs. It was a factual statement of what was going on; and if it had been delivered a year later, it would have been accepted without excitement. But in October, 1937, it caused a sensation:

Without a declaration of war and without warning or justification of any kind, civilians, including vast numbers of women and children, are being ruthlessly murdered with bombs from the air. In times of so-called peace, ships are being attacked and sunk by submarines without cause or notice. Nations are fomenting and taking sides in civil warfare in nations that have never done them any harm. Nations claiming freedom for themselves deny it to others. . . .

If those things come to pass in other parts of the world, let no one imagine that America will escape . . . that this Western Hemisphere . . . will continue tranquilly and peacefully to carry on the ethics and the arts of civilization. . . .

It seems to be unfortunately true that the epidemic of world lawlessness is spreading.

When an epidemic of physical disease starts to spread, the community approves and joins in a quarantine of the patients in order to protect the health of the community against the spread of the disease. . . .

The reaction to the speech was quick and violent—and nearly unanimous. It was condemned as warmongering and saber-rattling. The President was attacked by a vast majority of the press. It was charged that his statements were more likely to promote war than peace. There were some notable exceptions of course, like the Washington *Post*, which said editorially that this was the end of the flabby, vicious, humiliating doctrine that America could see no difference between a ruthless aggressor and the innocent victim of his aggression, and that the speech might well foreshadow a turning point in American history.

Telegrams of denunciation came in at once. I quote two, typical of scores of others:

1. If you "hate war" do not try to incite it by such appeals as that you made on the 5th in Chicago.

2. All right if you want peace keep the peace. No one is coming over here to attack us.

In Tokyo and Berlin it was not well received. In other foreign capitals it was hailed enthusiastically. A headline in a Chinese paper read, "Roosevelt's Roar of Justice." The typical foreign reaction was that of an article by Lord Lothian in the *Observer* in England, which stated:

President Roosevelt's speech in Chicago on October 5, will probably mark for the historian the point at which the United States definitely began to turn away from the isolation which had been its policy since the rejection of the League of Nations in the presidential election of 1920.

One person who definitely did not like it was the German Ambassador Dieckhoff. In a memorandum that he sent to the German Foreign Office October 15, 1937 (captured in 1945 among its archives), he wrote:

The draft did not, however, contain anything about a specific implementation of this cooperation, let alone a "quarantine" threat to foreign countries. These passages originated with the President himself and, as I learned, were not incorporated in the text of the speech until immediately before his arrival in Chicago. What induced the President to insert such a note into the original rather colorless draft is not quite clear. The intensification of the Japanese campaign in China probably alarmed him. Possibly it was an attempt to drown out or silence the public discussion of the Black case, which was embarrassing to Mr. Roosevelt, by a spectacular fanfare in the field of foreign policy. Roosevelt is a tremendously shrewd politician, and this might possibly have been his intention.

Sumner Welles has written me of the President's feeling about the reaction to his speech:

I also recall very well talking with the President about the public reaction to the Chicago speech. He was surprised by the volume of the attacks made upon it. I also remember that he spoke with great indignation of the failure of certain members of his Administration and of certain Democratic leaders in the Congress to come out with courageous and vigorous statements supporting his speech and clarifying the purposes he had had in mind. You yourself knew him so much better than most that you will understand what I mean when I say that I think that the negative course he pursued thereafter was due as much to his peculiar individual reaction of silence in the face of disaster or bitter disappointment—provoked in this case by the lack of vision as well as personal disloyalty of some of those who should have made themselves heard—as to any feeling on his part that politically it might be expedient to ride out the storm.

The speech was a milestone in the foreign policy of the United States. It was Roosevelt's first direct appeal in behalf of collective security as distinguished from isolationism and from impartial, blind neutrality.

But he had made a mistake that he seldom made—the mistake of trying to lead the people of the United States too quickly, and before they had been adequately informed of the facts or spiritually prepared for the event. On the other hand, a great deal more would have been accomplished and more public support would have been aroused if Hull and the Democratic leaders in the Congress had publicly backed the President up.

"It's a terrible thing," he once said to me, having in mind, I am sure, this occasion, "to look over your shoulder when you are trying to lead—and to find no one there."

Having gone too far out on a limb too fast, he decided the next day at his press conference that he had better get back, or at least not go out any further:

QUESTION: And you were speaking, as I interpreted it, you were speaking of something more than moral indignation. That is preparing the way for collaborative——

THE PRESIDENT: Yes?

QUESTION: Is anything contemplated? Have you moved?

THE PRESIDENT: No; just the speech itself.

QUESTION: Yes, but how do you reconcile that? Do you accept the fact that that is a repudiation of the neutrality—

THE PRESIDENT: Not for a minute. It may be an expansion.

QUESTION: Doesn't that mean economic sanctions anyway?

THE PRESIDENT: No, not necessarily. Look, "sanctions" is a terrible word to use. They are out of the window.

QUESTION: Right. Let's not call it that. Let's call it concert of action on the part of peace-loving nations. Is that going to be brought into play?

THE PRESIDENT: . . . I can't tell you what the methods will be. We are looking for some way to peace; and by no means is it necessary that that way be contrary to the exercise of neutrality. . . .

QUESTION: Wouldn't it be almost inevitable, if any program is reached, that our present Neutrality Act will have to be overhauled?

THE PRESIDENT: Not necessarily. That is the interesting thing.

QUESTION: You say there isn't any conflict between what you outline and the Neutrality Act. They seem to be on opposite poles to me and your assertion does not enlighten me. . . . How can you be neutral if you are going to align yourself with one group of nations?

THE PRESIDENT: What do you mean, "aligning"? You mean a treaty?

QUESTION: Not necessarily. I meant action on the part of peace-loving nations.

THE PRESIDENT: There are a lot of methods in the world that have never been tried yet.

QUESTION: But, at any rate, that is not an indication of neutral attitude— "quarantine the aggressors" and "other nations of the world."

THE PRESIDENT: I can't give you any clue to it. You will have to invent one. I have got one.

QUESTION: This is no longer neutrality.

THE PRESIDENT: On the contrary, it might be a stronger neutrality.

QUESTION: I mean as related to—— (Interrupted)

QUESTION: This is all off the record?

THE PRESIDENT: Yes, this is all off the record.

Whatever may be said of the tactical strategy and timing of the speech, it was a courageous and accurate appraisal of the world situation. The difficulty was that the country had not been sufficiently prepared. To the American people the clouds—so small and so far off on the horizon—were hardly noticeable.

During the years immediately preceding the war and after the war began, the President, with rare exceptions, was very careful never to recommend any drastic action without first informing the people of the facts as thoroughly as military security permitted. He knew that the American people, once fully informed, were willing to take whatever action was necessary—no matter what the price. But they had to know where they were going and why.

Two months after the "quarantine" speech, on December 12—as if to emphasize the speech—Japanese airplanes, without warning or provocation, bombed and sank the U.S. Gunboat *Panay* in the Yangtze River. Two weeks later the President sent a letter to the chairman of the Appropriations Committee of the House of Representatives requesting additional appropriations for combat ships. In it he said, "In speaking of my growing concern, I do not refer to any specific nation or to any specific threat against the United States. The fact is that in the world as a whole many nations are not only continuing but are enlarging their armament programs. I have used every conceivable effort to stop this trend, and to work toward a decrease of armaments. The facts, nevertheless, are facts, and the United States must recognize them."

Although he was not going to get out again on a limb in a speech, he was going to start to get the guns ready.

The years 1937 and 1938 were marked by Roosevelt's bitter and difficult fight with the Congress to obtain the passage of additional legislation—sometimes referred to as the Second New Deal. His popular appeal and prestige had been deeply hurt by the Court proposal; it was further hurt by the recession of 1937-1938. This was giving the President a lot of trouble and making him irritable. He had prided himself greatly on the economic recovery since 1933, and had referred to it repeatedly all through the recent campaign. His opponents were now blaming him personally for the recession, just as Hoover had been blamed in 1932. But the charge was not that he had done too little; it was that he had done too much—that his reforms were "strangling business," "ruining confidence," and "preventing full recovery."

Far from being intimidated into cutting down, Roosevelt was convinced that what was needed was more government action—not less. He also was determined not to let the recession slide into a panic; he knew that there was no reason for a panic, as there had been in 1933.

He was convinced that the recession was due to three things: the production of goods had been too high and had outstripped the purchasing power of consumers; industry had increased prices too much; government, in the mistaken belief that industry was ready to take up the slack of unemployment, had cut down its expenditures for relief and work relief too quickly and too drastically.

The speeches of the next two years—on the domestic side—had to do primarily with this fight. Roosevelt decided to take his case to the people.

The first thing he did, after the Congress adjourned in July, 1937, was to take a trip through the country and talk about the things he was trying to do in Washington. He knew how much his voice and smile and presence could do with the people. He had complete confidence that he could win—but he did not know how long and bitter the fight was going to be and how much it was going to take out of him.

The trip started from Hyde Park on September 22 and it extended to the Pacific Coast and back. Most of the speeches were extremporaneous. It was, as the President said, chiefly a "look-see" trip.

When he got back to Washington he called the Congress into Extraordinary Session to reconsider the legislation it had turned down in its regular session. Before it met, there were two speech-writing jobs to be done. One was the formal message to the Congress; the other was more important—an appeal to the people over the heads of the Congress, a fireside chat.

Tom, Ben and I worked on both these documents. Bullitt was in the country then and helped on the fireside chat. Some of the work was done at Hyde Park and some in Washington.

The fireside chat came first, October 12; a month before the date set in his proclamation for the Extraordinary Session of the Congress. He thought he could get the people to bring pressure on their Congressmen, who were then at home in their own districts. He hoped that by the time they met in Extraordinary Session, they would have been convinced that their constituents wanted action.

Consequently, in his chat he outlined the recommendations he expected to make in his message to Congress: the enactment of a new comprehensive farm program, legislation providing for minimum wages and maximum hours, the abolition of child labor in all interstate occupations, a plan of reorganization of the administrative agencies of the Federal Government, and a great expansion in the planning functions of government.

Referring to his Western trip, he said:

The other day I was asked to state my outstanding impression gained on this recent trip. I said that it seemed to me to be the general understanding on the part of the average citizen of the broad objectives and policies which I have just outlined.

Five years of fierce discussion and debate, five years of information through the radio and the moving picture, have taken the whole nation to school in the nation's business. . . .

It was an "impression" that gave him particular pride, for he felt that his previous fireside chats and other speeches were largely responsible for the people's lively interest in the affairs of their government.

One of the outstanding accomplishments of Roosevelt the statesman was his successful course of educating the American people in the uses of democracy, accompanied by practical examples of the doctrines he was teaching. In 1933 there were few books and no national precedents for the philosophy or legislation that came to be known as the New Deal. He had to write his own books in the form of speeches and messages, and then create the precedents himself to carry them out.

Back in the campaign of 1932 he had described the blueprint for this course, in his Commonwealth Club speech in San Francisco (largely the work of Berle, as revised by the Brain Trust):

"Government includes the art of formulating a policy, and using the political technique to attain so much of that policy as will receive general support; persuading, leading, sacrificing, teaching always, because the greatest duty of a statesman is to educate."

Roosevelt saw leadership in public life as the ability to see what is coming around the corner, to devise the best means of meeting it, and to win the people's approval to meet it. He sometimes failed to perform these tasks perfectly; but his successes overwhelmingly outnumbered his failures.

News of aggression abroad continued, and the chat of October 12, 1937, touched upon foreign affairs:

Nor can we view with indifference the destruction of civilized values throughout the world. We seek peace, not only for our generation but also for the generation of our children. . . .

I want our great democracy to be wise enough to realize that aloofness from war is not promoted by unawareness of war. In a world of mutual suspicions, peace must be affirmatively reached for. It cannot just be wished for. It cannot just be waited for. . . .

The President was still being criticized for his "quarantine" speech; the charge was still being made that he was seeking to entangle us in foreign disputes. In talking about this to us and to others, he spoke frequently of the events that had drawn the United States into World War I in 1917. He had great confidence that the mistakes of 1914-1917 could be avoided, and that profiting by them we could stay out of any war. One of the mistakes, as he put it, was to allow American vessels and citizens to get into combat zones. He was to learn that avoiding those mistakes was not enough, but in 1937 he was still confident. He wanted to tell the people that no matter what came, he had not intended to imply by the "quarantine" speech that we were going to get physically involved in any war. This is the way he wrote it himself; I remember that he was quite pleased with it. We did not think it was explicit enough, but he insisted on leaving it vague:

Meanwhile, remember that from 1913 to 1921, I personally was fairly close to world events, and in that period, while I learned much of what to do, I also learned much of what *not* to do.

The common sense, the intelligence of America agree with my statement that "America hates war. America hopes for peace. Therefore, America actively engages in the search for peace."

The radio speech did not have the effect the President hoped for. The Congress met; the President sent it the formal recommendations he had outlined in the fireside chat. But none of the recommendations was adopted.

The President did not stop.

In his message to the regular session of the Congress in January 1938, he repeated these recommendations and added two others: new tax legislation to prevent continued tax evasion and to further the principle of taxation according to ability to pay; and legislation to meet monopoly and the growing concentration of economic power. He made it quite clear in this message—as he had said so often in private conversation—that instead of pulling in or trimming sails, the way to beat the recession was to go ahead full speed.

As the 1938 session continued, the President continued his appeals to get his Second New Deal passed: in a speech on January 8 to a Democratic dinner to celebrate Andrew Jackson Day; in a speech at Gainesville, Georgia, March 23; in several press conferences. He was trying again to get a stronger public opinion in back of him.

In the meantime, the recession continued.

On April 14, the President sent to the Congress detailed recommendations on ways to meet the recession and to stimulate further recovery. That same night, he delivered a fireside chat.

Missy had phoned me the day before to come down, and I arrived at the White House in the late afternoon. The President had with him in his office a group of Congressional leaders and some members of his own official family. He had prepared a first draft of the message to the

Congress containing his recommendations; he was reading it to the group in order to get their reactions and suggestions. I waited outside and chatted with Missy. The continued recession, she told me, had produced some frayed nerves. The Secretary of the Treasury had gone so far as to threaten to resign because of the continued spending policy of the Administration. I do not know whether he was ever serious about it; the fact is that the policy was not changed, and he did not resign. The President was glad that he did not, for he had found his old friend Morgenthau a loyal supporter and good administrator of unquestioned integrity.

Missy gave us a copy of the draft of the message that the President was discussing with the group, and Tom and I went into the Cabinet Room to read it and work on it. That night after dinner, the President went over the draft again in his study. Jimmy and Betsy Roosevelt came in and sat around. The typing was done in relays by Grace and Dorothy Jones; for the message had to go up at noon the next day, and there was still the fireside chat to do for the evening of the same day. The work on the message was not completed until one o'clock in the morning.

The President was now tired—with good reason—and made ready to leave for bed.

"What about the fireside speech, Mr. President?" asked Missy firmly.

"Oh, I'm tired, let me go to bed," he said with mock entreaty, looking at the rest of us in the room.

"No," she said, "you just have to get something down on paper tonight."

He leaned back on the sofa with an air of resignation and shut his eyes for a long time. We sat there very quietly; after a while we thought he had actually fallen asleep. But finally he opened his eyes and, starting to dictate, said, "Mah F-r-a-a-nds" in such an exaggerated drawl of "My friends" (with which salutation nearly all his fireside chats started), and with such a comic expression, that we all broke out laughing. That perked him right up, and he dictated steadily until 2:15 A.M., when we let him at last go to bed.

Grace, Dorothy, Tommy and I went over to the Cabinet Room to revise the draft. The next morning, Harry Hopkins, Tommy and I put in some further work on it and the President worked with us in the afternoon. The final draft was not finished until 6 P.M. The President went in to take a nap, as he did frequently before a radio speech.

He had a light dinner in bed, and went downstairs to deliver his speech at ten-thirty. This was the quickest job of speech writing that I had ever had anything to do with. It was a fast pace for the President during those days, and a worrisome one. At breakfast Mrs. Roosevelt complained to me that "Franklin was getting very tired," but that apparently nothing could be done about it.

The purpose of the chat was to tell the people in very simple terms what was wrong, what he was doing about it, what he had recommended that the Congress do—and why. After enumerating his recommendations, he repeated one of his favorite themes:

Democracy has disappeared in several other great nations—not because the people of those nations disliked democracy, but because they had grown tired of unemployment and insecurity, of seeing their children hungry while they sat helpless in the face of government confusion and government weakness through lack of leadership in government. Finally, in desperation, they chose to sacrifice liberty in the hope of getting something to eat. We in America know that our own democratic institutions can be preserved and made to work. But in order to preserve them we need to act together, to meet the problems of the Nation boldly, and to prove that the practical operation of democratic government is equal to the task of protecting the security of the people. . . .

The speech is particularly impressive as showing how determined Roosevelt was not to let things slide. As we worked on it with him, it was easy to see this determination. He consulted with many people; he received and discussed all kinds of suggestions; he knew that forthright action was called for; and just as soon as he had decided on a program, he wanted to act.

Drawing on his navy experience, he had dictated this peroration for the speech:

I believe we have been right in the course we have charted. To abandon our purpose of building a greater, a more stable and a more tolerant America, would be to miss the tide and perhaps to miss the port. I propose to sail ahead. I feel sure that your hopes and your help are with me. For to reach a port, we must sail—sail, not tie at anchor—sail, not drift.

Another passage in the speech illustrates how effectively Roosevelt maintained contact with his listeners:

Finally I should like to say a personal word to you.
I never forget that I live in a house owned by all the American people and that I have been given their trust. . . .

And constantly I seek to look beyond the doors of the White House, beyond the officialdom of the National Capital, into the hopes and fears of men and women in their homes. I have traveled the country over many times. My friends, my enemies, my daily mail, bring to me reports of what you are thinking and hoping. I want to be sure that neither battles nor burdens of office shall ever blind me to an intimate knowledge of the way the American people want to live and the simple purposes for which they put me here.

In these great problems of government I try not to forget that what really counts at the bottom of it all, is that the men and women willing to work can have a decent job to take care of themselves and their homes and their children adequately; that the farmer, the factory worker, the storekeeper, the gas station man, the manufacturer, the merchant—big and small—the banker who takes pride in the help he gives to the building of his community, that all these can be sure of a reasonable profit and safety for the savings they earn—not today nor tomorrow alone, but as far ahead as they can see. . . .

I always try to remember that reconciling differences cannot satisfy everyone completely. Because I do not expect too much, I am not disappointed. But I know that I must never give up—that I must never let the greater interest of all the people down, merely because that might be for the moment the easiest personal way out.

I heard Roosevelt deliver this speech. His voice seemed to reach out right into every home in the United States. Those paragraphs, spoken badly, could have sounded very "corny"; but, as he delivered them, they expressed the deep, sincere, warm emotions of a leader who was terribly concerned about the millions of human beings whose welfare was so greatly affected by the policies of the government he led.

By the middle of 1938, much of the legislation the President had recommended was finally passed: a new farm program, minimum wages and maximum hours, outlawing of child labor, a commission for the study of monopolies and concentration of economic power. The statute permitting administrative reorganization was not passed until the next year.

By the end of the year, economic conditions began again to improve markedly.

What troubled the President most about the hard fight he had just been compelled to put up was that the opposition had come not alone from Republican Congressmen but from a substantial number of Congressmen of his own party. For by this time there had crystallized in the Congress a conservative bloc of Democrats, mostly from the South, who joined with conservative Republicans and voted consistently against the measures the President recommended. The same bloc is even more energetic, as this is being written, in 1952.

As this bloc crystallized, there also crystallized in the President's mind the idea that later came to be known as the purge.

"Purge" was the name given by Roosevelt's opponents to his efforts to let people know what representatives were supporting his program and what representatives were not. It was certainly a loaded word. The President did not desire to prevent any community from choosing its own representatives; but he did desire that the people should make an informed choice, that they should not necessarily assume that all Democratic representatives—just because they were called Democrats —were supporting the Democratic Administration or the Democratic platform. He hoped that, having the facts, the people would not return these men to office.

The purge had its birth in Roosevelt's personal resentment at the two major legislative defeats dealt him by members of his own party— the defeat of the Supreme Court plan in the spring and summer of 1937; and the defeat of two other pieces of legislation in the Extraordinary Session in the fall of 1937: the wages and hours bill and the administrative reorganization bill. There was no doubt of his animosity toward those who were willing to run on a liberal party platform with him and then vote against the very platform pledges on which they had been elected. I often heard him express himself about such "shenanigans" in a way that left no doubt about how he felt. But even deeper was his feeling—and I believe this was the fundamental reason for the purge —that the reactionary Democrats were doing a distinct and permanent injury to the nation. They were blocking the steps that he thought were essential to raise the American standard of living and make the nation strong enough to meet the growing menace from abroad.

The first factor—the personal one—was so strong that, in my opinion, it blinded the President to the great dangers to his own standing and prestige that were inherent in his entry into purely local primary party contests. His disregard of these dangers was also due to his confidence in himself and in the public support that he thought he could muster. Some of the people then very close to him whose judgment he trusted —notably Corcoran, Ickes and Hopkins—had been strongly urging this course. They had been active in trying to get the President's program through the Congress and had failed. Now they felt that the quickest way to remedy this failure was to prevent the re-election of some of those who had blocked him—with the idea that the other opponents would then capitulate. I heard the President express the same thought when it was suggested to him that a purge might be the wrong approach.

Nothing was more to Tom's liking than the political manipulation involved in trying to get votes for legislation pending in the Congress, trying to get recalcitrant Congressmen into line, and helping Congressmen who had incurred enmities by their support of the President. It was all strong food for his love of political excitement, his feeling for political power, and his satisfaction in promoting the aims of the New Deal without compromise or apology.

On the other hand, Farley and those most active in the Democratic National Committee did not want to pick and choose among Democrats as pro-New Deal or anti-New Deal. Indeed, I think Farley thought it was definitely no part of his function as chairman to interfere in these local fights. That is why Corcoran was in the purge fight and Farley out.

I am sure that by the end of the unsuccessful Extraordinary Session of 1937 the idea of the purge was rapidly forming in Roosevelt's mind, and that during the 1938 session it became fixed. For the first public announcement of it, he chose a fireside chat on June 24, 1938. The talk was ostensibly to discuss the accomplishments and failures of the Seventy-fifth Congress which had just adjourned. I was asked to come down to join with Tom and Ben on this speech.

Since the departure of High in early 1937, we three had become the regular speech-writing team; we were to remain as such until the 1940 Convention.

In this fireside chat—delivered on one of the hottest of Washington nights—the President did three things: first, he listed the accomplishments of the session of the Congress just ended; second, he pointed out the acts of obstruction by the Congress; third, he stated what he intended to do about the Congressmen who were repudiating the platform on which they had been elected.

Among the accomplishments, the President took quiet satisfaction in noting that "Because of increasing armaments in other nations and an international situation which is definitely disturbing to all of us, the Congress has authorized important additions to the national armed defense of our shores and our people." He had recommended these additions to the Congress.

Tom suggested the name "Copperheads" be used for those who were then urging the President to put an end to his program of liberal reforms and just coast along for the next four years.

Never in our lifetime has such a concerted campaign of defeatism been thrown at the heads of the President and Senators and Congressmen as in the case of this Seventy-fifth Congress. Never before have we had so many Copperheads—and you will remember that it was the Copperheads who, in the days of the War Between the States, tried their best to make Lincoln and his Congress give up the fight, let the nation remain split in two and return to peace—peace at any price.

His main topic—the proposed purge—was reserved for the end. He tried to soften it as much as possible by asserting that he was not "as President, taking part in Democratic primaries." What he was doing, he said, was this:

As the head of the Democratic Party, however, charged with the responsibility of carrying out the definitely liberal declaration of principles set forth in the 1936 Democratic platform, I feel that I have every right to speak in those few instances where there may be a clear issue between candidates for a Democratic nomination involving these principles, or involving a clear misuse of my own name.

The allusion was to those conservative Democratic candidates who used his name to help themselves get elected, saying that Roosevelt favored their election. He was particularly bitter about this practice, and said so frequently.

He tried in advance to shake off the charge—which he knew would come—that the basis of the purge was the vote on the Court bill, but he never succeeded; the "purgees" repeated it time and again. He invented a new word to describe the Congressman who publicly approved a progressive objective but who always found something wrong with any specific proposal to gain that objective—"a 'yes-but' fellow."

He urged that there was, or should be, a vital difference between the policies of the Democratic party and those of the Republican party. The Democratic and Republican parties should not "have different names but [be] as alike in their principles and aims as peas in the same pod." The voters should be given a clear chance to decide between the two. Above all, he argued, they should not be given the choice on election day between a liberal and conservative platform, and then find that the candidates they had voted for on a liberal platform refused to support the pledges and philosophy of that platform.

With these considerations and motives in mind, Roosevelt went out into the primary campaigns of 1938 in the home states of several Senators and Congressmen. It was a difficult, if not impossible, job that he had assumed. The men whom he tried to defeat were all popular in their own home states; they had all served for many years and had become firmly entrenched in their local political organizations. He was asking enrolled Democrats to reject these old officeholders; most of the voters to whom he was talking had voted for these same Congressmen time and again. Strong as the President's personal appeal and logic were, they were outweighed by the long personal relationships that these Congressmen had developed over the years with their constituents; by the entrenched political machinery which operated in favor of the Congressman in office; by the fact that generally the candidates Roosevelt backed did not have sufficient political following or standing to produce the votes. Besides, there was present the resentment which is nearly always aroused to some degree when a national figure interferes in a local political situation in a state where he does not live and vote.

From July 7 to August 12, the President took a long vacation trip across the continent and down the Pacific through the Panama Canal and up to Florida, Warm Springs and Washington. He made several speeches—some prepared and some extemporaneous. Tom did a great deal of the work on them. I had nothing to do with any of them, nor did Ben, who was in Europe at the time.

At Covington, Kentucky, on July 8, he urged the Democratic voters of Kentucky to vote for Alben Barkley in his primary contest with Governor Chandler. Both men were liberals, so this was not a purge speech. Here his choice was made on the basis of greater experience.

In Barnesville, Georgia, August 11, he urged the nomination in the coming primaries of Lawrence Camp, a liberal, over Senator Walter George, a conservative.

At a press conference, August 16, he urged the nomination of David J. Lewis, a liberal, over Senator Millard Tydings of Maryland, a conservative; and the nomination of James H. Fay over Congressman John J. O'Connor in New York for the same reason.

On September 5, at Denton, Maryland, he again took the stump for the liberal candidate in the Maryland primaries against Senator Tydings.

His speech against Senator George shows the approach Roosevelt made in each district in which he spoke during this campaign:

Let me make it clear that he [Senator George] is, and I hope always will be, my personal friend. He is beyond question, beyond any possible question, a gentleman and a scholar; but there are other gentlemen in the Senate and in the House for whom I have a real affectionate regard, but with whom I differ heartily and sincerely on the principles and policies of how the Government of the United States ought to be run . . .

Therefore, I repeat that I trust, and am confident, that Senator George and I shall always be good personal friends even though I am impelled to make it clear that on most public questions he and I do not speak the same language.

To carry out my responsibility as President, it is clear that if there is to be success in our Government there ought to be cooperation between members of my own party and myself—cooperation, in other words, within the majority party, between one branch of government, the Legislative branch, and the head of the other branch, the Executive. That is one of the essentials of a party form of government. It has been going on in this country for nearly a century and a half. The test is not measured, in the case of an individual, by his every vote on every bill—of course not. The test lies rather in the answer to two questions: first, has the record of the candidate shown, while differing perhaps in details, a constant active fighting attitude in favor of the broad objectives of the party and of the government as they are constituted today; and, secondly, does the candidate really, in his heart, deep down in his heart, believe in those objectives? I regret that in the case of my friend, Senator George, I cannot honestly answer either of these questions in the affirmative. . . .

The only contest the President won was in New York, in the defeat of Congressman O'Connor.

He never forgot the lesson of 1938—and never tried again.

The purge emphasized the great splintering that had developed in the Democratic party between the liberal and the conservative factions. Roosevelt came more and more to realize that there would always be this splintering as long as the party was organized along the same lines it had been for the last seventy-five years. His failure in the purge led him to begin to think about certain plans for the future of the Democratic party, which, as his emissary, I discussed with Wendell Willkie in secret in 1944, and about which I shall write later on in this volume.

Chapter XI

War on the Horizon, 1939

The President's speeches in 1939 reveal how quickly and how completely his emphasis, after the Munich Pact of 1938, began to shift to world affairs.

Munich convinced him that the foreign situation was heading to a crisis, that it was far more important than the impasse in which the New Deal legislation had bogged down, and that physical rearmament had to be pushed immediately and vigorously. Both convictions he expressed in his Annual Message to the Congress on January 4, 1939.

In a way, this message was the keynote of the President's program for 1939. That he spent many hours and days of thought on it I know, for Tom and Ben and I worked with him.

The President had come through a long series of setbacks in the domestic field in the last year and a half: the defeat of the Supreme Court bill, two defeats of the wages and hours bill before its final passage, the defeat of the reorganization bill, the 1937-1938 recession, the defeat in the purge, the loss of seats in the Congressional elections of 1938. His prestige at home and abroad had suffered a great deal. I do not know what course he would have taken in 1939 if events had not forced his major attention into international fields. I know of his feeling of frustration in pushing further reforms. I know that the fundamental solution he was thinking about was not a new third party of liberalism but a combination of the liberal forces then existing in each party. It may be that if international matters had not claimed his attention, he would have tried the task of realigning the two parties before his second term was over.

The fact is that he seemed to be much less interested in the domestic side of this January, 1939, speech than he was in the foreign side.

In the foreign field, he left no doubt that he was finally committed to a program of collective security in which all peace-loving nations would help victims of aggression. Neutrality alone was no longer the way to peace for anybody; and, under the concept of collective security, the United States had to become strong in a military sense as well as an economic sense.

He summed up the international situation and its threat to us and to world peace in a few paragraphs which he dictated himself, and which have often been quoted as showing the significance Roosevelt gave to religion in all American ideals:

> Storms from abroad directly challenge three institutions indispensable to Americans, now as always. The first is religion. It is the source of the other two—democracy and international good faith.
>
> Religion, by teaching man his relationship to God, gives the individual a sense of his own dignity and teaches him to respect himself by respecting his neighbors.
>
> Democracy, the practice of self-government, is a covenant among free men to respect the rights and liberties of their fellows.
>
> International good faith, a sister of democracy, springs from the will of civilized nations of men to respect the rights and liberties of other nations of men.
>
> In a modern civilization, all three—religion, democracy and international good faith—complement and support each other.
>
> Where freedom of religion has been attacked, the attack has come from sources opposed to democracy. Where democracy has been overthrown, the spirit of free worship has disappeared. And where religion and democracy have vanished, good faith and reason in international affairs have given way to strident ambition and brute force.
>
> An ordering of society which relegates religion, democracy and good faith among nations to the background can find no place within it for the ideals of the Prince of Peace. The United States rejects such an ordering, and retains its ancient faith.

The President felt the deep truth of that passage and he intended it to show the falseness of the philosophy of some of our industrialists that "We can do business with Hitler." His comment to us was, "We can do business with him all right but in the process we would lose everything that America stands for." That "everything" was encompassed in "religion, democracy and international good faith."

He pointed out the new things that we had learned about foreign affairs from recent events—referring, without naming them, to the mutilation of Czechoslovakia, Mussolini's conquest of Ethiopia, and Japan's aggression in China:

We have learned that effective timing of defense, and the distant points from which attacks may be launched are completely different from what they were twenty years ago.

We have learned that survival cannot be guaranteed by arming after the attack begins—for there is new range and speed to offense.

We have learned that long before any overt military act, aggression begins with preliminaries of propaganda. . . .

We have learned that God-fearing democracies of the world . . . cannot safely be indifferent to international lawlessness anywhere. . . .

These statements are all axiomatic in 1952; but in early 1939 they were new, and had to be said over and over again.

But what could we do to show that we could not be safely indifferent to aggression abroad? Fight? No! He used a new phrase to suggest the methods we could use:

"There are many *methods short of war*, but stronger and more effective than mere words, of bringing home to aggressor governments the aggregate sentiments of our own people."

The message contained his first determined attack upon the arms embargo provision of the neutrality law which was encouraging Nazi aggression. It was one of the things he had in mind when he used the phrase "methods short of war."

The President pointed to another truth we had relearned from events abroad: "the old, old lesson that probability of attack is mightily decreased by the assurance of an ever ready defense." And he said that he would later "send up detailed estimates of what was needed for adequate defense."

He took occasion to boast of how much the New Deal had done through its social and economic reforms to build up a defense "as basic as armaments themselves." During its first six years, his administration had developed new sources of power for the production of aluminum and other war materials in the Tennessee Valley and Columbia Valley; restored agriculture to a sound basis; established the dignity and bargaining power of labor and the assurance to them of a decent wage; protected the savings of investors who would be called upon to lend their capital to their country for purposes of defense; extended to the youth of the nation new opportunities for work and education; and,

above all, made the American people "conscious of their interrelation-
ship and their interdependence."

This is the way Roosevelt put it:

A dictatorship may command the full strength of a regimented nation.
But the united strength of a democratic nation can be mustered only when
its people, educated by modern standards to know what is going on and
where they are going, have conviction that they are receiving as large a
share of opportunity for development, as large a share of material success
and of human dignity, as they have a right to receive.

As he summed it up, "We have our difficulties, true—but we are a
wiser and a tougher nation than we were in 1929, or in 1932."

One week after the Annual Message he sent a message to the Congress asking for additional appropriations for national defense. And
two weeks after that he again asked for funds—to expand the air
forces of the United States. This time, except from extreme isolationists,
there were no cries of "warmonger." But the President had learned
how careful he had to be. The press had printed a story that he had
told some Senators whom he had called into conference that "the
American frontier is on the Rhine." At his press conference on February
3, 1939, the President showed how disturbed he was by this story; he
made quite a point of insisting to the newspapermen that he had never
said anything of the kind. He knew he could not move too fast or too
far ahead of the people, and he was determined not to let any fabri-
cated stories make him appear to be doing the very thing he was so
careful to avoid.

Events began to move faster in Europe.

On April 14, after Mussolini had invaded Albania, Roosevelt made
another try at peace—by words. He sent a letter to Hitler and Mussolini
suggesting that there be assurances "that your armed forces will not
attack or invade" the neutral nations of Europe and the Near East.
He offered to serve as "a friendly intermediary" in keeping each nation
informed of the declared policies of the others. Neither Hitler nor
Mussolini ever answered the President directly.

One of the major efforts of the Administration during 1939 was to
get the arms embargo provisions of the neutrality law repealed. On
July 14, the President stepped into the neutrality fight himself; he sent
a short message to the Congress urging the repeal of the arms embargo.
The message was prepared in the State Department; on this subject

Roosevelt and Hull saw eye to eye. With the message he enclosed a long and well-reasoned argument for repeal in the form of a statement by Hull which, the President said, "has my full approval."

This was an unusual device for the President to use in making a recommendation. Though it surprised me, I never asked him the reason for it. My surmise is threefold: Hull had been carrying on the fight for repeal in the Congress, and this was a way of strengthening his hand. Hull had always been very popular with the Congress and with the American people—especially the more conservative of both—and this method of recommendation used to the utmost Hull's personal strength. There were ill-founded rumors going around of a split between Hull and Roosevelt on the question of arms embargo repeal; Roosevelt wanted to spike them, and this was an effective way to do it.[1]

Four days later, in a desperate effort to speed repeal and perhaps prevent the war, the President called an evening conference at the White House of Congressional leaders of both parties. But he could not get approval. This was the famous conference at which Senator Borah flatly asserted that his private information from Europe was better than the State Department's, and that he knew there would be no war in 1939.

Although Hull had repeatedly invited Borah to examine the records and dispatches of the State Department showing the current state of affairs in Europe, the invitation had been ignored. The pleas of Roosevelt and Hull at the conference went unheeded. By midnight it was clear that there was going to be a rather solid Republican opposition to repeal of the embargo, and that, with the help the Republicans would get from some Democratic members, repeal was impossible during the current session of the Congress.

Roosevelt was extremely disappointed at the results of the conference. He had high hopes that a repeal of the embargo might actually discourage Hitler from war. He was coldly polite at the press conference three days later when the subject came up, but every newspaperman there could see the President's deep disappointment. Although he denied it specifically, I know from what he said frequently that he did feel a great deal of bitterness at the frustration of one of his last and best hopes to prevent the war.

[1] The President also took the unusual step of denying publicly and explicitly that there was such a split. See 1939 Vol., *Public Papers*, p. 380.

QUESTION: Mr. President, the isolation group in the Senate is predicting very freely that you are going to carry the neutrality issue to the country in your forthcoming Western swing. Can you comment on that?

THE PRESIDENT: On the neutrality issue?

QUESTION: The arms embargo.

THE PRESIDENT: Isn't that closed until January?

QUESTION: Well——

THE PRESIDENT: (interposing) By action of the Senate? I think that is the best way of handling it. There is no, and there cannot be any, immediate issue before the country because certain groups in the Senate just precluded any action until January, making it perfectly clear, of course—and they have accepted it—that the responsibility rests wholly on them. . . .

QUESTION: After the session on Tuesday, various participants, various Senators, gave their version of the meeting, what they had said to you, and more, what you had said to them.

THE PRESIDENT: It is like the old story of the Congressman that went in to see Mr. Hoover, I think it was, and was actually in Mr. Hoover's office by a stop-watch for a minute and a half and then went out into the lobby and took ten minutes to tell the Press what he had told President Hoover. I have always loved the story. You remember that?

QUESTION: Yes, and I remember the Congressman too.

THE PRESIDENT: Go ahead, I did not mean to interrupt.

QUESTION: That is a fitting story, and that is the way I meant it. But there was only one side of that conference came out, and I wondered if you had anything to say about the conference itself.

THE PRESIDENT: Except this, that any stories that there was any—I do not know—what is the term for it?

QUESTION: I used "clashes," "verbal clashes."

THE PRESIDENT: "Clashes"—right. I think it was John [Mr. O'Donnell] who said it was bitter. Did you ever see me bitter, John?

QUESTION: No, sir. [The President was frequently pretty bitter about many of the things that John O'Donnell himself was writing.]

THE PRESIDENT: There weren't any clashes. That part is entirely made up out of whole cloth. There was only one disagreement between two people in the conference, and that was due to the fact . . . that Senator Borah did intimate rather clearly and definitely that his information, his private information, from Europe was better than the information received by the United States Government from Europe. The Secretary of State asked him if he intended that as a suggestion that the State Department information was not as good as his own private information. He finally said that he had meant to infer that. It was all in very parliamentary language.

QUESTION: Did Vice President Garner step into that situation?

THE PRESIDENT: No, he did not.

QUESTION: Did the Vice President use this line, "Captain, we may as well be candid; you haven't got the votes"?

THE PRESIDENT: When it became perfectly clear from a statement by the

Republican Leader that the Republicans would vote en masse for postponement until January, and then Senator Barkley said there would probably be
sufficient Democrats to go along with them to prevent a vote being taken
if Congress stayed in session, nobody had to say anything more. That was
obvious. . . .

That was the last time the Congressional isolationist bloc defeated
Roosevelt on any question he submitted. He had to fight them repeatedly; and often his margin of victory was very small—as in the extension of the Selective Service Act in August, 1941. They certainly
slowed up his program; but they never again succeeded in definitely
defeating it. Some of the isolationist leaders—Senator Vandenberg, for
example—saw the light and changed their minds. But, more important
than that, the President by force of his leadership, speeches and other
means succeeded in winning the approval of the American people for
his own policy. The Republican party, as a party, never again publicly
supported an isolationist policy.

Again on August 24 and on August 25 he tried to persuade Hitler—
by words—to settle peacefully the question of Poland. He also wrote to
the King of Italy and the President of Poland.

But words could no longer stop Hitler's war. Hitler was determined.
Congressional refusal to repeal the arms embargo strengthened his
determination. The refusal also encouraged the Russians to enter into
the pact that assured Hitler that he would not have to fight a two-
front war.

One week after Roosevelt's last word to Hitler, Hitler invaded
Poland, and the war was on.

Chapter XII

War in Europe and Aid to Democracies, 1939-1940

When war began I was in the Adirondacks. Along with nearly every other American I listened to the President's fireside chat on the night of September 3.

Uppermost in everybody's mind was, of course, the question whether we could stay out of the war. As to this the President said what was in his own mind:

> I have said not once, but many times, that I have seen war and that I hate war. I say that again and again.
> I hope the United States will keep out of this war. I believe that it will. And I give you assurance and reassurance that every effort of your Government will be directed toward that end.

But in this, his first speech of the war, as part of his task of public enlightenment, he pointed out two hard facts. Both are accepted as obvious today; in 1939 they were not.

The first was that we could not shrug off the European war as none of our business:

> It is easy for you and for me to shrug our shoulders and to say that conflicts taking place thousands of miles from the continental United States, and, indeed, thousands of miles from the whole American Hemisphere, do not seriously affect the Americas—and that all the United States has to do is to ignore them and go about its own business. Passionately though we may desire detachment, we are forced to realize that every word that comes through the air, every ship that sails the sea, every battle that is fought, does affect the American future.

His second statement was more subtle:

> This nation will remain a neutral nation, but I cannot ask that every American remain neutral in thought as well. Even a neutral has a right to

take account of facts. Even a neutral cannot be asked to close his mind or his conscience.

Although the original draft of this speech was prepared in the State Department, this frank admission of unneutrality was Roosevelt's own insertion.

In line with this thinking, the President on September 13, 1939, called the Congress into Extraordinary Session; and on September 21, he appeared before them again to urge the repeal of the arms embargo.

Missy phoned me on the 19th and asked me to come down for the night of the 20th. When I arrived at the White House at 5:30 P.M., the President had about fifteen Democratic and Republican Congressional leaders in his office discussing neutrality legislation. Reporters were swarming around the entrance hall in the executive offices waiting for the conference to break up.

Missy gave me a draft of a speech that the President had dictated, and also one that Tom and Ben had prepared. I worked in the Cabinet Room, trying to combine parts of each into one speech, until the conference in the President's office broke up. I went in to say hello, and found him well satisfied with the conference, except that he was afraid Congressman Martin (the Republican leader in the House) was going to play politics with his proposal for repeal.

After a short discussion of the speech, he went over to the White House to take a brief rest, and I worked in the Cabinet Room until dinner was announced. At dinner with the President were Betsy (then James Roosevelt's wife), Grace, Missy and I. During the meal we talked about the series of magazine articles by Raymond Moley, who was by this time openly anti-Administration. Roosevelt asked me to read them carefully and mark any inaccuracies; he said he had asked Hull and others to do that too; he wanted at some time to make a public answer.

After dinner, Hull and Berle were announced. They had prepared a rewrite of the draft that the President had dictated. The four of us went over it carefully, and Hull and Berle left at 11 P.M. Shortly thereafter, the President went to bed; Grace and I worked on a new draft until about 2:30 A.M.

I was up again at seven, worked on the speech for a couple of hours, and then went into the President's bedroom, where we spent the rest of the morning on it. He did his work sitting up in bed; and we sent the pages over one by one to Grace, who rapidly typed a reading copy.

I talked with Hull by phone several times during the morning, reading him some new language and getting his suggestions.

By twelve-thirty the President had O.K.'d the last page. It was the deadline; the speech was delivered at 2 P.M. In it he acknowledged his mistake in signing the original neutrality act in 1935, which had the arms embargo provision in it:

"I regret that the Congress passed that Act. I regret equally that I signed that Act."

Many people have criticized Roosevelt for refusing to admit error. This was an example to the contrary, and the admission was wholly his own idea. We were talking about the original neutrality act, and the President said it was a mistake. He added that he was to blame as much as anyone, and that he wanted to say so.

The opposition to repeal had been led by Senator Borah, and the core of his following was Republican. The President had said frequently that he was not going to repeat what he thought was Wilson's mistake—leaving the Republicans out of the handling of the emergency. He started his bipartisan policy in this first wartime message to the Congress. It was an important part of his strategy, and he never altered it. First, however, he had a word for the isolationists, who were still against repeal and who were now calling themselves the only friends of peace. He dictated this passage himself, and was very pleased with it:

Because I am wholly willing to ascribe an honorable desire for peace to those who hold different views from my own as to what those measures should be, I trust that these gentlemen will be sufficiently generous to ascribe equally lofty purposes to those with whom they disagree. Let no man or group in any walk of life assume exclusive protectorate over the future well-being of America, because I conceive that regardless of party or section the mantle of peace and of patriotism is wide enough to cover us all. Let no group assume the exclusive label of the "peace bloc." We all belong to it.

He followed this up with his plea for nonpartisanship in the form of bipartisanship:

"These perilous days demand cooperation . . . without trace of partisanship. Our acts must be guided by one single hardheaded thought—keeping America out of this war. . . ."

The message was an exposition of the history of aggression by the Nazis and Fascists, the use of American influence to preserve peace, and the reasons for the repeal of the arms embargo. "I give to you my deep and unalterable conviction . . . that by the repeal of the embargo the United States will more probably remain at peace than if the law remains as it stands today. I say this because with the repeal of the embargo, this Government clearly and definitely will insist that American citizens and American ships keep away from the immediate perils of the actual zones of conflict."

But he had in mind an equally important reason for the arms embargo repeal: the desire to help Britain and France—which he knew was the desire of the overwhelming majority of the American people. This is what he said:

The enactment of the embargo provisions did more than merely reverse our traditional policy. It had the effect of putting land powers on the same footing as naval powers, so far as seaborne commerce was concerned. A land power which threatened war could thus feel assured in advance that any prospective sea-power antagonist would be weakened through denial of its ancient right to buy anything anywhere. This, four years ago, began to give a definite advantage to one belligerent as against another, not through his own strength or geographical position, but through an affirmative act on the part of the United States. . . . The step I recommend is to put this country back on the solid footing of real and traditional neutrality.

Legislation was passed and signed on November 4, revoking the strict arms embargo and permitting arms to be carried on the "cash and carry" principle, i.e., on non-American ships after title to the goods had passed.

The Congress reassembled in January, 1940, in a regular session. After the conquest of Poland, the German and French armies faced each other in a winter of inaction. In a general way the sympathies of the American people were with the Allies. But Americans, as a whole, were determined not only to keep out of the war but also to maintain a strict physical neutrality, no matter where their sympathies lay. The President clearly sensed and thoroughly agreed with this feeling. But he continued to express his disagreement with those who preached that the war was really no business of ours, and in his Annual Message to the Congress that year warned the country of the effects of a Nazi victory.

Tom and Ben and I worked on this speech. The President wanted to lay the major emphasis on foreign affairs; but the very discussion of foreign affairs almost inevitably led to a consideration of our own democracy and our own national strength, and the steps which we had to take to preserve both. As a result, the speech was devoted about equally to foreign and domestic matters.

It is difficult to remember in 1952 the force and volume of the isolationist propaganda in 1940. The isolationists were led by Lindbergh, Senator Wheeler, Congressman Fish and Father Coughlin, and had the backing of many papers such as those of Patterson, Hearst and McCormick. They had convinced many of our citizens that the European mess was none of our concern and that we had best stay out of it entirely. Even worse than that, they were preaching that the Axis powers were so far ahead in preparation that Britain and France were bound to be beaten; that there was nothing we could do to help anyway.

The President felt that his first and most essential job was to convince the American people of the folly and danger of isolationist thinking. His was the one voice that could cope with the strong emotional appeal being made to the parents of the nation:

We must look ahead and see the effect on our own future if all the small nations of the world have their independence snatched from them or become mere appendages to relatively vast and powerful military systems.

We must look ahead and see the kind of lives our children would have to lead if a large part of the rest of the world were compelled to worship a god imposed by a military ruler, or were forbidden to worship God at all; if the rest of the world were forbidden to read and hear the facts—the daily news of their own and other nations—if they were deprived of the truth that makes men free.

We must look ahead and see the effect on our future generations if world trade is controlled by any nation or group of nations which sets up that control through military force.

Therefore, he said: "I hope that we shall have fewer American ostriches in our midst. It is not good for the ultimate health of ostriches to bury their heads in the sand."

During the winter and spring of 1940, one of the matters that occupied the attention of the American newspapers and the American public was an important question closely related to the war itself: Was the President going to run for a third term? It was a matter that also absorbed the interest of the people who worked around the President. Very frequently as we met in the White House we would put the question to each other. Snatches of relevant conversation that one or another of us may have had with the President were repeated. None of these conversations was very convincing. But such as they were, they were pieced together. Notes were compared.

I formed my own opinion of the President's intention during the spring of 1940, from talks with him as well as with others who had discussed it with him. Since his death, I have talked with many people who had access to the President in those days. I was convinced during the spring months of 1940 that the President—at least up to April 9, the day that Norway was invaded—was absolutely determined not to seek a third term.

I talked with him about it early in 1940. Along with many other New Dealers, I wanted to see him run again, for I felt keenly that much at home and abroad depended upon a continuance of his leadership and his policies. But I found that it was impossible to persuade him. His mind was then made up; he was going to retire at the end of his second term.

I knew of the extensive plans that he was making for the Roosevelt Library at Hyde Park. I knew of the contract that he proposed to enter into for the publication of his autobiography and of the contract he had already made to write for a magazine for three years. I knew that he expected to work on the autobiography and on his papers at Hyde Park. He had told me that he wanted me to help him.

One week end during the fall of 1939 he had asked Mrs. Rosenman and me to come up to Hyde Park; we found, much to our surprise, that he had arranged with a real estate agent to pick us up directly after lunch to take us to see some Dutchess County property near his own place. At that time we had no thought of buying a country place. He said that he wanted us to have a country home up there as his neighbors. And he added significantly: "When I come back here next year, we can work on the papers together at Hyde Park." As late as February of 1940, Harry Hopkins talked to me about his own plan of buying a home and retiring in the neighborhood of Hyde Park. The President was building himself a hilltop cottage there for greater privacy.

I am sure that he did not change his mind until some time after the Nazis landed in Norway in April. Exactly how soon after, I do not know. It is my belief that up until the violation of the neutrality of Holland and Belgium and the invasion of France on May 10, he was still somewhat in doubt. After the evacuation by the British at Dunkirk, I am sure that his mind was made up to accept a third-term nomination.

The breakthrough by the Nazis at Sedan had an electrifying effect on the American people. Also on Roosevelt. On the day of the breakthrough, Churchill sent his first letter to Roosevelt asking for help.

The President determined to make unprecedented requests for appropriations for implements of defense. But he wanted to make very clear to the people exactly what the situation was in Europe, and he again wanted to impress upon them the kind of future we faced if Hitler finally won. He did not mean to mince words or spare feelings.

So on May 16, 1940, the President went up to the Congress. He pointed out that the Atlantic and Pacific oceans were no longer adequate defensive barriers; that it would be only a matter of hours to fly from certain bases in the Atlantic to attack some of the vital arteries of the United States; that by means of the Azores and Bermuda, modern bombers would find it easy to reach our shores; that the coast of Florida could be reached in short order from a base in the outer West Indies; that bombers working from the West Coast of Africa could approach us quite readily by a route over Brazil, Venezuela, Cuba, and the Canal Zone, then in a short time could be over Mexico, and then over St. Louis, Kansas City, and Omaha. On the other side of the continent, he pointed out how close we were to airplane attack through Alaska to Vancouver, Seattle, Tacoma, and Portland.

Citizens wrote to the White House complaining that he was unduly frightening them with these statements. To most Americans, the statements, while frightening, were also enlightening. The war in Europe seemed much closer to us as the President spoke. The American people were no longer merely interested spectators. Their attitude of sympathetic aloofness began to drop away quickly.

As Tom and Ben and I worked on the message we had one eye on the war cables of disaster and the other on the message. The Army and Navy furnished us with the material and statistics on military requirements. We had to call upon them quite frequently during the defense and war periods, for we wanted to make the statistics as accurate as possible. At the same time we did not want to reveal any information that might be helpful to the enemy. This was a feat that required at times all the ingenuity of the Chiefs of Staff.

The President was making a momentous decision in this speech. Many were advising him that the fight was hopeless so far as Britain and France were concerned; that he should not allow any more arms to go abroad; that he should keep them all at home to fight "in our own backyard if the Nazis came." This was not only the new line of the isolationists; it was the advice of many well-intentioned military men and civilians in high places.

It was a tremendous gamble to take but Roosevelt took it. He went further; he decided to give actual priority to shipping arms abroad—arms that he hoped would help the Allies hold Hitler back and thus give us time to prepare adequately.

"For the permanent record, I ask the Congress not to take any action which would in any way hamper or delay the delivery of American-made planes to foreign nations which have ordered them, or seek to purchase new planes. That, from the point of view of our own national defense, would be extremely short-sighted."

Until the end of the war he was to follow the strategy of using materials of war wherever they would count most—even if we were short of them ourselves.

This was the speech that set a goal of 50,000 planes a year—a goal that was ridiculed by Dewey, Lindbergh, and others but which was reached and later surpassed by a production in 1943 of 90,000 planes.

The isolationists shrieked louder than ever at this message and at its clear implications that Roosevelt was not only seeking to rearm the United States but preparing to rearm Britain also.

As disaster after disaster came to the Allied cause in Europe, and as the propaganda of the isolationists grew louder and more extreme, the President decided to talk to the people directly. He wanted to make sure that the country was behind him in his program of help to those fighting Hitler, for this was no longer being unneutral merely in thought; this was clearly unneutrality in deed.

He had no hesitation about the revolutionary steps he was taking. He saw the need for action; he saw the danger of sitting back and watching Britain fall. And, as in 1933, he was going to go into action.

Harry Hopkins and I worked on this speech with the President. Drafts had come in from the Army and the Navy separately at his request and he had given them to us to work on.

Although there had been a general rule in the White House not to broadcast on the Sabbath, he decided to make his speech on a Sunday night, May 26, when he would be assured of the largest possible audience.

I remember very well the small group in the President's study in the White House before dinner on the evening of this broadcast. Tonight there was no levity. There was no small talk. The President was reading dispatches which were being brought in to him from time to time by a White House usher. He mixed cocktails rather mechanically, as though his mind were thousands of miles away—as, of course, it was. The dispatches all painted a complete rout of the Allied armies.

"All bad, all bad," he muttered as he read one dispatch after another and handed them to Mrs. Roosevelt, who stood by his side. She read them and silently passed them on to us. It was a dejected dinner group.

It was a grim-looking President—but a very determined one—who took the microphone that night, and said, "Let us sit down together again, you and I, to consider our own pressing problems that confront us."

The President was worried. But he was not scared; he could not give the impression that he was scared. In fact I do not ever recall seeing the President scared at any time. He was a brave one.

> To those who have closed their eyes . . . to those who would not admit the possibility of the approaching storm—to all of them the past two weeks have meant the shattering of many illusions.
> They have lost the illusion that we are remote and isolated and, therefore, secure against the dangers from which no other land is free.
> In some quarters, with this rude awakening has come fear, bordering on panic. It is said that we are defenseless. It is whispered by some that only by abandoning our freedom, our ideals, our way of life, can we build our defenses adequately, can we match the strength of the aggressors.
> I did not share those illusions. I do not share these fears. . . .
> Let us not be calamity-howlers, and discount our strength. Let us have done with both fears and illusions. On this Sabbath evening, in our homes in the midst of our American families, let us calmly consider what we have done and what we must do.

The President then tried to give the American people the picture of what our armed strength was, in terms of the Army, Navy, and Air Force. He was deeply concerned by the claim of defeatists that we could never get ready in time to resist Hitler, and by the current charge that appropriations for defense had "gone down the rat hole." Our strength, as he gave it, might have seemed formidable before the invasion of Poland or even before the invasion of France. But in the face of what the German blitzkrieg had been able to accomplish, it seemed mighty weak—even though the President discussed it with great courage and confidence.

Still more disturbing was the fact that a good part of our combat equipment was then "on order." The more recent appropriations for defense had been used for war orders which, of course, had not yet been filled. We all thought it was perfectly legitimate to include these in the picture as long as we stated that they were on order, and so did the Army and Navy, who gave us the figures. But the phrase "on order" was seized upon by the President's opponents and ridiculed as an evasion.

The following memo from Major (now General) Bedell Smith of the Office of Chief of Staff came over the day before the speech; it is typical of the material which flowed into the White House while speeches were being prepared:

May 25, 1940

Memorandum for Judge Rosenman:

On the attached two sheets are correct revised figures of the data I gave you this morning, including items on hand for 1938. The cost of the more important or expensive items is also given.

Please note that the last column covers items *on hand* and *on order.* If limited to materiel actually on hand the figures would not be particularly impressive since we are just now beginning to get the benefit of the large appropriation for materiel authorized in 1940.

/s/ W. B. SMITH

Incls.

The President stated his armament plans for the immediate present and future, including the then bold project of having the government of the United States advance the necessary money to enlarge factories and war plants, to build new war plants, to develop new sources of supply for the hundreds of war materials required. He was not going to rely on private business to do it alone—indeed it would have been unfair to expect it to do so.

One of the President's concerns during this early defense period was that the emergency might be seized upon as an excuse to liquidate the New Deal and all that it had done for our citizens. There were plenty of people urging just that. He decided that this fireside chat was an appropriate opportunity to reassure the people on that point.

We must make sure, in all that we do, that there be no breakdown or cancellation of any of the great social gains we have made in these past years. We have carried on an offensive on a broad front against social and economic inequalities and abuses which had made our society weak. That offensive should not now be broken down by the pincers movement of those who would use the present needs of physical military defense to destroy it.

Finally, the President made a plea to the people above all to resist the divisive methods of the "fifth column."

"These dividing forces are undiluted poison. They must not be allowed to spread in the New World as they have in the Old. Our morale and our mental defenses must be raised as never before against those who would cast a smokescreen across our vision."

I still remember the satisfaction with which the President found the words to describe these activities: "undiluted poison."

The response to this speech was very pleasing; the President felt it showed that the people understood the urgency. Telegrams poured in offering personal services, plants, factories, etc.

Five days later he sent another message to the Congress asking for additional appropriations for national defense.

On June 10, the day Italy entered the war, the President made an address at the University of Virginia. He left Washington for Charlottesville with his speech fully prepared. We did not work on this speech at all; I think the draft came from the State Department. On the way down to Charlottesville, he inserted in his own hand the sentence that so dramatically highlighted the entry of Italy into the war. It was an example of the way in which the President could dramatize an event in a few words—words that would stick in the public memory long after the rest of the speech had been forgotten. Incidentally, these were words that gave concern to some of our political leaders, who felt that they might alienate part of the American-Italian vote in the coming election:

"On this tenth day of June, 1940, the hand that held the dagger has struck it into the back of its neighbor."

The speech came to be known as the "stab-in-the-back" speech. Those words were used in a cable that Paul Reynaud, Premier of France, had sent to the President earlier that same day, asking for help. The President inserted his own version of the phrase in the draft submitted by the State Department, but was persuaded by Sumner Welles to take it out of his reading copy. On the way to Charlottesville, he wrote it in again. His cold, biting tone as he read the sentence was even more eloquent than the language itself.

In the speech at Charlottesville, the President took another step forward. He said, "We will pursue two obvious and simultaneous courses: we will extend to the opponents of force the material resources of this nation; and, at the same time, we will harness and speed up the use of those resources in order that we ourselves in the Americas may have equipment and training equal to the task of any emergency and every defense."

This was the beginning of the policy of all-out aid to the democracies. It was still a "measure short of war"; it was a logical extension of the "quarantine" speech and the policy of collective security. The isolationists still shrieked; but the preponderance of American public opinion was rallying in back of the President. Events in Europe gave the President's bold policy its greatest support; as leader of the free world he could look over his shoulder now and see a nation following him.

A month later, on July 10, 1940, he sent another message to the Congress. In it he asked for an additional appropriation of $4 billion for national defense, and for the first time he came out for a system of selective service. No one knew better than he the political risks he was running—if he was again to become a candidate—in asking for a peacetime draft.

The Democratic National Convention was scheduled to be held only five days after this message and only about a month after the Charlottesville speech.

Chapter XIII

The Great Precedent Is Broken: The Third-Term Nomination, 1940

By the beginning of summer, 1940, I took it for granted that the President had decided it was his duty to accept the nomination.

There were reasons, of course, why he should not. First, there was the third-term tradition. True, he had broken many traditions and precedents before. But the third-term tradition was such a deep-rooted one! He knew the political dangers of breaking it, the political handicaps of a third-term candidacy.

The second reason was a personal one. He had felt the crushing physical and mental burdens that eight years in the White House could impose upon a President. He had smarted under the stings of the unjust criticism and unbridled abuse that our free press had directed at him continuously. He yearned for the leisure of Hyde Park, not for the sake of leisure alone, but for the opportunity it would give him to write the records of his times, and also to write on current affairs.

Third, he felt that his own position in history was already secure. He was certain that the New Deal program had not only saved the United States from a continued depression but had actually rescued the American system of free enterprise and private property from the danger of succumbing to an alien system of economics.

On the other hand there were, to his mind, compelling reasons why he should continue in the Presidency.

First, he was determined that if the next President was to be a Democrat, he should be a liberal Democrat. He was convinced that the continuance of his liberal program was essential to a continuance of recovery and indeed of our economic system. He knew also how important it was to his foreign program. And as a practical politician, he knew that a reactionary or conservative Democratic candidate would never receive the votes of labor, and that without the support of labor a Democratic victory would be highly improbable. The leading Presidential possibilities fell far short of filling this prime requirement of liberalism.

There were, of course, liberal members of the Democratic party who might measure up to the Presidency, but none who could muster enough delegates to be nominated. Roosevelt knew how little influence he would have on the nomination and on the platform of the convention once he had announced that he himself was not to be a candidate.

James A. Farley was perhaps the leading candidate. As one who had campaigned strenuously for Alfred E. Smith in 1928, Roosevelt knew too well the almost overwhelming and tragic handicap that a candidate of the Catholic or any other minority faith faced in a campaign for the Presidency of the United States. He had time and again denounced the religious intolerance of the Smith campaign in 1928. He had excoriated it in public statements, in interviews, in speeches. But although he hated religious intolerance, and did his best to combat it, he never was blind enough to ignore it as a factor in Presidential elections.

That was one of the reasons why he did not think that Farley, even if nominated, could be elected. That was not the most important reason, however, for his reluctance to have Farley as the candidate. What weighed more was that Farley was fundamentally not a New Dealer.

Farley's great help to the President before and after his election in 1932—and it was tremendous—had nothing to do with making policy or with carrying out policy. It had to do with organizing the party and getting out votes on election day; it had to do with patronage in levels below the policy-making offices; it had to do with party machinery and party leadership in various sections of the country. As far as actual policies were concerned, he was not at any time a part of the inner circle of advisers or consultants. As his writings later proved, his political and social views were more like Garner's than Roosevelt's. That is probably the chief reason why the President did not have Farley around as often as Farley, in his *Jim Farley's Story*, intimates that Roosevelt should have. Farley attributes this to some notion that the President thought Farley was not his social equal. To me that is just unbelievable. In all my long years with Roosevelt I never saw a single instance of his refusing to see people or to have them around because they might be considered social inferiors. I doubt whether the idea of social inferiority or superiority ever entered the President's mind at all in any connection.

Stanley High, who had plenty of opportunity to observe the President at work and at play, has described Roosevelt in terms very different from Farley's:

"Mr. Roosevelt, in his personal relationships, is wholeheartedly a democrat. His democracy, in fact, is of the genuine and uninhibited sort which sometimes appears in highborn people who have nothing to lose by friendliness and nothing to gain by patronizing. Snooty people are as much on his black list as prima donnas."[1]

As the years went by, the President's interest in day-by-day routine political activities—except actually at election time—diminished, and his interest in broad domestic and international objectives became even greater. He became less and less absorbed in the things that Farley had to do as a political leader, and more and more concerned that Farley was aligning himself with the conservative wing of the Democratic party. That, and not any consideration of social standing, was why during the second term their paths began to separate.

Senator James F. Byrnes was also an available candidate, and was very anxious for the nomination. He was from South Carolina, however, and for that reason would never appeal to the large Negro vote in the Northern cities. Labor was very lukewarm—if not actually opposed—to him. Besides, Byrnes had been born a Catholic but had changed his religion later in life. This was a double disadvantage politically; for not only would anti-Catholic bigots oppose him, but Catholics themselves might resent his change of religion.

The Secretary of State, Cordell Hull, was also mentioned as a candidate. He was getting fairly old at this time for first place, and would probably have made a poor showing in a hot, rough-and-tumble campaign with such a man as Wendell Willkie or Thomas E. Dewey. Besides, there was considerable doubt whether Hull really wanted the nomination, and on domestic issues he was too conservative for Roosevelt.

Harry Hopkins, whom Roosevelt at one time was seriously considering as a possible successor, was completely out of the running because

[1] Stanley High, *Roosevelt—and Then* (New York: Harper & Brothers, 1937), p. 63.

of his health and because he would not be able to get adequate political support.

Nearly all the other possible Democratic candidates—Jesse Jones, Speaker William B. Bankhead, Vice-President Garner—the President regarded as too conservative.

He was thoroughly frightened at the prospect of a Republican President who would be backed or controlled by the old leaders of the Republican party. He was convinced that a reversal or sabotage of the domestic reforms of the New Deal would lead to strife at home and to a split in the united strength of the American people—just when unity was essential in the face of increasing danger from abroad.

He knew also that a reversal of his foreign policy of all-out assistance to Britain short of war would deprive her of the arms she needed so desperately, and would cause a disastrous break in British morale. With Britain out of the way, he was sure that we were high on the list of nations, if not first on the list, that Hitler intended to attack.

Nevertheless, if France had withstood the Hitler attack in May, 1940, and if the war had then developed into a drawn-out stalemate as World War I did between 1915 and 1917, I am sure Roosevelt would not have consented to be nominated in July, 1940. If he had felt that a liberal, internationalist Democrat could have been nominated who had a fair chance of election, I am again sure he would not have consented to be nominated.

By "consenting," I mean that he was not an active participant or seeker for the nomination in 1940 in the sense that he was in 1932. He was not going to go out and actively seek delegates. He was not even going to ask any delegate to vote for him. As it later developed, he was going to tell the delegates in a formal fashion that those who had been pledged to him were released, and that they could vote for whomever they pleased.

On the other hand, although he felt that there was no such thing as a bona fide draft by a convention, he was confident that the American people wanted him to be President, and believed that they should be given a chance to vote for him.

Of course, if the President had really wanted to retire in any event, he knew how to do it. A simple statement that he would not accept the nomination if tendered would have been all that was necessary. It would have split open the convention in a struggle for the nomination by many candidates, and would have left the party thoroughly divided and weak —but there would have been a new Democratic candidate. The message he did send to the convention was not equivocal; but it did not shut the door, and it was not intended to do so.

Nor did he, to my knowledge, discourage the political leaders who were determined that he be the nominee. They of course were motivated by the desire that always motivates political leaders—the desire to win. They felt that their chances of winning with any other candidate were slim. They knew that with Roosevelt they had a fine chance. That is why I do not consider the third term-nomination of the President a draft in the literal sense.

I lived at the White House during the nine days from July 10 to July 19, 1940, during which the decisions were finally made in Washington and in Chicago. My plans had been made to take a Western vacation with my family starting on July 8. However, on July 5 I received a phone call from Missy saying that the President was anxious for me to come down and spend the convention period with him as I had in 1936 and 1932. I went down on July 10; my family went on ahead to Montana.

It was a very hot period in Washington. Fortunately my room was air cooled, and I could seek refuge in it from the terrible heat of the President's study and bedroom. The President did not like air conditioning. It seemed to affect his sinuses; so, on one pretext or another, he had the air conditioning in his room shut off even during the hottest summer days and nights. He did not even use an electric fan, except one on the floor in a distant corner of his study. It was quite a burden to work in the President's study at such times. However, he never seemed to mind the heat. He would take off his coat and tie, unbutton his collar and roll up his sleeves. Sometimes he wore a short-sleeved shirt. The trousers he wore during very hot weather were seersucker; they were cool, but quickly lost their shape and looked quite bedraggled. He perspired freely, and constantly mopped his brow. But he seemed to enjoy it—at least he seldom had the air conditioning turned on.

Among the infrequent memoranda which I made of my experiences in the White House, I find a rather full statement of this convention period.

The night I arrived we had dinner in the President's study in the Oval Room. The Oval Room was used for lunch or for dinner only when there were few enough people to sit around a portable extension table—never more than six. There were present that evening the President, Harry Hopkins, Missy, Grace and I. Strangely enough, there was no serious conversation about the approaching convention or anything connected with it. The President went to bed early. The rest of us played bridge. The next morning, Thursday, Harry came into my room from his room across the hall, and we had a long talk.

He brought me up to date on the various political conferences that had taken place in the White House during the past few days. We both assumed, although the President was making no effort to get delegates to vote for him, that he was going to be nominated and that he would accept, and we talked about whom he would prefer as his running mate for the Vice-Presidency.

Harry told me that the President had been discussing all the possibilities with him: Hull, Byrnes, Bankhead, Jones, Wallace. As far as the President was concerned, the choice had been boiled down to three: Hull, Byrnes and Wallace. The President was ready to back Hull if Hull wanted the Vice-Presidency, but he had become convinced that Hull did not want it. Harry told me that the President was going to have another talk with Hull, who could still have it if he wanted it.

Although Hull did not go along wholeheartedly with the President on all his domestic policies, he would have been a great asset to a ticket headed by Roosevelt. He had fine standing with the American people. He also stood ace-high with the Congress. He had been a member for many years, was highly respected there, and combined an ingratiating manner with a slow-moving soundness and humor in a way that was very appealing to Congressmen. He had long experience in public life, and was universally regarded as a man of unimpeachable integrity. His standing in the Democratic party was something like that of Henry L. Stimson in the Republican party; they were both men of great experience and imposing stature who had the confidence of members of both parties.

In the field of foreign affairs, Hull saw eye to eye with the President, although he was in favor of moving much more cautiously than the President and of using far less forceful language and tactics. The President had deep affection and admiration for Hull: he respected his opinion, and he also respected his high standing with the American people. In fact I think that Hull was the one man in public life who could give the President substantial concern by threatening, in a basic disagreement, to resign. There were many Cabinet officers who sought to gain their way with the President by threats of resignation. Harold Ickes did this quite often. The President, however, did not take such threats very seriously; Hull was the one exception. If at any time he had resigned as a result of a disagreement with the President—either personal or official—it would have hurt the President's prestige with the American people, and Roosevelt knew it. The President always had that in mind, and, for that reason, perhaps yielded to Hull's point of view more often than he otherwise would have.

The President, at this time, was very fond of Senator Byrnes, and if other things had been equal I am sure that he would have favored Byrnes for the nomination. Harry said that the President was also considering Wallace carefully and favorably. Wallace had made a good record as Secretary of Agriculture, and it was assumed that politically he would help in the farm states. But what appealed to the President more was that Wallace was then an out-and-out New Dealer, in whose hands the program of the New Deal—domestic and international —would be safe.

It had been arranged for Hopkins to leave that night for Chicago. He was not a delegate; he was going as the personal representative of the President—without, however, any specific credentials or instructions to that effect.

He told me that on the previous Monday night Mayor Kelly of Chicago, Edward J. Flynn of New York, Frank Walker, James Byrnes, the President and he had held a conference in the Oval Room. The President had announced that he wanted to send a letter to the convention to be read by Bankhead, who as the keynote speaker would make a speech on the opening night. The political leaders present urged him not to do it. They all wanted him to run, and they felt sure that if he kept quiet he would be nominated almost by acclamation. However, the President insisted, and did write a short letter in longhand to Bankhead, which he gave to Harry to take out with him.

Harry showed me the letter, and I made a copy of it:

DEAR WILL:

When you speak to the Convention on Monday evening will you say something for me which I believe ought to be made utterly clear?

You and my other close friends have known and understood that I have not today and have never had any wish or purpose to remain in the office of President, or indeed anywhere in public office after next January.

You know and all my friends know that this is a simple and sincere fact. I want you to repeat this simple and sincere fact to the Convention.

As it turned out, this statement was not used; a different method was adopted to do the same thing.

Just before Harry left for the train, he turned over to me copies of some rough drafts of platforms and a rough first draft of a proposed acceptance speech. We arranged to keep in touch with each other by phone so we would both know what was happening in Chicago and in the White House.

The afternoon that Harry left I had a swim with the President in the White House pool, and he talked quite frankly about the qualifications and drawbacks of the various Vice-Presidential candidates. For the first time I learned from his own lips how strongly he favored Wallace for the Vice-Presidency, and how opposed he was to the other candidates. He went over their qualifications and disabilities in detail in much the same terms that Harry had relayed to me before he left for Chicago.

The White House was always an exceptionally quiet place during National Democratic Conventions. Nearly every Washington official who would normally call on or phone the President was at the convention, or was at the radio in his own office or living room listening to the proceedings. Appointments and phone calls were kept at a minimum, and everybody tried to respect the President's desire to be as free from routine matters as possible during this period.

That night at dinner there were just the President, Missy and I. We had a movie after dinner; my notes say that it was *The Ghost Breaker*, but I do not have any recollection of what it was about. I could not get absorbed in a picture, as Roosevelt could, while such important events were in the making. The President again went to bed early. I spent a good part of the evening reading all the material that Harry had left with me.

On Thursday, Justice Felix Frankfurter came to swear in Colonel Frank Knox as Secretary of the Navy. We talked at length then and again the next day, and he mentioned some points he thought the President ought to make in his acceptance speech.

Frankfurter was a reliable source of ideas and language. Before he was appointed to the Supreme Court, Corcoran, Cohen and I used to consult him frequently on all kinds of matters, and I am told that Moley did also. After he became a member of the Bench his activities were necessarily circumscribed, and no one who knew him was left in doubt about his scrupulous observance of the restrictions of the Supreme Court Bench. But he continued to be very helpful to the President—

and also to Sherwood and me—in many ways. Frequently, while a speech was in the discussion stage, we would drive out to his house in Georgetown to exchange ideas about what it should contain. Our sessions often lasted until the early hours of the morning, and they were always fruitful. Occasionally, when speeches were in the writing stage, we sent him drafts for suggestion and criticism.

We were always careful—as was the President—never to discuss with him anything that might later embarrass him in his judicial capacity. I never knew him to offer any advice—or to be consulted—on any political question or on any matter that might possibly come before him later for judicial review.

I spent Friday working on a draft of some proposed paragraphs for the acceptance speech. We took it for granted that it was a speech that would be delivered. As things turned out, it looked for a short time in 1940, just as it looked in 1932, that an acceptance speech would be delivered by some nominee other than Roosevelt.

The next day the President decided to take a week-end trip down the river on the *Potomac*. I brought along all of my material, including drafts of the platform and acceptance speech. Other guests on the boat were Missy, Mr. and Mrs. Ed Bartlett (friends of Missy) and Dr. Ross McIntire.

We had a quiet, uneventful journey down the river and back. One would never imagine that significant political history was being made by the calm, thoughtful man sitting in the stern playing with his stamps or reading the newspaper. We did a little fishing. In the evening after dinner the President caught one rock bass and one eel. He was not always so lucky even as this in his fishing on the Potomac River. After a while, the others went above to an upper deck; and the President and I sat at the table in the dining cabin and talked about the convention which was to open in two days, and about his own nomination. He said that he did not want to give the appearance of making any effort for the nomination. He added that it was becoming apparent that Farley was going to make a convention-floor fight for the first place on the ticket, and that he did not want to exercise his prestige or influence as President to induce the delegates to vote one way or the other.

In order to make this attitude clear to the delegates, he said, he wanted to send a message to the convention which would be somewhat fuller and more definite than the one he had given to Hopkins to deliver. Knowing from previous talks with him that he might have this in mind,

I had already prepared a draft of such a message. I pulled it out of my brief case and showed it to him. He took it and, in longhand, wrote out a message of his own—a combination of the short cryptic one he had given to Hopkins and the longer one I had drafted. He then inserted a sentence specifically releasing his delegates.

The next day, Sunday, we cruised lazily back up the Potomac. For dinner that day we had the dish almost invariably served on the President's yacht on Sunday—one that he loved—chicken with curry. There was always quite a ceremony on board about this dish. The Filipino mess crew used to take great pride in preparing a dozen or more different side dishes for the curry, and the President used to overlook not a one of them. He thought that the food served aboard the boat by the Filipino crew was far better than the food served in the White House (and so it was). I suspect this was one of the reasons he so greatly enjoyed cruising on the yacht.

We got back to Washington about four. That night Tom and Ben came to dinner at the White House. There was no talk of the convention during dinner, but after a movie we discussed the draft of the President's message to the delegates. Up to this point the President had made no public statement of his third-term intentions. However, the newspaper stories at the time stated that my presence at the White House and on the *Potomac* indicated that an acceptance speech was being prepared, as it had in 1932 and 1936.

I was delighted that no work was attempted that evening, because it was oppressively hot in the President's study and in his bedroom. I was glad to be able to get to my own air-conditioned room where I continued to work alone on the acceptance speech. After I had gone to bed that night, I was awakened by a phone call from Chicago. Robert H. Jackson, who was then Attorney General, and Frank Walker were both on the phone. They said that the consensus of the political leaders in Chicago was that it would be a mistake for the President to send any message releasing the delegates and announcing that he did not desire to be a candidate. I have never discovered the reason for the great concern and nervousness of the political leaders in Chicago over this proposed message. Nothing that I have ever heard or read about the Chicago convention has led me to believe that Farley ever had enough delegates, or would have been able to get enough delegates, to make any serious showing against the President.

Whatever the reason, there was certainly strong sentiment against the message, because on the following morning, Monday, at about 7 A.M. I was again awakened by a phone call. This one was from Harry. He repeated what the others had said, and endorsed their opinion strongly.

I hurriedly dressed and went into the President's bedroom down the hall while he was still having his breakfast. He had apparently spent a restful night, for he looked very fit and was in a fighting mood. I told him that some of his friends in Chicago were going to call him soon to urge him not to send the message at all. They were also going to urge him, if he insisted on sending it, not to have it delivered by the key-noter, Bankhead. While I was still in the President's bedroom the call came through from Chicago, and the President asked me to listen in on the telephone extension in his bedroom. On the Chicago end of the wire there came consecutively Hopkins, Byrnes, Walker, and Mayor Kelly of Chicago.

The President insisted on sending the message. He put it on two grounds: first, a personal feeling that if he was to be nominated he wanted it to be a free and open nomination by delegates released from any pledge or commitment; second, for purposes of history, he wanted it made clear that he was not actively seeking a third term. He wanted this stated as a part of the permanent written record of the convention. Finally, after considerable argument, they asked him to postpone the message for one day and let it be read by Senator Barkley, who as permanent chairman was to make an address on Tuesday night.

I have never seen the President more stubborn—although stubbornness was one of his well-known characteristics. He continued to insist that the message ought to be read on the first day so that the delegates would have as much time as possible to make up their own minds what to do. However, one final argument from Chicago prevailed. Bankhead would not go on the air until 10 P.M. and probably would not finish until nearly midnight New York time. At that time very few people would be listening to the proceedings at the convention. On the other hand, Barkley's speech would be early in the evening of the second day's proceedings and would have a much more substantial radio coverage. On the basis of that, and that alone, the President gave in.

That afternoon Felix Frankfurter phoned, and read me some paragraphs MacLeish had written for the acceptance speech. I had Grace take them down on the telephone. During this period the split between Tommy Corcoran and the President was developing, and it produced a situation that I personally found uncomfortable. I asked the President whether I was to have Tommy and Ben collaborate in preparing the drafts of the platform and the message; and although he had had them both in to dinner the night before the convention started, he said I should not. Of course I could not tell Tommy this, and I am sure that both he and Ben must have considered it strange that they were not invited to the conferences which were taking place.

That Monday night we sat around—the President, Missy and I— listening to Bankhead's keynote speech. My recollection is that although he referred to the "Administration" and the "President" several times, he did not mention the President's name once. The tone of the speech showed that he certainly was no friend of the President in that convention, and that the leaders in Chicago were right in urging that the release of the delegates should be made through Barkley and not through Bankhead. During the evening, I had a long telephone conversation with Hopkins, who had become outraged at what he called the manipulations of Farley and his friends, who were spreading all kinds of stories about promises made to Farley by the President. It had now become clear that Farley was going to insist that his name go before the convention.

In the meantime the President had sent on to the chairman of the Resolutions Committee, Senator Wagner, the draft of the platform which had been prepared and revised in the White House. A bitter contest arose in the committee over the foreign affairs plank. A well-organized group insisted upon a statement that "We will not participate in foreign wars. We will not send our armed forces to fight in lands across the seas." I remember the President's great concern when I showed him this plank, which Senator Wagner had read to me over the telephone. No human being, no political party, could guarantee that we would not get involved in the war. On the other hand, Roosevelt realized that his opponents could make great political capital out of it if he were to insist that the plank be taken out entirely. His insistence could easily be misconstrued to mean that he was in favor of intervening in the existing war. We discussed this at great length and he talked about it with Harry, Byrnes, and others in Chicago. Byrnes was discussing it with Senator Wheeler of Montana and Senator Walsh of Massachusetts.

I suggested adding this proviso: "except where necessary to defend and protect our own American interests." The President was not satisfied with that. After some phone talks with Byrnes in the presence of Hull and me, he finally substituted in his own hand: "except in case of attack." (For a copy of this draft, see facsimile section following p. 336.)

That night, the 16th, the President's message releasing his delegates was read to the convention by Barkley as the last part of his address:

I and other close friends of the President have long known that he has no wish to be a candidate again. We know, too, that in no way whatsoever has he exerted any influence in the selection of delegates or upon the opinions of delegates.

Tonight, at the specific request and authorization of the President, I am making this simple fact clear to the Convention.

The President has never had, and has not today, any desire or purpose to continue in the office of President, to be a candidate for that office, or to be nominated by the Convention for that office.

He wishes in all earnestness and sincerity to make it clear that all the delegates to this Convention are free to vote for any candidate.

That is the message I bear to you from the President of the United States.

The next day, while we were working on the acceptance speech, the subject of the Vice-Presidency came up several times. The President was coming to the conclusion that Wallace was the man he would support.

That evening, Wednesday, July 17, Ross McIntire, his physician; Edwin ("Pa") Watson, his military aide; Steve Early; Captain Callaghan, his naval aide; Missy and Grace; Toi Bachelder, Louise Hachmeister ("Hackie") and Roberta Barrows, all White House staff assistants; and the President and I gathered in the Oval Room and again listened to the proceedings of the convention. Farley insisted on getting his name before the convention and on having a roll call. When the votes were finally counted, it was evident that he had made no impression upon the delegates except for a small number of personal friends and conservatives. Roosevelt got 946 votes, Farley 72, Garner 61 (omitting fractions). There was general satisfaction and relief, for that was not the kind of party split that might discourage the President from accepting the nomination or endanger the party's chances for victory in November.

That night, after everyone had gone home, Mayor Kelly of Chicago telephoned to the President, who asked me to remain while he took the call. The Mayor reported on the proceedings of the convention that evening; and the conversation then turned to the Vice-Presidential nomination which had to be made on the following day. That evening, for the first time, the President definitely stated that he favored Wallace. I could not hear the other side of the conversation; but from the President's expression I gathered that the name was not too enthusiastically received by the Mayor.

Apparently Kelly quickly spread the word among Roosevelt's friends at the convention. Very early Thursday morning, July 18, Hopkins called me to ask whether Wallace was still the choice.

I said, "Yes."

"There's going to be a hell of a lot of opposition," Harry said. "So far there must be at least ten candidates who have more votes than Wallace. It'll be a cat-and-dog fight, but I think that the Boss has enough friends here to put it over."

The President was having breakfast when I went to his room to tell him what Harry had said about the temper of the delegates. He did not seem surprised.

"Well, I suppose all the conservatives in America are going to bring pressure on the convention to beat Henry. The fellow they want is either Jesse [Jones] or Bankhead. I'm going to tell them that I won't run with either of those men or with any other reactionary—I've told them that before and I'll tell them again."

Then after a while, he added, grimly:

"I won't deliver that acceptance speech until we see whom they nominate."

The fighting soon broke out in Chicago. Among the first to call the President was Farley himself. The President took the call in the Oval Room. We were alone. Of course I could not hear what Farley was saying, but I learned later from the President—as well as from Farley's book—that he had said there would be great objection to Wallace because Wallace was a "mystic" and the delegates did not want to vote for him.

The President replied: "Jim, Henry's not a mystic, he's a philosopher, a liberal philosopher, and I'm sure that he'll be all right."

Farley was apparently quite aroused, because the telephone conversation ended abruptly. Farley was for Jesse Jones, Speaker Bankhead or Paul McNutt.

Soon thereafter a long telegram came in from Harold Ickes, who was at the convention, describing the opposition that was developing to Wallace, and suggesting that he himself would make a very good candidate for second place. The President handed me the telegram laughingly.

"Dear old Harold," he said. "He'd get fewer votes even than Wallace in that convention."

Ickes and Wallace had been enemies for a long time. After Wallace's nomination, Ickes nursed his grudge for four more years and then became one of the leaders in the movement to persuade Roosevelt to drop Wallace as his running mate. More of that later.

During the course of the day, Frances Perkins, the Secretary of Labor, who was also at the convention, phoned the President and told him there was a fight coming. She made a very constructive suggestion which the President adopted—that Mrs. Roosevelt go out to the convention and make a speech in the interest of harmony. Mrs. Roosevelt did fly out to Chicago and made such a speech; and while she was effective in smoothing down the tempers of some of the delegates, which by this time had risen to fairly feverish heights, she was not able to stop the fight.

In the midst of all the excitement and tension the President as usual found time for a joke. He was reading a paper when he came across a photograph of his Secretary of Labor and Jim Farley in a closely whispered conversation. He laughed, called for Grace and dictated and mailed the following note:[2]

THE WHITE HOUSE,
July 16, 1940

Memorandum for the Secretary of Labor:
After all these years of trusting you I believed that I could let you go to Chicago without a chaperone. You really must not let the camera men catch you when you are so truly coy!

F. D. R.

During the course of the afternoon, phone calls came in from Chicago at a great rate. Bankhead telephoned, and spoke very sharply with the President. He was angry that he had been passed over; he was angry that a liberal like Wallace—never an organization Democrat—might be nominated. Later Byrnes phoned, and argued with the President about the nomination. The President expressed great personal regret that he could not go along with Byrnes, for reasons with which he said he knew Byrnes was familiar. He added that he had given the matter a great deal of thought over many days and many weeks; that he was sure that the

[2] *F.D.R.: His Personal Letters*, pp. 1044-1045.

best candidate was Wallace; and that he hoped that Wallace would be nominated. Byrnes, unsuccessful in his argument, replied that if the President's mind was made up, he, Byrnes, would go down the line for his candidate and would try to put him over—but he was not sure that it could be done. Roosevelt thanked him for his loyalty and help, and hung up. By this time he was beginning to get quite concerned about what might happen that night at the convention.

Harry Hopkins later told the President and me that Byrnes had performed as he had promised. Although balked in his own ambitions, he went out among the delegates on the floor of the convention and used all the great force of persuasion and argument for which he was so well known in the Senate to help his successful rival. It was a fine display of political loyalty.

At the White House that night there was an unusually large crowd in the Oval Room with the President: Pa and Mrs. Watson, Steve Early, Ross McIntire, Dan Callaghan, Missy, Grace, and several others. The President had set up a card table; he sat there listening to the radio and playing a game of solitaire at the same time. His face was grim and set. The rest of us sat around in silence as the radio brought us the events in Chicago. Bankhead had insisted on running. The man who we feared would have the best chance of stampeding the convention against Wallace was Paul V. McNutt. However, when an attempt was made to nominate him, he made a short but forceful speech announcing that under no circumstances would he accept the nomination. The speeches nominating and seconding Bankhead were quite bitter. The radio commentators made it clear that a strong revolt was developing against the nomination of Wallace and that the President was being blamed for forcing his man upon the delegates.

As the fight got more and more acrimonious, the President asked Missy to give him a note pad and a pencil. Putting aside his cards he started to write. The rest of us sat around wondering what he was writing. We all felt a great desire to sneak around and read over his shoulders, but none of us succumbed to that temptation. Instead we continued to watch curiously while the President kept on writing in silence for five full pages.

Finally, he laid his pencil down, turned to me and said: "Sam, take this inside and go to work on it; smooth it out and get it ready for delivery. I may have to deliver it very quickly, so please hurry it up."

He then picked up his cards quietly and continued to play solitaire.

I walked out of the room into the hall with the sheets of White House notepaper. Pa and Missy followed very closely behind me; and as soon as I got into the hall and shut the door, they crowded up and said:

"What's in it? Let's see it!"

I went over to the desk that stood in the hall outside the President's study, where a lamp was lit, and sat down to read the pages. Missy and Pa, too anxious to wait, were bending over my shoulder reading with me.

It was a statement addressed to the "Members of the Convention" declining the nomination. It was obviously intended to be delivered if Wallace lost and Bankhead—who was the only one left in the fight against Wallace—were successful. This is what the President had written:

July 18, 1940.

MEMBERS OF THE CONVENTION:

In the century in which we live the Democratic Party has received the support of the electors only when the Party has been, with absolute clarity, the champion of progressive and liberal policies and principles of government.

The party has failed consistently when by political tricks it has been controlled by those interests, personal and financial, which think in terms of dollars instead of in terms of human values.

The Republican Party has made nominations dictated as we all know by those who put dollars ahead of human values.

The Democratic Party, as appears clear from the events of today, is divided on this fundamental issue. Until the Democratic Party makes clear its overwhelming stand in favor of liberalism, and shakes off *all* the shackles of control by conservatism and reaction, it will not continue its march of victory.

It is without question that certain influences of conservatism and reaction have been busily engaged in the promotion of discord since this Convention convened.

That being the fact and the case, I in all honor cannot and will not condone or go along with the fact of that party dissension.

It would be best not to straddle ideals.

It would be best for America to have the fight out.

Therefore, I give the Democratic Party the opportunity to make that historic decision by declining the honor of the nomination for the presidency. I so do.

I remember Missy's reaction. "Fine, I'm glad," she said, and returned to the Oval Room quickly, very pleased indeed.

Pa's reaction was quite different; he said, "Sam, give that damned piece of paper to me—let's tear it up."

I looked at him, thinking that he was joking and expecting to see his face wreathed in its usual smile. But he was in dead earnest.

"He's all excited in there now—and he'll be sorry about it in the morning. Besides, the country needs him. I don't give a damn who's Vice-President and neither does the country. The only thing that's important to this country is that fellow in there. There isn't anyone in the United States who can lead this nation for the next four years as well as he can."

Pa felt that every word of that was true—felt it with a religious fervor.

I said: "Pa, I hope he never has to read this speech; but if I know that man inside, he's going to read it if Bankhead gets this nomination, and nobody on earth is going to be able to stop him."

I went into my room to work on the draft that the President had written. First I had it typed by a stenographer. I worked on a carbon copy and after ten or fifteen minutes brought it into the Oval Room and gave it to the President with his longhand draft and the original typed copy.

He was still playing solitaire as I came in. Everyone in the room by this time knew what was up. They were standing around in groups of two or three discussing the situation. Missy was all smiles, saying that the President was doing the only thing he could do. Pa Watson was almost in tears, and looked at me angrily for bringing the sheets back. I suppose he had hoped I would run off with them and hide—as if that would have stopped the President. All of us except Missy were opposed to this course and told the President so. But if I ever saw him with his mind made up it was that night.

He took my typed suggestions silently, and copied most of them on the typewritten original; he added a full paragraph in his own hand. Steve Early had also suggested some corrections on another carbon and the President copied those also onto the original.

I took this new draft out, worked on it some more, and brought it back with some more corrections. He read it over and said:

"This will do; don't bother to retype it. I'll read it like this."

And he went back to his game of solitaire.

This is the way it read in final form:

MEMBERS OF THE CONVENTION: July 18, 1940.

In the century in which we live, the Democratic Party has received the support of the electorate only when the party, with absolute clarity, has been the champion of progressive and liberal policies and principles of government.

The party has failed consistently when through political trading and chicanery it has fallen into the control of those interests, personal and financial, which think in terms of dollars instead of in terms of human values.

The Republican Party has made its nominations this year at the dictation of those who, we all know, always place money ahead of human progress.

The Democratic Convention, as appears clear from the events of today, is divided on this fundamental issue. Until the Democratic Party through this Convention makes overwhelmingly clear its stand in favor of social progress and liberalism, and shakes off all the shackles of control fastened upon it by the forces of conservatism, reaction and appeasement, it will not continue its march of victory.

It is without question that certain political influences pledged to reaction in domestic affairs and to appeasement in foreign affairs have been busily engaged behind the scenes in the promotion of discord since this Convention convened.

Under those circumstances, I cannot, in all honor, and will not, merely for political expediency, go along with the cheap bargaining and political maneuvering which have brought about party dissension in this Convention. It is best not to straddle ideals.

In these days of danger when democracy must be more than vigilant, there can be no connivance with the kind of politics which has internally weakened nations abroad before the enemy has struck from without.

It is best for America to have the fight out here and now.

I wish to give the Democratic Party the opportunity to make its historic decision clearly and without equivocation. The party must go wholly one way or wholly the other. It cannot face in both directions at the same time.

By declining the honor of the nomination for the Presidency, I can restore that opportunity to the Convention. I so do.

(For samples of all these documents, see facsimile section following p. 336.)

The tenseness in the room mounted as the vote was taken. The President laid his cards aside and tallied the vote himself. It was close.

When it was over, and Wallace was announced as the winner, everybody relaxed. Somebody grabbed all the drafts of the declination statement in which all of us had suddenly lost interest. Who it was, I do not know. I had to make quite a search to find them. Even Grace Tully, who knew everything about the President's files, did not know what had happened to them. I finally located them in the Roosevelt Library at Hyde Park.

We phoned to the convention and had the chairman announce that the President would deliver his address accepting the nomination at 9 P.M. Chicago time.

The President by this time looked weary and bedraggled; his shirt was wilted from the intense heat of the Oval Room and he generally needed a freshening up. He was wheeled into his bedroom, where he washed, changed his shirt, combed his hair, and in a few minutes came out smiling, looking his usual, jaunty, imperturbable self.

We all went downstairs to the radio broadcasting room where everything had been made ready for the delivery of the acceptance speech. It was piped into the convention hall in Chicago, and simultaneously broadcast to the rest of the United States and the world. I looked around the room at the small gathering of close friends. We were all happy and smiling except one; Missy was in tears. I am sure that, with her fine loyalty and devotion to the President, she had almost hoped that the President would have to read the declination speech rather than the acceptance speech. She had seen the great toll that the President had paid in strength and health during his two terms in the White House. She felt that the convention not only should have nominated the President by acclamation, but should have accepted his choice for the Vice-Presidency likewise by acclamation. The haggling and the opposition and the political trading that was going on—above all the criticism of the President by the party reactionaries—made her feel bitter. It was hard enough for the President to carry on with the country divided on our foreign policy as it then was; it was too much for him also to carry on without the unanimous support of his own party. She knew that the coming struggle would sap the President's strength.

The President and I together had hammered out the acceptance speech during the week before, working a few hours at a time. Frankfurter and MacLeish had suggested some ideas and some paragraphs. The President relented on Tom, and he and Ben came in to help toward the end; it was the last speech that the three of us worked on together.

The President dictated a draft of what his personal feelings had been in the past few months on the question of the third term and any public announcement about it—a period, as he put it, of "conflict between deep personal desire for retirement on the one hand, and that quiet, invisible thing called 'conscience' on the other."

He knew that his motives would be misconstrued by some, and he said so; but he added that he "must trust to the good faith and common sense of the American people to accept my own good faith—and do their own interpreting. . . ."

When the conflict first broke out last September, it was still my intention to announce clearly and simply, at an early date, that under no conditions would I accept reelection. . . .

It soon became evident, however, that such a public statement on my part would be unwise from the point of view of sheer public duty. . . .

Every day that passed called for the postponement of personal plans and partisan debate until the latest possible moment. The normal conditions under which I would have made public declaration of my personal desires were wholly gone.

And so, thinking solely of the national good and of the international scene, I came to the reluctant conclusion that such declaration should not be made before the national Convention. It was accordingly made to you within an hour after the permanent organization of this Convention. . . .

Lying awake, as I have, on many nights, I have asked myself whether I have the right, as Commander-in-Chief of the Army and Navy, to call on men and women to serve their country, or to train themselves to serve and, at the same time, decline to serve my country in my own personal capacity, if I am called upon to do so by the people of my country. . . .

The right to make that call rests with the people through the American method of a free election. Only the people themselves can draft a President. If such a draft should be made upon me, I say to you, in the utmost simplicity, I will, with God's help, continue to serve with the best of my ability and with the fullness of my strength.

Leaving the personal side, the President then made it unmistakably clear that he would continue full blast his policy of helping Britain and resisting Hitler and all that Hitler stood for.

I would not undo, if I could, the efforts I made to prevent war. . . . I do not now soften the condemnation expressed by Secretary Hull and myself from time to time for the acts of aggression that have wiped out ancient liberty-loving, peace-pursuing countries. . . . I do not recant the sentiments of sympathy with all free peoples resisting such aggression, or begrudge the material aid that we have given to them. I do not regret my consistent endeavor to awaken this country to the menace for us and for all we hold dear. . . . So long as I am President, I will do all I can to insure that that foreign policy remain our foreign policy.

Certainly no one can deny that he plainly warned the people of the

United States from the very start of his campaign—right in the acceptance speech—that he was going to continue his anti-Hitler, pro-British policy of the preceding few months.

One thing, finally, he insisted on saying: that he was not going to have the time or the desire to campaign for re-election. That statement, however, would have caused him no end of trouble later, in September and October, if he had not added a reservation: "I shall never be loath to call the attention of the nation to deliberate or unwitting falsifications of fact, which are sometimes made by political candidates."

The day after the acceptance speech I went into the President's bedroom to say good-by, for I was leaving to join my family in Montana. I had nothing further to do with any of the events in Washington until September, when I was summoned back from vacation by a telephone call from Missy.

Chapter XIV

The Third Presidential Campaign, 1940

The summer of 1940 was a busy one for the President. Inspection trips to war plants and shipyards, speeches in various sections of the country, and countless other matters which the defense effort superimposed upon his regular peacetime duties engaged his attention the whole working day and late into the night. Willkie, his opponent, had no such duties or obligations. He was out campaigning—and campaigning as hard as he could.

The effect of Willkie's strenuous campaigning and Roosevelt's silence began to be felt by midsummer. Into the White House poured telegrams and telephone calls from all parts of the country, from political leaders and others interested in the President's candidacy, warning that Willkie was making great headway and that the President had better begin to do some campaigning. During the late summer political leaders started coming to Washington to the National Democratic Campaign Headquarters, and even to the White House, to urge upon the President the necessity of getting out among the people and discussing the campaign issues.

The political leaders were learning in their own local districts that, as far as votes for a President are concerned, the American people just naturally refuse to be taken for granted. They want to hear the campaign issues debated by the candidates. Fortunately for Roosevelt, the reports he was receiving made him realize this in time.

I cannot help but draw the comparison between that feature of the campaign of 1940 and the campaign of 1948 between President Truman and Governor Dewey. Dewey, starting with his acceptance speech at Philadelphia, refused to discuss any issues or to present a program of his own. Instead—convinced that the election was his—he went about the country in a self-confident, assured manner, and spoke platitudes and generalities which had not the faintest relationship to the vital issues of 1948. To all intents and purposes it was the same as if he had remained in the Executive Mansion in Albany all summer and fall waiting for the election to fall into his hands in November. On the other hand, his opponent, President Truman, did campaign—and very strenuously. He made hundreds of speeches in hundreds of places—big cities, villages, "whistle stops" all over the United States. He discussed the issues; he repeatedly denounced the failures of the Republican Eightieth Congress; and he clearly set forth his own objectives and program. The result was a complete surprise to nearly everyone, including Dewey. It showed that campaigning is necessary—even if the odds are overwhelmingly in your favor.

Willkie, in his zealousness, had made statements, as many candidates do from time to time in the heat of a campaign, that could legitimately be included under the "deliberate or unwitting falsifications of fact" which the President in his acceptance speech had reserved the right of answering. It was on the basis of this reservation that the President felt justified in taking an active part in the fight. I doubt very much, however, that he would have made the campaign he did in 1940 if Willkie had not been making such great headway.

I was in Portland, Oregon, when Roosevelt made up his mind to start campaigning. There, one night during the first week in September, I got a telephone call from the White House. Harry and Missy were both on the wire. I had been completely out of personal touch with Washington since the acceptance speech.

It was Missy who said: "Say, what are you doing all the way out there? We have tracked you down. Don't you know that F. D. has a campaign on his hands?"

"I thought the President said he wasn't going to campaign this fall," said I.

"Never mind about that," broke in Harry. "You better get on back. The President has to make a speech to Dan Tobin's union convention on the eleventh. How long would it take you to get here?"

I said: "I can get back in two days."

"Come on," said Harry.

In a day or two I was on a plane and headed for New York. That was the end of my 1940 vacation. Except for a few days snatched here and there, it was the last vacation I was to have until long after V-J Day in 1945.

Landing in New York City I learned that Roosevelt was at Hyde Park and immediately took the train up there.

Right after dinner Harry and I went up to my room, took off our coats and got to work. The President had given us very few instructions—the chief ones were to "take a crack" at the labor racketeers, and to assure the audience that defense preparations would not mean a wiping out of the social gains of the last seven years.

Harry had a draft which formed the general basis of the speech. I forget who he said had submitted it. On the way across the continent in the plane, I had written some paragraphs, which were also incorporated in it. They made the point that a strong, free labor union was in a real sense the same kind of stronghold of defense as the various plants and shipyards the President had just been visiting.

We went to Washington with the President on his train, and the speech was finished in the White House.

Speaking to an enthusiastic labor audience on the eleventh, he detailed the record of what his two administrations had done to raise the standard of living for workers in America.

For more than a month following this Teamsters' Union speech, the President did not make another political talk. However, he made three nonpolitical speeches. The President was very adept at using nonpolitical speeches—especially during his campaigns—to derive great political benefit. He frequently used a phrase he had coined in Albany, and about which Missy and Grace and I liked to tease him. He would say innocently in prefacing a speech that he was going to talk "government, not politics"—and then make what was in effect a fine political speech. It would not be in terms of political parties at all; rather it would contain generalities about government that would provide "kudos" (a common expression of his) for his own party and imply censure of the Republican party. After he had delivered one of these nonpolitical speeches, Missy or Grace would smile guilelessly and say: "That speech certainly was about government, not politics." This always drew a pleased laugh from the President, followed by a mock-indignant protestation of innocence and a vehement denial that he had intended any politics at all.

The first of the three nonpolitical speeches during this campaign was scheduled to be delivered at the University of Pennsylvania on

September 20. After the Teamsters' Union speech I had stayed on at the White House to work on it. However, on the 16th the President had to leave for Jasper, Alabama, to be present at the funeral of Speaker Bankhead, and he asked me to go along so we could do some more work on the speech. On the train, in the intervals between work, we talked of many things, including the Selective Service Act, which he had signed the day he left Washington. He had been urging the adoption of this peacetime draft for several months, yet he had not urged it too vocally. He did not want to suffer a defeat on this bill in the Congress; it would have been too encouraging to the Axis, too disheartening to Britain, and too harmful to his own prestige to make this act a matter of personal contest with the Congress and be defeated.

"From a political point of view, there couldn't have been a worse time for them to have passed this bill," I said. "The actual drawing of numbers will probably take place right smack in the middle of the campaign, and of course you are going to be blamed for it in a great many homes."

"I guess you're right," he answered. "But if we really do a job of telling American fathers and mothers how necessary this is—how much better it is to start training their sons now to protect themselves if we should ever be attacked than to have them go into battle as raw recruits—maybe it won't be so bad. The training itself, even if the boys never have to make use of any of it, will do them an awful lot of good. In fact, in a world like this, we ought to have universal military training for everybody in peacetime. Someday, if we can't get a permanent peace, I'm going to recommend that, too." Had he lived, I am sure he would have recommended it, as President Truman later did. In fact, I know it was on his mind just before he left for Yalta in 1945.

The University of Pennsylvania speech was concerned primarily with domestic affairs and democracy generally. In it, the President reaffirmed one of his deepest convictions.

"On candidates and on election issues . . ." he said, "I would rather trust the aggregate judgment of all the people in a factory—the president, all the vice-presidents, the board of directors, the managers, the foremen, plus all the laborers—rather than the judgment of the few who may have financial control at the time."

A free election by all the people, he said, is the greatest safeguard for democracy: "No dictator in history has ever dared to run the gauntlet of a really free election."

The second speech, on October 5, was at the dedication of three new schools which had been erected in the town of Hyde Park with the help of PWA funds. A draft for this speech had been sent over by the Office of Education, and I was called down to Washington on the 3rd to work on it. I rode up on the train with the President the next day.

While it was a nonpolitical speech in every sense of the word, the President took full political advantage of all that PWA and WPA had accomplished throughout the country, for he had suffered long from the bitter attacks upon the programs of these agencies as "boondoggling" and a waste of money.

There is not a single person in the United States who has not seen some new, useful structure—a hospital or a bridge or a town hall or a highway or an airport or a dam or a new waterworks or a sewage disposal system— one of the hundreds of thousands of new necessary improvements which were built recently in the United States—illustrations of the results of giving employment on useful projects that were approved by each community. . . .

Into every project went money for wages. Where did they go? Why, the wages were spent at local stores; the stores replenished their stocks; and the wheels of industry and business moved that much faster. Into every project went materials for construction—materials from every part of the United States. For example, right here, while our own local neighborhood provided the stone for these very schools, and perhaps the sand and the gravel for the concrete foundations, almost everything else, the steel and the lumber and the desks and the vocational training equipment and all the other things that are in these schools came here from other places in our country. . . .

Even in this speech he again took occasion to point out the horrors of foreign ideologies—for he always kept in mind during 1940 those in America who still felt that it might be better to make our peace with Hitler:

In the last decade, this right of free education, which has become a part of the national life in our land, has taken on additional significance because of certain events in certain other lands. For a large portion of the world that right no longer exists. Almost the first freedom to be destroyed, as dictators take control, is the freedom of learning. Tyranny hates and fears nothing more than the free exchange of ideas, the free play of the mind that comes from education. . . .

The third nonpolitical speech of this period was devoted exclusively to foreign affairs. It was on Columbus Day, October 12, 1940, at Dayton, Ohio. I remember this speech very well because it was the first one on which Robert E. Sherwood worked.

By this time the influence of the Corcoran-Cohen team was waning rapidly. Tom's disregard for bruised feelings had made him a lot of enemies, and his ruthlessness and aggressiveness had aroused the antagonism of important political leaders such as James Farley and Ed Flynn. In fact, nearly all the Democratic national political leaders in the country had become bitter at him. They resented the work he was doing in their field; they were jealous of his influence in Presidential appointments; they felt that he was hurting the party by his maneuvers. They carried their complaints to the President; several of them threatened to walk out unless Tom quit. And it is true that sometimes Tom's zealousness was embarrassing to the President. Finally Roosevelt decided that Tom should not be permitted to do all the things he had been doing; but knowing how unhappy Tom would be in Washington not doing them, he suggested that he go up to New York City and work with the Citizens' Committee for Roosevelt under the chairmanship of Mayor La Guardia. But Tommy had been fighting too long in the front lines to adjust himself to other work. In 1941 he left the government. He is now a prosperous Washington lawyer—quite a different person from the fighting, jolly New Dealer I used to know.

Ben stayed on in the government, but not in his old capacity. Beginning about this time, his main interest shifted to foreign affairs. He later became associated with Ambassador Winant in London and then with Justice Byrnes in OWM. Still later he served under Secretary of State Byrnes as counselor in the State Department. Now he is one of the United States delegates to the UN Assembly. After 1940, Ben continued to be a pillar of strength and wisdom for all who worked around the President, lending the same patient, studious co-operation as in the old days. He was, and still is, a kind of retired "elder statesman" in Washington, helpful to the many who come to him for advice and suggestions, respected and admired by all those who come to know him.

Except for Ben, then, the other members of the speech-writing teams with whom I had worked were no longer available. Ben did continue to help from time to time and we called upon him as often as we could get him away from his other duties in the government.

Bullitt, who had worked occasionally on speeches from 1933 on when he was in the United States, was particularly helpful during the summer and fall of 1940. However, he preferred to work alone, and was never a member of a writing team. In 1941 there came a gradual break between him and the President, and he was no longer asked to assist in speech preparation.

In the beginning of October, knowing that the campaign would soon develop full speed, and knowing how difficult, if not impossible, it was for one man to work alone on Presidential campaign speeches, I had a talk with Hopkins about getting some new blood for speech writing. We cast about for suitable people. The major requisites were to be able to write clearly and forcefully, and to be fully in sympathy with the domestic and international policies of the President. The first name that we agreed upon was Raymond Gram Swing, who was one of the outstanding radio commentators in America, a liberal and a supporter of the President's policies. Harry made some inquiries, and reported that Swing was then unavailable. He asked me if I knew the playwright, Robert E. Sherwood. I had met him personally only once, in a large gathering celebrating the opening night of his *Abe Lincoln in Illinois*; but I was, of course, familiar with his plays. I said that his plays certainly indicated a liberal point of view, and that his activities on the Committee to Defend America by Aiding the Allies showed that he shared the President's views on foreign policy.

As time drew near to prepare a draft for the Dayton speech, I suggested to Harry that he and Sherwood come up to have lunch with us one Sunday in our apartment in New York City.

That Sunday, as we sat down to dinner, there was organized the last speech-writing team that President Roosevelt was to have—the team that was to work on nearly all the major speeches from then until his death. At times one or the other of us was unavoidably absent, but I think that on every important speech and message after that Sunday, at least one of us was on hand to work with him. When we were all in the United States, we always kept closely in touch with one another. Harry worked on fewer speeches than Bob and I because he was out of the country more often than we were; also his constantly failing health often kept him in bed at home or—too frequently—in a hospital. Bob and I were the ones who worked on the early drafts of the speeches; Harry's most effective function was to look at the drafts Bob and I turned out, criticize them, and perhaps offer a fresh point of view on thought and language. He did not do as much original writing as we did. More useful as a destructive critic than as a constructive writer, he was excellent in tearing a draft apart to show its weakness and dangers, and always had good suggestions about what should be substituted. But he was not so useful at putting his ideas into actual words.

Harry was most helpful in our arguments with the President over what ought to go in or come out of a speech. I think that the President respected the judgment of each of us individually. Since he would respect the unanimous judgment of the three of us even more, we would try to reach unanimity among ourselves before presenting something for his consideration. I do not mean to say that he would necessarily accept even our unanimous judgment; there were many times when, after giving us a respectful hearing either on a question of policy or of language, he would calmly say that he was overruling us.

Many people in government in Washington used to complain that Harry, after agreeing with them in conference, would later secretly go around and see the President alone and argue for a different point of view. Unquestionably he did do this occasionally; it was one of the traits that made him unpopular with other officials, especially since it was his residence at the White House that made this tactic possible. While he did not do it very often with Bob and me, he did occasionally.

For example, in connection with the stabilization speech of October 2, 1942, which is discussed in detail later,[1] Bob and I felt that the President should proceed immediately to fight inflation by executive order and by such sanctions as he could legally muster apart from Congressional action. The Congress had continued to ignore his many requests for an effective anti-inflation bill. Many public officials in Washington had been urging this course upon the President. Harry was for giving the Congress another chance to pass a bill. And there was backing for this course, too, among the President's official family.

The President, Harry, Bob and I argued this matter out among ourselves for several days, enumerating all the pros and cons which we had gathered from all the interested agencies in Washington as well as our own personal views. We learned later, however, that Harry would go in by himself to see the President between these debates and seek to influence the President toward his point of view. He was convinced that it was the better course for the President to follow, and the President did.

In the last five years of the President's life—the most important years —Hopkins was unquestionably the most influential of those who worked with him. Sherwood's *Roosevelt and Hopkins* gives the story of this influence, how it was developed, and how it was exercised, and how it waned.

[1] See p. 336.

In many ways it was as strong as the earlier influence of Louis Howe; in many respects the two men were similar in character and in the way they worked. They were both extremely suspicious of people who sought access to the President, and jealous of almost anyone else who was close to him. I suppose that in all Presidential circles there always have been, and always will be, rivalries and jealousies. There seems to be something about a source of great power that makes it difficult for human beings to be really willing to share closeness to it. The Roosevelt administrations were no exception. As soon as one man was mentioned by the press as being particularly close to the President, many of the others who considered themselves close began to show jealousy. It was almost involuntary; I am sure that they would deny it and sincerely believe the denial. In turn, the victim of their jealousy generally became less tolerant of others and more protective of his own position. The President understood all this very well, and tried his best to prevent it from getting out of hand. When some Cabinet officer was petulant or irritable or threatening to resign, he could nearly always tell whether there was a real grievance or a substantial disagreement on policy, or whether it was merely the result of jealousy or hurt feelings.

"Something's eating so-and-so. Try to find out *who* it is," he would say.

The cure for "so-and-so" would generally be something to bolster his ego—like a luncheon with the President. Fortunately for the President's peace of mind, there was not too much of this; but there was enough of it to be very harassing to such a busy man. He once remarked that in this respect government was no different from large industrial corporations. There were the same kinds of rivalries there, too; but in government the conflicts—like everything else—were carried on in a fishbowl of publicity. The columnists and mischief-makers inside the government knew how to play on these natural emotions of jealousy and rivalry; and they used them frequently to create rifts between friends of the President who could have been more useful to him if dissensions had been avoided.

Both Louis and Harry served the President in the same way during their days of greatest influence. They were able to take hundreds of tasks from his shoulders. People who would formerly insist on seeing the President personally grew to be satisfied with seeing Howe or Hopkins—convinced that their message would reach the President. Each in turn lived at the White House. That kind of propinquity, which enabled them to see the President at almost any time, was the greatest possible assurance of influence and power.

Each of these men could sift the good from the bad, the sound from the unsound, before any matter was submitted to the President. But they were only human beings, susceptible to human error in judgment; and frequently it had to be their judgment that prevailed, without even a chance for the President to consider the matter fully on its own merits. This is one of the necessary drawbacks of any executive position where there is so much work in one day for one man. Reliance has to be placed on trusted people. In the majority of cases, the result is good. The occasional error cannot be avoided. Roosevelt, both as Governor and as President, liked to work that way—to have one man with whom he could exchange ideas at any time of day, whose judgment and loyalty he trusted, and whose disinterestedness he knew would make the advice impartial. In Louis and Harry he found such people. In the interval between Louis's death in 1936 and Harry's coming to live at the White House in 1940, he had no such help. There were many trusted people who worked with him during that period, but none in the same way.

On rare occasions the personal likes and dislikes of these men—their prejudices against certain people, perhaps their jealousies—kept from the President's side others who could have been of even greater service to him than they were. But this was not too high a price to pay for the years of loyal, patriotic, excellent assistance they gave the President, the work and worry they saved him, and the outstanding results they accomplished.

Harry's greatest disservice came from the fact that some of his decisions on problems and on people were too colored by his personal likes and dislikes. He did not like Baruch, for example, and was chiefly responsible for Baruch's absence from several situations where his services would have helped tremendously.

I am sure, for example, that if it had not been for Harry, Baruch would have been appointed the head of our industrial mobilization program—the chairman of the War Production Board—either when Nelson was appointed in 1942 or later when Nelson ran into trouble with the armed services in 1943.

When Harry left government in 1945 he was completely broke—financially as well as physically. He was determined not to take a job with some large corporation where he would be used as a "front" for public relations and official favors. When he got out of a sickbed on

May 23, 1945, to make his last mission for a President—to see Stalin in Moscow at President Truman's request—he still had no job to look forward to on his return. This fact seemed to me to be a most eloquent statement of the disinterestedness with which one of the most powerful and influential men of his times had lived his public life.

Of all the people with whom I worked in speech-writing during my seventeen years with Roosevelt, I enjoyed most working with Bob Sherwood. He never showed any pride of opinion or authorship. He was an excellent judge of the effect of words upon audiences—he had become one of the leading dramatists in the United States partly because of that ability. He was a burning enthusiast for the New Deal and for a strong international policy; if anything, he had to be restrained rather than encouraged. Of course he had had no experience at all in politics. When he began to work with us he was not yet as aware as he might have been that in order for Roosevelt to be able to do anything for the United States or for the world, he first had to get elected. He was sometimes too impatient at what had to be done in a political campaign or in any political fight. He soon learned, however.

His lessons, in a broader sense, may be said to have begun the day Harry first brought him to my apartment.

After lunch Harry had to take his usual rest. Sherwood, Mrs. Rosenman and I went into the library with a draft of the Columbus Day speech which had come up from the State Department.

"I have been reading a great many of the Presidential speeches and addresses as well as those delivered by Mr. Roosevelt when he was Governor," said Bob, "and I've been struck by the continuity and uniformity of style in them.

"I'm sure," he continued firmly, "that as Governor and as President, he must have written all his speeches and messages by himself; if there had been substantial assistance there would have been a mélange of style and quality which would have shown it right away."

Mrs. Rosenman and I looked at each other, quite surprised at this; but we said nothing.

I was very pleased to hear Sherwood's statement, the impression of an expert on prose style. It bore out two things: first, that those of us who had worked with the President on speeches had learned to imitate his natural style in the drafts we submitted to him; and second, that

Roosevelt worked so hard and consistently on his speeches himself, made so many corrections and inserted so many paragraphs of his own, that by the time a speech was delivered it was thoroughly impregnated with his own style and personality. There was something about working with the President on speeches, something about listening to him deliver them, something about listening to him dictate paragraphs time and again, that seemed unconsciously to color our style and manner of writing. I have noticed that fact even with Sherwood; his style for his own writings is quite different from the style in which he drafted for the President. All those who worked on speeches for any length of time came gradually and unconsciously to be able to imitate the President's style—some, of course, better than others.

When Harry came in from his rest we all started discussing the State Department draft—what we thought was the matter with it and what new ideas ought to be added. Finally, convinced that Sherwood was not only in full sympathy with what the President was doing and thinking but also that he knew how to say so with clarity and emphasis, I said: "Boys, there comes a time in the history of every speech when it's got to get written—that time for this speech is *now*. So let's get to work."

Bob had suggested that the draft was too cautious; that there ought to be a more forthright declaration about the isolationists in America. "Suppose, Mr. Sherwood, you go into the dining room," I suggested, "and write a couple of paragraphs along that line, so Harry and I can take a look at it. I'd like to write something on what Hitler is now trying to do here in America along the 'divide and conquer' line."

He looked at me, mystified, as if to say, "What in the world is the use of my writing a couple of paragraphs up here in this apartment in New York City? How is that going to do any good in a speech the President is now writing in Washington to be delivered in Dayton?" But instead of saying what I am sure was in his mind, he pulled his six feet six inches out of the chair, picked up a pack of cigarettes, and, with a shrug of the shoulders, went in to work.

He and I continued to work on the speech for several evenings; Harry returned to Washington.

We agreed on the new ideas that should go into it, and on the parts of the State Department draft that ought to come out or be reworded. We did our writing in different rooms and then got together to criticize each other's material. More ideas grew out of our conversation. What had been essentially a routine Columbus Day draft was converted into a speech in defense of the President's foreign policy.

On October 9, I took our latest draft down to Washington and went over it with the President, showing him the various changes we had made in the State Department draft. I returned the next day, and phoned Sherwood to come up and join us at the radio to listen to the speech on the 12th.

"What did the President think about our draft?" he asked eagerly.

"Well, he seemed pleased with most of it," I said. "He says there are some parts he wants to change. The best way for us to tell what he thinks of it now is to listen and see how much he uses."

"I'll be there."

As we sat at the radio that night waiting for the President to come on, I am sure that Sherwood was firmly of the opinion that our work had been a lot of wasted effort—that none of it would be used. He sat there with a carbon copy of the speech we had submitted, and as he compared it with the words the President spoke, I thoroughly enjoyed his expression of pleasure. He was getting his first thrill of hearing some of his words spoken by the President of the United States. That first thrill was always the deepest for each person who worked on a speech, but no matter how many times the experience was repeated the pleasure was always great. Since Sherwood was a playwright, he should have been used to hearing his lines spoken by others; but as he said to me, "When Roosevelt does it—it's different!"

The President had not changed our draft of this speech as much as he did most of our later ones, so for Sherwood it was a propitious induction into the work we were to do together for the next four and a half years.

The speech was definitely a step forward in Roosevelt's policy of resistance to Hitler and help to Hitler's enemies. It eschewed domestic politics completely.

In it the President made the point that the territory that the nations of the Western Hemisphere were determined to defend was not limited to the "territory of North, Central, and South America and the immediately adjacent islands."

"We include," he added, "the right to the peaceful use of the Atlantic and Pacific Oceans. That has been our traditional policy. . . ."

Again he announced that we were going to continue our policy of helping those who fought Hitler.

"No combination of dictator countries of Europe and Asia will stop the help we are giving to almost the last free people now fighting to hold them at bay. . . .

"We have learned the lessons of recent years. We know now that if we seek to appease aggressors by withholding aid from those who stand in their way, we only hasten the day of their attack upon us."

This—among the first of his allusions to Japan in this vein—was occasioned by the new alliance that had been formed just a few weeks before on September 27 by Rome and Berlin on the one hand and Tokyo on the other.

In the meantime the campaign of the Republican candidate was boiling along. Roosevelt decided to plunge into the fight. Not only Willkie but other Republican orators were making all kinds of statements, some of which Willkie later admitted to a Congressional committee were just "campaign oratory." The "falsifications" that the President most deeply resented were the statement that his policies were deliberately plunging us into war, and the charge that his election for a third term would mean the end of American elections and democracy.

In the light of Willkie's later role in international affairs, it is a little amazing to read some excerpts from his speeches during that 1940 campaign. For instance, at Coffeyville, Kansas, on September 16, he said:

Mr. Roosevelt's oratory, as the defender of democracy, conceals the fact that by his own meddling in international politics he encouraged the European conflagration. . . . And he was the godfather of that unhappy conference at Munich. . . .

I warn you—and I say this in dead earnest—if, because of some fine speeches about humanity, you return this Administration to office, you will be serving under an American totalitarian government before the long third term is finished.

Three days later Willkie spoke in Los Angeles:

"I hope and pray that he remembers the pledge [that America would fight in no European war] of the 1940 platform better than he did the one of 1932. If he does not, you better get ready to get on the transports. . . ."

It was this type of statement by Willkie and far more inflammatory ones by other Republican campaign orators that led Roosevelt to write to me after the election as follows:

THE WHITE HOUSE
Nov. 13, 1940

DEAR SAM:

Somehow, you and I made the same analysis of the votes on the fifth. In many ways, it was a narrow escape—not for personalities but for ideals. I wonder, with you, whether people will ever realize that. On Armistice Day, I tried to take the long-range view of the past and, at the same time, to imply that our type of civilization, though saved for a generation by the first World War, is again a world issue.

Furthermore, I have learned a number of things which make me shudder— because there were altogether too many people in high places in the Republican campaign who thought in terms of appeasement of Hitler—honest views most of them, and views based on the materialism in which they view not only themselves but their country.

So also in affairs at home, I live, as you know, in constant dread that the national security might, under remote circumstances, call for quick and drastic action. You and I have faced that possibility since 1928 and there have been a number of occasions when, both in Albany and Washington, it took real calm not to call out the troops. Little do people realize how I had to take abuse and criticism for inaction at the time of the Flint strike. I believed, and I was right, that the country including labor would learn the lesson of their own volition without having it forced upon them by marching troops.

No one can give guarantees for the future but I am certain that if the other crowd had won there would have been many more probabilities of drastic action by the government. Those newspapers of the nation which most loudly cried dictatorship against me would have been the first to justify the beginnings of dictatorship by somebody else.

I don't have to tell you how perfectly grand you were during those hectic weeks and how very much of a help you were, not only in the aiding of the draftsmanship, but also in helping me to keep both feet on the ground. I do hope to see you again very soon.

Why don't you and Dorothy come up for the Saturday after Thanksgiving? You can work on the papers in the library and I may be able to steal a few hours to help.

As ever yours,

F. D. R.

On October 18, Roosevelt announced that he was going to make five campaign speeches. These were scheduled for the weeks between October 23 and November 2. This meant working under great pressure.

The first speech was in Philadelphia, October 23.

After again explaining his personal entrance into the campaign, he referred to specific "falsifications" made by Willkie or his supporters:

But it is an entirely different thing for any party or any candidate to state, for example, that the President of the United States telephoned to Mussolini and Hitler to sell Czechoslovakia down the river; or to state that the unfortunate unemployed of the nation are going to be driven into concentration camps; or that the social security funds of the Government of the United States will not be in existence when the workers of today become old enough to apply for them; or that the election of the present Government means the end of American democracy within four years. I think they know, and I know we know that all those statements are false. . . .

The first "falsification" he took up and solemnly denied was the charge that he had made some secret treaties, commitments or under- standings to involve this nation in war. Prime Minister Churchill's *Their Finest Hour* has revealed how urgently the British and the French leaders had tried to get commitments of a much less serious nature from him, and how they failed. Up to now, no one has been able to disclose any commitments or understandings of such a nature before Pearl Harbor—because there were none.

But in the fall of 1940 these rumors and charges were alarming the American people, and Roosevelt knew how dangerous they were to his election.

The Democratic platform contained a solemn pledge not to get into any foreign war, with the proviso insisted upon by the President, "ex- cept in case of attack." Subsequent history has shown that in spite of repeated provocation, the campaign pledge was kept. Of course the President did many drastic things after the election to meet dangers from abroad; but none was more drastic in intent than the exchange *before the election* of United States destroyers for British bases. The people who voted for him in November, 1940, had been fully informed by this act alone—in addition to all he had said and done before—just how far he was prepared to go to make ready to repel any attack.

In this speech at Philadelphia, the President also answered another "falsification"—that the Administration had really accomplished noth- ing to improve the domestic economy. After citing many statistics to prove how far recovery had come, he quoted a *New York Times* financial writer, who said: "Dreams of business 'flat on its back' [as Republican campaign orators were saying] must come from smoking campaign cigars or else the speakers are talking about some other country." *The New York Times* was at this time ardently supporting Willkie. Some one had dug up this article and sent it to us. The President, in one of his typical clincher sentences, wrote an aside in the draft of the speech which, when delivered as only he could, made the hall ring with laughter and applause:

"Wouldn't it be nice if the editorial writers of *The New York Times* could get acquainted with their own business experts?"

There was another passage in the speech—aimed at the votes of labor, which Willkie, too, was courting assiduously—which the President delivered in so telling a fashion that Sherwood, whose profession required critical appraisal of actors' reading, said to me:

"That man would be one of the best actors on our stage with his fine sense of timing and the way he can modulate his voice and change his expression."

This passage, too, got applause and laughter:

The tears, the crocodile tears, for the laboring man and laboring woman now being shed in this campaign come from those same Republican leaders who had their chance to prove their love for labor in 1932—and missed it.

Back in 1932, those leaders were willing to let the workers starve if they could not get a job. . . .

Back in 1932, they met the demands of unemployed veterans with troops and tanks.

Back in 1932, they raised their hands in horror at the thought of fixing a minimum wage or maximum hours for labor; they never gave one thought to such things as pensions for old age or insurance for the unemployed.

In 1940, eight years later, what a different tune is played by them! It is a tune played against a sounding board of election day. It is a tune with overtones which whisper: "Votes, votes, votes."

Roosevelt was back on the stump!

The people loved it as he proclaimed: "I am an old campaigner, and I love a good fight." And as I watched Roosevelt write those words into a draft of the speech, as I saw his grim smile and set jaw, I knew that he was not exaggerating.

The next day there was a nonpolitical radio talk to the Herald Tribune Forum. Bob and I had helped on this—and in a hurry, because there was another campaign speech coming up in New York, at Madison Square Garden on October 28. At Madison Square, he set out to answer the charge that he had been slow and fumbling in preparing America for defense.

The President again used his own imagery to describe how he was answering these charges one by one. He referred to his boyhood days when he used to nail up the skins of foxes and weasels to the old barn door to dry (he mentioned to Bob and me another animal that he did not include in his speech—"skunks"). In the same way, he said, he was nailing these falsehoods to the barn door to dry. The audiences—even city dwellers who had never done any nailing to barn doors—seemed to enjoy this allusion.

This charge—that Roosevelt had delayed national defense—was an easy one to answer. The President had told us that he wanted to answer it in two ways. First, he wanted to state the facts about what he had done to prepare our defense. "But," he said, "in addition, I'd like to look up the voting records of the Republicans in the Congress. They opposed nearly everything we tried to do to strengthen our defenses. I'm sure that the voting record will show that if the Republicans had been in control of the Congress since 1933, we'd be as weak as a kitten right now." It was the best kind of defense in a political campaign to take the offensive, he said—and this was certainly taking the offensive.

The voting records were searched and tabulated; they bore out his claims.

"That's fine, fine," he said. "Put them all in the speech. The statistics may get to be a little dull after a while, but I want to get the whole record before the American people." Usually he disliked using statistics in a speech, but he loved these.

The record provided an effective counterattack. Taking up one after another—Hamilton Fish, ex-President Hoover, Senator Vandenberg, Senator Robert Taft—he quoted statements by all of them made *before* 1940 complaining that we were spending *too much* for defense.

There is the record on that; the permanent crystal clear record. Until the present political campaign opened, Republican leaders, in and out of the Congress shouted from the housetops that our defenses were fully adequate.

Today they proclaim that this Administration has starved our armed forces, that our Navy is anemic, our Army puny, our air forces piteously weak.

Yes, it is a remarkable somersault.

I wonder if the election could have something to do with it.

This was said in a voice of sarcasm which brought great applause and cheers.

But . . . [the President added] the printed pages of the Congressional Record cannot be changed or suppressed at election time.

He then cited by chapter and verse the votes of the Republican members of earlier Congresses *against* appropriations for national defense. In working on this part of the speech, the President himself inserted a phrase that found great response in the audience, taking it from an old song which had been revived and was very popular in 1940, "The Daring Young Man on the Flying Trapeze."

What did the Republican leaders do when they had this chance to increase our national defense almost three years ago? You would think from their present barrage of verbal pyrotechnics, that they rushed in to pass that bill, or that they even demanded a larger expansion of the Navy.

But, ah! my friends, they were not in a national campaign for votes then. In those days they were trying to build up a different kind of political fence.

In those days they thought that the way to win votes was by representing this Administration as extravagant in national defense, indeed as hysterical, and as manufacturing panics and inventing foreign dangers.

But now, in the serious days of 1940, all is changed! Not only because they are serious days, but because they are election days as well.

On the radio these Republican orators swing through the air with the greatest of ease; but the American people are not voting this year for the best trapeze performer. . . .

Coming to the Republican vote on repeal of the embargo, he pointed out that a majority of the Republican membership in both houses had voted against it, including many Republican leaders. Among these leaders were three Congressmen—Barton, Fish and Martin. In the first draft of the speech Bob and I prepared, we had them listed in that order. We sat around—I remember we were writing in my apartment in New York City—working on that paragraph. Then as we read those names, we almost simultaneously hit on the more euphonious and rhythmic sequence of Martin, Barton and Fish. We said nothing about it when we handed the draft to the President, wondering whether he would catch it as he read the sentence aloud. He did. The very first time he read it, his eyes twinkled; and he grinned from ear to ear. To use one of his own favorite phrases, he was "tickled pink." He repeated it several times and indicated by swinging his finger in cadence how effective it would be with his audiences. I saw that he was going to have a lot of fun with that one. And he did.

The phrase was used several times in New York and Boston. The audience howled with laughter the first time he used it at Madison Square Garden. After the second time, they began to expect it and listen for it. The people in the Boston audiences had heard it on the radio, so they repeated the phrase in time with him and yelled "Barton and Fish" as soon as he said "Martin."

Barton was then a candidate for United States Senator from New York. I have been told that he has said that one of the things that ensured his defeat was the President's effective use of that phrase. It took hold so strongly that Willkie is reported to have said later that it fastened around his own neck the isolationist, reactionary votes of all three.

The President then listed the things he had done—and not done—since 1933 to keep us out of war. His course was what he called an "affirmative, realistic fight for peace."

Though he was attacking Republican leaders he wanted to make sure —as always—that he would not alienate any Republican votes which might come his way:

"Remember, I am making those charges against the responsible political leadership of the Republican party. But there are millions—millions and millions—of patriotic Republicans who have at all times been in sympathy with the efforts of this Administration to arm the nation adequately for purposes of defense."

The political wisdom of this course was highlighted by the number of enthusiastic telegrams from people who said specifically they were Republicans that poured into the White House during October, 1940.

The day after this speech the President took part in a ceremony that any old-time politician would have said could never take place in the midst of a political campaign in peacetime—the drawing for the selection of draftees. It was just a week before election.

It had been suggested to the President, who had the discretion to fix the date of the drawing, that he set it after Election Day. He refused.

A speech had to be written for the occasion, and he asked Bob and me to submit drafts of what we thought he ought to say. He also asked MacLeish for a draft. He took very little from any of them, but prepared a statement himself. He had sought and obtained letters from spiritual leaders of the three principal religions in the United States— Protestant, Catholic, and Jewish. The speech was based in part on these.

In the statement he did not once use the word "draft" or "conscription." At the ceremony there were no drums beating or banners flying or men parading, as there would have been in any of the dictator countries. The atmosphere was that of a mustering of the human resources of the nation in a righteous cause. The President liked the word "muster" for this occasion, as it was used in the colonial and revolutionary days of this Republic.

You who will enter this peacetime army will be the inheritors of a proud history and an honorable tradition.

You will be members of an army which first came together to achieve independence and to establish certain fundamental rights for all men. Ever since that first muster, our democratic army has existed for one purpose only: the defense of our freedom. . . .

The next campaign speech was in Boston, October 30. Sherwood and I had worked on it in Washington, and we went on the campaign train to Boston to put on the finishing touches. Unfortunately, we could not get much time with the President because he had to make rear-platform speeches at New Haven, Meriden, and Hartford in Connecticut, and at Worcester in Massachusetts.

In the Boston speech he continued to answer "falsifications":

And while I am talking to you mothers and fathers, I give you one more assurance.

I have said this before, but I shall say it again and again and again:
Your boys are not going to be sent into any foreign wars. . . .

Every time the President had made this statement before Boston—and every time thereafter—he added to it the words he himself had so carefully added to the foreign policy plank: "except in case of attack." I suggested he add the same words this time but he suddenly got stubborn about it—I could not understand why.

"It's not necessary," he said. "It's implied clearly. If we're attacked it's no longer a foreign war."

That stubbornness was to cause him a lot of headaches later, because the Boston version was the one constantly thrown up to him. Whenever his opponents wanted to quote the phrase, they always quoted from the Boston speech rather than any other, since that was the only speech in which he omitted the limiting proviso.

The promise in the Boston speech—without the proviso—was over-simplified, but even that promise was kept. Certainly no one can say that the Japanese war was a "foreign" war after Pearl Harbor, or that the European war was a "foreign" war after Germany declared war upon us. The speech certainly made it clear, as had the acceptance speech and others, that if Roosevelt were re-elected there would be no letdown in our efforts short of war to help Britain defeat Hitler.

The American people knew the dangers of that policy, and with that knowledge they still elected Roosevelt.

Supplementing his Madison Square Garden speech of ten days before, he answered in further detail the charge that "we are not doing enough for national defense." Here he used a device that made his answer more dramatic to many millions of people. He referred to war plants in specific cities by name. In this way, he said to us, he could appeal to local pride and make his refutation more vivid.

You citizens of Seattle who are listening tonight—you have watched the Boeing plant out there grow. It is now producing four times as many planes each month as it was producing a year ago.

You citizens of Southern California can see the great Douglas factories. They have doubled their output in less than a year. . . .

But planes won't fly without engines. You citizens of Hartford, who hear my words: look across the Connecticut River at the whirring wheels and the beehive of activity which is the Pratt and Whitney plant which I saw today. A year ago that plant was producing airplane engines totaling one hundred thousand horsepower a month. Today that production has been stepped up tenfold, stepped up to one million horsepower a month. . . .

He also had to answer the charge the Republicans were making that the boys being drafted were not going to be housed and fed properly. For many days our political leaders throughout the country had been begging the President for a word of reassurance addressed specifically to the mothers of the nation. Edward J. Flynn, successor to Farley as the National Chairman, had been particularly insistent. The President did not want to do it. It seemed like getting down to the level of those who were playing upon maternal fears.

On the trip to Boston we again heard from Flynn; he sent us a telegram containing another urgent request for a special word to mothers. The President finally gave in, and Bob and I drafted a short paragraph. Then we sent Flynn a telegram: "Listen in tonight. 'Mother' is finally in. Congratulations!"

This is what the President said:

I cannot help but feel that the most inexcusable, most unpatriotic misstatement of fact about our Army—a misstatement calculated to worry the mothers of the nation—is the brazen charge that the men called to training will not be properly housed.

The plain fact is that construction on Army housing is far ahead of schedule to meet all needs, and that by January fifth, next, there will be complete and adequate housing in this nation for nine hundred and thirty thousand soldiers.

And so I feel that, very simply and very honestly, I can give assurance to the mothers and fathers of America that each and every one of their boys in training will be well housed and well fed.

Being in Massachusetts, the President paid special attention to Congressman Martin, the Republican leader in the House and later Speaker of the Eightieth Congress. He was a particularly conspicuous target, because Willkie had appointed him the Republican National Chairman and had publicly said, "For many years Joe Martin has represented all that is finest in American public life."

I am sure that Willkie—in view of Martin's completely reactionary and isolationist record—simply could not have believed that. It is an example of the kind of "campaign oratory" a candidate frequently uses in order to appeal to diverse elements in his party. A complete check had been made of Martin's public voting record. We wanted to disclose what Willkie thought was the "finest in American public life."

The President first quoted this statement by Willkie but without mentioning Willkie by name. It was the nearest that Roosevelt came to referring directly to his opponent in this campaign. Then he detailed Martin's almost unbelievable record of votes against every liberal measure of the last eight years. It led naturally into the repeated use of "Martin, Barton and Fish."

We always tried to put into a speech some late piece of news—war news or foreign news or news of production—that the President could himself announce. It added interest; it insured additional news coverage; it emphasized the President's position of leadership. Getting such a news story at just the right time, however, was not easy. Some of the best stories the President had were confidential. Frequently the British would break a story before we could, or our own War Department or Navy Department would release a good story before the White House heard of it.

We succeeded in getting a piece of news for the Boston speech— but the question immediately arose whether it could be told that night, since it was the story of a new order for war supplies placed in the United States by Britain. We had it typed on a separate piece of paper as a proposed insert, and not until the speech was almost completed was it finally cleared in Washington for release. The President prefaced the story by saying, "Tonight I am privileged to make an announcement using Boston instead of the White House."

The speeches were coming fast. The next campaign speech was to be in Brooklyn only two days later. In the meantime, the next day, October 31, the President was to dedicate the National Institute of Health at Bethesda, Maryland. Fortunately the Navy Department had prepared a draft for this occasion, and while the President was correcting it Sherwood and I went to work on the Brooklyn speech.

By this time John L. Lewis—whom many people considered a reckless labor leader because of his ruthless exercise of power to stop war production of coal—had come out for Willkie. At the same time, the Communists were also supporting him, even though Willkie did repudiate their support. During this period of the Hitler-Stalin pact, it was the Communist party line to support Willkie against Roosevelt because Roosevelt was so openly anti-Hitler and pro-British.

With this peculiar line-up in mind, the President had dictated a draft of thirteen pages. Where he ever found the time I do not know. He did not get around to the peroration, but he did dictate some suggestions even for that which I have before me. They are typical of the kind of suggestions Roosevelt would give us.

SUGGESTIONS FOR THE PERORATION

How can government of that kind function?

What will happen to nation if extreme right and extreme left join hands in matrimony?

Back of it all fear of those who obstruct and promise the earth and, at the same time, have only a record which shows their disbelief in democracy. These are first steps to dictatorship.

Unknown factor versus known factor.

F. D. R. could not be dictator, etc.

Sherwood and I went to work on this first draft. The President, who for years had been called by political enemies a Communist or a tool of the Communists, was now able to turn the tables on his Republican adversary, and attack the alliance of the Communists, the dictatorial labor leader Lewis, and the old-guard reactionary Republican leaders. This opportunity was unique in his political experience, and he cheerfully took full advantage of it.

There is something very ominous in this combination that has been forming within the Republican party between the extreme reactionary and the extreme radical elements of this country.

There is no common ground upon which they can unite—we know that— unless it be their common will to power, and their impatience with the normal democratic processes to produce overnight the inconsistent dictatorial ends that they, each of them, seek. . . .

In another example of vivid imagery, the President summed up this "unholy alliance" as follows:

We all know the story of the unfortunate chameleon which turned brown when placed on a brown rug, and turned red when placed on a red rug, but who died a tragic death when they put him on a Scotch plaid. We all know what would happen to Government if it tried to fulfill all the secret understandings and promises made between the conflicting groups which are now backing the Republican party.

In this speech Roosevelt had another glorious chance to turn the tables on his opponents—those who, ever since 1933, had been saying that he was inciting class against class.

One of the leading lawyers of the Philadelphia bar—a Republican campaign orator—had just made a speech in which he was quoted as having said: "The President's only supporters are paupers, those who earn less than $1,200 a year and aren't worth *that*, and the Roosevelt family."

Probably no one would have ever paid attention to that speech except for one unexpected circumstance. The sentence was quoted by Arthur Krock in his daily column in *The New York Times*, who pointed to it as one of the political blunders being made by Pennsylvania Republicans. That immediately gave the remark widespread publicity.

Sherwood and I were so busy that we had not even read Krock's column; but it was sent to us by one of Hopkins' economist assistants, Richard V. Gilbert. We discussed it with the President, who immediately saw the possibilities and was delighted to grab the opening.

After quoting the sentence, he said:

I think we might just as well forget the Roosevelt family, but these Americans whom this man calls "paupers," these Americans who, in his view, are not worth the income they receive, small though it is—who are they? They are only millions and millions of American families, constituting a very large part of the nation! They are only the common men and women who have helped build this country, who have made it great, and who would defend it with their lives if the need arose.

The demand for social and economic justice comes from those who receive less than $1,200 a year, but not from them alone. For I believe that when Americans cross this dividing line of $100 a month, they do not lose their devotion to social and economic justice. . . .

"Paupers" who are not worth their salt—there speaks the true sentiment of the Republican leadership in this year of grace.

The Republican leaders felt that this attack hurt. The alleged author of the statement denied that he had made it. Republican resentment against Krock for this piece of reporting caused the President much glee—for the President thoroughly disliked Krock.

After the Brooklyn speech, we all returned to the campaign train in Grand Central Station. It was about midnight, and as the President started for bed he asked:

"Have you boys got anything for Cleveland tomorrow night?" Cleveland was to be the last major speech of the campaign and was therefore considered very important. It was supposed to sum up all the issues. We looked at each other in embarrassment, and finally broke the bad news to him. We did not have a single word on paper—and the deadline was only seventeen hours ahead. But we hastened to promise that when he was ready for breakfast he would at least have a rough draft on which he could work.

That seemed to satisfy him, for with a cheery, "Well, don't stay up too late," he was off.

We were thankful that there was not the usual post-mortem discussion about the Brooklyn speech before he retired; we needed all the time we could get for the next one. Gathering in my compartment, Harry, Bob and I started to look through the material in the speech file. Most of it, of course, had already been used.

We had, however, some fine material submitted by Dorothy Thompson, Dean Acheson, and Archie MacLeish. Miss Thompson had been talking to Bob about certain ideas she had; Bob had asked her to send them in in writing; and she had submitted a draft of a complete speech, many parts of which we used. I had asked the other two to submit something we might use, for we were very much pressed for time. Their material proved to be most helpful, just when it was most needed.

We wanted to make this speech a summation of the President's position on the domestic and foreign issues, but we wanted to avoid repeating what he had already said in the campaign. By the time we had agreed on the general contents of the speech, Harry could not stay awake any longer and had to go to bed.

After he had gone to bed Bob and I fortified ourselves with many cups of coffee, and divided between us the speech material and the topics which we had agreed to include. Each of us in our separate compartments prepared a draft of our own subjects; then we met, reviewed,

and criticized what the other had written. There was some joint rewriting, and then some writing to make the different parts of the speech
flow together. Shears and paste were used plentifully and we were able
to get out a second draft in presentable shape by six o'clock in the
morning. A great deal of it was based on the draft Dorothy Thompson
had submitted.

We sent it into the President's car to be given to him with his breakfast, tumbled into bed, got a few hours of sleep, and were on hand to
greet him at about nine-thirty.

We all three were tired, but the President felt and looked completely
worn out. During the day, short as our time was, he had to make a
number of rear-platform talks as the train went through New York,
Pennsylvania and Ohio. In addition he left the train and visited two war
plants in Buffalo and made short talks there. After each of these speeches
there had to be handshaking and greeting, all of which took time and
effort and nervous energy.

The only chances he had to work on the evening's speech were in
between these various interruptions. Nevertheless, as the day went along
he seemed to gain more and more vigor. He enjoyed especially the inspection of the airplane plants, and he was looking forward to the end
of the campaign now drawing to a close. Although he was unable to
spend as much time as usual on this speech, the work that he did was
intensive and it was thorough. The deadline was made.

I have before me the draft on which he worked, with the longhand
changes he made in it. His handwriting was always hard to read at best;
and as he scrawled his corrections on the moving train, they could be
made out only by one with long experience with him, like Missy or
Grace.

The crowd at Cleveland was an enthusiastic one, and the President
was in his best oratorical form.

I heard Roosevelt make speeches for seventeen years—from 1928 to
1945. People have often asked me to name the speech I think his best.
This was it. As a political campaign speech it ranks second only to the
Teamsters' Union speech of 1944 (the "Fala" speech). Including all
the speeches, however—the nonpolitical as well as the political speeches
—this was his best. Although it was a campaign speech, it was pitched on
a level far above political battle. It expressed the President's hopes,
philosophy and aspirations; it laid out a blueprint for the America
of the future as he would wish it. As an example of what the President

could do in preparing a speech under great pressure of time and circumstance it was unequaled.

His delivery in this speech was better than in any other speech I have ever heard him make. It is difficult to analyze the oratory of a speaker to see what it is that makes his delivery of speeches effective and moving. Over the years I watched Roosevelt with ever-growing wonderment and admiration as he made speeches of all kinds with exactly the right effect. There were the homey fireside chats, the stirring campaign speeches of attack, the argumentative and persuasive addresses to the Congress, the extemporaneous informal remarks on the rear platform of a train, at a Thanksgiving dinner in Warm Springs, to a group of newspaper editors calling on him at the White House. Each speech seemed perfectly attuned to the audience and to the occasion.

Never was there the blustering or the posturing of Hitler or Mussolini. To make his points, he needed no gesticulations or shrieking or fist clenching. He substituted a glowing personality which got across the footlights or the ether waves with equal facility. A toss of the head, a tilt of the chin, a flash of the eye or a broad grin would drive home his point. He seldom appealed to the passions of his audience, nor did he ever seem to want to play on their emotions. He sought rather to appeal to their understanding; he sought to win their approval. He did not talk down to his audience; he tried to talk directly with them. And his voice, his tone, his countenance carried conviction.

One great advantage he had whenever he delivered a major speech—he knew it thoroughly from beginning to end. He had worked so hard and continuously on it that he knew it almost by heart. He knew the development of the theme, he knew always what was coming next, and the result was that his delivery progressed in solid logical fashion from one point to another, making it easy to follow and understand him. He could look away from the manuscript so much that many people did not even know he was reading.

And of course the attractiveness of his voice, its fine shadings and nuances, the infinite variety he knew how to give it—strength, sarcasm, humor, volume, charm, persuasiveness—all these would hold his listeners even when the content was dull. He read his lines like a finished actor, and they sounded the same when he delivered them to the public as they did when he read them later in private for the newsreels. He knew the proper emphasis for each phrase, the split-second timing required, the exact inflection called for. When his voice came over the radio it was as though he were right in the living room of his listeners discussing their personal problems with them—the cattle or crops of the farmer, the red ink of the shopkeeper, the loans of the banker, the wages and hours of each worker. He had a combination of familiar charm and deep dignity, of camaraderie and majesty, which enabled him to read a budget report aloud and almost make it seem interesting and alive.

The Cleveland speech began with one of Roosevelt's favorite themes: the vigor of democracy as a way of life—the best way of life. "The surge of events abroad has made some few doubters among us ask: Is this the end of a story that has been told? Is the book of democracy now to be closed and placed away upon the dusty shelves of time?" Then he continued:

My answer is this: All we have known of the glories of democracy—its freedom, its efficiency as a mode of living, its ability to meet the aspirations of the common man—all these are merely an introduction to the greater story of a more glorious future.

We Americans of today—all of us—we are characters in this living book of democracy.

But we are also its author. It falls upon us now to say whether the chapters that are to come will tell a story of retreat or a story of continued advance.

I believe that the American people will say: "Forward!"

He then turned to those who were attacking his foreign policy. Here is an example of the way the President could bring into sharp focus and emphasize points suggested to him. We had written: "We do *not* know what would be the foreign policy of those who are doubters about our democracy." He changed it to read:

"We *do* know what would be the foreign policy of those who are doubters about our democracy.

"We do *not* know what would be the foreign policy of those who are obviously trying to sit on both sides of the fence at the same time. . . ."

He then restated his foreign policy: first, to keep out of war and to keep foreign conceptions of government out of the United States; second, to keep war as far away as possible from the shores of the Western Hemisphere; third, to give all possible material aid to the nations which still resist aggression.

Then, turning to the domestic scene, he showed how the New Deal, "the creation of you, the American people," met the obligations of government in 1933, provided opportunity, and saved the American system of free enterprise. In this way, one by one, he covered all the major domestic accomplishments of his administration.

Now we are asked to stop in our tracks. We are asked to turn about, to march back into the wilderness from which we came.

Of course we will not turn backward. . . .

Neither will we be bribed by extravagant promises of fabulous wealth.

Those who offer such promises try to delude us with a mirage on the far horizon—a mirage of an island of dreams, with palaces and palms and plums.

And it is a curious fact of nature that a mirage is always upside down, above the horizon.

But then, the mirage—upside down or right-side up—isn't always there at all.

Now you see it—and now you don't.

The last three paragraphs were inserted by the President—and delivered by him—as a clincher.

Reminiscent of the last speech of the 1936 campaign—in which the repeated catch line was "For this too we have only just begun to fight" —was a new catch line for this last speech of the 1940 campaign. It occurred after each statement of continued New Deal policy, such as:

"Of course we intend to preserve and build up the land of this country . . .

"Of course we intend to continue to build up the bodies and the minds of the men, women and children of the nation . . ."

The catch line was:

"For there lies the road to democracy that is strong."

The President delivered this line as he had in 1936, with great force and deliberateness—and with great effect. Each time it was repeated it drew even greater applause than the more bellicose line of 1936.

With a number of paragraphs beginning "I see an America" the President painted his picture of the America of the future. This was the most moving passage of the speech, and among the most eloquent paragraphs in all Roosevelt's speeches. It was the synthesis of all his hopes for his country; it was the kind of future to which he said it was "the destiny of this American generation to point the road":

I see an America where factory workers are not discarded after they reach their prime, where there is no endless chain of poverty from generation to generation, where impoverished farmers and farm hands do not become homeless wanderers, where monopoly does not make youth a beggar for a job.

I see an America whose rivers and valleys and lakes—hills and streams and plains—the mountains over our land and nature's wealth deep under the earth—are protected as the rightful heritage of all the people.

I see an America where small business really has a chance to flourish and grow.

I see an America of great cultural and educational opportunity for all its people.

I see an America where the income from the land shall be implemented and protected by a Government determined to guarantee to those who hoe it a fair share in the national income.

An America where the wheels of trade and private industry continue to turn to make the goods for America. Where no businessman can be stifled by the harsh hand of monopoly, and where the legitimate profits of legitimate business are the fair reward of every businessman—big and little—in all the nation.

I see an America with peace in the ranks of labor.

An America where the workers are really free and—through their great unions undominated by any outside force, or by any dictator within—can take their proper place at the council table with the owners and managers of business. Where the dignity and security of the working man and woman are guaranteed by their own strength and fortified by the safeguards of law.

An America where those who have reached the evening of life shall live out their years in peace and security. Where pensions and insurance for these aged shall be given as a matter of right to those who through a long life of labor have served their families and their nation as well.

I see an America devoted to our freedom—unified by tolerance and by religious faith—a people consecrated to peace, a people confident in strength because their body and their spirit are secure and unafraid.

Finally, becoming personal, he expressed his pride in the fact that he had had the privilege of being the President "during these years while our democracy advanced on many fields of battle."

There is a great storm raging now, a storm that makes things harder for the world. And that storm . . . is the true reason that I would like to stick by these people of ours until we reach the clear, sure footing ahead. We will make it—we will make it before the next term is over. . . . When that term is over there will be another President and many more Presidents in the years to come, and I think that, in the years to come, that word "President" will be a word to cheer the hearts of common men and women everywhere.

By this time the audience was hanging on every word. When he spoke about "another President" there were shouts of "No! No!" I was worried that the radio audience might get the impression that a fourth-term demonstration was being started. The President told us later that he was worried too—but he was seldom at a loss about what to do in such an emergency. He raised his voice, got closer to the microphone, kept on talking, and finally drowned out the growing shouts from the audience.

I had considerable amusement watching Sherwood, who sat next to me on the platform. We were both enjoying this speech because our work for the campaign was practically over, and we were feeling quite relaxed. Sherwood, who knew the speech pretty well by now, was mouthing every word in unison with the President, completely oblivious of my stare. I leaned over and shouted into his ear, when the peroration had been delivered and the applause was at its height, that he ought to stand up and take a bow too because he had just delivered the speech himself, albeit inaudibly.

After it was over, we all gathered in the sitting compartment of the President's railroad car on the way back to Washington. Some of his other supporters had been in Cleveland, and they joined us. One of them was George Allen, who has been painted as a sort of White House jester but who is one of the shrewdest and keenest political thinkers I have met. He was telling some of his favorite stories. Suddenly, he turned to the President and said, "Mr. President, do you remember what you said tonight, 'When that term is over there will be another president'? Well," said he, laughing, "that's going to cost us a million votes in 1944."

In 1940, it seemed so ridiculous that anyone should think that the President would be running for a fourth term that we all burst out laughing. As shrewd as Allen was, I am sure he had not the faintest idea that Roosevelt would be the candidate again.

The President was relieved that his last major appearance in the ordeal of an American Presidential campaign was behind him. However, there still remained the usual nonpolitical speech that he delivered from his home on election eve. Bob and Harry and I worked on this speech with him, finishing it in Washington before he left for Hyde Park.

When the President delivered the talk from his library the night before election day, his words and his voice seemed to bring him right into the homes of his listeners. I am sure that, though there was not a single political argument in the speech or a single request for votes, it won him thousands and thousands of votes simply by establishing a close personal rapport with his audience. That was the purpose of this quadrennial election-eve talk; it was the effect he wanted—and the effect he usually got:

As I sit here tonight with my own family, I think of all the other American families—millions of families all through the land—sitting in their own homes. They have eaten their supper in peace, they will be able to sleep in their homes tonight in peace. Tomorrow they will be free to go out to live their ordinary lives in peace—free to say and do what they wish, free to worship as they please. Tomorrow, of all days, they will be free to choose their own leaders who, when that choice has been made, become in turn only the instruments to carry out the will of all the people.

And I cannot help but think of the families in other lands—millions of families—living in homes like ours. On some of these homes, bombs of destruction may be dropping even as I speak to you.

Across the seas life has gone underground. I think I speak the minds of all of you when I say that we thank God that we live in the sunlight and in the starlight of peace, that we are not in war and that we propose and expect to continue to live our lives in peace—under the peaceful light of Heaven. . . .

We vote as free men, impelled only by the urgings of our own wisdom and our own conscience.

In our polling places are no storm troopers or secret police to look over our shoulders as we mark our ballots.

Then followed a plea that everybody should go out and vote:

"Last Saturday night, I said that freedom of speech is of no use to the man who has nothing to say and that freedom of worship is of no use to the man who has lost his God. And tonight I should like to add that a free election is of no use to the man who is too indifferent to vote. . . ."

The next evening there was the usual election-night party of friends and neighbors at the President's home in Hyde Park, similar to the one in 1936. We listened to the returns for a while in the small family dining room with the President. There was the same general confusion and excitement. After a while Bob and I went upstairs to Hopkins' room and listened on a small radio. By midnight it was quite clear that Roosevelt had won. The usual torchlight parade came in; there was the usual homey talk by the President out on the front porch. The Sherwoods and the Rosenmans drove down to New York, listening to the late returns on the radio in the car. As the landslide for Roosevelt became certain, I said to Bob: "It looks as if you and I have four busy years ahead of us." That turned out to be an understatement.

He received 27,243,000 and Willkie received 22,304,000 votes. Roosevelt's electoral vote was 449 from 38 states and Willkie's was 82 from 10 states.

As the President pointed out in his press conference following the election, he had not thought he was going to do as well as this on his third try; his estimate was only 340 electoral votes.

Roosevelt was at one of the highest peaks of his career that night. He had won in spite of the ancient third-term tradition; he had won in spite of all the public irritations that had inevitably accumulated in eight years of officeholding; he had won in spite of the overwhelming majority of the press, in spite of vast campaign funds against him, in spite of the pent-up hatred of conservatives and isolationists, and in spite of the opposition of the richest and most powerful industrialists and financiers.

He had won because the American people, in the terribly dangerous days which they all knew lay ahead, were willing to rely on him for leadership. He was now the moral leader of that entire part of the world which hated Hitler and his works, and which yearned for peace, democratic government, and decent standards of living.

Chapter XV

Lend-Lease: Arsenal of Democracy, 1940-1941

The lend-lease program was one of the most brilliantly conceived and important contributions President Roosevelt made to ultimate victory. By late 1940, as the British needs for American material became ever more urgent, Britain's dollar and gold supply had become seriously depleted. It was apparent that her dollar resources could not last much beyond January, 1941. The President was well aware of this perilous economic fact and what it meant to the safety of the world.

Several weeks after his re-election, Roosevelt left on a cruise on the *Tuscaloosa*. In the course of this cruise, he had an opportunity to consider various expedients to continue the flow of American war materials to Britain.

He concluded that, without a long and dangerously bitter political fight, neither the Congress nor American public opinion would support an outright repeal of the provisions of the neutrality act. He felt that even if legislation could be enacted that would permit direct loans to Britain, it would be only a temporary stopgap and would raise the same diplomatic frictions which accompanied war-debt-settlement discussions following the First World War. Outright gifts of munitions and war matériel would be politically difficult if not impossible.

During his cruise, the President received a remarkable 4,000-word letter from Prime Minister Churchill, reviewing in some detail the British military position and financial situation. Churchill expressed faith that the people of the United States would not "confine the help which they have so generously promised only to such munitions of war and commodities as could be immediately paid for." It was not, Churchill said, "an appeal for aid, but a statement of the minimum action necessary to achieve our common purpose" of defeating Nazi and Fascist tyranny. But the letter—which Churchill has called one of the most important he ever wrote—offered no solution to the problem of how to alleviate Britain's financial squeeze.

Nevertheless, it was an important stimulus to the President's thinking during the quiet weeks he spent on the *Tuscaloosa*.

Toward the end of his cruise, the President one evening disclosed to Harry the answer he had arrived at—bold, ingenious, imaginative. It was his own device. What remained was to reduce the concept to legislative terms, and, much more important, to explain it to the country with simplicity and in a way that would capture its imagination—and obtain its approval. The former was accomplished with the aid of resourceful lawyers like Ben Cohen, Edward H. Foley, Herman Oliphant and Oscar Cox; the latter could only be done, and was done, by Roosevelt himself.

I remember talking with Lord Keynes in London in March, 1945, four years after the Lend-Lease Act was passed. We were discussing Britain's continued plight; and Lord Keynes said to me: "The only possible solution for Britain's problems today would be another brain wave by your President Roosevelt—like lend-lease." That is as good a word as I can find to describe the process by which Roosevelt hit on this conception: "brain wave." It was a solution that squared with every campaign pledge he had made—a solution which looked as though it might succeed in doing the job.

He first publicly mentioned the subject at his press conference on December 17, where he emphasized the argument that the more of our supplies Great Britain took, the more our productive capacity would be increased and the stronger our national defense would become. These war materials, he pointed out, would be more useful to the defense of the United States "if they were used in Great Britain, than if they were kept in storage here." The President again used his talent for homely simile to explain intricate and complicated theories. It was perhaps the most famous example:

"What I am trying to do is to eliminate the dollar sign," he said, and continued extemporaneously, "Suppose my neighbor's home catches fire, and I have a length of garden hose four or five hundred feet away. If he can take my garden hose and connect it up with his hydrant, I may help him to put out his fire. Now, what do I do? I don't say to him before that operation, 'Neighbor, my garden hose cost me $15; you have to pay me $15 for it.' What is the transaction that goes on?

I don't want $15—I want my garden hose back after the fire is over."

After the fire is put out, the President went on, he gets his garden hose back, and if it is damaged beyond repair in putting out the fire, "he [my neighbor] says, 'All right, I will replace it.'

"Now, if I get a nice garden hose back, I am in pretty good shape."

That simple concept of lending a garden hose to a neighbor to put out a fire—which, incidentally, might well spread to your own home—and later getting the garden hose back, or a duplicate, was lend-lease in its simplest terms. As complicated and as grandiose a scheme as lend-lease turned out to be, it could not have been more simply or effectively placed before the American people.

Were the American people ready for this step? Would they approve? The President felt sure that they would, but only if they were told all the facts showing how serious the danger was to the United States—how disastrous it would be for us if Britain were to fall.

That was his next task. First, at his press conference three days later, he announced the formation of the Office of Production Management for the purpose of speeding up war production.

Then, on December 29, he delivered a fireside chat—generally known as "the arsenal of democracy" speech.

Missy phoned me, and asked me to get Sherwood to come down with me the day after Christmas to help on this speech. Hopkins joined us and the three of us went to work. We all lived at the White House; it was during the Christmas holiday when a good part of official Washington was out of the city, and we were able to get long periods with the President.

We submitted an early draft to William Knudsen, then one of the directors of the Office of Production Management, for suggestions. I am printing his longhand note to the President returning the draft. It is typical of the kind of criticisms we looked for and would often get, and it also contains some fine phrases which we lifted out bodily and put into the next draft:

December 28, 1940

Pages #14 to #25 are just right and factual. Pages 1-2 a great introduction. For pages 2-14 stress should be placed on the fact that the honor of the soldier has been cast to the winds and the war of today has been transferred to the civilian and noncombatant population who are being driven into holes in the ground in order to glorify a so-called holy conquest. In all other wars men have fought and died for the protection of their women and children—in this war it is "kill women and children first." With all the vaunted efficiency in this war there is still the concentration camp in the background and the servants of God in chains. We do not have this in America and with God's help we are not going to have it. The activities of the Nazis in United States I would minimize or rather not acknowledge. The appeasers I would refer to Denmark, Norway, Belgium, France and England before she woke up. There can be no appeasement with ruthlessness. There can be no reasoning with an incendiary bomb. This is not a contest between the money dollar and the work dollar. This is a contest between earned and requisitioned dollars—between craft and whip. Then all help to Britain.

Sincerely and respectfully,

KNUDSEN

The President wanted to explain the crisis in as simple terms as he had the banking crisis in 1933, and the speech started by referring back to that fireside chat:

"I tried to convey to the great mass of American people what the banking crisis meant to them in their daily lives.

"Tonight, I want to do the same thing, with the same people, in this new crisis which faces America."

He explained the danger, which, he said, would never pass until "there is a clear intention on the part of the aggressor nations to abandon all thought of dominating or conquering the world." (That seems written for the present also.)

The President went on to explain what it would mean if Great Britain were to go down:

"If Great Britain goes down, the Axis powers will control the continents of Europe, Asia, Africa, Australasia, and the high seas—and they will be in a position to bring enormous military and naval resources against this hemisphere. It is no exaggeration to say that all of us, in all the Americas, would be living at the point of a gun—a gun loaded with explosive bullets, economic as well as military."

It is difficult to put ourselves back in the atmosphere of 1940 when so many people really believed—and did not hesitate to say so—that we were fully protected by the Atlantic and Pacific oceans; that with our natural resources, we could get along very well by ourselves even if all Europe fell; and that with our great strength Hitler and the Japanese would never dare attack us. Those who are now too young to have lived in maturity through those days will find it hard to realize how startling some of Roosevelt's statements sounded to a great many American people in 1940.

The American people now accept as almost axiomatic that they have a great stake in what happens even in far off Korea—so great that they are willing to send American boys there to protect that stake. We now realize that what happens way over there must intimately affect us over here; realize it well enough to take action about it—action that we hate to take.

But that kind of understanding did not exist back in 1940. Roosevelt's course was bold leadership then; but necessary leadership to awaken the American people to the danger abroad and to prepare them to meet it, even though it was still three thousand miles away.

No one could equal the President in making geography clear, and in this speech he showed how the Nazis could step from base to base right up to our borders. He always dictated such passages himself, and we used to marvel that he was usually able to do it without even looking at a map. Sometimes, after he had finished, he would pull down several of the roller maps in back of his desk and check on his dictation. I do not remember that he ever had to make any serious corrections.

Concerning those who preached appeasement of Hitler, he used a very striking paragraph, which came from Knudsen's suggestions:

"The experience of the past two years has proven beyond doubt that no nation can appease the Nazis. No man can tame a tiger into a kitten by stroking it. There can be no appeasement with ruthlessness. There can be no reasoning with an incendiary bomb. We know now that a nation can have peace with the Nazis only at the price of total surrender."

The President then came to his main point:

Thinking in terms of today and tomorrow . . . there is far less chance of the United States getting into war, if we do all we can now to support the nations defending themselves against attack by the Axis than if we acquiesce in their defeat, submit tamely to an Axis victory, and wait our turn to be the object of attack in another war later on. . . .

We must be the great arsenal of democracy. . . . No dictator, no combination of dictators, will weaken that determination by threats of how they will construe that determination.

The phrase "arsenal of democracy," which appeared for the first time in this speech, was coined by Jean Monnet, a representative of France then in Washington. In late 1940, he used it in conversation with

Justice Frankfurter, describing the most effective assistance the United States could provide in the world struggle against tyranny.

Frankfurter was struck by the phrase and told Monnet it was exactly right but that it ought to be given world currency by the person who could do it best—Roosevelt. He urged his friend not to use the phrase again lest someone else pick it up and repeat it in a speech—which would prevent the President from using it. The phrase was also mentioned to John J. McCloy, who was then an Assistant Secretary of War; and it was finally submitted to the President in a draft prepared in the War Department, which was sent over to me by General Edward S. Greenbaum, the Executive Officer of Under Secretary Patterson. As soon as the President saw it, he "loved" it. ("I *love* it" was a common phrase of Roosevelt's.)

In this speech, for the first time, Roosevelt presented a long-range plan of action for the United States. Up to now the help had been piecemeal, on an emergency, *ad hoc* basis. But he was now no longer a President whose term was about to expire, as he was when France fell in June, 1940. He had just been elected for four more years, and he was now in a position to lay long-term plans. I could not help but notice the difference that that fact made in the attitude and spirit with which he handled the job of helping the Allies. He even dared in this speech to express, for the first time, a faint hope of ultimate victory.

"I believe that the Axis powers are not going to win this war. I base that belief on the latest and best information."

That was a rash statement for December, 1940; and he made it only after careful consideration and after one of us had suggested that a little note of optimism, if at all possible, would be a great help.

The sixth draft of this speech had been sent over to the State Department for criticism, and was sent back with corrections and suggestions written in red pencil. I have that document before me, and I note that many of the corrections were adopted by the President. Sometimes the President compromised with the suggestions. For example, the draft had this sentence in it:

"The war needs of Britain and other free nations resisting aggression must be treated as an *integral part* of our own defense needs." The red pencil had struck out the phrase "integral part" which was the core, the "guts" of the idea; the sentence as corrected read:

"We are planning our own defense with the utmost urgency and in its vast scale *we must take care of* the war needs of Britain and other free nations resisting aggression."

The speech as delivered used the additional thought suggested by the State Department, but retained the central idea of integrated production by the two nations:

"We are planning our own defense with the utmost urgency; and in its vast scale we must *integrate* the war needs of Britain and the other free nations which are resisting aggression."

Another correction by the State Department irritated him. One sentence in the draft sent over to the Department read:

"There are also American citizens, many of them in high places, who unwittingly in most cases are aiding and abetting the work of these [Nazi] agents." He was referring to the extreme isolationist leaders in Congress and the America Firsters. But there were some people in the Department who were not in favor of his blunt language.

The draft came back with the words "many of them in high places" stricken out in red pencil. The President snorted and said forcefully: "Leave it in—in fact I'm very much tempted to say 'many of them in high places—*including* the State Department.'" We left it in, but not with the addition he suggested.

In his next speech, the annual message to the Congress of January 6, 1941 which he delivered in person, the President presented his lend-lease plan formally.

A very good draft of a proposed message had come over to the White House from the State Department. It had been prepared by Berle, who was most helpful on speeches during this period. He had a vast knowledge of both foreign and domestic affairs, and could write clearly and succinctly. It was always profitable to talk with him about a speech during its preparation. Ben Cohen, too, helped us a great deal on this speech. But the President had himself dictated five pages, and worked on it very hard through the various drafts—it went through seven—filling each of them with his handwritten corrections and insertions.

The passage for which the message is best known is that in which the President spoke about the four freedoms. Those paragraphs appeared for the first time in the fourth draft of the speech. We were sitting in the President's study one night grouped around his desk as usual—Harry, Bob and I. The President held the original of the third draft in his hand. Each of us had a carbon copy of the draft, and a yellow pad on his lap on which to make notes. Dorothy Brady was taking dictation this night; but by the time a speech had reached this stage there was not much dictation to take, usually only those inserts by the President which were too long for him to write out in longhand.

The President announced as he came near the end of the draft that he had an idea for a peroration. We waited as he leaned far back in his swivel chair with his gaze on the ceiling. It was a long pause—so long that it began to become uncomfortable.

Then he leaned forward again in his chair and said: "Dorothy, take a law."

And he dictated the following:

We must look forward to a world based on four essential human freedoms.

The first is freedom of speech and expression—everywhere in the world.

The second is freedom of every person to worship God in his own way—everywhere in the world.

The third is freedom from want—which, translated into world terms, means economic understandings which will secure to every nation everywhere a healthy peacetime life for its inhabitants.

The fourth is freedom from fear—which, translated into international terms, means a world-wide reduction of armaments to such a point and in such a thorough fashion that no nation anywhere will be in a position to commit an act of physical aggression against any neighbor.

Although he had mentioned these freedoms in a press conference on July 5, 1940, as an offhand answer to a question about his long-range peace objectives, the words seemed now to roll off his tongue as though he had rehearsed them many times to himself. A comparison with the final speech will show that his dictation was changed by only a word here and there, so perfect had been the formation in his own mind of the thought and phrases. He dictated the words so slowly that on the yellow pad I had in my lap I was able to take them down myself in longhand as he spoke. I was stirred recently—ten years later—to see that yellow sheet of paper in the speech file in the Roosevelt Library at Hyde Park.

When he had finished dictating he looked at us, inviting criticism or suggestions. That was his usual custom. Harry raised the question of the phrase "everywhere in the world" in the first two freedoms.

"That covers an awful lot of territory, Mr. President," he said. "I don't know how interested Americans are going to be in the people of Java."

"I'm afraid they'll have to be some day, Harry. The world is getting so small that even the people in Java are getting to be our neighbors now," said the President.

There was some discussion; Harry really was not very determined about it. He agreed with Roosevelt, but was wondering what effect it would have on the public. The phrase was not taken out; in fact it was later repeated for each freedom. And the American people approved it!

The President thought it necessary in this message to restate his foreign policy, which he was very anxious to make a bipartisan policy. In his restatement he took another bold step forward: ". . . we are committed to the proposition that principles of morality and considerations for our own security will never permit us to acquiesce in a peace dictated by aggressors and sponsored by appeasers. We know that enduring peace cannot be bought at the cost of other people's freedom."

In spite of his emphasis on war production and foreign affairs, Roosevelt did not neglect the domestic scene in this message. Indeed he pointed out that what we were fighting for was economic as well as political democracy; that our fighting men and those who produced behind the lines drew additional stamina and courage from the very knowledge that they were defending that kind of a way of life.

And again he outlined the objectives of a democracy:

For there is nothing mysterious about the foundations of a healthy and strong democracy. The basic things expected by our people of their political and economic systems are simple. They are:

Equality of opportunity for youth and for others.

Jobs for those who can work.

Security for those who need it.

The ending of special privilege for the few.

The preservation of civil liberties for all.

The enjoyment of the fruits of scientific progress in a wider and constantly rising standard of living. . . .

The basis for his renewed summation of the New Deal at this time was two items which he had filed in the "Annual Message File" for 1941. One was a letter from Harold Ickes dated September 27, 1940, calling Roosevelt's attention to the new book by Samuel Grafton entitled *All Out* and quoting the following passage from the book:

In September of 1940 the better sections of the English press began to debate the need for an "economic bill of rights," to defeat Hitlerism in the world forever by establishing "minimum standards of housing, food, education, and medical care," along with free speech, free press, and free worship.

This letter was marked by Roosevelt "G. T. [Grace Tully] Annual Message File. FDR."

The other item was an editorial of the New York *Post*, dated December 26, 1940, marked "S. I. R. Message to Congress File. FDR." It quoted five proposals recently made jointly in an unprecedented action by the leaders of both the Protestant and Roman Catholic Churches in England. The proposals were for a long-range program designed to banish hatred, mistrust, fear and the doctrine that might makes right. They were:

1. That extreme inequalities of wealth be abolished
2. Full education for all children, regardless of class or race
3. Protection for the family
4. Restoration of a sense of divine vocation to daily work
5. Use of all the resources of the earth for the benefit of the whole human race

One sentence in this speech shows how wrong we were at times about the value of phrases. Some phrases, to which we paid no attention at the time, caught on immediately, like "New Deal"; others, which we all thought wonderful, fell flat and were never heard of again. Sherwood had written a sentence about appeasers who wanted to do business with Hitler at the expense of American security: "We must especially beware of that small group of selfish men who would clip the wings of the American eagle in order to feather their own nests." The President and all of us thought it was fine; and it was beautifully delivered. But no one ever noticed the sentence, and, to our keen disappointment, it made no impression at all.

This was the last of the President's major speeches before he took the oath of office for the third term.

In the year and a half since the Congressional leaders met in the White House in July, 1939, and refused to repeal the Neutrality Law, the United States had come a long way out of its shell of isolationism.

The most important reason for this rapid development had been the world-shattering events abroad. But also there had been the voice, the skillful persuasion, the leadership and the grim determination of the man whom the people of the United States had decided to follow for a third term.

Chapter XVI

The Third Term: War on the Horizon, 1941

The tasks of leadership imposed upon Roosevelt as he entered upon his third term were formidable.

The American people always had been, were, and probably would always continue to be a war-hating and peace-loving people. In 1940 they were still—in general—a noninterventionist people. Many of them had become cynical about international affairs. Disillusioned by the events following the First World War, they were determined to keep out of this second war. The "stew-in-their-own-juice" philosophy of foreign affairs was widespread.

It was Roosevelt's first and primary task to convince the American people of the great peril which they faced if Britain were to fall as had the rest of Europe. He knew from experience as well as a sense of statesmanship how careful he had to be. He knew that he could not get out too far in front if he were to retain leadership. He knew that if he were defeated on any major proposal in foreign affairs by the Congress, his whole foreign policy would be endangered.

He had to wait until the facts of war impressed themselves upon the people's thinking. He could interpret events as they occurred, especially as they affected the geography and economics of the United States. But he had to be sure that the people had all the facts and that they fully understood the danger.

His second great task was to find a way to enable the Allies in Europe and in Asia to hold on until more help could come to them. This too called for effective explanation to convince the people of the United States that helping the Allies was the best way to serve American interests.

Third, to ensure that there would be equality of sacrifice by every citizen, he had to condition the American people willingly to accept restrictions and controls to which they had never been accustomed. These were measures in which all people had to co-operate, but they would co-operate only if they understood the necessity for them.

Roosevelt's fourth great task during the next four years was to act as the chief propaganda agent of democracy both at home and abroad. For in addition to the courage that our supply of planes and guns and tanks inspired in our Allies and in the occupied countries, there was also the confidence which came from the words of the President, his clear enunciation of our own war aims and objectives and of the kind of peace that we hoped to secure. Finally, as democracy's chief propaganda agent, he had to convince the enemy of America's determination to help our Allies and, later, to stay in the war until complete victory.

After Pearl Harbor the President had additional burdens of leadership. The first was his position as the Commander-in-Chief of the Army and Navy of the United States. The actual strategic and tactical conduct of the war was left, of course, to the professional soldiers who were trained for that purpose—the Joint Chiefs of Staff. But the accounts of General Marshall, Admiral King and General Arnold all show the great leadership furnished by President Roosevelt in planning and carrying out strategic moves all over the world.

One of the most vivid recollections I have carried away from my service in the White House is that of the three Joint Chiefs of Staff—Marshall, King and Arnold—coming over frequently to consult with the President on war strategy. As they would walk out of these conferences through the corridors of the White House, I remember distinctly the feeling of confidence that their calm, determined fighting faces inspired in those who had the privilege of seeing them. I know that a great deal of that calm confidence was a reflection of the spirit of the man inside the oval office whom they had just left. It would have been a great thing for the morale of the American people in the dark days following Pearl Harbor to watch these men as they entered and left the White House.

Then, starting in the days when victory began to look certain for the Allied cause, the President had to assume the ultimate task of leadership—to convince the American people that the future welfare of our country, as well as of the rest of the world, depended upon our continued co-operation in the affairs of the world. The concept of the United Nations has become a commonplace one with us now. But in the days when the President was re-elected for the third time, this concept was hardly acceptable to the American people.

These, then, were the tasks of leadership that President Roosevelt faced in 1941 as the third term began. They called for action; but they also called for words—words of information, argument, persuasion, morale, words of courage and inspiration and leadership.

As the date of the third inaugural approached, the President asked Sherwood and me to meet him in Washington to discuss the preparation of his address. Sherwood was unable to go because of illness; I arrived on January 17. Harry was in England, where he had gone for his first visit to the Prime Minister.

The President had written out in longhand on yellow legal cap paper what was really a first draft, which he handed me when I got there. At Roosevelt's suggestion, Archibald MacLeish had also submitted a very fine draft; this and the President's own formed the basis of the speech.

In the preparation of any speech or message, the most important document was generally the first draft. It set the tone, had much of the basic material, and indicated the purpose of the speech. It was usually easy to tell by the first or second draft whether the speech was going to be good or not. With rare exceptions, it was the earlier drafts that determined the essential quality of the final speech.

Whenever the President was able to take the time to isolate himself and write a longhand speech, as he occasionally did, the result was nearly always excellent. I know no one who could do a better job. It was generally simple, forceful, direct, and at the same time moving and eloquent. Rarely would any major revision be necessary.

Sometimes, the President dictated the first draft to his secretary. These dictated drafts were naturally much rougher than his longhand drafts, and frequently would have to be almost entirely rewritten. Sometimes it was necessary to revise only a part of what he had dictated. Very frequently, however, we did not have the advantage either of a draft dictated by the President or of a suitable draft submitted by someone else. In that event we would have to prepare a first draft ourselves, and would have a talk with the President about what he wanted to say. Our instructions were not always very clear. The President might merely say that he had not spoken to the American people for a couple of months, and that he wanted to tell them what was going on generally in the war, or how our production program was going. Once we had a good first draft—either as dictated by the President or prepared by us or someone else—the rest of the job was essentially one of addition, deletion, checking, rearranging, and polishing.

It was about the time of the Third Inaugural Address that MacLeish began to figure more prominently in the speech-writing picture. His first work of this sort for the President had been in connection with the laying of the cornerstone of the Jefferson Memorial in 1939. One day, after he and Roosevelt had been talking about Jefferson, Missy called him to say that the President would like him to submit a draft for the Jefferson speech. In answer to a letter of mine about further details of that speech, Archie wrote me in part: "All I'm certain of is that I worked like Hell for three days and that, although he never said a word to me, the President apparently liked the result."

After the third-term election we began to call on him more frequently for drafts, ideas, language suggestions and criticisms. He was an effective collaborator. He was particularly helpful in dealing with subjects like democracy or the Bill of Rights, and on speeches for Armistice Day, Jefferson Day and similar occasions, for he had a poetic eloquence that was moving and impressive. But he was also of great assistance on many of our more practical assignments. As he was later to demonstrate in the Office of Facts and Figures and the Office of War Information, he knew how to use facts as propaganda with telling effect. Not least important, he was easy to work with; he never quarreled over language. And he had a grand sense of humor—a real asset at three in the morning when ideas didn't seem to come, or when the President was getting, we thought, a little ruthless with our bright ideas.

I worked on the President's and Archie's drafts for the Third Inaugural most of the day on the 17th, and in the evening Archie joined me in the Cabinet Room.

The next morning I asked Justice Frankfurter to come over for breakfast and we discussed the speech at length before taking it into the President's bedroom.

The theme of the speech—which was contained in the President's original longhand draft—was that a nation, like a human being, has a soul or spirit, and that what the Nazis were attacking was not only the physical being of the United States but also its soul—its democracy. The Justice and I both thought that the President's draft had too much in it about "soul" and we went in to try to persuade him to leave some of the sentences out. We were only partly successful.

In the evening the President, MacLeish, and I worked on the speech together, polishing it. Short as it was, it went through seven drafts before it was finished. Even the fourth, fifth and sixth drafts at Hyde Park show corrections by the President.

Sherwood was still sick and did not get down until the 19th. That morning we all worked on the speech again, including the President.

At this time there was a best-seller book in circulation that was a powerful piece of propaganda for isolationism. It was written by Anne Lindbergh, the wife of one of the most prominent leaders of the isolationist group. It was called *The Wave of the Future.* In working on this speech Sherwood said to the President pointedly, "I certainly wish we could use that terrible phrase, 'the wave of the future.'"

"Why not?" said the President calmly, and he dictated the following:

There are men who doubt this. There are men who believe that democracy, as a form of government and a frame of life, is limited or measured by a kind of mystical and artificial fate—that, for some unexplained reason, tyranny and slavery have become the surging wave of the future—and that freedom is an ebbing tide.

But we Americans know that this is not true.

The speech was finished in the afternoon at about three o'clock, and I was free to join my family who had come down for the inaugural celebration.

The reading copy was the seventh draft. The speech, as delivered, after stating that a "nation, like a person, has a body" which must be fed and housed and clad in accordance with American standards, and that "a nation, like a person, has a mind" which must be kept informed and which must be understanding enough to be able to live with all other nations in the world, continued:

A nation, like a person, has something deeper, something more permanent, something larger than the sum of all its parts. It is that something which matters most to its future—which calls forth the most sacred guarding of its present.

It is a thing for which we find it difficult—even impossible—to hit upon a single, simple word.

And yet, we all understand what it is—the spirit—the faith of America....

The President made a slip in his delivery of the last word of one paragraph: "To us there has come a time, in the midst of swift happenings, to pause for a moment and take stock—to recall what our place in history has been, and to rediscover what we are and what we may be.

If we do not, we risk the real peril of inaction." He misread the last word as "isolation"; so he quickly added "the real peril of inaction." On his reading copy, after the speech had been delivered, he underlined the word "inaction" and wrote, "I misread this word as 'isolation,' then added 'and inaction.' All of which improved it!" The President was a careful and accurate reader generally; he also liked to make historical notes like this.

The speech was delivered in the usual inaugural setting, outdoors on the steps of the Capitol. It did not make much popular impression. The setting was not a very appropriate one for a philosophical theme of this kind. The President said that he was disappointed at its lack of impact. He felt very deeply that the struggle going on in Europe and in Asia was more than a struggle between armies and navies—that it was a struggle for fundamental human liberties and freedoms, for the kind of life which was written into the Constitution, the Declaration of Independence, the Gettysburg Address.

The President's major effort for the next two months after the third inaugural was to obtain the passage of the lend-lease bill. He felt that the fate of that bill would determine the future not only of Great Britain but of the United States and of the whole world. If the bill failed it would mean that isolationism had triumphed, and Britain would have to fight it out alone without adequate help from America. If it passed, the die would be cast for all time against isolationism and in favor of a system of collective security.

The President was very anxious that there be a full and unlimited debate. It was a bitter debate. Some, impatient at the long discussion and delayed action, urged him to try to cut short all the talk and to get some action. The need was so urgent abroad, and the time seemed so short. But the President refused. As he said in a speech at the Dinner of the White House Correspondents' Association, March 15, 1941, discussing the passage of the bill:

"Yes, the decisions of our democracy may be slowly arrived at. But when that decision is made, it is proclaimed not with the voice of any one man but with the voice of one hundred and thirty millions. It is binding on us all. And the world is no longer left in doubt."

On March 11, 1941, a little over two months after the measure was recommended to the Congress, the decision was made—the bill was passed and signed.

There are not many dates in the history of the world as important as that one. It is difficult for us, in 1952, to realize how important a decision that was back in 1941, and how extraordinary that such unanimity should have been achieved in reaching it at all. It is difficult to remember the great split among the American people of 1940 on how far we should go in helping the democracies.

The President always insisted on calling the act the "aid-to-democracies bill"; it never seemed to bother him that he was almost alone in that, since everyone else called it the "Lend-Lease Act."

The President summed up the significance of that decision as follows: "This decision is the end of any attempts at appeasement in our land; the end of urging us to get along with dictators; the end of compromise with tyranny and the forces of oppression." It was also the end of deviousness and evasion in sending help to the Allies. It was the beginning of forthright action.

The President lost no time in implementing the decision of the Congress. In the White House Correspondents' Dinner address, four days after the passage of the lend-lease bill—he told the American people how fast he worked as soon as the bill was passed:

> The-aid-to democracies bill was agreed on by both houses of the Congress last Tuesday afternoon. I signed it one half hour later. Five minutes after that, I approved a list of articles for immediate shipment; and today—Saturday night—many of them are on their way. On Wednesday, I recommended an appropriation for new material to the extent of seven billion dollars; and the Congress is making patriotic speed in making the money available.

The very first list of nonmilitary equipment suggested by the British under the Act brought out a strange coincidence. On that list there was an item of nine hundred thousand feet of *fire hose*.

The President also lost no time in warning the American people of the sacrifices that they were going to have to make, even though we were not *in* the war. He never let up on this theme—of sacrifice for war and the peace to follow—until his death. In his same speech he said:

> Whether you are in the armed services; whether you are a steel worker or a stevedore; a machinist or a housewife; a farmer or a banker; a store-keeper or a manufacturer—to all of you it will mean sacrifice in behalf of your country and your liberties. . . .
> You will have to be content with lower profits . . . obviously your taxes will be higher. You will have to work longer at your bench, or your plow, or your machine, or your desk. . . .
> We believe that the rallying cry of the dictators, their boasting about a master-race, will prove to be pure stuff and nonsense. There never has

been, there isn't now, and there never will be, any race of people on the earth fit to serve as masters over their fellow men. . . .

The President was in fine form the evening of the Correspondents' Dinner. I remember the great enthusiasm of the newspapermen and their guests, most of whom were hard-headed newspaper owners and editors. I remember the rousing applause which greeted the President time and again during the course of this speech. Newspapermen, especially those who practice their profession in Washington, are generally hard-boiled—almost to the point of cynicism—about eloquence from political leaders, even from Presidents. This occasion was different.

Roosevelt knew most of the newspapermen by their first names, and greeted them cheerfully as they came up to the table to congratulate him on winning the lend-lease fight. He was having a mighty fine time. It was the first evening out for him in many months, and he enjoyed it. And when he got home we all had a fine hour of post-mortems over a glass of beer, discussing the speech and how well it had gone over.

As finally delivered, the speech was utterly devoid of any of the bitterness which the President felt and often privately expressed during the debate on lend-lease. I know how he felt about that debate. He had been particularly incensed at a statement by Senator Wheeler that passing the bill meant "ploughing under every fourth American boy." And Wheeler was by no means the only one in the debate who used that kind of language.

One night during the preparation of this speech, the President let loose all his pent-up fury at the outrageous statements that had been made, and dictated page after page denouncing the men who had made them. This was a not unusual way he had of "letting off steam." I knew he was not going to use that material, and so did Grace, who conscientiously took it all down in shorthand. I am pretty sure the President, even as he dictated, knew that he would not use it. I know that Bob and Archie and Harry and I, who worked on this speech with the President, were all delighted that that vitriolic dictation was never heard of again.

I had seen him do that on several occasions. The first time I heard him dictate in that vein I was dismayed at the thought that he might really use it in the final copy—but I soon learned to relax, knowing that once it was "off his chest" (as he would say) the paragraphs would eventually come out.

It has been said by some that President Roosevelt was a callous man under criticism; that he was very thick-skinned and that attacks upon him dropped lightly off his back. I wish this had been wholly true; but it was not. Of course anybody in high political office who wants to retain his sanity must develop a high degree of imperviousness to criticism and public attack. If he were to feel bitter about every unjust criticism, his whole day—and much of the night—would be filled with bitterness. If he were to take the time to answer all the attacks upon him, he would not have enough time left to carry out the functions of his office. The President did not generally feel too bitter about attacks upon him, and certainly did not try publicly to answer them. Of all men in public life whom I knew, he was the least concerned about an adverse editorial, for example, if only it did not distort the facts.

However, at times, newspaper and radio criticism of the President was so obviously unfair, the Congressional attacks so unwarranted and the facts so shamelessly misstated, that he could not help feeling great bitterness and resentment. This was especially true when the attacks were directed at his wife or children. He seldom expressed his resentment openly and publicly; in private conversation, however, he gave it free rein. The occasions when he gave vent to it in dictation seemed to satisfy him greatly, even though he knew those paragraphs would never be used. He was presenting his side of the case as forcefully and tactlessly as he knew how—without an audience. Occasionally a paragraph would stick through several drafts in spite of our urging and arguing. Sometimes, as he crossed it out, he would mutter, "I'd like to say it anyway"—and grin. I might add that we too sometimes got a certain amount of satisfaction out of hearing the President's expressions of resentment and his answers to his critics. Those answers were usually pretty good, and had plenty of vitriol in them.

Two weeks later, March 29, on the occasion of the Jackson Day Dinner, the President was careful to point out that the decision which the American people had made by the passage of the lend-lease bill was not a partisan decision. He paid particular tribute to his old opponent, Wendell Willkie, who had helped secure the passage of the bill, and who, he stated, "in word and in action is showing what patriotic Americans mean by rising above partisanship and rallying to the common cause. . . ."

He never forgot the help that Willkie gave in getting lend-lease adopted by the Congress.

But the President did not believe, and did not mean to indicate, that all dissenters had been silenced.

"Sniping will still go on," he said to us during the preparation of the speech, "and I'm sure it will get worse and worse."

He warned some of the great industrialists of the nation—those who had suggested that we could still do business with Hitler; and he also warned some of the unionized workers of the nation—those whose unions were Communist-controlled—of the dangers of the propaganda both from Germany and Russia: "We have seen what has happened to the great industrialists of Germany who supported the Nazi movement, and then received their reward in Nazi concentration camps or in death.

"We have seen how the workers of France were betrayed by their so-called champions, the Communists. For no matter what Communist lips have said, their actions have proved that in their hearts they care nothing for the real rights of free labor."

Bob and I had prepared a draft of this speech and sent it by the White House mail pouch to the President, who was on a short vacation cruise on the *Potomac* in Florida. Recently I came across the little covering note we sent with it, which indicates the informality around the President even in the midst of serious business.

Bob Sherwood and I send you these suggestions. We hope they serve a better use than paper to write poker scores on—or for wrapping the small fish Hopkins catches. . . .

We have done our best on this; but, confidentially, we do not think it is worth $100 per throw [i.e., the price of admission to the Jackson Day Dinner] even with the food. S. I. R.

The President used a good part of our draft. He told us he did not want to make it a partisan speech—and it was not. In that it contrasts sharply with all previous Jackson Day speeches, which were expected to be—and always were—warmly partisan in tone. The President had always looked forward to these occasions, for then he was able to say exactly what he thought of the opposition. But this year he was too anxious for complete unity on foreign policy to make the traditional kind of Jackson Day speech.

In between speeches, the President was, of course, not only carrying on the kind of peacetime duties that had occupied his attention for eight years; he was also taking all the steps necessary to meet the thronging new emergencies.

Scores of executive orders were issued. Some divided new functions among Cabinet officers or agency heads; others consolidated functions formerly spread through many bureaus in Washington into one single new agency; others transferred to one department functions that had been exercised by another.

From time to time, the President asked me to work on these executive orders and to carry on the many conferences that were necessary before they could be drafted. I devoted all my three-months summer vacation periods in 1941, 1942 and 1943 to helping the President on these and other government matters, living temporarily in Washington for that purpose; I also spent nearly every week end there during the year. The story of these executive orders and the vast administrative changes they brought about for the more efficient conduct of the war does not fall within the general purpose of this book; I shall have little to say about them individually unless they were the subject of addresses by the President. Because some of them made fundamental changes in the daily lives of our citizens, the President felt called upon to explain them to the people as simply as possible, so that they would fully understand them and, understanding them, approve them and abide by them.

Each of them involved many conferences with many different people in the various departments of government in Washington; they involved consultations with Congressional leaders; very frequently they involved reconciling bitter differences among administrative heads. Ordinarily the President took little or no part in these negotiations, simply telling me in broad terms what he wished to accomplish. It was characteristic of him not to concern himself with the details of the subsequent negotiations unless some formidable snag or obstacle made his personal interference essential.

Usually, without taking much of his time, I was able finally to lay before him an executive order accomplishing the reorganization he wished to obtain. On some occasions, however, even after he was satisfied with an order but before he had issued it, an official whose powers were being cut would come in and, as Roosevelt liked to put it, "would cry on my shoulder" and ask him not to take away this or that function. Usually these pleas failed; but sometimes the President yielded, especially if a strong personal appeal was made. He would call me in and tell me to change the order, trying to justify the change with some of the arguments that had been used on him. I could tell by the expression on his face that he did not feel the slightest conviction about the strength of the arguments; that he had simply been unable to resist the pressure or importunities of an old associate, and was merely trying to rationalize his action. Fortunately, shoulder-crying was resorted to only rarely, and only by those close to him in the official family.

On one occasion, for example, he was about to take away some of Nelson Rockefeller's powers over information and propaganda in Latin America and place them in the Office of War Information where they belonged. In this case Roosevelt refused to change the order in spite of Rockefeller; and it was not until Rockefeller called in Hull and Welles as advocates for his point of view, and they came to see the President personally, that he finally gave in.

It happened again in the case of Henry Morgenthau, Jr., some of whose functions in the Treasury were going to be supervised by Byrnes, and later Vinson, as the Director of the Office of Economic Stabilization. Morgenthau came over several times to see the President to urge that Treasury be left out of such supervision. The President finally yielded, although he later admitted that it was a grave mistake.

But these instances of vacillation were so rare that they only emphasized to me the strength of the man who on thousands of other occasions could withstand pressures which were tremendous.

Anti-Roosevelt newspaper writers used to attack me frequently because of my activity in connection with these administrative reorganizations. Of course they had no interest in me; they were simply using me as they used many others—to level their gunfire on the President. Some of the writings of the more rabid anti-Roosevelt columnists are too ridiculous to quote. The following paragraph from a column dated May 21, 1942, by one of his more intelligent and moderate critics, Arthur Krock of *The New York Times*, is typical of the general line:

If you want to alarm any member of the Administration from the Cabinet level down just whisper in his ear one of two dread sentences: "Sam Rosenman is in town" or "The Chief has an executive order on his desk that affects you." Either whisper is calculated to pale the cheek of the most favored of administrators, and the fear has sound basis. . . . The alarum occasioned by news that Judge Rosenman is in town springs from the fact he has been called in by the President to draft orders which have sounded the doom of several official agencies. . . .

As the emergencies grew more acute in 1941, Roosevelt had to take new steps almost daily to meet them. But the most important problem that year was getting the lend-lease materials over to Great Britain. It was not easy. Most of the supplies went by the northerly route of the Atlantic. The Nazis of course realized the danger to them from the vast supply of materials that were being delivered over this bridge of ships. Their obvious job was to sink the materials before they could reach Great Britain. German submarines were sent out to do that job. The American people soon began to learn with dismay how large a part of the war materials they were producing at so great an expense of time, money and effort was being sunk. Not satisfied with the sinkings by their submarines, the Nazis sent battleships and cruisers into the Atlantic to prey on convoys. The new German battleship, the *Bismarck*, sneaked out from its port in Norway, and sank the British battle cruiser *Hood*. The *Bismarck* then disappeared into the Atlantic apparently bound for the shipping lanes; its mission was to do enough damage to convince the American people that they would never be able to get their supplies over to Britain.

The American isolationists and America Firsters—as Roosevelt had anticipated—were continuing their outcries against everything that Roosevelt was trying to do to get aid to Britain. Colonel Lindbergh and Senator Wheeler were going around the country declaring that he was dragging us into war. They represented only a very small minority in the United States; but they were quite vocal and efficient in their efforts to block Roosevelt's foreign policy.

The British land forces were not doing well in Africa, and the reports the President was receiving from the Prime Minister were alarming.

The President knew that Great Britain's fall or survival depended on whether the forces opposed to Hitler could maintain the freedom of the seas. If our lend-lease supplies could get to Britain, he felt confident that in the long run Hitler could be beaten. This had to be brought home clearly to the American people, so that they would understand the drastic steps our government was going to have to take to ensure that American-made supplies reached the battle lines of Britain.

During the month of May, 1941, as the news of submarine sinkings continued to get worse, the President said to us that we were approaching an unlimited national emergency. He said that the time was rapidly coming when he would have to declare such an emergency and explain to the American people how serious it was and that it called for equally serious action by us.

Arrangements had been made for the President to make a speech to the Pan American Union, as he did every year. In the past the speeches had been formal and routine pronouncements about Western Hemisphere affairs. This year the President decided to make it the occasion for what turned out to be one of the most important speeches he delivered in the pre-Pearl Harbor period.

On May 23 I came to Washington at the President's request and met Sherwood at the White House. Harry was quite sick, and was unable to work with us as much as usual. The President had already dictated a draft of part of the speech.

The President knew that his first dictation was generally pretty rough. We have his own authority for that. In a press conference on May 26, 1944, during which he spoke of the plans that the United States was drawing up for a world security organization, he was asked whether anything could be specifically said about the nature of the plans. He replied:

In those discussions, while . . . there was nothing on paper, we talked things over pretty thoroughly, and since then they have been reduced to first draft form. Well, I wouldn't give out a first draft any more than I would give out a first draft of one of my speeches. It would horrify you. Yes, it would horrify you. My fifth, sixth, or seventh draft you might say was at least worth listening to.

After dinner Bob and I took this first draft over to the Cabinet Room. My notes of this occasion show that we worked until 5 A.M.— and consumed a lot of sandwiches and coffee.

Mrs. Roosevelt told us at dinner the next day that she had seen our light in the Cabinet Room at 3 A.M., and scolded us for staying up so late.

"If I may say so, Mrs. Roosevelt, you were up rather late yourself," said Bob.

"I was working on my mail," she replied, and could not understand why the people around the table laughed.

The Pan American Union speech was bold, but not bold enough to suit some members of the President's Cabinet. The Secretary of War, for example, had been urging the President for more than a month to do something really drastic about the German destruction of our shipping in the Atlantic. He had, in fact, been urging actual convoying by American naval vessels and planes. The Secretary of the Navy was of the same view, as were some of the others. Roosevelt did not believe that the Congress would permit, or that the people would approve, such a course. This was no time to get out too far in advance of the American people—although with the *Bismarck* still on the prowl anything might happen to change public opinion. Nor was it a time to meet a defeat in the Congress at the hands of the isolationists—not so soon after the lend-lease victory. Such a defeat would have been hailed abroad by the Nazis, would have greatly discouraged the British, and would have provided a setback for the policy of helping the Allies by all means short of war.

On the other hand, the President did not agree with others who were urging greater caution, notably the Secretary of State. When an early draft of the speech was sent over to Hull on the 24th, the Secretary expressed misgivings. He asked that Welles, the Under Secretary, and Berle, the Assistant Secretary, be permitted to assist in later drafts. The President acceded to this; they worked with us on the draft practically all day and evening on Sunday, the 25th, including lunch with the President, and on most of the 26th. Fortunately, they were not so cautious as their chief.

Secretary Hull doubted the wisdom of declaring in this speech an unlimited national emergency, but both Welles and Berle were strongly in favor of it. They finally convinced Hull, and he reluctantly acquiesced. Hull did insist, however, on some deletions which weakened the effect of the speech. For example, while the President was not willing to go as far as Stimson and Knox were in the use of our naval vessels to convoy supplies, orders had been given to move some of our Pacific Fleet into the Atlantic. Although the President knew that this might embolden the Japanese, he wanted to announce the move in order to encourage the British and South Americans, and to warn Hitler. Accordingly an earlier draft had these sentences in it, but on Hull's strong urging they were deleted:

I am now ready to announce what is probably no secret to some foreign nations, that certain units of the American Navy have been recently transferred from the Pacific to the Atlantic, and that other units are in process of being transferred. These units are not considered vital to the maintenance of our operations in the Pacific Ocean, but will in the Atlantic perform duties now essential.

A compromise was reached on the following wording: "It is well known that the strength of the Atlantic Fleet has been greatly increased during the past year, and that it is constantly being built up."

On Sunday morning, May 25th, while we were working on this speech in the Cabinet Room, a letter was delivered from the Secretary of War to the President which he promptly sent over to us. I quote the letter in full, for it is typical of the kind of material that would arrive from department heads during the actual preparation of a speech, often within a few hours before delivery. Sometimes the material was used, even though it meant last minute revisions; sometimes it was discarded. But whether used or not, it was a great help to the President to receive a word of encouragement from men like Stimson about the policy he was following in a speech.

Sunday Morning
May 25, 1941.

Dear Mr. President:

The events of the past forty-eight hours have had their effect upon my judgment as to the character of your speech. I had hoped that before your speech was made the arrival at the Panama Canal of the first units of the Pacific fleet would speak more loudly than any words as to your purpose to defend the Western Hemisphere and to carry out the objectives of the Lease Lend Act. But it now appears that their arrival will not take place until after your speech is made, and the British disasters in Crete and in the North Atlantic have terrifically intensified the necessity of demonstrating that you have already taken command of the situation here.

In the hope of giving you some assistance in that demonstration, I have this morning hurriedly dictated a few paragraphs to indicate the line which seems to me most clear and effective in demonstrating your purpose. I feel confident that the great majority of your countrymen sympathize with that purpose, and I am also confident that by Tuesday night you will be able to successfully demonstrate to them that you are already engaged in piloting them along the only pathway that leads to safety and success.

Faithfully yours,
Henry L. Stimson

Stimson's suggestions covered three pages. They can be summed up in the following sentences—which, for the reasons above indicated, were not used.

For our own defense the secure control of that great ocean highway must be maintained by us and by those who are friendly to us. I have therefore directed that sufficient strength from our main fleet in the Pacific shall be brought into the Atlantic in order to secure beyond peradventure that great end. The vessels are already on their way. With our forces thus reenforced in the Atlantic, I shall take such further steps as are necessary to insure the carrying out of the mandate of Congress and, above all, to secure the safety of the shores of our hemisphere against the growing danger which has been now shown to confront them.

Sunday night, taking a break in our work to listen to a news broadcast, Bob and I were startled to hear the commentator, Raymond Clapper, announce that we were both at that moment in the White House helping the President on his forthcoming speech.

Believing violently in anonymity for speech writers, we had always tried hard to remain in the background and so far had succeeded in avoiding any real publicity about our work on the President's speeches. This search for anonymity, I want to make clear, was entirely a matter of our own volition and discretion; the President never asked us to make any secret of our comings and goings at the White House or the reason for them.

On this occasion, it seems that in answer to a query Steve Early had admitted to the press that Bob and I were around. The President, who was with us, enjoyed our discomfiture and, laughing, imitated the way we had looked when we heard our names mentioned in that fashion.

"You should have seen Sam's face," said the President; and he proceeded to imitate it—I must say very well. "As for poor Bob—he looked something like this."

Thereafter we began to get a great deal of unwelcome publicity.

On Monday the 26th Bob and I worked all day. Harry was still sick in bed, but we had our breakfast in his room and kept him informed of the changes being made. I had asked Sidney Hillman of OPM and William Davis of the National Mediation Board to come to see Harry and me to give us their ideas about how to handle the question of strikes, and we spent some time with them. We got a lot of time with the President on Monday.

The next day I phoned Mrs. Rosenman to come down for the broadcast. In order to work on the speech, the President cancelled all his afternoon appointments. Early reported to the press that 12,000 letters and telegrams had come to the White House from all parts of the United States in the last three days advising the President what to say.

The speech was intended to perform two functions. It explained to the American people the facts that made necessary the declaration of an unlimited emergency, and the drastic measures such an emergency equired. It was also a detailed argument which sought to convince the American people (and succeeded) that their very safety depended upon these drastic steps—even though they might increase the danger of our becoming involved in the war.

While the President had never told us directly that he wanted to use this occasion to declare an unlimited emergency, it was quite clear from his thinking and from his statements to us during the *Bismarck* episode that the time for it had come.

The *Bismarck* had disappeared, but all kinds of rumors of its whereabouts were flying in and out of the White House. Nobody knew and everybody wondered. The President was not only worried that it might show up in the Caribbean, for example—which was his guess; he was wondering what he should do about it if it did. Should he order the United States Navy submarines to attack it? What would the people say if he did? There would obviously not be enough time to ask the Congress. A declaration of an unlimited national emergency would at least create a better atmosphere for drastic action if he should decide to take it.

Luckily the *Bismarck* question did not have to be answered. On May 26, it was sighted by the British Air Force; and on the day Roosevelt delivered his speech, it was torpedoed and sunk by the British Navy.

When Roosevelt received this one bright piece of news by phone from the Navy Department, he hung up, turned to us and said:

"She's sunk!"

There could not have been more satisfaction in his voice if he had himself fired the torpedo that sank her.

There were many statutory powers which would vest in the President upon his declaration of an unlimited national emergency. These statutes dealt with a multitude of domestic and international matters. We had before us while we were working on the speech a printed Senate document containing a memorandum from the Attorney General dated October 4, 1939, outlining in full the extraordinary powers that would be available to the President in an unlimited national emergency. During the last few days, the President had studied this document with great care on several occasions—picking it up, laying it aside, picking it up again to read, almost wistfully.

In any case, we had taken the liberty of asking Jackson to prepare a draft of such a proclamation, and one of the early versions of the speech we submitted ended with the statement that a proclamation of unlimited emergency was being issued. The President affected to be greatly surprised when he read that last paragraph, but I doubt whether he really was. I remember his saying somewhat meditatively, after he had read it, as though he were thinking out loud: "There's only a small number of rounds of ammunition left to use unless the Congress is willing to give me more. This declaration of an unlimited emergency is one of those few rounds, and a very important one. Is this the right time to use it, or should we wait until things get worse—as they surely will?"

He was not fully decided until the last day, but the paragraph stayed in the speech and the proclamation was issued on the same day.

This was a dilemma in which the President frequently found himself in the months before Pearl Harbor. On the one hand, he wanted desperately to keep the United States out of the war if he possibly could; on the other, he knew that halfway methods were dangerous because they might not keep Britain's head above water. He was willing to fight with every weapon short of war—and he did. But these weapons were slowly and surely running out, so each time he took one down he had to decide whether this was the time to use it or whether he should wait until the enemy came closer.

The speech was delivered on May 27th—a very hot night indeed—before the Governing Board of the Pan American Union and guests in the East Room of the White House. The President sat at a small desk immediately inside the main door of the East Room. The small uncomfortable chairs that were used during White House musicales had been arranged in front of him. In this grim setting, the chairs were the only reminder of those lighter moments in Washington. The room gradually filled up with the representatives of the various republics of the Western Hemisphere. Canada, too, was represented. Many of the Cabinet members and other high officials were present. Bob and I had asked the President whether our friend Irving Berlin, who was then in Washington, could attend and he cordially said that he would like to see him very much.

The setting and the audience could not have been less appropriate for a speech such as this. But the speech was not directed at this audience. It was directed to all the American people, to all the peoples of the world—the neutral peoples, the enslaved peoples, the people of

Great Britain and Greece and China, even the people of the dictatorships.

The President began by giving a short history of the American role in the war. Speaking of our policy of aid to Britain, he said:

"We have made no pretense about our own self-interest in this aid. Great Britain understands it—and so does Nazi Germany."

I know that it was distasteful to the President to emphasize over and over again to the American people that the underlying reason we were helping Great Britain was our own "self-interest." It was the truth, of course. The American people understood the truth—so did the British and the Germans. And it was the only realistic explanation for the great calculated risks we were taking. I am sure, however, that Roosevelt would have preferred to put the emphasis on a nobler ground—that we wanted to help democracy anywhere in the world against those who sought to destroy it, and that we were determined to do so even though our own safety was not immediately in jeopardy.

After summarizing in simple terms how far the Nazis had already gone in their schemes of world conquest, and how closely "the war is approaching the brink of the Western Hemisphere itself," he came to the heart of the speech—the freedom of the seas:

> The Axis Powers can never achieve their objective of world domination unless they first obtain control of the seas. That is their supreme purpose today; and to achieve it, they must capture Great Britain. . . .
> But if the Axis Powers fail to gain control of the seas, then they are certainly defeated. . . . Both they and their people know this—and they and their people are afraid. That is why they are risking everything they have, conducting desperate attempts to break through to the command of the ocean. . . .

Recounting the many recent sinkings of merchant ships, he said, "The blunt truth is this—and I reveal this with the full knowledge of the British government; the present rate of Nazi sinkings of merchant ships is more than three times as high as the capacity of British shipyards to replace them; it is more than twice the combined British and American output of merchant ships today."

It took several days of discussion and conference with the Chiefs of Staff before this last quoted paragraph was permitted to go into the speech. The Chiefs of Staff were against it. They were more interested in keeping all information from the enemy than in the moral effect it might have on the American people. Undoubtedly it did furnish information of value to the enemy. However, it was argued that the enemy probably had a pretty clear idea of the number of ships they had sunk, so we were not telling them anything very new. It was decided also that the effect of this startling bit of information on the American public was well worth the risk of giving the Germans some information they might not have. When the decision was finally made, it had to be cleared, of course, by secret code messages with the British.

The President next made a very important announcement; he defined what was meant by the word "attack" in "the lightning speed of modern warfare." For, as he put it, "I have said on many occasions that the United States is mustering its men and its resources only for purposes of defense—only to repel attack." But he was also thinking of the statement in the Democratic platform—and in his campaign speeches—that our boys would not be sent to fight in any foreign wars "except in case of attack."

Some people seem to think that we are not attacked until bombs actually drop in the streets of New York or San Francisco or New Orleans or Chicago. But they are simply shutting their eyes to the lesson that we must learn from the fate of every nation that the Nazis have conquered.

The attack on Czechoslovakia began with the conquest of Austria. The attack on Norway began with the occupation of Denmark. The attack on Greece began with the occupation of Albania and Bulgaria. The attack on the Suez Canal began with the invasion of the Balkans and North Africa, and the attack on the United States can begin with the domination of any base which menaces our security—North or South . . .

We know enough by now to realize that it would be suicide to wait until they are in our front yard. When your enemy comes at you in a tank or a bombing plane, if you hold your fire until you see the whites of his eyes, you will never know what hit you.

When the President saw that line in one of the drafts, he immediately dictated the following sentence: "Our Bunker Hill of to-morrow may be several thousand miles from Boston."

That was a pretty good estimate—Pearl Harbor is about 5,000 miles from Boston. The speech continued:

"Old-fashioned common sense calls for the use of a strategy that will prevent such an enemy from gaining a foothold in the first place. We have accordingly extended our patrol in North and South Atlantic water. We are steadily adding more and more ships and planes to that patrol. . . ."

The American people never had to decide whether they should go to war on the basis of this broadened definition of "attack." The attack that came at Pearl Harbor was a physical attack about which there could be no doubt. I think, however, that the President would have been ready to ask for a declaration of war if an "attack," as he defined it, had occurred.

And so he announced as our national policy that "Our patrols are helping now to insure delivery of the needed supplies to Britain. All additional measures necessary to deliver the goods will be taken. Any and all further methods or combination of methods, which can or should be utilized, are being devised by our military and naval technicians, who, with me, will work out and put into effect such new and additional safeguards as may be needed."

The President knew that this kind of language and this policy would immediately be assailed. Some of the attackers he referred to as "the Bundists, the Fascists, and Communists, and every group devoted to bigotry and racial and religious intolerance." Others he referred to as the "small group of sincere, patriotic men and women whose real passion for peace has shut their eyes to the ugly realities of international banditry and to the need to resist it at all costs."

At no time during these days of bitter attack upon him did he ever indicate even privately to us the slightest wish that in some way the opponents of his policies—whether they were the sincere men or the wicked men—might be silenced. Though, of course, he was incensed at the misrepresentations of some newspapers and Congressmen, he was convinced that only through a full and fair and free debate could the American people ever be finally convinced and make their decisions felt.

Finally he stated: "I have tonight issued a proclamation that an unlimited national emergency exists and requires the strengthening of our defense to the extreme limit of our national power and authority. The nation will expect all individuals in all groups to play their full parts, without stint, and without selfishness, and without doubt that our democracy will triumphantly survive."

The audience was tense, and apprehensive.

The room had become excessively hot. After the speech there was a reception in the gardens of the south lawns of the White House. Unfortunately, I had to return to New York that night, so I missed the lawn party. My wife, who remained for the night, told me that after most of the guests had gone home, the President had a fine time listening to Irving Berlin play the piano and sing some of his old favorite songs.

This transition from an important, grim speech to a lawn party and popular music would have been difficult for most men. For the President, however, those who knew him thought it nothing unusual. I had seen him make this kind of easy transition many times, and was to see him make it on even more serious occasions. It was not callousness or indifference. It was the kind of relaxation that helped him to meet the terrible problems and burdens of the next day, and to live through twelve years of nerve-racking decisions.

Before the unlimited national emergency was proclaimed, a German submarine on May 21 had sunk an American ship, the *Robin Moor,* in the South Atlantic, en route to South Africa. The submarine set the crew and passengers adrift in· lifeboats, and two or three weeks later friendly vessels discovered and rescued them. It was not until then that the outrage became known.

When the President learned about it, he decided to use this incident as an illustration of what had been in his mind when he made his Pan American Union speech. Rather than repeat himself in another speech, however, he adopted the expedient of sending a message to the Congress, knowing that the people would read it in their newspapers or hear at least excerpts over the radio. Though the President never found this method as effective as a radio talk, he used it at times when he thought a speech would be inappropriate, as in this case it would have been so soon after the Pan American Union address.

In this message to the Congress on June 20, the President said: "The total disregard shown for the most elementary principles of international law and of humanity brands the sinking of the *Robin Moor* as the act of an international outlaw. . . .

"Were we to yield on this we would inevitably submit to world domination at the hands of the present leaders of the German Reich.

"We are not yielding and we do not propose to yield."

This last sentence was penciled in by the President in his own handwriting on the last draft. The message had been prepared in the State Department and bears the Department mark in its language, but the President put in the concluding wallop himself in the affirmative, positive fashion he liked.

Roosevelt had been urged by some to take a drastic course with respect to the *Robin Moor*. Stimson wanted him to ask the Congress immediately for authority to have the Navy convoy all vessels. But Roosevelt did not want to risk his whole policy of getting aid over to Britain by allowing the isolationists in the Congress to defeat him on such an important aid-to-Britain measure. He felt that he could not count too heavily on the Congress—and he was right. That was proved conclusively later by the close margin of one vote for the extension of the Selective Service Act in August, 1941.

The President was now traveling a narrow, dangerous ground between the more impatient of his associates, like Stimson and Hopkins, on the one hand, and the last-ditch isolationists in the country, on the other, who were eagerly looking for him to make some misstep which would enable them to scuttle his plans for defeating Hitler.

This does not mean that the President took no action as a result of the *Robin Moor* incident. Defending the freedom of the seas, he had explained in his May 27th speech, was more difficult in this war than in the last. In the last war the only danger was submarines; now the long-range bombers added a new menace. For this new danger, outpost bases were more important than naval escorts or convoys. The United States could not allow Hitler to get control of the seas by seizing "the island outposts of the Western Hemisphere."

Roosevelt was ready to seize the Azores as an "island outpost" if Hitler started to move through Spain down to Africa; he had prepared the plans and had issued the orders. This did not become necessary. But Roosevelt did arrange with Iceland to take over the protection of that island and to establish a base there for our forces. This movement was completed on July 7, 1941; and as soon as our Marines had landed there safely, the President notified the Congress of the arrangement. In his message he announced an additional step forward in his objective of getting the supplies across the Atlantic—that he had issued orders to the Navy to protect by any means necessary all convoys of American ships between the United States and Iceland, and between the United States and all the other forward bases which the United States had established. Because the water beyond Iceland was a combat zone under our neutrality act, any lend-lease cargoes in American ships had to be transferred to foreign ships in Iceland to complete the journey eastward.

During the summer of 1941 the most important utterance of the

President was the one that he and the Prime Minister issued jointly—the Atlantic Charter.[1]

While they were framing this declaration of principles to guide the postwar world, the Congress of the United States was debating whether or not service under the Selective Service Law should be extended for another year. The debate was bitter. The bill for extension of the law was almost lost; in fact, it was passed in the House of Representatives on August 12, 1941, by a majority of only one vote. The argument of the opposition—led by the Republican leaders—was that there was no danger of attack and that the situation was now very much better than it had been in 1940! This was four months before Pearl Harbor. The 203 votes in favor came from 182 Democrats and 21 Republicans; the 202 votes opposed came from 133 Republicans, 65 Democrats, 3 Progressives and 1 American Labor. One vote the other way and our Army, which was just beginning to take military form out of a mass of civilian selectees, would have been thoroughly disorganized and crippled.

On September 4, 1941, one of Hitler's submarines fired upon but missed the U.S. destroyer *Greer*, which was carrying mail to Iceland. The President was determined that no incident like this—illegal though it was—should lead him to ask for a declaration of war. Even when he later asked Congress on October 9 to amend the neutrality act to permit arming of our merchant ships and to allow them to enter belligerent ports, he said in his message: "The revisions which I suggest do not call for a declaration of war, any more than the Lend-Lease Act called for a declaration of war."

But he was not going to take the *Greer* incident lying down. He made up his mind to announce a new policy on convoys and patrols in a fireside chat.

The day after the attack on the *Greer*, the President called me into his office and said he wanted to make a speech on September 8 about the attack, and that he was determined to use any means necessary to get the goods to England. He had asked Hull to send a draft to him at Hyde Park, where he was going to be for the week end.

[1] For a description of this meeting and of the writing of the Charter itself see Sumner Welles: *Where Are We Heading?* (New York: Harper & Brothers, 1946); Basil Rauch: *Roosevelt from Munich to Pearl Harbor* (New York: Creative Age Press, 1950), pp. 358-374; Robert E. Sherwood: *Roosevelt & Hopkins* (New York: Harper & Brothers, 1947); Winston Churchill: *The Grand Alliance* (Boston: Houghton Mifflin Company), pp. 433-450.

"I'll have them send you a copy; maybe you'll come up to Hyde Park so we can work on it together."

The next day the speech was announced for the 8th; but on the 7th of September, during the President's visit at Hyde Park, his mother died.

Steve, Harry and I gathered in the White House when we received this news; we had several telephone talks with the President at Hyde Park. The question was whether it would be better for Hull to make the speech for the President or whether the speech should be postponed. We urged the President to postpone it and to make it himself later, and he finally agreed to put it off to the 11th.

The State Department turned out four consecutive drafts, which it sent to Hyde Park, copies of each of which it sent to us. Harry and I worked on our own draft for three days, using some material that the President had dictated at Hyde Park and had sent to Washington by wire.

Then, on the 9th, with the results of our labor we left Washington to spend the night in New York, meet the President at the Mott Haven yards of the New York Central Railroad, and ride with him to Washington. The three of us worked on the speech on the train down. A new draft had been finished by the time we arrived at the White House, about 9 P.M. The President knew how serious the speech was in the form we had cast it, how much more forceful than any of the State Department drafts, and he wanted to consult with others about it. Consequently, he asked Hull, Stimson, Knox, Hopkins and me to meet with him at nine o'clock. The President read aloud the latest draft of the speech. It was not very different from the final draft. Everyone approved it; though a few minor suggestions were made, which the President said he would adopt. After he and Hopkins had gone to bed, I went over to the Cabinet Room alone to prepare the last draft.

I had arranged in advance with Mr. Charles C. Wagner, who was in charge of the stenographic force, to have some stenographers report for duty at 11 P.M. The girls in the stenographic staff room were very efficient and willing. Sometimes during the day, when speed was necessary, Wagner would assign as many as ten girls to us. With each girl taking about two pages of the draft, a complete twenty-page speech might be turned out in fifteen or twenty minutes, and we could start working on the new draft almost without a break. Frequently, three or four stenographers had to stay until two or three o'clock in the morn-ing—or later—but I never heard a single complaint about it from any one of them. They always smiled when they went home, sleepy and tired, and generally expressed thanks for being allowed to be helpful.

The next morning, after breakfasting together in his room, Harry and I took the final draft to the President. He was going to read it to the Congressional leaders of both parties in his study at ten o'clock to get their reaction. It was important enough for that. I learned later from Harry that Hull, who had approved the speech the night before, and who had spoken even more forcefully about the matter in private conversation with the President, had come to the conclusion overnight that the speech was a little too warlike in its tone—especially that part of it that mentioned "shooting":

"We have sought no shooting war with Hitler. We do not seek it now. But neither do we want peace so much, that we are willing to pay for it by permitting him to attack our naval and merchant ships while they are on legitimate business."

The President rejected the advice of the State Department to tone down his language. The speech was delivered practically in the form in which it was read to the Congressional leaders.

As soon as the speech had been mimeographed, I went to the air-port and joined my family, who were on their way to visit the various projects of the Tennessee Valley Authority, many of which were later to play a most important part in winning the war. That night, while the President was broadcasting, we were driving in an automobile along the Tennessee River. We stopped the car and turned on the radio. I followed the President's delivery on a carbon of the reading copy which I had brought down with me.

The atmosphere was quiet and peaceful down there on the shores of the Tennessee River on that still September night. It seemed so far away from the world of conflict and destruction, from the mass killing of civilians and the cruelties of the Nazis, that the bold, resolute—almost belligerent—tones of the President seemed a little like a voice coming from another planet.

The President started by telling the people the facts: that a German submarine deliberately fired a torpedo at the United States destroyer *Greer* in full daylight while she was proceeding toward Iceland. She was carrying American mail to Iceland and flying the American flag.

The destroyer was in waters which the United States had declared to be "waters of self-defense—surrounding outposts of American protection in the Atlantic." He mentioned other acts by the Nazis showing that "the incident is not isolated, but is part of a general plan. . . . It is the Nazi design to abolish the freedom of the seas, and to acquire absolute control and domination of these seas for themselves.

"No matter what it takes, no matter what it costs," he continued, "we will keep open the line of legitimate commerce in these defensive waters. . . . When you see a rattlesnake poised to strike, you do not wait until he has struck before you crush him. These Nazi submarines and raiders are the rattlesnakes of the Atlantic. . . . Their very presence in any waters which America deems vital to its defense constitutes an attack."

The answer? "Our patrolling vessels and planes will protect all merchant ships—not only American ships but ships of any flag— engaged in commerce in our defensive waters. . . . From now on, if German or Italian vessels of war enter the waters, the protection of which is necessary for American defense, they do so at their own peril. . . .

"I have no illusions about the gravity of this step," he added. "I have not taken it hurriedly or lightly. It is the result of months and months of constant thought and anxiety and prayer. In the protection of your nation and mine it cannot be avoided."

Because of the orders he had given, the speech became generally known as the "shoot-on-sight" speech.

The origin of the rattlesnake simile was a memorandum Myron Taylor had sent the President after a week-end visit at Hyde Park. They must have talked about the submarine warfare; for, a day or so later, Taylor sent the President the following memo through Grace:

If I am armed and lawfully in a forest and suddenly along my path I hear the warning rattle of a rattlesnake, and though it has not otherwise disclosed itself, I would feel justified in discharging a shot into the apparent location of the snake. If I killed it, I would probably have saved my life, and no one would question my right to do so; no one would feel that I should wait until it had struck me, and bitten and perhaps killed me, before taking action.

One would consider this a parallel to the case of a vessel lawfully upon the high seas, which became aware of the underwater presence of any danger, be it submarine or other, and which used any instrument within its power to protect itself from attack.

In order fully to implement the new "shoot-on-sight" policy, the President, on October 9, 1941, asked the Congress to revise the neutrality act in two respects: first, to permit the arming of American merchant ships; and second, to remove the restrictions against sending American vessels and cargoes into belligerent ports. He used the medium of this message to restate generally the underlying purposes and reasons for the revision he was recommending.

He was determined, as he had said in his September 11 speech, that incidents like the *Greer* should not provoke us into war; but he was equally determined that we should shoot it out with the Germans if that was necessary to get the goods to England and Russia. The existing laws that prevented our ships from going into combat zones hampered our efforts to deliver the supplies; and they did not make it less likely that we would get into war, because the Germans were now sinking our ships even outside combat zones.

His request for authority to send armed ships with contraband cargo into Allied ports was in effect asking for Congressional approval and implementation of the shoot-on-sight order of September 11.

The President had been considering these recommendations during the entire summer of 1941. Hull had been urging him to discuss with the Congressional leaders at least an amendment of the act permitting American ships to carry supplies all the way to Great Britain. The leaders prophesied a long bitter fight, so Roosevelt did not formally act until October 9 to obtain modification of the act.

The message illustrates Roosevelt's strategy during this period: to keep one step ahead of public opinion, not to be stampeded in one direction or the other, and to encourage full debate before taking too drastic action.

The Congress complied with the President's recommendation on November 14—after two further incidents had occurred. Even then the vote was close: 50 to 37 in the Senate, and 212 to 194 in the House. The two further incidents both cost American lives. On October 17, a German submarine attacked the U.S. destroyer *Kearny*, and eleven of her crew were killed. This incident occurred three hundred and fifty miles southwest of Iceland. On October 31, a submarine sank the U.S. destroyer, *Reuben James*.

On Navy Day, October 27, Roosevelt explained his policy anew to the American people. He used the ship sinkings, not to suggest a declaration of war, but to justify the use of force to keep the sea lanes open. It was his strongest speech before Pearl Harbor. In it he made the flat declaration that we were in effect in the fight. At that time the phrase "cold war" had not been coined, but the words "shooting war" had, and it was a phrase that the American people dreaded.

Bob and I helped the President on this speech, which went through seven drafts.

He started with the blunt assertion that "America has been attacked."

"We have wished to avoid shooting. But the shooting has started. And history has recorded who fired the first shot. In the long run, however, all that will matter is who fired the last shot."

In an unusual effort again to impress upon the American people the great peril which civilization faced if Hitler were to win, the President revealed to an astounded world two startling bits of information contained in two separate Nazi documents which had come into our possession in some way. This was a somewhat dangerous thing to do because every time the Nazis learned that we had some of their secret data it made them more vigilant and increased their chances of ferreting out the sources of our information. The President told us, however, that the two documents were so startling that he felt he should disclose them so the American people and all the world might see the stark meaning of a Nazi triumph.

"I suppose the isolationists will say that these are none of our concern," he said to us, as he passed them over for us to read.

The first of these documents was a "secret map made in Germany by Hitler's government."

"It is a map of South America and a part of Central America, as Hitler proposes to reorganize it." In place of the fourteen separate countries of South and Central America were five new states.

"And," as the President put it, "they have also so arranged it that the territory of one of these new puppet states includes the Republic of Panama and our great life line—the Panama Canal.

"That is his plan. It will never go into effect.

"This map, my friends, makes clear the Nazi design not only against South America but against the United States as well."

That document had to do with military conquest. The other document was even more startling in its implications. To quote the President:

"It is a plan to abolish all existing religions—Catholic, Protestant,

Mohammedan, Hindu, Buddhist, and Jewish alike. . . . In the place of the churches of our civilization, there is to be set up an International Nazi Church—a church which will be served by orators sent out by the Nazi Government. . . ."

The President was using propaganda in this speech for three purposes: first to warn the Germans that we were preparing for a total defense for which we had issued orders to the Navy to "shoot on sight"; second, to convince the American people that the Allied cause was not hopeless, despite the propaganda of the American Firsters; and third, to sustain the morale of our Allies, and keep up the hope and spirit of the enslaved peoples of Europe.

He went out of his way to answer those who were willing—almost anxious—to have Russia go down to defeat, despite the fact that she was tying down and chewing up hundreds of Hitler's divisions on the Eastern front. The answer he made in October, 1941—without the benefit of hindsight knowledge of Russian intransigence—should serve as a strong defense in these recent years, when he is being attacked for the help we gave Russia. He said:

The other day the Secretary of State of the United States was asked by a Senator to justify our giving aid to Russia. His reply was: "The answer to that, Senator, depends on how anxious a person is to stop and to destroy the march of Hitler in his conquest of the world. If he were anxious enough to defeat Hitler, he would not worry about who was helping to defeat him."

The main point of the speech was, of course, the vital necessity of getting our supplies across to Britain and Russia:

It is the nation's will that America shall deliver the goods. In open defiance of that will, our ships have been sunk and our sailors have been killed.

I say that we do not propose to take this lying down.

That determination of ours not to take it lying down has been expressed in the orders to the American Navy to shoot on sight. Those orders stand. . . .

Our American merchant ships must be armed to defend themselves against the rattlesnakes of the sea.

Our American merchant ships must be free to carry our American goods into the harbors of our friends.

Our American merchant ships must be protected by our American Navy.

In the light of a good many years of personal experience, I think that it can be said that it can never be doubted that the goods will be delivered by this nation, whose Navy believes in the tradition of "Damn the torpedoes; full speed ahead!"

The President did not know that we were only a month or so from actual warfare. But he realized that we were already in an undeclared war when he said:

"Today in the face of this newest and greatest challenge of them all, we Americans have cleared our decks and taken our battle stations. We stand ready in the defense of our nation and in the faith of our fathers to do what God has given us the power to see as our full duty."

In my file, I find some of the speech material which was before the President while he was working on this speech. Among other items, there was:

1. A memorandum from Archibald MacLeish, then the Librarian of Congress, to the President giving a quotation from the papers of Alexander Hamilton with reference to the freedom of the seas. In the upper right-hand corner in Grace's handwriting appear the initials S. I. R., indicating that after the President had read this communication, he told Grace to send it to me.

2. A letter from a United States Senator enclosing a copy of the speech which he had made a few days before, entitled "The Defense of Our Country." In the upper right-hand corner in Grace's handwriting is the notation, "S. I. R. speech material."

3. A long memorandum from the Coordinator of Information, dated October 17, 1941, on the repeal of the neutrality act. This too has a notation on it, in the handwriting of Dorothy Brady, one of the secretaries who used to relieve Grace Tully during speech-writing periods, reading as follows: "H. Hopkins, Sam, Bob, for use in speech."

4. A communication to Mrs. Roosevelt from a friend, enclosing a memorandum prepared by a history professor on the "freedom of the seas." The letter to Mrs. Roosevelt says, "It occurred to me that in this memorandum there are pertinent phrases and some material which might prove of interest in assembling material for the President's statements on the subject." Attached to it is a memorandum, "October 23, 1941. For the President: E. R." (meaning Eleanor Roosevelt). In Dorothy Brady's handwriting appear the words, "Harry, Sam, Bob," indicating that the President was sending it to us for possible use.

5. A letter from a president of a bank in St. Louis, dated October 18, 1941, which stated that Pierre van Paassen had made a speech in St.

Louis urging the President to tell the American people "the whole truth about the terribly dangerous situation we are in, both internally and externally, unless you thought that the people could not stand the whole truth without a panic. . . . I will go further and state that I think our people should be told the whole truth . . . the time is now, before the Fascists in our midst soften us up any further. Tell them, Mr. President. Tell them now. Lead us! We will follow you as we have always followed you. May the everlasting arms uphold you!" In the upper left-hand corner of this document appear the words, in Dorothy Brady's handwriting, "Harry, Sam, Bob."

Scores of memoranda like these would come to the President at each speech time. As he picked them out of his mail basket and read them, if he thought that they contained usable material, he would tell his secretary to send them on to us. Sometimes, while he was doing other work some thought would come to him; he would dictate a few hundred words, and tell Grace to put it into the speech-material file. The following is an example:

March 19, 1943

Memorandum for Sam Rosenman

In my next speech I would like to say something like the following:

I get very many letters—too many—from boys in the Army and Navy who are under instruction and who complain that some of their instructors are hard-boiled reactionaries—exuding the spirit of isolationism, who pooh-pooh any idea of establishing a world peace, and scoff at any American attempt so to improve the lot of other nations that they will, in the future, resort to arms against their neighbors. I am told that these instructors talk of crackpot idealism and speak of giving away our prosperity.

In the conduct of any great war it is, of course, necessary to employ many thousands of instructors in the mechanics of war. In the course of such instruction it is inevitable that we find a certain proportion of men who are so hard-boiled that they have not changed their ideas in any way since the "get-rich-quick" days of fifteen years ago.

I like to think and believe that these are the exception to the rule. The best advice I can give to the boys in our services is to pay little attention to instructors who have never had a thought of a better world in which America can live in the future.

F. D. R.

All this material would be collected in a separate envelope marked "Speech Material"; and when we got to work on a speech, Grace or Missy would give us the envelope.

Out of this mass of material sometimes would come a thought, a phrase, a whole paragraph—sometimes the major part of a speech. Sometimes it became obvious later that the thought was inappropriate, or that it had been expressed many times before, or that it was too complicated. However, the speech-material envelopes were always very helpful, particularly in dictating a first draft. What was not used was sometimes returned to the general speech-material file to be re-examined on a future occasion. Most of the material submitted was not used, and could not be used for any speech. Generally such material was transferred to the regular files.

An effort was made to acknowledge the receipt of all material and to thank the sender for his interest and help. However, I have heard of people even recently who complain that they never received recognition or thanks for ideas submitted to and used by the President—they may even exhibit copies of their letters. Obviously, in the hundreds of letters and conversations in which ideas were submitted to the President there was bound to be duplication. Frequently someone would think an idea or a phrase was his own contribution when the President and his speech-writing assistants might never even have read his letter. Once in a while someone would send in an idea that we had already incorporated in a draft or had discussed time and again as appropriate for a speech.

There are now in the Hyde Park library a large number of these filing envelopes, entitled "Speech Material," containing thousands of similar items from all kinds of sources. Some examples:

1. A memorandum from Harry L. Hopkins to me, enclosing an eight-page memorandum from the Bureau of Labor Statistics on "Post War Wage Policies," dated August 24, 1944. Harry's memorandum says:

DEAR SAM:
   I think you ought to keep this in the speech material.
   I wish you would attach this note to it because I do not agree with the policy. [Here reasons are given.]
   I am all for the return of collective bargaining after the war.
                                        Sincerely yours, H. L. H.

2. A memorandum from the President to me, reading as follows:

                                        January 3, 1944
Memorandum for S. I. R.
   Will you keep in mind that I want to talk about certain types of Con-

gressmen, commentators, etc., in a speech along this line—"There are people who still think that this World War can be won with overwhelming supplies of hot air and no casualties."

F. D. R.

3. A memorandum from the President reading as follows:

January 24, 1944
SIR for Speech Material. "The Germans are not so much a people as they are a state of mind."

4. A telegram from a gentleman of whom I had never heard, named Gregory S. Drummen, of Greenville, Michigan, addressed to me, starting as follows:

Dewey's arguments are well described in the words of Abraham Lincoln who set up Stephen Douglas—"in every way possible he tries to prove that a horse chestnut is a chestnut horse."

This quotation was used by the President in his speech at Wilmington, Delaware, in 1944.

5. A memorandum from Cordell Hull to me enclosing two memoranda "on the subject of your inquiry yesterday afternoon relating to the Reciprocal Trade Agreements program." My inquiry had concerned the press conference Governor Dewey had held in which he claimed that the Reciprocal Trade Agreements had been a Republican program—whereas in reality the Republican party had tried to scuttle it several times.

There are also in my file a great many paragraphs and pages struck from drafts of other speeches. For as material was cut out of a speech, if I thought it was good and could be used some other time, I saved it. Bob did the same. The huge quantity of material in this file shows how ruthlessly the President cut material from his speeches; but I do not recall any instance where any of it was used in a later speech.

In addition, there were such things as campaign speakers' handbooks; copies of speeches of members of the Congress on all kinds of subjects which associates of the President would notice and send him; copies of newspaper editorials and of paid political advertising; copies of magazine articles of interest, political, economic or social; copies of speeches made by members of the President's Cabinet or heads of administrative agencies, discussing questions which might later be treated by the President.

Frequently personal friends of mine or of Bob or Harry would send ideas or suggestions, sometimes by mail, sometimes by phone. Some of them were used. They told me of their surprise and pleasure when one of their thoughts or phrases came back at them in one form or another over the radio from the White House microphone. From other people in government—Anna Rosenberg, Wayne Coy, William Hassett, Leon Keyserling, David K. Niles, Fred Vinson, Oscar Cox, Chester Bowles— would frequently come helpful suggestions either before or after they had seen a draft of a speech.

At times the head of a department or agency concerned with the subject matter of an imminent speech would send in an entire draft. Sometimes a draft would come from someone outside the government who was interested in the subject matter. Occasionally these drafts came in as a result of a request by the President; sometimes they were volunteered. If the President had time he would read the draft. More frequently he would ask one of the men helping him on the current speech to read it and see whether it, or any part of it, could be used. This was ticklish business because, while most people realized that someone had to do the job for the President, there were many who were quite sensitive about having their suggestions—on which they doubtless had spent much time and effort—rejected. We had to do the best we could and use our best judgment; the President would generally follow that judgment. Unfortunately, the author usually knew the identity of the person who was reviewing his draft; and it was not easy to make or keep friends when you were given that kind of job.

The following letter from one of Roosevelt's friends is an extreme example of the kind of hard feelings we tried to avoid arousing:

DEAR MR. PRESIDENT:

I enclose herewith a speech for this coming Saturday night over the air. It is a good speech. I did *not* write it.

Please be good enough to read it through fully before you start to change it. I am positive that, as it is, it will come over the air beautifully when delivered by you. A great deal of time and effort has been put into it.

Please, please, do not send it to your hackers to perform an OOPHOREC-TOMY on it. I just couldn't stand that!

Ex-Judge Rosenman telephoned me from Washington this morning stating that you had requested him to request me to send the speech to him in Washington "so that he could go over it and make whatever changes were necessary." When I finally ascertained that he really wasn't kidding me, I declined the offer.

Faithfully yours,

The fact is that the speech he sent in was a grandiloquent and super-rhetorical effusion which was so wholly different from Roosevelt's style of writing that it would have sounded strange indeed coming from lips so accustomed to simple phrasing. The speech referred to was unimportant, but it was going to be delivered over a national hookup.

The President laughed as he gave Bob and me the draft and the letter, and said:

"Boys, fix it up—and don't be too hard on ————."

We had to be hard—almost merciless. And whatever friendship existed toward us probably disappeared when the speech was delivered.

On occasion, some of the people in government after submitting suggestions used to call us up, argue for their point of view, and demand to know whether it had found its way into the President's speech, and if not, why not. I could not always be as frank as I should have liked; these people were nearly always well intentioned, and some of them would have felt badly if they were told bluntly how quickly the President had rejected their ideas.

Men in high-policy places in the government I would tell frankly whether the President had accepted their view or not. Sometimes they would go to the President directly in order to argue further.

The Navy Day speech of October, 1941, was enthusiastically received by the audience at the Mayflower Hotel. The dining room was so crowded that Bob and I had to listen standing up at the rear of the head table. It was also enthusiastically received by the people of the United States.

The speech was so warlike in tone that during the following week, on November 3, at a press conference the President was asked:

QUESTION: Lots of people who think just as you do on this war issue also think that a continuance of diplomatic relations with Germany is a form of dishonesty. Could you elaborate your thoughts for background?

THE PRESIDENT: No. Only off the record. I would have to make it completely off the record. [Then he talked about some of the dispatches which he had received, showing how Germany was trying to establish a kind of airline base in Liberia and also about "constant instances of trying to spread their power all over the world."] We don't want a declared war with Germany because we are acting in defense—self-defense—every action. And to break off diplomatic relations—why, that won't do any good. I really frankly don't know that it would do any good. It might be more useful to keep them the way they are.

QUESTION: There is the thought that in that way the situation would be brought home very directly to the American people.

THE PRESIDENT: Oh, I think the American people understand it pretty well. After all, in days like this, you don't do things for the sake of the record. And that is about all it would be.

No one can say how long this state of affairs between Germany and the United States would have continued without actual war. Most realists were convinced that sooner or later a general shooting war would develop; but no one could foretell how it would come, or when.

On the other side of the world, in the Far East, the President was facing the same kind of crisis. It was no secret that the Japanese forces were moving southward with the obvious intention of attacking either British possessions or Dutch or French possessions, or all. The President knew how dangerous such an attack would be to American interests, but he also knew how little concern the American people would feel about an attack six thousand miles away on some isolated British or Dutch possession.[2]

To keep the Japanese from open hostilities, and to buy time in which to gather our strength, we had gone to great extremes for more than a year—even sending them oil and steel. But Roosevelt had refused to appease Japan in its aims of aggression at the expense of other nations. In the last months before Pearl Harbor the talks with Nomura had convinced Roosevelt and Hull that Japan would never be satisfied with anything less than that kind of appeasement. Consequently it became the aim of diplomacy to hold off and postpone actual aggression by Japan as long as possible.

Hitler wanted Japan and the United States to go to war with each other, calculating that such a war would cut down the flow of supplies to Britain and Russia. Roosevelt understood that very well. His strategy, on the other hand, before and after Pearl Harbor, was to concentrate on Hitler as the Number One enemy who had to be defeated first. Therefore he was anxious to prevent the spread of the war to the Pacific Ocean area. Besides, from that area we were getting such scarce materials as rubber and tin, and England was getting a steady stream of these essentials and other supplies. The strategy of keeping Japan from

[2] A detailed account of the President's negotiations and efforts to prevent that attack is set forth in Rauch, *Roosevelt from Munich to Pearl Harbor*, pp. 375-408, 431-496.

starting a war in the Pacific worked for two long years, as the President put it, "for our own good."

On Thanksgiving of 1941 the President paid his usual visit to Warm Springs, Georgia. He made an informal extemporaneous speech to the patients there, similar to his Thanksgiving talks of other years.

Even while he was talking in the calm, secluded and peaceful atmosphere of the low hills of Georgia, the Japanese forces, by land and by sea, were treacherously moving to the attack.

Chapter XVII

On the Defensive, 1942

On December 7, 1941, the Japanese committed their act of infamy. It turned out to be also an act of unbelievable stupidity.

That sneak attack did our fleet the greatest damage in its history. But it did something else. It did something that the Nazis and the Japanese should have feared more than the American fleet and the British fleet combined—it created a unified, outraged and determined America. The dictators of the world could not have made a more serious blunder in their plans for world conquest than they did on that peaceful Sunday morning in December, 1941.

For months after Pearl Harbor, people used to tell each other how they got the news of the attack. Some were at a football game; others were at concerts or moving picture theatres. I was at home when the news came over the radio. My son Bobby, aged ten, was listening, as always, and rushed in to tell me the shocking news.

Almost immediately thereafter, Sherwood phoned me and we agreed that we ought to get down to Washington right away. I said that I would call the White House and find out if they wanted us. I did, and the President sent word through Grace that both Bob and I should come down as quickly as possible. I was scheduled to make a speech myself that night at a public dinner in New York City. I sent a telegram explaining why I would not be present, and Bob and I got on a plane which landed us in Washington at about 7:30 P.M. We learned, on phoning the White House, that the President had summoned the Cabinet for 8:30 P.M. that night and the Congressional leaders for 9:30. We went to the Willard Hotel, where the White House had reserved rooms for us, and listened to the news on the radio.

The President had decided to go to Congress the next day, and we learned later that evening that he had already prepared most of his speech. He had dictated it to Grace between his many conferences of the day with military leaders, with members of the Cabinet, with Congressional leaders, and with scores of other people. But though he had no need for us that night, Grace called us to say that the President wanted us to stand by since there was a "fireside" coming in a day or two.

Archie had heard we were at the Willard and came up with some paragraphs he had written during the afternoon, anticipating that a speech would soon be in the making.

The next morning, December 8, Bob and I went over to our usual speech workshop—the Cabinet Room. There was great excitement all through the White House; newspapermen had congregated in large numbers; there was much scurrying through the corridors. The secluded Cabinet Room, looking out over the peaceful rose garden and south lawn, was very quiet. We sat there discussing recent events, recalling the many conversations we had had with the President about how far the Nazis would have to go before the American people would be sufficiently aroused to the danger to be anxious to fight. And now this had come—with the enemy again choosing the time and place of attack.

The news soon began to come into the White House of how serious the damage had been at Pearl Harbor.

We were sitting there waiting for something to do when Mrs. Roosevelt telephoned over to the Cabinet Room and invited us to go with the President and his party to the Capitol to listen to the address. This was one of the rare occasions when we heard Roosevelt deliver an important speech without our being fully familiar with its contents in advance. Neither Bob nor I had seen any draft of it.

The speech was a telling one. It was a simple, straightforward, blunt statement of Japanese "infamy"; it was a frank disclosure that the attack had "caused severe damage to American naval and military forces," and ". . . that very many American lives have been lost." There was the flat prophecy that "the American people in their righteous might will win through to absolute victory" and that "we will gain the inevitable triumph—so help us God."

Instead of asking Congress for a declaration of war, he asked that "the Congress declare that since the unprovoked and dastardly attack by Japan on Sunday, December 7, 1941, a state of war has existed between the United States and the Japanese Empire."

The speech was very short—only about six and a half minutes long. Secretary Hull had urged the President to deliver a full-dress speech to the Congress, setting forth in detail the long history of Japanese-American relations, our efforts to attain a peaceful solution, and the final perfidy of the Japanese. The President preferred his own brief, dramatic message; but he told Hull that he would deliver a fireside chat on Tuesday, the 9th, in which he would make a more detailed statement.

I have recently examined the various drafts of that short message to Congress. In the first draft the first sentence reads: "Yesterday, December 7, 1941, a date which will live in world history, the United States was simultaneously and deliberately attacked by naval and air forces of the Empire of Japan." In the next draft, the President struck out "world history" and substituted "infamy"; he struck out "simultaneously" and inserted "suddenly."

The third draft has insertions in the President's handwriting, as follows:

"Last night Japanese forces attacked Hong Kong.

"Last night Japanese forces attacked Wake Island.

"This morning the Japanese attacked Midway Island."

Obviously, while he was waiting to go up to the Congress, the President had added to the speech the latest news as it came in from time to time during the morning.

Harry suggested, and the President just before finishing the final draft approved, the next to the last sentence expressing confidence that we would "gain the inevitable triumph—so help us God."

The remarkable thing is that on one of the busiest and most turbulent days of his life he was able to spend so much time and give so much thought to this speech.

In a memorandum which Hopkins attached to one of the drafts appears this paragraph: "The President was receiving the latest despatches this morning and the news is surely not good. But, as ever, he had a good night's sleep, although someone woke him up at 7:30."

I doubt whether many other Americans had "a good night's sleep" on December 7, 1941.

It was a most dramatic spectacle there in the chamber of the House of Representatives. On most of the President's personal appearances before the Congress, we found the applause coming largely from one side—the Democratic side. But this day was different. The applause, the spirit of co-operation, came equally from both sides of the chamber. I could not help but think back to the beginning of the year, to January 6, when I heard the President deliver his State of the Union Message to the Congress. The lack of enthusiasm and response on the Republican side of the chamber had been heartbreaking; it reflected the division and indecision that afflicted the United States. The new feeling of unity which suddenly welled up in the chamber on December 8, the common purpose behind the leadership of the President, the joint determination to see things through, were typical of what was taking place throughout the country.

Thirty-three minutes after the President had stopped speaking, the Congress, by a unanimous vote in both Houses (except for one lone dissent in the House), passed a resolution declaring that a state of war existed between the United States and Japan.

When we got back from the Capitol, Harry, Bob, Grace and I had lunch with the President in the Oval Room. There was no small talk; there were no jokes or quips; the coming events of the war were the topic of conversation. The President emphasized the fact that Hitler was still the first target, but he feared that a great many Americans would insist that we make the war in the Pacific at least equally important with the war against Hitler. Hitler had not yet actually declared war on us; but we assumed that that would come at any minute.

After a while, the conversation turned to the forthcoming fireside speech set for the next day, the 9th; and the President told us in a few minutes what he wanted to say. He wanted particularly to give the American people as complete a record as possible of the recent history of our Japanese and Far Eastern relations.

"I want to make it clear to them," he said, "that for more than a year we have been trying to prevent war in the Pacific. I want to make it clear that we were not appeasing Japan, but that the longer we could prevent war with Japan the stronger we could become and the more help we could send to the people fighting Hitler."

He told us that Sumner Welles had prepared a first draft of the fireside speech. Before news of Pearl Harbor came, the plan had been that in addition to making a last-minute appeal to the Emperor of Japan, the President was to send a message to the Congress on December 8 giving the full history of our negotiations with Japan to date. Hull and Berle had been working up the message on December 5 and 6, but the news of December 7 stopped them. Welles' draft of the proposed fireside chat contained a shorter rewrite of this historical material.

Bob and I went over to the Cabinet Room, got a copy of it, and went to work. At about six-thirty the President asked us to come over for cocktails and dinner with him. There were present besides the President, Harry, Grace, Bob, Elliott Roosevelt and two friends (all three of whom were in uniform), and I. After dinner the President worked on the speech in the Oval Room with Grace, Bob and me until about eleven-thirty. He went to bed, and the three of us went over to the Cabinet Room to continue work.

In the early morning MacLeish came into the Cabinet Room to talk to us. He urged very strongly that the President must tell the American people in great detail the damage that had been done at Pearl Harbor. There were many fine public officials in Washington at the time who, like Archie, deeply believed that the American public had to be given full information at once, and who urged the President to do so. Bob and I were opposed to this; Archie was very vehement, and there was a long discussion about it among us. The compelling argument against it was that we did not know whether the Japanese themselves knew how damaging a blow they had inflicted. Much of the damage had become apparent only after the Japanese planes had disappeared. To give them information about how many of our capital ships had been put out of commission and to what extent would have been folly if they did not already know the facts themselves.

Of course, only the President could decide this question. After consultation with the Chiefs of Staff, he finally decided that although he would in no sense minimize the gravity of the attack, he was not going to give any information which could possibly be useful to the enemy.

Bob and I continued working on the speech with MacLeish until about three o'clock in the morning. As was our custom, we left a draft with the White House policeman at the front desk of the White House, requesting him to give it to the White House usher in the morning, who would take it into the President's bedroom as soon as the President awoke.

We walked back the short distance to our hotel through the darkened streets of Washington. There had been wild rumors about a German air attack to be launched from submarines, and many cities in the United States had already instituted blackouts. Under the portico over the driveway leading from the Pennsylvania Avenue entrance to the White House, there had always burned a large lamp shedding a strong light over part of the White House grounds. The light was so strong that whenever I occupied one of the White House bedrooms facing the north, I found it necessary not only to pull down the shades but to draw the curtains closely in order to keep the light out of the room. As Bob and I walked along Pennsylvania Avenue that night of December 8, 1941, the light—for the first time—was out. There was complete darkness over the White House grounds.

"I wonder how long it will be before that light gets turned on again," I said to Bob.

"I don't know," he answered, "but until it does, the lights will stay turned off all over the world. That light has been the only ray of hope to millions of people, and those millions will still look to this house and to that man inside it as their only hope of deliverance."

The light did not go on again for three and a half years.

The next morning we went over to the Cabinet Room and started to reread the draft of the night before. It seemed very dull. It would seem even duller and more boring in a fireside chat. The President, who had read the draft with his breakfast, agreed with us that although there was not much time left, it would be better to try our hand at another quick draft and abandon the long history of our negotiations with Japan.

"Yes," he said, "I can send a message later to the Congress for purposes of the record; I can put all this historical stuff in that. Suppose you try to get up something else; let me have it by lunch, and we can all eat together and talk about it."

We did have something for the President by lunchtime. After the dishes were cleared away from the Cabinet Room table, where we all ate together, he went to work on the draft.

He made some suggestions and dictated some paragraphs; but soon had to return to his office to take care of innumerable military and other problems. We could not get in to see him with a new draft until about 5:30 P.M. The speech had to be delivered at 10 P.M., and before delivery it had to be mimeographed and distributed to the press. It was not easy to write under such pressure, but the President was calm and unruffled, as he generally was all through the trying days after Pearl Harbor. I do not once remember him getting impatient or irritated, in spite of the hundreds of things he had to do and the continuous bad news which was coming in in every dispatch. He stayed with us in his office until seven, correcting the draft, page by page. Usually we had the stenographers run off a new final draft before the reading and mimeograph copies were prepared. This was to enable us to take a fresh last look at it, to remove repetitious words or phrases or ideas, to make sure of logical sequence and development, and to make a general check. There was not time for that on this occasion. So as each page was corrected or passed by the President, it was taken out to Grace, who was in the next room typing his reading copy. This was the fastest job the President had done since the Cleveland speech during the 1940 campaign.

In the speech, the President spoke of how difficult the road ahead was going to be. It was the counterpart of the "blood, toil, tears and sweat" statement of Prime Minister Churchill a year and a half before. The future was not so bleak, of course, as the future that faced Great Britain in June, 1940; but the President warned the people that there would be many shortages, more taxes, fewer profits, longer and harder work, and dangerous service in the armed forces of the United States. The attack at Pearl Harbor had provided each nation in the world with a lesson that was not to be forgotten, namely:

There is no such thing as security for any nation—or any individual—in a world ruled by the principles of gangsterism.

There is no such thing as impregnable defense against powerful aggressors who sneak up in the dark and strike without warning.

We have learned that our ocean-girt hemisphere is not immune from severe attack—that we cannot measure our safety in terms of miles on any map any more.

Now in 1952 the American people and the people of all the United Nations are acting on that same lesson.

We are now in the midst of a war, not for conquest, not for vengeance, but for a world in which this nation, and all that this nation represents, will be safe for our children. . . . We don't like it—we didn't want to get in it—but we are in it and we're going to fight it with everything we've got.

Then a real note of optimism: "We are going to win the war and we are going to win the peace that follows." Only one half of that prediction of victory has as yet come true; but on December 9, 1941, even that one half seemed almost impossible.

After the speech was delivered, Mrs. Rosenman and I went up to say good-by to the President. He seemed quite surprised that I was leaving. He said that it was going to be necessary to prepare a message to the Congress to go up right away, forwarding all the material that the State Department had prepared about the history of our negotiations with the Japanese. He said it would be fine if I would stay over with Bob and help get that message out. I said that I would.

I drove out to the airport with Dorothy to put her on the plane. On the way back to the hotel, I thought I would stop at the White House and say good night to the President if he was still up. I inquired of the usher, and was told that he was still at his desk in the Oval Room. I walked up quietly, found the door to the Oval Room from the center hall open, and walked in.

This was almost the first time since the attack on Pearl Harbor that the President had been able to be alone for a few moments. As I entered the room I saw him there, sitting by himself. He was at work over his stamps. There was no excitement here now, no hectic atmosphere of false rumors; there was no fear—not even disquietude. There was a man at a big desk, smoking a cigarette, poring over his stamps. There was concern, yes, deep concern; but it was a calm concern. He was worried, deeply worried; but there was no trace of panic. His face was resolute, even grim; but it was confident and composed. He knew by this time all the damage that had been done to us at Pearl Harbor. Yet I felt, as I looked at him, that he was confident that ultimate victory, as he had said, was certain.

He was all alone. If Missy had been well, she would have been sitting up with him in the study that night. She always did in times of great stress, to see whether there was anyone he wanted to call or talk to, or whether he wanted to make any arrangements for the next day. But in June, 1941, Missy had suffered a stroke and was in Warm Springs attempting to recover. She never did.

The President looked up as I came in, and smiled. It was a sad and tired smile.

"Come in and sit down," he said. "Help yourself to a drink."

I took a glass of ginger ale from the tray which had been set up on a side table. I poured him a glass of beer. We talked about many things. Strangely enough, he seemed to avoid talking about the war. He began to talk about things of the past—about the speech he had just made, about the political situation in New York City, about the coming gubernatorial campaign in New York in 1942 and the possible candidates.

Pretty soon the telegrams began to come in about his speech. They always did after a radio speech; and until he went to bed, they would be brought over to him. Tonight, the usher brought them in large batches. During the time I was there, several hundred came. He read them hurriedly, and silently passed them over to me to read. Most of them congratulated him on the speech he had just made, and expressed confidence in his leadership. One telegram suggested, as a slogan for the war, "Remember the Oklahoma." Another suggested, "Remember Pearl Harbor." Although there were many who urged these and similar slogans reminiscent of "Remember the Maine" in 1898, none seemed to take hold with the people. They were all oversimplifications. The war was not about Pearl Harbor; it involved matters more fundamental than Pearl Harbor; it involved civilization itself.

After we had read the telegrams he began calmly to autograph a small pile of pictures of himself and Mrs. Roosevelt; they were to be sent to friends as Christmas presents. I got one myself. The President seemed to derive spiritual comfort and pleasure from doing this quiet Christmas chore after the three days of grueling work and nerve-racking responsibility through which he had just passed. As I watched, I hoped that the same spirit and fortitude he was showing that night would last during all the tragic days of the war.

Finally, long after midnight, I said good night to him, and he went to bed.

Bob was at the Willard when I got there, and we talked about various things, but mostly about the message to the Congress.

The next day I worked all day on Welles' draft. It had to be shortened and simplified considerably. Bob helped for a few hours; that evening we finished it, left it with the President, and both of us went home to New York.

On December 11, Germany and Italy made their expected declaration of war on the United States. On the same day Roosevelt sent a message to the Congress asking it to recognize a state of war between us and those two countries, saying:

"The long known and the long expected has thus taken place. The forces endeavoring to enslave the entire world now are moving toward this hemisphere."

On December 15 the message went to the Congress. It was a "historical summary of the past policy of this country in relation to the Pacific area and of the more immediate events leading up to this Japanese onslaught upon our forces and territory."

The President had laid down general principles about giving war information to the public: the information had to be accurate, and the information had to be of no use to the enemy. Now, on December 19, he appointed an agency to carry out those principles—the Office of Censorship. Under the very able leadership of Byron Price, the Office of Censorship, practically without any statutory powers—or any other powers for that matter except the moral right to demand voluntary co-operation—performed a remarkable job of preventing information from reaching the enemy. With one or two isolated exceptions, the press and radio co-operated on a voluntary basis with outstanding conscientiousness and loyalty.

On the night the Japanese struck at Pearl Harbor the President talked with Churchill by transatlantic telephone. He had been keeping in close touch with the Prime Minister since their Atlantic Charter meeting in August, 1941. The entry of the United States into the war called for a second conference.

On December 22, 1941, Churchill and his staff arrived in Washington. This conference, known as the Arcadia Conference, made possible full and free interchange of information, and the formulation of plans by the President and Churchill and their military, naval, production, and procurement staffs. It also reaffirmed the decision that Germany was to be target Number One. This conclusion was based on the fact that only in the European theater could the necessary build-up of forces be accomplished, air superiority be achieved, and British ground forces be committed along with the Americans. Because of sea distances, shipping difficulties, and an absence of nearby landing fields and staging areas, an early concentration of forces against Japan was out of the question. Furthermore, Germany possessed greater productive power and scientific genius than Japan, and therefore it was necessary to attack her before she became even stronger.

The operation against North Africa was discussed, and plans were laid for launching it as early as March, 1942, if the French invited it or if Hitler invaded Spain. 1943 was set as the most likely year for the assault on the European Continent. The Arcadia Conference also tackled the question of production goals to be met by the Allies.

An excellent detailed account of the negotiations during these weeks between the British and the American staffs, and between Churchill and Roosevelt, is contained in *Roosevelt and Hopkins.*

Those arrangements which could be announced, the President announced in his next major address—the State of the Union Message of January 6, 1942—which he delivered in person to the Congress of the United States.

It was Roosevelt's first major address to the American people since his fireside chat of December 9, 1941. I had gone to Atlantic City with my family for a short Christmas–New Year's holiday. While there I received a phone call from Grace asking that Bob and I come to the White House to work on the message. When we arrived we found that the President had already dictated a first draft, and we also found a very good memorandum submitted by Archie MacLeish.

All the war news that had been coming in since Pearl Harbor had been bad, and it was getting worse. The President said he wanted to tell the people how serious the danger was, but never would he allow any impression that he doubted for a moment our ultimate victory. He knew that the news would be bad for some time to come—in fact he said to us, "The news is going to get worse and worse before it begins to get better. The American people must be prepared for it and they must get it straight from the shoulder." He was going to have to call again for extreme sacrifice. He wanted to describe the strategic problems of the war in the Atlantic and Pacific; he wanted to state the objectives for which we were fighting; he was going to announce new and higher production figures and insist upon meeting them. Above all he must try to maintain the morale of our own people and of all people fighting Hitler.

The President knew how important this speech was, how desperately the world was looking here for leadership, and how essential that they should not look here in vain.

We prepared a new draft by midnight on the 2nd, and the next afternoon we went over to the President's study to work for about an hour with him. The Prime Minister was still a house guest at this time, and conferences had been going on every day and every night. It was hard to get time with Roosevelt.

Two days before, on January 1, the Declaration of the United Nations had been signed. This was a document subscribed to by all the nations then fighting Hitler. The text of it had been agreed upon with Churchill. The declaration was only a few paragraphs long. It reiterated adherence to the principles of the Atlantic Charter; it pledged the full resources of each signatory to fighting the Axis; and it guaranteed continued co-operation and refusal to make a separate peace.

The President was still full of exuberance about the signing. He spent a good part of that hour talking about it and about the great unity among all the Allies fighting the dictators. He told us with great satisfaction how he had finally convinced Litvinov of the importance of including the words, "religious freedom," in the Declaration.

The President had become quite sensitive about "religious freedom" because when he had returned from his meeting with Churchill in August, 1941, with the text of the Atlantic Charter, he had been severely criticized for the omission of "freedom of religion" from that document. I am positive that the omission was purely an oversight in drafting. However, it was an omission not generally condoned. The President was most anxious to have the phrase included in the Declaration of the United Nations, even though it was going to be signed by a government that was, in essence, antireligious.

Why the Russian leaders consented I do not know; nor, I suppose, does anyone other than the Russian leaders. The President used an ingenious argument, and he said he thought it worked. He explained to Litvinov how much he had been criticized and attacked because "freedom of religion" had been omitted from the Atlantic Charter; that he wanted the Russians to help him out in getting the phrase into this Declaration even though he knew that they might not like it. Instead of using the usual phrase "freedom of religion," which implied that everyone had a religion but was free to adopt the religion he wanted, the President suggested using the phrase "religious freedom." That phrase, he argued, meant just what the Soviet constitution meant, viz., freedom to have a religion, any religion, and freedom to have no religion and freedom to oppose religion. Litvinov accepted the argument, and cabled the Kremlin for authority to sign. This seems to me a rather naïve explanation for Soviet acquiescence, but the President told me—and I know he told several others—that that was the reason. Personally, I wondered whether he really believed it himself. At any rate he was pleased that the phrase got in.

He was also pleased—and proud—that it was he who had suggested the phrase "United Nations" to Churchill. Churchill, in public utterances, had referred to them as "Allied Nations" and "Associated Nations." The President thought of "United Nations," not as an analogy to

"United States," but rather as expressive of the fact that the Allies were united in a common purpose. Having hit upon that phrase one day, he immediately had someone wheel him right into Churchill's room, interrupting the Churchillian bath; and the two agreed then and there upon the name. The same name was used three years later to designate the formal worldwide entity, the United Nations Organization.

That same afternoon, January 3, I met Winston Churchill for the first time. It was in his bedroom in the White House. The Prime Minister was dressed in his famous one-piece woolen outfit, which was fastened by a long zipper. Lord Beaverbrook was with him. Churchill had his usual long black cigar in his mouth, and was holding a highball in his hand. He did a great deal of pacing about—as he always does.

This was a great moment for Bob and me. We had spoken and written so much about this indomitable spirit under whose leadership the British people were showing such civilian and military heroism. This short, almost pudgy man had come to typify the spirit of British resistance to Hitler—the bulldog determination of the British will.

Strangely enough, the conversation did not touch on the subjects that were really uppermost in our minds—the war and the survival of civilization, the plans and prospects upon which the future of the whole world depended. Instead, we talked, for example, about how cold it was to fly across the ocean in a bomber; we discussed the scarcity of English newsprint and the small size of the English newspapers compared with American newspapers; we discussed editorials in the English and American papers. Churchill said that the American papers were much kinder to President Roosevelt than the English papers were to him. This was indeed startling to us, who thought that it was well-nigh impossible for anyone to be more bitterly attacked by the press than Roosevelt.

We talked about the two recent speeches Churchill had made; he was obviously delighted at the very good press they had received. Then the conversation turned to Roosevelt's speeches. Churchill disconcerted us considerably by saying that the President had told him we were both of great help to him in the preparation of speeches. He asked us at length about the method Roosevelt followed in preparing his speeches, and spoke very glowingly of him as an eloquent and accomplished speaker.

While, as I have said, Bob and I—and most of the other speech assistants—tried to remain anonymous, the President never made any pretense that he wrote every word of his speeches and gathered all of the material himself. In fact, among his associates and friends, he frequently discussed the part that others took in the preparation of his speeches.

I recall my surprise about this during the visit to the White House of the King and Queen of England in 1939. The President, as he presented members of his Cabinet and others to the King, would explain in a few sentences the work that each one did for him. I was considerably taken aback to hear the President tell his Majesty that I had for many years helped him prepare his speeches and messages. Roosevelt never felt—nor did we—that someone who helped with the speeches was in any way a ghost writer in the popular conception of the word, that is, one who prepared a speech and turned it over to the orator, full grown and completed, to be delivered.

On several occasions during this visit and others, I had an opportunity to see the President and the Prime Minister together in serious conference, and also in lighter moments, in the White House and at Hyde Park. I tried at the time to make an appraisal of the President as he faced the man with whom he was joined in the most important partnership in the history of the world. By tradition, you would expect the Britisher to be tall, suave, guarded and reserved in his manner and speech, scintillating in his mastery of the facts of history and of geography. The traditional concept of an American diplomatic representative, on the other hand, would be one of blustering forthrightness, dogged determination to stick to unpleasant facts, complete disdain of the niceties of diplomatic usage. Tradition was not carried out in this case. Of the two men, the President was the more reserved, suave and diplomatic; he always had the facts of geography and history at his fingertips, and was ready to use them at any time to meet argument; he never seemed at a loss for ideas or words in any discussion about political events or international diplomacy or, indeed, about military or naval strategy. Although his experience in international affairs and in military affairs was not so great as Churchill's, no impartial observer could have detected it, either in the manner or substance of his speech.

I felt very proud of my President in the presence of this great leader from overseas—particularly proud of Roosevelt's charm and facility in conversation, his ability to match wits, to trade experiences, and to express ideas and hopes and aims for the new world the Allies were trying to build.

What a far-seeing Providence it was that supplied a Churchill for the

British people of 1940 and a Roosevelt for the American people of 1933 and 1941. Each seemed to fit so appropriately in his own place and in his own time. In the House of Commons in June, 1940, Roosevelt would not have been so magnificent as Churchill. During the first hundred days of the New Deal, or during the six months before and after Pearl Harbor, Churchill would not have equaled Roosevelt in the White House. I am not thinking of the difference in their political policies; I am thinking more of their general characteristics and personalities, of their particular kind of oratory and peculiar qualities of leadership. Churchill was made to order for Dunkirk. Roosevelt was made to order to lead his nation out of the panic of depression in 1933 into an era of confidence; out of the walls of isolationism into its rightful place among the nations of the world.

During the time that we were working on the State of the Union Message, the President had to interrupt frequently to carry on his conferences with Churchill. This was not easy. The two men had vastly different working habits, and those habits did not fit together smoothly. Almost every day Churchill used to take a long refreshing nap between 2 and 4 P.M. As a result, when he awoke he was ready for a day's work. Roosevelt, on the other hand, in addition to rounds of conferences with Churchill, had to carry on the thousands of exacting and difficult duties of a President running a nation at war. The Prime Minister was in fine trim to stay up discussing important matters until two or three o'clock in the morning. This routine was beginning to get Roosevelt down, and he laughingly remarked that he was looking forward to the Prime Minister's departure in order to get some sleep.

On Saturday, the third, Churchill had dinner at the British Embassy. Harry, Bob, Grace and I dined with the President. At dinner the conversation was mostly about Churchill—Roosevelt was most enthusiastic about him and praised his rugged, bold approach to the problems of the war. Right after dinner, Harry went to bed. Bob and I worked long past midnight.

On Sunday, the next day, Mrs. Roosevelt asked us to come over to lunch with Churchill and a few friends. This is one of the occasions when I was able to observe the President and Churchill in the presence of twelve or fifteen others. In addition to the President, Mrs. Roosevelt and the Prime Minister, there were Harry, Grace, Bob, several young friends of Mrs. Roosevelt's from the International Students Service League, Elliott's son by his first wife, and some others.

Here, too, the center of the stage was where the President sat. The Prime Minister was quite reserved—almost silent. The conversation was very general. I have been at several lunches and small gatherings where Churchill was present, and never did he try to make small conversation at table as Roosevelt always did. Maybe his reserve came from the fact that he did not know any of the guests well; but that would never have bothered Roosevelt. On the contrary, it would have stimulated him. In a small crowd of people, Churchill does not always give a hint of the great man he is; Roosevelt always did.

Churchill made one little "break" which gave us all a lot of silent chuckles at the table and many louder ones as we talked about it among ourselves later. The Prime Minister had apparently never heard of— or had forgotten—the busy public life that Mrs. Roosevelt had led ever since Roosevelt had become President: her constant travels away from the White House; her trips into city slums, devastated rural areas, poor mining towns and down into the mines themselves; her public speaking; her thousands of letters per week; her boundless energy and great activity on behalf of the underprivileged everywhere. At any rate, in answer to a question by Mrs. Roosevelt about what Mrs. Churchill was doing in the war, he proceeded to talk with great praise of his wife and the wives of his ministers at home—how wonderful it was that they did not engage in any public activities or appearances but always stayed at home. All of us—who admired and loved Mrs. Roosevelt because of the life she led—thought that this was strange talk at her table. Maybe our faces showed incredulity as he spoke; anyway, the Prime Minister stopped a little abruptly. Mrs. Roosevelt never "batted an eyelash" at this; later she told us she enjoyed it very much. We certainly enjoyed it at the time, and enjoyed the later retelling of it even more.

As we were breaking up after lunch the President whispered to me that he would like to have a copy of the latest draft of the speech because he wanted to read it to the Prime Minister. That afternoon and evening Bob and I continued to work over in the Cabinet Room, where we were joined by Archie, whom we had asked to come over and look at this draft.

During this time I was also working on a reorganization and unification of all the housing agencies of the United States. I had to spend several hours alone with the President that day going over the plans I had submitted to him, and also over the reports which different agencies of the government had sent him commenting on my plan of reorganization. He told me with great pride that Churchill "had loved the speech"; that he had suggested a few changes in wording, some of which the President had adopted and some of which he had not. During the preparation of an important speech like this, Sunday was a full working day. Indeed, there were few Sundays during the war that were not full working days for the President no matter where he happened to be —at Hyde Park, Washington or in his retreat in the Catoctin Mountains.

The next day, Monday, we did not have a chance to see the President at all until noontime, when he joined Harry, Bob, Grace, Dorothy Brady and me for lunch in the Cabinet Room. As we were finishing lunch, an amusing incident occurred; I tell it to show how easy it was for the President to relax and play jokes even in the midst of serious business.

Francis Biddle was announced; he had been asked by the President to get some information about something, and he was ready to report.

"Ask Francis to come right in here," the President told Pa Watson.

Then he turned to us, laughed and said:

"You know, Francis is terribly worried about civil liberties— especially now. He has been on my neck asking me to say that the war will not curtail them too much. Now don't laugh and give me away, but I'm going to hand him a little line."

After Francis had greeted us all and sat down, the President turned to him, and with a serious—almost solemn—face, said sternly:

"Francis, I'm glad you came. All of us have just been discussing here the question of civil liberties in the war, and I have finally come to a decision to issue a proclamation—which I am going to ask you to draft —abrogating so far as possible all freedom of discussion and information during the war. It's a tough thing to do, but I'm convinced that it's absolutely necessary and I want to announce it in this speech we are working on now."

We all sat there silent and serious. Not so much as a glimmer of a smile was on the President's face.

Biddle looked at us all, quite thunderstruck. Seeing that we all seemed to be in dead earnest, he immediately launched into a fervent argument against it. It was unprepared, but it was certainly vehement and, I must say, very persuasive. He stood up for greater emphasis and, pacing up and down, declaimed and declaimed against the idea. It went on for fully five minutes before the President and all of us burst out laughing. Francis took it in good spirit, but stayed around anyway for the balance of that afternoon speech-writing session. Maybe he thought there might be a germ of truth in it after all.

Whether it was a new joke going around Washington, or an amusing recollection of the President, or something funny that came to mind in connection with the language under discussion, or some anecdote or spicy gossip one of us had heard recently, the President was always eager for a laugh and always ready to supply one whenever he could. He never allowed the seriousness of the job in hand to become depressing. He enjoyed laughter, he enjoyed a good story, he enjoyed telling humorous incidents and anecdotes; he made these serious sessions pleasant, light and enjoyable experiences.

Once in a long while we would put a sentence or a phrase in a draft solely to amuse him, knowing full well that he could not use it.

Once—and only once—we put a sentence in that was a little bit off color. It was in the 1936 election eve speech which was being written at Hyde Park.

It really was not too much off color and it was an old, wormy chestnut. After a passage in the speech reading as follows:

> And when you go to the ballot box tomorrow, do not be afraid to vote as you think best for the kind of a world you want to have. There need be no strings on any of us in the polling place.
> A man or woman in the polling booth is his or her own boss. There once was a time when the ballot was not secret. That is not so today. How a citizen votes is the citizen's own business. No one will fire you because you vote contrary to his wishes or instructions. No one will know how you vote. And do not let anyone intimidate you or coerce you by telling you otherwise.
> "In the polling booth we are all equals"—

we had added the following:

> In the polling place, as in the men's room, all men are peers.

We inserted the line while he was out driving. When he came back it was chilly; he asked for some tea and said he would work on the speech at tea. Then he invited his mother to join us, saying that he wanted to read the speech to her. This pleased her no end, but it filled us with consternation as we thought of our little joke. As he settled down to read the speech over his teacup to his mother, we hoped that some interruption might come in time. It did not. The President plunged on, page by page, his mother smiling and nodding her head in proud approval. As he came to the paragraph, Missy had to go over and point to the passage in question and whisper to him not to read it. He read it to himself, however, smiled broadly, skipped it and read on. The gentle old lady never knew what had happened. And we never tried that again.

After the President had played his joke on Biddle, he resumed serious discussion of his State of the Union Message as easily as he had lapsed into his moment of fun. However, we did not get a great deal done that afternoon. Mrs. Henry Morgenthau, Jr., had sent over a tremendous bowl of pickled pigs' feet—which the President loved—for lunch for all of us. We ate too much, and had to stop work about three-thirty. The President and Harry went over to the White House, both to take a nap. Apparently the routine that Churchill was imposing upon them, plus the pigs' feet, was having its effect. In later years the President began to imitate Churchill and take a nap each day after lunch. Sometimes he would go back to the White House, but more frequently he would merely shift over to the long couch in his office and lie there with the shades drawn, and nap for an hour or so. He found, as Churchill had, that this gave him many more efficient working hours during the rest of the day and night.

That night, the 5th, we had dinner with Mrs. Roosevelt and the President in the West Hall; after dinner she left to keep a speaking engagement in Massachusetts. We all worked together in the Oval Room until about midnight; then Bob and I went over to the Cabinet Room and finished the final copy at about 2 A.M.

The next day the President asked us and some of the office staff to accompany him to the Capitol to hear the speech delivered. There, sitting in the Executive Box, we listened to him deliver this speech at noon to an enthusiastic and applauding Congress.

The President had put many hours into its preparation, and I think he knew it practically by heart. He was speaking not only to the Congress, but, much more important, to a worldwide radio audience as well. The speech was also to be rebroadcast during that evening, when it would have an even larger audience.

The entire body rose and applauded for several minutes as the President entered the Chamber on General Watson's arm. His face was sharp and stern, and never seemed to relent even into a faint smile until he had finished and turned to say good-by to the presiding officers on the rostrum. The members interrupted the speech frequently with applause. In press comments made after the speech was concluded, Congressmen of both parties expressed unanimous approval. This was the war leader talking now—and he was talking to a united Congress and a united country.

He started by pointing out that the attack by Japan was the natural culmination of the conspiracy among Hitler, Mussolini and the war lords of Japan which had been entered into in 1940. Japan's job in that conspiracy was "to cut off our supply of weapons of war to Britain and Russia and China—weapons which increasingly were speeding the day of Hitler's doom. The act of Japan at Pearl Harbor was intended to stun us—to terrify us to such an extent that we would divert our industrial and military strength to the Pacific area, or even to our own continental defense. . . ."

Here the President announced one of the important decisions that had been arrived at during Churchill's visit: that Hitler was to be treated by all the Allies as the principal enemy, and that the major part of our resources and manpower were to be directed at him. Referring to the necessity of concentrating on Hitler as Target Number One—a decision that resulted in our inability "to relieve the heroic and historic defenders of Wake Island . . . to land a million men in a thousand ships in the Philippine Islands"—he said: "Difficult choices may have to be made in the months to come. We do not shrink from such decisions."

The President then used two fine sentences of Bob's:

"The militarists of Berlin and Tokyo started this war. But the massed, angered forces of common humanity will finish it."

"Our own objectives are clear," he went on, ". . . smashing the militarism imposed by war lords upon their enslaved peoples . . . liberating the subjugated nations . . . establishing and securing freedom of speech, freedom of religion, freedom from want, and freedom from fear everywhere in the world."

"The world is too small," said Roosevelt, "to provide adequate 'living room' for both Hitler and God." I mention this sentence because Churchill in talking to us later said, "Whoever wrote that sentence I'd like to take with me to England." Neither of us said anything at the time; but it was Bob.

Turning next to the question of production, he said: "The superiority of the United Nations in munitions and ships must be overwhelming—

so overwhelming that the Axis nations can never hope to catch up with it. . . ."

Then came an enumeration of the production goals for 1942. These goals were so high and so unexpected that, while they produced great joy in the hearts of the victims of Hitler aggression abroad, they also raised incredulous eyebrows on many in the United States who doubted our ability to produce in such fantastic figures.

In fact, Roosevelt had quietly taken a pencil and raised the totals that had been given to him by his military and production staff as the maximum figures possible. When Hopkins questioned him on this, he said: "Oh, the production people can do it if they really try."

In the message, he spoke of 60,000 planes for 1942 and 125,000 planes for 1943. He spoke of 45,000 tanks for 1942 and 75,000 for the following year. He spoke of 20,000 antiaircraft guns and 35,000 for the next year. He spoke of 6,000,000 dead-weight tons of shipping and 10,000,000 for the following year. "These figures, and similar figures, for a multitude of other implements of war will give the Japanese and the Nazis a little idea of just what they accomplished in the attack at Pearl Harbor.

"And I rather hope that all these figures which I have given will become common knowledge in Germany and Japan."

Some of these production goals were later revised downward in the light of new developments and changing military needs; others were reached; and some were actually surpassed, notably shipping.

From production, the President's speech naturally turned to labor and the necessity for long hours and increased productivity; to raw materials and the necessity of curtailing civilian production; to the high cost of war, which "means taxes and bonds, and bonds and taxes. . . . It means cutting luxuries and other non-essentials. In a word, it means an all-out war by individual effort and family effort in a united country."

The President warned against the various facets of psychological warfare which he knew Hitler would use:

We must guard against complacency. We must not underrate the enemy. . . . We must, on the other hand, guard against defeatism. That has been one of the chief weapons of Hitler's propaganda machine—used time and again with deadly results. It will not be used successfully on the American people.

We must guard against divisions among ourselves and among all the other United Nations. We must be particularly vigilant against racial discrimination in any of its ugly forms. Hitler will try again to breed mistrust and suspicion between one individual and another, one group and another, one race and another, one government and another. . . .

Then the President announced his conception of the over-all strategy of the war—a strategy which was carried out until victory came.

"We cannot wage this war in a defensive spirit . . . we shall carry the attack against the enemy—we shall hit him and hit him again wherever and whenever we can reach him. We must keep him far from our shores, for we intend to bring this battle to him on his own home grounds."

Many people—frightened lest our own cities be attacked—were urging a very different kind of strategy. They urged that we bring back all our planes and ships; that we concentrate on the defense of our own shores. It is a testimonial to the leadership of Roosevelt and to his wisdom and the wisdom of his military advisers that such proposals never found acceptance with the American people.

Also there were many Americans who thought that Japan and not Hitler should be the object of our main offensive. The Hearst-McCormick newspapers urged this continuously, practically charging the President with a kind of treason in not sending enough force immediately to the Pacific to stop the Japanese and liberate the Philippines.

It was the President's job—in the face of the continuously bad war news—to bolster the morale of the American people and make sure that they never wavered for an instant in their determination to fight it out to an unconditional victory. The time was still far distant when he would be able to tell them of successes in the field. Now he could use only words of enthusiasm and hope, of courage and challenge:

"No matter what our enemies, in their desperation, may attempt to do to us—we will say, as the people of London have said, 'We can take it.' And what's more, we can give it back—and we will give it back—with compound interest. . . ."

He paid tribute to the courageous people of Great Britain, Russia, and China—a tribute which he repeated in nearly every wartime speech he made—and to the people of the other nations that had been overrun by Hitler.

He ended with these words:

"No compromise can end that conflict. There never has been—there never can be—successful compromise between good and evil. Only total victory can reward the champions of tolerance, and decency, and freedom, and faith."

Few, if any, of Roosevelt's wartime speeches failed to devote some time and attention to this type of propaganda: the promise of heavy attacks by land, sea and air, the statement of inevitable victory, the message of hope and faith to the people in the occupied countries, the triumphant recital of American production figures, the prospect of human freedoms throughout the postwar world. They were broadcast and rebroadcast throughout the world, they were put in leaflets which were dropped everywhere behind enemy lines—and they played no small part in gaining the ultimate victory.

As the President stood before the Congress on that day, the outcome of the war seemed terribly uncertain. Nineteen hundred and forty-two was to be the critical year. The President felt that the war job for 1942 was to hold—to hold the Japanese in the Pacific, to hold open our supply lines to Europe, to help the Russians hold the Nazis from the heart of the Soviet, to hold for another year all along the line until America could gather up her strength. The leadership in that job fell to Roosevelt. Sometimes it called for heartbreaking decisions in dividing and disposing our limited war supplies—decisions that would have broken a lesser man in that one year of 1942.

Within the next few months the President set up a number of those war boards with the strange-sounding names and initials which later became familiar to the American public. But before each of them was established, there were long conferences and negotiations, there were conflicts of personalities and personal ambitions, and there were many time-consuming and energy-consuming arguments.

On January 12 he established the National War Labor Board (NWLB).

On January 16 he established the War Production Board (WPB).

On January 26 he announced the creation of the Combined Raw Materials Board, the Munitions Assignments Board, the Shipping Adjustment Board.

On January 30 he signed the Emergency Price Control Act.

On February 7 he established the War Shipping Administration (WSA).

On February 24 he established the National Housing Agency (NHA).

On February 28 he announced the reorganization of the Army and the War Department.

On March 9 he established the Anglo-American Caribbean Commission.

On March 11 he established the Office of Alien Property Custodian (APC).

On March 12 he announced the reorganization of the Navy Department.

On March 18 he established the War Relocation Authority to take care of Japanese aliens, principally on the West Coast (WRA).

On April 7 he established machinery for rationing.

On April 18 he established the War Manpower Commission (WMC).

On May 15 he established the Women's Auxiliary Army Corps (WAAC).

On May 27 he asked the Congress for another $600 million for war housing.

On June 2 he asked the Congress to recognize a state of war between the United States and Hungary, Rumania, and Bulgaria.

On June 9 he announced the Combined Production and Resources Board, and the Combined Food Board.

During the early part of June he had conferences with Molotov, who had come to the United States from the Soviet Union to discuss the question of the second front and the continued supply of war munitions.

On June 12 he made a radio appeal to the nation asking the people of the United States to donate all of their scrap rubber to the service of the United States.

On June 13 he established the Office of War Information (OWI) and also the Office of Strategic Services (OSS).

During the latter part of June he spent several days in conference with Churchill.

On July 24 he appointed Admiral William Leahy Chief of Staff to the Commander-in-Chief in order to be more fully equipped to take his part in over-all strategy discussions.

On July 25 he established the War Relief Control Board.

On August 6 he set up the Baruch Board to survey and report on rubber.

On August 7 he received Queen Wilhelmina of Holland for a series of conferences.

On August 21 he issued a statement warning the Axis countries about the punishment in store for those committing war crimes.

On October 3 he established the Office of Economic Stabilization (OES).

Following the date of the State of the Union Message, the war was a series of disasters. The Japanese were spreading out successfully toward the mid-Pacific in the east, toward Australia in the south, and toward India in the west. Their march of conquest by land and by sea was so swift that it seemed to be almost unopposed. By the end of February, 1942, they had taken Singapore and had landed on Borneo, New

Guinea, New Britain and the Solomon Islands. The new territory acquired by conquest added to the old mandated islands, which they had illegally fortified, seemed to place them in an impregnable position. The lands they were seizing were rich with scarce raw materials sorely needed for war. A Japanese torpedo plane had sunk the *Prince of Wales*, one of Britain's mightiest and most modern battleships. Things were going so badly that the Prime Minister, in the face of grave criticism in the House of Commons, had to ask for a vote of confidence in his war leadership. The American troops in the Philippine Islands had retreated to Bataan, and although the news of their heroism warmed the hearts of the American people, there was no doubt that these men were doomed.

On the other side of the world, the Nazis had counterattacked in North Africa and were on a rapid march eastward. They were winning the Battle of the Atlantic. Their U-boats were operating with deadly precision practically within sight of our Eastern seaboard. Three German cruisers had managed to escape from a channel port through the English Channel—right under the nose of the British Navy and Air Force—and had found refuge in ports in Germany.

The President was beginning to feel concerned lest a spirit of defeatism settle over the American people. Americans had become accustomed to thinking that they could lick any nation with one hand tied behind their backs. Now, with all the resources and manpower of our Allies in the Pacific, we were being thoroughly smeared by the Japanese, about whose power and fighting ability a great many Americans had for years felt contemptuous. The Japanese and Nazi propaganda was taking full advantage of their victories.

It was in this atmosphere of black defeat that the President decided to make a fireside chat. The date selected was Washington's Birthday. To my mind it was an even more effective talk than that first fireside chat back in the dark days of 1933 during the banking crisis. His purpose then had been to inform the people about the complicated facts of finance and to reassure them that their government was taking any action necessary to protect them. This fireside chat in the dark days of February, 1942, had fundamentally the same purposes. The President wanted to explain to the people of the world the allied global strategy of the war, what the United Nations were doing to carry out that strategy, and just how the fortunes of war then stood. He wanted also, without giving information to the enemy, to tell as much as possible about our plans for the future. His second purpose was to give reassurance that, though the outlook seemed hopelessly dismal, liberation and victory were bound to come.

When we first talked about this speech, the President said, "I'm going to ask the American people to take out their maps. I'm going to speak about strange places that many of them never heard of—places that are now the battleground for civilization. I'm going to ask the newspapers to print maps of the whole world. I want to explain to the people something about geography—what our problem is and what the over-all strategy of this war has to be. I want to tell it to them in simple terms of A B C so that they will understand what is going on and how each battle fits into the picture. I want to explain this war in laymen's language; if they understand the problem and what we are driving at, I am sure that they can take any kind of bad news right on the chin."

This speech went through seven drafts before the President was satisfied with it. Bob and Harry and I worked on it with him. He himself had dictated a draft of thirteen pages. This was the speech I have discussed in Chapter I.

The newspapers, in response to his request, did print maps on which his radio listeners were able to follow his discussion of the war. As I sat in the basement room of the White House listening to him speak, I thought of the millions of families all over the country with their maps spread out in front of them locating the different parts of the globe to which he referred, and tracing the supply lines he described running from one side of the world all the way across the globe. And I thought also of those conquered and enslaved people all over the world who were listening at radios in dark cellars or concealed attics or in meeting places in the woods. This was the voice of the United States now, speaking with the strength of one hundred and thirty-five million people united in the struggle for democracy and human freedom. This was now the last best hope on earth. It was a voice that was to bring renewed courage to millions and millions of people all over the world. It was a powerful voice; and it would have been even more powerful if television had been in popular use during the war, so that the people could have seen the confidence and strength and determination of the man who spoke to them.

The President started on this Washington's Birthday by pointing out that in 1942 we were facing the "formidable odds and recurring defeats" that General Washington and his Continental Army faced nearly continually for almost eight years. And in Washington's day, as in 1942, "there existed fifth columnists—and selfish men, jealous men, fearful men, who proclaimed that Washington's cause was hopeless, and that he should ask for a negotiated peace."

He referred to those who thought that the over-all strategy of the war was wrong and "who still think in terms of the days of sailing ships. They advise us to pull our warships and our planes and our merchant ships into our own home waters and concentrate solely on last-ditch defense. But let me illustrate what would happen if we followed such foolish advice.

"Look at your map."

Step by step the President pointed out the great danger to us all if the United States, Britain, China and Russia were to isolate themselves, each from the other. There could be no aid sent to China, whose defense was keeping vast armies of Japanese troops away from other areas of combat, and was "one important element in the ultimate defeat of Japan." All the southwest Pacific, including Australia, New Zealand and the Dutch East Indies, would then fall under Japanese domination, which would enable Japan to "release great numbers of ships and men to launch attacks on a large scale against the coasts of the Western Hemisphere—South America and Central America, and North America—including Alaska." And also, Japan would "extend her conquests in the other direction toward India, and through the Indian Ocean to Africa, to the Near East, and try to join forces with Germany and Italy."

If we were to stop sending munitions to the British and the Russians, we would help the Nazis overrun Turkey, the entire Near East, the coast of North Africa, and West Africa, "putting Germany within easy striking distance of South America—fifteen hundred miles away." And "if by such a fatuous policy we ceased to protect the North Atlantic supply line to Britain and to Russia, we would help to cripple the splendid counteroffensive by Russia against the Nazis, and we would help to deprive Britain of essential food supplies and munitions."

He explained to those who were impatient about our failure to use our air power in the Pacific right away that although our heavy bombers could fly from here to the southwest Pacific, the smaller fighter and pursuit planes had to be crated and sent by cargo ships. On the map he pointed out the length and difficulties of this kind of transportation. He showed how the large number of bases the Japanese had seized and fortified made it easy for them to cover their transportation lines with air power; how their control of the air "has prevented us from sending substantial reinforcements of men and material to the gallant defenders of the Philippines."

The President answered the attacks of those who said that "Japanese gains in the Philippines were made possible only by the success of their surprise attack on Pearl Harbor."

"I tell you that this is not so," he said. "Even if the attack had not been made, your map will show that it would have been a hopeless operation for us to send the fleet to the Philippines, through thousands of miles of ocean, while all those island bases were under the sole control of the Japanese."

This was a fact not fully understood or appreciated by Americans in those days, and I doubt whether it is fully appreciated even now.

As the leading spokesman of all the people fighting the Axis, Roosevelt had to answer the propaganda pouring from the enemy radio:

Ever since this nation became the arsenal of democracy—ever since enactment of lend-lease—there has been one persistent theme through all Axis propaganda.

This theme has been that Americans are admittedly rich, that Americans have considerable industrial power—but that Americans are soft and decadent, that they cannot and will not unite and work and fight.

From Berlin, Rome, and Tokyo we have been described as a nation of weaklings—"playboys"—who would hire British soldiers, or Russian soldiers, or Chinese soldiers to do our fighting for us.

Let them repeat that now!

Let them tell that to General MacArthur and his men.

Let them tell that to the sailors who today are hitting hard in the far waters of the Pacific.

Let them tell that to the boys in the Flying Fortresses.

Let them tell that to the Marines!

The United States Marines were at that time performing indescribably brave and effective exploits, and this one-sentence combination of appeal to American pride and use of a common American colloquialism was a ten-strike (suggested by Bob).

Again, as the chief propagandist of all freedom-loving people, he envisaged the kind of world that would follow Allied victory:

We of the United Nations are agreed on certain broad principles in the kind of peace we seek. The Atlantic Charter applies not only to the parts of the world that border the Atlantic, but to the whole world; disarmament of aggressors; self-determination of nations and peoples, and the four freedoms—freedom of speech, freedom of religion, freedom from want, and freedom from fear.

The night that the President delivered this speech was the night that the submarine threw a few shells onto the shores of California. It was an abortive attempt to counteract the world-wide effect of the President's words of courage and hope.

Although during the months of March and April there were very exciting negotiations going on between the British and the Americans on military tactics, the next major Presidential speech had to do with what seemed on the surface to be a strictly domestic matter—the control of inflation. However, the President did not consider inflation to be a strictly domestic matter; he looked upon it as something inseparably bound up with winning or losing the war. This was a point he always stressed whenever he talked about inflation, privately or publicly. He was thinking not only of the greatly increased cost of war and the heavier debt burden which would result from inflated prices, but, even more, of the immediately devastating effect of inflation on the energies and morale of the American people. He was thinking of inflation's impact on wages and wage earners, of the vastly increased possibility of strikes, of the great diversion of energy from war production to the personal problems of making both ends meet. Nothing worried him more than the possibility of unrestrained inflation, and no nonmilitary problem took so much of his time and thought.

He finally decided to send a message to the Congress on April 27, 1942, in which he would recommend a fully worked out program to prevent inflation; and to go on the air the next night in a fireside chat to state the facts which made necessary the drastic program he was recommending.

In the early part of April, 1942, therefore, the President asked me to arrange a conference among the heads of the various agencies interested in economic stabilization in order to develop a co-ordinated program. As early as March 26, the Bureau of the Budget had been asked to prepare a confidential memorandum on the subject. The memorandum, consisting of about twenty-five typewritten pages, dealt with prices, wages and salaries, and with proposed fiscal measures to prevent inflation.

With that memorandum before me, I arranged for a conference in the Cabinet Room on April 10, inviting the various people of the government who were officially interested: Vice-President Henry A. Wallace, who was a member of the War Production Board; Henry Morgenthau, the Secretary of the Treasury; Marriner Eccles, the chairman of the Federal Reserve Board; Harold Smith, the director of the Budget; and Leon Henderson, the administrator of the Office of Price Administration.

I have a memorandum of that discussion; it lasted for several hours. There were expressions of opinion for and against all of the anti-inflation proposals which from time to time had been made by different officials. There was particularly sharp disagreement on one point: whether wages should be frozen along with prices of commodities or whether the adjustment of wages should be left to the process of collective bargaining. There was also considerable discussion about whether there should be a compulsory system of payroll deductions for war-bond purchases. On many of the proposals there was no agreement; and it was necessary for me to put some of them up to the President to decide. I prepared for him a complete memorandum of the case made by each of these officials, trying to report their arguments as fairly and fully as I could.

The interdepartmental conferences on some of the questions continued even while the anti-inflation message was being written. During its preparation, from the 10th to the 28th of April, I had many conversations, from time to time, with various people in the government. Some of the officials concerned conferred with the President themselves. There was marked opposition by the Secretary of the Treasury to some of the fiscal measures which were being suggested. While I tried my best to get agreement among the members of the President's official family, it was impossible. The President did not finally make up his mind on some of the disputed problems until he had the final draft of the message before him.

Neither the message nor the speech reflects in the slightest degree the weeks of debate and discussion and wrangling which went on before the final decisions were made.

My file on this subject is filled with memoranda from various officials, arguing their point of view more formally and not quite so lengthily as in the oral conferences. These too, as usual, I summarized for the President either orally or in writing before he made the final decision. I also consulted occasionally with people outside the government, including Mr. Baruch, who was the expert on this subject. He sent me some paragraphs which I had asked him to prepare.

Baruch was always helpful when asked to suggest ideas for speeches —especially speeches on foreign affairs, inflation, and war production. I suppose that nearly everybody in top Washington officialdom during the war could say that Baruch was of assistance to him at one time or another. Either on a sunny bench in Lafayette Park or in his suite at the Carlton Hotel, he was a kind of Mecca for troubled officials who wanted advice and encouragement, or for those who just wanted some wise and experienced but sympathetic soul to whom they could pour out their troubles.

I was no exception to the rule. I used to go over and talk with him by the hour on his park bench or in his rooms at the hotel, particularly when we were working on a speech or message dealing with war production, inflation, or finance. Frequently I took drafts over to show to him. He could always be counted upon for brutal frankness in criticizing speeches, and for keen wisdom in suggesting ideas. Sometimes, on request, he would submit a few original paragraphs himself. While we did not always use them as written, they helped to direct our thinking along sound economic lines. He was shrewd and farsighted about political matters and public reaction, more so than anyone but Roosevelt. He had great influence on the thinking and actions on Capitol Hill, and frequently used it to help pass legislation that the President needed or to kill legislation that might interfere with the President's objectives.

Roosevelt had deep confidence in Baruch's judgment on any subject on which he would express an opinion, for Baruch would not express an opinion on anything unless he knew exactly what he was talking about. He often would say that he would have to do a little further investigating before he could answer some question put to him. On economic and financial matters the President consulted him frequently; often he would tell me to go over and talk to "Old Bernie," as he affectionately called him, about some subject or other.

Baruch was helpful to the President in many other ways—sometimes anonymously and sometimes publicly. He was exceedingly helpful as an occasional intermediary between Roosevelt and Churchill, who was a very old friend of Baruch and respected his judgment. Mrs. Roosevelt sought his advice and guidance on all kinds of matters—public and private—and still does.

One incident in the summer of 1942 is typical of many and shows what Roosevelt thought of Baruch.

In the summer of 1942, the Congress passed a bill setting up a new independent agency charged with the duty of producing an adequate supply of synthetic rubber. The President vetoed the bill for several important reasons. In his veto message he announced the appointment of a board of three men to study the whole complicated question of synthetic rubber and to report all the facts. It was one of the most important problems in the war, for our source of natural rubber in the Far East had been cut off.

He had offered the chairmanship of the board to one of the Justices of the Supreme Court, who had declined it on the ground that his position on the Bench debarred him. The President then decided to offer it to Baruch. He asked me to take over to Baruch the following handwritten note, explain to him what he wanted done, and offer him the post.

DEAR BERNIE—

Because you are "an ever present help in time of trouble" will you "do it again"? You would be better than all the Supreme Court put together! Sam will tell you & I'll see you later.

As ever

FDR

That night, I had dinner with Baruch and Donald Nelson, then chairman of the War Production Board, who often sought Baruch out for advice. I explained what the President wanted, and Baruch accepted the post.

The President's sole reservation about Baruch was the great publicity that attached to his name. It was a publicity that Roosevelt thought Baruch sometimes courted, but on most occasions could not avoid. The public adulation which has been paid Baruch for many years sometimes made him stubborn in his views and ready to fight the President over them, though this happened rarely. Nevertheless, the two men sometimes fought and argued, as for example when they disagreed on SPAB in 1941, and on national service legislation in 1944. But both men were actuated only by what each thought was the best public interest. Occasionally they became quite angry with each other—but not for long. Nevertheless, Roosevelt avoided many mistakes, especially on matters of war production and inflation, just because of advice—and sometimes insistence—from Baruch. I know of no private citizen who,

These facsimiles represent the various drafts of the declination speech which Roosevelt intended to deliver to the 1940 Democrat National Convention in the event that the convention refused to nominate Henry A. Wallace for the Vice-Presidency and substituted some reactionary like Bankhead. See text pages 216-218. The first document is the first draft written in longhand by the President during the convention proceedings of the evening of July 18, 1940, while the debate on the Vice-Presidency was in progress. The second document shows Rosenman's corrections on the carbon copy of the first typed draft. The third document is the original of the first typed draft, to which Roosevelt in his own hand transferred the corrections which had been suggested by Rosenman, and wrote two new paragraphs in longhand. There is also one correction by Rosenman in the last line of page 1. The fourth document is the final draft, which the President was going to read to the convention, with handwritten corrections by Rosenman.

Document No. 1

Document No 1

THE WHITE HOUSE
WASHINGTON

4

the formation of discord
once this Convention was
convened.

That thing the fact that
the ones I cannot in
all honesty condone is
going with the fact
that party dissension.
It would be best not
to establish ideals.
It would be best for
America to have the
fight turn—

THE WHITE HOUSE
WASHINGTON

5

Therefore I give the
Democratic Party the
opportunity to make
that historic decision by
declining the honor of
the nomination for the
Presidency. I do so do.

Document No. 1

July 18, 1940.

MEMBERS OF THE CONVENTION:

In the century in which we live the Democratic Party has received the support of the electorate only when the Party stood, with absolute clarity, the Party champion of progressive and liberal policies and principles of government.

The Party has failed consistently when by political tricks it had been controlled by those interests, personal and financial, which think in terms of dollars instead of in terms of human values.

The Republican Party has made nominations dictated...

The Democratic Party, as appears clear from the events of today, is divided on this fundamental issue. Until the Democratic Party makes clear its overwhelming stand in favor of liberalism, and shakes off all the shackles of control by conservatism and reaction, it will not continue its march of victory.

It is without question that certain influences of conservatism and reaction have been busily engaged in the promotion of discord since this Convention convened.

That being the fact and the case, I, in all honor, cannot and will not condone or go along with the fact of that Party dissension.

It would be best not to straddle ideals.

It would be best for America to have the fight

end

Therefore, I give the Democratic Party the opportunity to make that historic decision by declining the honor of the nomination for the Presidency. I so do.

-2-

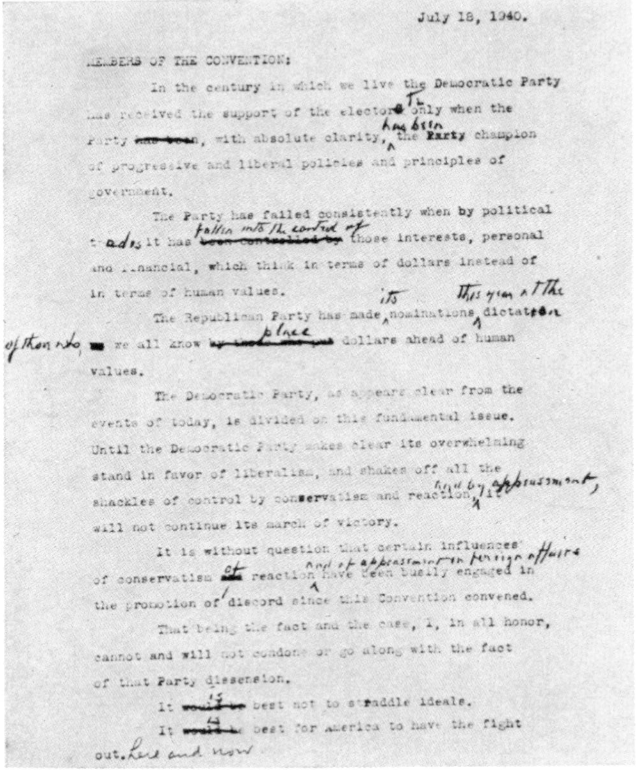

July 18, 1940.

MEMBERS OF THE CONVENTION:

In the century in which we live the Democratic Party has received the support of the electorate only when the party ~~has been~~, with absolute clarity, has been the Party champion of progressive and liberal policies and principles of government.

The Party has failed consistently when by political trades it has ~~been controlled by~~ fallen into the control of those interests, personal and financial, which think in terms of dollars instead of in terms of human values.

The Republican Party has made its nominations this year at the dictation of those who we all know ~~by their~~ place dollars ahead of human values.

The Democratic Party, as appears clear from the events of today, is divided on this fundamental issue. Until the Democratic Party makes clear its overwhelming stand in favor of liberalism, and shakes off all the shackles of control by conservatism and reaction, and by appeasement, it will not continue its march of victory.

It is without question that certain influences of conservatism ~~and~~ or reaction and of appeasement in foreign affairs have been busily engaged in the promotion of discord since this Convention convened.

That being the fact and the case, I, in all honor, cannot and will not condone or go along with the fact of that Party dissension.

It ~~would be~~ is best not to straddle ideals.

It ~~would be~~ is best for America to have the fight out. here and now

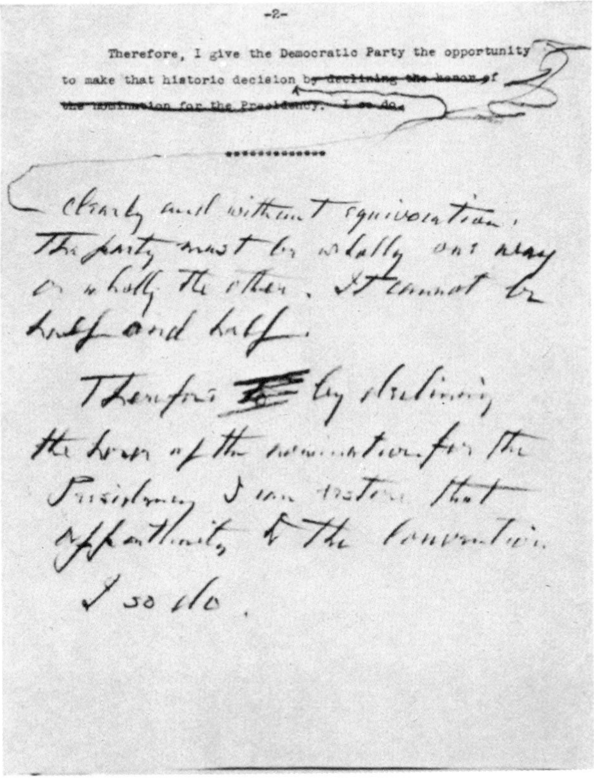

-2-

Therefore, I give the Democratic Party the opportunity to make that historic decision ~~by declining the honor of the nomination for the Presidency. I so do.~~

****

clearly and without equivocation. The party must be wholly one way or wholly the other. It cannot be half and half.

Therefore ~~I~~ by declining the honor of the nomination for the Presidency I can restore that opportunity to the Convention. I so do.

Document No. 3

July 18, 1940.

MEMBERS OF THE CONVENTION:

In the century in which we live, the Democratic Party has received the support of the electorate only when the Party, with absolute clarity, has been the champion of progressive and liberal policies and principles of government.

The Party has failed consistently when [through] political [trading] it has fallen into the control of those interests, personal and financial, which think in terms of dollars instead of in terms of human values.

The Republican Party has made its nominations this year at the dictation of those who, we all know, place dollars ahead of human [values].

The Democratic [Party] appears clear from the events of today, is divided on this fundamental issue.

Until the Democratic Party make clear its overwhelmingly... stand in favor of liberalism, and shakes off all the shackles of control by conservatism and reaction only by... appeasement, it will not continue its march of victory.

It is without question that certain influences pledged to conservatism of reaction and of appeasement in foreign affairs have been busily engaged in the promotion of

-2-

discord since this Convention convened.

[But being the fact and the case, I, in all honor,] cannot, and will not [straddle] ... the Convention.

It is best not to straddle it well.

It is best for America to have the fight out here and now.

[Therefore,] I give the Democratic Party the opportunity to make its historic decision clearly and without equivocation.

The Party must be wholly one way or wholly the other. It cannot be half and half...

Therefore, by declining the honor of the nomination for the Presidency, I can restore that opportunity to the Convention. I do so.

(A) In these days of danger when democracy knows more than vigilant, there can be no continuance with the kind of political situation internally and internationally... situations abroad ... keeps the enemy line attack from without.

Document No. 4

August 16, 1943

Dear Mr. President:

So much of the attached as refers to the proceedings now going on in Quebec is based entirely on crystal-gazing by the firm of Sherwood and Rosenman, New Deal astrologers. If any of it is correct, we shall be surprised. We do not guarantee its accuracy; it comes from sources not deemed to be very reliable; and any resemblance to any of the actual facts of the case is purely coincidental.

Frankly, we hope you will say: "The boys have done a lousy job with this draft. Maybe they could do better if they were on Canadian soil."

In which case, we'll be right up.

WASHINGTON AIRPORT
PLANES FOR QUEBEC AND POINTS WEST

Typical of the spirit of informality which prevailed around the President. A note from Sherwood and the author. See text page 386.

Dear Bob:

You have written me about Harry Truman and Bill Douglas. I should, of course, be very glad to run with either of them and believe that either of them would bring real strength to the ticket.

Always sincerely,

FDR

Hon. Robert Hannegan

FDR's longhand note in favor of Truman, which Hannegan carried to the 1944 Convention. See text page 446.

Convention
Draft of Major Plank *"except in case of attack*

The American people are determined that war, raging in Europe,

Asia and Africa shall not come to America.

We will not participate in foreign wars.

We will not send our Army, Naval or Air Forces to fight in

foreign lands outside of America / *except to defend and protect*
our own American interests

The direction and aim of our foreign policies have been

and will continue to be the security and defense of our own land

and the maintenance of its peace. To that end we favor and shall

enforce the rigorous application of the Monroe Doctrine. For years

our President has warned the nation that organized assaults against

religion, democracy· and international good faith threatened our own

peace and security.

...en blinded by partisanship brushed these aside these warnings

as war-mongerings and officious intermeddling.

The fall of twelve nations was necessary to bring their

belated approval of legislative and executive action that the

President had urged and undertaken with the full support of the

people. It is a tribute to the President's foresight and action

that our defense forces are at the peak of their peace-time

effectiveness.

A partial reproduction of an early draft of part of the foreign affairs plank of the 1940 Democratic Platform. The isolationists at the Democratic Convention wanted to provide that no American troops would ever be sent to fight in foreign lands. The President insisted on the now famous reservation "except in case of attack," and inserted the words in his own hand. The other handwriting is Rosenman's. See text pages 211-212.

in an unofficial capacity, rendered greater service than Baruch did during the war.

Though I had been carrying on interdepartmental conferences on inflation since the beginning of April—going back and forth between Washington and New York—we did not begin the intensive preparation of the President's message and speech until the evening of April 22. As early as April 11, however, I had prepared a very rough draft of a message. Bob Sherwood and I worked on that draft, and by April 22 we had a fairly substantial first draft which we submitted to the President. We worked first on the message to the Congress. That was the usual procedure where a message to the Congress and a fireside chat were to be used consecutively. On April 23 the President took our draft, and in our presence dictated a first draft of his own, using ours as a basis. This was one of the ways in which he frequently prepared the first draft of a speech.

Both Bob and I were very anxious to get into the message a recommendation for freezing of wages and for fixing farm prices at the levels then in effect rather than allowing them to rise to parity. Baruch had publicly urged, and privately convinced us, that that was the only realistic way to fight inflation successfully—straight across the board. Of course, the labor and farm leaders were opposed to this; but we based our arguments on the memoranda favoring such a course which had been submitted to the President. For this first draft, however, the President refused to insert anything of the kind.

On the next day, Friday, Bob and I worked on the message nearly all day. We could not get much time with the President because both a press conference and a Cabinet meeting had been scheduled. That frequently happened on a Friday: the press conference in the morning and the Cabinet meeting in the afternoon. We did have dinner with the President in the evening, and discussed the message carefully with him. Then Bob and I went over to the Cabinet Room and worked quite late. Before we went home we sent copies of the latest draft to the Secretary of the Treasury, the director of the Budget, and the administrator of the Office of Price Administration.

We worked all the next day, Saturday. Morgenthau brought over some proposed substitute pages which had been drafted in his department on taxes and the purchase of war bonds.

That night at dinner there were the President, Hopkins, Grace, Dorothy Brady, Bob and I. In the movie shown afterward, *Yankee*

Doodle Boy, Roosevelt was impersonated as the President. It was interesting to watch the man and the impersonator together in the same room. We felt the voice was very good, but the President did not think so. Bob said he thought that Roosevelt was a better actor than the man on the screen—and I think that the President silently agreed with him. He had a substantial amount of the actor make-up in him, and he liked it.

After the picture we worked some more with the President on the message. During the evening Crown Princess (now Queen) Juliana of Holland came in with her husband. Work stopped, refreshments were called for, and we all talked for an hour about the war news of the day. It seemed so easy for Roosevelt, in spite of the great press of time and the necessity of getting a message and a speech ready by a certain deadline, to drop work for an interlude of light (and unimportant) conversation, as though he had nothing at all to do.

The next day, Sunday, Leon Henderson, the administrator of the Office of Price Administration, met us by appointment in the Cabinet Room at eleven. He was boiling over with vehement protest about one part of the message, which he claimed would drastically raise the cost of living. The farm groups were operating under a statute which, by a complicated formula, would have permitted some farm prices to rise to 110 per cent of parity before being frozen. The New Deal policy had always been to restore parity prices to the farmers, but not to procure prices in excess of parity. This was one of the subjects about which there had been so much disagreement at the earlier interdepartmental conferences. Henderson urged that farm prices should be frozen as soon as they reached parity—otherwise, he argued, they would create a justifiable demand for further wage increases, and stabilization would become increasingly difficult. The current draft of the message did not include what Sherwood and I had been arguing for, namely, a return to parity. It merely read as follows:

Some of the products of the farms have not yet reached the stage of parity. Others have exceeded parity. Under existing legislation a ceiling cannot be placed on certain products until they reach a level somewhat above parity. I am confident, however, that with price ceilings imposed in accordance with law, the average of all farm products can be kept at a parity ceiling.

This was the passage about which Mr. Henderson was complaining so bitterly. We phoned to get Harry Hopkins out of bed and over to

he Cabinet Room to listen to Henderson's argument. We also phoned
Harold Smith, the Budget Director, to come over. There was a long
discussion among the five of us which was broken up finally only by a
telephone call from the White House usher to come over to the White
House for lunch.

At lunch there were the President, Harry, Sherwood and I. We had
already been turned down two or three times in our efforts to get the
President to insist that farm prices should not rise above parity; but,
bolstered by the arguments of Henderson, whom we had just left, we
all went at him again right after lunch. He was hard to convince.
He was sure, from his conferences with Congressional leaders, that
the Congress would not amend the law to permit price ceilings to be
imposed at parity, and he feared that if Congress did refuse the labor
leaders might refuse to agree to stabilize wages. In other words it
might give the labor groups an excuse to be as stubborn as the farm
groups. Our argument was that the President in his recommendations
to the Congress ought to be right in his economics, irrespective of what
Congress did with them afterward. We argued that if the Congress
refused to accept the perfectly fair and traditional New Deal policy
toward farm prices, the burden of the blame would be on the Congress,
and not on him.

Finally the President acquiesced, and dictated that part of the message which dealt with parity. After striking out the last sentence from
the paragraph of the earlier draft quoted above, he added the following:

This calls for the second legislative action which I have mentioned.
Under a complicated formula in the existing law, prices for farm products—
prices which housewives have to pay for many articles of food—may rise
to 110% of parity or even higher. It is the fault of the formula. In the case of
many articles this can mean a dangerous increase in the cost of living for
the average family over present prices.

In fairness to the American people as a whole, and adhering to the purpose
of keeping the cost of living from going up, I ask that this formula be
corrected, and that the original and excellent objective of obtaining parity
for the farmers of the United States be restored. . . .

As a national policy, the ceiling on farm products—in other words, the
maximum prices to be received by the producers of these products—should
be set at parity.

And that is the way it read in the message as delivered.

I have taken the space and time to discuss this technical question of
parity in order to show some of the work, discussion, and conferences

that often went into the writing of a speech. They involved not words alone but the establishment of fundamental policy.

On Sunday afternoon my wife came down and joined us at dinner with the President. After dinner the President worked for a while, and after turning out another draft in the Cabinet Room we all went back to the hotel.

On the next day, Monday the 27th, the President made a few last-minute changes in language. At noon, when the message went up to the Congress, Harry, Bob and I were already at work on the fireside chat for the next night.

That message to the Congress set the anti-inflation policy for the rest of the war. It presented a seven-point program of stabilization: to increase taxes and keep down war profits, fix price ceilings on commodities and rents, stabilize wages, stabilize farm-products prices, induce larger purchases of war bonds, rationing, and finally limit credit and installment buying.

Although the nation became accustomed to these controls as the war went on, it was a startling and drastic program in 1942, and shocked a good many Americans. It was extraordinarily successful in checking inflation. As compared with World War I, the increase in the cost of living after 1942 was negligible. It was not until after Roosevelt's death, when the Eightieth Congress removed controls and wiped out the program, that living costs began to get substantially out of hand.

In this message he also asked, for the first time, that a limitation of $25,000 after taxes be placed upon income of all kinds for every American citizen:

Some have called this an "economy of sacrifice." Some interpret it in terms that are more accurate—the "equality of sacrifice." I have never been able to bring myself, however, to full acceptance of the word "sacrifice," because free men and women, bred in the concepts of democracy and wedded to the principles of democracy, deem it a privilege rather than a sacrifice to work and to fight for the perpetuation of the democratic ideal. It is, therefore, more true to call this total effort of the American people an "equality of privilege."

At this time the Allies were still on the defensive and losing side of the war. In discussing with us his fireside chat which he was to make the night after the message, the President said, "I certainly would like to tell the people something about what is going on at the fighting fronts. I'd like to show them the kind of sacrifice their sons are making

—maybe in that way we can get them to realize how important it is to back up those boys by any sacrifice necessary."

Since our armed forces were still fighting a rear-guard action, it was difficult to dramatize the courageous job they were doing. The President conceived the idea of singling out a few individual exploits of outstanding American heroes; he believed that a recital of some of their incredibly brave acts would also bolster American morale, which had been badly damaged by the growing list of Allied defeats and withdrawals. He suggested that we could get some examples from the Army and the Navy.

We asked the President's naval aide, Captain (now Admiral) John L. McCrea, to get from the official records of the War and Navy Departments some of the outstanding instances of personal bravery during the past three or four months that would make inspiring stories for the American people. McCrea brought over several official records of thrilling valor and courage. We selected three of the best ones for the coming speech; the choice was a difficult one, for there were so many amazing incidents from which to choose.

The speech was not finished until 6 P.M. on the day of delivery. Of course, its tone and language were quite different from the formal message to the Congress. But its chief subject was the same—inflation.

The President started with a brief résumé of what was happening in the war, pointing out that American forces were fighting in all parts of the world. By way of propaganda both for the Russians and against the Nazis, he complimented the "crushing counteroffensive on the part of the great armies of Russia against the powerful German army. These Russian forces have destroyed and are destroying more armed power of our enemies—troops, planes, tanks, and guns—than all the other United Nations put together."

Then by way of propaganda for the French people he condemned the acts of the Vichy collaborationists and said: "Our victory means the restoration of a free and independent France—and the saving of France from the slavery which would be imposed upon her by her external enemies and by her internal traitors."

In these speeches the President was always careful to make sure, if he was praising one nation for resisting Hitler, that he included all of them. So, after pointing out how badly the war was going against us in the Far East, he took occasion to state, by way of propaganda for the Chinese people: "We remember that the Chinese people were the first to stand up and fight against the aggressors in this war; and in the future a still unconquerable China will play its proper role in maintaining peace and prosperity, not only in eastern Asia but in the whole world." At this writing this appears to be one of his least accurate prophecies— but it certainly was one of his most fervent hopes.

Pointing out how the worldwide war was bound to create civilian shortages and at the same time increase spending power, he repeated the stabilization recommendations he had sent to the Congress the day before. He bluntly said that every single person in the United States would be affected by this program—businessman, farmer, wage earner, landlord—and he explained what difference it was going to make to each one personally.

He went on:

The price for civilization must be paid in hard work and sorrow and blood. The price is not too high. If you doubt it, ask those millions who live today under the tyranny of Hitlerism.

Ask the workers of France and Norway and the Netherlands, whipped to labor by the lash, whether the stabilization of wages is too great a "sacrifice."

Ask the farmers of Poland and Denmark, of Czechoslovakia and France, looted of their livestock, starving while their own crops are stolen from their land, ask them whether "parity" prices are too great a "sacrifice."

Ask the businessmen of Europe, whose enterprises have been stolen from their owners, whether the limitation of profits and personal incomes is too great a "sacrifice."

Ask the women and children whom Hitler is starving whether the rationing of tires and gasoline and sugar is too great a "sacrifice."

We do not have to ask them. They have already given us their agonized answers.

Then he used the stories of heroism which we had prepared for him.

One of the anecdotes had to do with a Doctor Wassell, and his exploits in taking care of twelve badly wounded men, moving them out of Java and over to Australia. I have since received a letter from Commander (later Rear Admiral) Wassell in which he gives the following account of how he learned about the world-wide mention of his name and his exploits by the President of the United States:

On the morning of April 28th, 1942 (you know we are a day ahead of you out there) I started my regular morning rounds. First to the Hollywood Hospital near Perth, where I had my wounded. One of my Corps boys said to me "Did you hear the President talk about you last night?" I said, "Now you had just better take care of your work and not bring the President into your conversation."

My next regular stop was my Medical Store House half way between Perth and Fremantle. Here my old chief said to me "Well, Commander, what did you think of the President's speech last night?" My answer was "Oh, yes, George Washington used to speak about me in his younger days." . . .

Wassell would not believe the story until he saw it in a West Australian paper.

The President also told the gallant story of Captain Hewitt T. Wheless of the Army Air Forces, the pilot of one of our Flying Fortresses operating in the western Pacific.

His bomber developed engine trouble and lost contact with the other bombers with which he had started out on the mission. By the time it arrived at the target the other bombers had already dropped their bombs, and a hornets' nest of eighteen Japanese fighter planes had been stirred up. They attacked in mass the single bomber under the command of Captain Wheless. In spite of the attack, he kept on to the target, dropped his bombs, and started back.

The President described the fight:

As it turned back on its homeward journey a running fight between the bomber and the eighteen Japanese pursuit planes continued for seventy-five miles. Four pursuit planes of the Japs attacked simultaneously at each side. Four were shot down with the side guns. During this fight, the bomber's radio operator was killed, the engineer's right hand was shot off, and one gunner was crippled, leaving only one man available to operate both side guns. Although wounded in one hand, this gunner alternately manned both side guns, bringing down three more Japanese "Zero" planes. While this was going on, one engine on the American bomber was shot out, one gas tank was hit, the radio was shot off, and the oxygen system was entirely destroyed. Out of eleven control cables all but four were shot away. The rear landing wheel was blown off entirely, and the two front wheels were both shot flat.

The fight continued until the remaining Japanese pursuit ships exhausted their ammunition and turned back. With two engines gone and the plane practically out of control, the American bomber returned to its base after dark and made an emergency landing. The mission had been accomplished.

The name of that pilot is Captain Hewitt T. Wheless, of the United States Army. He comes from a place called Menard, Texas—with a population of 2,375. He has been awarded the Distinguished Service Cross. And I hope that he is listening.

He also told the story of one of our submarines and what it had been doing in the Pacific, the U.S.S. *Squalus*. It had been sunk in 1939 by accident; but it had been raised, put back into commission, renamed the U.S.S. *Sailfish*, and even as the President spoke it was busy sinking Japanese ships in the Pacific.

The President summed them up—these three exploits and the fighting spirit they typified—as follows:

These stories I have told you are not exceptional. They are typical examples of individual heroism and skill.

As we here at home contemplate our own duties, our own responsibilities, let us think and think hard of the example which is being set for us by our fighting men.

Our soldiers and sailors are members of well-disciplined units. But they are still and forever individuals—free individuals. They are farmers, and workers, businessmen, professional men, artists, clerks.

They are the United States of America.

That is why they fight.

We too are the United States of America.

That is why we must work and sacrifice.

It is for them. It is for us. It is for victory.

It was going to be a long time before the President would be able to tell the American people of victories.

Only a small group listened to that broadcast; it included two representatives of the British Political Warfare Agency who were Bob's guests, the Rosenmans and our son Jimmy, then fifteen years old, Leon Henderson and Frances Perkins. After the broadcast was over, we went up to the Oval Room to talk and to read the inevitable telegrams which had begun to arrive.

The next major speech of the President was not delivered until more than four months later.

In the meantime, and even during the preparation of his inflation program and speeches, many military problems and negotiations absorbed the President's time and attention. They had to do largely with the opening of the second front. The War Department was planning a full-scale offensive in Europe with concentrated American forces of men and weapons. The only place where this force could be built up in great quantity was the British Isles. The plan then being discussed was for a direct cross-Channel invasion of France by American and British forces. It called for invasion in the spring of 1943 across the narrowest part of the Channel rather than where the assault actually occurred in 1944. The invasion plan was originally known by the name of ROUNDUP; it was later changed to OVERLORD. The process of building up a sufficient force of American strength in Great Britain had the code name of BOLERO. There was also a supplementary plan: if the resistance by the Russians were broken in 1942 there would be an earlier token bridgehead invasion of the continent by a limited force of Americans and British. This proposed alternative operation was known as SLEDGEHAMMER.

These plans were worked out by the American Army, and by April 1 the President had approved them. The decision was all-important for two reasons: first, it was a clear and definite seizure by us of the initiative; second, it was a final reaffirmation that Hitler was to be the main target, and that there were to be no diversionary movements of American troops in other parts of the world which might interfere with hitting this main target just as hard as possible. On April 4 the President sent Harry Hopkins, General Marshall and several others to London to obtain the final approval of the Prime Minister and the British War Cabinet. This mission remained in England for several weeks, and, after full discussion, the British agreed.

In June, 1942, however, the Prime Minister came to the United States for a second wartime conference, mainly to re-examine the question of the second front and when and where it would be established. In the midst of these conferences news came that Tobruk had fallen to the Germans on June 21. Churchill had to return hurriedly to England to answer attacks in the House of Commons on his conduct of the war, and to engage in military conferences to find ways to counteract the successes of the Germans in North Africa.

In July, word was received in Washington that the Prime Minister was urging that ROUNDUP be abandoned as a major operation in favor of an invasion of North Africa, then being discussed under the name of GYMNAST. The President had always been sympathetic to the idea of a North African invasion. It seemed to be the quickest offensive that the Allied nations could take to relieve some of the pressure on the Soviet Union. For the President had been insisting right along that there be some offensive operation in 1942. By the end of July—after another trip by Hopkins, Marshall and King to London—a North African invasion in the fall of 1942 was finally settled upon. The operation was given the new name of TORCH, and replaced in priority BOLERO and SLEDGEHAMMER.

Although it takes only a short time to mention these military discussions and decisions, these missions overseas, and these exchanges of messages, the amount of the President's time and energy they consumed can only be appreciated by those who were working with him.

The responsibility resting upon Roosevelt in making these decisions was tremendous. Hundreds of thousands of lives were involved. If the first offensive were to prove unsuccessful, the crumbling of American and Allied morale would be disastrous.

During the summer of 1942 the President said several times that he would like to make a special radio address to all the youth of the nation —those in our armed forces and those at home—not only because recognition of their work was due them but because they had a particular interest in the kind of world in which America would have to operate after the war.

An appropriate time for this kind of speech came in the early part of September when the so-called International Student Assembly held a three-day convention in Washington and invited the President to speak to them. Before we started writing, knowing that Mrs. Roosevelt was very much interested in this organization, Bob and I discussed the speech with her and with a group of the young people in the organization.

Mrs. Roosevelt was very helpful on certain kinds of speeches. Because of her extensive travels and correspondence with people in all sections of the United States, she had acquired a deep insight into the thinking and reactions of the American people, especially the housewives and youth of the country. In her travels she always made a special effort to talk to young people—soldiers, sailors, WACS, WAVES, and civilians. She invited some of them to Hyde Park and to the White House, and encouraged them to write to her. At times she drove the Secret Service to distraction by her invitations to unknown soldiers who had expressed views to her she thought the President should hear. We never knew when one would show up, and she was always amused at our fears for her safety and the President's. Out of all this she had learned as much about the thinking and the emotions of the average American citizen as anyone with ready access to the President. She could fill the great gap which every President has in his contact with the people—a gap that arises from the fact that he cannot mingle with them as he would like.

Consequently, on speeches involving youth, education, and consumer interests, we would try to get her ideas on the best general line of approach, and at times would show her drafts of a speech. Once, while we were talking with her about a speech, she pulled a letter out of the pile of mail she was answering and from it we got an idea which we used.

She was helpful to the President in hundreds of ways. Her indefatigable energy made it possible for her not only to act as White House hostess, but to travel around the country, engage in nationwide activities, and meet the American people as none of her predecessors had ever done.

She never hesitated to express her views to the President, no matter how much she knew he would disagree with them. She was invariably frank in her criticism of him—and of his speeches. Sometimes I thought that she picked inappropriate times to discuss matters with him—as when he was engrossed in some other problem or perhaps during a social and entertaining dinner. Even she, however, was not always able to catch the President in a free moment, and frequently had to take what opportunity she could. Occasionally I felt that she pressed her point too hard; and sometimes I thought that she used to bring strange company to dinner to meet the President—company we knew he did not relish. But I am sure it was because she believed it would be to the President's own benefit, and of course the nation's, to hear what they had to say. Once in a while, the President, in self-defense, would decide not to come down to talk with them, but would take his meal up in his study with two or three friends. She understood, and was always pleasant and good-natured about this kind of obstinacy. As she later discovered herself, some of these people imposed upon her generosity and on her desire to help the President; but that did not discourage her in her search for facts and for the best means of attaining the President's objectives.

Her objectives were the same as his. She had none of the give, however, that is one of the great essentials of a successful political leader. It was hard for her to compromise, and she frequently disagreed with the President when he was willing to. She advocated the direct, unrelenting approach. If she had had her way, there would have been fewer compromises by Roosevelt, but also, I am afraid, fewer concrete accomplishments.

The President not only welcomed her advice and criticisms; he invited them—even when he knew he was going to disagree with them. He used to encourage her into heated discussions with others at the table or in the study in order to get the benefit of the clash of ideas among them. He would often ask me and others to talk to the "Missus," as he called her, to get her views and suggestions.

She is, of course, best known for her own activities outside the White House and, more recently, in the United Nations. There she has taken a role of democratic leadership, has promoted extensive international understanding and co-operation, and has earned for herself a reputation as one of the outstanding women of the world. Only those who were privileged to know her personally and to see the life she led in the White House can appreciate her feminine grace, charm, simplicity and tolerant understanding. No act of kindness and courtesy ever seemed too trivial for her personal attention. No act of helpfulness and encouragement seemed too difficult for her to undertake. Her instinct to help others often embarrassed her—especially when a government official would do something inadvisable because of a letter which she had received and, as a matter of routine, had sent over for his attention. She felt that he would exercise his own discretion in the matter, never quite realizing that he might construe her very transmission of the letter as a request that he do something about it. As a result, things were sometimes done for those who wrote to her that should not have been done, and that she would not herself have done had she known the facts. However, when one considers the many thousands of requests that came to her, the mistakes made were rare indeed.

Sometimes her insistence on listening to every point of view from all kinds of people put her into embarrassing situations. Coupled with the strong maternal instinct which made her happy to act as mother, guide, and adviser to the young people of her acquaintance, this intellectual curiosity and open-mindedness got her into occasional trouble with the hostile press. In the main, however, the attacks on her, like the attacks on all people around Roosevelt, were intended primarily to hurt "that man in the White House."

In any account of those associated with Roosevelt in his work in the White House who helped, encouraged, and advised him, Eleanor Roosevelt must be high on the list.

The youth speech was broadcast in the United States and also by short wave to the members of our armed forces all over the world. It was also broadcast in translation to the young men and women of the occupied countries who were the backbone of the resistance movement in Europe. The occasion had been well publicized and the Axis radio was giving it a lot of attention in advance with all kinds of ridiculous propaganda.

In this speech, the President contrasted the kind of world offered by dictatorships with that offered by democracies. Addressing the young men—the young fighting men—of our own forces, he had words of praise and encouragement, and also words of promise for the kind of world the Allies were trying to build.

During the summer of 1942, when the Allies were still on the defensive and Roosevelt was sorely beset by multitudinous problems, he set aside for himself in the Catoctin Hills in Maryland a simple week-end retreat. During the war it was difficult for him to go to Hyde Park as he delighted to do. It was an overnight trip, and it consumed manpower and fuel. The Presidential yacht had been laid up for the same reason, and also because it was considered too vulnerable to attack. The retreat in the Catoctin Hills, once a summer vacation camp for boys and girls, was now being used as a training camp for some U.S. Marines and some OSS men scheduled for overseas service. It consisted of a number of rudely constructed, small pine cabins, each of two or three rooms. The principal cabin of the camp was used by the President and his guests. It had a combination living and dining room, a kitchen, four small bedrooms and two baths. It was furnished with the most rudimentary kind of secondhand furniture, most of which had come from a navy storehouse where unwanted and well-used furniture had been accumulated over the years. The rugs had come from the same place and were in a bad state of repair.

The President occupied a bedroom looking out through the woods over a beautiful valley. To it was attached one of the two bathrooms. The other three bedrooms were double bedrooms but none of them had space for more than two simple metal beds, a dresser, and a chair. These three bedrooms were all served by one bathroom. The door to the bathroom never closed quite securely, and the President laughingly used to warn each of his guests of that fact; but the door never was repaired. There was practically no decoration on any of the walls except a few cartoons—including the President's favorite. This hung just outside his door so that each morning when he came out of his bedroom he had to pass right by it. It was a picture of a small girl running to tell her mother standing in the doorway of a prosperous and fashionable house: "Look, mama, Wilfred wrote a bad word." The bad word which Wilfred wrote on the sidewalk in front of his house was "Roosevelt."

Six or seven other cabins in the simple, almost bare camp were used by the members of the President's staff who accompanied him on these week-end trips. In addition there were the buildings and quarters of the training camp for the Marines, some of whom also acted as guards.

The President had selected the place because it was only about a two-hour drive from Washington, and was cool enough and secluded enough to afford him a two-day surcease from the depressing heat and humidity and the unending pressure of official business and visitors in the Capital. He had given the place the name "Shangri-la." The name expressed his appreciation of the reinvigorating effects of the few hours spent there each week; because of the strict wartime secrecy that enshrouded the President's whereabouts, it also was an apt name for a secret spot.

Not only the locality of the place but its very existence was a secret fairly well kept during the war by the newspaper correspondents in Washington, who of course knew about it—as they seemed to know about nearly everything. There was a direct telephone line to the White House switchboard so that Roosevelt was able to keep in immediate touch with anyone and any place in the world. And it was near enough to Washington to make it easy for the military and civilian officials whom he wanted to see to drive out to consult with him.

The housekeeping was done by the crew of Filipino boys who used to serve on the President's yacht.

A good part of the time at Shangri-la he spent on a screened-in stone porch at the edge of the woods overlooking the valley, arranging stamps or playing a game of solitaire, going over official memoranda, reading, talking with guests, or just sitting there looking over the valley, thinking. He nearly always brought a few guests, generally people whom he knew well and who knew him well, and knew his ways of working. Whether he was thinking, playing solitaire, or arranging his stamps, they never interrupted him with conversation.

The most restful aspect of these week-ends trips was that no one felt he should try to make conversation or small talk. Everyone did more or less as he pleased, as if he were off by himself. There was no effort to entertain anybody, and the spirit and tempo were of complete relaxation and detachment. Life was very informal. There never was any attempt at formal dressing; sport shirts and slacks were the custom. Certainly that was the President's habit—and old slacks his were. There were some fishing spots on the grounds which were sometimes used, but the President seldom left his porch during the daytime or his combination living and dining room after dinner.

Occasionally the President and I put in some work on a speech, discussing and outlining it, or perhaps even writing several drafts. Most times I was at Shangri-la, however, I simply joined in the chief order of business—resting.

On one of the first trips that Mrs. Rosenman and I made to Shangri-la with the President—on a purely social and restful, rather than working, week end—she made some notes. It was her first trip to the place, and it was the only time either of us kept any record of the many week ends we spent with him. I reproduce them here practically as she wrote them, for they describe a typical Shangri-la week end—indeed a typical week end of rest at Hyde Park, too.

Left the White House Saturday, August 8, 1942, at 2:00 P.M. The President, Ada and Archie MacLeish, Margaret Suckley, Grace Tully, Secret Service men. There was no motorcycle escort; the White House low license plates had been changed to high numbers not easily identified (as they have been since the war). It had been pouring rain in Washington. We drove two hours to "Shangri-la" where it continued to rain heavily. Driving as private citizens, we stopped for all traffic lights. We drove slowly through little villages, and the President was seldom noticed. Occasionally, the line of four cars would attract attention, particularly since the three or four Secret Service men, while going through a crowded street, would get out of their own car and ride on the running board of the President's car, watching the people. That attracted people's attention.

We reached Shangri-la about four. It was pouring too hard to sit on the lovely stone-floored screened-in porch which overlooks the valley which can be seen through an opening cut in the deep forest. The President was wheeled through the little house so he could show us to our rooms, and see where the pictures he had just sent up from Washington had been hung. He turned to the Filipino boys who had hung the pictures, and sweetly said, "Fine," and then added in an aside to us, as a casual afterthought, "I may make a few changes tomorrow." In fact, they had been hung very badly by the staff of the *Potomac*, who are in charge of this cottage now that the President does not use the *Potomac*.

The President very gleefully told us that all of us in the guest rooms would have to share one bathroom. I had had an account of this from Sam who had been here two weeks ago.

He then sat down in an easy chair in the living-dining room and I gave him the box of cheeses, cocktail appetizers and candy we had brought. He had a boyish glee in opening each package within the box, and then told Isaac, the Filipino who is in charge, just when to use each item during the week end. We all sat around chatting—sometimes about matters of importance but mostly about trivialities. The President, Archie and Sam would slide from serious talk to comedy with each other, and the President was thoroughly relaxed. At six o'clock he asked when I would suggest we eat. It was made a question of great moment. I was hungry and suggested some speed. So with much seriousness we all discussed dinner timing, and he finally decided that cocktails would be had at 6:40 and dinner at 7:00, and that he would take a little nap before 6:40.

During cocktails Daisy Suckley took flashlight pictures of us, and she also took several at dinner. At dinner the President asked for his little radio so he could hear the seven o'clock news. [The Commander-in-Chief of the most far-flung intelligence service in the world used to get a great deal of his war news this way. S.I.R.] Before we sat down to dinner, the White House, from which a direct wire runs, called and gave the President some more of the latest news. When he finished talking he said, "I've just read my newspaper," but made no comment of what he had "read."

During dinner he told story after story—things that had happened in the past. Some of the stories dealt with cases of executive clemency upon which he had passed and Sam had worked on when he had been Governor and Sam had been Counsel. Many I had heard before but had forgotten. He told each dramatically, and with every little detail. One case was that of a forger who had just taken the check of any convenient bank, written it up and passed it off. He told how the forger had left New York after he became too well known and went to Pittsburgh, and then later turned up in Cleveland. Sam told me later that he had remembered every little detail correctly—even the cities were the right cities. He also told an old French story, which he thought was written by Dumas but never translated into English. It was the story of a barber during the last desperate days of the siege of Paris in 1870 when the Parisians were starving. This barber used to supply delicious "veal" to the local butcher. It was suspected that the "veal" came right from the barber's chair, because several of the barber's customers had been missing for weeks. He told all the details about how the "veal" was butchered and delivered, until Ada shivered. She said she thought she might make excellent "veal" because she is a little plump— but pleasingly plump.

These gruesome stories were inspired by the fact that the six German saboteurs had been put to death that noon. Sam and Captain McCrea had reviewed the record of their trial for the President, as had been Sam's custom with executive clemency cases when the President was Governor. The telling of many of the old cases which had occupied his attention more than ten years before in Albany, with all details is indicative of the way the President does his job. Although someone else may do all the spade work of study and review, he grasps the facts that are analyzed for him so clearly and so thoroughly that they remain with him for years afterward.

After dinner the President worked on stamps; Daisy (as Miss Suckley was familiarly known) read, and I knitted. The President warned us that Grace would gradually have every one of us playing "gin"—which she finally did. Sam and Archie, Ada and I took turns playing with her—all losing to her. It was a very peaceful scene. After working on stamps awhile, the President started a detective story. About ten o'clock we all went to bed.

The next morning it again rained heavily. The President did not come out of his room until noon. He had been on the phone frequently during the morning. He went out on the porch. Grace had come over from her cottage a short distance away, and as he came out on the porch he started singing "Happy Birthday to you." It was Grace's birthday.

After some pleasantries, he started to work. He had dictated a draft of a message to Churchill on the first anniversary of the Atlantic Charter. He showed it to Archie and Sam for their comment, and asked what they thought of including the 28 nations in the message instead of just Great Britain. They discussed it for a while. He then read mail from the basket and dictated answers.

About 12:45 Captain McCrea (the President's Naval Aide) came up from Washington with war news that he said he did not want to discuss over the phone. We all rose to leave; but the President told us to remain where we were, saying, "We have no secrets to talk about—but if we have," he smiled, "we'll talk in a low voice—we'll whisper." As a matter of fact they did whisper most of the time.

McCrea had brought a large map which they unrolled and examined together. They talked for a half hour and we knew they were speaking of the big battle raging on and off shore of Guadalcanal in the Solomon Islands. The Marines had just landed there two days before.

They pointed to places on the map and you could see that they were following the course of what had happened. They talked to each other in soft voices, and I—for one—have no knowledge of what actually was discussed though I was not six feet away from them. The President asked McCrea to stay to lunch when they finished, but the Captain rolled his map, said he could not, and left. Later, when we went in to dinner the President said, "Things are not going so well in the Pacific. There are heavy losses on both sides." Nothing more was said. He was referring, I learned later, to the disastrous naval engagement near Savo Island where the Allies lost four heavy cruisers.

We changed the subject after a short silence, and I asked where the Nazi saboteurs were being buried. The President said that was one of the things he had discussed with Captain McCrea, and that they had not yet made up their minds. We discussed the various possibilities, and then he told two stories which Sam and I had heard him tell many times but could enjoy hearing him tell many more times. He tells them so well.

One story was of a famous English general who was killed in the battle of New Orleans. The English wanted to take him to England for burial—so they put him in a barrel of rum and lashed it to the deck. One of his descendants had shown the President his burial place in England. The President inquired as to the state of the body upon arrival. Descendant said, "It would have been all right, but some of the crew got thirsty and used an auger on the way over."

The other story was about a wealthy Chicago widow who was on in years, but insisted upon seeing the world. So she went traveling about until she finally reached Moscow. There she died. Her family cabled and asked that her body be sent to Chicago for burial. When it arrived they opened the casket to take one last look at "Dear Mama"—and much to their horror found a Russian General, with white pointed beard, in full military regalia, etc. They frantically cabled the Embassy in Russia, and received the following reply: "Suggest you close the casket and proceed with the funeral. Your grandmother was buried in the Kremlin with full military honors."

Some of the White House staff had planned a surprise birthday party for Grace at the Marines' mess hall, and had asked the President to come. The President was delighted and organized us all (including Grace) into a fake auto ride. When we got to the mess hall we stopped and Grace thought the President was going in to inspect it. He got out and was taken in. Grace said she thought she wouldn't go in as she had seen it many times; but Archie told her it would be impolite not to go in. When she got in, the young Marine lieutenants and other officers sang "Happy Birthday." Grace was much surprised. We were all introduced. They served cocktails and birthday cake—they even had chocolate ice cream for Sam. Ada MacLeish played the piano and sang most charmingly. The Marines sang. The President sang an old Marine song, and everyone joined in. He had a grand time, and it was a novel experience for the three young lieutenants. It was such an easy, natural atmosphere.

Before going back to the cottage we did go for a little drive. The President then planned a longer drive into the countryside for the next afternoon.

That evening, the President worked on his stamps, read a little, and we all went to sleep early.

Monday, the President stayed in bed until noon. He had been on the phone a great deal. The Solomon Islands battle was continuing.

Under Secretary of War Patterson and Mrs. Patterson came to lunch. Mrs. Patterson had come down from Putnam County where she was running their farm herself—without any help.

Before lunch the President and Bob Patterson discussed the Civil War, as some of it was fought in the neighborhood of Shangri-la. Bob Patterson is a great authority on battles of the Civil War. In this, of course, we were all present and took part. After lunch the President and Patterson talked in the living room for several hours while we all talked on the porch.

When the conference was over, we all went for the drive planned the previous day. The Pattersons went part way, and then drove on to Washington. The country was lovely. Few people recognized the President, but they were amazed at the cavalcade of cars—four of them—a lot for the area. Sometimes we thought children recognized the President (he drove in an open car with top down); but they just stood in the fields or on the road where they were and stared. I think they could not believe their eyes. One old man recognized him just as he had gone past and his face was fun to see. We were in the third car and got a fine sight of it.

We left at ten Tuesday morning to go back to Washington.

The President was able to relax completely, or the job would have killed him earlier. He could take bad news on the chin. He never lost his human touch, or his desire to share in the joys and sorrows and experiences of those around him, even in the midst of momentous events. He was expert at dividing his day into periods of work and play, of excitement and relaxation, of importance and minutiae—enjoying to the utmost every minute of every period.

His pleasures were always of the simple kind. He loved to drive through the countryside, observing the crops and stopping to look at old houses. He loved trees; he enjoyed planting them and he admired outstanding specimens when he passed them.

When he was out in the country, he would ask for a picnic whenever it was possible: sandwiches or a simple roast of frankfurters or hamburgers out in the woods. He would fish whenever he could—for large fish or small—and he continued the sport patiently whether he was catching anything or not. I have seen him hold a line in the Potomac River for hours and silently sit on fishing after all the others had put away their lines in disgust at the absence of a nibble. He enjoyed playing "Twenty Questions" on the rear deck of the Presidential yacht for hours at a time.

He dressed simply, too. That helped considerably to put me at my ease once. It was on one of my first overnight visits to the White House after the 1933 inauguration. I had brought my dinner jacket, but I was dismayed to learn that the only other guest at dinner—Premier Ignace J. Paderewski of Poland—was wearing tails and a white tie. Embarrassed, I sat downstairs stiffly with the Premier, waiting for the President to be wheeled in. When he finally appeared I was relieved to see him dressed in an unpressed seersucker suit! But despite his own informality, he never failed to admire a pretty dress or coat or trinket worn by a wife of a guest or associate or one of the young ladies in a group.

In social hours he liked informal company—people who would not insist on talking continuously about affairs of state or other serious matters. He preferred people who could relax the way he did and be gay when there was time for it. But even in company of this kind he often brought up a serious subject to get the viewpoint of one or more people. He liked to chat with people informally in all walks of life to see what they were thinking about. In Hyde Park, he would frequently stop his little car and talk with his own farm manager and with farmers he knew along the dirt highways in the remote parts of the country. He could not, of course, talk with taxi drivers, but he did try all other cross sections of the American public that happened to be close at hand when there was time for even a brief exchange.

Only four days after he spoke to the International Student Assembly he made another major speech. It was occasioned by his continued anxiety over the rising cost of living and the threat of inflation. The Congress had ignored the recommendations about parity prices and higher taxes that he had made in April. Elections were coming, and many of the Congressmen were loath to impose price ceilings upon farm products and levy higher taxes upon their constituents generally.

In view of Congress' laxity, many of Roosevelt's advisers were urging him to rely upon his war powers and—without waiting further for the Congress—to proceed by executive order to place into effect all the points of the stabilization program. I joined in this recommendation. In fact, after consulting with the Solicitor General, I had drafted an executive order which would have this effect; and it was on the President's desk.

Other advisers were suggesting a contrary course: that he send another message to the Congress urging the enactment of his program, and that he appeal once again to the American people in a fireside chat for their support.

This dispute and disputes about other features of the anti-inflation program had been going on for a good part of the summer. The President had asked me to talk to all the people involved. My records show that during the summer (which I spent in Washington during the court recess) I discussed the problem with Leon Henderson and David Ginsburg of OPA; William Davis, Wayne Morse, and Frank Graham of the National War Labor Board; Donald Nelson of the War Production Board; Fowler Harper and Anna Rosenberg of the War Manpower Commission; Frances Perkins, Secretary of Labor; Claude Wickard, Secretary of Agriculture; Vice-President Henry Wallace; Alben Barkley, the Democratic leader of the Senate; Henry Morgenthau, Randolph Paul, and Herbert Gaston, all of the Treasury; Justice James F. Byrnes; Benjamin V. Cohen; Isador Lubin, commissioner of the Bureau of Labor Statistics; Philip Murray of the C.I.O.; and William Green of the A.F.L.

It was proving impossible to stabilize wages while food and farm prices were being allowed to rise way above parity. Labor was becoming quite vehement about it.

There was also the usual violent disagreement between Harold Smith, the Director of the Budget, and Henry Morgenthau, the Secretary of the Treasury, on the fiscal policies involved in the fight on inflation. Time and again, each carried his arguments to the President. Finally the President sent me the following memo; I showed it to each of them, and it stopped their running to the President:

Memorandum for S. I. R.
Get Harold Smith, usually known as "Battling Smith," into a room with the Secretary of the Treasury, usually known as "Sailor Morgenthau," lock them in and let the survivor out.

F. D. R.

The course the President finally adopted was a compromise; a compromise in such a situation was not unusual for Roosevelt. In a message to the Congress dated September 7, 1942, and in a fireside chat the same night, he pointed out that although he had the power to take action himself, he was loath to do it and was submitting the question again to the Congress. He added, however, that unless some definite action was taken by the Congress by October 1, which was a little less than a month off, he would take the necessary steps himself under his war powers.

The fact that the President was ready only four months after his first message and speech on inflation to send another message and make another speech on the subject shows how important he thought it was. And it is a fact that he used to talk about it almost constantly, in terms that revealed his genuine fear and concern. Those critics who used to refer to him as a reckless, deficit spender to whom inflation meant nothing would have been surprised if they could have heard him on the subject. It was as much on his mind during 1942 as war production itself.

Work on this message and fireside chat consumed many days—in Washington, in Shangri-la, and at Hyde Park—at the same time that we were also working on the youth speech. The message to the Congress was forceful and unusually long. Since the President did not deliver it in person, he was not so particular about its length.

In it he pointed out that the pressure on prices had increased drastically since his last message in April. The chief difficulty, he said, was the lack of authority to stabilize farm prices, which were continuing to rise. As the President said:

> You cannot expect the laborer to maintain a fixed wage level if everything he wears and eats begins to go up drastically in price. On the other hand, it is impossible to keep any prices stable—farm prices or other prices—if wage rates, one of the most important elements in the cost of production, continue to increase. . . .
>
> Therefore, I ask the Congress to pass legislation under which the President would be specifically authorized to stabilize the cost of living, including the prices of all farm commodities. The purpose should be to hold farm prices at parity, or at levels of a recent date, whichever is higher. . . .
>
> In the event that the Congress should fail to act, and act adequately, I shall accept the responsibility, and I will act.
>
> At the same time that farm prices are stabilized, wages can and will be stabilized also. This I will do. . . .
>
> There may be those who will say that, if the situation is as grave as I have stated it to be, I should use my powers and act now. I can only say that I have approached this problem from every angle, and that I have decided that the course of conduct which I am following in this case is consistent with my sense of responsibility as President in time of war, and with my deep and unalterable devotion to the processes of democracy.

In view of the fact that the President was asking for legislation which adversely affected the farmer—at least in the first instance—he took this occasion to add to his recommendation "legislation which would place a floor under prices of farm products, in order to maintain stability in the farm market for a reasonable future time."

This was the farm support program, which was one of the most important causes for the unbelievably immense production of farm products during the war.

He next turned to the question of tax legislation which he had asked for in April, and recommended heavy taxes "on everyone except persons with very low incomes." Again the President repeated his suggestion that "the tax rate should be such as to give the practical equivalent of a top limit on an individual's net income after taxes, approximating $25,000."

In his fireside chat the same night the President now had some American victories in the Pacific to talk about, such as the Coral Sea, Midway and Guadalcanal. Nevertheless, he still wanted to tell a few stories of individual heroism. Bob and I gathered some more data and picked several examples from the many scores that were available.

The President began his talk with one of them, using it very skillfully to lead into his theme: the necessity of sacrifice by the "folks back home." He quoted a sentence from a little talk that the hero delivered to his bomber squadron just before he left for his mission—and death: "Remember, the folks back home are counting on us. I am going to get a hit if I have to lay it on their flight deck."

The President then said: "He said that we counted on him and his men. We did not count in vain. But have not those men a right to be counting on us? How are we playing our part 'back home' in winning this war?

"The answer is that we are not doing enough."

One of the things we could do, he said, was to see that inflation, or, as he preferred to call it, the "rise in the cost of living," was controlled.

Knowing that the American people, with all the stirring military news they were now receiving daily through their newspapers and radio, would not be satisfied with merely a discussion of domestic problems, the President had decided also to present the picture of the worldwide war as he saw it at that moment. He had told us to prepare a review, and with the assistance of the War Department we had gotten it ready.

He divided the global war into "four main areas of combat" and described each of them in a paragraph: "the Russian front," "the Pacific Ocean area," "the Mediterranean and Middle East area," and "the European area." Not a hint did he drop, of course, about the project for the invasion of North Africa, which was even then being rushed forward with feverish haste.

In discussing the European area, he used his usual tactic of keeping the Nazis guessing: "Here the aim is an offensive against Germany. There are at least a dozen different points at which attacks can be launched. You, of course, do not expect me to give details of future plans, but you can rest assured that preparations are being made here and in Britain toward this purpose. The power of Germany must be broken on the battlefields of Europe."

The fact is, of course, that the invasion of Europe had already been subordinated to the invasion of Africa—but the President was not going to let the Nazis get an inkling of this if he could help it. And besides he wanted to let everyone know—enemy and ally—that he did not subscribe to the comparatively easy theory that Germany could ever be bombed into submission from the air alone. He felt certain that Germany could be beaten finally only on the ground, and he was never persuaded to the contrary.

Then, again tying up the exploits of our soldiers and sailors with the necessity of sacrifice and more sacrifice by our people at home, he said:

"Battles are not won by soldiers or sailors who think first of their own personal safety. And wars are not won by people who are concerned primarily with their own comfort, their own convenience, their own pocketbooks. . . ."

This time the President was successful. The Congress passed the necessary legislation, and on October 3 the Office of Economic Stabilization was established by executive order. James F. Byrnes, Associate Justice of the Supreme Court, resigned from the Bench at Roosevelt's request and accepted appointment to this top economic job on the home front.

In the meantime, while Congress was debating the stabilization program, the President made one of his "secret" inspection trips throughout the United States—looking at factories, shipyards, training camps, and other installations having to do with the war. After his return he decided to make another fireside chat, giving his impression of what he had seen, bringing into the living rooms of his audience a general picture of the country's activity in producing materials for war. He delivered this speech on Columbus Day, October 12, 1942.

Even as he was delivering it, tens of thousands of American soldiers and sailors were on their way to North Africa from the United States. Other tens of thousands were making ready to sail from England on the same mission.

The speech was the speech of a military leader who knew that, for the first time since Pearl Harbor, the Allies had at last taken the offensive. In the Coral Sea and at Midway, the Japanese had been stopped; and, starting with our landings at Guadalcanal, we had taken the offensive from them. Roosevelt had just come back from a trip which convinced him that we had taken the lead in war production. The Russians had finally repulsed the Nazis at Stalingrad. And the opening of the long-debated second front was now only a matter of days. The surging confidence this knowledge gave him was in his voice as he spoke that night; it poured out of him and transmitted itself to the American people.

The President had dictated a first draft of about twenty-one pages which he had given to Harry and Bob and me to work on, asking us to add some words of praise for the many volunteers in selective service and civilian defense.

He had two grave problems to discuss in that speech: how to get adequate manpower for civilian production, and where to find more young men for our fighting forces. The solution was going to be difficult and unpopular; but the President wanted to give the people the facts.

The problem of manpower was acute. Paul McNutt, chairman of the War Manpower Commission, had sent us several memoranda, including a suggestion calling for compulsory methods of allocating manpower.

In this speech in October, 1942, the President urged voluntary measures of rationing our manpower. In 1944, as the needs grew worse, he recommended compulsory measures. But for the present he was satisfied with only a hint of its possible necessity.

By this time he had come to the conclusion—on advice from his military chiefs—that it was necessary to reduce the age for selective service, and he took this occasion to announce this very unpopular decision.

During this period some of the military writers in the newspapers of the country were criticizing the conduct of the war—especially the fact that nothing was being done to mount a second front or a diversionary offensive in Europe. Some attacked the President himself, saying that he insisted on making his own decisions without consulting others. Of course, they knew nothing of his long negotiations and arguments with the British on the subject; nor did they know that an offensive operation in great force was even then being carried out. The President had several times expressed to us his bitterness about this criticism, especially since his critics did not have and necessarily could not have the essential facts. He decided to let loose in this speech in a few well-chosen paragraphs of his own:

I can say one thing about these plans of ours: They are not being decided by the typewriter strategists who expound their views in the press or on the radio.

One of the greatest of American soldiers, Robert E. Lee, once remarked on the tragic fact that in the war of his day all of the best generals were apparently working on newspapers instead of in the Army. And that seems to be true in all wars.

The trouble with the typewriter strategists is that, while they may be full of bright ideas, they are not in possession of much information about the facts or problems of military operations.

We, therefore, will continue to leave the plans for this war to the military leaders. . . .

The reference to Lee was the result of a letter which the President had received early in March, 1942, from his friend R. C. Leffingwell. It had been reposing in the speech-material file since then. The letter quoted from page 235 of *Lee the American* by Gamaliel Bradford: "And laughing at them, in his own sunny, kindly fashion, he told B. H. Hill that the great mistake of the war was in making all the best generals editors of newspapers."

The President had dictated another insert, which we finally persuaded him was too rough, and he took it out. It read: "A very long experience before and during the last war, and before and during this war, leads me to make the flat statement that one arm-chair civilian strategist or commentator is more harmful to victory in a democracy than ten so-called 'brass hats.' "

Throughout his talk he hammered away on the enemies' morale:

They are proclaiming that a second front is impossible; but, at the same time, they are desperately rushing troops in all directions, and stringing barbed wire all the way from the coasts of Finland and Norway to the islands of the eastern Mediterranean. . . .

The strength of the United Nations is on the upgrade in this war. The Axis leaders, on the other hand, know by now that they have already reached their full strength, and that their steadily mounting losses in men and material cannot be fully replaced. Germany and Japan are already realizing what the inevitable result will be when the total strength of the United Nations hits them—at additional places on the earth's surface.

Roosevelt was reluctant to talk much about the role of the United States in the postwar world. As long as the dictators were sweeping to repeated victories, the time was not very appropriate. As things got a little brighter in 1942, he began to think and talk about it more and more. No reference to the subject appeared in this speech until the fifth draft. From now on, he undertook whenever he could to build up popular acceptance of the idea that America henceforth had an international role to fill and a part to play in a postwar international organization. How much of our willingness in 1945—and the willingness of the other nations—to work in co-operation toward a peaceful world was due to his constant repetition of this theme in speech after speech, and in one international conference after another, no one can accurately measure. Although in 1942 little progress had been made on a world organization, and although the wording and tone of his speech were therefore less definite and certain than in later speeches, it is nevertheless typical of scores that followed:

There are a few people in this country who, when the collapse of the Axis begins, will tell our people that we are safe once more; that we can tell the rest of the world to "stew in its own juice"; that never again will we help to pull "the other fellow's chestnuts from the fire"; that the future of civilization can jolly well take care of itself in so far as we are concerned.

But it is useless to win battles if the cause for which we fight these battles is lost. It is useless to win a war unless it stays won.

We, therefore, fight for the restoration and perpetuation of faith and hope and peace throughout the world.

There were no major speeches for the rest of the year. Instead, there was action. On the morning of November 8, 1942, the long-planned and much-discussed landings on North Africa began.

I saw the President the day before the troops landed, just before he left for Shangri-la. He knew what was coming. He knew that it was largely because of his own insistence that this invasion was taking place; that on the next day many American lives might be lost. Yet in spite of his terrible responsibility he was calm. Of course he was concerned—deeply. But there was no brooding, no undue nervousness, which might interfere with efficient, clear thinking.

The landings were successful; but the politics of administration in North Africa were not. The President was soon swamped with bitter criticism of American deals with Darlan, Peyrouton and others. He was criticized most sharply by many of his own liberal adherents, who did not have all the facts, and who were unwilling to recognize that many thousands of American lives had been saved by our military and political deals in North Africa. Much of Roosevelt's time was taken in meeting these attacks and in backing up General Eisenhower's administration of political matters in the invaded area. He strongly resented this criticism—indeed I do not remember his ever being more deeply affected by a political attack—especially since it came chiefly from those who usually supported him. He so sincerely detested Fascism and Nazism that the charges of undue and unnecessary collaboration with some former Fascists in North Africa were painfully distressing. He showed more resentment and more impatience with his critics throughout this period than at any other time I know about. At times he refused to talk about the deals in North Africa at all; at times he bitterly read aloud what some columnist had written about them, and expressed his resentment.

The story of those landings and the events—military, political, and psychological—that followed is not a part of this story. There is one exception. On the night of the landings, a speech by the President in French, which had been secretly recorded under military auspices, was broadcast at frequent intervals to the people in France and in the invaded areas of North Africa. It was an explanation to them of the American landings:

> We come among you to repulse the cruel invaders who would remove forever your rights of self-government, your rights to religious freedom, and your rights to live your own lives in peace and security.
> We come among you solely to defeat and rout your enemies. Have faith in our words. We do not want to cause you any harm.
> We assure you that once the menace of Germany and Italy is removed from you, we shall quit your territory at once.

Pamphlets reproducing the speech were dropped from the air. The propaganda aspects of the African landings had been planned long in advance, and were efficiently carried out.

This was the beginning of the turn of the tide. Everybody felt better. New Year's Eve in the White House was a much more cheerful affair than it had been in 1941. Mrs. Rosenman came down for dinner and the usual midnight celebration; the Sherwoods were there, and the Hopkinses, the Morgenthaus, and some other relatives and friends of the Roosevelts. Champagne was served at midnight; it had been omitted in 1941. We drank first to the President's customary toast on New Year's Eve: "To the United States of America." Then the President added a new toast for this annual custom: "To the United Nations." Then there was a toast "To the President of the United States"; then, at the suggestion of Mrs. Roosevelt, "To those members of the family and friends who are in other parts of the world and unable to be with us tonight"; then to the toast of the President: "To the person who makes it possible for the President to carry on," pointing out Mrs. Roosevelt.

The movie that night must have been selected by someone who knew about Roosevelt's plan to leave within ten days to meet Churchill in their next war conference in North Africa; it was *Casablanca*.

Chapter XVIII

The Tide Turns, 1943

Roosevelt's first address of 1943—his State of the Union Message on January 7—reflected the improved morale and heightened confidence that our successes in North Africa had brought not only to our armed forces but to all Americans. For the first time since Pearl Harbor he wanted to make a speech that was affirmatively optimistic. First of all, he wanted to give a comprehensive review of the fighting in all the theaters of war. Second, he wanted to report what America had done in the way of production. Although he was never fully satisfied with the rate of our war production—and always wanted to "put a burr," as he used to say, under those responsible for production—he now knew that American industry was beginning to accomplish the almost unbelievable goals he had set in 1941 and 1942. He wanted to boast about that accomplishment. He still remembered some of his critics back in 1941 who referred to his production goals as "fantastic" and "demagogic." Now the goals were being reached, and some were even being surpassed. But he was not so much interested in refuting his former critics—although that always pleased him no end—as he was in the propaganda value of telling the Germans and the Japanese about our production miracles. Third, he wanted to talk again about America and the postwar world.

The speech went through nine drafts; he dictated the first draft himself. Harry, Bob and I worked with him. It took many days of active preparation, and the President spent a great deal of time on it. Although few people knew it, he was also preparing for his departure two days after the speech for the Casablanca conference with the Prime Minister.

The message was delivered in person. In his review of the war, the President spoke of "the implacable defense of Stalingrad; and . . . the

366

offensives by the Russian Armies" as the "largest and most important developments in the whole worldwide strategic picture of 1942."

In the Eastern theater he pointed out that "The period of our defensive attrition in the Pacific is drawing to a close. Now our aim is to force the Japanese to fight. Last year, we stopped them. This year, we intend to advance."

He spoke proudly of the landings in North Africa, which compelled "Germany to divert part of her manpower and equipment to another theater of war," and prophesied that the Axis would be "driven from the whole of the south shores of the Mediterranean." He said the landings not only opened to attack the "underbelly of the Axis" but removed "the always dangerous threat of an Axis attack against . . . the continent of South America itself."

Then he let loose a fusillade of propaganda:

I cannot prophesy. I cannot tell you when or where the United Nations are going to strike next in Europe. But we are going to strike—and strike hard. I cannot tell you whether we are going to hit them in Norway, or through the Low Countries, or in France, or through Sardinia or Sicily, or through the Balkans, or through Poland—or at several points simultaneously. But I can tell you that no matter where and when we strike by land, we and the British and the Russians will hit them from the air heavily and relentlessly. Day in and day out we shall heap tons upon tons of high explosives on their war factories and utilities and seaports. . . .

Yes, the Nazis and the Fascists have asked for it—and they are going to get it.

Reviewing next our progress on the production front, he gave some detailed figures on different weapons:

"These facts and figures . . . will give no great aid and comfort to the enemy. . . . I suspect that Hitler and Tojo will find it difficult to explain to the German and Japanese people just why it is that 'decadent, inefficient democracy' can produce such phenomenal quantities of weapons and munitions—and fighting men." The sarcasm at this point was dripping.

He paid enthusiastic tribute to "those responsible for our American production—to the owners, managers, and supervisors, to the draftsmen and the engineers, and to the workers—men and women—in factories and arsenals and shipyards and mines and mills and forests—and railroads and on highways. We take off our hats to the farmers . . . to all the loyal, anonymous, untiring men and women who have worked in

private employment and in government and who have endured rationing and other stringencies with good humor and good will."

Note the all-inclusive list of people in this paragraph. Whenever the
President wanted to pay tribute to groups of citizens or to our Allies
or to the people of occupied countries, he was extremely careful to
make sure that no one was overlooked. He spent much time on this,
and would often repeat, "Let's make sure we're not leaving anyone
out"—and would look inquiringly around to see whether any of us
could think of some omission. The list would grow in each draft until
we were sure that all were included. Occasionally in the very last draft
one of us might think of another person or group, and the President
was always very pleased. I must say we got few or no complaints
about omissions.

Getting down to cases about the kind of America we were fighting
for, he said:

The people at home, and the people at the front, are wondering a little
about the third freedom—freedom from want. To them it means that when
they are mustered out, when war production is converted to the economy
of peace, they will have the right to expect full employment. . . .

. . . but that with the opportunity for employment they want assurance
against the evils of all major economic hazards—assurance that will extend
from the cradle to the grave. And this great Government can and must
provide this assurance.

I have been told that this is no time to speak of a better America after
the war. I am told it is a grave error on my part.

I dissent.

The President also got more specific about the postwar world:

"Today the United Nations are the mightiest military coalition in all
history. . . . [They] can and must remain united for the maintenance
of peace by preventing any attempt to rearm in Germany, in Japan, in
Italy, or in any other nation which seeks to violate the Tenth Com-
mandment—'Thou shalt not covet.' "

With all this optimism, however, he was not ready to predict when
victory would come. This is as far as he would go:

"I tell you it is within the realm of possibility that this Seventy-eighth
Congress may have the historic privilege of helping greatly to save the
world from future fear."

He missed it by eight months.

Two days later, the President was on his way by airplane to Casablanca to meet with Prime Minister Churchill. It was the first of the

several wartime conferences that the President was to hold on foreign soil. For the first few days of such trips his absence from the White House was not noticed. However, after a few days went by without visitors and without the usual daily announcement of appointments, it would become obvious to the White House reporters that the President was away from Washington. Censorship regulations permitted no one to speak or write about it publicly; and, with very rare exceptions, no newspaper or radio did. Occasionally, some of the people who knew about it simply could not refrain from whispering mysteriously that "The President is off on one of those trips," and in this and other ways people in many parts of the United States would get to know of his absence. The exact place, however, even the approximate place, was seldom known to more than a few.

The President would take along, at most, only the three newspapermen who represented the three major press associations, and one photographer, who furnished copies of all pictures to all the other photographers covering the White House. Sometimes the President did not take any newspapermen or photographers with him, but arranged to have them come on later to meet him. The press always objected to this treatment; it was the cause of many harsh disputes, hurt feelings, and bitter words during the war. However, great care was taken to see that all the papers were treated fairly, no matter which reporters or photographers were actually taken along on the trip. News releases were always so arranged that no one newspaper had a time advantage over the others.

The President's flight to the conference at Casablanca was the first time that he had traveled by air since he flew from Albany to Chicago to accept the Presidential nomination in 1932. He did not like it. He said that he did not enjoy flying over the ocean, that it was too monotonous, that there was no scenery, and that everything seemed so confining. He never did grow to like airplane travel; and whenever he could conveniently make a journey by train or ship, he did.

The principal purpose of the Casablanca Conference was to determine where and when and how the next attack on the Axis was to be made. The President tried twice to get Stalin to join them in this conference—Khartoum was suggested as the meeting place—but Stalin both times pleaded that he was absorbed in activities on the Russian front. The Allies had to decide whether the much-discussed plan to invade France during 1943 was to be carried out, or whether it was to be delayed until greater Allied air and ground forces could be established in Britain. The alternative was to proceed from North Africa against Sicily. This, of course, would be easier since troops and ships were already available in the Mediterranean in great numbers. It had other great military advantages: the capture of Sicily would eliminate a serious Axis threat to Allied shipping in the Mediterranean; it would provide fine air bases from which to protect Mediterranean shipping; and it would be an important step in knocking Italy out of the war.

At Casablanca it was decided to proceed against Sicily, and at the same time to accelerate the build-up of strength in the United Kingdom, and to continue to weaken Germany by increased strategic air bombardment.

It was inevitable that the tangled French political situation should come into the Casablanca discussions. Indeed Roosevelt and Churchill arranged for the two rival French leaders, De Gaulle and Giraud, to join them at Casablanca and take part in some of the talks.

Of course, the official communiqué of the Casablanca conference was couched in very general terms to give not the slightest hint of the decisions which had been reached. The President used to delight in the uninformative language of these communiqués. He loved mystery in all forms, and he knew it would baffle the enemy and give them what he called the "jitters."

This communiqué, for example, said: "The entire field of the war was surveyed theater by theater throughout the world, and all resources were marshaled for a more intense prosecution of the war by sea, land, and air." That was as much as the enemy learned about all our military plans.

It was at this conference that the famous "unconditional surrender" terms were imposed upon all our enemies. The President, at a joint press conference held by him and Churchill at Casablanca on January 24, 1943, announced the terms:

Some of you Britishers know the old story—we had a General called U. S. Grant. His name was Ulysses Simpson Grant, but in my, and the Prime Minister's early days, he was called "Unconditional Surrender" Grant. The elimination of German, Japanese, and Italian war power means the unconditional surrender by Germany, Italy, and Japan. That means a reasonable assurance of future world peace. It does not mean the destruction of the population of Germany, Italy, or Japan, but it does mean the destruction of the philosophies in those countries which are based on conquest and the subjugation of other people. . . .

I am sure that the gist of this statement had been carefully thought out. The President had said practically the same thing a few weeks before, in his State of the Union Message, although he did not use the actual words "unconditional surrender" before the press conference at Casablanca.

Churchill has stated that Roosevelt had mentioned the phrase in informal talks with him at Casablanca. Not only did Churchill know about the idea, but in an earlier, more formal talk at Casablanca, he and Roosevelt had decided to make a formal unconditional surrender demand, excluding Italy. Churchill telegraphed the British War Cabinet their intention.[1] The official communiqué of the Casablanca Conference did not use the words; but the phrase popped up in the President's mouth during the press conference. Churchill used the same phrase at this press conference when his turn came to speak.

In his first speech after his return from Casablanca he tried to make it clear to the enemy countries that he was interested only in the "unconditional surrender"—and punishment—of their leaders; that he was not concerned in inflicting harm or punishment upon the people themselves.

The President on several occasions during the rest of the war re-affirmed the terms of unconditional surrender, and they became the established policy of the United Nations. In spite of protests by some that such a policy would prolong the war, I do not remember any time when the President wavered on it.

In a much later press conference, on July 29, 1944, in Oahu, the President, talking about the use of this phrase at Casablanca and its implications, had this to say:

QUESTION: At your conference at Casablanca, you gave us a very fine phrase about unconditional surrender. Are we going to make that our goal out here in the Pacific? I wonder if you could tell us anything about that from your talks here?

THE PRESIDENT: There is nothing I can tell you, except that at Casablanca I made no differentiation between our European enemy and our Far Eastern enemy. The same thing applies to Japan.

QUESTION: And the goal with Japan is still unconditional surrender?

THE PRESIDENT: Still is with everybody. There has been a good deal of complaint among some of the nice, high-minded people about unconditional surrender, that if we changed the term "unconditional surrender," Germany might surrender more quickly.

---

[1] Churchill, *The Hinge of Fate* (Boston: Houghton Mifflin Company, 1951), pp. 685-687.

Mr. Churchill and I have made no modification of the terms of unconditional surrender.

They complain that it is too tough and too rough. I will explain it a little this way.

Back in 1865, Lee was driven into a corner back of Richmond, at Appomattox Court House. His army was practically starving, had had no sleep for two or three days, his arms were practically expended.

So he went, under a flag of truce, to Grant. Lee had come to Grant thinking about his men. He asked Grant for his terms of surrender.

Grant said, "Unconditional surrender."

Lee said he couldn't do that, he had to get some things. Just for example, he had no food for more than one meal for his army.

Grant said, "That is pretty tough."

Lee then said, "My cavalry horses don't belong to us, they belong to our officers and they need them back home."

Grant said, "Unconditional surrender."

Lee then said, "All right. I surrender," and tendered his sword to Grant.

Grant said, "Bob, put it back. Now, do you unconditionally surrender?"

Lee said, "Yes."

Then Grant said, "You are my prisoners now. Do you need food for your men?"

Lee said, "Yes. I haven't got more than enough for one meal more."

Then Grant said, "Now, about those horses that belong to the Confederate officers. Why do you want them?"

Lee said, "We need them for the spring plowing."

Grant said, "Tell your officers to take the animals home and do the spring plowing."

There you have unconditional surrender. I have given you no new term. We are human beings—normal, thinking human beings. That is what we mean by unconditional surrender.

The allusion to spring planting was a splendid way of showing that unconditional surrender did not mean starvation and extermination. The conference continued:

QUESTION: The fact is that unconditional surrender still stands?

THE PRESIDENT: Yes. Practically all Germans deny the fact they surrendered in the last war, but this time they are going to know it.

And so are the Japs.

This was one of the very few times that the President made a serious error in American history. It was not at Appomattox but at Fort Donelson that Grant demanded unconditional surrender; it was not of Robert E. Lee but of S. B. Buckner—in 1862.

The President arrived home in Washington on January 31, 1943. In a press conference in Washington two days later he described the Casablanca meeting as "essentially a military conference . . . a conference to win the war."

Roosevelt told us that he wanted to make a radio speech about the meeting. This became a regular custom upon his return from each of his international conferences. For obvious reasons, he never disclosed in these speeches the really important decisions reached. The enemy and the American public both used to learn about them later and at the same time—when bombs were dropped or landings made on enemy territory.

The President decided to make his Casablanca report on the anniversary of Lincoln's birthday, and he chose as his audience the White House correspondents, whose annual dinner was slated for that night.

I came down to the White House on February 9 to help on the speech. The usual team collaborated—Harry, Bob and I. The President had dictated a two-page statement of what he wanted to talk about. It was more usual for him to give us his instructions orally, but on this occasion he had found a few minutes to dictate them to Grace, and he had asked her to hand them to me when I arrived.

Because they are typical of the kind of instructions we would sometimes get about a coming speech, I am printing these two pages just as he dictated them.

I want to speak of two subjects which are based on my trip.

1. The atmosphere when you get closer to the fighting is a very different atmosphere from that which you get back home. One doesn't hear in places where they have been short of this or that—things that are essential to their living—the people grousing in the same terms that people back home are grousing about having their supply of butter cut down by a quarter or a third.

2. There are a great many people—to use a hunting expression—who are rushing their fences. They are demanding now that I come back and tell them what the boundaries of France, or the Netherlands or China or Russia or any other place in the world are going to be after the war is won. I cannot tell. Nobody can tell. It is all right to think about it, but to rush into print and have an argument about it now is about the greatest loss of energy, useless running up and down the field, that one can imagine; taking away of mental effort and getting the people all excited about something that is not yet ripe.

The country has got to get a better sense of proportion. Just for example: We read headlines about general charges of this and charges of that. It is perfectly all right to make general charges but if the people who make general charges would make specific charges about running the war, we would get a great deal further. I wish they would be more constructive and then we might get at some things in trying to run the war better which would be useful.

Just the same way that there is a habit in this country about talking about Brass Hats. Who are Brass Hats? It is an unfair term to apply to top people in the Army and Navy. (Perhaps use the Jeffers episode.) People have got to be specific. It doesn't pay to call a man a Communist in this country and throw him out if he has belonged to some liberal organization which is trying to do some good for some downtrodden part of the community.

On the back of the original pages Grace gave me appear the notes I jotted down during a conference I had with the President when I arrived, in which he amplified the things he wanted to say. They, too, are typical of the oral instructions he would give us before we started to work on a speech—that is, when he himself had not already dictated a regular first draft—and typical of the notes we used to take as he talked. I am quoting these fragmentary notes just as they appear in my handwriting in pencil. They may not make much sense to a reader ten years later, but to me they recall the things he spoke about at length while I jotted down the essence of what he was saying. As soon as a draft was prepared we nearly always threw away these cryptic notes; but in this instance I placed them in my file—probably because they were on the back of what the President had himself dictated.

Dictated by
FDR to me

| Efficiency ⎫
good order ⎬
adaptability ⎪
high morale ⎭ | | of Army and
Navy and
Merchant
Marine. |

Efficiency and common sense of our supply
    system—right kinds of
    material—right place and
    right time.

Always room for improvement—like
mail delays—trying to correct them.

Men at front understand
   1) Need of winning war
   2) What it means if we win
       1) Must work with rest
          of world to prevent
          Fascism and Nazism

3) Risking their lives to see that
   we accomplish something.
   They see both the forest *and* the trees.
Civilian populations recognize the problem.

Nearer home, we here do not see the whole of the
   forest because of magnifying trees and
   bushes, shrubs and branches

Great number here are still thinking in
terms of politics and personal convenience.
   Example (a)   Priority on a commodity—big
                   file—first goes to war
                   effort, on war front—if needed
                   to kill Germans with that is all—
                   irrespective of personal convenience.
                   That is a 2nd priority.
            (b)   People often look for
                   chance to say something to
                   hurt something.
                   Look at press clippings.
            (c)   People shooting off mouths—like
e.g. about Stalin and Chiang—Reason is Japan not fighting
Russia, China is not fighting Germany.
Can't send any to China—can use only transport
planes—not enough now—we send supplies.
Same thing with Russia—can't send troops—only
   equipment.
   Each—Russia, China and we—have our own theater.
   There *is* an Allied Council—each Republic doing part.
But cannot all sit on military council.
   The 4 nations have a council and
we keep the other nations informed.
   De Gaulle and Giraud. Talking about it
widens the breach. Churchill and I
trying to bring them together—Prisoners
have been released—
   Do you really think Giraud is pro-Nazi?
   Do you really think majority of North Africa is
        pro-Laval? They have not
        been able to fight Nazis.
   Peyrouton—minister in Paris, then
        Bordeaux, then Vichy. Vichy
        Cabinet tried to keep France. Peyrouton
        arrested Laval—Resigned gov.
        and left for Brazil.

The speech as delivered followed some of these general thoughts; but, as usual, other ideas were developed and added during its preparation.

In addition to these preparatory instructions, the President later dictated a rough first draft. Not much of it was used. Some of it was dictated in the process of "letting off steam." He never seriously intended that it should be retained, and we lost no time in deleting it. I print that part here as a milder example of what, on rare occasions, he might dictate to relieve himself of some of the outraged resentment he occasionally felt:

A newspaper owner, who is a professional sower-of-discord in our midst, recently tried to sell the American people the idea that the recent rationing of shoes to three new pairs a year would soon make every American child go barefooted—and all with the objective of providing nice new shoes for the civil population of Britain under the Lend-Lease Act. He was dishonest enough to omit the fact that under Lend-Lease we are not sending shoes to the population of Britain but that we are providing shoes for the many thousands of British soldiers on the fighting front—on the same fighting front that our own boys are fighting on. He was dishonest enough to try to throw an unnecessary and false scare into the families of America.

Few Americans can look at these men, soldiers or sailors without great emotion and great pride and a very deep sense of responsibility to them. I say few Americans, yet you and I know some Americans who, in seeing our soldiers and sailors at the front, have one paramount thought—the thought "How can I make political capital or selfish gain of one kind or another out of this war?"

Some snob asks glibly "Why should we give a quart of milk a day to every Hottentot?" First of all that type of man would have you people think that that is the great American aim in life. Secondly, he deliberately omits the fact that if the population of Dakar, and the population of Morocco and the population of Algiers and even the Hottentots could be helped to get a better standard of living, each one of them would have greater capacity to participate more greatly in the trade of the world and by that create employment needs among nations and, incidentally, assure greater markets for producing for the manufacturing nations of the world, including the people of the United States of America.

It might be illuminating to compare several paragraphs of the speech as Roosevelt finally delivered it with the notes from which they were developed. For instance, Block 4 of my notes, headed "Men at front understand," came out like this:

Ask them what they are fighting for, and every one of them will say, "I am fighting for my country." Ask them what they really mean by that, and you will get what on the surface may seem to be a wide variety of answers.

One will say that he is fighting for the right to say what he pleases, and to read and listen to what he likes.

Another will say he is fighting because he never wants to see the Nazi swastika flying over the old First Baptist Church on Elm Street.

Another soldier will say that he is fighting for the right to work, and to earn three square meals a day for himself and his folks.

And another one will say that he is fighting in this world war so that his children and his grandchildren will not have to go back to Europe, or Africa, or Asia, or the Solomon Islands, to do this ugly job all over again.

But all these answers really add up to the same thing: every American is fighting for freedom. And today the personal freedom of every American and his family depends, and in the future will increasingly depend, upon the freedom of his neighbors in other lands.

Block 6 of my notes—dealing with the selfishness of those who complained of hardships at home—became this:

Many of our soldiers and sailors were concerned about the state of the home front. They receive all kinds of exaggerated reports and rumors that there is too much complaining back here at home, and too little recognition of the realities of war; that selfish labor leaders are threatening to call strikes that would greatly curtail the output of our war industries; that some farm groups are trying to profiteer on prices, and are letting us down on food production; that many people are bitter over the hardships of rationing and priorities; and especially that there is serious partisan quarrel over the petty things of life here in our Capital City of Washington, D.C.

I told them that most of these reports are just gross exaggerations; that the people as a whole in the United States are in this war to see it through with heart and body and soul; and that our population is willing and glad to give up some of their shoes, and their sugar, and coffee, and automobile riding—and privileges and profits—for the sake of the common cause.

I could not truthfully deny to our troops that a few chiselers, a few politicians, and a few—to use a polite term—publicists—fortunately a very few—have placed their personal ambition or greed above the nation's interests.

The final draft of the speech then departed from the dictated notes and went into a description of war in Europe, in Africa, and in the Pacific.

For the first time the President boldly spoke of an Allied victory in Tunisia, and pointed out its military consequences:

"The consequences . . . are the actual invasions of the continent of Europe. And we do not disguise our intention to make these invasions . . . The enemy must be hit and hit hard from so many directions that he will never know which is his bow and which is his stern."

The President liked to make such statements of future plans, threatening the enemy without giving any information away. It was probably this kind of propaganda—backed by skillful deception on the part of our armed forces—that drove Hitler to complain publicly that if he were fighting experienced and trained military leaders, he could guess their future plans; but since he was opposed by lunatics and idiots like Roosevelt and Churchill who did not know traditional military tactics, he never knew what to expect from them—or where.

This speech also indicated—following again the longhand notes—the President's great concern over the criticism of the way we had handled political affairs in North Africa. As soon as France is liberated, he said, "Frenchmen will be represented by a government of their own popular choice." This was directed not only to Frenchmen, but to those who were fearful that the dubious French characters with whom we were working in North Africa would be able to seize control of the French Government after liberation. A memorandum of suggestions for the portion of the speech dealing with France had come to the President from Jean Monnet.

For the Japanese, the President had this to say:

"We do not expect to spend the time that it would take to bring Japan to final defeat merely by inching our way forward from island to island across the vast expanse of the Pacific. It would take too many years. . . . Remember that there are many roads that lead right to Tokyo. And we are not going to neglect any of them."

This speech, in my opinion, was one of his best wartime speeches from the point of view of building morale among our own troops, among our Allies, among the occupied and enslaved countries, and among the American people themselves.

Shortly after it was delivered I became ill. Since Pearl Harbor I had been commuting weekly between Washington and New York, taking care of my judicial duties during the week and spending all vacations and week ends in Washington. In the month of January, 1942, I was assigned to a part of the Court that heard appeals from lower courts. The nature of this assignment gave me the opportunity to spend more time in Washington. As a result, however, of the constant traveling back and forth and the double work I was doing, one of my eyes became temporarily blind. In April I was in Johns Hopkins Hospital in Baltimore for four weeks and thereafter had to remain in Baltimore for observation for another two weeks.

While I was at the hospital one of the President's little jokes nearly caused me some extra medical discomfort. He sent me several letters of sympathy and encouragement; in one he suggested that my ailment might possibly be due to too many chocolate sodas. The doctors had been giving me all sorts of tests and thorough examinations to try to find the root of my trouble. When one of them saw this letter, he suggested that maybe this one time the President might be right (he was strongly anti-Roosevelt) and that a stomach pump should be used to find out. I had quite a time convincing him that the President was only joking, and that he ought to forget about the stomach pump.

Fortunately the sight in the eye was completely restored. However, Dr. Alan Woods, who had treated me, warned me that I could not continue at the same pace; that it was overwork and nervous strain that had affected the nerve and temporarily destroyed the sight of the eye; that continued work at the same rate might cause a recurrence in both eyes, and that I would have to give up one of my two duties, either my judicial place or my war work in Washington.

When I told this to the President, he said that he would prefer to have me resign from the Court and come down to Washington full time for the duration of the war. I complied with that request.

Until my resignation in October, 1943, I could render only part-time service in Washington—for which, of course, I received no compensation except the consciousness of doing some small bit to help the President carry the great burdens of his office and of contributing something to the defense and war effort of the United States. When I resigned my judicial post and was appointed Counsel to the President, I became, for the first time, a part of the federal payroll (at less than one half my former judicial salary). Bob, too, received no compensation for his work on speeches. Only for a part of the time he was on the team did he receive any government pay at all—and that was for his services with the Office of War Information.

After I left the hospital, the President suggested that I spend the summer at Hyde Park. It would be easier to work because I could go back and forth on the train with him whenever he traveled between Hyde Park and Washington. Dorothy Schiff generously offered to let us use for the summer her unoccupied cottage near the President's hilltop cottage.

While I was still in the hospital, the President was called upon to make a major radio address, on which I was unable to do any work at all.

It was a unique Roosevelt speech in that it was addressed to one comparatively small segment of the American people. It was occasioned by a strike in the bituminous coal mines on May 1. Although the President had made several requests that the United Mine Workers under the leadership of John L. Lewis submit their dispute to the National War Labor Board, like all other labor disputes, his plea had been ignored. Accordingly, on May 1, as soon as the strike began, he issued an executive order directing the Secretary of the Interior to seize the coal mines on behalf of the United States.

On the following night, May 2, he made a radio speech to explain to the American people why he had taken this drastic step. Bob worked on this speech with the President. Roosevelt's hope was to bring the force of public opinion to bear upon the mine workers and their leaders to induce them to return to work. As he was on his way downstairs at the White House to deliver the speech, word came that Lewis had agreed that the miners should return to work in two days. There was a rapid discussion about whether the speech should be made anyway, and the decision was that it should.

After the successful completion of the Tunisian campaign early in May, 1943, the American and British leaders and their staffs met at the Trident Conference in Washington to agree upon next steps and future plans. During the two weeks it lasted, they set the target date for the invasion of France (now called Operation OVERLORD) at May 1, 1944, agreed on the details of the air offensive against Germany, and mapped out the future campaign against Japan, both from the Chinese mainland and from the sea approaches to the south and to the east. Finally, the conference directed General Eisenhower to push his campaign in the Mediterranean area until Italy was forced to withdraw from the war.

Ever since the first of the year, the President had been busily occupied by many domestic problems and difficulties arising out of the war in addition to carrying on the normal peacetime routine of his office.

On February 5 he established an interdepartmental committee to consider cases of alleged subversive activities by federal employees.

On February 6 he sent a message to the Congress asking it not to repeal the $25,000 net salary limitation which was part of his stabilization program.

On February 9 by executive order he established a minimum wartime work week of 48 hours.

During February he held a series of conferences with Mme. Chiang Kai-shek on aid to China.

On March 10 he sent a message to Congress transmitting the National Resources Planning Board reports on postwar plans, which had been developed at his request.

During March he held a series of conferences with the Foreign Minister of Great Britain, Sir Anthony Eden.

On April 2 he vetoed, as inflationary, a parity computation bill.

On April 7 he set up the Committee for Congested Production Areas.

On April 8 he issued the "hold-the-line" order on prices and wages.

On April 19 he set up the Solid Fuels Administration for War.

During April he took inspection trips through a number of war plants and training camps, etc., extending into Mexico.

On May 13 he sent a message to the Congress urging additional funds for war housing.

On May 26 he had to intervene in a rubber strike in Akron.

On May 27 he established a new Committee on Fair Employment Practices as an independent unit.

On May 27 he established the Office of War Mobilization to obtain greater speed and unity in the work of the war agencies.

On June 7 he addressed the delegates of the United Nations Conference on Food and Agriculture.

On June 21 he had to intervene in race riots in Detroit.

On June 25 he vetoed the Smith-Connally Bill—which was passed over his veto.

On July 2 he vetoed a bill imposing restrictions on the Commodity Credit Corporation.

On July 15 he intervened and silenced the public dispute between the Vice-President and the Secretary of Commerce over economic warfare measures.

These matters were popularly referred to as part of the "home front," as distinguished from the fighting front. But the President refused to distinguish between the two fronts. He insisted, and repeatedly asserted, that there was only one front. Whoever was engaged in the home front was as much a part of the war as any fighter. It was part of Roosevelt's job to get this concept over to the people. It was not too easy a task; but to a great extent he succeeded. That success was largely responsible for the high morale and efficiency of American industrial management and labor and of American farmers.

The identity of fronts was well explained by Roosevelt himself in a press conference on July 27, 1943. It was an extemporaneous statement evoked by a question:

QUESTION: Mr. President, can you give us any guidance on your speech tomorrow night—the scope of it?

THE PRESIDENT: It is going to be about the war.

QUESTION: Abroad, or at home, sir?

THE PRESIDENT: You know, I hoped you would ask that question just that way. This doesn't really apply to you personally, but I am just thinking about the general lines of thought.

There are too many people in this country who go after a slogan, who simplify things down, who are not mature enough to realize that you can't take a piece of paper and draw a line down the middle of it and put the war abroad—or the war front—on one side of the line, and put the home front—so called—on another side of the line, because after all it all ties in together.

When we send an expedition into Sicily, where does it begin? Well, it begins at two places, practically; it begins on the farms of this country, and in the mines of this country.

And then the next step in getting that army into Sicily is the processing of the food, and the processing of the raw materials into steel, and then the munitions plants that turn the steel into tanks or planes or the aluminum, whatever it may be. And then, even during that process and a long time afterwards, a great many million people in this country are engaged in transporting it from the plant, or from the field, or the processing plant to the seaboard.

And then it's put on ships that are made in this country, otherwise you couldn't get it over there at all. And it gets on board ships that you have to escort and convoy with a lot of other ships, and a lot of other planes that are based, most of them, in this country. And finally, when they get to the other side, all these men go ashore. . . .

But all through this we have to remember that there is just one front, which includes at home as well as abroad. It is all part of the picture of trying to win the war.

By the middle of July, so much had happened in the war, especially in the Mediterranean theater, that the President decided to make another report to the people in a fireside chat.

He did not deliver the speech until July 28, but as early as July 11 he had dictated a few short notes of what he wanted to talk about. They were some more of the kind of "steam" I have described before. Of course, they were not used in any speech.

For example, they contained an attack on those pre-Pearl Harbor isolationists—"a small and noisy minority"—who had urged that the war in Europe and Asia was none of our business and that "the government of the United States was made up of a bunch of crackpots, wild-eyed dreamers, communists and incompetents" who were urging that we were in great danger and should get prepared. And even after Pearl Harbor, he continued, there were "a lot of know-it-alls" who said that the production goals he had set were unrealistic.

On July 19, he dictated to Grace some more notes "to be incorporated in radio address," which he later gave to Sherwood and me when he asked us to accompany him to Shangri-la to work on the speech. In the meantime we had obtained from General Thomas T. Handy, Chief of the Operations Division of the War Department, and Colonel William T. Sexton, Secretary of the General Staff, a memorandum draft of their ideas for a possible speech. From this, which contained many interesting facts about the recent landings in Sicily, and from the President's notes (the later ones), we worked out a first draft.

In July, working at Shangri-la was much pleasanter than working in Washington. At anytime it was also more efficient than working in Washington. The President had few if any callers; he was not distracted by telephone messages except those of great urgency; he could work out in the open air on the screened porch; and, above all, he was available to us for longer stretches of time than in the White House.

The speech had begun to take final form by Sunday, July 25, when word was flashed to the President from the White House that Mussolini had resigned. The flash was in a radio report, which, in turn, was based upon an announcement from the Rome radio. To that extent it was not entirely reliable—although we could think of no reason for such a misstatement coming from an Italian-controlled source. Both Sherwood and I got on different telephones trying to get some definite and official confirmation from other sources, but we were not successful. However, pending further news, the speech had to be changed a little to include a discussion of this most important item and its effect on the war. Only two weeks before, on July 16, the President and the Prime Minister had issued a statement to the people of Italy, which had been transmitted to them by radio and by airborne leaflets, urging them to throw off their Fascist leaders and save themselves from the future horrors of war. Now, if Mussolini had actually resigned, the President wanted to push the advantage and get the Italian people to surrender unconditionally without more loss of life on their part—or ours. The news was not fully confirmed officially until we returned to Washington that Sunday night after dinner.

As finally delivered three days later on the 28th, the speech started off with a discussion of the resignation of Mussolini as the Number One war item:

"The first crack in the Axis has come. The criminal, corrupt Fascist regime in Italy is going to pieces." Then, to try to split the Italian people from their ally Hitler, he said: "Hitler refused to send sufficient help to save Mussolini. In fact, Hitler's troops in Sicily stole the Italians' motor equipment, leaving Italian soldiers so stranded that they had no choice but to surrender. Once again the Germans betrayed their Italian allies, as they had done time and time again on the Russian front and in the long retreat from Egypt, through Libya and Tripoli, to the final surrender in Tunisia."

The President announced that the terms for Italy were still "unconditional surrender"; that we would "have no truck with Fascism in any way" and would "permit no vestige of Fascism to remain." However, to encourage the Italians to force their government to surrender, he added:

Eventually Italy will reconstitute herself. It will be the people of Italy who will do that, choosing their own government in accordance with the basic democratic principles of liberty and equality. . . .
We are already helping the Italian people in Sicily. With their cordial cooperation, we are establishing and maintaining security and order—we are dissolving the organizations which have kept them under Fascist tyranny—we are providing them with the necessities of life until the time comes when they can fully provide for themselves.

The President believed that this speech helped to bring about the final surrender of Italy.

For the first time, the President announced in some detail the plans that were being made for "the return to civilian life of our gallant men and women in the armed services. They must not be demobilized into an environment of inflation and unemployment, to a place on a breadline, or on a corner selling apples. We must, this time, have plans ready —instead of waiting to do a hasty, inefficient, and ill-considered job at the last moment." This point had been covered in the notes the President had dictated. He then set forth a five-point program—the minimum program—which he hoped to accomplish for returning veterans. By the time Roosevelt died, most of this program had been enacted.

As 1943 progressed, Roosevelt had increasingly to warn the American people against overconfidence in victory. It was quite different from 1942, when his task was to bolster the nation against total despair and hopelessness and to try to keep alive its faith and confidence.

In this speech he put it this way:

The next time anyone says to you that this war is "in the bag," or says "it's all over but the shouting," you should ask him these questions:
"Are you working full time on your job?
"Are you growing all the food you can?
"Are you buying your limit of war bonds?
"Are you loyally and cheerfully cooperating with your government in preventing inflation and profiteering, and in making rationing work with fairness to all?"
Because—if your answer is "No"—then the war is going to last a lot longer than you think.

The new situation in Italy obviously called for a rapid meeting between the British and the Americans. Churchill and the President met at Quebec on August 17, 1943, in a top-level conference that was given the name Quadrant.

The decisions reached were as follows:

1. That the invasion of France in 1944 through Normandy should be supplemented by an invasion of the southern shores of France in the Toulon-Marseilles area.
2. Although negotiations were going on for the surrender of Italy, General Eisenhower was directed to seize Corsica and Sardinia.
3. That a four-power declaration should be worked out (including the Soviet Union and China) providing for the establishment of an effective international organization after the war.
4. That the supreme command in the Normandy invasion should go to an American.
5. To create a Southeast Asia Command under Lord Louis Mountbatten. General Joseph W. Stilwell was designated as Deputy Supreme Allied Commander in the area.

A general air of optimism prevailed at this first Quebec Conference. In addition to the imminent fall of Italy, the naval picture in the Atlantic had brightened perceptibly, and it was possible for Roosevelt and Churchill in a joint statement to report that the British Navy and the United States Navy definitely had the upper hand in the war against the U-boats. Furthermore, the shortage of escort vessels was being relieved by superhuman production efforts.

The communiqué issued after this conference was particularly un-informative. The press complained so bitterly about the censorship and secrecy that at a press conference in Quebec on August 24, following the conference, both Churchill and Roosevelt apologized for the lack of news.

While the President was engaged in the conference in Quebec, Bob and I received word by phone from Grace that he wanted us to prepare a draft of a speech which he could deliver at Ottawa as a report on the conference. We suggested that since we were several hundred miles from the conference, it might be a good idea for us to come up to Canada and learn something about what had happened.

Grace called back and told us that the President was very busy attending meetings, and that he would probably not be able to give us much time in Quebec; that we should go ahead and draft something and send it up to him.

We knew the general background and purposes of the conference. We had not the faintest idea, however, of the extent of agreement or whether any new subjects had come up for discussion. But we knew that the nature of the decisions at these conferences precluded giving any exact details about them. We proceeded to prepare a draft as best we could. The distance seemed, at first, too much of a mental hazard, and we felt a little like Cinderellas left behind. Over the phone, we hinted broadly to the other members of the President's party that we could do a much better job if we were up in Quebec; but the hints never took effect. Finally Sherwood and I sent a draft of a speech up to the President, with a covering letter reading as follows:

DEAR MR. PRESIDENT:
So much of the attached draft as refers to the proceedings now going on in Quebec is based entirely on crystal-gazing by the firm of Sherwood and Rosenman, New Deal astrologers.
If any of it is correct, we shall be surprised. We do not guarantee its accuracy; it comes from sources not deemed to be very reliable; and any resemblance to any of the actual facts of the case is purely coincidental.
Frankly, we hope you will say: "The boys have done a lousy job with the draft. Maybe they could do better if they were on Canadian soil."
In which case, we'll be right up.

It was signed with a drawing (by Sherwood) of a tall thin man—Sherwood; and a short fat man—Rosenman. (See facsimile section, p. 336.)

The summons to Quebec never came; so we settled back, thinking that the speech was either all right or had been thrown bodily into the wastepaper basket. What happened was that the President worked on it very carefully, making many changes in language here and there, which strengthened it. But except for the final pages, the draft we sent up was used rather extensively.

We congratulated ourselves that through long experience we had become pretty well able to guess in a general way what the President was going to want to say. By experience, too—and by watching our words frequently go into the wastepaper basket—we came to know even the kind of expressions and language which were his.

The Ottawa speech was not a major policy speech in any sense of the word. It was, however, important. As I have indicated, the President discarded the last few pages of our draft and wrote a new conclusion with an optimistic note:

Surely by unanimous action in driving out the outlaws and keeping them under heel forever, we can attain a freedom from fear of violence.

I am everlastingly angry only at those who assert vociferously that the four freedoms and the Atlantic Charter are nonsense because they are unattainable. If those people had lived a century and a half ago they would have sneered and said that the Declaration of Independence was utter piffle. If they had lived nearly a thousand years ago they would have laughed uproariously at the ideals of Magna Chàrta. And if they had lived several thousand years ago they would have derided Moses when he came from the Mountain with the Ten Commandments.

We concede that these great teachings are not perfectly lived up to today, but I would rather be a builder than a wrecker, hoping always that the structure of life is growing—not dying. . . .

After the Quebec Conference the Prime Minister and his daughter Mary went to Hyde Park to spend a few days with the President. While they were there the Roosevelts gave one of their usual picnics on the hilltop. The hamburgers and hot dogs, which generally formed the *pièces de résistance* of Roosevelt picnics, were present in profusion. The dessert was watermelon served in large slices. This was all a new kind of luncheon fare to the Churchills, and they enjoyed it. I recall the President admonishing Mary, who was having her first taste of watermelon, to be sure not to swallow any of the pits lest they grow into watermelons in her stomach.

The Prime Minister's cheerfulness revealed more eloquently than the formal communiqués how much better we were doing in the war. The President, too, was in a cheerful mood—although even during the darkest days of the war he never seemed so worried or so downcast as did the Prime Minister. But at the picnic, the change in the fortunes of war could likewise be seen in his face. Also, as I learned later, progress was being made in arranging for a Big Three conference; this was something the President had long been pushing, and it added to his satisfaction.

During that summer I saw a great deal of Roosevelt at Hyde Park. Our cottage was only a short distance from his home. I was recuperating from my eye illness, and the President, who enjoyed nothing better than riding through the countryside of Dutchess County in his small automobile, came over frequently for lunch or dinner. Our cottage was on the top of a hill, with a distant unobstructed view for miles on all sides. The President loved to sit on our terrace silently looking over the scenery of his native and beloved Dutchess County. It was always very peaceful and quiet there. No one felt the need of making conversation. There was only one source of noise and conflict. The President always had his dog Fala with him. The Rosenmans had a wire-haired terrier by the name of Spotty. Spotty and Fala became implacable enemies—nobody knows why—and they did not care who knew it. After a while we had to lock Spotty up in one of the bedrooms whenever Fala was about the premises.

On September 17, the Congress, which had been in a two months' recess, returned to Washington. The President on that date sent it an unusually long and complete report on the state of the war. He had spent a good deal of time on the message himself, and it went through several drafts. It was intended to be as informative as military security would permit. In the course of his review, he pounded away again on what was becoming one of his favorite themes: that the war was far from won and over. He was now genuinely worried that Americans might grow complacent about the war and thus prolong it and even endanger the ultimate victory. It was a concern that he also expressed again and again in private conversation.

He made another plea for "greater economic protection of our returning men and women in the armed forces—and for greater educational opportunities for them," and urged a study of legislation necessary to meet the problems of eventual demobilization. Here again he wanted to make sure that his recommendation would not be misconstrued:

"I do not mean that this statement should be regarded in any way as an intimation that we are approaching the end of the war. Such an intimation could not be based either on fact or on reason. But when the war ends, we do not want to be caught again without planning or legislation, such as occurred at the end of the last war."

The next important message to the Congress was on October 6, 1943, requesting authority to proclaim a free Philippine Government. The President was particularly interested in the Philippines at this time, for two reasons:

First, he wanted to do something to keep up the morale and fighting spirit of the Philippine people, who had been subjected to the harsh rule of a Japanese puppet government for nearly two years. Second, he hoped that the treatment of the Philippines by the United States— including the granting of final independence—would serve as a model and example for the European powers who had colonies in the Far East.

Since Pearl Harbor the President had been giving assurance and encouragement to the Philippine people. As recently as August 12, 1943, he had made an address in which he said, "I give the Filipino people my word that the Republic of the Philippines will be established the moment the power of our Japanese enemies is destroyed. . . . You will soon be redeemed from the Japanese yoke and you will be assisted in the full repair of the ravages caused by the war."

Nevertheless, despite his promises and encouragement, the morale of the people of the Islands was—perhaps understandably—low. Japanese propaganda and disloyal native collaborationists had combined to make many of the otherwise loyal Filipinos skeptical of the plans and promises of the United States. On September 11, the matter was brought to the President's attention anew by a letter from President Quezon, who was being treated for advanced tuberculosis at Saranac Lake, New York.

OFFICE OF THE PRESIDENT
OF THE PHILIPPINES

CAMP McMARTIN
SARANAC LAKE, N. Y.
September 11, 1943

MY DEAR MR. PRESIDENT:

When Secretary Stimson came to see me just before going to Quebec, I spoke to him of my very serious concern over the effect in the Philippines of the Japanese plan to grant her so-called "independence." I therefore requested him to submit to you the idea of having Congressional action that would, in effect, confirm everything you have said and done in reference to the Philippines since the outbreak of the war.

After Secretary Stimson's visit, Senator Tydings, in company with his father-in-law, former Ambassador Davies, came to see me. In view of the fact that Senator Tydings is the chairman of the Senate Committee in charge of Philippine legislation, I discussed with him this matter, and he informed me that he would cooperate to the fullest. He said he would be ready to introduce any resolution which you approve. Commissioner Elizalde feels that the sentiment in the House is in accord with the attitude of Senator Tydings.

Mr. President, I earnestly request that you send a message to Congress recommending Congressional action that would declare the Philippines as an independent nation in line with the policy you have adopted to regard, in practice, the Government of the Philippines as having the same status as the governments of other independent nations.

Since I cannot be in Washington to discuss this matter further with you, Vice President Osmeña, if you so desire, will more fully present to you our views on this subject.

Faithfully and respectfully yours,

/s/   Manuel L. Quezon

This letter was routed to me, with a notation in the handwriting of Dorothy Brady, "SIR to prepare the message."

There was, however, a difference of opinion among the War Department, State Department, Department of the Interior, President Quezon, and Senator Tydings about what the President should recommend to the Congress: whether the complete independence of the Philippines should be proclaimed at once, or whether the proclamation should await further talks between the President of the United States and the President of the Commonwealth of the Philippines after the freeing of the Islands. The purpose of their talks would be to agree on what bases the United States should keep as "necessary for the mutual protection of the Philippine Islands and of the United States."[2]

The difference of opinion is shown in a memorandum sent to me during the period of our conferences by General Watson, the President's secretary:

September 27, 1943

Memorandum for Judge Rosenman:
Dear Sam—

I have tried unsuccessfully to get you on the 'phone several times this morning. I understand you called me back but at that time I was busily engaged. I wanted to tell you this:

Secretary Stimson is very much upset on account of his understanding

[2] This quotation is taken from the final resolution as passed, Public Law 380 of the Seventy-eighth Congress.

that Senator Tydings is going to introduce a bill for immediate independence of the Philippines. Secretary Stimson says that he, the War Department and Ickes, oppose this immediate granting of independence, as they believe a lot should be done before this is given to the Philippines. Secretary Stimson has been requested to appear before the Committee on Insular Affairs of the Senate tomorrow morning, and he wants to know the White House viewpoint so he will not appear to go contrary to their views. The President told me to take this matter up with you for action this afternoon.

/s/   E. M. W.

PA

To straighten out these differences and to get agreement on a plan of action, the President asked me to get together Stimson, Tydings, Ickes and Quezon, who had come to Washington, and try to work out a compromise satisfactory to all of them.

These conferences were among the most dramatic episodes of my years in Washington. They were held at the Shoreham Hotel in Quezon's apartment—at his bedside. His small body, his tiny, emaciated, flushed face seemed to make his large bed seem larger. His wife and nurse were constantly about, as were his military aides, except only during the actual conferences. He was tensely holding on to life, determined to carry on in the cause to which he had dedicated his whole career—the independence of the Philippine Islands. He seemed to be impatient to see the job done before his eyes were closed, for he knew he was a very sick man. And, of course, the crowning glory would come if he could live long enough to become the first President of the Republic of the Philippines as he had been the first, and only, President of the Commonwealth of the Philippines.

Vice-President Osmeña took an active part in the negotiations. He too was ambitious to become the first president of the new republic; at the same time he tried to be loyal to his chief. The differences between them got to be very embarrassing. Neither of them attained his ambition.

On October 4, after many conferences, the differences were ironed out by compromise around Quezon's bedside, and the policy of the message was agreed upon.

I immediately sent the President the following memorandum enclosing a draft of the message:

October 4, 1943

Memorandum for the President

We had a conference this afternoon on the matter of Philippine independence at President Quezon's apartment. Present: President Quezon, Vice-President Osmeña, Secretary Stimson, Secretary Ickes, Under Secretary Fortas, Senator Tydings and I.

After a long discussion everybody present agreed, subject of course to your approval, on the attached draft of a message to the Congress.

As a compromise between "immediate independence" and "independence after the Japanese have been expelled," the resolution would provide that the President of the United States after consultation with the President of the Commonwealth of the Philippines would have the authority to advance the date of independence to a date as early as feasible.

This would give you the discretion as to when independence is physically possible.

The resolution would also provide that the President of the United States and the President of the Commonwealth of the Philippines enter into negotiations to provide military security for the Philippines. President Quezon is perfectly agreeable to this and affirmatively desires it; but he asked us to leave out the reference to actual military and naval air bases because of the unfavorable propaganda which might follow. Secretary Stimson has agreed to the language as changed.

It was the consensus that the necessary economic adjustments and the physical and economic rehabilitation of the Philippines be in a separate bill so it would not delay the passage of the independence resolution. The independence resolution will, however, provide for the joint commission to make for economic adjustments.

The attached message is, therefore, agreed upon and as soon as you approve we can send it up and Senator Tydings will amend his resolution to conform with it.

S. I. R.

P.S. Senator Tydings was most co-operative in reaching agreement.

The President signed and sent the message to the Congress two days later.

The gallant leader Quezon was denied by death the privilege of seeing the promise to his people finally kept. I can still see the flushed face of the small wiry man on that bed, the wan but confident smile, when I paid him a final visit to tell him that the message had been sent to the Congress, and that it was going to be broadcast to his people overseas. Senator Tydings was with me, and assured him that the Congress would do its part too.

The message did a lot to maintain the splendid resistance of the Philippines—which was one of the President's chief reasons for sending it at that particular time. A few weeks later he stated formally that the Government of the United States would never recognize the puppet government which the Japanese had set up in the Philippines.

The next message to the Congress was also aimed at bolstering the morale of one of our fighting Allies—this time the people of China. Dated October 11, 1943, it urged the Congress to correct the "historic mistake" that the United States had made in enacting the Chinese exclusion laws—a mistake that was helping the Japanese convince the Chinese that we really did not mean to help them. "Nations, like individuals, make mistakes. We must be big enough to acknowledge our mistakes of the past and to correct them." The President said that "I regard this legislation as important in the cause of winning the war and of establishing a secure peace." The legislation proposed by the President was passed by Congress about two months later with a minimum of debate— showing how the events of the war were accelerating the attainment of equality and justice among nations.

Although the President still consistently refused to make any prediction about when the war would end, he felt very confident after Italy had surrendered that our final victory in Europe was certain. He also felt confident of ultimate victory in Japan; but this he considered a much more distant prospect.

With victory perceptibly in the air, starting in October, 1943, he began in great earnestness to make plans and formulate policies for the postwar domestic economy. His first step, on October 15, was to establish an advisory unit headed by Baruch in the Office of War Mobilization to deal exclusively with postwar problems. In a statement issued at that time, he said: "The unit will study and consider the whole range of problems which will ultimately arise out of the termination of war contracts . . ." But again to make sure that no one would think he was taking this step because he believed that the war was over, he added: "While we must prepare for necessary postwar adjustments, this preparation must not interfere with the long and hard war programs which are still ahead of us."[3]

The next big step in postwar planning was his message to the Congress on October 27, recommending legislation to provide education for returning veterans.

Frequently at dinner and in informal moments the President talked with his associates and friends about what the United States should do

[3] In February, 1944, the advisory unit published its "Report on War and Postwar Adjustment Policies," dealing with surplus property disposal, curtailment of war production and resumption of civilian production, disposition of wartime controls, the human side of demobilization and the termination of war contracts.

to compensate its veterans at least in part for what they would lose by their years of service. His ideas ran something like this:

The American who has given his services to the United States does not expect and does not want bonuses and handouts when he comes back. He is not interested in a few hundred dollars. Money will not begin to pay for the loss of job opportunities or job advancement, or for the loss of educational opportunities. What the American soldier wants when he comes home is the opportunity to train for a better job than he had when he went away, or to train for some kind of skilled occupation or profession. The most important thing we can do for our veteran is to provide a sound economy for him when he comes home, free from the kind of inflation and wild speculation which characterized the early 1920's. The second most important thing is to give him an opportunity to get the education and training he missed because he was in the armed forces.

The President's concern about the loss of educational opportunities had increased when in November, 1942, it became necessary to extend the draft to young men of eighteen and nineteen years. At that time he had announced the appointment of a committee of educators to devise a comprehensive program for the education and training of returning veterans.

This committee sent the President a preliminary report in August, 1943. After studying it very carefully, he directed me to prepare a draft of a message transmitting it to the Congress and urging strongly that its recommendations be adopted. Thus was born the GI Bill of Rights, conceived by Roosevelt long before the Normandy invasion, two years before V-J Day, and still in operation for the soldiers in Korea. It was one of the greatest examples of statesmanlike vision during the war. No postwar problem was of greater moment to him; as he said in his message:

"This is a good time not merely to be thinking about the subject, but actually to do something about it. Nothing will be more conducive to the maintenance of high morale in our troops than the knowledge that steps are being taken now to give them education and technical training when the fighting is over."

There was another reason for this message—a reason influenced by his early impressions and resolves. On his first trips to Warm Springs, Georgia, the President had been gravely disturbed by the poor educational facilities in many counties in the South. In private conversation he often made it clear that he felt strongly that there was no reason why a child born in some county too poor to sustain a good school system should have to start life in competition with children from sections of the country that had fine schools. If the states were not themselves willing or able to provide enough money to help, he felt that the only way to equalize educational opportunities was through the resources and Treasury of the United States.

However, he knew, as did everyone interested in federal aid to education, that this idea had always been resisted by "states'-righters" and many others, who for years had successfully used the argument that federal aid to schools or teachers would lead to federal interference with education, curricula and content. But he was also sure that even the most rabid opponent of federal aid to education would not dare raise his voice against federal financial aid for educating GI's. He saw this proposal as a kind of entering wedge, feeling that if he could once get this piece of legislation on the books it would be much easier thereafter to get more and more federal aid for all children in states that could not provide decent educational facilities out of their own resources.

Subsequent events have proven him right. The successful administration of the GI education program has broken down much of the resistance to federal aid. It has been shown by actual experience that the federal government can help financially to provide education without interfering with local autonomy in education.

The next subject to which the President devoted a major speech was food. Ever since the early days of the war there had been recurrent criticism of the way the Administration was handling our supply of food. The constantly increasing needs of our Army, Navy and Air Forces and of our Allies, in addition to the abnormally high consumption of food by the American people, were resulting in shortages, rising prices, and sometimes inequitable distribution. In an effort to remedy these evils, the Administration had fixed the price of food, established a system of rationing, and by support prices and subsidy programs induced the farmers to raise farm products in greater and greater amounts.

These steps all had to be imposed upon a normal peacetime economy with great speed. They had to be co-ordinated with other government activities, some of which pulled in opposite directions. For example, men were needed on the farms to produce food—but they were also needed in the armed forces, in war factories, and for other manpower requirements. Steel and chemicals were necessary for farm machinery and fertilizer materials—but they were also desperately needed for war weapons and ammunition. With hundreds of such conflicting demands, there were bound to be cases of maladjustment. Some of these maladjustments became acute before they could be corrected. By the fall of 1943 criticism ran high. Time and again the voices of influential newspapers, radio commentators and Congressmen were raised in favor of appointing a "food czar" with "full" power to handle food. It was often the easy suggestion of critics during the war, whenever a shortage of any specific item—food, rubber, ships, freight cars, or oil—began to create an unbalance in our complicated economy, to call for a "czar" over that particular commodity.

The President had on many occasions pointed out that if any "czar" were appointed for any one commodity, like food, he would immediately run up against the needs of other commodities governed by other agencies. For example, if a "food czar" called for more freight cars to transport food to the large cities, he would be met by resistance from the "transportation czar," who had to meet the demands of the Army for more freight cars to transport tanks. Both "czars" could not possibly have their way. There had to be someone over both of them to apportion the freight cars between them. And as soon as someone was put over them, they were, of course, no longer "czars."

As the criticism increased during the summer of 1943, there were many discussions among the President and the various agencies of the government concerned with raising, distributing, selling and transporting food. It was finally decided that what was needed was a clear, definite statement by the President to the American people of exactly what was involved in the whole farm and food problem, and what we were trying to do to meet it.

I started to collect material for such a speech; but it soon became obvious that to discuss the whole program comprehensively would require many more than the thirty minutes the President had set as the maximum for a radio speech. Accordingly, instead of making a radio talk, he decided to prepare a message to the Congress going into all the phases of the food problem. As more and more material was gathered, the message became longer and longer. Each time I submitted a draft to the President he would follow his custom of looking at the number on the last page to see how long it was, and "rib" me about its ever-growing length. But although he tried to shorten it, he could suggest no major cuts; and he finally gave up and said: "Go ahead, put it all in; maybe nobody will ever read the whole thing, but the whole story will be there. You'd better put in a table of contents— and an index, too."

It did grow and grow—until it became the longest message the President ever sent to the Congress. It was sent up on November 1, 1943, and consisted of more than 10,000 words. Usually, when a speech or message was too long, Roosevelt would write alongside the paragraphs he thought should be shortened his favorite speech-writing direction— "Boil." I have many pages with that word written in the margin. His most tactful way of saying he did not like a part of a speech was, "Let's save this for some later speech." We knew that that was a polite "ax."

The President could generally gauge within a matter of seconds how long a speech would take to read and how much time would be taken up in applause; so it was seldom that he did not finish within exactly the allotted time, with no seconds to spare, but none lost. When we got down to the final drafts of a speech, the words were counted one by one so that the President would know exactly how much had to be cut out. This last process, just before the final reading copy, of cutting out 314 words, for example, was most difficult. By this time every sentence had been gone over eight or nine times; the speech had been "boiled" and "boiled" until it seemed that no water was left in it. But the 314 words had to come out—and finally did.

In the message on food he explained that the aims of his farm program were: first, to increase production of food so as to have enough to go around in fair proportions; and second, to keep the price of food down.

Even here, he pointed out, there was conflict at times. For example, one of the ways to get increased production was to pay the farmer more; this in turn raised prices in the retail stores. Conversely, if the price of food in the stores was so low that the butcher or grocer could not pay the farmer enough, the farmer would not raise as much food as was needed. The job of government was to devise means to achieve both objectives that did not counteract each other.

In order to induce farmers to increase production and at the same time to keep the cost of food down, "it will be necessary to increase the amount of government funds which were used for these purposes in 1943," that is, for support prices and subsidy programs. "We cannot and should not expect the farmers of the nation to increase their production all over the United States if they face the definite risk of loss by reason of such production. We do not expect industrial war plants to take such risks, and there is no reason why the farmers should."

It was the same kind of subsidy program that had been so effective in the production of other war materials, such as copper, lead, zinc, aluminum and others.

"The subsidies that are used cannot properly be called producer subsidies or consumer subsidies. They are war subsidies. The costs which they cover are war costs."

It was essential to keep the cost of food down, he said, if we expected wage earners to stabilize their own wages. And he proudly added: "Since August, 1939, the month before the war broke out in Europe, the total cost of living in the United States has increased not quite 26 per cent, as compared with an advance of 53 per cent in the same period [46 months] in the last war."

This information came from a memorandum prepared by the Office of Price Administration. It was sent to me on July 13, with a chit by the President reading as follows:

Memorandum for S. I. R.
For use in my next speech—and be very careful of it.

F. D. R.

Perhaps the greatest criticism of the food program had to do with rationing. In his food message the President explained the need for it, but conceded that mistakes had been made: "Control and distribution by rationing has involved many difficult administrative problems, most of which have been solved by experience. No one would contend that mistakes were not made. Nevertheless, there has been steady improvement. A recent survey has shown that 93 per cent of American housewives agree that a good job—a job fair to all—has been done.

"Unfortunately, the 7 per cent who are not satisfied are more vocal than the 93 per cent who are."

Finally, taking up the "loose talk in some quarters about the need for a food 'czar' to have full control of food—including not only production and distribution, but prices, rationing, and transportation," the President explained why it was impossible to give one man power to "encroach upon other war agencies which deal with such separate but relevant subjects as price control, transportation, etc."

After this message, the criticism did die down a little, but not entirely. Whenever criticism appeared from any responsible source, the President used to refer the critic to parts of this food message for his answer.

Another example of the way in which the President, early in the war, looked ahead to the problems the end would bring was the organization of the Office of Foreign Relief and Rehabilitation Operations (OFRRO) in December, 1942, less than a month after the North African invasion. It was the forerunner of the United Nations Relief and Rehabilitation Administration (UNRRA). The President visualized the chaos and the suffering, the shortage of food, clothing, and shelter, which would afflict the people of the occupied countries even after they were liberated from their conquerors. The basic idea underlying the relief and rehabilitation of the countries of Europe was not only humanitarian; there was also the selfish realization that a chaotic, disorganized, and starving Europe would be dangerous to peace and democracy.

In deciding upon someone to head the American OFRRO, the President had in mind that his selection would unquestionably be chosen later to head the international UNRRA, which would take over all rehabilitation operations, including OFRRO. He was looking for a man of unquestioned integrity, accustomed to administering large affairs.

One day he told me that he had decided to ask Herbert Lehman, who was then serving in his fourth term as Governor of New York, to take this job.

"As you know, he's a fine administrator and executive with experience in this kind of work. But there is another reason. After all that Hitler has done to the Jews of Germany and of every nation he has conquered, I think it would be wonderful, poetic justice if we could get a Jew to head the agency which is going to feed and clothe and shelter the millions whom Hitler has robbed and starved and tortured— a member of the group Hitler first selected for extermination. It would be a fine object lesson in tolerance and human brotherhood to have a Jew head up this operation, and I think Herbert would be fine."

Herbert Lehman got the job.

In the fall of 1943 the feeding and rehabilitation operation was turned over to the international organization of UNRRA. On November 9 the representatives of 44 nations—members of the United Nations and those associated with them—gathered in the White House to sign the agreement which set up the organization.

The President took much pleasure in preparing and making his address to the delegates. UNRRA was a heartening result of a belief he had long preached: that, as he said, "nations will learn to work together only by actually working together. Why not? We nations have common objectives. It is therefore, with a lift of hope, that we look on the signing of this agreement by all of the United Nations as a means of joining them together still more firmly."

He made a point that has been made time and again since the end of the war, when many of the prostrate nations of the world became targets for Communist propaganda and aggression.

It is not only humane and charitable for the United Nations to supply medicine and food and other necessities to the peoples freed from Axis control; it is a clear matter of enlightened self-interest—and of military strategic necessity. . . . When victory comes there can certainly be no secure peace until there is a return of law and order in the oppressed countries, until the peoples of these countries have been restored to a normal, healthy, and self-sustaining existence. This means that the more quickly and effectually we apply measures of relief and rehabilitation, the more quickly will our own boys overseas be able to come home.

In a message on UNRRA which the President sent to the Congress a week after this occasion, he made another point which is still being repeated—that the United States cannot do the job alone:

"UNRRA will be able to make only a beginning in the vast task of aiding the victims of war. The greatest part of the job will have to be done by the liberated people themselves. What UNRRA can do is to help the liberated peoples to help themselves. . . ."

Chapter XIX

The First Big-Three Conference: Teheran, 1943

For more than two years Roosevelt had tried unsuccessfully to arrange a conference of the Big Three—Churchill, Stalin and himself. He tried first in 1942 during the negotiations leading to the Casablanca Conference; he tried again in May, 1943, when he and the Prime Minister met in Washington. He tried another time at the time of the first Quebec Conference in August of that year. When at length Stalin agreed to a meeting and suggested that it be held at Teheran, Roosevelt tried vainly to get him to fix on some other place. He pointed out that Teheran was so isolated and so surrounded by mountains that access by airplane was difficult, and that the distance would make it hard for him to handle Congressional bills within the constitutional period of ten days. Stalin refused to budge, except to suggest that the conference be postponed until the next spring and then held in Alaska. Roosevelt, however, wanted no further delay; he was convinced that the sooner the meeting was held the better; and he finally agreed to Teheran.

The very code name of the conference—Eureka—seemed to indicate how anxious the President was to find the place and the time and the means for a meeting with all three leaders sitting around one table. The need to formulate joint strategic plans with the Russian war leaders was immediate, for the repeated postponement of the cross-Channel invasion had led to some rather acrimonious talk by the Russians. Roosevelt had in mind, also, the necessity of getting the Soviets to join in the war against Japan as soon as it became advisable. His military experts in 1943 were advising him that Soviet participation might save hundreds of thousands of American lives when the time came to invade Japan.

In addition to these overriding military considerations, the President was eager to get top-level discussions started about a postwar peace organization. He had already discussed this at length with Churchill, and had found that there was substantial agreement between them. He had also talked about it with Anthony Eden when Eden was in Washington in March. And to get the ball rolling at once he was ready to travel halfway around the world to meet Stalin face to face.

Roosevelt's feeling of urgency was expressed at a press conference held on March 30, 1943, after Eden left:

THE PRESIDENT: Anthony Eden has left, and we decided that it was probably better not to give out one of those formal statements by the two of us. And he asked me to just talk to you all informally about it. . . .

We talked about the practical problems that will arise on the surrender of the enemy . . . primarily in safeguarding the world from future aggression.

I think I ought to make it clear that these conversations are exploratory. The object of them was *not* to reach final decisions, which were, of course, impossible at this stage; but to reach a large measure of general agreement on objectives. . . .

If some of you go back . . . to 1918, the war came to a rather sudden end in November. And actually it's a fact that there had been very little work done on the postwar problems before Armistice Day. Well, between Armistice Day and the time that the nations met in Paris early in 1919, everybody was rushing around trying to dig up things.

And the simile I used to Mr. Eden the other day was that—I was here at the time—the tempo seemed to be that of the lady who is told at noon that she is to accompany her husband on a month's trip on the three o'clock train that afternoon. Well, I have seen ladies trying to pack for a month's trip in three hours, and that was a little bit the situation over here and everywhere else in making preparations for the Versailles Conference. Everybody was rushing around grabbing things out of closets and throwing them into suitcases. . . .

I have forgotten how many experts we took to Versailles at that time, but everybody who had a "happy thought," or who thought he was an expert got a free ride.

And that is why I think that this whole method that is going on now is a very valuable thing, in an exploratory way, and incidentally—as I remarked the other day—in the process of getting to know each other.

If you want to be didactic and put it in terms of figures, I would say that so far, in all of the conferences that we have held with other members of the United Nations—not just the British . . . we are about 95 per cent together. Well, that's an amazing statement. It happens to be true. I wish some people would put that in their pipes and smoke it.

So it was a very good conference. . . .

QUESTION: Could you tell us anything about that 5 per cent?

THE PRESIDENT: Well, every additional conversation eliminates a little bit more of the 5 per cent.

QUESTION: Mr. President, when you say it applies to the others as well, that includes Russia, does it not?

THE PRESIDENT: Yes.

QUESTION: And China?

THE PRESIDENT: And China.

QUESTION: Mr. President, you spoke of plans to have conversations with Russia in the near future. Is there anything more specific we can have on that? This summer, do you plan——

THE PRESIDENT: No—not today.

QUESTION: Is hope still "springing eternal" about Mr. Stalin? [Meaning the arrangement of a meeting with him.]

THE PRESIDENT: Yes.

Roosevelt prepared for Teheran with high hopes. He had great confidence in his own ability to sway people if given an opportunity to talk with them—he had seen it work so many times. And, in spite of the difficulty of exchanging ideas through an interpreter, he felt the same self-confidence regarding Stalin. Few of us who were familiar with his charm and skill in negotiation had any doubts on the score. Before he left, he made a point of asking people who had met Stalin about Stalin's characteristics and the way his mind worked. He was reasonably sure that he and Churchill, who generally agreed with him on postwar plans, could persuade Stalin to join them, not merely in lip service but in a genuine meeting of the minds. Roosevelt knew that there would have to be compromises, that a willingness to give as well as to take was essential; but on the overall objectives of the four freedoms and on the creation of a formal organization to further their attainment, he was quite confident of unanimity. It was a meeting he looked forward to with relish.

Again it is illuminating to quote the President himself on his conception of what can be done at an international conference. In Washington on October 29, 1943, he was discussing with the newspapermen the recently concluded Moscow Conference of the Foreign Ministers of Great Britain, the Soviet Union, and the United States. What he said about that Moscow Conference he felt to be true about the impending meeting of the Big Three:

QUESTION: Mr. President, in a good many quarters of late, there has been expressed the feeling that in view of the developments some sort of redefinition or restatement in more explicit terms of this country's foreign policy as a whole might be in order, particularly with reference to what those objectives at Moscow might be. I know that's a large order, but is there anything that could be said at this conference about it?

THE PRESIDENT: Well, I suppose the easiest way to answer it is this, that when we went to this Conference all three Nations had a thing called an agenda, and in that agenda were many matters of general policy. Well, if at this particular time, when our delegation went over there, Mr. Hull had been bound not merely to the general policy but certain more specific things, and the British had been bound to theirs, what would have been the use of a conference? You learn a lot in a conference, both sides.

The ultimate objectives—we all know pretty well what they are. The first desideratum is peace in the world and the end of aggression. That is far and away the most important thing. But the idea of a conference is to confer, get the other fellow's point of view. It is quite possible that you might get a good idea from somebody else outside of our own borders. It is quite possible that you might persuade the other fellow that some idea that you had was a pretty good idea. I think we have all lost sight of the fact that the main practical point at the present time is to sit around the table and see if we can't agree, and swap various kinds of language.

Now, in conferences, domestic, or foreign, you draw up a document. Well, it's done by some draftsman, and they agree that is pretty darn good language, and you get a general agreement on the language. And then you bring it into the whole conference, before all the conferees.

And somebody says, "Don't you think it would be better to put it this way, in the light of all the circumstances?" And the others say, "Well, that's a good idea. Let's change those few words, here or there." Or they say, "No. No, I don't think that is so good. Let's try a third method."

And finally you get a document which has been gone over with a good deal of care and agreement. You can't just go in and say didactically, "Take this language. We won't consider any other language."

If Roosevelt had lived, I am sure he would have had many more personal conferences than his successor has had with the leaders of the Soviet and other governments. He was sure that misunderstandings could best be straightened out in the kind of meeting that he described at this press conference. For, as I have said, he was so firmly convinced of his own ability to get along with people and to work out acceptable agreements with them. Whether he would have succeeded any better than President Truman has without personal meetings with Stalin—who knows?

Before Roosevelt left for Teheran, he talked with me about making some arrangements for forwarding any bills that the Congress (then in session) might pass and send to the White House for approval or disapproval. The Constitution of the United States provides that if a bill is not returned by the President within ten days after it is presented to him (if the Congress is in session), it becomes a law without his signature.

Normally a bill is delivered to the White House by the Congressional messenger, who is given a dated receipt. The ten days allowed the President start to run from the date of that receipt.

An airplane carrying bills from Washington to Teheran might find it hard to get there and back within the ten days, especially if it ran into bad weather or mechanical difficulties. Consequently, on the basis of a legal memorandum from the Attorney General, Roosevelt took the position that under a broad interpretation of the Constitution he should have ten days after a bill was presented to him in person wherever he might be. Therefore, while Roosevelt was away on this trip and on subsequent trips, whenever a bill was presented to the White House, there were added to the usual form of receipt the words "For forwarding to the President."

There was the added difficulty that the President's trip had to be kept a secret. We were fearful that any unusual form of receipt might cause some indiscreet inquiry in the office of the clerk of the House of Representatives or the Senate. I talked about this with the Speaker, Sam Rayburn; the presiding officer of the Senate, Vice-President Wallace; and the president pro tempore of the Senate, Senator Barkley. I explained the difficulty to them, and they arranged with the clerks of the Congress to handle the matter as discreetly as possible.

Of the 44 bills that were receipted for in this unusual way and forwarded to the President on his trip to Teheran, he vetoed only two. It so happened that he was able to return the vetoed bills to the Congress within ten days from the time they were delivered to the White House, so no questions were raised; and it never become necessary to put our constitutional theory to the test.

Before the President left for Teheran he had prepared a message to the Congress recommending legislation for additional help for our veterans on their return to civilian life. At first he was going to send this to the Congress before he left; but he decided to sign it and leave it behind to be sent up a week or ten days after his departure. It might help, he thought, to keep his absence from the country a secret.

The President sailed from Hampton Roads, Virginia, on November 13, but transferred to a plane at Oran on the 20th. He stopped off at Cairo for four days of conferences with Churchill and Generalissimo Chiang Kai-shek. The meetings with the Chinese leader did not produce many results. What military arrangements were made had to be canceled after Teheran because the commitments entered into there for the cross-Channel invasion of France made it impossible to carry on the full-scale operations necessary to relieve the Chinese. It was, however, stated in the formal joint communiqué on this Cairo Conference that: "The aforesaid three Great Powers, mindful of the enslavement of the people of Korea, are determined that in due course Korea shall become free and independent."

At the Teheran Conference with Churchill and Stalin, the President, with apparently unanimous consent, occupied the head of the table—although it was a circular table. The Prime Minister said so publicly and, on innumerable occasions, privately. The President said so, too—but he put it on the ground that he was not only the representative of the United States but also "an elected head of a State." Theoretically, King George, not Churchill, was "head" of the British State; and President Kalinin, not Stalin, was "head" of the Soviet Union. Of course, this was not the explanation. The United States was the leader of the world in so many ways—military, productive, moral, and spiritual—that it was automatically assumed among the three participating nations that the head of the table was the logical place for the representative of the United States. As Stalin himself said at this conference, without American production the war would have been lost on all fronts.

The President, very early in the conference, gave Stalin the news that Stalin was so anxious to hear—that OVERLORD, the trans-Channel invasion, had been definitely set for May 1, 1944. At this first plenary meeting Stalin also gave Roosevelt the military assurance that Roosevelt wanted to hear—that although the situation on the German front prevented the Soviet Union from entering the war against Japan right away, she would eventually do so. This was wonderful news to a President who had been advised by his highest military experts that he was facing a long war against Japan, and that Russian intervention would help to shorten it and save American lives. It was wonderful news indeed—and would have been to every father and mother in the United States if they had heard it.

There was a great deal of discussion about OVERLORD. The Prime Minister, while agreeing to the cross-Channel invasion, continued to spend much time talking about the possibility of other military operations along the "soft under belly" of Europe. The President remarked to us once rather tartly after he got back that "Winston has developed a tendency to make long speeches which are repetitious of long speeches which he has made before."

The President and Stalin were insistent that OVERLORD be settled once and for all at this conference, in such a way that there never would be any further question about it from anyone, including Churchill. It was. The President had come to the definite conclusion that the only way Germany could be defeated was by an army of invasion. He refused to place any reliance upon the probability of an internal revolution in Germany. I was with him on the U.S.S. *Baltimore* on the way to Pearl Harbor in July, 1944, when the German generals' uprising against Hitler was tried and suppressed.

"If we can get rid of Hitler this way," he said when the news came in, "and still get unconditional surrender from any responsible German government, it would be fine because it would save many lives. I don't think we will."

Stalin expressed disagreement with the President's doctrine of "unconditional surrender." He wanted to define unconditional surrender in more definite terms so that the German people would know exactly what they could expect, but he did not convince the President.

Roosevelt soon got around to the subject that to him was second in priority only to beating the Japanese and the Nazis—the future peace of the world. He discussed at length with Stalin the highlights of the organization of the United Nations, to which he was looking forward as a means of enforcing peace. Stalin indicated clearly that such an organization must be prepared to enforce the peace by arms, and Roosevelt stated that he was in complete agreement with him on this.

This was almost seven years before the armed conflict broke out in Korea in 1950; but there was a meeting of the minds at Teheran that the use of force was the only way to ultimate peace in a situation like Korea.

Other military matters were discussed. On repeated occasions Stalin attempted to pin the President down to name the general who would command OVERLORD. Although during the conference Roosevelt felt that this command would probably go to General Marshall, then Chief of Staff, he refused to make a definite commitment to Stalin at the time. It is not clear exactly when he changed his mind about this and named Eisenhower.

Before the President left for this conference, it was fairly well understood in Washington circles that the appointment would go to Marshall, though there had been some difference of opinion among the President's advisers. Then the anti-Roosevelt newspapers began to protest against the appointment of Marshall as the supreme field commander. One of them concocted the preposterous story that Harry Hopkins, Justice Frankfurter and I were engaged in a traitorous plot to have Marshall removed from Washington and kicked out as Chief of Staff. We wanted him out, the story went, so that some other favorite of ours (I forget the name of the man they mentioned—a man whom I had never even heard of before) could be made Chief of Staff. The President used to kid me a good deal about this. He himself used to be attacked so frequently and so outrageously in the press that I think he enjoyed it a bit when some of us who were not out on the firing line were singled out for this kind of treatment. I must confess that although some of the attacks on me by the anti-Roosevelt press during the war years got under my skin, this particular charge was so fantastic and unbelievable that it left me cold. Every once in a while the President would greet me by saying: "I'm sorry, Sam, I still have to keep Marshall in as Chief of Staff—you can try again some other day."

Long after this episode—three years later—after President Roosevelt had died and after General Marshall had retired as Chief of Staff, President Truman asked the General to undertake a mission to China for him as his special representative. President Truman had frequently joked with me about the Frankfurter-Hopkins-Rosenman cabal to get Marshall out of the country. I was no longer officially connected with the White House when I read about this new mission for Marshall; but one day I came into the President's office and said: "Well, Mr. President, you might joke about that plot of mine to get rid of Marshall and send him out of the country, but you must admit that, although it took a little time, I finally got my man."

At one time during the Teheran Conference Churchill spoke of Russia's need for warm-water ports. The President mentioned the possibility of access to the port of Dairen in Manchuria. This suggestion has been mentioned frequently and erroneously by some writers as having been first made at Yalta.

The conferees at Teheran also discussed other things, such as the division of the Italian fleet; the western and eastern frontiers of Poland; and how Germany should be dismembered after the war. On the first of these matters they reached a preliminary agreement.

The Declaration of Teheran, the official communiqué, did not reveal much. As to the military plans, its chief statement was quite cryptic: "We have reached complete agreement as to the scope and timing of the operations to be undertaken from the East, West, and the South."

About international accord for the future it was a little more expansive:

> We are sure that our concord will win an enduring peace. We recognize fully the supreme responsibility resting upon us and all the United Nations to make a peace which will command the good will of the overwhelming mass of the peoples of the world and banish the scourge and terror of war for many generations. . . .
>
> With our diplomatic advisers we have surveyed the problems of the future. We shall seek the cooperation and active participation of all Nations, large and small, whose peoples in heart and mind are dedicated, as are our own peoples, to the elimination of tyranny and slavery, oppression and intolerance. We will welcome them, as they may choose to come, into a world family of democratic Nations. . . .

It was a bold statement that these three men signed. Only Stalin and the top Russians with him know whether the Soviet representatives really meant what they signed. The President told us on his return that he was sure Stalin meant every word of it. The communiqué contained the essence of what Roosevelt had for many months planned and patiently strived to accomplish. The Declaration of Teheran had in it everything necessary for world peace—everything except the willingness of the Soviet to carry it out. In December, 1943, it was to Roosevelt, and to all other men of good will, a glowing milestone on the way to permanent international accord and peace.

Next on the trip was the meeting at Cairo with the President of Turkey and Prime Minister Churchill. There was some inconclusive talk about Turkey's getting into the war. Churchill had urged this before, and at Teheran. During this second Cairo Conference, the President made an informal extemporaneous speech to a group of MP's who had been guarding his villa in Cairo:

> These conferences here, and up in Iran, have been very satisfactory—extremely so. Real accord has been reached. After all, the Russians, the British, the Chinese, and ourselves—collectively we represent and are fighting for nearly three-fourths of all the people in the world. That is something for us to realize. It means without doubt that even if we have to keep peace by force for a while, we are going to do it. But that does not mean that you are going to have to stay overseas all your lives.

The speech was not published at the time, for obvious reasons. Roosevelt's extemporaneous—almost casual—remark about keeping "peace by force for a while" was so important and so new that the staff accompanying him wanted to have it released back home as soon as made. The President, however, said that it was too important an announcement to be made in this offhand way. He directed instead that a typewritten copy of this remark should be forwarded to me, to be included in the formal report he was going to make later to the American people on the Teheran Conference.

From the second meeting at Cairo the President flew to Malta. For many terrible months this small island had been subjected to continuous and terrific Nazi bombing. It refused to surrender. Two or three days before he left for the Teheran Conference, the President had called me in and said that he wanted to present a scroll to the inhabitants of Malta expressing the appreciation of the people of the United States for the gallant part the Maltese had played in the war. Sherwood and I prepared a short text for the scroll, which the President changed a little and approved. The question then arose how to get it appropriately engraved without revealing the coming trip. I called in Mr. Augustus E. Giegengack, the very competent and discreet gentleman who was then in charge of the Government Printing Office, and explained the problem to him. He undertook to get it done in a way that would not reveal the proposed trip to more than one man. This took much more time than it would have normally, so it was not ready for the President to take with him when he left. It had to be sent on after him by plane. The Government Printing Office did a most beautiful piece of scroll-work, and the document is now one of the treasured possessions of Malta. There have not been many statesmen who in the midst of the kind of activities that beset Roosevelt in November, 1943, would have thought of presenting the Malta scroll and have taken the time and trouble to do so.

On the way home from Teheran, the President received the sad news of the third casualty that had occurred among the small group of his close friends and advisers since he became President. The first had been the death of Louis McHenry Howe in 1936; the second had been Missy LeHand's stroke in June, 1941. Now came the death of Marvin H. McIntyre, a loyal friend for over twenty-five years.

McIntyre had been with the President during his Vice-Presidential campaign in 1920, and had served as his secretary in charge of appoint-

ments since the day Roosevelt entered the White House. In that capacity, his sound judgment about whom the President should see and
whom he should not had made him particularly valuable. He had a
wide circle of acquaintances in Washington, and was able to pick up
much news about people in official and semiofficial circles that never
got into the papers. Unswervingly loyal, he was one of the few men
who would frankly speak his mind to the "Boss" even though what he
had to say was thoroughly unpleasant. In later years he became quite
ill and should have cut down on his work; but he refused to take his
doctor's advice and, as a result, shortened his own life.

The President returned to Washington on December 17. The entire
Cabinet and all the agency heads had been informed of his expected
arrival, and they were all on hand to meet him at the south entrance to
the White House. I do not remember ever seeing the President look
more satisfied and pleased than he did that morning. He believed intensely that he had accomplished what he had set out to do—to bring
Russia into co-operation with the Western powers in a formidable
organization for the maintenance of peace—and he was glad.

He looked a little tired; but there was none of the drawn and hag-
gard expression that he brought back from Yalta a year later. He looked
robust and healthy. He was indeed the "champ" who had come back
with the prize. I had seen that expression many times before; but, except for a few exhilarating moments during the campaign of 1944
when the fighting got tough, I never saw that same expression again.

As a result of Teheran, the health of all three leaders seemed to
suffer. The Prime Minister developed a case of pneumonia which for
a time seemed quite serious—serious enough to have the President remark in his report on Teheran that "the heartfelt prayers of all of us
have been with this great citizen of the world in his recent serious illness." From behind the veil of censorship that covered Russia, there
came reports that Marshal Stalin had a heart attack which required
weeks of recuperation. The President developed some sort of bronchial
affliction in Teheran which gave him a racking cough. As the cough
persisted, Dr. McIntire called in some medical consultants, but they
found no unusual condition for a man of his age except his cough and
his sinuses. It took him a long time to shake it off. While Teheran was
a high point in the President's career as Commander-in-Chief of our
armed forces and as our leader in foreign affairs, it seemed to me to be
also the turning point of his physical career. I think that his physical

decline can be dated from Teheran, although at the time we did not see it. Bronchitis was not an uncommon disease, nor was it unusual to hear a man cough. For a man who had spent an average of sixteen hours a day for a period of three years or more thinking, working, writing, speaking and acting to meet terrible and recurrent crises, the Teheran Conference must have been a terrific strain. We did not realize it at the time; and if it had been suggested to the President, he would have conscientiously denied it.

As soon as the President got settled in his chair in Washington he began to talk to the Congressional leaders about his report to the American people. He also held a press conference. He opened it by saying that he thought the trip to Teheran "was in every way a success, not only from the point of view of the conduct of the war, but also for the discussions that I hope will have a definite and very beneficial effect for the postwar period." He had no doubt or reservation about that in his own mind.

After the press conference he talked with us about his report to the people. The Congressional leaders had suggested that he go up to Capitol Hill to deliver it, but he had other ideas. He wanted to make it in a fireside chat on Christmas Eve, and tie in the objective of permanent world peace discussed at Teheran with the natural message of Christmas—peace on earth, good will to men.

The President spent a great deal of time on that fireside chat. And it was the eighth draft that was finally delivered from his home at Hyde Park.

On this Christmas Eve, the President said, we can at last "look forward into the future with real, substantial confidence" toward peace.

He showed his satisfaction at the agreement which had been reached at Teheran: "We had planned to talk to each other across the table at Cairo and Teheran; but we soon found that we were all on the same side of the table. We came to the conferences with faith in each other. But we needed the personal contact. And now we have supplemented faith with definite knowledge."

He talked of the military situation in the Far East and of our future plans, which "will spell plenty of bad news for the Japs"; of the agreements on future war strategy in Europe; of the personalities of Stalin and Chiang, about whom he knew the people would be curious; of the new Supreme Commander and his deputies; of the plans to take effect "following Germany's defeat"; and of agreement on basic principles of future international relationships. He continued:

> Britain, Russia, China, and the United States and their allies, represent more than three-quarters of the total population of the earth. As long as these four nations with great military power stick together in determination to keep the peace there will be no possibility of an aggressor nation arising to start another world war.
>
> But those four powers must be united with and cooperate with all the freedom-loving peoples of Europe, and Asia, and Africa, and the Americas. The rights of every nation, large or small, must be respected and guarded as jealously as are the rights of every individual within our own Republic.
>
> The doctrine that the strong shall dominate the weak is the doctrine of our enemies—and we reject it.
>
> But at the same time we are agreed that if force is necessary to keep international peace, international force will be applied—for as long as it may be necessary.

The President felt that he had come really to know Stalin at this conference, and that their personal contact had done a great deal to break down the barriers of distance and language differences: "To use an American and somewhat ungrammatical colloquialism, I may say that I 'got along fine' with Marshal Stalin. He is a man who combines a tremendous, relentless determination with a stalwart good humor. I believe he is truly representative of the heart and soul of Russia; and I believe that we are going to get along very well with him and the Russian people—very well indeed."

If there was any doubt about the future position of the United States in the field of foreign affairs, the President bluntly stated that the general objectives of Teheran meant the definite end of isolationism in the United States:

"The well-intentioned but ill-fated experiments of former years did not work. It is my hope that we will not try them again. No—that is putting it too weakly—it is my intention to do all that I humanly can as President and Commander-in-Chief to see to it that these tragic mistakes shall not be made again. . . ."

Then a warning: "The war is now reaching the stage where we shall all have to look forward to large casualty lists—dead, wounded, and missing.

"War entails just that. There is no easy road to victory. And the end is not yet in sight."

A speech of major importance during the war, like this one, was given worldwide coverage by radio and newspapers and also by all the government facilities of the Office of War Information, for the aim was to have it reach every part of the globe—to encourage those who were fighting in the open, those who were fighting in the underground, and those who were living under the conqueror in fear of their lives; to spur on those who were working to produce the food and materials and weapons of war, to give renewed faith to those whose freedom had been snatched from them, to those who were cynical about the aftermath of the war, and to those who held high hopes that this war might really be the last one.

Throughout the fall and winter of 1943, domestic problems continued to pile up on Roosevelt's desk:

On September 14 he sent a message to the Congress on the segregation program of the War Relocation Authority.

On September 25 he established the Foreign Economic Administration.

On September 28 he sent a message to the Congress recommending self-government for Puerto Rico.

On October 5 he made a radio address on the opening of the National War Fund Drive.

On October 15 he established a unit in OWM to deal with postwar and conversion problems.

On October 27 he·sent a message to the Congress on education of war veterans.

On October 29 he seized the coal mines, on behalf of the United States. They had been shut down by a labor dispute.

On November 23 he sent another message to the Congress on measures to help veterans returning to civilian life.

On December 27 he seized the railroads, on behalf of the United States, in order to prevent their shutdown by strike.

At the year's end, on December 28, the President held a now famous press conference in which he discussed the future of the reform program of the New Deal, the pace of which in the midst of war and international matters had slowed down to a practical standstill. At the close of the previous press conference one of the reporters had stayed behind after the others had gone, and had asked the President what had happened to the New Deal. The President had made an offhand answer which indicated that the pressure and necessities of war had caused it to be laid aside temporarily. The answer was given publicity, and it caused a flurry of excitement. So at his next press conference the President explained extemporaneously in more detail what he had meant. He prepared for the conference by asking me to get up a concise list of New Deal agencies and accomplishments. He knew that he would be asked about the subject.

How did the New Deal come into existence? It was because there was an awfully sick patient called the United States of America, and it was suffering from a grave internal disorder—awfully sick—all kinds of things had happened to this patient, all internal things. And they sent for the doctor. And it was a long, long process—took several years before those ills, in that particular illness of ten years ago, were remedied. But after a while they were remedied. . . .

And there were certain specific remedies that the old doctor gave the patient, and I jotted down a few of those remedies. [The President listed the remedies—they were all New Deal remedies—a sound banking system, the FDIC, the HOLC, the AAA, the SEC, decent housing and slum clearance, reduction of farm tenancy, old age and unemployment insurance, PWA, WPA, FERA, CCC, NYA, reforestation, abolition of child labor, FHA, reciprocal trade agreements, TVA, REA, crop insurance, drought and flood relief, soil conservation, conservation of natural resources. He mentioned about thirty of them.]

I am inclined to think that the country ought to have it brought back to their memories, and I think the country ought to be asked, too, as to whether all these rather inexperienced critics shouldn't be asked directly just which of the remedies should be taken away from the patient, if you should come down with a similar illness in the future. It's all right now—it's all right internally now—if they just leave him alone.

But since then, two years ago, the patient had a very bad accident—not an internal trouble. Two years ago, on the seventh of December, he was in a pretty bad smashup—broke his hip, broke his leg in two or three places, broke a wrist and an arm, and some ribs; and they didn't think he would live, for a while. And then he began to "come to"; and he has been in charge of a partner of the old doctor. Old Dr. New Deal didn't know "nothing" about legs and arms. He knew a great deal about internal medicine, but nothing about surgery. So he got his partner, who was an orthopedic surgeon, Dr. Win-the-War, to take care of this fellow who had been in this bad accident. And the result is that the patient is back on his feet. He has given up his crutches. He isn't wholly well yet, and he won't be until he wins the war. . . .

But at the present time, obviously, the principal emphasis, the overwhelming first emphasis should be on winning the war. In other words, we are suffering from that bad accident, not from an internal disease.

And when victory comes, the program of the past, of course, has got to be carried on, in my judgment, with what is going on in other countries—

postwar program—because it will pay. We can't go into an economic isolationism, any more than it would pay to go into a military isolationism. . . .

It seems pretty clear that we must plan for, and help to bring about, an
expanded economy which will result in more security, in more employment,
in more recreation, in more education, in more health, in better housing
for all of our citizens, so that the conditions of 1932 and the beginning of
1933 won't come back again.

Dr. New Deal and Dr. Win-the-War soon became very well known
and oft-mentioned practitioners.

Chapter XX

Troubles with Congress, 1944

Although the President kept hammering at his theme that the war was not over, there were large numbers of people who were not convinced. The manpower resources of the nation, already drained by the draft for military service, were further curtailed by the growing tendency of war workers to drift away from war plants and seek more permanent jobs in civilian industry. This tendency worried the President greatly. It was the subject of much discussion among him and his advisers—particularly the Secretary of War, who was urging drastic action upon him.

Action came in his next annual State of the Union Message to the Congress on January 11, 1944. It was the most drastic recommendation he ever made with respect to American labor. The message was important in other vital respects; but his recommendation to provide a continued and adequate war labor supply took all the headlines and set off a long and bitter public debate.

The President considered this one of his most important messages and, for emphasis, planned to deliver it in person. It was to be broadcast simultaneously to the American people. However, because of an attack of the "flu," he had to send the message up to the Hill in writing. On the same night, January 11, he read it over the air as a fireside chat. As he explained, only a few newspapers in the United States were equipped to print the message in full, and he was anxious "that the American people be given the opportunity to hear what I have recommended to the Congress for this very fateful year in our history—and the reasons for those recommendations."

Hopkins was unable to work at all with us on this message. On New Year's Day of 1944 he had been taken ill again, and was not able to do any substantial work on speeches until sometime during the campaign of 1944, ten months later.

Sherwood and I prepared the first draft; it went through eight before the President was satisfied. He himself labored hard and long on it; a good part of the work was done with us sitting around his bed, to which he was confined with a bad cough.

The first thing in the message was a further report on what the President believed was the important and over-all result of Teheran—the end of isolationism for the United States and the beginning of formal world co-operation for future peace. Then he continued: "And an equally basic essential to peace is a decent standard of living for all individual men and women and children in all nations. Freedom from fear is eternally linked with freedom from want." That too had been discussed at Teheran—largely on his initiative. It was the same idea that was later expanded and is now being put into effect under the name of "Point 4" in President Truman's program.

The President had proclaimed this objective before and had been attacked by many people who spoke caustically of "a quart of milk every day for every Hottentot." Now he took cognizance of that kind of criticism:

There are people who burrow through our nation like unseeing moles, and attempt to spread the suspicion that if other nations are encouraged to raise their standards of living, our own American standard of living must of necessity be depressed.

The fact is the very contrary. It has been shown time and again that if the standard of living of any country goes up, so does its purchasing power—and that such a rise encourages a better standard of living in neighboring countries with whom it trades. That is just plain common sense—and it is the kind of plain common sense that provided the basis for our discussions at Moscow, Cairo, and Teheran.

The use of the word "moles" in this quotation was the President's. His original dictation read "there are within our nation a group of people called moles who circulate constantly in the dirty darkness and insist that if outside nations are encouraged to raise their standards of living, our American standards of living must of necessity go down hill." We persuaded him to soften that paragraph a little—but it was a hard job.

Then he went after those who were letting down in the war effort either because of selfishness or complacency:

. . . while the majority goes on about its great work without complaint, a noisy minority maintains an uproar of demands for special favors for special groups. There are pests who swarm through the lobbies of the Congress and the cocktail bars of Washington, representing these special groups as opposed to the basic interests of the nation as a whole. They have come to look upon the war primarily as a chance to make profits for themselves at the expense of their neighbors—profits in money or in terms of political or social preferment. . . .

Overconfidence and complacency are among our deadliest enemies. Last spring—after notable victories at Stalingrad and in Tunisia and against the U-boats on the high seas—overconfidence became so pronounced that war production fell off. In two months, June and July, 1943, more than a thousand airplanes that could have been made and should have been made were not made. Those who failed to make them were not on strike. They were merely saying, "The war's in the bag—so let's relax."

That attitude on the part of anyone—government or management or labor—can lengthen this war. It can kill American boys.

When aroused, this usually affable and agreeable man could really swing his fists, and did not hesitate to do so. The lobbyists and other "pests" that infested Washington had aroused his indignation for a long time—especially in the face of growing casualty lists. There were those who counseled softer words in the interest of unity; but the President, who had frequently fought with bare knuckles on all kinds of domestic and foreign policies, said he was not going to put on silk gloves for this one.

Now came the controversial core of his message—his recommendations for handling the manpower shortage. They were not impulsively or lightly made. I have a memorandum from him which shows that even as far back as November, 1942, he had been worrying about the problem and considering how best to deal with it. At that time he was strongly in favor of continuing with the system of voluntary co-operation.

November 11, 1942

Memorandum for

> *Hon. Bernard M. Baruch*
> *Hon. James F. Byrnes*
> *Hon. Samuel I. Rosenman*

Following the suggestion of B. M. B.'s memorandum, I approach manpower needs somewhat as follows:

Needs up to January 1, 1944:

1. For the armed forces 4,500,000 additional men.
2. For additional workers—men or women—(excluding agriculture) in

munition and equipment factories to supply them, 5,500,000. (This is by no means B. M. B.'s figure of 4¼ men behind the front to every man in uniform, but is based on an estimate of actual factory needs by January 1, 1944, this being based in turn on using existing factories to limit and manning of new factories.)

3. For additional agricultural workers, including transportation of agricultural products, 2,000,000 men or women (this is based on a pure guess, and I am told by some that an additional 1,000,000 would cover the situation).

I like B. M. B.'s conclusions:

1. No further laws.
2. Voluntary cooperation.
3. Central authority.
4. No further enlistments. (I question this.)
5. Improved administration.
6. Length of work week.

But on this latter I call attention to the fact that this whole hullabaloo is not aimed at long hours. It is aimed solely at time-and-a-half for overtime. I am convinced that the most efficient production standard is forty-eight hours a week (except in a few exceptional cases where that is over-long, and a few other exceptional cases where fifty-two or fifty-four hours can be used effectively).

F. D. R.

As time went on and more men were drafted, the need for manpower in war factories and farms became greater and greater. In 1943, Secretary of War Stimson urged Roosevelt to recommend a national service act which would give the President the power to conscript workers into civilian war work. As the shortage became more acute the Secretary pressed more forcefully.

When I came to draft some paragraphs covering this part of the message, I had before me two strongly worded memoranda that Stimson had sent the President. The first was dated March 19, 1943. The second, dated July 1, 1943, advised "immediate and forceful advocacy of the Austin-Wadsworth National War Service Bill which would impose on every adult man and woman, with appropriate exceptions and safeguard, the equal obligations to aid the war effort by noncombatant work." Five pages long, it set forth forcefully Stimson's reasons for thinking this legislation was imperative. The President had sent it to me with a note:

July 21st, 1943

Memorandum for S. I. R.
Will you talk with me about these matters on Friday?

F. D. R.

It is a fact that the United States was the only major power in the war that did not have such a law. Stimson was soon joined by Knox, the Secretary of the Navy, and Land, the chairman of the Maritime Commission. Still the President hesitated to take this unprecedented step.

Previously that year he had set up a very informal group—consisting of Bernard Baruch, James F. Byrnes, Admiral William Leahy, Harry Hopkins, and me—to make a thorough study of available manpower resources and the foreseeable demands upon them, and to report our recommendations to him. No publicity was ever issued, and none appeared, about this informal committee and its activities. Together we consulted with all the government experts on the subject, with the heads of the government agencies concerned, and also with some of the labor leaders. We held six meetings, in which we interviewed representatives of the War Manpower Commission, the Department of Agriculture, the Army, the United States Employment Service, the Selective Service System, the War Production Board, the American Federation of Labor, and the C.I.O. After a very extensive examination of government statistics and reports, we unanimously reported to the President that, although the situation was very tight, we did not think it critical enough to justify at that time so drastic a law.

But the armed services continued to press, and by September the President had gone so far as to direct that a tentative bill be drawn. He was seriously thinking of recommending it in the fall of 1943. However, he changed his mind. There was very little support for it from any of his Cabinet members or advisers, except the armed services; labor was clearly opposed to it. Baruch on September 8, 1943, had written him a strong memorandum against it. The President wanted Baruch's support for the measure, for he recognized the effect that Baruch's opinion would have on the Congress and on the public generally. Baruch suggested that the proper way to control manpower was by use of priority of materials—allocating materials only to the industries useful to the war. As a result manpower would have to shift to those industries in order to get employment.

Roosevelt left for Teheran without taking action. But when he returned, his mind had apparently been made up. He had seen our fighting men at close hand, their hardships and danger and sufferings—and those neat but crowded American cemeteries. He came back determined to see that the people back home did their share too. One of his first acts when he got back was to take over the railroads to prevent their stoppage by strike. He had not only made up his mind to ask for national service; he had made up his mind that he would not again change his mind. When Roosevelt's mind was once made up as firmly as this, he was stubborn and inflexible, and would become irritated at continued argument.

On this occasion he went out of his way to avoid any further argument on the subject. Very firmly, almost grimly, he told us one day while we were working on the message: "I have just dictated an insert, asking for a national service act. I have made up my mind on it, and I don't want to argue about it any more with anybody. Therefore I want you both to keep it a complete and absolute secret—tell nobody about it. I don't want to be talked out of it again and I am going to ask the Congress for it. So Grace will hand you what I have dictated, and I want you boys to go to work on it, and—remember—keep it quiet."

"But, Mr. President," I said, "does that mean that I shouldn't take it up with Jimmy [meaning James F. Byrnes, who was then the director of the Office of War Mobilization]?" He was the one official in the government most entitled to know about the President's plan in advance. He should be getting ready immediately to push the legislation on the Hill as soon as the message was delivered. "Shouldn't I tell Bernie or the other people who have been working on this problem with me?"

"No," said the President. "I don't want you to tell it to anybody. As soon as it gets around, I know they will try to argue me out of it. I just want it kept right here in the room just between us boys and Grace" —and he smiled in a way that I had come to know meant business.

Sometimes the President, out of his love of mystery and surprise, went to extreme lengths to keep proposed actions secret. He delighted in springing things on people, and he would chuckle with glee when he succeeded. This was especially true where the press was involved. Most times it seemed to me to make little practical difference if a leak occurred—but it made a great difference to the President. On this occasion, however, he wanted secrecy because he had grown tired of the continued argument and indecision. It was another instance of his dislike of unpleasant scenes and discussions, which he knew were inevitable if he had to argue it all out again with all his close associates who were opposed to the course he was taking.

Sherwood and I took all possible precautions to prevent a leak. That is not easy in Washington, as anyone with experience there can testify. The insert that the President had dictated and the subsequent drafts of that insert we labeled, humorously, "Project Q 38." They were not typed upstairs in the staff room in the White House with the rest of the message, but were done separately by Grace herself, and each draft of the insert bore the label "Project Q 38."

In reading through my copies of the various drafts of the message, I notice that "Project Q 38" did not appear until the third draft. The President was apparently still doubtful even then whether he would use it, because at one point on page 15 of the third draft there appears this statement in parentheses: ("Here would come 'Project Q 38' if you decide to use it").

Our efforts at keeping it a secret were successful. I am not sure that even Hopkins knew about it. I know that he never mentioned it to us. Nor did I discuss it with Byrnes or Baruch or Stimson or Knox or any of the people with whom I had been talking about the subject almost every week. It was an extremely embarrassing situation for me, but the President's emphatic instructions about secrecy left me no choice.

The message—also for reasons of secrecy—was not mimeographed until the last possible minute. Consequently, until it was actually read in the Congress, neither Baruch nor Byrnes had the faintest idea that a recommendation for national service was to be included. I was informed that as soon as he heard of it, Byrnes stalked into the President's office and resigned. The President persuaded him to remain, but there was a bitter scene between the two. It caused very strained relations for a short time between the President and Byrnes, and between Byrnes and me, and even between Baruch and me. They both thought that I should have kept them informed, but of course they did not know until much later, when I told them the whole story, how strictly I had been enjoined to silence. They both certainly should have been told what was coming; in view of all the discussions the President had carried on with them during the past year he should have told them himself. But under the circumstances there was nothing that I could do. No one, incidentally, was more surprised at the message than the man who had been the most strenuous in pushing it—Stimson.[1]

This was one of the instances where those working with the President had to take criticism and abuse for doing their job as they were told to do it. Everybody who worked closely with him understood that there would be occasions when "they would have to take the rap for

[1] Henry L. Stimson and McGeorge Bundy, *On Active Service in Peace and War* (New York: Harper & Brothers, 1948), p. 483.

the President." This was one of the many times when I had to take it—
in this case from people who had been close associates of mine.

In his message the President put forth every argument he could to
justify the passage of a national service act at this time:

I am convinced of its necessity. Although I believe that we and our
Allies can win the war without such a measure, I am certain that nothing
less than total mobilization of all our resources of manpower and capital
will guarantee an earlier victory, and reduce the toll of suffering and
sorrow and blood.

I have received a joint recommendation for this law from the heads of the
War Department, the Navy Department, and the Maritime Commission.
These are the men who bear responsibility for the procurement of the
necessary arms and equipment, and for the successful prosecution of the
war in the field. . . .

National service is the most democratic way to wage a war. Like selective
service for the armed forces, it rests on the obligation of each citizen to
serve his nation to his utmost where he is best qualified. . . .

Experience in other democratic nations at war—Britain, Canada, Australia,
and New Zealand—has shown that the very existence of national service
makes unnecessary the widespread use of compulsory power. . . .

It is argued that we have passed the stage in the war where national service is necessary. But our soldiers and sailors know that this is not true. We
are going forward on a long, rough road—and, in all journeys, the last
miles are the hardest. And it is for that final effort—for the total defeat of
our enemies—that we must mobilize our total resources. The national war
program calls for the employment of more people in 1944 than in 1943. . . .

It will give our people at home the assurance that they are standing four-
square behind our soldiers and sailors. And it will give our enemies demoral-
izing assurance that we mean business—that we, 130,000,000 Americans, are
on the march to Rome, Berlin, and Tokyo.

But he was not willing to call for a national service law by itself,
feeling that this would be a highly inequitable burden on one single
class of our citizens—labor. Consequently, he also asked for four other
items in conjunction with national service:

(1) A realistic tax law—which will tax all unreasonable profits, both
individual and corporate, and reduce the ultimate cost of the war to our
sons and daughters. . . .

(2) A continuation of the law for the renegotiation of war contracts—
which will prevent exorbitant profits and assure fair prices to the government. . . .

(3) A cost of food law—which will enable the government (a) to place
a reasonable floor under the prices the farmer may expect for his produc-

tion; and (b) to place a ceiling on the prices a consumer will have to pay for the food he buys. . . .

(4) Early reenactment of the stabilization statute of October, 1942. . . .

These five measures together form a just and equitable whole. I would not recommend a national service law unless the other laws were passed to keep down the cost of living, to share equitably the burdens of taxation, to hold the stabilization line, and to prevent undue profits.

Then, after making a plea that the Congress facilitate absentee voting for the men in the armed services, the President launched into the "plans and . . . strategy for the winning of a lasting peace and the establishment of an American standard of living higher than ever before known":

This Republic had its beginning, and grew to its present strength, under the protection of certain inalienable political rights—among them the right of free speech, free press, free worship, trial by jury, freedom from unreasonable searches and seizures. They were our rights to life and liberty. . . .

We have come to a clear realization of the fact that true individual freedom cannot exist without economic security and independence. . . .

In our day these economic truths have become accepted as self-evident. We have accepted, so to speak, a second Bill of Rights under which a new basis of security and prosperity can be established for all—regardless of station, race, or creed.

The phrase "Economic Bill of Rights" immediately became one of general usage. It was not one of those spontaneous phrases. Its background is interesting. It came originally from a report of the National Resources Planning Board transmitted to the Congress by the President on January 14, 1942. The board had discussed this subject with the President as early as 1941, following his "four freedoms" speech. As originally drafted, chiefly by Luther Gulick, the Bill of Rights contained some international items too—such as free access by all nations to raw materials. When the President saw the first draft in July, 1941, he extracted some of the international ideas and they found their way into the Atlantic Charter the next month.

In December, 1943, when I was talking to Louis Brownlow about the forthcoming annual message—principally about long-range domestic policies—he reminded me of the Economic Bill of Rights in the report of the National Resources Planning Board. At about the same time, Chester Bowles, the director of the Office of Price Administration—an

outstanding liberal who was very helpful to me on occasional speeches
—sent me an excellent memorandum about what he called a "Second
Bill of Rights" and an outline of a proposed speech. He urged strongly
that this was the time for Roosevelt to reannounce his liberal program
and his determination to push it as soon as the exigencies of war
permitted.

When we were discussing the Annual Message of 1944, I showed the
President that part of the report of the National Resources Planning
Board and Bowles' memorandum and draft. He told me he wanted to
include the subject in his message.

This is the way he phrased the Second Bill of Rights:

The right to a useful and remunerative job in the industries or shops or
farms or mines of the nation;
The right to earn enough to provide adequate food and clothing and
recreation;
The right of every farmer to raise and sell his products at a return which
will give him and his family a decent living;
The right of every businessman, large and small, to trade in an atmosphere
of freedom from unfair competition and domination by monopolies at home
or abroad;
The right of every family to a decent home;
The right to adequate medical care and the opportunity to achieve and
enjoy good health;
The right to adequate protection from the economic fears of old age,
sickness, accident and unemployment;
The right to a good education.

The President wanted to impress upon the Congress that the people
of the United States—especially the returning veterans—would certainly
expect the Congress to do something about this program. As has been
seen, the President seldom hesitated, when necessary, to go over the
head of the Congress and appeal directly to the people. In this instance
he practically threatened in advance to do so if the Congress did not
enact his program. True, his threat was couched in an outstanding bit
of understatement, but it was there:

"I ask the Congress to explore the means for implementing this economic bill of rights—for it is definitely the responsibility of the Congress
so to do. . . . In the event that no adequate program of progress is
evolved, I am certain that the nation will be conscious of the fact."

The Eightieth Congress—the first elected after the end of the war

(1946)—turned its back completely on the Economic Bill of Rights. In the national election of 1948—waged chiefly on this issue—the American people spoke clearly and emphatically. Roosevelt's prophecy was correct: the nation was certainly "conscious of the fact" of the Congress' failure to enact an "adequate program of progress."

All told, the State of the Union Message was unusually bellicose. The President was in a fighting mood, and in short order got into some bitter fights with the Congress: one on soldier voting, one on national service, and one on taxes. The fights showed that on domestic, civilian issues the President had lost control of the Congress, and indeed of his own party in the Congress. The small reactionary wing of the Democratic party, principally the Southern members, was working in coalition with the Republican party. It was the same combination that opposed Roosevelt at the polls in 1944, and Truman in 1948; and has been blocking Truman's Fair Deal ever since.

These unsuccessful fights with the reactionary forces in his own party were, I believe, the last straws which convinced him that the time had come for a new alignment of political forces in the United States. Six months later they induced him to open the negotiations with Wendell Willkie that are described in a later chapter.

The Presidential elections were coming in November. Quite apart from any personal or political considerations, Roosevelt was concerned about the inadequacy of the existing absentee voting laws, for he knew that the men and women in the armed services would resent losing their Presidential vote.

On January 25, 1944, he sent a message to the Congress asking for new legislation. There was then pending in the House a bill that had already passed the Senate. This the President characterized in language that caused great resentment in the Congress. In fact it started the Congressional pot boiling.

"I consider such proposed legislation a fraud on the soldiers and sailors and marines now training and fighting for us and for our sacred rights. It is a fraud upon the American people. . . ."

The subject had become so involved in politics that it had been rumored that the Congress was going to pass a soldiers' vote bill without a roll call; this would mean that the people would never know how their Representatives or Senators had voted. In a passage unique for Roosevelt, he urged the Congress to abandon this proposal:

I have hesitated to say anything to the Congress on this matter for the simple reason that the making of these rules is solely within the discretion of the two Houses of the Legislative Branch of the Government. I realize that the Executive as such has nothing to do with the making or the enforcement of these rules. Nevertheless, there are times, I think, when the President can speak as an interested citizen.

I think that there would be widespread resentment on the part of the people of the nation if they were unable to find out how their individual Representatives had expressed themselves on this legislation—which goes to the root of the right of citizenship. . . .

His recommendations were in the main ignored. Many of the grave defects that he had detailed in his message remained in the final legislation. His admonition about a roll call was, however, heeded.

The fight with the Congress on this subject left substantial scars; they were soon reopened. The occasion was the passage of a bill by the Congress on February 17, which extended the life of the Commodity Credit Corporation but took from it its power to grant subsidies on any agricultural commodity, including milk and livestock. The previous July, the President had vetoed a similar bill. He promptly returned the new bill without his signature, saying that "This bill, like that bill, is an inflation measure, a high-cost-of-living measure, a food-shortage measure."

To dramatize the effect of this legislation on the pocketbooks of the people, he asked that figures be compiled on what it would mean in the cost of milk, bread, butter, ham, etc.

"I'm going to put it right up to the housewife who understands such things better than she understands the cost-of-living index in the Bureau of Labor Statistics," he said to us. "Maybe she can hold the boys in line better than I can. At any rate she'll know who voted against her."

That is what he did. He itemized them in his veto message by pennies per pound. He had done this kind of thing successfully before—for example, in the old "waffle iron" campaign for the Governorship in 1930. He also warned that if the price of food went up wages could not be held—and the whole cost of living and of fighting the war would spiral in a vast inflation.

This time he won. Although the bill had passed with more than a two-thirds vote, there was not the two-thirds vote necessary to repass it over his veto.

The climax to his fight with Congress came on February 22, when he vetoed a revenue bill which fell ludicrously short of providing the additional $10½ billion for which he had asked. Purportedly, it would increase the revenue by about $2 billion; actually it would "in its net result enrich the Treasury by less than one billion." In addition the bill granted "relief from existing taxes which would cost the Treasury at least $150,000,000, and possibly much more."

The President branded the bill as follows: "In this respect it is not a tax bill, but a tax relief bill providing relief not for the needy but for the greedy. . . . The bill is replete with provisions which not only afford indefensible special privileges to favored groups but set dangerous precedents for the future. . . ."

It was a very bitter veto message; it had bitter results. The Congressional pot, which had been boiling since the President's caustic reference to the soldier voting bill, now exploded.

The veto message had been drafted in the Office of War Mobilization under Justice Byrnes, and the President had signed it pretty much in the form in which it had come to him from that office. Much to the President's amusement, although I had not even seen the veto message before it was issued and had had nothing at all to do with its preparation, I was immediately accused of being the author of the phrase that became quoted all through the nation: "a tax relief bill providing relief not for the needy but for the greedy." In fact, after a few days, Steve Early took the unusual step of denying formally to the White House correspondents that I had anything to do with it. Of course he did not state who had prepared it, for he took the position flatly that once the President had signed it the identity of the drafter was immaterial. The hostile press was interested because it could concoct all kinds of stories about some anonymous drafter which it could not about the President himself. In fact, neither Steve nor I knew where the original draft had come from until, when the criticism reached a great height, we examined the file to satisfy our own curiosity.

The bill, with all its inequities and inadequacies, was promptly passed over the President's veto. And violent tempers had been aroused. Shortly after the veto message had been read in the Congress, the Senate majority leader, Alben Barkley, who had favored the legislation, submitted his resignation. The President thought that his veto was a wise one and that the legislation fully justified his language. But he was extremely distressed that he should have so deeply hurt Senator Barkley, whom he had helped make majority leader of the Senate in 1937 and who had been his loyal supporter in the Congress.

The President was in Hyde Park when he learned about the resignation, and immediately sent the Senator a telegram, part of which read:

You and I may differ, and have differed on important measures, but that does not mean we question one another's good faith.

In working together to achieve common objectives we have always tried to accommodate our views so as not to offend the other whenever we could conscientiously do so. But neither of us can expect the other to go further.

When on last Monday I read to you portions of my tax message and you indicated your disagreement, I made certain changes as a result of our talk. You did not however try to alter my basic decision when you realized how strongly I felt about it. While I did not realize how very strongly you felt about that basic decision, had I known, I should not have tried to dissuade you from exercising your own judgment in urging the overriding of the veto. . . .

With the many serious problems daily confronting us, it is inevitable that at times you should differ with your colleagues and differ with me. I am sure that your differing with your colleagues does not lessen their confidence in you as Leader. Certainly, your differing with me does not affect my confidence in your leadership nor in any degree lessen my respect and affection for your personally.

The telegram asked the Senator to withdraw his resignation, and expressed the hope that if he did not do so the Senate would immediately and unanimously re-elect him.

The President's telegram was spontaneous and heartfelt. He was generally a most tolerant man, not only about such matters as race, religion, nationality, social and financial status but also about differences in opinion. But not always. When he felt that he was right in a political or economic view, and that the opposition was coming from people who were actuated by selfish economic or political considerations, he was bitter, vindictive and unforgiving, and became personally unfriendly toward those who led the opposition. There were many examples of this: Senator Wheeler and others in the Supreme Court fight; Senator George, Vice-President Garner and others in the attempted "purge" of 1938; Jesse Jones and the preconvention fight in 1944; Wheeler and Lindbergh in the America First isolation fight; Governor Dewey in the 1944 campaign; Congressmen like Representative John J. O'Connor in the wages and hours bill fight and the reorganization bill fight of 1937-1938.

Sometimes this vindictiveness was costly to the nation. For example, because of a very old feud (started in the days of Louis Howe in Albany) between him and Robert Moses, one of the most capable, conscientious and effective public servants of our day, the President not only failed to avail himself of Moses' services but actually excluded him from opportunities for service. Fortunately, such examples were rare.

Some people charged that the President's unusual solicitude for Barkley on this occasion was due only to the fact that the elections were close and he did not want the party split wide open. While I am sure that he was not wholly oblivious to the political implications of Barkley's resignation, I am equally certain from the way he talked at the time that he was very fond of Barkley and appreciative of his loyal record as the Democratic leader of the Senate—in a sense his own spokesman on the floor—and that he was deeply distressed by the incident.

The Senator did resign; but he was immediately re-elected. The breach between the President and the Congress on domestic affairs had widened. Everybody's nerves had become tense and jittery in this trying wartime period of unremitting work and anxiety.

Early in February, 1944, Bob Sherwood went to Great Britain. As head of the Overseas Branch of OWI, he had to be there before, during, and after the cross-Channel invasion. Harry Hopkins was then still in the hospital or convalescing. In addition to my regular work as Counsel to the President, I was therefore left quite alone to work with him on speeches and messages. I did not try to build a new team again, and the President did not suggest it.

During the first six months of 1944 there was growing excitement in Washington arising from the knowledge that the great invasion of Europe was in the making. Although few people knew when and where, a great many knew that a direct strike at the fortress of Europe was imminent. Nobody talked about it. But, as the weeks went by and the summer approached, the atmosphere in official Washington got more and more tense.

On June 5, the President made a radio address on the fall of Rome. In a direct appeal to the Italian people, he pointed to their great early history, and looked forward to the days ahead when "We want and expect the help of the future Italy toward lasting peace." He listed what the Americans were doing to save the Italians from the starvation with which the Nazis were threatening them. And then he continued: "Our victory comes at an excellent time, while our Allied forces are poised for another strike at western Europe—and while the armies of other Nazi soldiers nervously await our assault."

He knew full well that our Allied forces were *not* "poised for another strike" but were actually *striking*. Even as he spoke, they were crossing the Channel on their way to the beaches of Normandy.

Chapter XXI

Victory in Europe Assured, 1944

Originally planned at Teheran for early May, the invasion—or, as the President preferred to call it, the liberation—had been postponed by bad weather. When finally, on June 6, our troops landed, the President again went on the air. It was a far cry from the kind of speech Hitler would have made if his troops were landing on the beaches of England. Indeed it was not a speech at all, but a simple prayer in which the President asked his "fellow Americans" to join. It was written with the assistance of his daughter Anna and her husband at the home of Pa Watson in Charlottesville, Virginia, where they were spending the week end.

While the President was not a regular churchgoer, I always thought of him as a deeply religious man. That he should turn to prayer instead of oratory on this most important day of the war since Pearl Harbor was not surprising; Roosevelt felt a veneration for his Creator which expressed itself often. It was this feeling that made him ask for special church services on particular occasions, such as inauguration days. He was deeply moved during these services, and you could see the effect of them on his face as he left the church to go to the Capitol to take his oath of office. His references to God, so frequent in his speeches, came naturally to him; they were prompted by the same feeling. I have often thought that his deep concern for his fellowmen—even those whom social and financial tradition might call the meanest and the lowliest—had its roots in his religious conviction of the innate dignity of every human being.

I watched him read that D-Day prayer over the air; deep religious faith was apparent in his voice and in his countenance:

Almighty God: Our sons, pride of our Nation, this day have set upon a mighty endeavor, a struggle to preserve our Republic, our religion, and our civilization, and to set free a suffering humanity.

Lead them straight and true; give strength to their arms, stoutness to their hearts, steadfastness in their faith.

They will need Thy blessings. Their road will be long and hard. For the enemy is strong. He may hurl back our forces. Success may not come with rushing speed, but we shall return again and again; and we know that by Thy grace, and by the righteousness of our cause, our sons will triumph.

They will be sore tried, by night and by day, without rest—until the victory is won. . . .

Some will never return. Embrace these, Father, and receive them, Thy heroic servants, into Thy Kingdom.

And for us at home—fathers, mothers, children, wives, sisters, and brothers of brave men overseas—whose thoughts and prayers are ever with them—help us, Almighty God, to rededicate ourselves in renewed faith in Thee in this hour of great sacrifice. . . .

Give us strength, too—strength in our daily tasks, to redouble the contributions we make in the physical and the material support of our armed forces. . . .

And, O Lord, give us Faith. Give us Faith in Thee; Faith in our sons; Faith in each other; Faith in our united crusade. . . .

With Thy blessing, we shall prevail over the unholy forces of our enemy. Help us to conquer the apostles of greed and racial arrogancies. Lead us to the saving of our country, and with our sister Nations into a world unity that will spell a sure peace—a peace invulnerable to the schemings of unworthy men. And a peace that will let all of men live in freedom, reaping the just rewards of their honest toil.

Thy will be done, Almighty God.

Amen.

That was all.

All day through D-Day and the next few days reports kept coming into the White House. Roosevelt read them all with grim satisfaction. He stopped in each day at the Map Room in the basement of the White House on his way to and from the office to get the latest bit of news they had there. As the news got better day by day, the tenseness lessened. The President did not talk much about the military events with anyone except his military leaders; but the men in Normandy were constantly on his mind—as was obvious to anyone who spent time with him.

Later on D-Day the President held a press conference. During the course of it, he was again careful to warn that this was not the end of the war, using one of his convenient fictional "friends" for his purpose:

A fellow came in some time ago whom I have known for quite a while —near home—and he had come—oh, this was several months ago, at the time we took Sicily—and he had had a mighty good job out on the Pacific coast. I don't know what he was—a welder or something like that.

I said, "What are you doing back home?"

"Oh," he said, "the war's over. I am going to try and get a permanent job before everybody quits working on munitions."

He just walked out, quit his job—and he was a good man, he was a munitions worker—because when we took Sicily he said to himself the war's over.

Now, that's the thing we have got to avoid in this country. The war isn't over by any means. This operation isn't over. You don't just land on a beach and walk through—if you land successfully without breaking your leg—walk through to Berlin. And the quicker this country understands it the better.

The "people" who so frequently used to come in to see the President about some problem or other in their daily lives were usually average citizens—typical Americans. The newspapermen would listen to these stories, knowing quite well that the person mentioned was entirely fictional, but knowing also that the fictional conversation with the fictional person would drive home the point that the President wanted to make. Sometimes I thought that he talked so often about these men and women who dropped in to see him at the White House (apparently without any appointment or prior notice, and with enough prestige to get quickly by all the guards) that after a while he began to believe himself that they really existed. Anyone who saw the earnestness with which he told the stories would have thought so, too.

He made use of another "old friend" in a press conference a few days before (May 30, 1944), in which he was pointing out that frequently when people complained about the high cost of living, they were complaining about the price of luxuries rather than necessities.

A friend of mine, a foreman in one of the substantial trades, came in last January, and said to me, "I have an awful time when I go home." He says, "My old lady is ready to hit me over the head with the dishpan."

I said, "What's the trouble?"

"The cost of living."

"Well," I said, "what, for instance?"

"Well, last night I went home, and the old lady said, 'What's this? I went out to buy some asparagus, and do you see what I got? I got five sticks. There it is. A dollar and a quarter! It's an outrage.'"

Well, I looked at him, and I said, "Since when have you been buying asparagus in January—fresh asparagus?"

"Oh," he said, "I never thought of that."

"Well," I said, "tell that to the old lady, with my compliments."

QUESTION: (interposing) Mr. President, is that the same foreman you mentioned in a press conference some time ago who bought the strawberries in the winter? (Much laughter.)

THE PRESIDENT: It happened to be a different one, but it's all right. Still makes a true story.

There was a "businessman" who used to come in once in a while—anonymously. He used to complain to the President about things. But his arguments were always pretty weak, because as soon as the President pointed out the most obvious answer, his visitor would mutter, "I never thought of that," and walk out completely convinced and satisfied.

Another amusing example occurred back in 1938 when there was some discussion about taking a national census of all the unemployed in order to get reliable statistics. The President was making the point that it was impossible to define "unemployed."

"For example," he said, "take the case of a piano teacher I know at Hyde Park. She lives at home and her parents are able to house and feed her. She does not have to work, but used to give five or six lessons a week. She has no pupils now, so she does not work. Would you call her unemployed?"

The piano teacher got to be quite a joke among Hopkins and other of the President's associates, for he insistently referred to her time and again when discussing the need to get a good definition of unemployed.

One morning I was up at Hyde Park, working, when I saw Hopkins come downstairs, all dressed up for the outdoors.

"Where are you going?" I asked.

"I thought I'd take a walk around a bit for some exercise," Harry said, and then as he opened the door, he added, laughing, "While I'm out I'm going to try to locate that piano teacher I've heard so damned much about. I know her intimately by this time, and there are a couple of things I'd like to say to her."

These instances illustrate how completely the President looked at problems of government in terms of their impact upon human beings rather than as abstract questions. Inflation meant less milk for some baby; drought meant a bankrupt farmer; water power and irrigation developments on the Tennessee, Columbia or Missouri River meant more prosperous farm families, safe from flood and drought; cheap electricity meant that some farm family's living standards would go up;

federal aid to education meant a better school for some poor children he had seen in Georgia; public housing meant better homes for people he had seen in rural shacks or city tenements. Then he multiplied the effect by millions of people—but always the problem stood out in his mind as something associated directly with human beings.

Chapter XXII

Fourth-Term Nomination: The New Vice-President, 1944

By this time it had become quite evident that the President intended to run for a fourth term. In July, the chairman of the Democratic National Committee, Robert E. Hannegan, reported that more than a majority of the delegates were already pledged to him. The President wrote Hannegan that, while his personal preference was to retire and drop the responsibilities of his office, he was ready "as a good soldier" to continue to serve if "so ordered by the Commander-in-Chief of us all, the sovereign people of the United States."

In contrast with the period before the third-term nomination in 1940, there was very little debate around the White House—or anywhere else, for that matter—about the fourth-term nomination. Everyone seemed to take it for granted. The President wanted to see the invasion through to victory; he thought the Japanese war would be over before the end of the next term; and he was confident that by then he could lay firm foundations for peace.

The big question in 1944 was, Who is to be the President's running mate? Great opposition had developed in the party to Henry A. Wallace as Vice-President. He had incurred the enmity of a great many important and powerful people by his lack of tact. The many interdepartmental disputes in which he had engaged had not only greatly embarrassed the President, but had hurt Wallace's own standing with the American public. While the hullabaloo of 1940 about the so-called Guru letters had died down, he was still suspected of being something of a mystic and supernaturalist. Many of his progressive and well-meaning speeches about improving the standards of living in backward

438

areas of the world had been so unfortunately phrased that they were distorted by the isolationist press into a statement of readiness to embark on crackbrained and unrealistic projects of worldwide charity handouts.

More important than all this was the fact that the delegates to the Democratic Convention—backed by their political leaders and associates—were simply going to refuse to nominate him. Political leaders from all parts of the country had been telling Hannegan that it would be fatal to the party in November if Wallace were renominated. They argued with the President that many of the more conservative voters behind Roosevelt—especially those who were supporting him in spite of his domestic policies and only because of his foreign policy—would desert him if Wallace were on the ticket.

On the other hand, Wallace had the strong backing of organized labor and many independent liberal groups. A turndown of Wallace at this time was sure to displease a great number of his followers, and some people thought it might endanger the election.

Hannegan came to the White House late in June, and with complete candor told the President what he had learned from the various Democratic political leaders throughout the nation. I was present at one of these conferences. The President became convinced that in order to nominate Wallace as Vice-President for a second term he would have to go through the same "knock-down and drag-out" fight that he did in 1940. He did not want to do that again.

"I am just not going to go through a convention like 1940 again," he said. "It will split the party wide open, and it is already split enough between the North and South; it may kill our chances for election this fall, and if it does, it will prolong the war and knock into a cocked hat [a common expression of the President's] all the plans we've been making for the future."

The President in his own mind saw as the big task for his fourth term the creation and successful functioning of the United Nations Organization. This would require not only the complete co-operation of his own party but the co-operation of the Republican party as well. He was determined not to repeat the mistake of Woodrow Wilson and try to frame the future peace of the world by himself or with his own party alone. Congressional leaders were to be called in for assistance and collaboration, and both parties were to be invited to join in the effort. This bipartisan approach was already in operation. In all the conferences then going on in the State Department about the postwar organization Republican Congressmen and outside Republican advisers were participating. Roosevelt had no intention of jeopardizing this precious bipartisanship or the unity of his own party.

This conclusion raised two questions: how to tell Wallace; and who was to be Wallace's successor?

The first question would seem to be an easy one—Roosevelt would simply tell him himself directly. But that was the one kind of thing Roosevelt hated to do. He always had. He could be cruelly blunt to adversaries in any kind of fight, political or personal. But when it came to hurting friends, he put it off as long as he could; and, not too unlike other men, he preferred to do it at a distance or through an intermediary rather than face to face.

His unwillingness to be unpleasantly frank was notorious among those who knew him well. But it was a characteristic that visitors who came to see him with new ideas or suggestions sometimes had to learn the hard way. They often left his office thinking they had convinced him of the soundness of their views, when what had happened was that he had refrained from telling them frankly that he disagreed with them. By smiling and nodding, and saying, "I see," or "That's very interesting," or "Thanks for taking the trouble to come in and give me your slant on this" (another common expression of his), he would give them the impression that he had been completely convinced. Later, when they learned that he had not, they would complain that the President did not know his own mind, and that the last person who saw him was the one who prevailed.

I, who had worked with the President for a long time, had grown used to this trait; but his performance in 1944 on the Vice-Presidential nomination was the most extreme expression of it I ever experienced. The President liked Wallace—he liked him as a person and as an outspoken liberal and internationalist. This was four years before the days of 1948 when Wallace was to startle and disgust most of his liberal followers by his attitude toward Communist Russia at a time when she was deliberately trying to tear down the foundations of peace.

The President wanted Wallace to know his views about the Vice-Presidency before he took any formal action. Wallace, at the President's request, had gone on a mission to China; and at the time of these conferences with Hannegan he was on his way home by plane.

"Someone will have to go out and meet Wallace and tell him," said the President. "In that way he will be prepared for the action which I am sorry I have to take."

Who was to go? He looked at me, smiled and said: "You remember how in our Albany days whenever I had some unpleasant message to deliver to the political leaders or officials in New York City, I used to let you have the pleasure of bearing the bad news? I am going to let you have that pleasure again. I'd like you to go out and meet Wallace when he lands at Seattle, and fly back with him. I want you to tell him all you heard Bob Hannegan say. Tell him that I'd like to have him as my running mate, but I simply cannot risk creating a permanent split in the party by making the same kind of fight for him that I did at the convention four years ago. I am sure he will understand and be glad to step down."

I had grown to know Wallace better during the past four years. I knew enough about him to feel sure that he would not be glad to step down—in fact I had great doubts whether he would be willing to withdraw at all. But I had to accept the assignment, unpleasant as it was.

When I called his office in Washington I learned that he was expected in Seattle in a few days. I told his secretary that I had been directed by the President to fly out to meet him in Seattle and return with him in his plane, but that nobody was to know about it. I asked him to communicate with the Vice-President and then let me know just when and where I could meet him.

Whether Wallace and his office staff became suspicious at this request, I do not know. They must have got some wind of the purpose of my mission. Either the Vice-President or his staff in Washington made up their minds that I should not see him until after he had himself seen the President. They probably thought that he would be able to talk the President out of his position. At any rate, they were not very cooperative, and I had to call them several times and remind them that I was making this trip at the express direction of the President.

In due course they informed me that the Vice-President did not expect to come home by way of Seattle but by way of Chicago. I told them that I would meet him in Chicago at any place he selected, and that they should ascertain his wishes.

Unfortunately, during this delay Harold Ickes—I do not know how or why—had somehow talked the President into letting him go with me to meet Wallace. Had I known about this in advance, I should have objected strenuously, because Ickes and Wallace had been bitter enemies for a long time and I knew that any chance of persuading Wallace to do anything voluntarily would be wiped out if Ickes joined the conference. To make matters worse, it soon became known that Ickes was himself receptive to a nomination for the Vice-Presidency; this certainly was not going to be helpful.

Ickes had always been a tower of strength for the liberal forces in the Administration, and the President had great regard for him. He had been a political progressive long before the days of Franklin D. Roosevelt, and was among the most ardent and effective New Dealers in his administrations. He was also one of the earliest and the most outspoken critics of Hitler and Mussolini. At campaign time he could always be counted on for forceful support; his use of ridicule and invective was especially effective. The President used to love to listen to him "lay it on." Above all the President felt great comfort and easiness with Ickes as Secretary of the Interior because of his rugged honesty and incorruptibility. However, Roosevelt did not think that he could ever be nominated.

To add to my difficulties, we got word that the plane bringing Wallace and his party back from China had been forced to land in Canada because one of the pilots had become ill. The illness turned out to be scarlet fever, and there was immediate talk of quarantining all the members of the crew and all the passengers. This would mean that I would not see Wallace in time. I phoned his office and told them the President wanted Wallace to come on home as quickly as he could. Apparently the Vice-President was able to arrange it; but instead of stopping at Chicago, he came directly to the Washington airport. In the meantime, he had sent me a wire reading: "Believe I should see President before the meeting you mentioned. H. A. Wallace." I ignored his wire, and said that I would go out to meet him; but word came back that he wanted us to meet him instead at his apartment at the Wardman Park Hotel for breakfast.

I shall not soon forget that breakfast. Wallace's face can be as immobile as stone when he wants it to be—and he certainly wanted it to be during that conference. Both Ickes and I tried our best to explain the reasons in back of the President's determination. He seemed not even to be listening. When he did finally talk, he merely said: "Sam, I've just come back from a country where people are dying by the hundreds of thousands because of lack of food. They and their children and grandchildren have nothing to look forward to in the future but a continuance of that kind of life—whether there is war or peace. In the face of my experience in China I have no interest now in discussing political matters. I shall do so eventually with the President."

To say that my mission to Wallace was unsuccessful is an understatement. I went back to the White House with Ickes, and we reported to the President our complete failure.

Wallace had already phoned the White House for an appointment that very morning, and the President had invited him to lunch. I never was able to find out exactly what transpired between the two men at lunch. I asked the President, but he merely said that he thought it had gone very satisfactorily. Knowing Roosevelt, however, I had my doubts about whether Wallace was really made to understand what was in his mind. Subsequent events at the convention proved that my doubts were well founded. I am sure that the President did not put it as frankly and bluntly to him as he had to Hannegan and me, or as I had to Wallace. However, Wallace probably understood that there was to be no down-the-line fight by Roosevelt on his behalf as there had been in 1940. He probably told Roosevelt he was going to make the run on his own for the nomination, and induced the President to write the letter which is later set out in full (page 449). I also suspect that he persuaded the President to promise to make room for him in his Cabinet if Wallace did not succeed—a promise that, at great political cost, Roosevelt later kept.

The next job was to choose a new candidate for Vice-President. There were many—some very active and some merely receptive. Among the active candidates for the nomination, the one farthest out in front was James F. Byrnes. Many people had spoken to Roosevelt about various candidates, but he had come to no conclusion. Byrnes had discussed his own candidacy with him more than once. Although the President did not think that Byrnes was in all respects a New Dealer, he never told him that he did not want him to make the try. He felt, as he had with Farley in 1940, that he had no right to tell anyone not to enter the contest in a convention. His refusal directly to discourage Byrnes led Byrnes to redoubled efforts.

The President wanted to make sure above all that the candidate nominated was a liberal in complete sympathy with the New Deal and with the Administration's foreign policy and postwar program. He was considering several possibilities, which he discussed from time to time with different people. He weighed carefully not only the political philosophy of each candidate but also the potential political strength that each might add to the ticket. There was one man who seemed to combine political liberalism and political strength to a greater degree than anyone else, and the President was about ready to decide on him. He did not make up his mind definitely, however, until the close of a conference in the White House held on July 11, 1944.

At this conference there were present the President, Hannegan; Frank Walker; Mayor Kelly of Chicago; John Boettiger, the President's son-in-law; George Allen, then an official of the Democratic National Committee and a friend of the President; and Ed Flynn. Although Hannegan had suggested that I be invited and had told me to be ready to come, I was not asked. I do not know why, and never inquired. But I soon learned from several of those present exactly what happened at the meeting.

Several possibilities, including Rayburn, Barkley, William O. Douglas, Byrnes, Truman and others, were discussed. As each name came up, it was appraised coldly and calmly; the merits and demerits of each were measured from the point of view of political strength and sympathy with the President's program. When discussion about one man was ended, they passed on to the next. Some of those present urged favorites of their own. Hannegan, who would be responsible for getting the man they decided on nominated by the convention, strongly favored Truman, who had befriended him; but leaned over backward to be fair to the other candidates. The President turned to each of his guests and asked him to express an opinion about each name under discussion.

The political weaknesses of Byrnes were gone over in great detail: the fact that labor was only lukewarm, if not slightly hostile, to him; the fact that the Negroes would oppose him because of his Southern political and social background; the effect of his Catholic birth and later adoption of the Protestant faith. Some of the conferees thought that the matter of religion would not be important, but all agreed that the antipathy of the Negroes and the lack of enthusiasm on the part of labor would hurt the ticket in the larger Northern cities. These latter considerations weighed more heavily with the President than the religious one. He knew that labor had the same doubts about Byrnes' liberalism that he had.

Everyone seemed to take for granted that Wallace was out; not much time was spent discussing him. They all knew that Roosevelt's mind had been made up about him for several days. The President mentioned the names of John Winant and Justice Douglas as possibilities, but the conferees had no enthusiasm for either of them, feeling that neither would add any vote-getting strength to the ticket.

When Truman's name came up, it seemed to find favor with every one present. His qualifications as a candidate and as a prospective Vice-President were discussed fully and frankly and approvingly; no one could find any major disqualification. The President spoke very highly of him—of his ability and his liberalism and his loyalty.

When all the names had been fully canvassed the President said with an air of finality: "It's Truman." The conference was over—the next President of the United States had been selected.

There were several reasons for Roosevelt's decision. First, Truman had been an undeviating supporter of the President's domestic and foreign policies. A check of Truman's voting record in the Senate showed that he was a thorough New Dealer. With only one or two exceptions, he had supported the President in every legislative matter. His service as chairman of the Congressional Committee Investigating the National Defense Program—popularly known as the Truman Committee—had been thorough, dignified, and painstaking. It had not been used—as so many Congressional committees are used—for political propaganda or to garner headlines for its chairman; it had been devoted scrupulously to obtaining the greatest efficiency and economy in the conduct of the war. Truman was an authority on the history of the Civil War, and knew how badly President Lincoln had been handicapped by a Congressional Committee during that conflict. And so, instead of trying to interfere in the conduct of the war as did the Civil War Congressional Committee, he concentrated on trying to break bottlenecks in production and transportation, and on preventing waste and misuse of public funds. His Committee had made none of the mistakes of the Civil War Committee. Its work had built up vast public support and good will for Truman. Coming from the central part of the country, he was geographically very acceptable as a candidate. He was from a border state which was politically doubtful in 1944, and he could be expected to win its fifteen electoral votes. He was a combat veteran of World War I, active in veterans' affairs, and would appeal strongly to the soldier vote.

The President's judgment of Truman's liberalism has been thoroughly justified by later events. Truman the President has been a New

Dealer in every sense of the word, as was Truman the Senator. Almost every one of his legislative recommendations would have been signed by Roosevelt. In many fields of reform Truman has moved even more quickly and more drastically than Roosevelt would have. In the fields of civil rights and health insurance, for example, Truman has not only followed the philosophy of Roosevelt; he has gone much further and has tried to act with greater speed. Perhaps it was Roosevelt's sense of timing which made him move more cautiously in these fields. As for Byrnes, his speeches since 1949 and his assumption of the leadership of the Southern opposition to Truman and to his policies have shown how shrewd and accurate was the President's measure of his conservatism.

As the White House conference broke up that hot July night, Hannegan whispered to Walker: "I'm going to stay behind and ask the Boss to give me a letter saying 'It's Truman'—I may need it to put him over at the convention. You wait for me downstairs, and I'll ride home with you." They were all anxious to leave, for the President's study was stifling. As the group was breaking up, the President called Walker over and said:

"Frank, will you go over tomorrow, and tell Jimmy [Byrnes] that it's Truman, and that I'm sorry it has to be that way." This again was one of those pleasant chores Roosevelt often handed out to his friends, like my assignment to tell Wallace that he was out. Frank was as used to this as I was; he just grinned and said, "O.K.," and went downstairs to wait for Hannegan.

When Hannegan came down, the rest of the group was waiting for him curiously, but Hannegan never vouchsafed a word about what had transpired between him and the President after the others had left. As they all were getting into their cars under the north portico of the White House, he nudged Walker and said, "I got it." He never told any of the others that he had "got it" until he actually used the letter more than a week later in Chicago.

What he had got was the following, written on a piece of scratch paper in the President's handwriting:

July 19

DEAR BOB,
You have written me about Harry Truman and Bill Douglas. I should, of course, be very glad to run with either of them and believe that either one of them would bring real strength to the ticket.

Always sincerely,
FRANKLIN ROOSEVELT

This letter was written on July 11 but the President dated it the 19th, which was the opening date of the convention and about the date when it probably would have to be used.

The next morning, July 12, Hannegan and Walker came to the White House, on different errands. Hannegan came to ask the President to have Grace Tully type on White House stationery the scratch-pad note of the preceding evening. This was done. He also agreed with the President that the letter should be used at Chicago only if necessary. Walker's errand was to deliver the President's oral message to Byrnes. But Byrnes was not convinced. He said that the President had given him the green light, and that he was going ahead and run. And he did!

The President's letter named both Truman and Douglas, and in that order. He told me later than he had used two names to avoid the impression that he was dictating to the convention. But he left no doubt in the mind of Hannegan (or of anyone else at the conference of July 11) that Truman was his first choice, and that is why he placed Truman's name first. There have been stories that the original handwritten note named Douglas first, and that Hannegan induced the President a few days later in the railroad yards in Chicago to change the order. So far as I have been able to learn by examining the documents and by talking to the few people who knew about the letter (including Hannegan a few weeks before his death), this is not so. The only handwritten note I have been able to find is the one set out above. The original of it is now in the possession of Mrs. Hannegan. Hannegan turned it over to her on their way to Chicago, and she tells me that, at his request, she kept it in her pocketbook until he finally decided he had to use it, and asked her for it.

No more than three or four people knew about this letter before the convention opened. Truman, Roosevelt's first choice, was not among those who knew. He not only did not know about the letter; he did not even know until the following week that he was the President's first choice. But before Truman left for Chicago, Byrnes phoned him and asked him for his support for his own candidacy. Truman, in ignorance of what had happened, promised Byrnes his support, and agreed to make the nominating speech for him at the convention.

Having committed himself to Byrnes, Truman loyally stuck to that commitment until Byrnes finally withdrew. He probably would have made the promise to Byrnes even if he had known about the President's decision in his own favor, because he definitely did not want the nomination for himself. Apparently no one told him that he was the President's choice—I do not know why—until after he arrived in Chicago.

Byrnes went to Chicago, set up headquarters, and began actively to gather delegates behind him. The political handicaps that had convinced the President that Byrnes should not be the choice soon began to plague him. A number of labor leaders announced that they were opposed to his nomination. While there was nothing distinctly antilabor in his past record, the labor leaders wanted someone whose liberalism had been more pronounced. They came to see Truman in Chicago to tell him that they would enthusiastically back him for the nomination but not Byrnes. To them Truman repeated what he had already told others in Chicago who had urged him to make the run: that he did not want the nomination even if the President did want him to take it, that he preferred to remain in the United States Senate, that he was committed to Byrnes anyway, and that he expected to support him to the end.

Again the national political leaders, especially Flynn, went over all the political handicaps that Byrnes had against him. Byrnes, however, kept assuring Hannegan that he was going to be able to get the support of labor.

Hannegan had plenty of trouble trying to stop Wallace and at the same time get Byrnes to withdraw. But his chief difficulty came not from Wallace or from Byrnes. It came from his own candidate—Harry S. Truman. Truman was adamant, not only in his refusal to run but in his intention to make the nominating speech for Byrnes. He rejected all suggestions from labor leaders and political leaders that he should be the candidate. He tried to get the Missouri delegation behind Byrnes. He tried to get labor leader Sidney Hillman to support Byrnes; but Hillman said he was for Wallace, Douglas, or Truman—and for no one else. Murray and Whitney and other labor leaders also rejected Truman's approaches in behalf of Byrnes. Green of the American Federation of Labor said he was for no one but Truman. Truman turned aside the political leaders' insistence that he was the President's choice. Hannegan showed him and others the President's note; but he still declined. As he stuck to his determination Hannegan was almost ready to quit the fight in despair. As he said to Walker, "It's all over; our candidate won't take it—we have no candidate."

In the meantime, on July 13, the President left Washington for a transcontinental train trip to San Diego, via Hyde Park and Chicago. He intended to make his acceptance speech at San Diego on July 20, and there embark on a cruiser for Pearl Harbor and Alaska. He asked me to accompany him on the trip, saying that we would prepare the acceptance speech on the way. Of course, the whole trip was officially a secret at the time. However, by the time the convention opened, it was generally known in official circles that the President was not in Washington. This was the first Democratic National Convention where he was a candidate which he did not watch carefully from his study and with which he was not in constant communication.

When we reached Chicago on Saturday, July 15, the President's train was shunted into the freight yards before being switched to the tracks going west. There Hannegan came aboard. Mrs. Roosevelt and I were finishing lunch with the President in the dining compartment of his private car. We excused ourselves, and left Hannegan alone with the President for about an hour.

He had come to the train to give the President a firsthand report on the convention—particularly to tell him about the impasse caused by Truman's determination to support Byrnes and his refusal to become a candidate himself. Affairs were further confused by the letter that the President had written to the convention—I assume in accordance with his promise to Wallace. It read as follows:

HYDE PARK, N. Y.
July 14, 1944

MY DEAR SENATOR JACKSON:

In the light of the probability that you will be chosen as permanent chairman of the convention, and because I know that many rumors accompany all conventions, I am wholly willing to give you my own personal thought in regard to the selection of a candidate for Vice President. I do this at this time because I expect to be away from Washington for the next few days.

The easiest way of putting it is this: I have been associated with Henry Wallace during his past four years as Vice President, for eight years earlier while he was Secretary of Agriculture, and well before that. I like him and I respect him and he is my personal friend. For these reasons I personally would vote for his renomination if I were a delegate to the convention.

At the same time I do not wish to appear in any way as dictating to the convention. Obviously the convention must do the deciding. And it should —and I am sure it will—give great consideration to the pros and cons of its choice.

Very sincerely yours,
FRANKLIN D. ROOSEVELT

On the strength of this letter and with his strong following of liberal supporters Wallace was rapidly gaining ground. The atmosphere of the convention was quite different from 1940, when there was so much hostility toward Wallace. This time his supporters were getting ready to pack the galleries and to try to stampede the convention for him. If Truman stayed out of the race it looked like a close fight between Wallace and Byrnes. And if Byrnes stayed in and Truman was induced also to become a candidate, Wallace might prevail over the split strength of the other two. However, I have grave doubts that Truman would ever have become a candidate if Byrnes had stayed in. Hannegan's job was to get Byrnes out of the contest and Truman in—so that Wallace could not win.

As Hannegan left the train, he had Roosevelt's encouragement and support; but he still had grave misgivings about ever inducing Truman to change his position.

The Presidential train continued on its journey to San Diego. The President ordered it to move very slowly since he did not want to arrive at San Diego until July 19. He never did like speed anyway, either in an automobile or on a train.

During the campaign of 1944, for example, we were preparing a speech to be delivered at Chicago, and the President was dictating a word picture of the United States of the future as he saw it—with increased tempo of production, increased standards of living, better health, expanded education, etc. I suggested that perhaps we might include faster transportation. We were then on a train moving rather rapidly toward Chicago. As the train lurched around a curve, he frowned and said: "Better leave out faster transportation; the trains go too fast already." The only place he liked speed, apparently, was in his small wheel chair going between his residence and the offices at the White House; we used to wonder how he stayed on going around curves!

At operating stops on our way to San Diego, or at stations where a delay of a few minutes was necessary, the President spoke by telephone with Washington and occasionally with leaders at the convention. He kept urging them to induce Truman to run, and they kept reporting their failure.

The trip was still supposed to be a secret, and, of course, none of the newspapers mentioned it until the news was finally released. I am sure that it was no secret at any station where we stopped. It was a special train, and it arrived at unscheduled hours. As if to remove any doubt about who was aboard, there would descend from the train as soon as it pulled into a station a lady easily recognized as Mrs. Roosevelt, leading by a leash a little black Scottie dog easily recognized as Fala. They would walk up and down the platform while the train went through its inspection or fueling or icing. Although the curtains were tightly drawn in the President's own car, I was always sure that the crowd which gathered at each stop had a pretty good idea who was sitting behind the curtains. I would saunter over to mix with them, and their conversation never left any doubt.

By the time we got to San Diego on July 19, the convention was in a state of confusion. Many delegates had been flocking to Byrnes. Wallace was pushing hard. Truman was still for Byrnes.

Word had gotten around generally by now that the President wanted Truman, but whenever asked about it Truman said, "I am for Byrnes." Finally, on Thursday, the 20th, Hannegan got some of the leaders together in a room at the Blackstone Hotel—Walker, Flynn, Kelly—and phoned Roosevelt at San Diego. Truman was with them.

After some discussion the President said: "Have you got that fellow lined up yet?"

The answer was "No."

"Well, tell the Senator," said the President, "that if he wants to break up the Democratic party by staying out, he can; but he knows as well as I what that might mean at this dangerous time in the world. If he wants to do it, anyway, let him go ahead." Truman finally gave in and said: "I guess I'll have to take it."

Byrnes, finally realizing he could not get the support of labor, had withdrawn. That was the end of it. Although on the first ballot Wallace got 429½ votes, on the second he got only 105.

Truman was the candidate.

President Truman has been good enough to read this account of his nomination at the Chicago Convention, and has authorized me to state that to the best of his knowledge and information it is factually correct.

On the trip across the continent the President occasionally worked on various drafts of the acceptance speech. Bob was still in London; Harry was still sick. On the train, however, was Elmer Davis, the head of the Office of War Information; and he assisted in the preparation of the speech.

The train, from which the speech was delivered, stood on a well-concealed and well-protected siding in the naval reservation at San Diego, and the President spoke from a car specially equipped for that purpose. There was room for only a few people; moving-picture and still cameras and radio broadcasting equipment cluttered up almost the entire car.

In the speech the President said that he was talking from a naval base, but he did not say where. He did not disclose that he was on his way to Pearl Harbor for conferences with Admiral Nimitz and General MacArthur on the future conduct of the war in the Pacific; but he did say that his presence at the naval base was "in the performance of my duties under the Constitution. The war waits for no elections. Decisions must be made—plans must be laid—strategy must be carried out."

He indicated, as in 1940, that he did not expect to conduct a campaign "in the usual sense." He did not consider it fitting, and he did not think he would be able to find the time. He did say again, "I shall, however, feel free to report to the people the facts about matters of concern to them and especially to correct any misrepresentations." It is fortunate that he made that reservation again; for he was to have occasion in the campaign—many occasions—to correct misrepresentations by the opposition.

It was a political speech, of course—even in the midst of war. We were winning the war by now, and had already begun to lay the foundations on which the peace might be built. The question for the electorate was, Why change? The President was not satisfied merely to argue that there was no need for a change; he urged that a change would be harmful—that it would put in power the very leaders who had opposed the measures that were proving so successful. That was to be the theme of the campaign, and he wanted to strike it right away.

For his peroration, he drew on history. This was the first wartime election since the Civil War. He had asked me to bring along on the train the famous Second Inaugural Address of that earlier President.

The peroration of Lincoln's Second Inaugural delivered in 1865 fitted the occasion of 1944 as though it had been written specially for it. The President, saying it set the goal of today in "terms which the human mind cannot improve," quoted it in full as his own peroration.

. . . with firmness in the right, as God gives us to see the right, let us strive on to finish the work we are in; to bind up the nation's wounds; to care for him who shall have borne the battle, and for his widow, and his orphan—

to do all which may achieve and cherish a just and lasting peace among ourselves and with all nations.

Many orators like to close their speeches with a well-known quotation. Roosevelt did not; this is one of the rare exceptions.

After the formal delivery of the speech, the President, as usual, reread selected portions while the photographers and movie cameramen took the inevitable pictures. One of the pictures was a most unfortunate one. It was snapped while the President, with his head bowed over the printed page, was pronouncing a broad vowel, so that his mouth was wide open at the click of the camera. The result showed a tragic-looking figure; the face appeared to be very emaciated because of the downward angle and open mouth; it looked weary, sick, discouraged, and exhausted. The picture was completely distorted, bearing no resemblance to the man I watched deliver that speech that night.

Unfortunately, Steve Early was not aboard the train; for he always took great pains to see that that kind of unfair and distorted picture was not distributed. However, in his absence the undeveloped film, along with the others, was flown out from San Diego. It was later published with great glee by enemies of the President, who urged it as proof of their charge that he was no longer physically or mentally competent to manage his office.

I was very sorry that Steve was not along on this trip—not only because of the incident of the photograph but also because I was deprived of his good sound judgment about the speech. He was one of our most helpful critics during the final stages of speech preparation. We generally did not show him the early drafts for two reasons: he wanted to be able to say truthfully to newspapermen who might ask him about a forthcoming speech that he did not know its contents; and second, we wanted to reserve his judgment and criticism for the nearly finished product.

He was one of the most capable men in the Administration in forecasting public reaction to a speech or indeed to any proposed course. He was very frank in his criticism, and never hesitated to tell the President or us what he thought of a speech or any part of it.

Throughout his terms of office, the President, with rare exceptions, had a fine relationship with the reporters at the White House. Most of this was due to the President himself. But a great deal of it was due to Steve. The White House correspondents admired Steve's ability, respected his integrity and honesty, and loved him personally. He never lied to them, and they knew it. He might decline to answer a question, but he never deliberately gave a reporter—even a hostile one—a false lead. At times, when the President became irritated with the correspondents, especially in his later years when they insisted on going with him on his wartime trips, it was Steve who would patch things up. He would argue at length with the President to let them go along; he knew, as an old newspaperman himself, the importance of covering the President at all times and in all places. The President was occasionally vexed with Steve for his continuous defense of the White House reporters and for his unfailing advocacy of their cause when he thought it was right. But he realized that Steve was only doing his job, and his vexation would soon disappear. He leaned heavily on him in many things and trusted him without reservation. There was a closeness between them that went back to 1920 when Steve was with Roosevelt in his unsuccessful Vice-Presidential campaign. When he finally resigned after thirteen years of service, the White House lost one of its ablest men.

Chapter XXIII

To Hawaii and Alaska, 1944

At midnight on July 21 we sailed from San Diego on the cruiser *Baltimore* for Pearl Harbor. The ship, which had been in many Pacific battles, was ordered back to San Diego for this voyage. Few of her officers and men suspected the purpose for which she was being sent back. They began to suspect, I suppose, when they saw a ramp being constructed on the ship, and they must have been convinced when they saw Fala come aboard several hours in advance of his master.

It was an uneventful voyage. The cruiser was preceded by six destroyers, and she also had a complete air cover. By means of radar it was possible to observe any approaching enemy. The ship traveled under rigid wartime conditions, no lights showing. On ocean voyages such as this the President was able to snatch some sustained rest. Although the ship's radio received news and messages which kept him in touch with all worldwide occurrences, messages were sent from the ship only in extreme need, because the signals might help a watching enemy locate the ship. The President read a great deal, slept late in the morning, took a nap in the afternoon. Movies were shown after dinner every evening. The grim appearance of the trimmed-down ship, the absence of chairs on deck, the repeated lifeboat drills, the well-manned guns, the presence of the six destroyers—all reminded us that this was no pleasure cruise but part of the business of war. I like to sit on deck, so I used to drag up a straight-backed cabin chair and sit out on the middle of the quarter-deck, much to the amusement of the old salts aboard, especially Admiral Leahy.

Fala became quite a pet of the crew on this voyage. Their affection for him soon resulted in a near mishap. Fala, like his master, loved people; and would quickly begin to fraternize in almost any company.

It was his custom, as soon as he was permitted on deck in the morning, to scamper forward and find his way below to the seamen's quarters. This was not just natural canine curiosity. He had learned quickly that little scraps of delicacies would be fed to him on these forays below. It soon became a steady habit. Unfortunately, one day, a sailor got the idea that his younger brother back home would be pleased to receive a small lock of the famous dog's hair. With his scissors, he snipped off a little bit of Fala's shaggy black coat. Other sailors had little brothers, too, and followed suit. Pretty soon the absence of hair on Fala's back became quite noticeable; the poor dog was in danger of being completely shorn. At first, the President was mystified; but soon the truth was discovered. Instructions had to be given to the men to confine their demonstrations of affection to petting, and to discontinue feeding and clipping. While Fala's hair grew back by the time he returned to the States, he was for a short time a strange-looking dog.

We reached Pearl Harbor on the 26th.

We assumed, as we neared our destination, that our expected arrival had been kept a secret. Imagine our surprise, therefore, when we steamed into the harbor and up toward the dock, to see all the Navy ships with the men in whites at attention at the rails. At the dock an area of about two acres had been cleared off; a tremendous crowd stood in back of this space. They cheered as the gangplank was lowered to receive on board Admiral Nimitz, General Richardson and some fifty other high military and naval officers. The officers came aboard to greet the President on the quarter-deck.

One officer was conspicuously absent. It was General Douglas Mac-Arthur. When Roosevelt asked Nimitz where the General was, there was an embarrassed silence. We learned later that the General had arrived about an hour earlier, but instead of joining the other officers to greet the Commander-in-Chief, he had gone by himself to Fort Shafter.

After we had waited on the *Baltimore* some time for the General, it was decided that the President and his party would disembark and go to the quarters on shore assigned to them. Just as we were getting ready to go below, a terrific automobile siren was heard, and there raced onto the dock and screeched to a stop a motorcycle escort and the longest open car I have ever seen. In the front was a chauffeur in khaki, and in the back one lone figure—MacArthur. There were no aides or attendants. The car traveled some distance around the open space and stopped at the gangplank. When the applause of the crowd died down, the General strode rapidly to the gangplank all alone. He dashed up the gangplank, stopped halfway up to acknowledge another ovation, and soon was on deck greeting the President.

He certainly could be dramatic—at dramatic moments.

"Hello, Doug," said the Commander-in-Chief. "What are you doing with that leather jacket on—it's darn hot today."

I understand that the MacArthur jacket was still nonregulation.

"Well I've just landed from Australia," he replied. "It's pretty cold up there."

Greetings all around—and we proceeded to leave the ship.

The President made several inspection trips through the island of Oahu. He went to the shipyards, to the jungle training grounds and other training camps, to the hospitals and to the flying fields. We were all lodged in a beautiful villa on the shore near Waikiki Beach. In the evenings, Admiral Nimitz, General MacArthur, Admiral Leahy, and the President spent many hours in military conferences. The non-military members of the party would go out and sit under the palm trees along the beach; from our chairs we could look through the glass doors into the living room of the villa. There we could see the four of them studying maps and going over the plans for the next move in the Pacific.

That was the chief purpose of the President's trip to Pearl Harbor. Of course, MacArthur and Nimitz could have been recalled to the States to consult with him, but this was no time to call them away from their all-important posts in the Pacific. Besides, the President found it useful to make these trips. You could nearly always tell when he was going off on one of them. He looked it. He would become as excited as a boy. Preparations, laying out the routes on the map, figuring distances and fixing times of arrival and departure at various places—these were all given his personal, loving attention, no matter how busy he was. His visits to the training camps gave him a closer feel of the conduct of the war, and getting out of Washington, he said, always gave him a better perspective. He also was convinced that visits to military installations in different parts of the world helped the morale of the troops—not only those he was visiting, but those elsewhere who would later read about it. And they made the parents back home feel that the President was making personally sure that everything possible was being done for the safety and welfare of the men and women at the fronts. In a smaller measure, Roosevelt felt that a visit by his wife served the same ends.

On the President's inspection trips to different parts of Oahu, the streets of the cities and villages were lined with residents of the island. I thought that this was taking unnecessary risks. Many of the inhabitants were pure Japanese or descended from mixed marriages of Japanese. The President, however, insisted on riding through these crowds—and in an open car. Frequently, Admiral Nimitz, General MacArthur, and Admiral Leahy were in the car with him. Following behind in the procession, I could not help thinking how dreadful a toll one well-placed bomb would take. The Secret Service men were worried to distraction. It was another display of the President's personal courage. Although he knew the danger (and had once narrowly escaped an assassin's bullet in a crowded city street in Florida), you would never have thought so as you saw the calm joy with which he waved to the crowds, or the lightness with which he talked and laughed with the people in his automobile.

At one of the hospitals in Oahu, the President did something which affected us all very deeply. He asked a Secret Service man to wheel him slowly through all the wards that were occupied by veterans who had lost one or more arms or legs. He insisted on going past each individual bed. He had known for twenty-three years what it was to be deprived of the use of both legs. He wanted to display himself and his useless legs to those boys who would have to face the same bitterness. This crippled man on the little wheel chair wanted to show them that it was possible to rise above such physical handicaps. With a cheery smile to each of them, and a pleasant word at the bedside of a score or more, this man who had risen from a bed of helplessness ultimately to become President of the United States and leader of the free world was living proof of what the human spirit could do to conquer the incapacities of the human body. I had seen him try to give the same sort of encouragement and example by cheerful conversation with young folks in Warm Springs and elsewhere who had been stricken by polio. Here, in the presence of great tragedy, he was doing it on a grand, heroic scale. The expressions on the faces on the pillows, as he slowly passed by and smiled, showed how effective was this self-display of crippled helplessness.

I never saw Roosevelt with tears in his eyes; that day as he was wheeled out of the hospital he was close to them.

Later that day the President boarded the *Baltimore* and left for Alaska. I returned to Washington by airplane.

Two days later, on July 31, the sad news came of the death of Marguerite A. LeHand. She had been an invalid since her stroke in the summer of 1941, and during the last three years the President and all of us had felt the great loss of her services. She was one of the most important people of the Roosevelt era. She sought to remain out of the limelight—and succeeded. I doubt whether her real contribution to the work of the President and to her country will ever be adequately understood except by those who personally knew her and watched her in the White House. She had worked with Roosevelt since 1920, and had become one of his most trusted and efficient associates, living with the Roosevelt family both in Albany and in the White House. To the Roosevelt family, to her friends, and to all official Washington which had business with the White House, she was affectionately known as "Missy."

In hundreds of ways, as the personal secretary to the President, she was able to lighten the burdens of his office, and to steer details away from his desk. She had unbounded charm and an appealing personal vivacity. Her loyalty toward Roosevelt was unshakable, her devotion to his interests unfailing. Her feminine instinct, with few exceptions, was quick to distinguish between those who were seeking out the President for selfish reasons and those who wanted to be of service to him and to the nation. She was the frankest of the President's associates, never hesitating to tell him unpleasant truths or to express an unfavorable opinion about his work or about any proposed action or policy. For that reason and because of her sound common sense and good judgment, he had a deep respect for her opinion about persons and events.

While the President was around, she was always within call, seldom taking any time off for herself unless he was away on a trip. She could with equal facility be the efficient secretary, the helpful and lively participant in a policy conference, or the gracious hostess at the Roosevelt table. She could read the President's mind correctly and anticipate his wishes. She never broke a confidence, and could relay messages for the President, pleasant and unpleasant, with just the right amount of tact, firmness, and courtesy.

She understood his political and social objectives, and knew all about his methods of work. She would suggest that certain people be invited to tea or dinner who she thought would have helpful ideas about problems he had on his mind. When the strain of the daily work and grinding routine became too tough, she would get his permission to ask some of his friends to come in for cocktail pleasantries or a game of poker in the evening. And when sometimes he would seek to put off some decision or some action, she would stand there firmly but pleasantly and keep reminding him to do it.

She frequently would hold up a letter the President had written in anger, and beg him the next day not to send it. In most cases the President's anger had subsided overnight and the letter would be torn up. If he persisted, I have known her to put the letter away in her desk again and try once more in a day or two to persuade him not to send it.

She was struck down just when she could have been of greatest service, six months before Pearl Harbor. Those who knew of her great work realized what a loss her country had sustained. After so many years of responsibility and association she was able to assume, and Roosevelt was willing to delegate to her, an infinite variety of details. She took care of them with such lightness that he never fully realized himself how much work she saved him. I feel that had she lived she could have so lightened his wartime burden that his own life would have been prolonged.

Grace Tully, who had been Missy's assistant and constant friend and companion since 1928, was asked to take over her desk as soon as Missy became incapacitated. Grace had served the President and had worked with Missy so long that she knew exactly how the President thought, worked, and lived. For years she had taken the President's dictation for correspondence and for speeches, relieved only occasionally by Dorothy Brady, her assistant. Missy used to dictate letters for the President's signature and for her own signature as personal secretary; but seldom did any typing herself. As a result Grace had been thoroughly trained, and it was fortunate for the President and for the country that she was there, ready to step in. She remained with the President to the end, and was at Warm Springs with him when he died. She, too, was a great master of detail and had a machinelike efficiency which was amazing. At the same time, she had a friendly charm and warmth, and a never-failing sense of humor and gaiety of laughter; the President loved to have her around. No one else could have filled as much of the void left by Missy's passing as she did.

Grace had come with us on this trip across the country and had typed the acceptance speech delivered at San Diego, as she typed nearly every speech the President made. She did not go to Hawaii; she waited on the West Coast until the President came back from Alaska, and met him for the return train trip from Bremerton, Washington, to the Capital.

The President had transferred in Alaska from the cruiser to a destroyer and had traveled down to Bremerton on the destroyer.

On his arrival at Bremerton, Roosevelt delivered a speech at the Puget Sound Navy Yard. I am informed by Commander (then Lieutenant) William Rigdon, who generally acted as secretary when the President was aboard American combat ships, that the President dictated this speech to him when the destroyer was two or three days out of Bremerton. None of those who usually worked on speeches was aboard, and the President apparently asked no one for suggestions or help. The speech was intended to be a report on his trip. After the first draft, he neglected the speech entirely until Rigdon asked him what he wanted done about mimeographing and releasing it. Then, on the night before the day set for the speech, he made the first and only revision of the draft himself, and sent it to the mimeograph room.

While this was not an important speech, it was a major one; and deserved much more attention than that. The people had not heard the President since the acceptance speech of July 20; he had in the meantime journeyed out to Hawaii and Alaska; Dewey had been out strenuously campaigning. The American people expected that the President had something to say and would say it. But the speech had nothing to say, and said it poorly.

He delivered it standing on a deck of the destroyer before a large crowd of navy-yard workers gathered on shore. It was the first time that he had used his braces in many months. Although he had made many speeches during that time, he had delivered them sitting down. In the days before the war, he had insisted on wearing his braces whenever he was to appear before any large group. As the stress of events increased, he would not take the time or trouble to put them on. He made no effort, as formerly, to appear to be less handicapped than he was. During the year since he last stood on his braces, he had lost considerable weight; as a result the braces no longer fitted him. Even when they had, his position as he rested on them had not been secure. And, on this occasion, there was a marked curve on the first super-structure of the destroyer where he stood. A fresh wind was blowing. The curve and the wind increased the insecurity of the braces. His audience was too far away from him to permit the feeling of contact which is so helpful to effective delivery. All this affected the President's manner of speaking—making it hesitant, halting and indecisive. He told me about these things later in Washington, as he did others, to explain what he knew was a very bad performance. The reaction of the audi-ence—which the President was always quick to sense—was so unfavor-able that it made his delivery even worse. The speech at best was a rambling account of his journeys and experiences during the past month, and he ad-libbed a great deal in a very ineffective manner. It was a dismal failure.

That speech, together with the unfortunate photograph of the President in San Diego a few weeks earlier, started tongues wagging—friendly and unfriendly tongues—all through the United States. His enemies concluded that "the old man is through, finished." His friends and supporters of many years shook their heads sorrowfully and said, "It looks like the old master has lost his touch. His campaigning days must be over. It's going to look mighty sad when he begins to trade punches with young Dewey."

I must admit that as I sat at my radio and heard that speech delivered, I too had a sinking sensation of concern that something must have happened to the President since I had left him in Hawaii. His voice and delivery seemed so different. Many were the comments about it in Washington, New York, and all over—at dinners, at cocktail parties, and official conferences.

I was mistaken—just as all his other friends were—just as his enemies were. Six weeks later, he was to deliver the greatest political speech of his career—in his most vigorous and effective form.

Chapter XXIV

A New Alignment of Parties for the Future: Roosevelt and Willkie, 1944

Before leaving on the trip to Hawaii, I took part at the President's direction in a discussion that, but for the death of the two leading political figures of America within six months of each other, might have led to a fundamental change in the political history of the United States.

One day during the last week in June, 1944, the President called me into his office, and said:

"Governor Pinchot has just been in to see me. He has had a meeting recently with Willkie. They talked about the possibility of a new setup in American politics. It was Willkie's idea. Willkie has just been beaten by the conservatives in his own party who lined up in back of Dewey. Now there is no doubt that the reactionaries in our own party are out for my scalp, too—as you can see by what's going on in the South."

He was referring to the bitter revolt then flaring up in Texas and in a few other Southern states against Roosevelt and the principles of the New Deal. The revolt was finally carried right into the Democratic Convention of 1944. It continues to this day.

"Well," he continued, "I think the time has come for the Democratic party to get rid of its reactionary elements in the South, and to attract to it the liberals in the Republican party. Willkie is the leader of those liberals. He talked to Pinchot about a coalition of the liberals in both parties, leaving the conservatives in each party to join together as they see fit. I agree with him one hundred per cent and the time is now—right after election. We ought to have two real parties—one liberal and the other conservative. As it is now, each party is split by dissenters.

"Of course, I'm talking about long-range politics—something that we can't accomplish this year. But we can do it in 1948, and we can start building it up right after the election this fall. From the liberals of both parties Willkie and I together can form a new, really liberal party in America."

Since the "purge" of 1938, he had frequently talked about a new alignment of political parties in the United States; this was the first time he had actually got down to naming a Republican leader that he thought was qualified to join him in the project. And Willkie's talk with Pinchot was the catalytic agent which produced this call for action now.

"What I want you to do is to go up to New York to see Willkie and tell him how I feel about this whole idea and get his reaction."

"Do you suppose he'd be willing to talk to me just now?" I asked.

Ever since Willkie had been defeated by Dewey for the Republican nomination, the Dewey forces had been trying to get him to join them in the campaign against Roosevelt. On the other hand, many Roosevelt followers—and many Republican liberals who were strenuously opposed to Dewey—had been urging Willkie, privately and publicly, to come out for Roosevelt. In this tug of war to get his support, Willkie had remained silent and had given no hint of what he proposed to do in the campaign, if anything.

"He might think," I continued, "that this is another effort or subterfuge to get him to come out for you—and apparently he is not yet ready to come out for anyone. At any rate, I can phone him and see whether he'll meet me."

"Better explain to him in advance that what you want to see him about has nothing to do with the coming election," he warned as I left the office.

I reached Willkie on the telephone. I explained to him that the President had asked me to go to New York to see him about something in which I was sure he would be interested. I hastened to add that it had nothing to do with the coming election and that I did not intend to talk to him at all about the election. With this assurance, he expressed a willingness to see me; and I arranged to meet him for lunch at the St. Regis Hotel in New York City on July 5.

The meeting obviously had to be a complete secret; so I had lunch served in a private suite in the hotel. So far as I know, on our side only the President knew about this meeting. Several years later, when I first began to gather together my notes for this book, I learned that Willkie had told two or three of his close associates about it. I have checked their recollection with mine, as well as with some notes which I dictated on my return to the White House.

At the appointed hour Willkie arrived. So anxious were we for no leak to occur about this meeting that when luncheon was served, Willkie stepped into the bedroom of the suite so that the waiter would not recognize him.

He told me that over the week end he had been subjected to terrific pressure to come out for Dewey—pressure from Dewey himself, and from others who were house guests with him over the holiday; that the pressure on him from our side was also substantial and was growing. He frankly said he was not ready to announce any stand on 1944, and gave me the impression, without so saying, that he had not yet made up his mind what to do. He repeated his wish not to discuss it with me, and I repeated the President's insistence that that was to be left out of the conversation entirely.

I told him that Roosevelt was delighted to learn from Pinchot the way Willkie's mind was working, because it agreed so thoroughly with what was in Roosevelt's mind.

"Ever since the unsuccessful 'purge' of 1938," I said, "the idea has been growing in the President's mind that the real future of progressivism in American politics lies in a realignment of the parties rather than in intraparty conflict. The trouble is that all Democrats get together in a convention hall and the majority adopts a good liberal platform; then, after election, the Southern conservatives, who do not depend for election on anyone outside their own conservative districts, just run out on the platform. The President learned in 1938, the hard way, that he cannot beat them in their own districts. He is now ready to form a new grouping, leaving them out of the new liberal party. You see, you both are thinking along the same lines. He wants to team up with you, for he is sure that the two of you can do it together; and he thinks the right time to start is immediately after this election. If it is impossible for you to start talking with him about it before election, then you can wait until later; but he wants to do it—whether he wins or loses in November."

This meshed exactly with his own thinking. He said that it was obvious from the recent preconvention fight in his own party and from the proceedings at the 1944 Republican National Convention that his party was completely in the control of the reactionary leaders. It was also clear to him that the reactionary elements of the Democratic party —especially in the South—had nothing in common with the liberalism of the Administration.

"Both parties are hybrids," he said.

He felt that after the war the political conflict in the United States with respect to both national and international affairs would be clear-cut: it would be between all the liberal forces on one side and all the conservative forces on the other, rather than between Democrats and Republicans.

He expressed great satisfaction at the prospect, for he loved a good fight almost as much as Roosevelt did—and I think he rather liked the idea of fighting for the first time with, rather than against, Roosevelt. He was particularly concerned about foreign affairs and the kind of internationalism that could be brought about by the new political group. He talked about this at great length.

"You tell the President that I'm ready to devote almost full time to this," he said. "A sound, liberal government in the United States is absolutely essential to continued co-operation with the other nations of the world. I know some of these reactionaries—especially those in my own party. They'll run out on the other nations when the going gets tough—just as soon as they can."

We went over the groups of people who would fall naturally into a cohesive liberal party: labor, racial and religious minorities, small farmers, students, small shopkeepers and businessmen, progressive intellectuals. We mentioned some of the more outspoken Republican liberals, who naturally felt out of place in the old party, and who would probably be willing to join in a new division of political forces. We went over the names of the leaders in the Democratic party who were completely out of sympathy with the Democratic platform and with the policies of the Administration, and who would feel more at home in a conservative party.

Willkie said he was deeply interested in meeting the President personally and discussing the plan more fully. But he was convinced that the meeting should not take place until after election day. He did not want to have it appear that he was trading or being traded with; and a meeting between the two before election—which could not possibly be kept secret—would give rise to many conjectures.

Here were the two men in all the United States who had the leadership and prestige to do this job. The facts of political history in 1944 made them naturals for it. One was the undisputed leader of liberal democracy in the United States; he had seen the Democratic platform sabotaged time and again by conservative Democrats lining up with his Republican opponents; in 1938 he had tried unsuccessfully to clear the Democratic party of those conservatives. The other man was the great liberal leader in the Republican party; he had always been regarded with suspicion by the old-guard reactionary Republicans; he had unsuccessfully tried to lead his party up the progressive path.

As Willkie left after about a two-hour conference I felt sure that he was as enthusiastic as Roosevelt in wanting to get the movement started right after the election. I told him that the President would communicate with him in due course, now that it was clear that Willkie would be willing to discuss it more fully.

I returned to Washington immediately and reported to the President in detail. He was pleased and excited at the prospect of this fundamental political fight of nationwide proportions.

"Fine, fine," he said. "I'll arrange to get together with him at the proper time."

I assumed that the "proper time" would be right after the election. But apparently the President could not wait. Maybe the prospect was too thrilling; maybe he thought that the discussions should be started right away; maybe his motive was—as his hostile critics urged at the time—to give the impression that Willkie was going to support him in the coming 1944 election. Whatever the reason, the fact is that on July 13, just as his train was to pull out of Washington en route to San Diego, he dictated and mailed with great secrecy the following letter:

July 13, 1944

Personal
DEAR WENDELL:

I will not be able to sign this because I am dictating it just as I leave on a trip to the westward.

What I want to tell you is that I want to see you when I come back, but not on anything in relationship to the present campaign. I want to talk with you about the future, even the somewhat distant future, and in regard to the foreign relations problems of the immediate future.

When you see in the papers that I am back, will you get in touch with

General Watson? We can arrange a meeting either here in Washington or, if you prefer, at Hyde Park—wholly off the record or otherwise, just as you think best.

Always sincerely yours,
FRANKLIN D. ROOSEVELT

Although I was on that trip with the President across the continent and on to Hawaii, I did not know until more than a month later that he had written such a letter. I doubt whether anyone knew about it at the time it was sent except Grace, who typed it. Why he kept it a secret from me—who was, I think, the only person in the White House besides himself who knew about the St. Regis meeting—I shall never know. As I have said, he loved mystery and secrecy; he was fond of the dramatic and climactic; and having learned that Willkie was receptive to his plans, he apparently decided to play it from then on all alone.

This kind of thing had happened before. About some matters, for some reason that none of us understood and that I am sure the President could not himself have put into words, he seemed not to want any one person to know the whole story. At times he seemed to delight in having two or more people do different but related parts of a single job which could better have been done by one person. Sometimes I thought it was because it gave him a sense of power—which he loved— to be the only person who knew everything about a project. After a while you accepted this failing of his even though it was an inefficient way of doing things and frequently led to duplication of effort, and sometimes to argument and conflict. It perhaps explains why several of the recent writers of memoirs about Roosevelt differ so thoroughly on what Roosevelt had in mind when he did certain things. Each one is giving his own conclusions as he gleaned them from the particular role he played or from the part of the story the President told him. Not that Roosevelt sought to deceive; he just did not let them in on the whole tale.

On this occasion, however, he could not keep the secret himself. He must have talked to someone about the letter, for the fact that it had been sent began to "leak." The Willkie adherents charged that the President had deliberately let it leak; the President's supporters insinuated that Willkie had let it leak.

Although Roosevelt loved secrecy, he was often the one guilty of letting facts get out about which he had sworn others to silence. While this never happened in military matters, we could often trace a news leak to some casual remark that the President had made to a visitor or dinner guest. My own guess is that that is how word of the letter to Willkie got out.

The President tried to explain the leak in a second letter to Willkie, after a very embarrassing press conference on his return from Alaska. A newspaperman asked him flatly whether he had written to Willkie, and he answered that he had not. By this time, however, a great many people had heard of the letter, and Willkie's friends were threatening to publish it.

So the President wrote Willkie again:

August 21, 1944

Personal
DEAR WENDELL:—

A most unfortunate thing happened at my Press Conference on Friday. I had written you on July thirteenth, just as I was leaving for my trip to Hawaii and Alaska—a purely personal note telling you I hoped much to see you on a non-campaign subject sometime after I got back. Quite frankly when I was asked—in a series of questions about foreign affairs—whether I had written you to invite you to Washington, I said "No." That afternoon Steve Early said to me "Are you sure you did not write to Wendell Willkie?" And it flashed into my mind then that I had written you before I left.

The interesting thing is how word of my note to you got out to the Press. I have been trying to find out where the leak was down here, as I regarded it as a purely personal note between you and me. As far as I can remember I said nothing about it to anybody, though it is possible that I told Leo Crowley that I was going to ask you if we could talk the subject over. I am awfully sorry that there was any leak on a silly thing like this—but I still hope that at your convenience—there is no immediate hurry—you will stop in and see me if you are in Washington or run up to Hyde Park if you prefer.

I hope you have had a good Summer. My trip in the Pacific was extraordinarily interesting. I hope to be able to tell you about it and about how I am trying to keep China going. Our friend, Madame Chiang, is in Brazil with her sister, Madame Kung, and I hope they will both come here before they return home.

Always sincerely,
FRANKLIN D. ROOSEVELT

Willkie, however, had made up his mind that the meeting between them should not take place until after election. In fact, it appears that on receipt of the first letter from Roosevelt, he drafted, but did not mail, a reply which showed his interest in the subject matter of the proposed meeting but indicated his disagreement with the proposed timing of it. The unsigned, unmailed reply read as follows:[1]

MY DEAR MR. PRESIDENT:

I have your gracious note of the thirteenth. The subjects concerning which you suggest we have a talk on your return from the West are, as you know, subjects in which I am intensely interested. I am fearful, however, that any talk between us before the campaign is over might well be the subject of misinterpretation and misunderstanding. And I do not believe, however much you and I might wish or plan otherwise, that we could possibly have such a talk without the fact becoming known.

Therefore, if it is agreeable with you, I would prefer postponement of any such talk until after the November election.

I hope you will understand that I make this suggestion solely because you in a great way, and I in a small one, have the trust and confidence of people who might see in the most innocent meeting between us at this time some betrayal of the principles which each of us respectively holds so deeply.

Believe me, with great respect,

Sincerely yours,

By Election Day, Willkie was dead. Five months after Election Day, Roosevelt was dead.

The project was never even discussed between them directly. It was a herculean task that these two political leaders had thought of undertaking. No combination other than Roosevelt and Willkie could have done it. And 1948 would have been the most opportune time to do it. Nineteen hundred and forty-eight was the year of the Dixiecrats, the year that the most reactionary of the Democratic leaders seceded from the party on the ground that it had become too liberal and progressive. President Truman, then the leader of the party, refused to compromise with them. He won without them! But in 1948 there was no Willkie, and no one to take his place. There was no Republican leader ready or able to lead the liberal Republicans of the nation. Had Roosevelt and Willkie lived, their political alliance might have been so firmly cemented by 1948 that the great schism and realignment might have taken place that year.

As this is being written it is becoming more and more obvious that the Dixiecrats intend to carry on their fight against the New Deal. The need for a realignment of political forces continues—and, as the record of the last five years shows, becomes more acute. Even if Truman were willing, where is there another Willkie?

[1] Roscoe Drummond, "Wendell Willkie: A Study in Courage," in *The Aspirin Age 1919-1941* (New York: Simon & Schuster, 1949), p. 473.

Chapter XXV

The Last Political Campaign, 1944

By the time Roosevelt made his Bremerton speech, the armed forces of the United Nations were beginning to sweep through Europe. Paris was liberated on August 24, 1944. Luxembourg and Belgium were liberated in September. Allied troops entered Holland on September 18.

In August the President announced that on September 23 he was going to make a speech which he frankly labeled as political, though "not very political." The occasion was a dinner of the International Brotherhood of Teamsters at the Statler Hotel in Washington. It was unusual for the President to announce a speech this far in advance. The circumstances, however, made an early announcement appropriate.

The President, as he had promised in his acceptance speech, had remained quite aloof from the campaign. But Dewey, an active, spirited and able campaigner, had begun quite early to make campaign trips around the country. At the start, the wise political prophets gave him a slim chance of winning. However, as the summer wore on, and as the stories continued to spread about the President's bad health, his weariness of mind and body, and his general disinterest in the political campaign, Dewey's chances brightened. From the very beginning, Dewey leveled his attack on the "tired old men" who were running the government, and on the frequent bickering among members of the Administration. He argued that the "time for a change" had come, and that the affairs of government should be turned over to fresh, younger and more enthusiastic hands.

In one of his first major campaign addresses, Dewey seized upon a chance remark of General Hershey, the director of the Selective Service System, that in order to prevent unemployment after the war the United States would have to keep its men in the armed forces even after the military need for them had passed. Hershey had no authority to make such a statement. It involved matters with which he had no official concern and over which he had no control. It did not represent Administration policy. The Administration policy was exactly opposite; it called for preparing a sound postwar economy with full employment to which veterans could be returned immediately after the need for them had passed. The Army had officially stated that its policy was to discharge men as soon as they were not needed for military reasons. However, there was the statement by Hershey, the director of the Selective Service System. Nobody paid much attention to it when it was made, but it now became the principal issue of the opening days of the campaign. Dewey kept repeating it and repeating it, calling it high Administration policy, until the charge began to take hold—especially among many American fathers and mothers who were anxious to get their boys home as soon as possible.

In addition to this kind of misrepresentation, Dewey made several misstatements of fact in the early days of the campaign. He also made statements that were not direct falsifications, but rather distortions of the truth, in that phrases and sentences in speeches and statements made by the President and his supporters were pulled out of context in a way that twisted their meaning. As statement after statement of this kind appeared in Dewey's speeches, I prepared a memorandum pointing out in what respect they were false and where the proof of their falsity could be found. The President did not want the White House to become engaged in a direct controversy with Dewey over the veracity of his statements. Accordingly, my list, consisting of several typewritten pages, was given to the reporters by Steve Early, not as a White House statement or release but as a memorandum for their guidance to help them in writing their stories. Many of them used it; and later, in his own speeches, the President with effective sarcasm made veiled but telling references to this practice of Dewey's.

As Dewey continued vigorously to campaign and as the President continued to remain silent, the same thing began to happen among the voters that had happened in 1940. Sentiment began to rise for Dewey and to fall for the President. Again, Democratic political leaders, friends, and visitors at the White House urged the President to start campaigning. Many of them, even as they urged him, felt great doubt whether he was physically up to campaigning in his old style.

The President soon began to realize that it was necessary for him to get out again and fight hard. He also realized that it was up to him to prove that he could stand the physical and mental rigors of a political campaign. Accordingly, in August, he announced that he was going to open his campaign on September 23; and, before he went to Canada for the second Quebec Conference, he asked me to prepare a draft of the speech. I had to start on this speech unassisted, because Sherwood was still in England, and Harry was still sick. Bob did get back a few days before the speech was delivered and was able to work on the later drafts with us. While the President was at Quebec, I worked on the early drafts down in Maine, where my family and I were spending a week. Busy as he was in Quebec, however, the President found time to turn out a few paragraphs. What he told me on the phone was that Grace was sending down some pages he had dictated "just as a happy thought"; that he did not think too much of them but I should see whether they could be used some place or other. In those pages, however, there was included the part of the speech that everyone long remembered and many people still remember—the paragraph about Fala, the President's dog.

Some Republican Congressmen had started to circulate the ridiculous story that on the President's trip home from Alaska it was discovered after the ships were a couple of days out that by inadvertence Fala had been left behind. Whereupon, so the tale went, one of the destroyers was sent back to Alaska to pick the dog up, at a cost to the taxpayers of some absurdly large sum of money. There was, of course, not a single bit of truth to any part of the story, but some of the anti-Roosevelt papers played it up as though it were gospel.

When the President returned from the conference I showed him a revised draft of the speech, including his immortal paragraph about Fala. He spent many days working over the subsequent drafts, for he realized how important this speech was going to be politically. He wanted to prove—and had to—that he was still the old master at campaigning. He also wanted to inject more excitement into the campaign, for he knew that the larger the number of voters, the greater were the Democratic chances. The Teamsters' Union speech was written primarily to stir up some interest. It succeeded.

I never saw President Roosevelt in better form than he was that evening. The scene was a crowded banquet hall in the Statler Hotel in Washington. The audience was composed largely of members of the Teamsters' Union and other supporters of the President. It was an enthusiastic, friendly audience—the kind most conducive to effective delivery—an audience that was rooting for him and hoping that he would make a telling speech.

After his unfortunate experience with his braces at Bremerton, the President decided that he would make his major political campaign speeches sitting down. His braces had become painful and, apparently, they could not be readily adjusted. The physical exertion and mental strain of standing with his torso resting on a circle of padded steel were so great that he decided not to undergo them further. His speeches during this campaign, therefore, were scheduled either at dinners such as this one, where he could speak naturally from his seat on the dais, or in a large field, like a baseball park, where he could speak from the rear seat of an open automobile—the technique used in Chicago, Boston and Philadelphia.

We were apprehensive that there might be an adverse reaction to the fact that the President remained seated during his speech. To our relief, there was not much comment. The people had come to take his disability for granted and seemed to understand the difficulty he had in drawing himself to his feet and remaining there for a half hour or more.

The only time during his campaign that he had to stand to speak was on the rear platform of the train when he addressed crowds at railroad stations. This was an ordeal that would have made any ordinary man hesitate. I was struck by the patient determination with which the President went through it. At no time during my long association with him did I feel more admiration for his fortitude and perseverance, or more deeply grieved by the sight of his severe physical handicap, than during this campaign. One day in September, before he gave up the idea of standing during his speeches, I went into his bedroom and found him with his braces on walking up and down, leaning on the arm of Dr. McIntire. He was literally trying to learn to walk again! During the last three years he had found little or no time to exercise those leg muscles which still functioned, and they had become weakened from disuse. In spite of the almost overwhelming amount of work that faced him daily in late 1944, he had made up his mind that he was going to learn to walk again—and he did. I never saw such a display of guts.

At the Teamsters' Union dinner, his sitting position certainly did not deprive him of any of his usual force and incisiveness. The speech was spiced with biting sarcasm, pleasant ridicule, bitter denunciation; but it expressed his deep conviction of the soundness of American democracy, and a fixed determination to keep peace in the world. In all these moods the President that night was the perfect campaigner.

The most dangerous and effective weapon in a political campaign is ridicule. Nothing is so successful in a political fight as to get the voters laughing at your opponent. "Martin, Barton and Fish" was the outstanding phrase of ridicule used in the 1940 campaign. The "Fala" speech was the outstanding example in 1944.

I doubt whether the President himself foresaw the effect the speech would have.

He started by ridiculing Dewey's charges that he was "a tired old man":

Well, here we are together again—after four years—and what years they have been! You know, I am actually four years older—which is a fact that seems to annoy some people. In fact, there are millions of Americans who are more than eleven years older than when we started in to clear up the mess that was dumped in our laps in 1933.

The misrepresentations of Republican campaign orators he took up one by one. Some of the more fantastic he met by sheer ridicule, which is all that they deserved. Others he met directly by citing chapter and verse of the truth.

It was a labor union dinner; so he dealt first with the Republican claims that the real friend of labor was the Republican and not the Democratic party.

We all know certain people who make it a practice to depreciate the accomplishments of labor—who even attack labor as unpatriotic—they keep this up usually for three years and six months in a row. But then, for some strange reason they change their tune—every four years—just before election day. When votes are at stake, they suddenly discover that they really love labor and that they are anxious to protect labor from its old friends.

I got quite a laugh, for example—and I am sure that you did—when I read this plank in the Republican platform adopted at their National Convention in Chicago last July:

"The Republican Party accepts the purposes of the National Labor Relations Act, the Wage and Hour Act, the Social Security Act and all other Federal statutes designed to promote and protect the welfare of American working men and women, and we promise a fair and just administration of these laws."

He read that paragraph with such exaggerated solemnity that it sounded even more ridiculous than it was.

You know, many of the Republican leaders and Congressmen and candidates, who shouted enthusiastic approval of that plank in that Convention Hall, would not even recognize these progressive laws if they met them in broad daylight. Indeed, they have personally spent years of effort and energy—and much money—in fighting every one of those laws. . . .

The whole purpose of Republican oratory these days seems to be to switch labels. . . .

Can the Old Guard pass itself off as the New Deal?

I think not.

We have all seen many marvelous stunts in the circus but no performing elephant could turn a hand-spring without falling flat on his back.

There were jibes at the charge being made that the President had not tried to prepare the United States for war and that he was not competent to carry on a sound foreign policy:

There were some—in the Congress and out—who raised their voices against our preparations for defense—before and after 1939. . . . We remember the voices. They would like to have us forget them now. But in 1940 and 1941—my, it seems a long time ago—they were loud voices. . . .

What the Republican leaders are now saying in effect is this: "Oh, just forget what we used to say, we have changed our minds now—we have been reading the public opinion polls about these things and now we know what the American people want." And they say: "Don't leave the task of making the peace to those old men who first urged it and who have already laid the foundations for it, and who have had to fight all of us inch by inch during the last five years to do it. Why, just turn it all over to us. We'll do it so skillfully—that we won't lose a single isolationist vote or a single isolationist campaign contribution."

Becoming serious, he praised the workers of America for their war production and defended them against the charge that there were too many strikes in wartime.

But a strike is news, and generally appears in shrieking headlines—and, of course, they say labor is always to blame. The fact is that since Pearl Harbor only one-tenth of one per cent of man-hours have been lost by strikes. Can you beat that?

Dealing with the fantastic charge that the depression of 1933 belonged properly on the doorstep of the Democrats, he said:

. . . although I rubbed my eyes when I read it, we have been told that it was not a Republican depression but a Democratic depression from which this nation was saved in 1933–that this Administration . . . is responsible for all the suffering and misery that the history books and the American people have always thought had been brought about during the twelve ill-fated years when the Republican party was in power.

Now, there is an old and somewhat lugubrious adage that says: "Never speak of rope in the house of a man who has been hanged." In the same way, if I were a Republican leader speaking to a mixed audience, the last word in the whole dictionary that I think I would use is that word "depression."

The audience howled at that one.

For several weeks Roosevelt had ignored Dewey's use of the Hershey statement. This was, as I have pointed out before, Roosevelt's usual tactic in the face of campaign charges. But in this case Dewey's vigorous repetition and the fact that the charge was seemingly based on the assertion of a high government official were having a steadily increasing effect. So now he made an exception—and answered it directly and flatly. He said that on the very day this fantastic charge was first made, the War Department had publicly announced an entirely different plan for demobilization—"a plan based on the wishes of the soldiers themselves"—and that the charge was a "callous and brazen falsehood . . . to stimulate fear among American mothers, wives and sweethearts."

Then as a climax of ridicule came the defense of Fala which he had written during the Quebec Conference. No one could have delivered this short passage more effectively. His mock-serious face and his sad tone of voice set the audience shouting with glee, but he continued through the statement with the same serious note of righteous indignation, never cracking a smile until the end.

These Republican leaders have not been content with attacks on me, or my wife, or on my sons. No, not content with that, they now include my little dog, Fala. Well, of course, I don't resent attacks, and my family doesn't resent attacks, but Fala *does* resent them. You know, Fala is Scotch, and being a Scottie, as soon as he learned that the Republican fiction writers in Congress and out had concocted a story that I had left him behind on the Aleutian Islands and had sent a destroyer back to find him—at a cost to the taxpayers of two or three, or eight or twenty million dollars—his Scotch soul was furious. He has not been the same dog since. I am accustomed to hearing malicious falsehoods about myself—such as that old, worm-eaten chestnut that I have represented myself as indispensable. But I think I have a right to resent, to object to libelous statements about my dog.

The rest of the speech was a serious enumeration of the tasks ahead—winning the war, setting up a durable peace, demobilization into a sound postwar economy of full employment.

"The fruits of victory this time," he said, "will not be apples sold on street corners."

The applause and cheers when he finished were startling even to those of us who had seen him out campaigning in 1932, 1936 and 1940. Never had there been a demonstration equal to this in sincerity, admiration and affection. In the mind of every friend and supporter who stood and cheered and applauded in that large dining hall was the same thought: "The old maestro is back again—the champ is now out on the road. The old boy has the same old fighting stuff and he just can't be licked." Many expressed that thought as they clapped one another on the shoulder.

Roosevelt was at his vigorous best—taunting his opponents, ridiculing their misstatements and exaggerated charges, and inspiring his listeners throughout the nation by his eloquent delineation of his aims for the future of the world.

I was at a table with some of his family and closest friends. As the audience all rose to applaud at the end of the speech, there were tears in the eyes of many, including his daughter Anna. After the Bremerton speech, she too had secretly expressed to me her apprehension about whether her father would still have enough of his old campaign fire to meet the young and forceful Dewey. She had watched the daily preparation of this speech, and had read and offered helpful suggestions for each of the drafts. She had seen how hard the President and I worked on it, and she knew how important a speech it was.

"Do you think that Pa will put it over?" she asked nervously during the dinner. "It's the kind of speech which depends almost entirely on delivery, no matter how good the writing—if the delivery isn't just right, it'll be an awful flop."

"No doubt in the world he'll get it over fine; don't you worry," I answered—doubting and worrying.

As the speech went on and the old champ delivered his telling blows, she smiled at my wife and me; and finally with great relief broke out in laughter.

The speech had just the effect we had hoped for. Bremerton was forgotten. The campaign was jolted out of its rut. The Democratic forces were electrified. Dewey was made fighting mad, and showed it in his next few speeches by swinging wildly in a way that damaged himself rather than the champ. Dewey was too smart a campaigner not to realize how much he had been hurt by the Fala speech. But it was the kind of political speech which was so hard to answer that he should simply have ignored it.

Shortly after the speech, I got a letter from Paul A. Porter, then director of publicity of the Democratic National Committee, giving me his ideas about several themes for future campaign speeches. The postscript to the letter reads as follows: "P.S. We have a new slogan in headquarters now—the race is between Roosevelt's dog and Dewey's goat."

The President followed up by a radio address from the White House on October 5. Again it was a frankly political speech, designed to get out as large a vote as possible and to answer at length some of Dewey's charges.

He made a strong plea for "every man and every woman in this nation—regardless of party—who have the right to register and to vote" to fulfill "the sacred obligation to register and to vote." He pointed out that the strength of American democracy depended upon the use of the ballot box, and said that he personally would be sorry to be elected President on a small turnout of voters. By the same token, he said that if he were to be defeated he would be much happier if he were defeated in a "large outpouring of voters." Striking at the poll tax, he said: "The right to vote must be open to our citizens irrespective of race, color, or creed—without tax or artificial restriction of any kind."

In this campaign, as in previous ones, the Republican leaders tried to fasten the label of communism on the New Deal. Roosevelt met the charge head on this year, as he had in the past:

. . . . Labor-baiters, bigots, and some politicians use the term "Communism" loosely, and apply it to every progressive social measure and to the virtues of every foreign-born citizen with whom they disagree.

This form of fear propaganda is not new among rabble rousers and fomenters of class hatred—who seek to destroy democracy itself. It was used by Mussolini's black shirts and by Hitler's brown shirts. It has been used before in this country by the silver shirts and others on the lunatic fringe. But the sound and democratic instincts of the American people rebel against its use, particularly by their own Congressmen—and at the taxpayers' expense [referring to franked propaganda].

I have never sought, and I do not welcome the support of any person or group committed to Communism, or Fascism, or any other foreign ideology which would undermine the American system of government, or the American system of free competitive enterprise and private property.

Roosevelt was beginning to get quite angry at the kind of campaign being waged against him; in fact the first and second draft of this speech contained a ringing denunciation of the Republican tactics. He finally decided to delete it, and it was never used in the speech; but I am printing it to show how he felt at the time:

> In accepting the nomination in this campaign I said: "I will not campaign, in the usual sense, for the office."
>
> Apparently the Republican campaign orators came to the conclusion that meant that they were free to say anything they wanted without contradiction; that they could make up any kind of misrepresentation without fear of having their falsehoods exposed.
>
> But in their habit of tearing sentences from their context, which they seem to do in their campaign speeches with great facility, they decided to overlook what I said in the same paragraph. It was this: "I shall, however, feel free to report to the people the facts about matters of concern to them and especially to correct any misrepresentations."
>
> So last week, I exposed their misrepresentations. And the people understood. And the campaign orators got very angry and complained that I had not let them get away with it. . . .

We were all glad he did not insist on using that kind of language in the speech.

On October 20, the President issued a statement hailing the landing of the American troops in the Philippines under General MacArthur. While the statement was nonpolitical, it had substantial political repercussions. Governor Dewey, just a short time before, had charged that insufficient supplies and equipment were being sent to General MacArthur. Right after this the General landed in the Philippines fully supplied and equipped for all military needs. It was clear that the Republican candidate did not know what he was talking about, and that in the heat of the campaign he would not hesitate to make charges he could not substantiate. To that extent this dramatic military event had great political significance in the campaign.

The President's next campaign speech was on foreign policy, and was delivered in New York City on October 21. He spent a great deal of time on it. Harry, Bob and I worked with him and were helped greatly by Ben Cohen and by "Chip" Bohlen of the State Department. Some valuable material and suggestions were submitted by MacLeish, Berle, Russell Davenport, another well-known Willkie follower, Dorothy Thompson and Raymond Swing.

There were four preliminary drafts drawn before the President could get down to work, and six drafts afterwards. At first it looked as though it were going to be difficult to write a political speech about foreign affairs. Since Governor Dewey, at least to all outward appearances, had dropped any semblance of isolationism, there seemed to be very little difference between the parties on foreign policy. Indeed, extensive campaign use had been made of the slogan that politics should stop at the "water's edge."

However, while the speech was being written, an issue did arise—an important issue. On it, the two parties fell into their natural grooves. It was raised first by the Republican Senator Joseph H. Ball. He had been actively associated politically with Willkie, who had died two weeks before, and he was generally regarded as the spokesman for those who had followed Willkie in 1940 and since. His support, therefore, was deemed very important, and both parties were trying hard to get it. Ball had publicly asked several pointed questions which sought to clarify important aspects of the foreign policy of each candidate, and had indicated that his own support would be determined by the candidates' answers. The most important question was whether or not the candidate was prepared to recommend that our representatives on the proposed Security Council of the United Nations should be authorized in advance by the Congress to vote to commit us to the use of force against an aggressor nation without having to wait for further Congressional action.

Before Ball propounded the questions publicly, he had talked with Ben Cohen in New York on the day of Willkie's funeral, and had told him what he intended to do. Ben said that he would take it up with the Administration immediately, reported the conversation to Harry Hopkins, who then also talked with Ball at length. Ben discussed the question with the State Department and brought it up with me during the preparation of the foreign policy speech. We then explored it fully with the President.

On several occasions since the Teheran Conference the President had publicly stated his belief that if force were necessary to maintain the peace of the world, then force—united force—should be used. He felt strongly that it would be useless for the nations to reach decisions and then rely upon everybody's good will to carry them out. He also felt that the Congress should commit the United States in advance to the use of such force so that it would not have to pass on the question again each time force had to be used. He told us to prepare an answer

to Ball for the speech, but he did not consider that he was saying anything new. Indeed the passage probably would not have provoked any
great comment had Governor Dewey been willing to announce the
same conclusion. However, in a major speech on October 18, hoping
to catch what remained of the isolationist vote in this country, Dewey
avoided the issue.

We considered this a lucky break, and decided to take full advantage of it in the foreign policy speech. After it was over, Ball announced
in Roosevelt's favor.

The President had one other lucky break on the speech—the weather.
It had become almost axiomatic that whenever the President made
public outdoor appearances the weather was fair. At times, on a rainy
day the skies almost miraculously cleared just before he appeared. This
had occurred so many times that we used to refer to fair weather as
"Roosevelt weather." The day of the Foreign Policy Association dinner
the President was scheduled to make a long trip all around the city of
New York, visiting and making short speeches in each of the boroughs.
His route through the city had been fully publicized, and it was
expected that millions of New Yorkers would be lining the streets to
get a glimpse of him. We all hoped that the weather would be fine.
Contrary to the usual Roosevelt luck—or so we thought—it turned out
to be a cold, rainy, bone-chilling day. Although we did not realize it
at the time, that kind of weather on that particular day was the best
thing that could have happened—politically. The members of the President's party, including his physician, urged him not to venture out, to
cancel all his outdoor appearances for the day, and to confine his
speechmaking to the one major speech scheduled for the evening at
the hotel.

The President would not hear of it. Rumors about his health and his
inability to withstand the strain of a campaign had been cropping up
again; there were whispers that bad health was the reason he had
stopped active campaigning since the night of the Teamsters' Union
speech. He decided to show everyone that the rumors were false. He
took his seat in the open car, and, with his navy cape wrapped around
him, traveled through the cold, driving rain, greeting in his usual
enthusiastic and friendly manner the millions of people waiting for a
glimpse of him. For fifty miles he drove all around the city in that open
car. Some of the newspapermen and others who rode behind him have
told me that only a momentous occasion like this could have made

them continue that drive for more than five minutes. They were amazed, as I am sure millions of others were, at the great stamina the President showed and the glowing exhilaration with which he went through the ordeal. He knew very well what was going through the minds of many of the people who waved to him in the rain. After this, the rumors about Roosevelt's bad health became less audible.

The President showed no ill effects from the drive; and after a hot bath and a few drinks, he was ready to proceed to the banquet room and his foreign policy speech.

The President delivered the speech that night from his seat on the dais. He opened it with the statement that World War II was providing a second opportunity to organize a peaceful world for future genera- tions, and he warned that the opportunity might not knock a third time.

Detailing some of the acts that the United States had taken in the interest of world peace, he spoke with pride of our conduct of Philip- pine affairs—an actual practice of the philosophy "that animated the Good Neighbor policy." To indicate the path he hoped the other great powers would follow—and which some of them have—he repeated what he had said two years earlier: "I like to think that the history of the Philippine Islands in the last forty-four years provides in a very real sense a pattern for the future of other small nations and peoples of the world. It is a pattern of what men of good will look forward to in the future."

He cited as another illustration of our good neighbor policy some- thing he was "proud of"—American recognition in 1933 of the Soviet Union. At this point he bluntly ad-libbed several paragraphs about Russia.

While working on the second draft, the President had dictated a story Mrs. Roosevelt had told him about a visit she had once made to a rural schoolhouse. In a history class for children about ten years old, there hung a map of the world. Where the Soviet Union should have been on the map there was only a big white space without any name or designation. The teacher explained the map to Mrs. Roosevelt by saying that the school board had decided that nothing about Russia should be taught to the children.

The first time the President dictated this material for the speech we tried to talk him out of using it on the ground that it was irrelevant and that it distracted attention from the main outlines of the speech. We were unable to persuade him. On reading the draft over, we decided to leave it out of the next one and to discuss it again with the President. We failed again; he asked that the material he had dictated be put back in the next draft. We all felt so strongly about this that we left it out a second and third time—each time, of course, calling the President's attention to the omission and raising the point again.

Since it was apparently making us all very unhappy, he finally grinned, and said: "All right, boys, leave it out of the speech if you want."

We all smiled contentedly.

Then he added: "I'll just ad-lib it."

We thought he was joking.

So I was genuinely surprised as I sat listening on the radio when I heard him use extemporaneously all that old material about the map with the white space on it. I think that in back of his head he had an idea—which he did not want to express too fully—that the long years of suspicion shown by many people toward the Soviet Union even after official recognition were going to have their effect on international relationships after the war, and that it was going to be difficult to convince the Russians now that we genuinely trusted them and sincerely desired full international co-operation.

The President's concern has been justified by later events. But what he feared has not been the whole trouble—or even half the trouble. The real trouble, of course, has been that Russia has refused to be convinced of our peaceful intentions, she has refused to keep an open mind on our sincerity, she has refused to meet us even part of the way, and—disregarding all our acts of good faith—she has proceeded on her own along the path of aggression and war.

With damning detail, Roosevelt traced the long history of isolationism among the Republican leaders, and contrasted it with the internationalist record of his own Administration. Nothing could have emphasized more dramatically the great danger of having such men as Joseph W. Martin, Hamilton Fish, Gerald P. Nye, and Hiram Johnson, by virtue of their seniority in length of service, become chairmen of the important Congressional committees that dealt with various aspects of foreign affairs—as they would if the Republicans won. Calling these men by name, he asked: "Can anyone really suppose that these isolationists have changed their minds about world affairs? . . . Politicians who embraced the policy of isolationism, and who never raised their voices against it in our days of peril—I don't think they are reliable custodians of the future of America."

Coming down to the present, he answered Senator Ball's question directly, thus making an issue between himself and Dewey even in the field of foreign affairs.

Peace, like war, can succeed only where there is a will to enforce it, and where there is available power to enforce it.

The Council of the United Nations must have the power to act quickly and decisively to keep the peace by force, if necessary. A policeman would not be a very effective policeman if, when he saw a felon break into a house, he had to go to the Town Hall and call a town meeting to issue a warrant before the felon could be arrested.

So to my simple mind it is clear that, if the world organization is to have any reality at all, our American representative must be endowed in advance by the people themselves, by constitutional means through their representatives in the Congress, with authority to act. . . .

His answer was hailed by all the sincere internationalists in the United States, just as it was condemned by those who delighted in paying only lip service to the cause of internationalism. How strong a structure of internationalist philosophy has been built in the United States on the foundations laid by Roosevelt in 1944 is shown by the almost unanimous popular approval of armed intervention by the United Nations in Korea.

Turning to the future, he uttered a note of caution which has been thoroughly justified by events since his death:

The kind of world order which we the peace-loving nations must achieve, must depend essentially on friendly human relations, on acquaintance, on tolerance, on unassailable sincerity and good will and good faith. . . .
If we fail to maintain that relationship in the peace—if we fail to expand it and strengthen it—then there will be no lasting peace.

The President was frank about the difficulties:

The task ahead of us will not be easy. Indeed it will be as difficult and complex as any task that has ever faced any American administration.
I will not say to you now, or ever, that we of the Democratic party know all the answers. I am certain, for myself, that *I* do not know how all the unforeseeable difficulties can be met. What I can say to you is this—that I have unlimited faith that the task can be done. . . .

The President, now thoroughly angry at Dewey's continued habit of quoting him out of context, referred to it in this speech:

"I am quoting history to you. I am going by the record. And I am giving you the whole story and not merely a phrase here and half a phrase there"—and he was about to continue to read the rest of the sentence: "picked out of context in such a way that they distort the facts." However, before he could finish, there were loud outbursts of laughter as the audience guessed what he had in mind. So he continued by saying: "In my reading copy there's another half sentence. You've got the point and I'm not going to use it."

Roosevelt's ad-libbing about Russia that evening did not add to the speech as some of his extemporaneous insertions in other speeches had. The business of ad-libbing had always been a source of amusement as well as concern among us. Harry, Bob and I had organized what we called the "Society for Prevention of Ad-Libbing." We always urged the President not to do it in any major speech. Every word he said had direct repercussions all through the United States and, particularly after 1939, throughout the whole world. We knew how easy it was for even the most accomplished orator to choose unfortunate words on the spur of the moment and thus give a wrong impression of what he meant.

The President understood and agreed with all this in theory; but he enjoyed ad-libbing—and he did a lot of it. After any speech in which he had done it extensively, we would report to him very solemnly the next morning that the "Society for Prevention of Ad-Libbing" had held a meeting immediately upon the conclusion of his speech and had decided to expel him from membership. He would then seek to gain readmission to the society by promising not to ad-lib again—but it was always a tossup in every speech whether he would violate the pledge or not. Jocosely one day he said that the one advantage he felt in going up to the Congress to deliver a message in person rather than sending it up by messenger was that it gave him an opportunity to ad-lib. One of us suggested that he might overcome this seeming difficulty by typing in red the parts of the message that he wanted ad-libbed, so that the clerk of the Senate or House could ad-lib them on the President's behalf. It was remarkable how little trouble he got into—considering how much ad-libbing he did.

The next speech was delivered in Shibe Park, a baseball park in Philadelphia, on October 27. It was the President's first experiment at making a major speech outdoors seated in an open automobile. There were many misgivings about the reaction of the audience. A large platform with a ramp leading up to it had been constructed in the middle of the field. The President's automobile was driven up on this. A battery of microphones was placed on a board across the car directly over the President's lap. He could thus sit in the back seat of the car with the microphones in front of him and his manuscript in a position to read.

Strangely enough, and to our great relief, the audience seemed to pay no attention to the fact that the President remained seated. The entrance into the park of the long cavalcade of cars led by the President's—the bright lights, the red torches, the loud band—all this was very dramatic. The audience seemed so thoroughly absorbed in the spectacle and so busy cheering and applauding that most of them probably never even thought of the fact that the President was not standing up for his speech.

The speech had been carefully worked out over many days. Roosevelt wanted to talk about the strenuous and exacting role that a President has to carry as Commander-in-Chief of the Army and Navy in the conduct of a war. The political point was obvious even though unspoken: that the man who since 1937 had been preparing the country physically and mentally for what was coming, who had been conducting a successful global war for almost four years, should be continued in office to finish the job; that it would be inadvisable to turn it over to inexperienced and untried hands.

He started off by recounting with pride—arousing at the same time the pride of his audience—the victories attained by the American forces on both sides of the world. In this way he was able to associate himself with those victories without actually saying so. He spoke of the fact that within the last year our armed forces had made twenty-seven different landings in force on enemy-held soil; that major offensive operations had been carried on in both Europe and the Philippines, 13,000 miles apart from each other.

"And," he added, "speaking of the glorious operations in the Philippines—I wonder whatever became of the suggestion made a few weeks ago, that I had failed for political reasons to send enough forces or supplies to General MacArthur?"

This, of course, was direct reference to the reckless charge made by Dewey a few weeks earlier to which I have already referred. At Roosevelt's sally, yells of "pour it on" came from the bleachers in the ball park.

He pointed out that under the Constitution it was the Commander-in-Chief who had to appoint the civilians and the military men who had immediate charge of production and fighting in the war. He could well boast of his appointments. His war experience as President was vastly different from that of Lincoln, who had to endure the heartbreaking failures of many generals before he picked the right one. From the very start, Roosevelt had reached down, and without regard to seniority picked the right military commanders. He made a point of this in his speech and he took advantage also of the great popularity of the men whom he had appointed. But like the good orator he was, he did it by understatement; he said: "I feel called upon to offer no apologies for my selection of Henry L. Stimson, the late Frank Knox, and Jim Forrestal, or of Admiral Leahy, General Marshall, Admiral King, and General Arnold."

On this occasion, as on many others, we were plagued by having to cut short the list of names we wanted to mention. The President could have gone on and named at least Eisenhower and MacArthur; but to do that would have meant that in fairness he should include many other American generals. We always considered carefully whether the President could justify including one name and omitting another. In the quotation above, for example, he mentioned only the Cabinet defense officers and the Chiefs of Staff—and he mentioned all the men in both categories. If he had gone down one more level he would have had to name all the men on that level, and the list would have been too long. He was meticulous in giving no possible ground for offense by unfair discrimination.

He continued with his list of the demanding tasks that fell to the Commander-in-Chief—for instance, the allotment of our resources among our land, sea, and air forces, and among the different theaters of operation, and the decision about what portion should be turned over to our Allies.

To emphasize the great difficulties of the job was the most emphatic way of driving his point home. Not only was it the most emphatic; it was the least embarrassing. It would have been vainglorious and boastful for Roosevelt to point out directly how much more qualified he was than Dewey. It might even have alienated many voters on the theory that the young man should be given a chance to show what he could do. But to enumerate the soul-searching responsibilities of the Presidency— the awful decisions on each of which so many hundreds of thousands of lives might depend, the quick judgments in the face of crisis which called for soundness, maturity, experience and long seasoning—was to emphasize the very qualities the voters would recognize in Roosevelt and would not see in the brash, untried, though forceful, Dewey. That, the President had concluded, was the way to put it over.

The Republican orators had charged that "there are not five civilians in the entire national government who have the confidence and respect of the American people," and that the present Administration was "the most spectacular collection of incompetent people who ever held public office."

Roosevelt now leaped happily to the counterattack:

"Well, you know, that is pretty serious, because the only conclusion to be drawn from that is that we are *losing* this war. If so, that will be news to most of us—and it will certainly be news to the Nazis and the Japs."

Again the audience shouted with laughter. Not satisfied with ridicule, Roosevelt turned seriously to the record, pointing out that almost from the first minute of the Administration in 1933 he had started to rebuild the Navy, which had been neglected during the previous Republican Administrations. And to bring it home—as Roosevelt always tried to do by specific reference—he added that of the ships in Admiral Halsey's powerful Third Fleet, which "just the other day" had "helped to give the Japanese Navy the worst licking in its history," every battleship had been authorized between 1933 and 1938, and that construction had begun on every one of them well over a year before Pearl Harbor; that all but two of the cruisers had been authorized between 1933 and 1940, and construction on all but one of them had begun before Pearl Harbor; that all of the aircraft carriers had been authorized before Pearl Harbor, and half of them were actually under construction before Pearl Harbor.

These statistics had been carefully worked up by us with the Navy; they made a telling story, after which the President could say: "There is the answer—just a little part of it—once and for all—to a Republican candidate [Dewey] who said that this Administration had made 'absolutely no military preparation for the events that it now claims it foresaw.' "

Then followed other statistics about the Army, Navy and Air Force which effectively refuted the charges of incompetence.

When we wanted to use statistics of war production we would prepare the paragraph with blank spaces for the actual figures, and send a carbon copy over to the War and Navy Departments to be filled in with the latest figures. However, the President used as few statistics as he could, and only when absolutely necessary, as here, to make his point. They made a speech dull; but sometimes there was no escape. Pa Watson used to open the door to the Cabinet room from time to time while a speech was in progress, stick his head in, and say with a laugh: "Now, Sam, go easy on those statistics." Then he'd wink and, before I could answer, close the door and disappear.

In the next part of his speech the President discussed the over-all strategy of the war. This always made a deep impression on his audience, though of course he never told anything secret. Nevertheless, his voice, his manner, his words, all seemed to make his audience feel that he was letting them come in and sit around the planning table with him and look at the war maps over his shoulder. And he had the ability to state war strategy in such simple terms that the average layman was able to grasp and understand its broad outline. At Shibe Park, he spoke of the involved advance planning behind every one of the major operations of the war.

It has meant planning in terms of precisely how many men will be needed, and how many ships—warships, cargo ships, landing craft—how many bombers, how many fighter planes—how much equipment—food—what types of equipment down to the last cartridge. And, it has meant getting all of them to the right place at the right time. . . .

The whole story of our vast effort in this war has been the story of incredible achievement—the story of the job that has been done by an Administration which, I am told, is "old, and tired, and quarrelsome."

The Republican strategists wanted to keep the war out of the campaign, ostensibly on the ground that the war was nonpolitical. But they knew, of course, that any discussion of it could only be to the advantage of the man who had served so successfully as Commander-in-Chief. For just that very reason, the President insisted on talking about the war:

"Now, of course, I realize that in this political campaign it is considered by some to be very impolite to mention the fact that there is a war on."

And all through the campaign he continued to talk about it. While he believed that the conduct of the war had to be nonpolitical, he knew that the fact of war was definitely political; for this political campaign would determine who was to be the Commander-in-Chief in the war for the next four years.

The greatest single factor in Roosevelt's effectiveness as a public speaker was his ability to associate himself closely with his listeners. He could give them the impression that they were all sitting down together discussing common problems, common successes, and common failures. I never saw the President make better use of that ability and technique than he did in this speech at Philadelphia under the worst possible physical conditions—a huge outdoor baseball park with the audience a great distance from him, their faces practically invisible in the darkness. When I first saw the speaking arrangements, I was afraid that he would never be able to bridge the distance from second base where his car was parked to the vast audience around him in the grandstand and the bleachers. But he did. He did it best when he came to the part of the speech where he spoke of his own four sons in the war. He was able to associate himself and Mrs. Roosevelt, as an ordinary American father and mother, with the mothers and fathers in the ball park and with the millions of fathers and mothers all over the country who had boys fighting away from home. The President's four sons already had enviable war records—which they were to improve before the war was over.

It was a question that came up often during the campaign: should the President mention the service of his own sons? This was tied up with the question of what he should say about the charges being made in veterans' quarters that Dewey, as a younger man, should have taken a more active part in the war. Some people had urged the President to point out that Dewey, in spite of his comparative youth, had not gone into military service. Roosevelt consistently refused to do this. He felt strongly that government was an essential industry; that service in government by those who were not actually drafted was in the public interest. This did not apply, however, to anyone of draft age who had been called up by a draft board. Roosevelt was tough in refusing deferments to men solely because they were in federal service. He would not take the recommendations of his own department heads for deferments on that ground. He set up an independent board to pass on these cases. I used to review the findings of this board, on appeal, and knew how harsh a policy Roosevelt insisted be followed. But he certainly did not think that all high public officials should resign and dash into military service. And in any case, he felt that such an attack on Dewey might be considered unfair.

He had said little up to now about his own sons. In speaking about them at Philadelphia he did not appear boastful, or even proud; he simply indicated that all fathers and mothers in America were now in the same boat.

> Mrs. Roosevelt and I hear very often from a great many of these women who live in loneliness and anxiety while their men are far away.
>
> I can speak as one who knows something of the feelings of a parent with sons who are in the battle line overseas. I know that, regardless of the outcome of this election, our sons must and will go on fighting for whatever length of time is necessary for victory.

After the speech, relaxing in his train over a glass of ginger ale, the President spoke to us about its effect. He was satisfied that it had provided a full answer to the charges of mismanagement in preparing for and conducting the war, and that they were now out of the campaign. I always thought that October, 1944, was a particularly unfortunate time for the Republican candidate to attack the handling of the war. The United Nations were winning on all fronts. The President was very proud of his record as Commander-in-Chief, and the attacks upon his conduct in this capacity had made him genuinely angry. It was more than a personal resentment; he realized that if the charges took hold they might have a devastating effect upon the morale of the American people.

From Philadelphia we traveled to Chicago for the next major campaign speech, arriving the following evening about six o'clock. The main part of the speech had been prepared in Washington before we left, but a great deal of polishing and filling in still remained to be done. On the train between Philadelphia and Chicago we prepared two new drafts, with the President taking a continuous and active part.

There had not been enough time in Washington to have facts and statistics checked as carefully as usual. Therefore I had left with Isador Lubin one copy of the latest draft, and had asked him to have it all carefully checked by the agencies concerned. With the new Signal Corps car on the train, he would be able to communicate with us directly and send what corrections were necessary. Longer telegrams could be sent to stopping points so as to leave the wire free for official messages.

I told Lubin that we would probably keep sending him additional statistics for checking, and asked him to keep in constant touch with the White House telegraph office night and day. He was to act as a clearinghouse; as soon as he got a query from us he was to call the proper agency for the answer. Otherwise we would have been sending telegrams to agencies all over Washington.

"Lube" (as he was called by his friends) probably got very little sleep between the day we left Washington and the time the Chicago speech was delivered, for we kept him constantly on the alert with all kinds of requests. While we worked on speeches in Washington, we verified our facts by telephone, or if time was short we asked the government officials concerned to come over to the White House and check the drafts. The Chicago speech is one of the few of which any written record of the checking process exists. I am reproducing a few of our many exchanges, for they indicate the kind of detailed, meticulous checking and cross-checking that was always done on Presidential speeches.

For example, at Pittsburgh a six-page telegram was delivered to us. It was Lubin's first check on the draft we had left behind in Washington. The telegram was dated the night of the day we had left, October 27:

Deliver care of Mr. Linkins, Western Union Representative for Judge Rosenman from Mr. Lubin:

1. Sheet 1 first draft. Change figure on productive jobs from sixty (60) to fifty-seven (57) million.

2. Sheet 2. Change figure on increase in employment to ten million (10,000,000).

3. Sheet 2. Change increase in farm income to read "we almost tripled . . ."

6. Sheet 4. Blandford and D. R. suggest following as substitute for fourth sentence in paragraph on housing . . . etc. [This was in answer to a wire I had sent him from Philadelphia: "Please check the following paragraph with National Housing Authority and with Mrs. Rosenman, etc., etc." Blandford was the head of the National Housing Agency, and "D. R." stood for Dorothy Rosenman, my wife, who was an expert in the field of housing.]

7. Section on social security has been approved by Arthur [meaning Arthur Altmeyer, chairman of the Social Security Board].

8. Material on taxation has been approved by persons designated by you, etc., etc.

Many more items were included in the message; they were all of a similar nature.

On the way to Chicago, the President dictated an insert reading:

Emerson said to young men: "Hitch your wagon to a star." He knows and we know that we cannot attain this star while we live. But this teaching, and it is the teaching of Christianity, holds out hope—yes, the star of hope. Let us join in making some progress. Yes, more progress while we live.

This insert was finally discarded in the speech as delivered. Although I felt from the indifferent way the President dictated it that it would be dropped in a later draft, I thought I'd better check the authorship of the well-known quotation, since none of us aboard the train were too sure of it. As soon as I had a chance, while the President was still working on the draft, I sent the following wire to Lubin—just in case:

Please check whether it was Emerson who said: "Hitch your wagon to a star." Wire immediately giving exact quotation.

The answer came back quickly:

For Judge Rosenman from Lube. The statement "Hitch your wagon to a star" appears in an essay entitled "American Civilization" by Ralph Waldo Emerson. Boy, I am proud of this one. Please remember that I am an economist who has had some statistical training. I am neither a littérateur, poet or playwright. What in hell have you got Bob [Sherwood] there for?

The President had a good laugh at this answer, and was not at all put out that I had checked on his literary allusion. He knew that we checked on everything, and I am sure that that knowledge gave him a feeling of confidence and security.

Checking was more difficult on a moving train, especially when we had such a short time. Even in the midst of dictation by the President we might be opening a telegram and, then and there, correcting one figure or another. The President never got flustered or excited by this sort of thing, even if the deadline was getting dangerously near—as it did on this trip—before the final draft was finished. He took it all coolly; would joke as we went searching through the pages for the right paragraph to correct; would even calmly stop to wave a return greeting to a group of people at a station or siding. The speech-writing team would get more excited and anxious as the hours went by and as the speech got pulled apart and rearranged. But Roosevelt always seemed confident that when the hour came to speak, the reading copy would be there, and the press copies would have been distributed to the newspapermen. It was a deep unspoken compliment to his speech-writing helpers, but it was often nerve-racking. Frequently I had grave doubts that all would turn out well—and I expressed my doubts. Fortunately, my fears never materialized: the reading copy was always ready; the press copies had always been properly distributed.

On this occasion, we were fortunate in being able to spend almost an entire day with the President on the speech. He was interrupted only once, at Fort Wayne, Indiana, where he made a rear-platform speech directed particularly at the large number of railroad workers employed there.

Speaking briefly and extemporaneously, he again referred to Dewey's practice of twisting words out of context:

I have heard some rather irritated comment by Republican campaign orators about taking a campaign trip.

They don't like it.

They seem to believe that I promised them . . . that I was not going to campaign under any circumstances, and therefore that they could say anything they wanted to about my policies and my Administration.

However, they conveniently overlook what I actually said in my speech of acceptance last July . . . I am going to quote from that speech very briefly—and I am sure you will pardon me if I quote it correctly—because, you know, a long time ago, when I was Governor of New York, I formed the habit of quoting correctly. I said I wasn't going to conduct the usual campaign. I said, however: "I shall, however, feel free to report to the people the facts about matters of concern to them and especially to correct any misrepresentations."

So that is why I am going out to Chicago for another similar speech tonight.

The President was very careful about the contents of the Chicago speech. He had told us in Washington that he wanted to make it a well-reasoned résumé of his political and economic philosophy. He had already delivered one major speech on foreign policy, and one on the conduct of the war. He now wanted to talk about the domestic policies he expected to follow after the war and the kind of expanding postwar American economy he envisaged generally.

I had asked economists and statisticians in Washington to make surveys to determine what we could reasonably expect in the way of an expanding economy after the war. The most optimistic of the projections indicated something around 57 or 58 million jobs, and some of them cautioned against overoptimism. One day, after studying these memoranda, the President put them down and said: "We are going to shoot for a sixty-million-job peacetime economy. Some of the reactionaries will laugh at us just as they did when we talked about a fifty-thousand-plane production, but they're going to be just as wrong about jobs as they were about planes." They were—the goal was reached even before the new war economy which started with the outbreak in Korea.

No one who was at Soldiers' Field in Chicago that night will ever forget it. I was informed that the ordinary capacity of Soldiers' Field is about 100,000 persons. No fewer than 125,000 persons were there that night, to say nothing of the uncounted thousands who were outside the walls of the field. Here as in Philadelphia a large platform and ramp had been constructed in the center of the field. The President's car, followed by a dozen others, entered the field at one end and amidst enthusiastic shouting and applause drove across the field; then his car went up the ramp and onto the platform alone. On the platform a small number of invited officials and dignitaries were seated. The arrangements for broadcasting were similar to those in Philadelphia; the President was able to deliver his speech from his seat in the open automobile. A cool, stiff wind was blowing in from the lake, but the President was bareheaded. Speaking conditions were very difficult. His words had to travel the great distance from the center of the field to the outer edge of the audience, and there was a distinct echo which clashed with his voice. The reception in most parts of the field must have been extremely bad. But it was a Roosevelt crowd, and it never left any doubts about how it was going to vote.

To me, the speech at Soldiers' Field was the most dramatic example of the range and power of the President's speaking ability. It was far from the best of his orations; it had too many statistics; in some parts it was downright dull. In spite of all that, he held those 125,000 people completely; they seemed intent on catching every syllable; they voiced their approval and encouragement at just the right moments; their attention never seemed to lessen for a second.

Early in the speech the President stated its general text: "Tonight I want to talk simply to you about the future of America—about this land of ours, this land of unlimited opportunity."

His economic philosophy was succinctly stated. It was nothing new; there had been no substantial change since the first year of the New Deal. There was the underlying belief that all the segments and groups in our economy are interdependent. There was the concept of ever-expanding economic opportunity, embodied in the Economic Bill of Rights which he had enunciated almost a year before and which, he said, provides "a new basis of security and prosperity [which] can be established for all. . . ."

Some people—I need not name them—have sneered at these ideals as well as at the ideals of the Atlantic Charter, the ideals of the Four Freedoms. They have said that they were the dreams of starry-eyed New Dealers— that it is silly to talk of them because we cannot attain these ideals tomorrow or the next day. [This is where the President had dictated and later deleted the insert from Emerson about hitching one's wagon to a star.]

The American people have greater faith than that. I know that they agree with these objectives—that they demand them—that they are determined to get them—and that they are *going* to get them.

The President argued that these rights did not interfere with private enterprise; that they were essential to a system of real private enterprise; and that without them, enterprise could no longer be private but would become monopolistic.

I believe in free enterprise—and always have.
I believe in the profit system—and always have.
I believe that private enterprise can give full employment to our people....
I believe in exceptional rewards for innovation, skill, and risk-taking by business.

In his campaigns of 1932 and 1936, Roosevelt had made a major speech on agriculture in the Middle West, and others in the Northwest and Southwest. But because of the war he did not this year want to go further west than Chicago; consequently, he decided to say what he had to say about farmers as a part of this speech.

He pledged that his Administration policy of conserving the natural resources of the country would be continued. He pledged a continuance of the policy that had "put into the law of the land the farmers' long dream of parity prices," and the policy of "giving to as many farmers as possible the chance of owning their own farms." He promised a program of genuine crop insurance.

On the fulfillment of all these policies he based his idea of the "America of tomorrow." What did it include? It included, of course, American homes, decent homes, "well-built homes, with electricity and plumbing, air and sunlight . . . well over a million homes a year for at least ten years. . . .

"In the future America that we are talking about, we think of new highways, new parkways . . . thousands of new airports . . . new planes, large and small, new cheap automobiles . . . new hospitals and new health clinics . . . a new merchant marine for our expanded world trade.

"In the America of tomorrow . . ." said the President, "our Economic Bill of Rights . . . must be applied to all our citizens, irrespective of race, or creed or color. . . . I believe that the Congress of the United States should by law make the [Fair Employment Practice] Committee permanent." The FEPC was a committee which had been created by the President in 1941 to prevent discrimination against Negroes and other minority groups in war industry and government employment.

And in that future America ". . . small business will continue to be protected from selfish, cold-blooded monopolies and cartels. Beware of that profound enemy of the free enterprise system who pays lip-service to free competition—but also labels every anti-trust prosecution as a 'persecution.' You know, it depends a good deal on whose baby has the measles." This last phrase is one which the President used quite frequently in conversation.

The program painted in the Chicago speech was a complete statement of the New Deal of 1944, and that is why I have quoted from it so extensively. It was a program in which the President believed. It was the program he had brought to Washington with him in 1933—expanded and developed to meet new conditions. As enunciated in 1944, it was not the program of a beginner in the Presidency. It was a program that Roosevelt as President had followed successfully for eleven years, and that which millions of Americans—the majority of Americans—enthusiastically supported.

After the success of the Chicago speech, many of the President's friends wanted him to go into some of the other states, particularly Ohio. This he stubbornly refused to do, although the political leaders in Ohio and elsewhere were confident that with one speech there he would not only carry the state for himself but would defeat one of the major opponents of his program in the Congress, Senator Robert A. Taft. The President thought it was hopeless, however, and did not want to take the time. Later he regretted his stubbornness; for Taft won his Senate race by only a small majority, and the President felt that he could have overcome it had he gone into Ohio.

He did yield, however, to the importunities of his campaign advisers, who urged him to make another campaign speech before going to Boston, where the next one had been scheduled. But with the war reaching a climax both in the Pacific and in Europe, he did not wish to leave Washington for it; so he made a political radio address from the White House.

Among the suggestions that came in for this speech was a proposed draft by Max Lerner, the well-known liberal teacher and writer.

I have always felt that a radio address without a visible audience is an inappropriate vehicle for a campaign speech. There is something about the spirit and tempo of a political speech that requires an audience. The enthusiasm of the crowd and its reaction to the candidate's words create an atmosphere that a cold microphone in a secluded room cannot furnish. As I reread this address of November 2, my conviction is strengthened. As a campaign speech, it seems dull, stuffy, and ineffective. Nevertheless, it did serve to show that the candidate was "in there pitching." That is always important in political campaigns. The head of the ticket can never himself relax and expect the campaign workers to carry on. They are generally exactly as enthusiastic and energetic as the candidate himself; if he stops working, there is a letdown all along the line.

This radio speech was a fairly complete summary of the war situation as it stood, and dwelt at length on the vast amount of preparation and planning that this kind of war called for. The President's purpose was obvious: to drive home again the idea expressed in Philadelphia—that a war of this magnitude required a Chief Executive with war experience.

He also made a point of paying special tribute to the women of the country—in the services, in the war industries and on the ration boards. He knew, of course, that his mention of all these women specifically would bring him votes. But that was not his sole motive. He did the same thing even when there was no political campaign on, for he knew that it helped to build up their morale. That was part of his job of leadership as he saw it.

In this radio speech the President denounced some of the whispered rumors that had been going around; but he reserved his real attack on the rumormongers for his next speech at Boston.

The night after the radio address, November 3, we left for Boston on a campaign trip through New England. With three rear-platform speeches—at Bridgeport, Hartford, and Springfield—and the major speech at Boston to be delivered all in one day, Sherwood and I were kept busy. Hopkins was unable to go. We worked most of that night and all through the next day, practically up to the moment we had to leave the train for the ball park in Boston.

The President had told us he wanted to answer in kind a vitriolic attack that had been made upon him by his opponent at Boston a few days before. By now, he was altogether fed up with the attacks on him and the rumors being spread about him, which he said were below the belt. He considered this the meanest campaign waged against him during his entire political life.

As he put it at Bridgeport, Connecticut, on November 4:

There are a few politicians . . . who work themselves into such an emotional state that they say things I hope they will be sorry for before they die. . . .

In this campaign, of course . . . I can't talk about my opponent the way I would like to sometimes, because I try to think that I am a Christian. I try to think that some day I will go to Heaven, and I don't believe there is anything to be gained in saying dreadful things about other people in any campaign.

After next Tuesday there are going to be a lot of sorry people in the United States.

At Hartford, the President answered some of the campaign charges about his attitude toward business. Hartford, Connecticut, is essentially an insurance city, and the insurance business is particularly sensitive to any government policy that might affect the purchasing value of the dollar. Insurance executives—members of the Republican party—had spread rumors that if Roosevelt were elected again they would have to go out of business because the dollar would lose its value.

The President referred to this at the beginning of his extemporaneous speech:

I am glad to come back here. Four years ago I was told terrible things were being circulated all over the country. People all over the United States were being told that if I got reelected, all of the Hartford insurance companies would go broke. So, coming in here, I expected to see vast, empty buildings not being used and employing no people. . . . And yet they are still here. And the joke is that the insurance companies, not only of Hartford but of other places, are better off than they ever have been before. . . .

And they are making the fantastic claim this year that your government is now engaged in some deep-dyed plot to take over the insurance business. . . .

I know that the workers and managers in that business cannot be easily fooled by that type of propaganda.

Why, the insurance policies of the United States and your savings are safer than they ever were in the whole history of the United States—and so is the insurance business. That was not true in 1933 when I took office.

Since a great many of the voters in Hartford were white-collar workers, the President seized the opportunity to discuss their particular problem:

> There is one thing that I have meant to say for the last two months, and haven't had a chance. It's a word about a group of our citizens that have been pretty hard hit by the war. They have not been able to earn the high level of wages that have been paid in shipyards and war factories—and yet, with amazing patience and fortitude they have continued in their essential jobs—carrying on as best they can. And those are the white-collar workers of America.
>
> I think, however, that . . . they realize that this Administration had done a pretty good job in keeping down the cost of living—in protecting the purchasing power of their dollars in terms of rent and other necessities of life. Compared with the skyrocketing cost of living in the last war—twice as much of a rise as in this war—our record in this war, on the whole, has been very good. And I want you—as they used to say—to give a hand to the white-collar workers of the United States.

One of the President's political axioms was never to go on the defensive in a campaign speech. He used to say that if it was at all possible, always carry the attack to the enemy. A defensive or explanatory speech, he felt, was always taken as a sign of weakness.

In the Hartford speech he carried out this axiom boldly. In 1944, as from time immemorial, the Republican party claimed to be the party of sound money, and accused the Democratic party of unsound monetary policies. The President took the offensive and charged that it was the Republican party that was the party of unsound money. To substantiate this unusual charge, he called as witness the record of Republican votes in the Congress:

> Time and again the Republicans in the Congress voted overwhelmingly against price control, and in favor of letting prices go skyrocketing.
>
> So I make an assertion. The Democratic party in this war has been the party of sound money. The Republican party has been the party of unsound money.
>
> If the Republicans had had their way, all of us—farmers, white-collar workers, factory workers, housewives—we would all have had our dollars cut by inflation and a higher cost of living.

It gave the President a lot of satisfaction to make this point, and he chuckled about it in advance.

Only a few days before, in Boston, Dewey had accused the President of leading the country into the paths of communism. Republican leaders were also doing their best to create the impression that Sidney Hillman, the well-known labor leader, who as co-chairman of the Office of Production Management had done much to help prepare the United States for war, was the predominating influence in the Democratic party and in the 1944 campaign. The charge had its genesis in a column written a few days after the convention by Arthur Krock in *The New York Times*, saying that the President had told Hannegan during Hannegan's visit to the train in the Chicago yards to "clear everything with Sidney." Krock later stated that the source of this story was "two defeated aspirants for the Vice-Presidential nomination."

Although Krock insisted that he meant to include in those instructions only the Vice-Presidential nomination, and although Hannegan vehemently denied that any such direction—or anything like it—had been given to him by the President, the Republican Campaign Committee insisted on circulating and exaggerating the canard into a statement that Roosevelt had thus given Sidney Hillman complete charge of "everything" in the campaign. No proof was ever offered to substantiate the charge, but it was spread throughout the land in paid newspaper and billboard advertisements, by radio, and by campaign speeches. Coupled with a widely circulated description of Hillman—his parentage, birth and religion—this part of the Republican campaign was obviously an unvarnished, unabashed appeal to anti-Jewish prejudices.

The President decided to wade in on all this at Boston. He started by referring to his own efforts to elect Alfred E. Smith President of the United States; and, just as he did in 1928, he let loose on the whole subject of religious intolerance. He said:

When I talked here in Boston in 1928, I talked about racial and religious intolerance, which was then—as unfortunately it still is, to some extent—"a menace to the liberties of America."

And all the bigots in those days were gunning for Al Smith.

Religious intolerance, social intolerance, and political intolerance have no place in our American life. . . .

Today, in this war, our fine boys are fighting magnificently all over the world and among those boys are the Murphys and the Kellys, the Smiths and the Joneses, the Cohens, the Carusos, the Kowalskis, the Schultzes, the Olsens, the Swobodas, and—right in with all the rest of them—the Cabots and the Lowells. . . .

It is our duty to them to make sure that, big as this country is, there is no room in it for racial or religious intolerance—and that there is no room for snobbery.

It will be noticed that there was nothing defensive in this type of treatment. The President did not try to defend Sidney Hillman, or say that there was no truth to the charge that things had to be "cleared with Sidney." Instead, he carried the attack right to his opponent. Later in the speech he did something that he did not do more than once or twice in all his political campaigns. He actually quoted what Dewey had said about communism's taking over control of the New Deal. But here again he did not go on the defensive:

Just the other day you people here in Boston witnessed an amazing demonstration of talking out of both sides of the mouth.

Speaking here in Boston, a Republican candidate said—and pardon me if I quote him correctly—that happens to be an old habit of mine—he said that, quote "the Communists are seizing control of the New Deal, through which they aim to control the Government of the United States." Unquote.

The President delivered that "and pardon me if I quote him correctly" with such telling effect that the audience—immediately getting the significance of the reference to Dewey—broke into a great howl of laughter which stopped his delivery for a while. He continued:

However, on that very same day, that very same candidate had spoken in Worcester, and he said that with Republican victory in November, "we can end one-man government, and we can forever remove the threat of monarchy in the United States." Now, really—which is it—Communism or monarchy? . . .

Everybody knows that I was reluctant to run for the Presidency again this year. But since this campaign developed, I tell you frankly that I have become most anxious to win—and I say that for the reason that never before in my lifetime has a campaign been filled with such misrepresentation, distortion, and falsehood. Never since 1928 have there been so many attempts to stimulate in America racial or religious intolerance.

Roosevelt's estimate of this last campaign against him appears in a letter he wrote a friend, Mrs. Rupert C. King, a few weeks after election. She had knitted a new pair of socks for the President at the time of his previous inauguration, and had asked him what color socks he wanted for the fourth inauguration.[1]

---

[1] *F.D.R.: His Personal Letters, 1928-1945:* Vol. II, p. 1563.

Dec. 21, 1944

DEAR GRACE:

That is a grand thought about another pair of socks and in regard to color, I would suggest either black or blue because that is a little bit the way I felt after going through THE DIRTIEST CAMPAIGN IN ALL HISTORY.

I hope all goes well with you and that I shall see you one of these days soon.

With all good wishes of the Christmas Season,

As ever yours.

In some of the more populous sections of the country, Dewey had been making speeches that at times sounded almost like New Deal speeches. At the same time, the Republican Vice-Presidential candidate, Bricker, was going through the country making violent anti-New Deal speeches. The President referred to these strange goings on, using again his most deadly political weapon—ridicule:

> The American people are quite competent to judge a political party that works both sides of a street—a party that has one candidate making campaign promises of all kinds of added government expenditures in the West, while a running mate of his demands less government expenditures in the East.

A charge frequently made by Roosevelt's enemies was that he had such a "swelled head" that he never would admit he was mistaken. I do not think it was "swelled-headedness," but I would say that he was frequently just plain stubborn about realizing and admitting that he had made a mistake. Of all the charges leveled at him, I think this one had more truth in it than most all the others combined. On the other hand, very frequently his mistakes would right themselves in time. This gave rise to another saying about Roosevelt: that he had "pulled another rabbit out of the hat."

Ever since 1933 he had been carrying on a social and economic program, parts of which he had designated as "bold experimentation"—a series of experiments and day-to-day improvisations designed to meet unprecedented conditions in American history. In such a program, he was bound to make a number of mistakes. But in spite of advice and arguing to the contrary, he was not, as I have said, too fond of admitting them, except in a general way. Seldom did he get as specific as he had back in 1939, when he admitted having made a mistake in signing the neutrality law.

In Boston, for example:

But—despite these campaign promises [by the Republicans] of wholesale housecleaning—have you heard one word of specific criticism of any of the progressive laws that this Administration has proposed and enacted?

Have you heard any talk of sweeping out any of these laws—or sweeping out any of the agencies that administer them?

Oh, no, on that subject the Republican politicians are very uncharacteristically silent.

This Administration has made mistakes. That I freely *assert*. And I hope my friends of the press will not change that to *admit*.

But, my friends, I think it is a pretty good batting average. Our mistakes have been honestly made during sincere efforts to help the great mass of citizens. Never have we made the inexcusable mistake—we know some who have—of substituting talk for action when farms were being foreclosed, homes were being sold at auction, and people were standing in breadlines. . . .

The evening before Election Day the President gave his usual "non-political" fireside chat from his library at Hyde Park. Sherwood and I were there to help with the writing, but most of it was the work of his daughter Anna and his son-in-law John Boettiger.

In the later years of the President's life, after Anna became a resident of the White House, she was frequently very helpful in making suggestions about speeches. Like her mother, she had a fine sense of what the American public was thinking. She had a facile pen herself, and actually wrote parts of several of the President's speeches, including this one and the D-Day prayer in June, 1944.

This election-eve speech was a plea that at least fifty million voters go to the polls the next day to show the world the strength of our democracy. It was also a plea that this time the world find a way to avoid the possibility of a third war:

When we think of the speed and long-distance possibilities of air travel of all kinds to the remotest corners of the earth, we must consider the devastation wrought on the people of England, for example, by the new long-range bombs. Another war would be bound to bring even more devilish and powerful instruments of destruction to wipe out civilian populations. No coastal defenses, however strong, could prevent these silent missiles of death, fired perhaps from planes or ships at sea, from crashing deep within the United States itself.

This time, this time, we must be certain that the peace-loving nations of the world band together in determination to outlaw and to prevent war.

Most of us who had been active in the campaign believed that the vote for Roosevelt would be greater than he did. A few days before election, six of us, including Roosevelt, had entered into a five-dollar pool on the forthcoming electoral vote. Watson had guessed 400, Hopkins 440, Early 449, Sherwood 484, and I 431. The President was not so confident even as Watson. In fact his guess was so low that as soon as he paid his bet he insisted on tearing up his slip. The actual number of electoral votes was 432, which meant that I collected the twenty-five dollars.

On election night, I was at Hyde Park as the returns came in, as in the previous years. By this time the procedure had become somewhat routine. The results seemed fairly certain. Victory was clearly indicated in the very early returns. Roosevelt won the electoral votes of 36 states. His oft-repeated wish that 50 million voters go to the polls was not quite fulfilled; only 48 million went. Of the 48 million, Roosevelt received 25,600,000 and Dewey received 22 million.

Chapter XXVI

The Last Annual Message and Inaugural, 1945

The military successes of the summer and fall continued to build up the confidence of official Washington that the end of the war was approaching. It became so pronounced that on December 1, 1944, the President found it necessary to send a letter to the heads of government departments and agencies to refrain from public statements indicating an early end of the war.

About this time he also ran into trouble over some appointments he had made in the State Department. On November 21, Cordell Hull, who had been Secretary of State ever since the first day of the Roosevelt Administration, resigned because of ill health. The President appointed as his successor the then Under Secretary of State, Edward Stettinius. He also appointed as Assistant Secretaries of State a number of men who could never have qualified as New Dealers. The announcement of their names caused dismay among liberals in Washington. The President had gone to Warm Springs for a rest; but many of his friends and supporters, including myself, wrote him about our uneasiness at the fact that the State Department had been turned over to men whose philosophy was at variance with his own domestic policies. His campaign had been conducted on so liberal a plane that these appointments were even more noticeable than they would have been if made a few months back. The grumblings and dissatisfaction became so pronounced that the subject was a matter of discussion at the first press conference after his return to Washington, December 19:

MAY CRAIG: Mr. President, there's a good deal of question as to whether you are going right or left politically, and I would like your opinion on which way you are going?

THE PRESIDENT: I am going down the whole line a little left of center. I think that was answered, that question, eleven and a half years ago, and still holds.

MAY CRAIG: But you told us a little while ago that you were going to have Dr. Win-the-War and not Dr. New Deal.

THE PRESIDENT: (interjecting) That's right.

MAY CRAIG: (continuing) The question is whether you are going back to be Dr. New Deal after the war——

THE PRESIDENT: (interposing) No, no, no. Keep right along a little to the left of center, which includes winning the war. That's not much of an answer, is it?

MAY CRAIG: No. (Laughter.)

THE PRESIDENT: However, you have broken the ice, May.

QUESTION: Mr. President, if you are going down a little left of center, how does that match with the six appointments you sent up to the Hill on the State Department?

THE PRESIDENT: Very well.

QUESTION: Would you call them a little left of center?

THE PRESIDENT: I call myself a little left of center. I have got a lot of people in the Administration—oh, I know some of them are extreme right and extreme left, and everything else—a lot of people in the Administration, and I cannot vouch for them all. They work out pretty well, on the whole. Just think, this crowd here in this room—my gracious, you will find every opinion between left and extreme right.

I am sure that the President realized he had made a mistake in these appointments. But here again he would not admit it, not even to us, who were close to him, when we renewed our complaints.

The rumor of an impending second meeting among Churchill, Stalin, and the President was also agitating the press at this time. He was questioned about it at this same press conference. Naturally he evaded the query. At a later press conference, on December 22, when he was pressed again about the prospective meeting, he pointed out that the element of security precluded any statement about it. Finally he said this:

QUESTION: Mr. President, is there anything that could be said to further our understanding as to what has held up this meeting up to this point? Since you have said you were anxious to meet, Mr. Churchill has said the same thing.

THE PRESIDENT: Well, again, I have got to tell you off the record. It's largely a question of geography. There aren't three people in the same place. You can't hold a conference in several different places. There has got to be one place. That has to be off the record, too. In other words, to find a place that three of us can go to.

QUESTION: Does the fact that the Premier of Russia is also actively at the head of the armed forces have a bearing on that?

THE PRESIDENT: Oh, yes. Oh, yes. Oh, all kinds of factors.

The question of the place of meeting was always a serious and difficult one whenever Stalin was concerned. At this time, the Russians were engaged in a great offensive against Germany, moving westward at a swift pace, and Stalin had this additional reason for being unwilling to leave Russia. Both Churchill and the President were deeply anxious, however, to have another meeting with him. Their anxiety increased as our armies and the Russian armies began to crowd in against the heart of Germany. Many problems were pressing for solution, and the solution could be arrived at only by a personal conference among the Big Three. There were still no agreements on how to deal with Germany after surrender. Our Chiefs of Staff, with the approval of the President, had determined upon a landing upon the Japanese mainland to take place about November 1, 1945. The date of Russia's entry into the Japanese war, the extent of her participation, and the terms on which she would participate were all matters that still had to be determined around a conference table.

Agreements also had to be arrived at regarding the frontiers and government of Poland. The position of France in German affairs and in European affairs generally, the question of zones of occupation and of possible dismemberment of Germany, reparations from Germany, the treatment of Nazi war criminals, the form of the United Nations Organization—all these were still open for discussion.

As early as September, 1944, plans for a conference were being considered and discussed; even while he was working on the political campaign the President was trying to arrange the meeting. It took a long time and much negotiation to agree upon a place. The Crimea was the final selection—Yalta. But it was not selected until some time after the election. A great many of Roosevelt's advisers urged him not to put himself in the position of going so far around the globe to meet Stalin. The President felt that so much depended upon this meeting that he would have gone almost any place to bring it about. He was working toward the most cherished objective of his eventful life—a chance at permanent world peace.

As soon as the place had been agreed upon, it seemed as though a great load had been lifted from his shoulders. He began to plan and look forward to the trip with all the enthusiasm and exuberance of the days of 1933.

The annual message to the newly elected Congress, to be delivered on January 6, 1945, was prepared as the President was getting ready to leave for Yalta.

He started very early on this task. I have a memo from him dated December 12, 1944, in which he asked that I start gathering material and working up a draft of a message. Although in this memo he suggested that I "try to hold it to 3,000 words," it turned out to be the longest of his State of the Union messages.

Sherwood and I worked up a draft for him based on material and suggestions that we had requested from various agencies and departments, including State, War, and Navy. Ben Cohen, Archibald MacLeish, and Harold D. Smith of the Budget Bureau had all submitted drafts and suggestions. In our conversations with the President he had said that he wanted this speech to cover a very wide field: the status of the war, the international situation during and after the war, the formation of the peace and the United Nations Organization, and the future of America. He wanted it to synthesize everything he had said and promised during the campaign. He also wanted it to be a message from which all the freedom-loving peoples of the world could draw confidence and hope for the future.

Reading this message, particularly those parts which have to do with the future international organization, one is struck by how closely it follows the pattern of the discussion that Roosevelt was to lead at Yalta.

We had obtained a written memorandum containing an over-all review of the war from both fighting services. We also had an eighteen-page memo from General Marshall. On the basis of these we prepared a draft of what we thought the President might want to say about the war. He revised it carefully.

The keynote of the war part of the message was set immediately at the beginning of it: "We have no question of the ultimate victory. We have no question of the cost. Our losses will be heavy. We and our Allies will go on fighting together to ultimate total victory."

The Germans were then engaged in their counterattack through Belgium in the Battle of the Bulge, and the American people were worried. The President wanted to give them the facts, and felt that he could reassure them in the face of this new threat. He did.

He then launched upon a review of the "basic strategy which has guided us through three years of war, and which will lead, eventually, to total victory." This part of the speech was based upon the memorandum General Marshall had sent over to us, and was a broad over-all review of the war from the days of Pearl Harbor to date.

This kind of statement of our long-range strategy and ultimate aims was one of the most potent instruments the President employed in the development and exercise of war leadership. From the very beginning he used the radio and newspapers continuously to explain his policies directly to the people. He was able to make them understand—better than any other President in our history. So long as the people understood and approved his long-range objectives, whether in war or peace, tactical setbacks and incidental mistakes along the road took their proper subordinate place in perspective. The loss of a battle considered all by itself might assume disastrous proportions in the public mind, but viewed in the light of long-range military strategy it looked entirely different. Roosevelt always had great confidence that the mass of American people could understand long-range objectives just as thoroughly as immediate problems. "Give them all the facts," he would say, "and I would much rather trust the judgment of 130,000,000 Americans than I would that of any artificially selected few."

Still faced with the problem of how to combat the spread of overconfidence in early victory, the President skillfully tied his call for renewed effort by all Americans to the need to support the Americans fighting at the front. This was no mere oratorical device. To him, a weapon of war was not an abstraction—he visualized it in the hands of an American boy. A B-29 was something that an American crew would be flying; a destroyer the fighting home of American boys. So it was natural for him to tie in his new appeal for stepped-up war efforts with the support of American soldiers and sailors.

He outlined what full support meant.

First it required increased production of all articles of war.

Second, it required more Army and Navy nurses; and in order to secure them, the President recommended that the Selective Service Act "be amended to provide for the induction of nurses into the armed forces. The need is too pressing to await the outcome of further efforts at recruiting."

Third, it required the production of "new types of weapons, for we cannot afford to fight the war of today or tomorrow with the weapons of yesterday." He described some of them, but not the atom bomb.

But, though it was never mentioned among us during the preparation of the speech, he certainly had the possibility of the atom bomb in mind when he said: "If we do not keep constantly ahead of our enemies in the development of new weapons, we pay for our backwardness with the life's blood of our sons."

"Then," continued the President, "the only way to meet these increased needs for new weapons and more of them is for every American engaged in war work to stay on his war job—for additional American civilians, men and women, not engaged in essential work, to go out and get a war job." Men and women who had begun to leave war jobs and rush for civilian jobs he criticized as "quitters."

Fourth, in order to provide these new weapons in increased amounts, the President repeated to the Congress his recommendation of the year before for the adoption of a national service act "for the total mobilization of all our human resources for the prosecution of the war."

Fifth, pending the passage of such a law, the President recommended that the Congress immediately enact legislation which "would be effective in using the services of the four million men now classified as 4F in whatever capacity is best for the war effort."

These were indeed drastic recommendations—made at a time when a great many Americans thought that the war was already won; when a great many workers were actually leaving their war jobs to return to peacetime industry. These were the drastic recommendations of a President who had been advised by his military experts to expect and be prepared for several bloody years of war with the suicide battalions of Japanese. And they were based on the same deep concern as his resolve a month later at Yalta to make sure that the Soviet Union got into the war against Japan at the earliest possible moment.

Turning from a discussion of the war, he said:

In the field of foreign policy, we propose to stand together with the United Nations not for the war alone but for the victory for which the war is fought.

It is not only a common danger which unites us but a common hope. Ours is an association not of governments but of peoples—and the peoples' hope is peace. . . .

It will not be easy to create this peoples' peace. We delude ourselves if we believe that the surrender of the armies of our enemies will make the peace we long for. The unconditional surrender of the armies of our enemies is the first and necessary step—but the first step only.

We have seen already, in areas liberated from the Nazi and the Fascist tyranny, what problems peace will bring. And we delude ourselves if we attempt to believe wishfully that all these problems can be solved overnight.

Speaking of the kind of international problems he anticipated, he pointed out the resemblance between the days ahead and the days immediately following our own Revolutionary War. Many difficulties arose then—"lawlessness and disregard of human life"; separatist movements of one kind or other started in the various states; even open or threatened insurrections in some, as in Massachusetts and New Hampshire.

This was a theme on which Roosevelt often dwelt in private conversation. I am told by Anne O'Hare McCormick that even in March, 1945, just before he left for Warm Springs—at a time when the Soviet Union, to his knowledge, was already beginning to make trouble—he spoke to her of the great similarity between the two situations. And as he said in this State of the Union Message:

These difficulties [of our own post-Revolutionary days] we worked out for ourselves, as the peoples of the liberated areas of Europe, faced with complex problems of adjustment, will work out their difficulties for themselves.

While it might be comforting and encouraging, when we see the international discord of today, to reflect that our own post-Revolutionary days were not marked by too much co-operation between the States, I have always thought this analogy was oversimplified and misleading. But the President seemed to be convinced that it was quite apt.

Roosevelt was realistic and farsighted enough to foresee that the nearer we came to defeating our enemies, the more conscious we would become of differences among the victors. Pointing out that "international co-operation on which enduring peace must be based is not a one-way street," he urged strongly that "we must not let those differences divide us and blind us to our more important common and continuing interests in winning the war and building the peace."

Warning that international organizations were bound to contain many imperfections, he said: "Let us not forget that the retreat to isolationism a quarter of a century ago was started not by a direct attack against international co-operation but against the alleged imperfections of the peace."

He mentioned his "concern about many situations, the Greek and the Polish, for example," pointing out how difficult these problems were. As if he were already sitting around the conference table at Yalta, he said:

> We and our Allies have declared that it is our purpose to respect the right of all peoples to choose the form of government under which they will live . . .
> During the interim period, until conditions permit a genuine expression of the people's will, we and our Allies have a duty . . . to use our influence to the end that no temporary or provisional authorities in the liberated countries block the eventual exercise of the peoples' right freely to choose the government and institutions under which, as free men, they are to live.

One of the major problems that he knew he was going to have to face at Yalta was the role of France in the postwar world. It was to be a problem for a long time. But he wanted to discuss it in this speech and I know he talked about France with State Department officials several times during the weeks this message was being prepared. Roosevelt said that "we fully recognize France's vital interest in a lasting solution of the German problem and the contribution which she can make in achieving international security."

These friendly words for France were written largely by Hopkins, who was very anxious that the President use them. Harry was about to leave for Paris, en route to Yalta, and was going to see De Gaulle. He thought that Roosevelt's expressions of friendship would help him defrost De Gaulle, but they did not.

Turning finally to postwar America, Roosevelt said: "I am clear in my own mind that, as an essential factor in the maintenance of peace in the future, we must have universal military training after this war, and I shall send a special message to the Congress on this subject."

Perhaps in January, 1945, universal military training had a better chance in the Congress than it did during the seven years that followed. Certainly it had a better chance before the explosion of the atomic bomb on Hiroshima than it had later. However, the President died before he could prepare the message; President Truman sent one later.

Roosevelt called again for the enactment of the Economic Bill of Rights which he had set forth in his State of the Union Message a year before, and stated that he would communicate further with the Congress on each of its provisions at a later date.

As a matter of fact, before he left for Yalta several weeks later he asked me to begin to get the material together for three of these promised messages to the Congress: one on an expanded social security program, one on education, and one on health.

Later, after President Roosevelt died and President Truman requested me to stay on as Counsel to the President, he asked me what unfinished business I had in hand. I told him of the three messages Roosevelt wanted to deliver. Truman directed me to go ahead with them, and I did. The messages that Roosevelt promised to send to the Congress were later all sent by the man he had picked as his successor.

The State of the Union Message was favorably received. Roosevelt's election, his platform and campaign pledges, this message—all made it quite clear that liberalism and internationalism were to be the program for the next four years. The only possible stumbling block was the Soviet Union, and Roosevelt was hopeful that the Soviet would cooperate in peace as well as it had in war. In order to defeat the Nazis, he had taken a great gamble in his wartime dealings with Russia. He had furnished the Soviet with arms and weapons and supplies in spite of the grim prophecies of many people that as soon as the Nazis were off Russian soil she would make a separate treaty with Hitler. Roosevelt had gambled on this—and had won. Russia was still a loyal ally. And in January, 1945, Roosevelt was hopeful that she would remain an ally after the war, too.

On the same day that the Annual Message was delivered in writing to the Congress, the President over the radio delivered a shortened version of it to the people of the United States. It was very difficult to decide what to cut out of the written message to get it down to radio-speech proportions. I took a carbon copy of the original message and put brackets around the portions I thought should be omitted. Some new sentences had to be written so that the shortened material would run smoothly. The President approved or disapproved the cuts. Some entirely new paparagraphs were written to make the radio speech a little more interesting, especially the parts that included statistical information.

The President, convinced that the war still had a long way to go, kept hammering for national service legislation even while he was getting ready for Yalta. On January 17, 1945, he wrote and publicized a letter to the chairman of the House Military Affairs Committee reemphasizing the need. In it he enclosed a letter signed by General Marshall and Admiral King, pointing out that national service legislation was necessary to ensure that war production would be maintained at an uninterrupted rate. The Battle of the Bulge made the need even more pressing.

On the same day that the President made his second request of the Congress for national service legislation, January 6, 1945, a bill was introduced in the Congress to carry out his recommendations. It provided that any draft registrant between eighteen and forty-five who left an essential job without good reason, or failed to take an essential job within a specified time, should be immediately classified as available for induction into the armed forces. This measure was popularly known as the "work or fight" bill. It passed the House of Representatives on February 1 by a vote of 246 to 167. In the Senate, it became bogged down in a number of substitute proposals and amendments. As finally written by the Conference Committee, the bill provided, among other things, fines and jail sentences for workers who voluntarily left jobs in war-essential activities without the approval of the director of the Office of War Mobilization and Reconversion. Organized labor protested strongly against these "job freeze" provisions. But the Conference Report was adopted in the House of Representatives on March 27 by a narrow vote.

By the time the Conference Report came to a final vote in the Senate, the American armies were across the Rhine River in full force, racing their way through Germany. Russia was hammering westward toward a meeting with the Allied troops. The Senate became convinced that the need for this drastic manpower legislation had passed; it rejected the Conference Report and the legislation was dead. The incident is important, for it shows the great concern Roosevelt and his military experts felt, just as he was leaving for Yalta, about the future length of the war in the Pacific.

For his last inauguration, the President insisted upon a simple ceremony without parades or display of any kind. It was his first wartime inaugural. When asked at a press conference about a parade, he poignantly replied: "Who is there here to parade?" He wanted also to save the materials, the manpower and the money. Accordingly the ceremonies took place on the south porch of the White House; they consisted of prayer, the singing of the national anthem, the administration of the oath of office to the President and Vice-President, and the delivery of the inaugural address.

The address took less than five minutes. Drafts had been submitted

to the President by MacLeish, by Sherwood and by me. Hopkins took
no part in the preparation of this Inaugural Address. The President
did not write out his own draft in longhand as he had for the first and
third Inaugurals. But at different times as thoughts came to him he
had dictated some paragraphs. For example, on January 6, he dictated
one page of material, which is headed "Some thoughts for inaugural
speech," containing a paragraph about something his old schoolmaster,
Dr. Peabody, had once said. This passage remained in the speech. A
week later, he dictated two pages of material entitled "Other thoughts
for inaugural speech." The President took all the drafts, including his
own dictation, and combined them into a speech that was shorter than
any of the three drafts.

The speech was essentially a plea for patience and faith. He quoted
his old schoolmaster's comment that "things in life will not always run
smoothly. . . . The great fact to remember is that the trend of civilization itself is forever upward. . . ." He recalled again that "our own
Constitution of 1787 was not a perfect instrument; it is not perfect yet.
But it provided a firm base. . . ." He said that we were determined in
1945 to build upon a similar firm base—striving always with patience
and faith for perfection, but knowing that it will not quickly come
to pass.

It was also a plea that the American people remember the lesson they
had learned through the years of war at such fearful cost—that "we
cannot live alone at peace, that our own well-being is dependent on
the well-being of other nations far away . . ." that "we have learned
to be citizens of the world, members of the human community"; and
that "as Emerson said . . . 'The only way to have a friend is to be one.'"

It was deeply moving to watch him standing there in the cold winter
air, without overcoat or hat, delivering these simple words. Oblivious
of the people in front of him or the people all over the world who were
listening to him, he seemed to me to be offering a prayer. It was a
prayer—on the eve of his departure for Yalta—that all the peoples of
the world, and their leaders, be endowed with the patience and faith
that could abolish war. When he came back from Yalta, I think he was
certain that his prayer had been answered.

Chapter XXVII

Yalta and After, 1945

On January 22, 1945, the President secretly left Washington for the Crimea. Shortly before he left, he asked me to take a trip to Europe. He had two purposes in mind. Allied troops had nearly reached the Rhine and were moving forward in France, Belgium, Holland, and Germany. To meet their needs, a constant flow of supplies had to be kept moving across France and Belgium. But the people of these countries, as well as Norway and Denmark, were suffering bitterly from lack of food, coal, transportation and other civilian supplies and services. The President realized, as did our Chiefs of Staff, that the lack of supplies for the civilians behind our lines created a great hazard for our troops. In addition to the military hazard, there was, of course, a humanitarian incentive for getting additional supplies into the liberated areas. Consequently, at the President's direction, I organized a small group to take with me—consisting of representatives of the State Department, the Foreign Economic Administration, and the Army—to make a thorough study of the civilian needs of western Europe and the possibility of supplying them.

The second purpose of my trip was to discuss with the appropriate British authorities the question of the procedure and timing of the trials of Nazi war criminals, some of whom had already been captured. At the President's direction I had called together a small group in Washington—representatives of the War Department, Navy Department, and the Department of Justice—to study the question. The President, the Prime Minister and Stalin had each on different occasions publicly proclaimed that the Nazi war criminals would be brought to quick justice and punishment. The President had told me that he did not want to see the record of the First World War repeated, where it had taken years after the end of hostilities before anyone was ever brought to trial. The trials had then bogged down in questions of procedure. The result was that practically every war criminal of the First World War—and there were plenty—got off free. "This time," he said, "let's get the trials started quickly and have the procedures all worked out in advance. Make the punishment of the guilty swift."

He realized that there would have to be international action, and said that he wanted me while over there to take the question up with the British first; we would take it up later with the French and the Russians.

The President had already issued orders that the Army, as it advanced, should arrest war criminals whenever they were found and gather whatever evidence it could. An International War Crimes Commission had been operating in London for some time, and had prepared a long list of Nazis who were suspected of criminal activities. The list was growing daily. I gave the President, to read on his way to Yalta, a memorandum on "Punishment of War Criminals" which came out of the conferences I had been having in Washington.

Our supply mission (known as the Rosenman mission) arrived by plane in London on February 10. As soon as I arrived at my hotel I telephoned our Ambassador, John G. Winant, an old friend of mine from the days of the first Social Security Board. He greeted me cordially, but told me not to unpack my things; that I was to continue journeying eastward.

"I can't talk with you about it over the phone," he said; "better come around to the Embassy as soon as you can."

I immediately went around the corner to the Ambassador's small flat which he occupied in a building adjoining the American Embassy.

"The President wants you to join him," he said, "and go back with him to Washington on the *Quincy* to help prepare his report to the Congress on the results of the Yalta Conference. I guess I had better arrange to get you a plane so that you can leave right away."

He then handed me a message from the President reading as follows (paraphrased):

February 9, 1945

Personal and Top Secret.

The President wants you to meet him about February fifteenth in the Mediterranean area. You are to proceed to Naples and there communicate with the Commander of the United States Eighth Fleet, Admiral Hewitt. He will arrange for your transportation to meet the President. The President wishes you to assist in preparation of speech to be delivered on his return. As soon as the President gets home, you may return to Europe on your mission. Communicate through Map Room, White House.

WILSON BROWN (*Naval Aide to the President*)

"What about the members of my mission?" I asked.

"I guess you will have to leave them here," said Winant, "and I will see that they get all possible preliminary information. For example, they can survey the amount of civilian supplies now in the British Isles which could be transferred, without hardship to the British, over to the liberated areas of western Europe. They can also make some preliminary studies with the representatives of those liberated countries who are now in London. At any rate, I think you'd better get going pretty quickly."

I got going the next day. The Army Transport Command furnished a C-47 for me at the Ambassador's request. I flew to Marseilles; from Marseilles over to Naples. It was my birthday. As we flew over Corsica, within easy range of enemy fighter planes on the mainland, I nervously engaged my two young pilots in conversation. There were just the three of us in the plane. One of them told me that this day was his wedding anniversary. I had some chocolate bars in my bag. He had some soft drinks in the plane. Between us we broke out a joint birthday–wedding anniversary feast. It was fun, but I was glad when the airfield at Naples came into view.

As soon as I landed, I reported to Admiral Hewitt. He suggested that the most convenient way for me to join the President would be to leave with him on his flagship *Memphis*, which was about to proceed to Algiers, there to wait for the President.

By this time the joint communiqué had come out of Yalta; and I was therefore fully informed on what had been done, so far as the facts had been made public. However, as I was to learn after I boarded the *Quincy*, there were some agreements reached at Yalta that were not to be made public until much later.

I was hoping that if I could prepare a good first draft, and if the President would go right to work on it, we would be able to finish the speech by the time the *Quincy* reached Gibraltar on its homeward voyage. Then I could disembark at Gibraltar and rejoin my mission in London. I remembered many speeches done in less time in the past, and knew that if the President were willing this one could be finished in a couple of days. In order to save time, I started work on it as soon as I reached Naples. What I wrote in this first draft was based on the communiqué and on what I had learned from the President, while he was still in Washington, of the purpose and background of the Yalta Conference. By the time Admiral Hewitt and I arrived in Algiers aboard his flagship, I had a complete draft ready. It was typed for me by Admiral Hewitt's aide on stationery of the United States Navy.

As we drove from the pier to the navy officers' villa in Algiers, where the Admiral had invited me to stay until the arrival of the President, we passed the Hotel Aletti. There, on the lawn, I saw three familiar American figures waving to me in great excitement. They were Merriman Smith, Douglas Cornell, and Robert G. Nixon, White House correspondents for the UP, AP, and INS. They had been summoned from Washington by the President to meet him and to accompany him home on the *Quincy*. They had been directed from place to place in North Africa until they were finally ensconced in the Hotel Aletti and told to wait. There they had waited for several days, but they still did not know where the President was or where they were to meet him. As Mr. Smith has said in his book, *Thank You, Mr. President,* for all they knew the President may have already steamed by the Algiers breakwater, leaving them behind. When they saw me, however, they were quite elated, for they knew they would soon be joining the President.

On Sunday, February 18, the *Quincy* steamed into Algiers; and, to quote the official log of the voyage for that day, at 10:30 A.M., "The Honorable Samuel I. Rosenman came aboard and joined the President's party for the return trip to the United States." The newspaper correspondents also came aboard, as did several others. Among them was Ambassador Jefferson Caffery (Ambassador to France), who informed the President that General de Gaulle, who had been invited to confer with the President at Algiers, had declined the invitation out of pique at not having been invited to Yalta. This was quite a disappointment to the President, for he had gone out of his way in the last State of the Union Message to include France in his plans for the control of Germany and for a major role in the United Nations. He had also just succeeded at Yalta in having France invited to take a control zone in Germany and to join with the Big Three powers in sponsoring the San Francisco Conference. He took it philosophically, as part of the De Gaulle enigma; in typical fashion he dismissed it for the present as something that would have to be taken care of later and separately.

As soon as I got aboard, I went to the President's cabin to say hello. It was approximately one month since I had seen him last; I was disheartened by his physical appearance. I had never seen him look so tired. He had lost a great deal more weight; he was listless and apparently uninterested in conversation—he was all burnt out. He slowly and silently went through the process of signing some bills and some correspondence to be dispatched home by air.

After I greeted him and his daughter Anna, who had come with him on the trip, Admiral Leahy said that we ought to have a hurried conference with Harry Hopkins, Charles Bohlen and Steve Early, all of whom were going to leave the vessel at Algiers. They each wanted to give me some background information and "fill-in" to help me prepare a draft of the President's report. I was shocked to learn that Pa Watson had suffered a stroke a few days previously and was lying in a coma in one of the cabins. Harry, too, had become quite sick and was being taken to Marrakech by Bohlen for a few days' rest. All in all, it was a sorry ship.

Bohlen, who had possession of all of the signed agreements and initialed memoranda of Yalta, turned them over to me during the course of a two-hour conference which we held in Hopkins' cabin. We went over the notes and memoranda of all that had taken place not only among the Big Three at Yalta but among the three Foreign Ministers as well. Bohlen had acted as our Russian interpreter at all the conferences at Yalta. He had dictated a six-page memorandum for me, which was transcribed and turned over to me, after he left the ship.

At four o'clock in the afternoon the *Quincy* got under way from Algiers. There was a full twenty-four hours before we reached Gibraltar. I still figured hopefully that I could rewrite my draft on the basis of the latest information I had received, go over it with the President, leave it with him, and then get off the ship at Gibraltar and return to London. I soon saw that that was going to be impossible, and after the first few hours I gave up the idea and resigned myself to the long trip home.

The hard voyage to Yalta and the shattering responsibilities of the conference seemed to have sapped a substantial part of the President's remaining reserves of strength. All the buoyancy of the campaign, all the excitement of arranging and preparing for the conference, had disappeared; in their place was gray fatigue—sheer exhaustion. The wild tales being circulated today by some of the more fanatical Roosevelt-haters—the isolationists and the reactionaries—that Roosevelt was mentally unfit at Yalta are, of course, just so much nonsense. But the conference did leave him physically and nervously spent, and it took the whole trip home to refresh him. Usually, after the most brain-racking ordeal his resilient body and mind would freshen up in a few days. This time it took a long while. Yalta was, in a sense, the climactic project of his life—to arrange for a permanent peace. He knew what it would mean if he succeeded—and he knew also what it would mean if he should fail.

I could not get the President to go to work on the speech at all that day or the next day. In fact, though the speech was scheduled to be delivered immediately upon his return, almost a week went by before I could get him to give any serious attention to it. He would stay in bed most of the morning, reading the books he had brought with him or looking over official reports. After lunch, which we usually took with him in his cabin, he would go above to sit with his daughter on the top deck in the sun, quietly reading or just smoking and staring at the horizon. Sometimes Admiral Leahy and I went above to join him. Most frequently we left him alone with his book—and his thoughts.

When the sun began to sink, the President would retire to his cabin for a nap before dinner. Dinner was served in his cabin. It was preceded by the usual cocktail ceremony during which he made the cocktails, and we all partook generously of the rare caviar that Stalin had given him. While he was comparatively gay and animated during this period and during dinner, I could not get him to work on the speech after dinner, as we used to do so frequently in Washington. Instead, we would all go into Admiral Leahy's cabin to see a moving picture. I prepared some revised drafts of the speech, based upon the documents and memoranda which I had by now had time thoroughly to read, and upon more detailed oral reports of the conference which I got from Admiral Leahy.

I have recently re-examined the official log of this journey home. On the day we left Algiers we went to movies in the flag cabin to see *Phantom Lady*. The next day, February 19, the President held a brief informal press conference in his cabin with the three White House correspondents. That night we attended movies, at which *Janie* was shown.

On February 20, the President was further deeply depressed by the death of General Watson from a cerebral hemorrhage. Pa's death increased the President's reluctance to go to work. The two had become intimate friends. The President was very fond of General Watson, whose devotion and loyalty to the President were well known all over Washington. The General had insisted, against medical advice, on accompanying the President on this trip.

Watson's rugged, soldierly figure and warm personality were known to everyone who visited the White House offices, and he was loved by all those who worked with the President. He was discerning and intelligent in handling Presidential appointments. His buoyant sense of humor frequently relieved tense and embarrassing situations, and was always a source of great comfort and amusement to the President. Many people in Washington considered him merely a jovial companion to the President. He was much more. Like Missy, he had an uncanny instinct for distinguishing between the fake and the genuine in human beings and human conduct. He knew which visitor to the President was on a selfish mission, and which one was interested in the welfare of the United States or of the President. He served as eyes and ears for Roosevelt in many places in Washington that Roosevelt could not himself cover. While he knew nothing—and cared less—about the details of legislation, he knew what the social policy and objectives of the President were. Whether he agreed with them or not, he was ready to do anything to help him achieve them. His was the kind of loyalty that is met with very seldom in human affairs, and practically never in political life. He was a blunt soldier; he never hesitated to tell people what he thought of them. He always expressed his frank opinion to the President without reserve. However, once Roosevelt made a decision, there was as little likelihood of Pa Watson's disputing it or holding back any punches in executing it as there was of his debating the wisdom of the Ten Commandments. His passing left a deep void in the President's life. The President had seen many of his friends die; but in his weakened and tired condition, the death of Watson seemed to have a more depressing effect upon him than the death of any of the others. Although he said very little about Pa at lunch or dinner that day or later, it was plain to all of us how deeply affected he was.

Day after day as the *Quincy* steamed westward, the same routine was followed. The President rested continuously through the day, and went to the movies at night. Since I could not get him to work on the speech, I continued, with Admiral Leahy's and Anna's assistance, to turn out additional drafts, polishing and changing where we thought it advisable.

On February 23, the President again called the three press correspondents into his cabin. Much of the discussion concerned the future of the people of the Pacific, who for generations had been governed by European powers. The President showed his eagerness to apply the principles of the Atlantic Charter to all the colonial peoples in that area as soon as they were ready for self-government, just as we had done in the Philippines. The following excerpt from that press conference shows the differences of opinion between him and the Prime Minister in this field:

QUESTION: Is that Churchill's idea on all territory out there, he wants them all back just the way they were?

THE PRESIDENT: Yes, he is mid-Victorian on all things like that.

QUESTION: You would think some of that would be knocked out of him by now.

THE PRESIDENT: I read something Queen Wilhelmina said about the Dutch East Indies. She's got a very interesting point of view. I think it was a public statement concerning the plans about her islands; they differ so from the British plans. The Javanese are not quite ready for self-government, but very nearly. Java, with a little help by other nations, can probably be ready for independence in a few years. The Javanese are good people—pretty civilized country. The Dutch marry the Javanese, and the Javanese are permitted to join the clubs. The British would not permit the Malayans to join their clubs.

The Queen's idea for some of the Dutch possessions is eventually to give them their independence. When Java is ready for independence, give her help and make her a member of a federation. Sumatra the same.

I asked her "What about Borneo?" She said, "We don't talk about that very much. They are still head-hunters. It might be one hundred years before we could educate and civilize the Borneo head-hunter. . . ."

QUESTION: This idea of Churchill's seems inconsistent with the policy of self-determination?

THE PRESIDENT: Yes, that is true.

QUESTION: He seems to undercut the Atlantic Charter. He made a statement the other day that it was not a rule, just a guide.

THE PRESIDENT: The Atlantic Charter is a beautiful idea. When it was drawn up, the situation was that England was about to lose the war. They needed hope, and it gave it to them. We have improved the military situation since then at every chance, so that really you might say we have a much better chance of winning the war now than ever before. . . .

QUESTION: Do you remember the speech the Prime Minister made about the fact that he was not made the Prime Minister of Great Britain to see the empire fall apart?

THE PRESIDENT: Dear old Winston will never learn on that point. He has made his specialty on that point. This is, of course, off the record.

Occasionally the President would interrupt his reading or thinking to talk to me about what had happened at Yalta. But according to the official log and my own recollection, it was not until February 26 that he actually began to work on the speech. He worked that afternoon, and, instead of going to the movies after dinner with the rest of the party, we continued to work on it that evening.

He went over the minutes of the various meetings in order to refresh his recollection. The record of those meetings has now become public and has been fully discussed in books by Byrnes, Stettinius, and Sherwood; I shall not attempt repetition here.

The President told me that his role at the conference frequently had been that of a mediator between Churchill and Stalin; that many times the differences between them had become very wide, and the two men had turned to him expecting him to suggest a compromise. The record shows that these expectations were sometimes fulfilled; at other times settlement was simply postponed.

The President made it clear, not only when we were working alone on the speech, but in luncheon and dinner conversation, that he was certain that the Yalta Conference had paved the way for the kind of world that he had been dreaming, planning, and talking about. He felt that he understood Stalin and that Stalin understood him. He believed that Stalin had a sincere desire to build constructively on the foundations that had been laid at Yalta; that Stalin was interested in maintaining peace in the world so that the Soviets could make the industrial and social changes he thought necessary. The only reservation Roosevelt had was whether or not the others back in the Kremlin would sincerely go along with what Stalin had signed at Yalta. He did not doubt that on the surface they would subscribe to the Yalta agreements; he did have doubt whether, when the chips were down, Stalin would be able to carry out and deliver what he had agreed to. He was also worried about what would happen if Stalin should die or be stripped of his power. But there was no doubt in his mind that if the Soviet leaders would back Stalin, a new era in world peace was at hand.

Roosevelt was prone to jealousy of competitors in his field. He liked flattery, especially as he grew older, and seemed frequently to be jealous of compliments paid to others for political sagacity, eloquence, statesmanship or accomplishments in public life. He liked so much to excel that he took almost as much pleasure in being told he was a better poker player than someone else as he did in being told that Willkie was not as good an orator as he was, or that he, Roosevelt, was a better politician than Farley. Churchill seemed to be an exception to this. It may be because they never really competed with each other, but always seemed to be collaborating. It was also because of his real, deep affection and admiration for Churchill as Prime Minister, as war leader, as a courageous and magnetic human being.

So it was with the kindliest of feelings that he mentioned to me on several occasions that "dear old Winston" was quite loquacious in these conferences; that he liked to make long speeches—sometimes getting into irrelevancies; that he quite obviously irritated Stalin by these long discourses; and that at times he, Roosevelt, had to get Churchill back to the subject at hand. Now that victory seemed pretty close and the time was drawing near for carrying out some of the tough principles contained in the Atlantic Charter, the President was beginning to feel that the traditions of British imperialism were playing too heavy a part in Churchill's thinking. In this area the President knew that he and Churchill were going to have deep-seated differences of opinion.

The President and I finished the second and third drafts of the speech on the cruiser; but we began work on it none too soon, for we arrived the next day at Hampton Roads and entrained at once for Washington. Almost immediately we went to Arlington for the funeral services for General Watson.

Afterward, the President worked on later drafts of the speech, and asked his son-in-law John Boettiger to work with us in the preparation of the fourth and fifth drafts. Sherwood was out of the country and Harry was still too sick to participate. The fifth draft was put into a reading copy, but the President made so many corrections in the reading copy that it was retyped as a sixth draft.

I went up to the Capitol to hear him deliver his report to the Congress on March 1. I was dismayed at the halting, ineffective manner of delivery. He ad-libbed a great deal—as frequently as I had ever heard him. Some of his extemporaneous remarks were wholly irrelevant, and some of them almost bordered on the ridiculous—as, for example, his statement:

For instance, on the problem of Arabia, I learned more about that whole problem—the Moslem problem, the Jewish problem—by talking with Ibn Saud for five minutes, than I could have learned in the exchange of two or three dozen letters.

This was a thought that must have popped into his head at just that moment, for I never heard him say anything like that on the way home from Algiers.

It was quite obvious that the great fighting eloquence and oratory that had distinguished him in his campaign only four months before were lacking. The crushing effect of twelve years of the Presidency was beginning to be more and more evident. For the first time, in an ad-lib, he admitted it in public:

I hope that you will pardon me for this unusual posture of sitting down during the presentation of what I want to say, but I know that you will realize that it makes it a lot easier for me not to have to carry about ten pounds of steel around on the bottom of my legs; and also because of the fact that I have just completed a fourteen-thousand-mile trip.

The keynote of the speech was in his statement near the very beginning: "I come from the Crimea Conference with a firm belief that we have made a good start on the road to a world of peace." He believed that—fully.

He then proceeded to discuss the "two main purposes in this Crimea Conference." The first was "to bring defeat to Germany with the greatest possible speed and the smallest possible loss of Allied men." The second purpose "was to continue to build the foundation for an international accord that would bring order and security after the chaos of the war, that would give some assurance of lasting peace among the nations of the world."

The military part of the conference resulted in "a closer tactical liaison" between the American and British on one hand and the Russians on the other. He repeated that the terms of surrender were still "unconditional surrender." He again explained that "unconditional surrender does not mean the destruction or enslavement of the German people." The meeting at Yalta made clear "just what unconditional surrender does mean for Germany": temporary control and occupation by the four great powers, each with a separate zone; the end of Nazism and of the Nazi party; the end of militarism in Germany; speedy and severe punishment for the Nazi war criminals; complete disarmament of

Germany; the destruction of its capacity to produce armaments; the dispersal of its armed forces; the permanent dismemberment of the German general staff; and reparations by Germany in plants, machinery, rolling stock, and raw materials.

He described the kind of destructive "reckless senseless fury" that comes out of German militarism, which he saw during his stay at Yalta and Sevastopol. "I know that there is not room enough on earth for both German militarism and Christian decency."

Taking up the second purpose of the Yalta Conference—building world peace—the President spoke of the agreement reached on the United Nations Organization and voting procedure, and of the conference of all the United Nations scheduled to meet in San Francisco on April 25, 1945.

This time we are not making the mistake of waiting until the end of the war to set up the machinery of peace. This time, as we fight together to win the war finally, we work together to keep it from happening again.

In some detail he discussed the various problems which had been taken up at Yalta: the occupation zones in Germany, the problem of the liberated areas, Poland and Yugoslavia, France.

He pointed out that many of the decisions reached at Yalta were the result of compromise, of give-and-take; and he warned that future decisions also were going to be made jointly and "therefore they will often be a result of give-and-take and compromise. The United States will not always have its way one hundred per cent—nor will Russia or Great Britain. We shall not always have ideal answers—solutions to complicated international problems, even though we are determined continuously to strive toward that ideal."

On the way home the President had told me that he wanted to use this speech to "put in a plug" for Senate ratification of the charter which was to come out of the San Francisco Conference. This is the way it appeared in the speech:

This is our chance to see to it that the sons and the grandsons of these gallant fighting men do not have to do it all over again in a few years.

The conference in the Crimea was a turning point—I hope in our history and therefore in the history of the world. There will soon be presented to the Senate of the United States and to the American people a great decision that will determine the fate of the United States—and of the world—for generations to come.

There can be no middle ground here. We shall have to take the responsibility for world collaboration, or we shall have to bear the responsibility for another world conflict.

In some anti-Roosevelt quarters today the Yalta Conference has become a symbol of sinister politics, secret sellouts, appeasement, and abject subservience to the Soviet Union. Ardent Roosevelt-haters, perpetual isolationists, and many well-meaning people who simply have been misled have sought to draw a picture of President Roosevelt at Yalta as too sick and weary adequately to protect the interests of the United States. Neither the symbol nor the picture is warranted by the facts.[1]

Many issues and problems, other than military ones, confronted the conferees and were discussed: the formal organization and "voting formula" in the United Nations, Poland's boundaries and her form of government, French participation in the government of postwar Germany, reparations from Germany, the treatment to be accorded liberated areas, the form of government for Yugoslavia, the Soviet Union's claims concerning the Dardanelles, foreign access to the oil of Iran, territorial trusteeships, and the Soviet Union's claims with respect to Sakhalin, the Kurile Islands, Dairen, Port Arthur and other territories in the Far East which she had lost to Japan forty years before.

And underlying all these problems was one all-important military question: the time of the Soviet Union's entry into the war against Japan and the conditions upon which she would participate.

I was not at the Yalta Conference. However, I knew something of what Roosevelt hoped to achieve there; and I know what he felt he had achieved.

About some of the questions considered there, no decision was reached. They were left substantially where they were found. For example, the matter of the Soviet claims concerning the Dardanelles was referred to a future meeting of the Foreign Secretaries. There was

---

[1] For an excellent description of the Yalta Conference, see *Roosevelt and the Russians; The Yalta Conference*, by former Secretary of State Edward R. Stettinius, Jr.; also Robert E. Sherwood's *Roosevelt and Hopkins*, Chapter 33. Other descriptions which help to bring the events and agreements at Yalta into proper perspective are James F. Byrnes' account in *Speaking Frankly*; Sumner Welles' statement in *Where Are We Heading?*; and the statement of W. Averell Harriman ". . . regarding our wartime relations with the Soviet Union, particularly as they concern the agreements reached at Yalta" to the Senate Committees on Armed Services and Foreign Relations, released August 17, 1951.

flat disagreement over the question of foreign access to the oil of Iran; that was left open. The discussion concerning territorial·trusteeships was inconclusive; but it was agreed that provision for them would be made in the United Nations Charter.

On reparations, Churchill and Roosevelt disagreed in many respects with Stalin. In a rather typical Rooseveltian device for avoiding a deadlock—which at Yalta might have been dangerous not only to world peace but to the winning of the war—the issue was postponed by referring it to a British-American-Soviet commission "to consider the question of the extent and methods of compensating damage caused by Germany to the Allied countries." Although the conversation at Yalta plainly involved no definite commitment that the Soviet would receive any fixed sum, and indeed clearly excluded any such commitment, the Soviet has always stubbornly insisted upon taking the contrary point of view.

On other problems, the conferees were able to reach definite agreements. They reached them, as the President told the Congress, by give-and-take compromises. And the record shows that greater concessions to the United States and Great Britain were made by the Soviet Union than were made to the Soviet by the other two powers.

Regarding the formal organization of the United Nations, it was agreed (as announced in the communiqué) that a conference would be held at San Francisco on April 25, 1945—a date that Churchill had initially opposed as too early. Russia agreed to follow the American formula for selecting the countries to be invited to attend the San Francisco Conference, viz., all the Allied nations that had declared war on the Axis by March 1, 1945. This extended date allowed a number of Latin-American nations to come in and participate. This was a definite concession on the part of the Soviet Union.

Another concession by the Soviet was the agreement on the voting procedure in the Security Council of the United Nations. The discussions on this point concerned chiefly the extent of the permissible use of the veto by any one of the major powers. The compromise reached at Yalta was substantially the proposal made by the United States. This same proposal had been submitted to Stalin in December, 1944, when he had flatly rejected it. At Yalta he finally agreed. It provided that procedural questions should be determined by a vote of any seven of the eleven members of the Council, but that substantive questions would require a vote of seven members including the affirmative votes of all the five great powers (United States, Britain, Russia, France, and China). It was further agreed that any Security Council member that was itself a party to a dispute should not be permitted to vote unless the matter involved enforcement action or sanctions.

This was the formula finally adopted at San Francisco. After extended consideration and discussion at San Francisco, and after conversations between Stalin and Hopkins in Moscow (where Hopkins had been sent by President Truman in May, 1945, to try to iron out differences which had arisen with the Soviet Union), it was also agreed that the question whether a certain topic or complaint could be discussed would be considered a procedural question.

There was another aspect of United Nations procedure concerning which agreement was reached. It involved giving two additional votes in the General Assembly to the Soviet by treating the Ukraine and Byelorussia as separate entities, and giving each of them one vote. The Soviet asked for this at Yalta, and Great Britain supported her. The President had been informed in advance that Great Britain was going to take this position because of the problem of India, which at that time was not independent and had no separate Foreign Office.

Roosevelt finally agreed at Yalta that if the Soviet would submit her demand for decision by the nations gathered at San Francisco, the United States would also support the Soviet position. Stalin agreed in return to support two additional votes for the United States if we should decide to ask for them at San Francisco. Roosevelt insisted upon this reciprocity, remembering the debates about the League of Nations in 1919 and 1920 and the strong popular reaction against any charter that gave the United States fewer votes than any other country. The United States, however, never made the request at San Francisco. This agreement concerning the Soviet's additional votes in the United Nations Assembly was not announced in the communiqué; it did not become public until the information "leaked" on March 29, 1945.

The three votes of the Soviet in the Assembly have never played any part in United Nations decisions or made any difference one way or the other. Where the United Nations has been ineffective, it has been owing to Soviet intransigence and her veto power in the Security Council—not to her three Assembly votes. They have served chiefly to help Soviet propaganda and to give a fictitious cloak of independence to the Soviet republics, which, in fact and in law, have no independence at all.

Another very important area of agreement at Yalta concerned the postwar treatment of liberated European countries. The agreement is eloquently expressed in the communiqué.

The Declaration on Liberated Europe was prepared in the United States State Department and submitted at Yalta as an American proposal. It was modified only slightly at Yalta—and not at Soviet suggestion. In fact, making another concession, Stalin withdrew two amendments proposed by Molotov to which the President objected. The Declaration is a direct answer to charges made by Roosevelt-haters that Roosevelt agreed at Yalta directly or indirectly to some arrangement for spheres of influence that would give the Soviet Union control in eastern Europe. The words and spirit of the Declaration are exactly to the contrary—against the formation of any exclusive spheres. The Declaration states that the three great powers will jointly assist the people in the liberated and Axis-satellite countries "to create democratic institutions of their own choice" with the right—which is expressly stated to be "a principle of the Atlantic Charter"—"to choose the form of government under which they will live." And they agreed jointly to assist in holding the earliest possible free elections for that purpose. No language is less susceptible of any implication of spheres of influence.

Present-day failure in this area is not due to anything that happened at Yalta. The principles and formula reached there were unassailable. What has happened is a result of the Soviet's refusal to carry out the agreement it made; the present Soviet position is a square repudiation of Yalta. And the Soviet was emboldened to take this stand by the speed with which our armed strength was scuttled as soon as victory had been won—a speed which American mothers and fathers loudly demanded of their Congress and of their Executive.

Stalin made other concessions at Yalta.

The agreement to grant an occupation zone to France, for example, represented a concession by the Soviet Union. And, although at the start of the Yalta Conference the Soviet vigorously opposed the inclusion of France on the German control commission, she later yielded to American and British pressure on this point as well.

Then there was the agreement on the reorganization of the government of Poland as suggested by the Americans and British. Although the Soviet initially argued for a mere enlargement of the Polish Provisional Government, both the President and Prime Minister Churchill insisted on a genuine reorganization of the Provisional (Lublin) Government so as to include democratic leaders from outside Poland. As stated in the communiqué, Stalin finally agreed at Yalta to go along with full reorganization. The Red Army at the time was occupying practically all of Poland; and although the Soviet almost immediately repudiated its agreement on Poland, it was at the time a major concession in an area where she was in complete *de facto* control.

She conceded another point when she agreed to leave the Polish western boundary to be settled at the peace conference. The President and Prime Minister Churchill refused to accept the Soviet request that the Neisse River be made the western bounary of Poland.

Finally, at the request of President Roosevelt, Russia agreed to coordinate her military activities with those of the western Allies. For the first time, she made a frank statement of her future offensive plans, and the United States Army Air Forces were given Soviet air bases near Budapest. The record therefore is very clear, and very full, on the major concessions which Stalin agreed to at Yalta.

The part of the Yalta Conference that has given rise to most criticism concerned Soviet participation in the war against Japan and her claims to certain territory and concessions in the Far East. These items were embodied in a separate agreement—secret. The matter was treated more as a military than a diplomatic one, and the issues were not discussed at the plenary sessions. In substance, it was agreed that the Soviet would join the Allies in the war against Japan "two or three months after Germany has surrendered and the war in Europe has terminated"; in return, "the former rights of Russia violated by . . . Japan in 1904 shall be restored." This "restoration" was to include the return of the southern half of Sakhalin Island, the return of the use of Port Arthur as a naval base, internationalizing the commercial port of Dairen, and the joint control with China of the Manchurian Railroad and Chinese-Eastern Railroad. In addition, the Soviet Union was to get the Kurile Islands.

The agreements described in the preceding paragraph were not included in the public communiqué, for obviously it could not be revealed in advance that Russia had agreed to enter the war against Japan or when she would do so. Nor could China be apprised of these decisions in advance, because by long experience it had become common knowledge how easily and quickly news leaked out of Chungking. Those who complain that these agreements were secret ignore the facts of the military situation.

At Teheran, more than a year before Yalta, the Soviet had already indicated her intention to come into the Japanese war, but had not disclosed when she would or what she wanted in return. The great military concern now was the timing of her entry. The President's top military advisers at Yalta were eager for Russia to come in as soon as possible. The *Forrestal Diaries* indicate that General MacArthur—who was not at Yalta—also wanted to commit the Russians to an active campaign against the Japanese in Manchuria in order to pin down a large part of the Japanese Army. Though victory seemed fairly certain in Europe, it still appeared to be far away in the Pacific—and it was going to be bloody and costly. The operations at Iwo Jima and Okinawa were yet to get under way. An invasion of Japan was being planned for November, 1945. Our manpower resources were beginning to feel the pinch. The potential—almost certain—loss of American lives weighed heavily on Roosevelt's mind. Our military experts anticipated the probability of one million casualties in the invasion and mopping up of Japan;[2] and the Japanese war was generally expected to be over no earlier than the end of 1946—almost two years after Yalta. Because of Russia's ambitions in the area, there is little doubt that she would have moved in—no matter what was done or not done at Yalta—when she found it easiest and most profitable to do so. The object was to get the Soviet committed to join in time to shorten the war and avoid those million American casualties.

Above all, neither the President nor anybody else at Yalta, in February, 1945, or elsewhere, knew that the atomic bomb project was going to be successful. It was not until three months after Roosevelt's death that our atomic experiments ended successfully in the desert of New Mexico.

There are those who now argue that the Japanese were beaten and ready to surrender before the atomic bomb was dropped on Hiroshima on August 6, 1945. Indeed on July 1, 1946, the United States Strategic Bombing Survey, conducted long after Japan surrendered, concluded that "certainly prior to December 31, 1945, and in all probability prior to November 1, 1945, Japan would have surrendered even if the atomic

[2] Stimson and Bundy, *On Active Service*, p. 619.

bombs had not been dropped, even if Russia had not entered the war, and even if no invasion had been planned or contemplated."

Assuming that this hindsight conclusion is correct, no evidence exists that the Japanese had been so beaten that they were ready to surrender at the time of Yalta—nine months earlier. Indeed the report of the Strategic Bombing Survey is itself to the contrary. And, as clearly stated by Secretary of War Stimson[3] there was "no indication of any weakening in the Japanese determination to fight" even as late as July, 1945, when the plans for the land invasion of Japan were completed and approved. He adds that "it was emphatically *not* the fact that Japan had decided on surrender before August 6, 1945," and that no intelligence report "was made" or "could have been made" that any such decision had been reached in Japan.

The vast damage in Japan inflicted by our strategic bombing came months after Yalta, and particularly after our occupation of Okinawa in June, 1945. Far from advising the President at Yalta that Japan was already beaten, the Joint Chiefs of Staff in an official memorandum made the flat statement to Roosevelt on January 23, 1945, that they were "working towards U.S.S.R. entry into the war against Japan" on the basic principle that "Russia's entry at as early a date as possible consistent with her ability to engage in offensive operations is necessary to provide maximum assistance to our Pacific operations. . . ."

That was the military picture before Roosevelt at Yalta.

In these circumstances, whatever concessions were made by President Roosevelt at Yalta to get the Soviet into the Japanese war quickly must be balanced against the overriding war necessity as our military leaders saw it. And if, as anticipated at Yalta, we had invaded Japan and the Soviet Union had joined us, she undoubtedly would have occupied all the territory given her at Yalta—and probably would have claimed much more. Even without the invasion, there was not a single territorial concession made at Yalta, with the possible exception of the Kurile Islands, that the Soviet could not have moved in and taken at any time with the greatest of ease—without the consent of the United States, Great Britain or China.

President Roosevelt may be criticized for not being psychic enough to foretell that the Japanese war was going to end in six months—in spite of all military estimates to the contrary—but he cannot fairly be

[3] *Ibid.*, pp. 618, 629.

criticized for surrender or appeasement, for inept bargaining, or for lack of good sense or good faith. The Far Eastern agreement reached at Yalta cannot be considered exclusively as an item of foreign policy. It was essentially a military measure, executed in time of war emergency, and the *quid pro quo* was American lives.

Now that we know how soon after Yalta the atomic bomb was developed, now that we know how deadly our strategic bombing was to become on Japanese cities, war plants, and morale, now that we know how much Japanese shipping we had destroyed, it is easy to criticize this *quid pro quo* military arrangement. But what American mother or father whose boy was in uniform (or about to be) in 1945 would have criticized it then?

The fact is that the Yalta Conference produced the United Nations Organization, committed the Soviet firmly to the war in the Pacific at at early date, and agreed to apply sound principles to the solution of many of the problems facing the Allies after the war.

Had the Soviet carried out the letter and spirit of the Yalta agreements, that conference would have been the greatest step in history toward a lasting world peace.

In preparing his speech to the Congress, the President made one of his few major mistakes in public relations. He decided to keep secret one of the Yalta agreements, although it had nothing to do with military security. It was the agreement about three votes for the Soviet and the United States in the Assembly. His decision not to disclose it in his speech was the kind of mistake he had never made before, and I have never been able to understand the reason for it in this case. The whole matter was bound to come out shortly in San Francisco when the Soviet would make her demand. Besides, anyone with any experience in Washington should have anticipated that the matter would soon leak out anyway, even before the meeting at San Francisco. But the President insisted that it should not be mentioned in the speech.

The matter did soon leak, prior to the San Francisco Conference; and Roosevelt was justifiably attacked for trying to keep the arrangement secret. Had he taken the American people into his confidence he could have explained how unimportant a concession this was; but, having kept it from them, he never was able adequately to justify his action.

Shortly after the President's report it became evident that the frank and forthright spirit of co-operation that had prevailed at Yalta was breaking down. During the two months he lived after Yalta, the

President began to get glimmerings of the dangerous new attitude of the Soviet Union. To several people he privately voiced his growing reservations and doubts about the good faith of the Soviet rulers and their willingness to live up to their agreements.

On March 27, he expressed to Churchill his "anxiety and concern" over "the development of the Soviet attitude." The Soviet Union was showing that she did not intend to respect either the spirit or the letter of her agreement regarding Poland. At Yalta, a commission representing the three powers had been set up to consult with Polish leaders in and out of Poland, and to carry on the reorganization agreed upon and announced in the communiqué. The Soviet member of the commission continued to insist, as Stalin had unsuccessfully insisted at Yalta, that the new Polish Government should merely be an enlarged edition of the Provisional Government; furthermore, he seemed determined to reject the suggestion that any but Communists and their sympathizers should constitute the new Polish Government.

Disturbed over this turn of events, Roosevelt on April 1, 1945, cabled Stalin that he was disappointed in "the lack of progress made in the carrying out, which the world expects, of the political decisions which we reached at Yalta, particularly those relating to the Polish question." He warned Stalin sharply against the plan merely to enlarge rather than to reorganize completely the existing Polish Provisional Government. The President also said that "any such solution which would result in a thinly disguised continuation of the present government would be entirely unacceptable, and would cause our people to regard the Yalta agreement as a failure." Marshal Stalin replied on April 7, admitting that the Polish issue had reached an impasse, but he evaded the question by charging that the impasse was due to the British and American Ambassadors. Before a reply could be prepared, Roosevelt was dead.

A few days before his death, the President received a request from Churchill asking what he might say to the House of Commons on the Polish question. From Warm Springs, Georgia, on April 12, 1945—the day the President died—he sent the following message to Churchill: "I would minimize the general Soviet problem as much as possible, because these problems, in one form or another, seem to arise every day, and most of them straighten out as in the case of the Berne meeting. We must be firm, however, and our course thus far has been correct." There is no question from the correspondence that the "course" the President was referring to was not the general wartime policy toward the Soviet

Union but the firm, even tough, position that he and Churchill had taken with Stalin on Poland.

The President's reference to the "Berne meeting" in his April 12 message to Churchill concerned another irritating episode in Roosevelt's post-Yalta relations with Stalin. Here too the President had to take a firm stand. Stalin had charged that Allied and German officers, without consulting the Soviet Union, were meeting in Berne to arrange for the surrender of the German Army in Italy. The President had previously assured Stalin that no such negotiations were taking place. Now, in reply to Stalin's repeated charge, the President stated that he resented the "vile misrepresentations" of Stalin's informants, who apparently were trying to destroy friendly relations between the two countries. Stalin then replied in a more conciliatory tone.

What the President did at Yalta indicates an attitude of patient, tolerant effort to co-operate with the Soviet Union. That was clearly his attitude on February 12, 1945, when the Yalta communiqué was issued. That was also his attitude on March 1, when he made his report on Yalta to the Congress. The President lived too short a time after March 1 to give any clear official indication of his reaction toward the changing behavior of the Soviet Union. Certainly Roosevelt was not one to consider himself bound, no matter how the Soviet acted, to persist in his attitude of February 12. It is easy to estimate how he would have reacted to the kind of Russian treaty-breaking that occurred after his death—indeed his last few messages to Stalin indicate plainly what his attitude would have been.

He clearly was puzzled by what was happening. He was not yet ready to believe that Stalin had practiced pure deceit at Yalta. He was under the impression that Stalin had been meeting stiff resistance from the Politburo since his return from the conference, and that he was yielding to it. The gradual breaking down of the close co-operation that had developed at Yalta had a depressing effect on the President. I am sure it hastened his death.

On the morning following his speech to the Congress, I went into the President's bedroom for the usual staff conference; and when it was over, I told him I was going to leave that morning to return to London, where the members of my mission were still waiting for me. I asked him whether he had any further instructions.

The President shook hands with me and said: "The only further instructions I have for you, Sam, are these. It is very rainy and wet in

London the early part of March. Be sure to take your rubbers with you."

Those were the last words I heard the President speak.

My mission in Europe carried me from extended conferences with members of the War Cabinet in London to many conferences with the officers of SHAEF in Paris, to talks with many of the French ministers in Paris, on to Luxembourg, Belgium and Holland, and up to the front lines as far as Cologne in Germany.

After my visit to Cologne, I returned to London for further conferences with the British, and to prepare my report. I also wanted to carry on discussions with the Lord Chancellor and others in London who would be authorized to make arrangements for the trial of war criminals.

While I was there, the President, on April 5, held a press conference at Warm Springs. The leak about the three votes for Russia in the United Nations Assembly had already occurred and the reporters questioned him about it. In response, the President offered the following explanation of the three votes, but no explanation of why he had insisted that the arrangement be kept secret:

THE PRESIDENT: As a matter of fact, this plea for votes was done in a very quiet way.

Stalin said to me—and this is the essence of it—"You know there are two parts of Russia that have been completely devastated. Every building is gone, every farmhouse, and there are millions of people living in these territories—and it is very important from the point of view of humanity—and we thought, as a gesture, they ought to be given something as a result of this coming victory. They have had very little civilization. One is the Ukraine, and the other is White Russia. We all felt—not any of us coming from there in the government—we think it would be fitting to give them a vote in the Assembly. In these two sections, millions have been killed, and we think it would be very heartening—would help to build them up—if we could get them a vote in the Assembly."

He asked me what I thought.

I said to Stalin, "Are you going to make that request of the Assembly?"

He said, "I think we should."

I said, "I think it would be all right—I don't know how the Assembly will vote."

He said, "Would you favor it?"

I said, "Yes, largely on sentimental grounds. If I were on the delegation—which I am not—I would probably vote 'yes.'"

That has not come out in any paper.

He said, "That would be the Soviet Union, plus White Russia, plus the Ukraine."

Then I said, "By the way, if the Conference in San Francisco should give you three votes in the Assembly—if you get three votes—I do not know what would happen if I don't put in a plea for three votes in the States." And I said, "I would make the plea for three votes and insist on it."

It is not really of any great importance. It is an investigatory body only. I told Stettinius to forget it. I am not awfully keen for three votes in the Assembly. It is the little fellow who needs the vote in the Assembly. . . .

QUESTION: They don't decide anything, do they?

THE PRESIDENT: No.

Although I have recently discussed the matter with many people who might have known what the President had in mind, I am still in the dark about why he made the obvious mistake of trying to conceal this harmless and easily explainable arrangement.

Chapter XXVIII

The End of an Epoch

Before starting my journey on the Continent through the liberated areas, I had several conferences with the Prime Minister. He was afraid that the President was thinking of diverting to the Continent some of the food that was scheduled to be shipped to the British Isles. He pointed out that although the British people had enough to eat in the way of calories, they had been on a dull, monotonous diet for six years. In my trips about England I had learned how right he was. On my return to England, Churchill asked me to come down to Chequers overnight to discuss both civilian supplies and the trial and punishment of war criminals.

In my talks with other officials of Great Britain it was made clear that the British wanted to dispose of the six or seven top Nazi criminals —Hitler, Goering, Ribbentrop, Goebbels, Himmler, Streicher, and one or two others—without trial. They feared that an open trial would provide too loud a sounding board for Nazi propaganda.

Roosevelt was determined that a speedy but fair trial should be accorded all the war criminals. I told the British that, and gave them his reasons as he had given them to me:

"If those men are shot without any trial," he had said, "there'll soon be talk stimulated by Nazi adherents about whether they were really guilty of any crimes at all." He felt that instead of being recognized as criminals they might be ultimately mourned as martyrs. Tradition and legend would grow up about them, much as they now have about the memory of Napoleon. He was determined that the question of Hitler's guilt—and the guilt of his gangsters—must not be left open for future debate. The whole nauseating matter should be spread out on a permanent record under oath by witnesses and with all the written documents;

there should be in one place—easily accessible in the future—a full statement of their guilt. In short, there must never be any question anywhere by anybody about who was responsible for the war and for the uncivilized war crimes.

I passed these views on to the Lord Chancellor and to Anthony Eden and others of the British War Cabinet, telling them how strongly the President felt about it. But they were just as determined in their opposition to a trial—they wanted to take the top Nazi criminals out and shoot them without warning one morning and then announce to the world that they were dead. Apparently this difference of opinion was reported to Churchill.

I motored down to Chequers, arriving there in the late afternoon. I got a first-hand picture of the way in which the Prime Minister worked at home.

Perhaps a letter which I wrote home the next day while the visit was still fresh in my mind will best describe it:

Monday Apr. 9

Dear Dorothy,

. . . . Chequers is an old estate with a house started in 1430 and reconstructed and added to through the centuries. Some of the original walls are still there. Shades of temporary housing! It is forty miles, about, from London, in the most beautiful rural area you have ever seen. I assure you it bears no resemblance to the retreat in the Maryland mountains except, perhaps, in the paucity of bathrooms. . . .

I was asked for dinner last night and to spend the night. As per instructions, I arrived at 7:45. The guests were there in country attire except the P.M., who was, I suppose, sleeping in preparation for the evening. Guests were Mr. Fraser, the P.M. of New Zealand; Major Churchill, the P.M.'s brother; Lord Cherwell, the P.M.'s economist and statistician; Mrs. Sarah Oliver, the P.M.'s daughter; and a few other men.

At 8:15 I was told to go up and dress for dinner. For me this meant a clean shirt and a black tie, for I was wearing my blue suit. But for the other men, it meant dinner coats. Mine was a good substitute with the black bow tie. The P.M., however, pulled an F. D. R.[1] In fact he went him one better. He came down in one of those air-raid zipper overall affairs with his shirt collar unbuttoned—and *no* tie. I must add that I was forced to take a bath before dinner by the valet announcing very firmly that my bath was ready. It was way down the cold and drafty hall.

The house—every part of it—was freezing unless you hugged the great big fireplaces, in which event you broiled.

We sat down to dinner at 9:00 P.M. Sarah Oliver, about the soup course,

[1] This referred to the incident with Premier Paderewski, previously mentioned.

announced loudly and abruptly that she understood that my wife was *the*
U.S. authority on housing. That created quite a sensation. . . .

Dinner was over at 10. Brandy was over at 10:30. I began to envisage bed
because I was tired and was trying to keep up the appearance of drinking. I
could have slept.

But at 10:30 the P.M. turns to Sarah and says: "What is the film for
tonight?" I thought I had misheard; but the answer was clear—*A House of
One's Own*—and she added, turning to me, "Put on your overcoat, because
it's cold in the cinema room."

I put on my overcoat. The P.M. put on a loud bathrobe, and we all trotted
to the refrigerator where the movie was shown. There were thirty or forty
soldiers, sailors, maids, butlers, etc., seated there—as at the White House.
Our procession moved in. The P.M. sat down with a whiskey and soda, and
I had one forced into my hand too.

The movie was a British film, long and dull and very badly acted. We
stumbled downstairs at about 12:30. By this time in addition to being
sleepy, I was cold and hungry.

Sarah was smart; she went to bed. The P.M. really was very entertaining.
He held the floor, reciting poetry and talking generally until 2:15 A.M.,
when he suddenly turned to me and wanted to know what I was putting in
my food report and whether I was going to take any British food away
from them.

Thereupon followed serious discussion with which I will not bore you.
At 3:00 A.M. someone (bless his soul) suggested bed. The P.M. displayed
surprise at the lateness of the hour, but I knew that he was not surprised.

I had heard from F. D. R. and from Harry about this performance but
this is the first time *I* was the victim.

Somebody carried me to bed, for I was too tired to walk—and a comfortable one it was. It was a good thing I had not tried to keep up with
the drinking or the word "carried" would have been literal.

I had a date today with the Lord Chancellor so, I got up at 8:30. At 9:30
I went in to say good-by to the P.M. and he was having breakfast in bed—
very chipper and gay.

We had a talk about war crimes and then I drove in to London. I'm
going to try to catch up with some sleep tonight.

Before going down to Churchill's I had lunch at Dr. Weizmann's house,
and tea with the Lunts (the actors) at the Savoy. . . .

Just got your letter dated Easter Sunday.

Hope to leave about the 15th.

Good night and much love. It was quite an experience at Chequers, but
protect me from it as a steady diet. I would not have missed it for the
world.

                                        Devotedly,

                                                    SAM

During the evening conference mentioned in this letter, Churchill, prompted now and then by Lord Cherwell, his economist, poured onto me statistics of foodstuffs shipped to England, shipped out of England and consumed in England—all to prove that it would be cruel for the United States to divert a substantial amount of the food in the British Isles to the Continent.

Armed with the statistics I had gathered during my weeks of study, I did my best to cope with his arguments at that late hour. I was armed also with firsthand knowledge of the tragic suffering of the people in the cities of France, Belgium and Holland. While there was an adequate supply of foodstuffs in many of the rural areas of western Europe, the lack of fuel and transportation and the instability of the currency had almost stopped the flow of food from the country into the cities.

I am afraid that I did not acquit myself very well that night, but I managed to give the Prime Minister a brief review of what I intended to report to the President. He seemed fairly well satisfied.

At our breakfast conference the next morning, the Prime Minister repeated the same views about war criminals that I had heard everywhere in official London: that long-drawn-out trials would be a mistake and that the best thing to do was to dispose summarily of the six or seven top men. I told him that I was sure that the President would never agree with that; but I suggested that the matter might properly be a subject of discussion at the United Nations Conference at San Francisco starting on the 25th.

However, when I later went out to San Francisco at the direction of President Truman in May, 1945, to continue discussions on the subject with Britain, France and the Soviet, I found that the British were ready to abandon their insistence on direct action and to join us in international trials. Two years later, in 1947, I saw Churchill for the first time since my visit to Chequers. It was at a small dinner given to him in New York by Mr. Baruch. When I shook hands to say good night to him, with typical Churchill frankness, he said:

"Rosenman, do you remember our talk at Chequers when I argued so strenuously against trying those Nazi war criminals? Now that the trials are all over, I think the President was right and I was wrong."

But at breakfast at Chequers he was quite determined about it. After a while he began to talk at length about the President. The look which came into Churchill's eyes as he talked showed the strong bond of affection that had grown between these two great leaders.

"There are two things which I wish you would convey for me to your great President—both matters of personal interest to me," he said. "First, as you know, the President and Mrs. Roosevelt have accepted the invitations of their Majesties to make a visit to England during the month of May."

I had not yet heard this; but there was no reason why I should have during my absence from Washington. He continued, "Will you tell him for me that he is going to get from the British people the greatest reception ever accorded to any human being since Lord Nelson made his triumphant return to London?"

I could not gauge the extent of the welcome which was in store for the President. But it was obvious that he would be received by the British people with all the enthusiasm, affection and adoration which his leadership and steadfastness and friendship for Britain during the dark early days of the war had earned for him.

"I want you to tell him that when he sees the reception he is going to get, he should realize that it is not an artificial or stimulated one. It will come genuinely and spontaneously from the hearts of the British people; they all love him for what he has done to save them from destruction by the Huns; they love him also for what he has done for the cause of peace in the world, for what he has done to relieve their fear that the horrors they have been through for five years might come upon them again in increased fury.

"Here is the second thing I want you to tell him," he said, a bit sheepishly.

"Do you remember when I came over to your country in the summer of 1944 when your election campaigning was beginning? Do you remember that when I arrived, I said something favorable to the election of the President, and immediately the associates of the President sent word to me in no uncertain terms to 'lay off' discussing the American election? Do you remember I was told that if I wanted to help the President get re-elected, the best thing I could do was to keep my mouth shut; that the American people would resent any interference or suggestion by a foreigner about how they should vote?"

I was a little embarrassed, because I did remember the vehemence with which we all urged the President to get word to the Prime

Minister to keep quiet and act as though he did not know that an American election was about to be held. I suppose the Prime Minister noticed my embarrassment because he immediately said with one of his most engaging laughs:

"Now what I want you to tell the President is this. When he comes over here in May I shall be in the midst of a political campaign myself; we shall be holding our own elections about that time. I want you to tell him that I impose no such inhibitions upon him as he imposed upon me. The British people would not resent—and of course I would particularly welcome—any word that he might want to say in favor of my candidacy." He chuckled, and as I shook hands with him to say good-by I felt anew the glow of his warm personality—frank, blunt and direct.

No one can tell what Roosevelt would have said in England that May about the British elections. I am sure, however, that having worked so hard and so long in building this international team for war and peace, he would have been sorry to see it broken up, especially before the foundations of the peace were made secure.

As I left Chequers and drove up to London, I thought of the overworked and harried man whom I had seen last in his bedroom reminding me to take my rubbers to London; and I felt happy at the thought of the great physical and spiritual lift he would get from the welcome of the British people.

A few nights later, on April 12, just before going to bed, I stopped in to say good night to Baruch, whose rooms were on the same floor as mine at Claridge's.

Baruch was in London on behalf of the President to discuss with Churchill and the British War Cabinet various matters of industrial, financial and economic importance. He had come over in the President's private plane, the *Sacred Cow*, and expected to return to Washington the next morning. He had invited me to go back with him; but I still had work to do in London, and I had to decline. After a few words with him I went to my room.

I was working on some of the memoranda and documents from which my report was being prepared when the phone rang. It was one of Baruch's assistants.

I recognized the voice, which said: "Judge, have you gone to bed yet?"

I answered: "No," and was told that Mr. Baruch would like me to put on my bathrobe and come to see him right away. I asked whether he had been taken sick. I was informed that he had not; but that he was quite anxious to talk with me at once.

When I entered Baruch's bedroom, he said to me: "Now, Sam, steady in the boat! Brendan Bracken just phoned. He said that the radio has announced that the President is dead."

We sat there in silence for a while, each with his own thoughts and memories.

From the radio we learned some of the details. It was at about 1:15 that afternoon, Warm Springs time, that the President had made his last statement. It was a simple one:

"I have a terrific headache."

A few hours later he was dead.

I sat on the edge of Baruch's bed, and said, "Bernie, I guess I will be going back with you after all. I think we ought to start first thing tomorrow, and we can probably get there in time for the funeral."

He said, "I think that's wise. Let's see whether Ed Flynn and Elliott Roosevelt would like to join us. We can take them with us; there is plenty of room." The next day, at noon, we four were off on our last visit to the President. The members of my mission (which seemed fairly unimportant to me now) were to follow and join me in Washington to complete our report. We were in Washington by midnight, Washington time.

The next morning my wife and I were at the railroad station waiting for the funeral train to come in from Warm Springs, Georgia. All of official Washington was there and many of his personal friends, too. Even more marked than their sadness and grief was their appearance of complete bewilderment, as though, having lost the leader to whom they could always turn, they felt uncertain—almost frightened.

The funeral procession finally formed, and behind the caisson on which lay the flag-draped body of the Commander-in-Chief we all rode in silence through the lines of hundreds of thousands of Washington residents. Many were crying aloud or weeping quietly. Many just stood there, dazed. It was hard to believe he was dead.

All through the United States there was the same kind of public reaction, the same sense of personal loss. Millions of people in America, and in the rest of the world, seemed to have lost a close relative or dear friend—even though they never laid eyes on him.

What was the source of this intimate contact which one man had been able to cement with so many millions of human beings in widely scattered parts of the world, of different races and religions, of different trades and occupations?

As I watched those miles of mourning faces along the sidewalks of Washington, I thought about this unique phenomenon in American political life.

There was something more to it than an eloquent, moving radio voice. There was something more than a smile, than friendliness, warmth—something more even than the fighting desire to bring a better life to the many who needed help. There have been, and still are, many statesmen who have spent their political lives in the same kind of fight in behalf of the forgotten man. Yet none of them evoked the kind of affection that I saw in those faces.

I think that the great reason for Roosevelt's place in the hearts and heads of people was his ability to make them feel that he associated himself personally with each of them in each one's aspirations for something better in life. He did not seem to be someone far removed, fighting their battles in a rarefied atmosphere. He was right down in the sweaty arena with them, side by side, expressing what they were thinking, doing what they wanted done, taking his strength and his boldness from their strength and their support—making them feel that he and they were all doing it together.

He could identify himself with each individual worker in the sweatshops as he led the fight to build up trade unions and brought about better working conditions, higher wages, shorter hours, and a higher dignity for labor. The worker thought of him as a sympathetic and understanding friend who was fighting shoulder to shoulder with him against all labor baiters and exploiters.

The farmer recognized in him a warm human being to whom relief of agriculture did not mean dry statistics and economic charts. Here was a President who seemed to be personally interested in the mortgage on each farmer's farm, who was fighting to reduce his interest rate so he could buy more shoes and schooling for his children, to get rural electrification so that the farmer's wife could lead an easier life, to promote soil conservation so that the farmer would not see his old farm go to pieces. It was in terms of the members of the farm family, of human beings, that Roosevelt thought and talked, and he was able to make each farmer who listened to him think that he was the specific farmer the President had in mind.

Roosevelt was also able to do this with the small businessman who was looking for some protection from his monopolistic competitors; with the housewife and schoolteacher who saw their money melting away in inflation; with the wage earner who wanted protection against unemployment, old age, and sickness.

As a war leader and as a builder of peace, he never seemed to be talking down to the people, enunciating theoretical principles and precepts as Wilson did; he seemed to be expressing in simple terms the unexpressed yearnings of each man, woman and child who listened to him. The Atlantic Charter and the four freedoms were not presented by Roosevelt as something from on high; instead he spoke of them in terms of the desires and needs of all human beings in the world, and each person who heard the President talk about them could feel: "Yes, that's what I'd like to see happen myself."

And in the same way, the poorest and lowliest of the starving millions of India and China and Iran, the refugee in the hot streets of Tel Aviv, the Frenchman, the Italian, the Dutchman picking his way through the rubble of his destroyed city—each person in the great masses of people all over the world felt that here was a man who was fighting not only *for* him but *with* him: fighting for some peace and security for him as an individual, for some better food and shelter and clothing for him and his family.

How was Roosevelt able to do this? The answer is difficult—as difficult as the answer to any question of personality. This much is sure. Roosevelt thought in terms of human beings rather than of abstract problems. To him every problem was defined in terms of effect on people. And since he did think in those terms, it was natural that the people should come to realize it—to recognize him as an associate in their struggles for a better life and in their aspirations for a better world. And now that he was dead, it seemed natural that they should mourn him as a departed ally and friend, without whom they would have to get along somehow as best they could.

As my wife and I passed under the portico of the White House and through the door we had entered so many times since March 4, 1933, she whispered to me: "This is the end of an epoch in our lives!"

And as we sat through the funeral services in the East Room that afternoon, and as we rode up on the funeral train to Hyde Park, and as we stood beside the grave in the rose garden that I had watched and admired so frequently with Roosevelt, I kept thinking to myself, "This is the end of an epoch for the United States too—and for the entire world."

Roosevelt, in his last few days, had written a speech for delivery on April 13, Thomas Jefferson Day. A draft of the speech was prepared by someone on the staff of the Democratic National Committee. A copy of that draft was given to Jonathan Daniels, then acting as press secretary, who sent it to Bob. I was still in Europe and Harry was in the Mayo Clinic. Bob prepared a new draft in New York and sent it on to Warm Springs. The President, alone, had started intensive work on the speech, using Bob's new draft as a basis.

The Jefferson Day speech was never fully finished, and of course was never delivered; it still required final polishing and correction. The last two paragraphs of that speech should have been included in the prayers at his grave. They were the President's last message to America and to the world—a message that was uppermost in his mind as he died. The last sentence of these two paragraphs—a basic creed with him—was his own addition to the draft in his own handwriting:

Today, as we move against the terrible scourge of war—as we go forward toward the greatest contribution that any generation of human beings can make in this world—the contribution of lasting peace, I ask you to keep up your faith. I measure the sound, solid achievement that can be made at this time by the straight edge of your own confidence and your resolve. And to you, and to all Americans who dedicate themselves with us to the making of an abiding peace, I say:

The only limit to our realization of tomorrow will be our doubts of today. *Let us move forward with strong and active faith.*

Index